I0313586

HEBREW ORIENTALISM

Hebrew Orientalism

JEWISH ENGAGEMENT
WITH ARABO-ISLAMIC CULTURE
IN LATE OTTOMAN
AND BRITISH PALESTINE

MOSTAFA HUSSEIN

PRINCETON UNIVERSITY PRESS
PRINCETON & OXFORD

Published by Princeton University Press
41 William Street, Princeton, New Jersey 08540
99 Banbury Road, Oxford OX2 6JX

press.princeton.edu

GPSR Authorized Representative: Easy Access System Europe - Mustamäe tee 50, 10621 Tallinn, Estonia, gpsr.requests@easproject.com

ISBN 978-0-691-28070-7
ISBN (pbk.) 978-0-691-20203-7
ISBN (e-book) 978-0-691-28003-5

Library of Congress Control Number 2025937659

British Library Cataloging-in-Publication Data is available

Editorial: Fred Appel and James Collier
Production Editorial: Jill Harris
Jacket Design: Katie Osborne
Production: Erin Suydam
Publicity: William Pagdatoon
Copyeditor: Cindy Milstein

Jacket image: *Jerusalem (El-Kouds). Street scene inside the Jaffa Gate.* Courtesy of the G. Eric and Edith Matson Photograph Collection / Library of Congress, Prints & Photographs Division, LC-DIG-matpc-06546.

This book has been composed in Minion Pro and Universe

10 9 8 7 6 5 4 3 2 1

To Basma, Nour, Malek, and Dania

CONTENTS

List of Illustrations ix
Acknowledgments xi
Note on Translation and Transliteration xiii

Introduction 1

PART I. SHARED HOMELAND: LATE OTTOMAN PALESTINE, 1882–1917 17

1 Ambivalent Encounters: Jews and Arabs in Late Ottoman Palestine 23

2 Writing the Landscape, Writing the Homeland 61

3 Constructing Jewish Indigeneity through Arabic Language and Literature 95

PART II. THE CONSTRUCTION OF A NATIONAL HOME IN MANDATE PALESTINE, 1917–48 139

4 The Ethnonationalization of the Palestine Landscape 147

5 The Hebrew Construction of an Arabo-Islamic Literary Past 183

Conclusion 225

Notes 247
References 297
Index 319

ILLUSTRATIONS

1.1. The cover of Abraham Shalom Yahuda's *Ḳadmoniyot ha-'Aravim* (The antiquities of the Arabs). 29

1.2. Israel Belḳind's *Erets Yisrael shel zemanenu* (The land of Israel in our time) contains not only a natural description of Palestine but also of its inhabitants. 33

1.3. Cover of Isaac Yahuda's *al-Maḍnūn bihi 'ala ghayr Ahlih* (That which is to be withheld from those unworthy of it). 43

1.4. *Filasṭīn* (Palestine) newspaper, August 5, 1911. 48

1.5. Menashe Meirovitch's Arabic letters published under the title *Rasā'il fallāḥ* (A fellah's letters). 51

2.1. Cover of *Kitāb al-rawḍa al-Mu'nisa fī waṣf al-'arḍ al-Muqaddasa.* 64

2.2. Cover of Abraham Moshe Lunts's yearbook *Yerushalayim* (Jerusalem). 68

2.3. Cover of Eliezer Ben-Yehuda's *Sefer Erets Yisrael.* 71

2.4. The front page of Menashe Meirovitch's series of articles, "Tsimḥe erets ha-tsevi," on the flora of Palestine. 81

2.5. David Yellin's article "Yerushalaym li-fnay arba' Me'ot shanah" (Jerusalem four hundred years ago). 85

2.6. Cover of David Yellin's *Rabenu Mosheh Ben Maymun* (Our master Moses Maimonides). 89

3.1. A list of plant names in Palestine appears in Eliyahu Sapir's series of articles "Tsimḥe Erets Yisrael" (Plants of the land of Israel). 112

3.2. Eliyahu Sapir's geographic book *Ha-arets* (The land). 116

3.3. The front page of A. S. Yahuda's essay on "Nedive ve-gibure 'Arav." 129

4.1. Cover of Israel Belḳind's *Erets Yisrael shel zemanenu* (The land of Israel in our time), published in British Palestine in 1928. 152

4.2. Cover of Israel Wolf Horowitz's encyclopedic work *Erets Yisrael u-shekhenoteha* (The land of Israel and its adjacent countries). 158

4.3. A list of Arabic place-names along with their Hebrew equivalents and their references in the Hebrew Bible in Eliyahu Sapir's *Ha-arets* (The land). 160

4.4. Cover of Isaac Yahuda's book *Ha-Kotel ha-Ma'aravi* (The Western Wall), published in Jerusalem in 1929. 169

4.5. David Yellin's testimony to the British Commission of Inquiry published in Jerusalem in Arabic in 1930. 171

4.6. Cover of Aḥmad Zakī Pasha's *Taṣḥīḥ al-Aghlaṭ* (Correcting errors). 178

5.1. Cover of Isaac Yahuda's book *Mishle 'Arav* (Proverbia Arabica). 188

5.2. Cover of David Yellin's *Sipure Elef Laylah va-Laylah* (The thousand and one nights). 207

5.3. Cover of Yosef Yo'el Rivlin's *Elef Laylah va-Laylah* (One thousand and one nights). 212

ACKNOWLEDGMENTS

WORKING ON THIS BOOK has been a challenging endeavor, as its topic and theme lie at the crossroads between two cultures, two national movements, two languages, and two worlds often perceived as separate as the East Coast is from the West Coast. This book would not have come to fruition without the unwavering encouragement and support I received from numerous friends, colleagues, and institutions throughout the writing process. I am profoundly grateful to all who helped make this book a reality.

The genesis of this work traces back to 2011, when I began my graduate studies at Brandeis University as a Fulbright scholar. During my time as a PhD candidate at Brandeis, I received support from numerous mentors, whose wisdom has guided my academic journey. My gratitude goes to Jonathan Decter and Eugene Sheppard for guiding me through the earlier stages of this project. Ilan Troen, both a mentor and colleague, provided invaluable advice, while Susannah Heschel's unwavering support from the outset helped me navigate key aspects of the project. I also benefited greatly from the mentorship of Carl Sharif El-Tobgui and Joseph Lumbard, whose contributions enriched my academic journey at Brandeis.

The Judaic Studies Department at the University of Michigan has been a scholarly home to me over the past several years, offering an environment of intellectual rigor and camaraderie. During my fellowship year at the institute in 2016–17, I received invaluable comments and suggestions on the project in general as well as on significant portions of the book from an inspiring group of colleagues, including Naomi Brenner, Liora Halperin, Noah Hysler-Rubin, Lior Libman, Aviad Moreno, Shachar Pinsker, Bryan Roby, Gavin Schaffer, Rachel Seelig, Shayna Zamekanei, and Yael Zerubavel. Their comments were crucial in refining various chapters of this book. I am especially grateful to Jeffrey Veidlinger, whose steady support, insightful advice, and accessibility were instrumental in advancing this project. Maya Barzilai also offered valuable feedback, reading portions of the manuscript and providing sharp suggestions. My gratitude extends to Deborah Dash Moore and Scott Spector for their encouragement and thoughtful engagement at various stages of this process. Additionally, Evyn Kropf and Gabriel Mordoch at the University of Michigan library were immensely helpful in retrieving primary and secondary sources crucial to this project.

As a fellow in the Society of Fellows at the University of Southern California, I benefited from the feedback of colleagues, whose comments and suggestions helped me improve the book's chapters. My gratitude extends to Lisa Bitel, Cavan Concannon, the late Thomas Habinek, Sherman Jackson, Jessica Marglin, James McHugh, and Lori Meeks for their encouragement and incisive comments.

This book has also benefited from the many conferences and workshops where portions of it were presented. Discussions at the Association for Israel Studies, Association for Jewish Studies, and Middle East Studies Association proved invaluable in refining its ideas. The excitement and encouragement I received at these conferences helped shape certain aspects of the book. I am grateful to the conference organizers for welcoming my participation, and the copanelists and scholars for their comments and suggestions. Special thanks go to David Myers for inviting me to present parts of this work at his graduate seminar at the University of California at Los Angeles, as well as to Stephanie Kraver and Elena Hoffenberg for hosting me at the Jewish Studies Workshop at the University of Chicago. I am thankful to the participants at these events for their feedback, which greatly enriched the manuscript. My gratitude extends to Orit Bashkin, who despite her inability to attend the workshop in person, was generous with her suggestions and comments, which enriched and advanced the manuscript's discussion. Hilary Kalisman's careful reading of an earlier draft, along with her insightful comments, played a crucial role in refining the work.

Fred Appel has been supportive of this book project from its early stages. When I contacted Fred in 2018 with a book proposal, he showed great excitement and support for the project. From that moment until the publication of this book, we met several times virtually and in person to check on my progress and help me sharpen the central ideas of the book. His support, along with that of his team at Princeton University Press, has been pivotal. Gratitude goes to James Collier for his assistance, including reading earlier versions of the book, sharing his comments at the Middle East Studies Association annual conference in Denver, Colorado, in November 2022, and providing guidance throughout the publication process. Appreciation is also extended to Joanna Rutter for taking on this book project, and collaborating to enhance its quality and accessibility to a broader audience. Her editorial suggestions have greatly improved the book.

Finally, I would like to thank my family for their support throughout this book's journey. My parents and siblings have followed the progress of this project, eagerly anticipating its completion. To my wife, Basma Emam, and my children, Nour, Malek, and Dania, I am forever grateful for your unwavering love and support. This book is dedicated to you, as a testament to the sacrifices you made and the love that has carried me through. I hope it serves as a reflection of the cause that temporarily pulled me away from our shared moments of joy and achievement.

Ann Arbor, Michigan
April 2025

NOTE ON TRANSLATION AND TRANSLITERATION

Unless stated otherwise in the footnotes, I have personally translated all primary or secondary sources cited throughout this book.

I have used the *International Journal of Middle Eastern Studies* transliteration system for Arabic and the Library of Congress transliteration system for Hebrew.

HEBREW ORIENTALISM

Introduction

THIS BOOK EXAMINES how Arabic and Islamic culture was used to advance Zionist ideals in late-nineteenth- and mid-twentieth-century Palestine through the activities of a group of culturally influential and ethnically diverse Jewish intellectuals. While Arabic and Islamic culture includes Palestinian culture and ways of life, it also encompasses constituents shared by other adjacent Arab communities. Like the identities of people in many other Arab contexts in the modern era, Palestinian identity is complex due to its intricate connections with broad and influential transnational identities, particularly Arabism and Islam.[1] Some members of this group were Palestine-born Jews who grew up in mixed cities like Jerusalem, Haifa, and Jaffa, and acquired knowledge of Arabic through their daily contact with Palestinian Arabs as well as in educational settings, studying with local Arab or Jewish teachers. They were either Sephardi, or of hybrid Sephardi and Ashkenazi origin, such as David Yellin, Abraham Shalom Yahuda, Isaac Yahuda, Eliyahu Sapir, or of only Ashkenazi descent, like Israel Horowitz and Yosef Yo'el Rivlin. Other members of this cohort included Ashkenazi Jewish immigrants who were born in eastern Europe and settled in late Ottoman and British Palestine, such as Eliezer Ben-Yehuda as well as the Bilu members Israel Belḳind and Menasche Meirovitch.

In scrutinizing Hebrew Orientalism, I diverge from two dominant methodologies: the ideological critique of Orientalism as presented by the scholar and literary critic Edward Said, and the defense of Orientalist studies, practices, and activities based on their contributions to scientific progress or national enterprise. In examining practices of Hebrew writers in this book, I refer to the actual activities, methods, and routines of Jewish individuals who engaged in the formal or informal pursuit of Arabo-Islamic culture and language in Palestine long before the opening of the School of Oriental Studies (*ha-makhon le-limude ha-mizraḥ*) at the Hebrew University in Jerusalem in 1926, and mainly functioned outside this academic institution. This approach is contrasted with investigating the Hebrew perception of Islam and the Arab, which would focus more narrowly on how Hebrew writers conceptualized and portrayed Islam, Arab culture, and the Arab. Instead, I advocate for a detailed exploration of the day-to-day work as well as scholarly and quasi-scholarly practices of those Jewish individuals in their cultural and social environments.

The justification for the above-mentioned "third way" or alternative method lies in its ability to bypass the dichotomy inherent in either purely ideological critiques or defenses of Orientalism's scientific merits.[2] By concentrating on the tangible practices—such as learning languages, translating texts, producing scholarship, and engaging in fieldwork—I aim to uncover the nuanced realities of how Hebrew Orientalism functioned in the context of the creation of Hebrew culture and the advancement of Zionist aspirations in Palestine. This includes understanding the motivations, ambitions, and prejudices of the scholars as well as the broader institutional and cultural contexts in which they operated.

I believe that recognizing and analyzing these practices can shed light on the complexities and contradictions within the field of Hebrew Orientalism. It allows for a critical history that acknowledges the contributions while also being mindful of the power dynamics and prejudices embedded in the discipline. This approach seeks to provide a more balanced understanding that informs contemporary discussions on postcolonialism, settler colonialism, and global history, highlighting how past scholarly practices have shaped and prepared the ground for current academic and ideological trends.

This book explores the complexities and nuances of the engagement with Arabo-Islamic culture in the formative period of modern Hebrew culture through the knowledge-making practices of this cohort of Jewish writers who were widely recognized as authorities on the religious, cultural, and historical significance of Arabic and Islamic culture. Their works were instrumental in the indigenization of Jewish settlers by virtue of bolstering and reinvigorating Jewish ties to their perceived ancestral homeland, excavating the place of Jews in the literary and historic legacy of the Orient, while promoting the return to origins and adopting Orientalist attitudes.

The shared experience of living in the Ottoman homeland encouraged Jews and Arabs to seek common ground rather than focus on differences. One of the main foundations for common ground was Islamicate civilization: a culture to which Muslims, Christians, and Jews contributed. Interconfessional relations between Jews, Christians, and Muslims from late Ottoman Palestine until World War I fostered a sense of Ottoman fellowship that created by and contributed to an ecumenical framework in which these various communities could retain their distinctiveness, while making possible a bridge between all parties. Although Orientalism informed Hebrew works on Arabo-Islamic culture in the Ottoman era, and guided their settler colonial practices and activities, as the political landscape shifted into the British Mandate period, the Jewish settler community, centered on its project of national reclamation along with elevating and advancing Jewish indigeneity in Palestine, amplified Orientalist views about Palestinian Arabs that both reified differences and denigrated their Palestinian neighbors.

Hebrew writers' knowledge of Arabic and Islam was instrumental in advancing the Zionist project as a settler colonial enterprise, and reconciling Zionism with Ottoman citizenship. This book explores the sorts of knowledge of Arabic and Islam that were vital to their evolving perception of their own heritage in relation to the long Arabo-Islamic history of the region. The transmission of Islamic culture—through language, literature, religion, and knowledge of the natural world—into the modern Hebrew culture taking shape in Palestine was made possible through the practices and activities of the aforementioned Jewish intellectuals.

The British conquest of Palestine brought about drastic changes in the relative political and social status of Sephardi and Oriental Jews as well as Ashkenazi Jewish communities. With the termination of the Ottoman state, Sephardi and Oriental Jews lost the superior status granted to them by the Ottoman authorities, with the power balance now tipped in favor of Ashkenazi Zionists, whose hegemonic leadership marginalized the Sephardi and Oriental Jewish communities. The latter adapted to this new reality by continuing to play their historical role as mediators between Ashkenazi Zionists and Arabs, while demonstrating their loyalty to the Zionist movement and commitment to solving "the Arab question"—a notion that emerged only after the decline of the Ottoman state and loss of Arabs' hope for a unified independent Arab state.[3] While other studies have exposited the mediatory role played by Sephardi and Oriental Jews in building bridges between Jews and Arabs on the political, sociocultural, and security levels, this book concentrates on the intellectual history of the period, arguing that these mediatory agents also contributed to shaping the emergent Jewish culture by adopting and adapting elements from Arabo-Islamic culture.[4] This book shines light on the dual role a group of Sephardi and Oriental as well as some Ashkenazi Jews played in connecting Jews to the cultural sphere of the East, on the one hand, while expressing their commitment to the Zionist movement, on the other.

The Sephardi and Oriental Hebrew authors examined in the pages that follow present several unique problems regarding their position in British Palestine, ranging from Zionism to the native Palestinian Arab population. As supporters of the Jewish national home enterprise pledged in the Balfour Declaration of 1917, they ultimately went from being natives to be seen by their Palestinian Arab fellows as settler colonists in their own land, as it will be explored further in chapters 4 and 5. Their knowledge production likewise went from advocating coexistence with Arabs to stigmatizing the native Palestinian Arabs in service of Jewish nationalism. In other words, their participation in the production and dissemination of Hebrew Orientalism caused the instability of their own indigeneity, and placed them into the settler category in British Palestine. This book identifies specific patterns of thought that the authors employed to craft social spaces circumventing the rigid colonial dichotomy, thereby enabling them to maintain a native identity.[5] At some point, these patterns of thought necessitated that they align with the colonial dichotomy of native versus settler—an alignment that ultimately disempowered the Palestinian Arab population. The book posits that their adoption of Orientalist practices played a role in reinforcing their perceived settler colonial identity during the Mandate era when Palestinian Arabs sought the revocation of the imperial British pledge and the invitation of native Jews to join their national movement in seeking independence from the British. It considers the possibility that native Jews adopted Orientalist expressions and styles in their writings to make their discourse more palatable to their European-oriented Jewish audience, which had already internalized Orientalist ideas. By distributing negative representations of the land and its people, they sought acceptance among Zionist European Jews, reinforcing rather than challenging stereotypes, and therefore solidifying the Jewish community's distinctiveness in contrast to Arabs.

The Jewish discourse on Arabo-Islamic culture in Palestine revolved around Palestine's territory and encompassed contradictory attitudes ranging from reconciliation to instrumentalization, from romanticization to denigration, and centered around subjects such as *yedi'at ha-arets* (knowledge of the land), the Hebrew Bible, the creation of the "New Jew," and the revival of modern Hebrew. All figures featured within the book came of age in the Ottoman era, and continued to write and influence during the Mandate period, drawing on their Ottoman experiences to advocate for their belonging, nativity, and a Jewish national homeland under British rule while counteracting Palestinian nationalist aspirations.

In what follows, the relational history between Jews and Arabs in Palestine is refocused away from aggressors and victims, toward settlers and natives where settlers sought self-indigenization influenced by Orientalization. The settler's main interest is in territory—a desire for land that propelled and guided the appropriation of Arabo-Islamic knowledge to enhance the settlers' connection to the land even as it advanced their claims to long-standing ties to it. This analytic framework reveals the depth of the Hebrew scholarship and investment in Arabo-Islamic culture in a way that challenges the conventional impression that Hebrew scholars in Palestine were dismissive of as well as uninterested in Arabo-Islamic culture. Thus the book charts the growth of Hebrew works drawing on Arabo-Islamic materials (textual and oral) paralleled by the evolution of the Jewish settlement in Palestine, beginning with the early influx of a small group of Jewish settlers committed to residing there and leading up to the establishment of a Jewish state within the boundaries of historical Palestine. The book looks at the ways in which Arabo-Islamic knowledge practices by Hebrew scholars and educators helped in the advancement of belonging in the land of Palestine, creation of the New Jew, and production of distinct understanding of the Hebrew Bible within the national context taking place in the East, and built familiarity with and othering from the Arab. This discussion moves beyond native Palestinian Hebrew writers to include Ashkenazi Hebrew writers who were no less interested in the cultural currents of their place and time.

The life and work of Yellin (1864–1941) provide a uniquely opportune vantage point from which to investigate the influence of Arabo-Islamic thought on the Jewish culture evolving during the formative years of both the Zionist and Palestinian national movements. As a central figure whose life and activities spanned the period from the late Ottoman Empire to British Palestine and witnessed various forms of Jewish-Arab relations (from amity to discord and tension to enmity), Yellin epitomized the intersection of Jewish renewal centered on Zionism with the broader cultural, political, and social landscapes shaped by centuries of Arabo-Islamic presence in the region. His hybrid identity—his mother was an Iraqi Jewess, and his father was born in Jerusalem to a Jewish Polish immigrant—enabled him to mediate between Arabs and Ashkenazi Jews.[6] Yellin's promotion of Zionism and engagement with Arabo-Islamic culture rendered him the perfect tour guide through the intellectual and sociopolitical complexities that emerged during the period in question.

In a speech delivered to the Twelfth Zionist Congress in September 1921 in Czechoslovakia—an event held in the shadow of the May 1921 riots in Jaffa that led to dozens of deaths in both Jewish and Palestinian communities—Yellin commemorated the Jewish victims of the riots in Jaffa earlier that year by citing the following lines from "To Zion" by eleventh-century Jewish poet Yehuda Halevi (1075–1141): "When I weep about your sorrow, I turn into a wolf / when I dream of you, freed / I became a harp that accompanies your song."[7] Although Yellin's speech, with its medieval poetic reference, was met with favor by the assembled delegates, it was vehemently criticized by members of the Muslim-Christian Association (Al-Jam'iyya al-'Islāmiyya al-Masiḥiyya) (MCA), founded in 1918 in opposition to the Balfour Declaration and Zionist movement. For MCA members, Yellin's remarks were seen as evidence of his intent to incite Jews against Arabs for nationalist objectives. Indeed, MCA members claimed that the speech led to further clashes between Jews and Arabs in Jerusalem on the fourth anniversary of the Balfour Declaration, on November 2, 1921.[8]

In response to the MCA public statement, Yellin sent an Arabic translation of his speech along with a letter to the editor in chief of *al-Ṣabāḥ*, then the organ of the Arab Executive Committee.[9] In his letter, Yellin complained that the MCA had taken his quotations from Halevi's famous poem "Zion" out of context. As he wrote at the end of this letter,

> For my entire life, I have been a lover of the Arab people (*ohev ha'am ha-'aravi*), occupied with learning their language, reading their literature, and always encouraging my people to study it. It would not be an idle boast on my part to say that most Arab leaders in our land recognize me, thank God, as a man who at all times loves peace (*ohev shalom*). [This is the way of all Zionists ever since the appearance of this movement until today.] They are the same people who elected me before the Great War as a delegate in the Provincial Council (*Majlis 'Umūmī*) of the land of Israel.[10]

To counter the MCA's depiction of him as a provocateur who incites violence between Jews and Arabs, Yellin portrays himself as a cultural intermediary with longstanding affection toward Arabic language and culture, and someone who encourages other Jews to likewise learn the language and acquaint themselves with the culture.

At the same time and in the same letter, Yellin makes a crucial distinction between contemporary Arabs and Arabs of the past, noting that "there is difference between Arabs and Arabs." Yellin rejected the claims of Palestinian nationalists to continuity with the legacy of Saladin (ca. 1137–93), the Muslim leader who reconquered Jerusalem from the medieval Crusaders.[11] Yellin argued that contemporary Arab nationalists' opposition to mass Jewish immigration and land purchases severed their link to the more welcoming spirit of their Arab forebears. He criticized the nationalists for allegedly straying from the inclusive legacy of figures such as Ḥātim al-Ṭā'ī, celebrated for his generosity, and Saladin, who welcomed Jews back to Jerusalem following his triumph over the Crusaders. While Yellin appears to show respect for Arabs through the advocacy of learning their language and culture, he seems inclined to appreciate the cultural dimension of the native Arab population without heeding the invocation of past Arab and Muslim figures for the assertion of political aspirations. Even though Yellin's interest in Arab culture may seem positive, studying the language and literature of a people without engaging with their political aspirations or social realities reflects a superficial commitment to their identity. The Arabic culture that Yellin praised, appropriated, and borrowed from, in other words, was not to be found among the Arab inhabitants of the Palestine of his day. He found it, rather, in the cultural production of the pre-Islamic and medieval historical periods as well as preserved in the physical landscape of Palestine.

Yellin's professed love of Arabic language and literature, and premodern Arab rulers, combined with his refusal to recognize contemporary Arabs as social and political actors worthy of respect, is characteristic of other members of the aforementioned cohort of Jewish writers and intellectuals.

These Jewish writers interacted with and transformed an imagined and reclaimed Orient located largely in the past, and preserved, frozen, into the present in the character and customs of Arab peasants and Bedouins. This view aligns with the prevailing Orientalist framework through which earlier Jewish settlers regarded Arab inhabitants of rural settlements as "primitive, dirty, noisy, and chaotic."[12]

Zionist settlers drew on local cultural components that facilitated their indigenization into the region, while maintaining aspects from their home culture to preserve their Europeanness. Examples of this cultural selection include the adoption of certain foods and clothing styles from the Bedouins and fellahin (local Arab peasants) by the early Zionist pioneers during the First and Second Aliyah. The *Ha-shomer* (Watchmen's Association), a defense organization responsible for guarding Jewish settlements, for instance, donned keffiyeh and agal as their uniform. These adoptions, however, were not simply straightforward borrowings from neighboring cultures; they were complex reinterpretations filtered through existing models and stereotypes of the "Orient." The settlers' perspective was influenced by nineteenth-century Romantic views and contemporary portrayals, which often linked Bedouin attire to the biblical ancestors of the Jewish people. This reshaping of reality allowed the settlers to create positive connections with the cultural items they embraced. Despite this, the local Palestinian Arab populations—the Bedouins and fellahin not Arab city dwellers—were perceived ambivalently. On the one hand, they were viewed as noble and heroic individuals deeply connected to the land, and on the other, as primitive and culturally backward. The settlers' assimilation of Arab culture was akin to translating the new reality into an old, familiar Eastern European cultural framework. This was done by mapping familiar archetypes onto the new context: the Bedouin replaced the Cossack figure, and the fellah the Ukrainian peasant. Symbolically, the keffiyeh replaced the rough Cossack chokha, and local Hebrew songs that are based on Arabic tunes such as "Yafim halelot Bicen'an" (How beautiful are the nights of Canaan) took the place of Eastern European folk tunes. This cultural adaptation allowed the settlers to understand and incorporate the new experiences into their existing worldview while building a distinct Jewish cultural identity in Palestine.[13]

In their encounters with Palestine's landscape, Hebrew writers drew on their own firsthand experience with the land, Arabs' individual and collective experience of the land, and textual representations of the land produced by medieval Arab geographers and botanists. Hebrew texts on Palestine's landscape and Arab culture reflect the flow of ideas and views from the Arabo-Islamic to the Jewish realm, and back again, with transformations along the way. These writings do not reflect a purely Jewish experience of Palestine but rather a hybrid experience that has absorbed Arabo-Islamic knowledge in the construction of Jewish indigeneity through the connection to the natural and human landscape. These works enrich our understanding of how this knowledge was used by both Jewish and Arab intellectuals in the construction of their selfhood within a society whose nature and structure were highly fluid.

Some of the thinkers we will consider held attitudes that profoundly linked Jews and Arabs into one race (the semitic race), acknowledging that they shared not only the land of Palestine but also key parts of biblical scripture, cultural values, language, and histories. It is too simplistic to claim that they always thought of themselves as a united group over and against "the Arab other." In some contexts, they rendered Arabs as others, and in other circumstances as kin, though notably "cousins" in need of tutelage, according to Jewish Palestinian journalist and translator Nissim Malūl (1892–1959).[14] With that in mind, one needs to appreciate the richness and complexity of Jewish relations to Arabo-Islamic culture through the lens of these Jewish scholars without imposing binary distinctions that distort our understanding of the complex social as well as cultural life of the nineteenth- and twentieth-century Jewish writers studied here.

The depth of Yellin's scholarship and investment in Arab culture challenges the conventional impression that Jewish intellectuals of the Hebrew revival movement were incurious about Arabo-Islamic culture. Yellin and others not only demonstrated curiosity about Arabo-Islamic culture but also advocated for and promoted Arabic culture, language, and literature. Yellin's involvement in the diffusion of Arabic culture is attested to by his translation of major Arabic literary works into Hebrew in addition to the incorporation of Arabo-Islamic cultural constituents into many of his writings, whether those on medieval Hebrew poetry or biblical interpretations.

Sephardi and Oriental Jews such as Yellin and his Jerusalemite contemporaries, as the historian of Sephardi and Oriental Jewish communities Yitsḥaḳ Bezalel has shown, were involved in Zionism from its infancy onward. Yet due to their familiarity with the physical and cultural landscape of Palestine, their notion of Zionism was importantly distinct from that held by their Ashkenazi counterparts.[15] During the Ottoman period, they did not see a contradiction between supporting Zionism and belonging to the Orient. Sephardi and Oriental Jews' affiliation with Zionism, as historian Michelle Campos has observed, did not impugn their Ottomanism.[16] This view continued in British Palestine, and reverberated in Sephardi and Oriental Jews' efforts to mediate between Arabs and Zionists, as has been recently shown by historians Abigail Jacobson and Moshe Naor in their study *Oriental Neighbors*, despite the tremendous pressures they faced from members of both national movements to pledge allegiance exclusively to one or the other.[17]

Yellin and his Jewish contemporaries were clearly following the major polemics and intellectual currents of their time and place, where ideas of modernity and national identity swept al-Mashriq (Orient) in the aftermath of European encroachment, particularly the Napoleonic invasion of Egypt in 1798. The essential preoccupations of these Jewish figures resembled to a striking degree those of the Arab scholars of the *nahda* movement (Arab cultural renaissance). Christian and Muslim Arab members of nahda were deeply engaged in the construction of a modern selfhood that was in dialogue with the Arabo-Islamic past, as in the case of Buṭrus al-Bustānī and his work *Khuṭba fī adab al-ʿArab* (Discourse on Arab culture), published in Greater Syria, in which he provides a commentary on Arab culture past and present.[18] Meanwhile, as these debates swept the intellectual spheres of the Middle East, Jewish intellectuals in Palestine appropriated aspects of the Arabic heritage to fulfill their own objectives in accordance with their own religious identity and political inclinations.

The reform movement (Tanzimat or reorganization) led by the Ottoman sultan in 1839, included the February 1856 issuance of the Hatt-i-Humayun (Noble Rescript), a decree that granted equal rights to non-Muslim minorities in the Ottoman Empire. The imperial rescript eliminated all forms of discrimination based on language, religion, or race, with the goals of undermining nationalist separatist efforts, promoting loyalty to the sublime porte, and forging better connections between imperial subjects and their homeland.[19] Three decades later, all subjects of the empire became Ottoman citizens, regardless of their religious identity. With the rise of Zionism in the late nineteenth century, some Jews became Ottoman citizens and Zionists simultaneously. The love of homeland promoted by the Ottoman authorities, which echoed a major Zionist principle regarding Jewish people's connection to their perceived ancestral land, encouraged Jewish intellectuals in Palestine to enhance their relationship with the surrounding landscape and promote Jewish immigration to it.

Jewish settlers in late Ottoman Palestine, in their efforts to establish a unique Jewish culture distinct from their diasporic origins, and especially from eastern European traditions, selectively adopted features from the local Arabo-Islamic culture and infused them with Zionist ideology. This created what Israeli culture scholar Itamar Even-Zohar has called an "alternative system" within their emerging culture. In their project to reject the cultural trappings of the Diaspora in favor of a newly constructed culture of the old-new homeland in Palestine, the origin of the adopted cultural constituents was secondary to their capacity to "fulfill new functions," in Even-Zohar's framework.[20] Looking closely, one finds that this resonates with the notion of authenticity, not as a singling out of what is mine and nobody else's, but as that "which is original and pristine to us, stripped of all later accretions, and therefore 'true,' 'genuine,' and 'real.'"[21]

Hebrew Orientalism

The "mediation practices" of the Hebrew writers examined in this book revolved around producing texts pertaining to the physical, linguistic, and human landscape of Palestine, and in particular the history, geography, and flora and fauna of the land, and at other times by providing Hebrew translations of Arabic sources treating Palestine's physical, linguistic, and human landscape. This "textual attitude" to Palestine rendered the land open to Hebrew readers' scrutiny, particularly those of European origins who were gazing at Palestine and aiming to settle in it. When Ashkenazi Jews planned to immigrate to Palestine, they built their imagination of the land and its people based on what they found in these Hebrew corpora.

If Orientalism is based on a stark distinction between West, as the subject, and East, as the object, this dichotomous model is not entirely applicable to the group of Hebrew authors explored here, considering the various ways in which they connected with the Orient. Hence in the assessment of these individuals' Orientalism as representation or notion, we must go beyond simplistic dualism. As literary critic Homi Bhabha has insisted, the images that Easterners and Westerners have of themselves and one another, while ostensibly separating people into distinct categories, are inherently multivalent. Bhabha's insight, as Harvey Goldberg has pointed out, provides "an appreciation of 'hybridity' as cultural creativity, transvaluing the perception of some cultural processes and thus adding a positive perspective missing from Said's assessment."[22]

The usefulness of the notion of Orientalism in construing the ways in which Hebrew writers encountered Arabic and Islamic culture as well as mobilized it to a Hebrew-reading audience is complicated by these individuals' entangled and enmeshed relationship to the Orient. The Jewish community in late Ottoman Palestine can be divided generally into two groups: Sephardim and Oriental Jews, on the one hand, and Ashkenazi Jews who had settled in Palestine since the eighteenth century, on the other. The presence of the latter intensified with the eruption of pogroms in eastern Europe and Russia coupled with the rise of Zionism along with calls to emigrate and settle in Palestine, identified by those settlers as their ancestral homeland. The Hebrew scholars examined in this book reflect the ethnic diversity of the Jewish community of Palestine. They were embedded in a diverse and intertwined relationship with the Orient through birth, immigration, affection, and learning, and with the West through origins, education, and exposure to acculturation to Western society.

"Eastern" or "Oriental" was the identifier that Sephardi and Oriental Jews chose for themselves. According to historians Ivan Davidson Kalmar and Derek Jonathan Penslar, "The [Western] Jews are identified, both by themselves and by the Western world, with the ancient Israelites who established themselves and the monotheistic tradition, in the same 'Oriental' location. It is this latter identification with the Biblical lands that allowed Jews to be seen during the centuries as an 'Oriental people,' a perception challenged only in the twentieth century as the result of Jewish-Arab strife in the Middle East."[23] For European Jews, identifying as Oriental and disseminating Orientalist knowledge about Islam in the West did not entail an identification with the colonizer. As historian John Efron explains,

> For many central European scholars, among them Jews, orientalism was more than a system of domination. It could be genuinely celebratory and inspirational, as orientalism sometimes entailed a valorization of the Muslim Other. For Jews, such an exercise was often tantamount to a search for roots, for authenticity, and for oriental role models. Thus, rather than a straightforward means of asserting colonial, corporeal, and cultural authority, orientalism could be a profound expression of one's own cultural anxiety and insecurity, one that could provoke deep-seated fears of inferiority. Such is a far cry from the overconfidence and feelings of cultural superiority that Said and his followers attribute to all orientalists.[24]

In the following look at the Hebrew Orientalism that emerged in prestate Palestine, we discover how the Jewish communities' relationship with the East differed from that with the West. Ashkenazi Hebrew Zionists recognized the centrality of the Arab figure and Arab culture in the construction of a Hebrew national culture in Palestine. In the process of transforming "the exilic Jew" into a New Jew, early Zionists were fascinated with the image of the Bedouin, Oriental city, and lifestyle of local peasants.[25]

Settler Colonialism

A recent strain of scholarship in the field of Palestine-Israel studies has enriched our understanding of the evolution of the Zionist enterprise within the framework of a settler-native narrative.[26] Approaching the linkages between the two paradigms helps illuminate the distinctiveness of Hebrew Orientalism and its contribution to Jewish indigeneity as well as its impact on Indigenous Palestinians.

At the heart of "settler colonialism" lies the issue of territory, where "land is life," in the words of English historian Patrick Wolfe.[27] Unlike other settlement movements that chose their target lands on the basis of their political, geographic, and economic availability, "Zion"—a name that denotes the promised land, which is Palestine in the Jewish religion—as Israeli sociologist Baruch Kimmerling has indicated, "was *a priori* the territory" where the Zionist movement found the political answer to an ethnic-religious minority that "could not be absorbed or assimilated as a group within the so-called 'host' societal systems."[28] In contrast to European colonial movements, historian Gershon Shafir has shown that Jewish settlers could not claim the land under the "right of discovery," "right of conquest," or "right of protectorate" since they lacked military power as well as governmental support to expropriate and transfer land in favor of their ancient claims. Thus to acquire the land, Jewish settlers and their philanthropists had to purchase it primarily from absentee landlords, not the Palestinian farmers who were cultivating it. Late Ottoman Palestine was not a tribal society but rather a sedentary agrarian community that was part of the Ottoman Empire. As Shafir indicates, the settlement pattern of the Palestinians made them vulnerable to outside penetration. Concentrated primarily in the hilly regions, they had only started expanding into the coastal zones and inland valleys a generation or two before the onset of Jewish immigration. These areas were already inhabited, and their populations opposed the Jewish settlement.[29]

Jewish settlers aimed to, as historian and prominent scholar in the field of settler colonialism Lorenzo Veracini has argued, delegitimate the Indigenous population by asserting their inauthenticity. From a Zionist perspective, Palestinians could never be accorded the status of one of the "first nations" that inhabited the land.[30] The Zionist settlers' project can thus be described as one of surpassing the native population in terms of authenticity and legitimacy.[31] Settlers sought the replacement of Indigenous Palestinians in several ways: superseding Palestinian farmers in cultivating the land and ridiculing their cultivation techniques, replacing the Arab geographic imagination with a Hebrew map, and claiming to be more native than native Palestinians. Palestinian sociologist Areej Sabbagh-Khoury, in her study on Zionist settlements in Mandate Palestine, demonstrates how interactions between settlers and Palestinian cultivators led to a lasting structural change, with settlers replacing the farmers. This process of supersession did not always progress unhindered. She highlights, for example, the contingency of settler colonial practices, noting that the resistance of Palestinian farmers (fellahin) sometimes slowed down the eliminatory aspect of settler colonialism.[32] Supersession could also mean reducing the Indigenous presence in favor of the exogenous settlement and replacing the former's geography with that of the latter. In the wake of the 1948 war, for instance, Palestinian place-names were effaced and replaced with Hebrew toponymy.[33] The efforts of Hebrew writers who operated from both within and outside Zionist institutions to replace the Palestinian presence on the land by hebraizing the land's map must be understood in the context of a project of replacing the existing natives with settlers who claimed to be the prototype native who, based on religious texts, had inhabited the land of Palestine a long time ago.

Recognizing settler colonialism's enduring nature—its temporal quality—offers a valuable lens through which to examine the proliferation of Hebrew

Orientalism. This long-term perspective allows for a comprehensive evaluation of how Hebrew writers utilized their understanding of Arabic and Islamic culture over time, particularly as the Zionist project progressed in Palestine. By focusing on the evolving relationship between these writers and the local culture, insights can be gained into the changing dynamics of cultural integration and appropriation within the broader context of the Zionists' ongoing settlement activities.

In indigenizing themselves, European Jewish settlers mimicked the lifestyle of the native Palestinian population to emulate their biblical ancestors who had lived and toiled on this land millennia ago. Consequently, the categories of settler and native are not only socially constructed but also strongly contested in the Israeli-Palestinian context. In both the construction of Jewish settlers' indigeneity and the contestation of that of Palestinian Arabs, the Hebrew writers explored in this book resorted to Arabic and Islamic sources in seeking textual evidence to recuperate their nativity. For example, Hebrew writers disseminated narratives drawn from Arabic culture in which the Jewish presence is attested to, as in their Hebrew-language versions of *The Arabian Nights* and Arabic proverbs. Concurrently, Hebrew writers investigated the origins of the Palestinian Arabs, and produced narratives that sometimes indicated the commonalities between both people, and at times contested the indigeneity of the Palestinian Arabs, who for their part, vehemently opposed Zionist claims to the land and asserted their precedence as inhabitants.

This book investigates the positionality of Hebrew writers in the settler colonial context along three axes. The first is these writers' contribution to the indigenization of the settlers—that is, their project of turning European Jewish settlers into "natives." The survivability of Jewish settlers in Palestine was contingent on instrumentalizing Arab culture and at the same time avoiding complete assimilation into it. Second, these writers promulgated histories and institutions that led to land possession for Jewish settlers coupled with the dispossession of the native population, in the erasure of the native presence on the land and the marginalization of their presence by replacing Arab place-names with Hebrew ones. And finally, these writers exploited the Arabic language to advance the revival of Hebrew. Understanding the positionality of Hebrew writers necessitates turning to Palestinian narratives that interacted with the Zionist movement as a settler colonial enterprise and reflect the experience of the Palestinian people. The interrogation of the positionality of Hebrew writers against the history and experience of the Palestinian people gives a voice to Palestinians, and as such, provides "a writing and a righting of Palestinian history through purposely elevating Palestinian indigenous experiences and narrative."[34]

The examination of Hebrew writers' positionality within the settler colonial context allows us to explore how Arabo-Islamic knowledge became a crucial instrument for advancing various dimensions of their efforts. First, in the discourse on *yedi'at ha-arets* (knowledge of the land), Jewish intellectuals harnessed Arabo-Islamic insights to strengthen the ties between Jewish settlers and the Palestinian landscape. Next, the Hebrew Bible served as a foundational text for constructing a national identity, with Hebrew writers integrating Arabo-Islamic interpretative traditions to align Jewish heritage with Zionist ideologies. Additionally, the concept of the New Jew emerged as a redefinition of Jewish identity, drawing from Arabo-Islamic cultural elements to connect modern aspirations with ancestral roots. Finally, the utilization of Arabic, termed *sefat ha-arets* (language of the land), highlights how Hebrew writers saw Arabic not only as a means to reconnect with the land but as a vital resource for reviving the Hebrew language too. These dimensions collectively illustrate the pivotal role that Arabo-Islamic knowledge played in the Hebrew scholars' strategies to establish and legitimize a Jewish presence in Palestine, while simultaneously shaping the cultural and political dynamics of the settler colonial project.

The broader settler colonial endeavor in late Ottoman Palestine was marked by a complex interplay of cultural adaptation and self-indigenization, driven by both national and colonial impulses. This duality is evident in the settlers' pursuit of Jewish national aspirations on a land they believed belonged to their ancestors based on biblical narratives. Yet this self-indigenization process also carried a colonial dimension, involving the marginalization and dispossession of the Indigenous Palestinian population. This colonial aspect has continued to manifest in the Israeli government's expansionist policies in the West Bank, Gaza, and southern Syria. These policies jeopardize not only the fulfillment of justice for the Palestinian people, but more dangerously the acceptance of Israel in the Middle East, despite earlier efforts at the construction of Jewish indigeneity. And these policies contradict the early settlers' hopes for self-indigenization, as they perpetuate a system of occupation and dispossession that undermines the very foundation of a just and equitable society—a society where both Jews and Palestinians can live as equals as well as exercise their right to self-determination.

The book is divided into two parts. Part I traces the evolution and appropriation of Arabo-Islamic knowledge in late Ottoman Palestine, while part II addresses similar issues in British Palestine. Although the book progresses chronologically from the late Ottoman period to the establishment of the state of Israel, the chapters are not rigorously chronological as they treat various central themes (knowledge of Palestine's landscape, the Hebrew Bible, the New Jew, the Palestinian Arab, and Arabic language and literature) with which Hebrew writers of different periods interacted. The chapters of part I look at discussions of people, land, and language in the Ottoman era. Chapter 1 delves into the complex dynamics between Jewish settlers and Palestinian Arabs in both rural and urban settings during the late Ottoman period. Chapter 2 explores the interconnectedness between human identity and the natural landscape, particularly in the context of the Zionist imagination of Palestine. Chapter 3 focuses on the role of Arabic language and literature in the revival of modern Hebrew along with the construction of Jewish indigeneity in Palestine. Part II revolves around the construction of a national home in Mandate Palestine. Chapter 4 turns to the emergence of polemical discourses surrounding landownership based on a reliance on Arabo-Islamic sources to strengthen Zionist objectives. Chapter 5 examines how Hebrew writers studied Arabic folkloric literature based on their translation of works like Arabic proverbs and the *Nights* to gain insights into Arab culture as well as aid in the creation of a Jewish homeland in Palestine, enriching Hebrew with Arabic language and customs.

This book is based on evidence drawn from primary sources published in the late Ottoman period through British Palestine and during the first decade of Israel as well as the work of contemporary scholars in this field. The primary sources are mainly published Hebrew textual materials from various books and journal articles pertaining to the geographic and botanical world of Palestine. Some of these textual materials treat topics within Arabic literature such as pre-Islamic Arabic poetry, medieval, premodern and modern Arabic proverbs as well as topics within Islamic urban history. Some of these works are original publications whereas others are Hebrew translations of Arabic texts such as the *Nights*.

PART I

Shared Homeland: Late Ottoman Palestine, 1882–1917

AT THE CENTER OF OUR look at the ways in which Arabo-Islamic knowledge was instrumentalized to both realize and advance the Zionist enterprise stands the relations between Jewish scholars and Ottoman and British rules in Palestine. Assessing the relations between these scholars and the Ottoman and British governments helps us address the contextual pressures, political projects, and intra-Zionist debates these figures are engaging in. The complex relationship between Zionism and empire, as Israeli sociologist Yehudah Shenhav has shown, moved between fruitful cooperation, on the one hand, and rejection, on the other, while trying to maintain the portrayal of Zionism as an anti-imperial movement.[1] These paradoxical relationships are exemplified in the ways Jewish figures related to the Ottoman and British rules in Palestine.

As a former Ottoman citizen, David Yellin's invocation in British Palestine of his past membership in Majlis 'Umūmī (Provincial Council) in Jerusalem—which is highlighted in the book's introduction—indicates his involvement in the Ottoman imperial system and testifies to his cooperation with the Ottoman authorities through the participation of the parliamentary elections of 1908.[2] Still, he was not above circumventing the Ottoman land laws to help Jewish settlers purchase plots of land to found Jewish colonies. While Ottoman laws prohibited the acquisition of lands by Jewish settlers, Yellin took advantage of his Ottoman citizenship privileges to do so, calling into question his loyalty to the Ottoman regime, and thus to his Arab fellow citizens who objected to land sale to Zionists and demanded the Ottoman authorities put an end to it.[3]

Yellin's celebration of the Balfour Declaration and exchanges with the secretary of the Mandate government speak to his collaboration with the British Empire in Palestine. Meanwhile, other Sephardi and Oriental Jews, while supporting the declaration, were attentive and sensitive to the Palestinians' opposition to it.[4] Many Muslims and Christians who had grown up in the late Ottoman environment regarded the post-Ottoman order and colonial period as, in Middle East historian Michael Provence's words, "inferior, less free, and less representative than what had come before."[5] Isaac Yahuda (1863–1941), a Jewish former Ottoman citizen as well as a Jerusalemite writer and manuscript and book trader, voiced his concerns about British colonial rule as divisive, sowing discord and hostilities between the three large constituent communities of Muslims, Christians, and Jews. With the shift in power, according to his reading of the intercommunal relations in British Palestine, Christians felt uplifted, believing in the beginning of a favorable era for them, Muslims saw it as an opportunity for retribution against other groups for past grievances, and Jews demonstrated restraint and a desire for cohabitation with other groups. Consequently, divisiveness resulted from the differing reactions and expectations each religious community had following the British takeover of Palestine in 1917. While initial Christian sentiments may have exacerbated tensions with Muslims, in Yahuda's assessment, the Jews' measured approach helped foster some unity between them and the Arabs. The Christians, however, eventually realized that these dynamics had widened the gap between them and other groups, potentially paving the way for a closer relationship between Muslims and Jews, which they had not anticipated. Yahuda had hoped that the leaders of the Zionist movement would join forces with Muslims in Palestine to stand against the British government's colonial policy of "divide and rule."[6] Jerusalemite Christian author Wāṣif Jawhariyyeh recounts in his diaries a similar critique of the ways the British colonial policy negatively impacted intercommunal relations between Jerusalem residents of Abrahamic religions.[7]

The Ecumenical Frame

The imperial Ottoman proclamation of nondiscrimination between Muslims and non-Muslims in 1839, the official announcement of equal citizenship among the empire's subjects irrespective of religious identity, and promulgation of the Ottoman Constitution of 1876 all marked the transition to a new political system that would absorb the multireligious, multiethnic, and multilinguistic landscape of the vast Ottoman Empire into what Campos describes as "civic Ottomanism."[8] This new era witnessed the participation of ethnically, religiously, and linguistically diverse intellectuals (Muslims, Christians, and Jews) in what historian Ussama Makdisi identifies as the "ecumenical frame." Within this frame, individuals from various confessional groups retain their religious affiliation and religious identity, while simultaneously searching for ways to overcome religious differences and denounce religious extremism.[9]

The relevance of religion in defining the relations between Muslim and non-Muslim communities in the late Ottoman era delineated, to a noticeable extent, the relations between Zionist intellectuals and Arab elites in Palestine. In his study on the relationship between Zionist writers and Arabs in late Ottoman Palestine, historian Jonathan Gribetz indicates that the two sides did not view each other as competing nations with opposing political agendas. Rather, they saw themselves as citizens of a larger nation, the Ottoman nation, in which they represented different religious categories.[10] Through the ecumenical frame, these distinct and separate religious communities come together to compose a mosaic of the Ottoman nation as a whole.[11] Jewish communities, including Sephardi and Oriental as well as Ashkenazi Jews, enjoyed religious and civil autonomy in return for their political subordination to the Ottoman Empire.[12]

Coexistence in the Ottoman Empire since the mid-nineteenth century was predicated, as Makdisi further explains, "on the deep formal inequality within *every* community of the empire and, of course, on the Muslim-dominated spaces of most cities in the empire."[13] Coexistence then was a given, a reality, and hence there was no need to celebrate it. It informed the everyday lives of most of the empire's subjects and was evident in the urban geography of most major cities, where churches, mosques, and synagogues stood in proximity to one another.[14] This multivalent atmosphere is evident in the diaries of Wāṣif Jawhariyyeh, an Orthodox Christian Arab who attested to the religious and cultural pluralism in late Ottoman Jerusalem.[15]

One of the chief tensions within the ecumenical frame is the central tenet of the superiority of Islam over Christianity and Judaism.[16] As Provence explains, while the nineteenth-century European state "fostered a range of public rituals, origin stories, and invented traditions intended to cement loyalty, allegiance, and compliance with the state . . . these [public rituals and traditions] in the Ottoman state centered around Islam and the person and the office of the Sultan-Caliph."[17] *Nahdawi* (a progenitor of Arab cultural renaissance) Arab Muslim thinkers who supported ecumenism nonetheless endorsed this principle of the superiority of Islam. Likewise, thinkers, reformers, and communal leaders such as Muḥammad 'Abduh, Rashīd Riḍa, and Shakīb Arslān simultaneously accepted and promulgated a pluralist *Umma 'Uthmaniyya* (Ottoman nation) defined by the constitutional equality of its citizens regardless of their religious affiliation, and emphasized the "assumption that the essential sovereign core of this nation had to remain Muslim."[18] Writing about the Islamic character of Egypt and the Ottoman nation as opposed to Christian Europe, lawyer and nationalist Muṣṭafa Kāmil stressed that non-Muslim subjects were well treated, and in return, recognized their place and were content with it. Regarding Christian subjects of the empire, he writes, "If the European states were just to an extent, they would recognize the manifest truth which indicates that Christians are no less than

Muslims with regard to how well they are treated, if they were not treated even better." Then Kāmil turns to Jews, underlining their loyalty to the modernizing Egyptian and Ottoman states as a testament to their nondiscriminatory treatment by the authorities: "There are the Jews. They neither rebel nor complain. Rather, they praise the state day and night, in prosperity and adversity. At all times, they hymn the praise of the state and her good protection." He then invokes the Armenian case, and accuses Armenians of allowing European powers to manipulate and use them against the Ottoman state. In Kāmil's view, Jews receive protection and good treatment in return for their recognition of Muslim sovereignty along with their refusal to make themselves pawns in the hands of European powers. In his words, "That is because there is no state among the European states that claims to protect Jews and work for their benefits. Therefore, [Jews] are not an instrument within the state against her. They know deep within themselves that they are Ottoman citizens who enjoy all the Ottoman rights."[19]

Thus Arab Muslims, Christians, and Jews participated in the articulation of the ecumenical frame. The participation of Ashkenazi Jewish writers who denounced their foreign citizenship in exchange for becoming Ottoman citizens and were at the same time supporters of the Zionist idea merits special consideration. These ethnically diverse Jewish individuals recognized that they lived in a predominantly Arab and Islamic environment, and processed this fact either politically or intellectually. I suggest, then, the extension of the ecumenical frame as an antisectarian and anticonfessional framework to assess the coexistence among Jews, whether Ashkenazi or Sephardi Jews, and Arabs, whether Muslim or Christian. The application of this frame opens before us other possibilities of political imagination forged by both sides in their interactions. It also allows us to look for the bases on which this multiethnic and multireligious frame took shape. In this ecumenical age, Hebrew writers and intellectuals grappled with issues that reflect living in a shared national homeland that resembled the similar preoccupations of nahdawi Arab intellectuals. Chief among these subjects was Semitism and Arabic language. Even though Jewish writers perceived late Ottoman Palestine as a shared homeland under the Ottoman sovereignty, their writings embodied Orientalist ideas that patronized local Arab populations (peasants were backward, Bedouins were part of the natural landscape, and Arab elites were motivated by self-interest and greed. They embraced European values, appreciated European modernity and demoted tradition, and amplified the notion of Jewish indigeneity in Palestine. The following chapters include depictions of real human relationships between Jews and Arabs in late Ottoman Palestine. These accounts, however, contain a substantial amount of Orientalist fantasy too—even among native-born Sephardim—about what "coexistence" would or should look like. This occurs particularly in the context of the emergence of Jewish political claims on land, especially rural land, in late Ottoman Palestine.

Semitism in al-Mashriq

No less than religion, the concept of race played a significant role in the texts of Hebrew scholars from the late nineteenth to early twentieth centuries. Their discussion of Semitism paralleled a similar scholarly discourse among nahdawi Arab intellectuals. In response to the creation of "Semites" as a racial category by Western historians and biblical scholars, both Jewish and Arab intellectuals adopted this category to fulfill certain self-serving objectives. In their embrace of Semitism, both Hebrew and Arab writers, as scholar Yoni Furas has shown, sought self-redemption from the inferior status that the West imposed on them with the help of a racial category that was primarily developed in opposition to the conceptualization of an Aryan race.[20] In rejection of this externally imposed inferiority, Hebrew and Arab intellectuals inverted Semitism as a racial category, turning it into a source of pride by defining the Semitic nation as the birthplace of human civilization, subsequently bestowed on Europeans.[21]

The adoption of Semitism by scholars such as Buṭrus al-Bustānī, Jurjī Zaydān, and Shāhīn Makāryūs, and Palestinian Hebrew writers like David Yellin, Isaac Yahuda, and Abraham Shalom Yahuda, and Jewish writers of Arabic such as Murād Farag in Egypt as well as Eastern European writers like Moshe Leib Lilienblum, Moshe Eismann, and Rabbi Binyamin testifies to the fact that Semitism was not only a local concern that triggered the attention of Hebrew intellectuals in Palestine but also was alive in the discussions of other scholars in the region and beyond.[22] Nor was Semitism an exclusive racial category that included either Jews or Arabs.[23] These writers' conscious use of Semitism as a racial category that comprised the children of Shem, according to the table of nations in Genesis 10, reflects their understanding that the category included both Jews and Arabs. The idea of Semitism explicitly controverted nineteenth-century French philologist and Orientalist Ernest Renan's theory of Aryan racial superiority over an inferior Semite race that included Jews and Muslims.[24]

Within the boundaries of the ecumenical frame, the Hebrew discourse on Semitism, while it chastised manifestations of European anti-Semitism, and perceived it as a phenomenon that targeted both Jews and Arabs, discerned negative representations of Jews in Arabic texts in the Middle East at the time, largely as manifestations of foreign views that penetrated Arabic thought and contradicted the core principles of Arabo-Islamic culture.[25] For their part, Arab nahda intellectuals in the Levant were not idle before the penetration of these negative Jewish portrayals. Instances of the circulation of anti-Semitic views among Arab readers in the late Ottoman era, as historian Orit Bashkin has explained, were condemned by Arab intellectuals who refuted these depictions along with the adoption of conspiratorial theories against Jews as something that undermined and ran counter to the spirit of nahda.[26] A relevant case in point with regard to

Palestine, as Emanuel Beška observes, is the condemnation of the ritual murder accusations against Jews in Ukraine by editor in chief Yūsuf al-ʿIsa, who in 1913 ran the unambiguously anti-Zionist newspaper *Filasṭīn* (Palestine), and yet defended Jews and Judaism against this slander.[27]

Arabic and the Bible

Hebrew intellectuals emphasized the role of language in the rejuvenation of the Jewish nation in late Ottoman Palestine. Studies have shown the efforts of Sephardi and Oriental as well as Ashkenazi Jewish thinkers regarding the use of Hebrew as a spoken language along with its vital role in connecting the Jewish people and Palestine, a land that they considered their ancestral homeland.[28] Endeavors to renew Hebrew and adapt it to fulfill the needs of modernity were in tandem with the efforts of nahdawi Arab intellectuals to reinvigorate Arabic.[29] In a multireligious community such as that of the Ottoman Empire, religion played a significant role in building self-realization as well as defining the relations between one religious community and another. Hebrew scholars such as Eliezer Ben-Yehuda and Yellin attributed great significance to the Hebrew Bible as a legitimate source for the revival of modern Hebrew, just as nahdawi Muslim, Christian, and Jewish Arab intellectuals promoted and recognized the Quran and Bible, respectively, as legitimate sources for the renewal of modern standard Arabic *fuṣḥa*. Buṭrus al-Bustānī's lexicographical enterprise *Muḥīt al-muḥīt* (1869) aspired "to strengthen, improve, and preserve" knowledge of Arabic language.[30] Additionally, it aimed, as scholar Rana Issa has shown, at the articulation of the biblical origins of key Arabic words and simultaneously put forward a narrative about the biblical origins of the Arab civilization. Issa demonstrates that al-Bustānī did so by using etymology to decenter the Arabo-Islamic myth of the origins of Arabic from the narrative of the land of the Bible in the Levant. He also uses biblical terms in rewriting older lexical definitions and invents new terms. Finally, he defocuses the Arabo-Islamic identity that considered the Arabian Peninsula as the *terra prima* of Arabo-Islamic civilization by stressing a Syro/Christian-Arab composite.[31]

1

Ambivalent Encounters

JEWS AND ARABS IN LATE OTTOMAN PALESTINE

FROM THE BEGINNING, encounters between Jewish settlers and Palestinian Arabs in rural settings were characterized by ambivalence. On the one hand, Jewish settlers viewed the Arabs with admiration for "their valor, hospitality, and attachment to the land," as noted in Moses Smilansky's novel *Ḥawaja Nazar* (1912)—traits that Jews would emulate in their effort to re-create the lives of the Israelite patriarchs.[1] On the other hand, and at the same time, they viewed village-dwelling Arabs as backward, and their villages "themselves . . . 'folded back' upon themselves, frozen in time and space . . . densely populated and spatially underdeveloped."[2] Bilu members, who spearheaded the first wave of Jewish immigration to late Ottoman Palestine, had a clear objective, articulated in their manifesto:

> What we want: (1) A Home in our country. It was given to us by the mercy of God, it is ours as registered in the archives of history. (2) To beget it of the Sultan himself, (3) and if it be impossible to obtain this, to beg that at least we may be allowed to possess it as a state within a larger state; the internal administration to be ours, to have our civil and political rights, and to act within the Turkish Empire only in foreign affairs, so as to help our brother Ishmael in his time of need.[3]

The creation of this Jewish state grew from the grassroots up. On settling in Palestine, these immigrants acquired land and worked as farmers on European-style agricultural Jewish settlements, or *moshavoth*. Within these agricultural communities, they employed Palestinian farmers, thereby creating a hierarchical socioeconomic and cultural framework in which Jewish landowners assumed a superior position, while the Palestinian Arab farmers were relegated to an inferior status, receiving lower wages than their Jewish counterparts.[4] This dynamic exemplified the unequal power dynamics and economic disparities within the colonial context of European Jewish settlement in Palestine.

In 1881, following the assassination of Czar Alexander II, violent anti-Jewish riots erupted across the southern and western regions of the Russian Empire, lasting until 1884. Amid this turmoil, several Jewish families, some with financial resources, relocated to Palestine. Before embarking on their journey, they sought guidance from Yehiel Michael Pines (1843–1913)—a Russian-born rabbi, writer, and ardent supporter of Jewish nationalism through settlement in Palestine and who settled in Jerusalem in the nineteenth century—on the best way to create a new settlement in Palestine.[5] In his response, Pines advised them on how they should treat Arabs as they establish themselves in the land:

> Across the Jordan River to the Sea, there are no raiders. The farmers there are content and peaceful, submissive, and accepting mastership from those who know how to impose it upon them [in what is right] with length, weight, and capacity. Therefore, guarding against robbery depends solely on the Jewish settlers knowing how to behave towards their neighbors to instill in them respect and fear of punishment, and how to behave among themselves so as not to be contemptible in their neighbors' eyes.... The government of the land cares only about the existence of harmony and it will not pay attention to anything else.[6]

Pines thus advises Jewish settlers to behave in a way that is both respectful and respectable toward their Palestinian neighbors. Understanding how to exert control and authority in a just manner, they will ensure that the Palestinians perceive them as authoritative and formidable figures. By doing so, the settlers can instill a fear of consequences in their neighbors, thereby reducing the likelihood of theft or aggression. At the same time, Pines underlines the superiority inherent in calling the Palestinian farmers "submissive and accepting mastership" as well as the notion of instilling "fear of punishment," all of which is said from the perspective of the presumptive master.

Encounters between Jewish settlers and the Palestinian Arab population in the late nineteenth century took place primarily in rural areas due to the involvement of early Jewish settlers in farming, and were characterized by ambivalence toward Arab farmers.[7] In the colonies associated with the First Aliyah, the initial wave of Jewish immigration to the country (1881–1904), a system of "hierarchical coexistence" emerged in which the Arab workers provided services and cheap manual labor for Jewish settler-landlords.[8] The earlier Jewish settlers received agricultural training and learned various tasks from Palestinian Arabs, reflecting an initial phase of cooperation. Jewish settlers at first lived in Arab caravansaries or large houses, as in the case of Bilu members, purchased essentials (such as vegetables, milk, and eggs) from neighboring Palestinian villages, and sold some of their produce (especially oranges) to Arab merchants. Palestinian labor played a significant role, as Arabs, Bedouins, Maghrebis, and

Circassians served as guards and workers for Jewish settlements. In some cases, Jewish settlers were unable to fully cultivate their new land and continued to lease parts of it back to previous Palestinian cultivators, maintaining a degree of economic interdependence.[9] Members of the First Aliyah typically viewed cooperation with Palestinian peasants as a practical necessity. This pragmatic approach was critiqued, however, by the more ideologically driven Second Aliyah Jewish settlers (second wave of Jewish immigration to Palestine between 1904 and 1914), who saw it as an undesirable dependency that contradicted their vision of Jewish labor and self-sufficiency. Bilu member Israel Belḳind (1861–1929) built an agricultural school called Ḳiryat Sefer in 1907 with the ethos of fostering direct Jewish connection to the land through farming, as he sought to train Jewish orphans from the Kishinev pogroms to become skilled farmers. Yet Belḳind's project faltered due to financial constraints, leading to the closure of the school in 1909. The critique from the Hebrew newspaper *Ha-Po'el Ha-Tza'ir* blamed the failure of Ḳiryat Sefer on Belḳind's willingness to work with Arabs. It was asserted that by leasing part of the Ben Shemen estate to a wealthy Arab and hiring Arab farmers to work the land, Belḳind had strayed from the ideal of independent Jewish labor and maintained the type of dependence that the Second Aliyah settlers sought to eliminate.[10] This situation epitomized the ideological divide between different waves of Jewish settlers: whereas the First Aliyah settlers were sometimes pragmatic in their relations with Arabs due to practical considerations, the Second Aliyah envisaged a new social order based on Jewish agricultural labor and the building of a self-sustaining Jewish economy in Palestine.

Notwithstanding Jewish settlers' economic dependence on local labor, Arab agricultural techniques provoked ridicule, which was expressed in contemptuous and dismissive language in the settlers' writings. In the settlers' view, the Arab farmers' relationship with the land was one of primitive subjugation to the land as opposed to the domination of it. Dominating the land required such interventions as intensifying the production of crops using fertilizers or altering the traditional cycle of planting crops. A settler from Rishon Le-Zion summarizes this worldview as follows:

> We looked down upon the Arabs, saying that they would not teach us but rather we would teach them. These primitives would see what a European could do in this forsaken land using proficient tools and rational farming methods. However, the catch was that we ourselves only knew from hearsay about European farming.[11]

Thus given the limitations of their own agricultural expertise and despite their negative perception of Arab agricultural techniques, Jews reluctantly drew on traditional agricultural knowledge possessed by the local population, and in some cases, even "hired local peasants as agricultural instructors." Consequently, Jewish settlers ultimately adopted various "traditional local agricultural practices and crops."[12]

This duality in relating to Palestinian Arabs emanates from the polarity characteristic of Zionism as a movement that comprises features of both nationalism and settler colonialism in combining "the image of . . . the powerless with the powerful, the victim with the victimizer, the colonizer with the colonized," to which I add the Orientalized with the Orientalizer.[13] The unique aspect of the Orientalist approach taken by Hebrew writers in late Ottoman and British Palestine lies in the way they balanced their sense of national allegiance with their portrayal of Palestinian Arabs.[14] These writers managed to depict the Palestinian Arabs as both competitors and individuals with an innate connection to the land, captured by the Hebrew phrase *ʿam ha-arets* (people of the land), which Hebrew authors used often to describe the local Arab populace.

Sociologist Aziza Khazzoom claims that early Zionists' Orientalization of others derived from their own experience of stigmatization and trauma in Europe. The internalization of this stigma and will to self-modernize compelled them to Orientalize as well as "other" the weaker group in their environment. Khazzoom notes a pernicious hierarchy of stigmatization: Jewish immigrants of eastern European origins, themselves Orientalized by their Western European coreligionists, Orientalize Sephardi and Oriental Jews, who in turn Orientalize the native Palestinian population.[15]

This chapter investigates Hebrew writers whose interactions with the local Palestinian population were imbued with Orientalist views. These views found expression in several ways. First, these writers assumed and asserted Jewish superiority over Arabs racially, religiously, and/or culturally. Second, they promulgated the theory of benefits—that Jewish immigration would benefit Palestine by civilizing its population and modernizing its land. Third, they categorized Palestinian Arabs variously according to their religious identity, social status, or geographic location, imposing a set of reductive stereotypes and narratives on the Indigenous people who erased the complexities of the natives' own cultures, histories, and perspectives. Fourth, Hebrew writers acknowledged the right of individual Palestinian Arabs to live on the land, but denied them a collective national identity. Fifth, they either silenced the voices of native Palestinian intellectuals and politicians who opposed the increase of Jewish immigration and the sale of lands to Jews, or demonized them by portraying them as exploitative and manipulative individuals who took advantage of the rural population to build their social prestige, accumulate wealth, and increase their political power. And finally, these writers undermined Palestinians' sense of national identity by claiming discontinuity with ancient and medieval Arab culture.

Jewish Views on the Origins of Palestinian Arabs

As will be discussed in chapter 2, the Jewish immigration to and settlement in Palestine was accompanied by efforts to interpret the physical landscape according to biblical and postbiblical sources. But the human landscape of Palestine was equally scrutinized by Jewish settlers. Menashe Meirovitch and Israel Belḳind, members of the Bilu agricultural movement of Russian Jews, demonstrated how settler Jews perceived as well as appropriated the Palestinian Arab in their cultural enterprise.

The Biluim who sought to establish a Jewish presence in late Ottoman Palestine subscribed to the image of Arabs derived from the Bible. In their manifesto, issued from Constantinople en route to Palestine, the Biluim identify Arabs, holistically, irrespective of their lifestyle and geographic locations, as the descendants of Ishmael.[16] The use of the term "our brother Ishmael" aims to foster a sense of kinship and shared ancestry between Jews and Arabs, despite their distinct national and religious identities. It attempts to contextualize the Zionist desire for a homeland in a way that acknowledges the presence of the Arab population already living in the region. This familial affinity is attested to by late Ottoman Palestinian intellectuals. In his letter to the founder of political Zionism Theodor Herzl (1860–1904), prominent Palestinian politician Yusūf Ḍiya al-Dīn al-Khālidī (1842–1906) stressed that Jews were "our cousins" with a reference to Abraham as the father of both nations.[17] While it shows affinity with Palestinian Arabs, this ascribed genealogy reveals how the Bilu members perceived themselves as inherently superior to Palestinian Arabs. The depiction of the Arab inhabitants as the progeny of Ishmael while Jews claim descent from Isaac invokes the biblical image of Ishmael as a marginalized figure.[18] The son of the maid Hagar "is not the son of the covenant." As scholar of religions Carol Bakhos explains, "He is part of the family, yet he is excluded. His presence is felt, yet his actions are few. He is spoken about, yet never speaks. God hears his voice, but the reader hears his silence."[19] The invocation of the brotherly connection between the two groups, therefore, by no means renders them equal partners. Furthermore, the sons of Ishmael are depicted as desperate for help that only their "advanced and modern" cousins can provide. This depiction of Arabs as in need of help for which they have not asked conformed in many ways to the colonialist and Orientalist sensibilities of late nineteenth-century European society, as noted by historian Derek Penslar. Zionism contained, Penslar writes, "a powerful *mission civilisatrice* to awaken the Middle East from its narcotized Levantine torpor, to shatter the fossilized soil of the Holy Land with European tools and technology."[20]

Another aspect of Jews' presumed superiority was their adherence to the productivization ethos among Russo-Polish Jewry during the nineteenth century—an ethos "that valued occupational transformation as a vehicle of economic improvement, moral regeneration, and social integration."[21] In their application of this ideology to Palestine, Bilu members believed that they were more capable than the native Palestinian Arab population of extracting profits from land through technology and innovation.

The juxtaposition of the superior eastern European Jew against the imperfect or inferior Arab was propelled by the Bilu members' self-realization as the avant-garde of a national resurrection that should culminate in the foundation of a Jewish state.[22] As laid out succinctly in their manifesto, their political scheme was either to establish an autonomous Jewish state with the permission of the Turkish government or found a state within a state.[23] This process necessitated a cultural learning curve with respect to Arabic and Islamic culture as Bilu members and other Hebrew scholars sought to understand matters pertaining to Arabs and their culture, including fundamental questions such as the origins of the Arab people.

The Jerusalemite Abraham Shalom Yahuda (1877–1951) was an early Jewish theoretician of Arab origins. He won recognition in Zionist circles as a young man for a book titled *Ḳadmoniyot ha-ʿAravim* (The antiquities of the Arabs), which treats the history of Arabs from antiquity up to the rise of Islam, based on historic and literary narratives from pre-Islamic Arabia that were codified by early ninth-century scholars such as Hishām Ibn al-Kalbī (d. 819) in his book *al-Aṣnām* (The idols) and tenth-century scholar Abū al-Faraj al-Iṣfahānī (d. 972) in *Kitāb al-Aghānī* (The book of songs).[24] Yahuda also traces the circulation of Jewish traditions in the works of medieval Arab and Muslim historians and genealogists, such as *Murūj al-Dhahab* (Meadows of gold) by al-Masʿūdī (896–956) and *Ansāb al-Ashrāf* (Genealogies of the notables) by al-Balādhurī (806–92). His own work is based on pre-Islamic Arabic poetry and other sources.

In *Ḳadmoniyot ha-ʿAravim*, whose title might have been inspired by first-century Roman Jewish historian Flavius Josephus's (ca. 37–ca. 100 CE) *Antiquities of the Jews*, Yahuda draws a sophisticated picture of Arab origins, adopting medieval Arab Muslim historians' division of Arabs into two groups: the Arab *bā'ida* (Extinct Arabs), who lived in ancient times and then disappeared, leaving little available information about their origins, and the Arab *Bāqiyya* (Extant Arabs), who comprise two groups mentioned in the Hebrew Bible that were linked through their Semitic origins.[25] The first of these, called the Arab *ʿāriba* (Arabian Arabs), includes the descendants of Joktan, the son of Eber (Genesis 10:25), who inhabited the southern part of the Arabian Peninsula and became associated with the Yemenites as well as those who lived in the northern parts of Ḥijāz and Syria. The second group is known as the Arab *Mustaʿriba* (Arabicized Arabs), associated with the people of the central and eastern parts of Arabia. Members of this division are the descendants of ʿAdnān, one of the children of Abraham's son Ishmael. The difference between the two groups is well

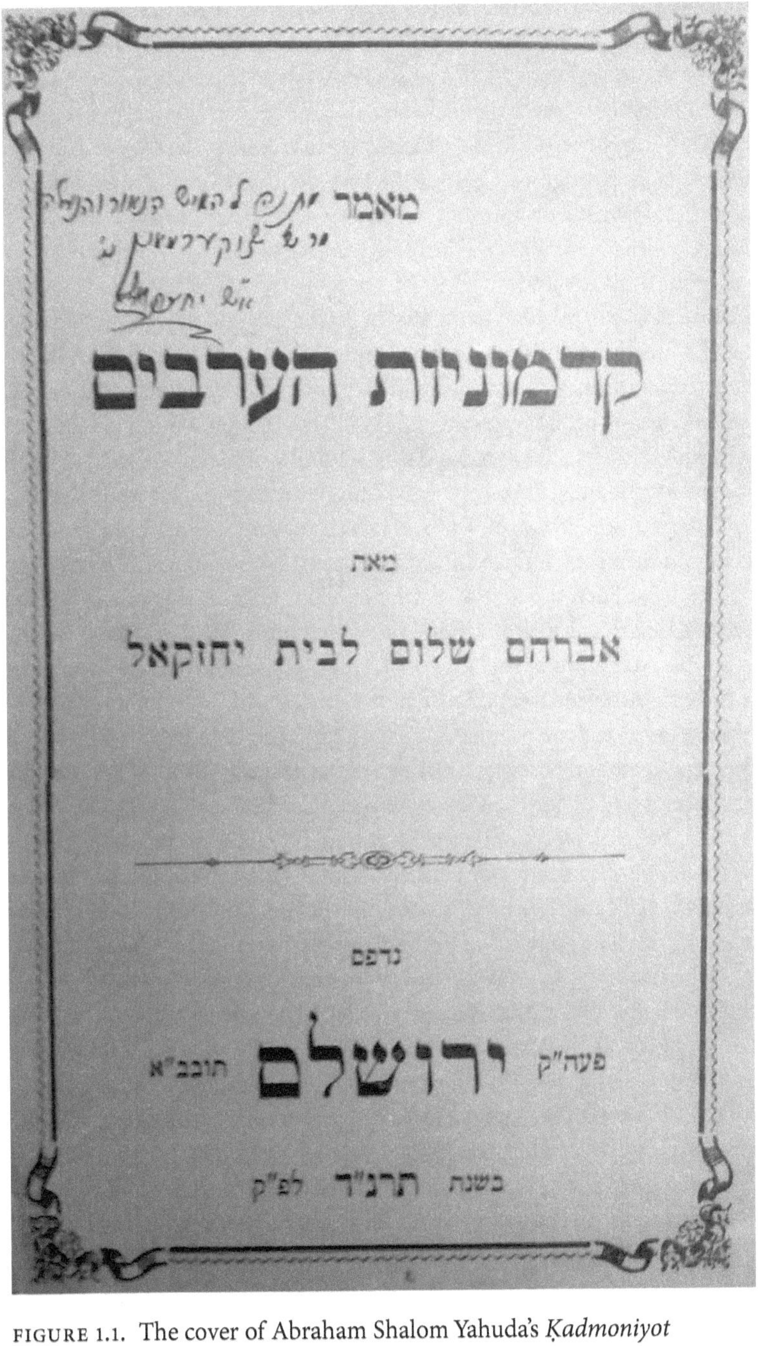

קדמוניות הערבים

מאת

אברהם שלום לבית יחזקאל

נדפס

פעה"ק ירושלם תובב"א

בשנת תרנ"ד לפ"ק

FIGURE 1.1. The cover of Abraham Shalom Yahuda's *Ḳadmoniyot ha-ʿAravim* (The antiquities of the Arabs). The book was published in Jerusalem in 1894.

established in early Arabo-Islamic sources: while the former are considered the "real" or genuine Arabs, the latter are considered newcomers to Arabia.[26] Adopting this division, Yahuda's historical survey leads to the conclusion that unlike the word "Hebrew," which denotes the ancient Israelites as an ethnic entity, the word "Arab" does not stand for an ethnic entity. Nevertheless, Jews and Arabs are connected through the kinship tie between Ishmael and Isaac, and both groups are of Semitic origins.

Hebrew writers emphasized the linkage between Arabs and Ishmael by drawing on both Arabo-Islamic and Jewish sources. The association between Arabs and Ishmael was explicitly highlighted in Arabo-Islamic sources. In the Quran, Ishmael is identified not as an Arab but instead as a son of Abraham, and appears most often in prophetic lists along with Abraham, Isaac, Jacob, and the Israelite tribes, and assists his father, Abraham, in raising the foundation of "the house," which is identified as the Meccan Ka'ba (Quran 2:127). Nowhere in the Quran is Ishmael identified with Arabian tribal communities or genealogy. In the Islamic exegetical tradition, however, Ishmael is transformed into an Arabian prophet: he is buried in Mecca, married a woman from the Yemenite tribe Jurhum, is reported to have been the first man who spoke Arabic, and is portrayed as the father of Arabs. In historical Arabo-Islamic literature, the like of which Yahuda cited in his excavation of the origins of Arabs, Ishmael is often associated with the northern "Arabized Arabs," whereas the tribe of Jurhum is associated with the "Arabian Arabs" or "the original Arabs."[27] Similar to the Quran, in the Hebrew Bible, the connection between Ishmael and the Arabs is not emphasized. Rather, it was developed outside the Hebrew Bible. According to S. D. Goitein, scholar of Jews in the medieval Islamic world, although there is no mention in the Hebrew Bible of Ishmael as the forefather of Arabs, this connection was treated as an established fact in Jewish literature since the Second Commonwealth (ca. 515 BCE–70 CE).[28] The association between Ishmael and Arabs is based on an ethnological Midrash of Genesis 25, in which, according to Israel Eph'al, a link is established between the sons of Ishmael and tribes known as "Arabs" in Assyrian sources.[29] Initially, this established association in the Jewish tradition was espoused by Jewish figures seeking commonalities between Jews and Arabs. Jerusalemite David Yellin, for example, stressed the familial affinity between the two groups, as evidenced in his reference to Arabs as *bene dodenu* (our cousins).[30]

Viewing the Arabs of Palestine through a biblical lens resonated with Eliezer Ben-Yehuda (1858–1922), whose trip to Jerusalem in 1881 constituted his first encounter with the native population.[31] His lack of experience with contemporary Arabs allowed Western accounts as well as biblical and postbiblical representations of the local Arab population to strongly influence his first encounters with actual Arabs. His first meeting with "our cousins Ishmael," as he relates, challenged his perceptions and filled him with *magor*, a word that connotes dread and fear, according to Ben-Yehuda's own definition.[32] This meeting took place aboard a ship on its way to Palestine and clearly left a negative impression on the ambitious young man. At the sight of "tall, strong, and customarily dressed" Arab travelers, growing in numbers as the ship approached the shores of Jaffa, Ben-Yehuda felt himself a stranger in what he regarded as his ancestral land:

> I felt that they considered themselves the citizens of that very land that had been my ancestral land, and I, I the son of these ancestors, came to this land as a stranger, as a foreigner, as the son of a foreign land, a son of foreign people, and I have, in my forefathers' land, neither political nor citizenship rights. I am a foreigner in the land and a stranger!

Encountering a native population that saw themselves as the legitimate inhabitants, the true citizens of the land who were "all cheerful, rejoicing, happy, laughing, and reveling," Ben-Yehuda experienced a profound sense of alienation and displacement. Despite his perceived historical and ancestral connection to the region, he felt himself an outsider. His description reveals a poignant awareness of his lack of political and civic standing in what he imagined as his ancestral homeland; he came to the land of his forebearers and yet was treated as a foreigner *ger*, without official status. His culture shock seems to arise from his having imagined a land devoid of any people or government, just waiting for him and his fellow Jews. He could not easily accept that Arabs were rooted in the very land he believed to be that of his ancestors; he reports that the thought deprived him of sleep some nights.[33]

The sight of "tall, strong, and customarily dressed" Arabs boarding the ship in their expensive and elegant clothes, evoked in Ben-Yehuda feelings of rootlessness and alienation, which he refers to as *nokhri*.[34] In addition to connecting his present-day Arab with Ishmael, Ben-Yehuda associates Arabs with Esau and depicts the meeting with them after a long period of living in the diaspora with feelings of disappointment and despair:

> I was not prepared for this feeling; I did not expect to feel such a thing on meeting Esau, my brother. Suddenly I felt broken, and thoughts of regret began to rise from the depths of my soul: perhaps, in truth, everything I planned to do is futile and worthless; maybe the dream I dreamed about the revival of Israel on the land of our ancestors has no place in reality.[35]

The association of Ishmael and Esau with present-day Palestinian Arabs incited feelings of desperation and sorrow for him, as though, despite their proclaimed kinship, Ishmael and Esau were the cause of Ben-Yehuda's suffering.[36] Although his first meeting with Palestinian Arabs was peaceful, it raised doubts about the implementation of his national project in his "ancestral homeland."[37]

In addition to stressing the familial affinity between Jews and Arabs, evidenced in connecting them with Ishmael and Esau, Jewish figures espoused other theories about the origins of the Palestinian people. Belḳind, for instance, noting the ethnic connection of Palestinian Arabs and Jews, came to the conclusion that the Arab inhabitants of Palestine were descendants of Jews who had converted to Islam to remain in the land after the destruction of the Second Temple in Jerusalem.[38] This theory remained in circulation decades into the poststatehood era to help solve what some Jews perceived as the "mysterious origins" of the Arabs and assimilate them into Israeli society.[39] He supported his theory by observation of the lifestyle of the various segments of the Palestinian Arab population he met in his travels throughout Palestine, learning about their manners and customs through their daily interactions among themselves along with the landscape surrounding them. In late 1893, he embarked on a walking tour that lasted thirty-six days, meeting Bedouins in their tents, and exploring their culture and folklore. He also toured Arab villages, witnessing and documenting aspects of their encounters with the land as well as their views on the Jewish newcomers.[40] Through his interactions, as historian Shmuel Almog has shown, Belḳind formulated perspectives on the origins of Palestine's Arabs and their views of the landscape, and the way Jews should interact with them.[41] Belḳind writes,

> If we look deeper into history, [we] will find the story of the complete exile of the people of Judea from their land does not suit the fact entirely. The Arabs who inhabit our land are not Arabs, but Hebrews, who accepted Islam and the language of the followers of that religion, the Arabic language.[42]

Belḳind supports his theory by claiming that despite the Jewish oppression under Roman rule, Jews continued to live in Judea (southern Palestine as a Roman province) in great numbers according to historical sources until the conquest of Palestine by Muslims. While Belḳind was apparently seeking to highlight the connection between Jews and Arabs, he simultaneously discredits Palestinian Arabs' claims to ethnic purity and identity. If other constructions of the superior Jew versus the inferior Arab were based on connecting the Arab population to Ishmael, the marginalized biblical figure, Belḳind's perspective assigns Arabs to another marginalized category: the convert. These apostate Jews, the supposed forebearers of the Palestinian Arabs according to Belḳind's theory, left the circle of the unique and divinely chosen people to remain on their land. Per Belḳind's theory, they did not belong to the Jewish nation for they were insincere Jews, nor did they belong to the Arab nation for they were clandestine Jews.

What, then, is Belḳind's proposal to deal with Arabs? He proposes neither the assimilation nor Judaization of Jewish converts to Islam and their descendants. Instead, he believed that through education, Jews and Arabs could live in peaceful cooperation with each other. Arabs who converted to Islam to stay in the

FIGURE 1.2. Israel Belḳind's *Erets Yisrael shel zemanenu* (The land of Israel in our time) contains not only a natural description of Palestine but also of its inhabitants. Belḳind here brings an image of an Arab shepherd dressed in the traditional garb and that of a peasant riding the back of a donkey.

land need not give up their culture and language: "God forbid that we damage their religion that is their ancestors' legacy that passed to them from generation to generation." But adherence to their faith and language should not hinder their modernization and development: "We must influence them by means of our culture. Through it we will elevate them so that we can work together to live together.... [T]he path to our culture is through our school which we must open widely before them."[43] Belḳind's statement reflects a Eurocentric view that positions European Jewish culture as being superior to Arab culture—a perspective that was common among some Jewish settlers of the Bilu movement and underscored in their manifesto referenced earlier. The belief that one's own culture can "elevate" another suggests a hierarchy of cultures, with European Jewish culture at a higher level and Arab culture below, needing upliftment or improvement. The idea of influencing the native Arab population "by means of our culture" implies a one-directional imposition of European Jewish cultural values and norms on the Indigenous population that does not recognize the validity or richness of the existing Arab culture, and instead assumes that it requires transformation according to European Jewish standards. The language of "elevating them so that we can work together to live together" echoes the "civilizing mission" rhetoric often used by colonial powers, which justified their domination by claiming they were bringing civilization to the "uncivilized" or "backward" cultures. The assumption here is that interaction and coexistence can only occur on the terms of the more "civilized" European Jewish settlers. Belḳind's educational program, while hopeful and forward-looking, was founded on the belief that Arabs needed cultural elevation to be on the same level as their neighbors, the European Jewish settlers; in other words, it took as its premise Arabs' cultural inferiority. Belḳind's emphasis on schools as the pathway to imparting culture is indicative of a broader strategy where education is used as a tool for cultural assimilation. The notion that schools must be "opened widely before them" bespeaks cultural generosity, but the unidirectional flow of cultural transfer highlights the perceived need for the Arab population to be taught and guided rather than engaged as equals. Belḳind's view can be interpreted as being paternalistic, assuming a position of benevolent authority over and responsibility for the Arab population's cultural advancement that is fundamentally rooted in the superiority complex of the European Jewish settler.

Jewish Insights on Arab Discontent

The first wave of Jewish immigration to Palestine was marked by rivalry and hostility between settlers and Palestinian Arabs across cultural as well as religious classes, but scholars differ as to the reasons underlying these tensions. Scholars have argued that before World War I, Arab hostility toward Jewish settlers in Palestine was primarily motivated by anti-Zionism as opposed to anti-Semitism. The Palestinians distinguished between Jews as a religious/ethnic group that had been living in the country before the emergence of Zionism, and Jewish settlers who followed a political movement seeking to establish a Jewish homeland in Palestine, as evidenced in Yusūf Ḍiya al-Dīn's letter to Herzl from 1899, and the Palestinian deputies Sa'īd al-Ḥusseinī's (1878–1945) and Muḥammad Rūḥī al-Khālidī's (1864–1913) opposition to Zionism in the Ottoman Parliament in 1911.[44] Given that most Palestinians were peasants, their primary concern was with losing their land to the influx of Jewish immigrants due to Zionist activity during the First (1881–1903) and Second Aliyah (1904–14). Palestinian peasants' hostility was rooted in the fear of being dispossessed of their land and becoming a minority in their homeland, rather than based on innate religious or ethnic animosity. The purchase of lands led to the eviction of Palestinian peasants, created clashes with Jewish settlers, and united different strata within Palestinian society, including Bedouins, urban leaders, intellectuals and journalists, and politicians in the Ottoman Parliament, to block Zionist land purchases and the growth of Jewish settlements.[45]

One of the earliest cases of clashes between Palestinian peasants and Jewish settlers is the case of Petaḥ Tiḳva's settlers and al-Yahudiyya's village farmers. In 1886, the establishment of the Jewish settlement of Petaḥ Tiḳva sparked tensions with local Palestinian peasants over competing claims of landownership. The land, which had been purchased from Christian Orthodox merchants by Jewish settlers, was previously tenanted by Arab farmers from nearby villages who claimed legal rights to portions of it due to the imprecise Ottoman land registry system (*tapu*). Conflicts erupted when new Jewish settlers insisted on cultivating fields that Arab farmers expected to plant based on traditional crop rotation rights. This clash over rightful land use and ownership led to an attack by Arab peasants from al-Yahudiyya's village on Petaḥ Tiḳva, culminating in a violent confrontation. The incident was settled by the intervention of Ottoman troops, arrest of many peasants, and death of a Jewish settler. It was covered in a Hebrew newspaper at the time as a dispute over land entitlements rather than outright nationalistic hostility.[46] In 1913, representatives of certain Bedouin tribes aligned themselves with peasants concerned by the growing influence of agricultural Jewish colonies in Jaffa and their effect on the rural population. Representatives from villages in the northern part of the district (*kaza*) of Gaza and the Abū Kishk Bedouin tribe from the nearby subdistrict of Jaffa came together to submit a collective petition. This act indicates an unusual level of coordination and solidarity between the rural villagers and nomadic or semisedentary Bedouin tribes, which typically had different lifestyles and interests, but found common cause in opposing the Jewish colonies. In their petition to the grand vizier, the rural and Bedouin petitioners accused the nearby Jewish colonies of Rishon Le-Zion and Reḥovot of harsh treatment toward the local population. Specifically, they alleged that the colonists attacked travelers, employed aggressive Jewish and foreign guards, and illegally possessed weapons. These grievances underscored the sense of threat felt by the local population in the face of the expansion of the Jewish colonies that was encroaching on their way of life and security.[47]

As reports of incidents and petitions by rural villagers and Bedouin nomads began to resonate within urban centers, a chorus of intellectuals, journalists, and politicians emerged in the press, articulating heightened concerns over the adverse impacts Jewish settlement activities were having on the rural population. This altered the discourse from localized rural resistance into a broader, urban-centered critique, in which anti-Zionist views became increasingly vocal. Scholars have argued that the anti-Jewish sentiments voiced by Palestinian Arabs in urban centers were also nurtured by a fear of the political motives behind Jewish colonists' growing presence in Palestine and their increasing land purchases, especially with the influx of Second Aliyah Jewish settlers, at which point the discourse transitions from anti-Jewish to anti-Zionist. Similarly, political scientist and historian Alan Dowty contends that Arabs were hostile toward Jews in late Ottoman Palestine because they took the aspirations of Jewish settlers and immigrants seriously.[48] In urban areas, Palestinian local elites, including merchants and craftspeople, felt threatened by the economic competition brought with the settlement of Jews in urban communities like Jerusalem and Jaffa.[49] Still, being taken seriously, as Dowty asserts, was far better than the persecution and oppression Jews were fleeing.[50] Historian Neville Mandel maintains that Arabs were also influenced by the imported Christian anti-Semitism during this period that penetrated Muslim Arab circles.[51]

While the growing presence of Jews in Ottoman Palestine elicited fears and hostilities among various rural Palestinians, a nuanced perspective based on conciliatory intellectual engagement was emerging among the Arab intelligentsia that distinguished between anti-Zionism and anti-Semitism. The literary and cultural activities of *al-nahda* in late nineteenth-century Egypt, Syria, and Palestine were led by members of an educated elite who demonstrated an interest in, among other subjects, Jewish culture and history, including the waves of oppression and anti-Semitism Jews were experiencing in Europe.[52] Building on intellectual historian David Nirenberg's insight that writing about Jews is often detached from the presence of Jews in a particular place, Orit Bashkin argues that nahdawi Arab intellectuals' interest in anti-Semitism correlated with discourse on the protection of the rights of ethnic and religious minorities in the Ottoman Empire.[53] This discussion took place within what Ussama Makdisi called, as noted earlier, the "ecumenical frame" of the late Ottoman era in which individuals, while conscious of their religious affiliation, invested in a culture of coexistence that sought to overcome religious differences and denounced religious extremism.[54] Indeed, Makdisi points to "the rich diversity of al-Mashriq that has stubbornly refused repeated attempts to reduce the region to one religious hue."[55]

Transitioning from the nuanced engagement with Jewish culture demonstrated by the Arab intelligentsia, this complex interplay between anti-Zionism and anti-Semitism inevitably influenced the Jewish community's self-perception and response. Local Jewish intellectuals took it on themselves to challenge and address the negative portrayals circulating in the broader Arab society within and outside Palestine. Eliyahu Sapir (1869–1911), a writer from Jerusalem, highlighted the importance of Jews learning Arabic, and leveraging their Arabic linguistic capabilities and direct interactions with Arabs to counteract the diffusion of anti-Jewish tropes derived from European anti-Semitism within nineteenth-century Arabic literature. He dedicated an article to dissecting these representations, emphasizing the necessity for proactive Jewish engagement to understand and address the underlying misconceptions fueling the Arab community's negative views.[56]

Sapir recognized that the spread of negative portrayals among the Palestinian educated elite, which in part emerged as a reaction to the rural population's distress over Jewish immigration and land acquisitions, required vigilant opposition. He thought it was crucial as well as possible to counter these narratives promptly to prevent anti-Semitism from taking deeper root in the region, potentially jeopardizing the peaceful coexistence of mainly Muslim Arabs and Jews in Palestine.[57] Sapir remained convinced of the foreign origin of anti-Semitism and refused to interpret Palestinian Arab opposition to Jewish immigration as manifesting a native anti-Semitism. Even when a group of Arab notables in Palestine stood against Jewish immigration, signing a petition in 1891 to the Sublime Porte to ban Jews from immigrating to Ottoman Palestine, Sapir did not see this as an embodiment of Islamic-based antagonism.[58] Rather, he viewed it as stemming from the influence of Christianity, particularly the Catholic Church.[59] He defended "Muḥammadan [Muslim] Arabs" as "one of the peoples—or the only people—who are close to us and to our hearts. In times we [Jews] lived well. Their love and closeness to us are still possible in the future." Muslim Arabs' tolerance toward Jews, as opposed to that of their Christian counterparts, in his analysis stemmed from the similarities between Jews and Muslims, such as Semitic ties and the valorization of similar moral qualities. These values, in his assessment, led to friendly behavior toward Jews that passed from one generation to another in contradistinction to the inherited anti-Semitism characteristic of Christian culture.[60] Sapir is at pains to rationalize the antipathy toward Jews expressed in certain Muslim literary texts as historically contextualized rather than dogmatic.[61] An example of this is his reading of medieval Muslim historian Ibn Khaldūn's (1332–1406) assessment of Jews in his renowned work *al-Muqaddima* (Introduction). At the outset, Sapir makes a general exculpatory comment about Arab culture as "possess[ing] a pronounced inclination toward critique and skepticism of others. [Arabs] are known for their piercing examination and pointed commentary when they perceive faults, no matter how small or imagined." With this in mind, Sapir highlights Ibn Khaldūn's nuanced understanding of the Jewish experience as both a historical and sociopolitical phenomenon. Ibn Khaldūn considers both internal factors (such as loss of unity) and external factors (including oppression by other groups) as influences on the history and behavior of Jewish communities. Sapir writes,

> The eminent historian Ibn Khaldūn offers a largely positive portrayal of Jews in his seminal work, *al-Muqaddima*. He approaches instances mentioned in the Bible with a critical eye, mirroring the scrutiny of modern biblical scholars. In one place, Ibn Khaldūn commends the Jewish people, holding them up as an exemplar of political acumen and intellectual vibrancy. He attributes the decline of Jewish prominence to a loss of unity, positing that their

> historical greatness waned when they ceased to be bound together by a strong, common force—a central ideal that they will follow out of love and respect. Elsewhere, he discusses the Jewish tendency towards rebelliousness and subterfuge, suggesting it stems from the longstanding pressures and oppressions imposed upon them by non-Jews. This harsh treatment, he hypothesizes, left the Jews in a state of perpetual fear of theft and injustice, leading them to strategies of avoidance and evasion.

Comparing anti-Jewish views in historical Arabic literature such as those expressed by Ibn Khaldūn with what is found in European literature, Sapir observes that "in historical Arabic literature, there is no hatred of Israel at all in the way that we are accustomed to seeing in the literature of European nations. A few mocking words occasionally slip in casually and incidentally, and sometimes infrequently."[62] Hence the level and severity of anti-Jewish sentiment within the historical Arabic literary corpus is significantly less than that which is typically found in European texts. Sapir's contention that Jewish-Muslim relations have historically been less fraught with animosity than the Jewish-Christian relationship in Europe implies that European Jews seeking to settle in Palestine could anticipate a relatively more tolerant environment among the Arab majority compared to their European homelands.

Sapir concludes his comparative discussion on Jewish animosity in Europe and the Middle East with the following:

> In Europe, our efforts to eradicate the deeply rooted hatred against us prove fruitless, as it is ingrained in the psyche of its peoples. Thus, our only recourse to preserve our dignity and maintain our resilience is to detach ourselves from this pervasive "consensus." However, in the regions [the East] I have alluded to, we must actively ensure this pernicious sentiment is not adopted by others. In our ancestral homeland and its adjacent territories, we must assert our value. Our presence and actions there should stand as a vivid repudiation of the defamation and vilification aimed at us. Above all, it is crucial to foster a sense of belonging, to feel truly at home, not as outsiders, engaging fully with the local languages and cultures of these lands.[63]

Sapir was born in Jerusalem as a descendant of a Lithuanian family that had settled in Ottoman Palestine in 1830. In appealing to mostly European Jewish immigrants, Sapir stresses his European connection with them, which is discernible through his use of the collective "our" when referring to experiences in Europe, indicating a shared identity with European Jews despite his Middle Eastern birth and upbringing. Moreover, Sapir's emphasis on "detaching" from the European "consensus" reflects a critical view of European society's norms and an alignment with Zionist ideology, which advocated for a return to the ancestral homeland as a solution to the Jewish plight in Europe. Sapir's use of language suggests he embraces a dual identity that is both rooted in Palestine and connected to the broader Jewish experience in Europe. He uses this standpoint to argue for a proactive and confident Jewish presence in Palestine, contrasting it with the situation in Europe and urging European Jews to establish a new life in a region he views as historically more receptive to Jewish existence. By advocating for a strong and unapologetic Jewish presence in the Middle East, "in our ancestral homeland and its adjacent territories," Sapir is calling for hands-on engagement with the culture and language of the region. This engagement is seen not only as a means of affirming Jews' place in these societies but also as a strategic move to prevent the spread of European anti-Jewish prejudices to their new surroundings.

The juxtaposition of anti-Jewish Arab attitudes with European anti-Semitism is taken up in Ben-Yehuda's writings too, but unlike Sapir, his perspective is characterized by ambivalence and inconclusiveness. While Arabs do not regard Jews as their foes per se, he writes, perhaps because the latter did not constitute a threat, neither do they approach them with amicability or respect. On his arrival in Palestine, he notes,

> There was one thing I felt inside me in the few days following my arrival to the Land of Israel, and that was that Arabs, at least Muslim Arabs, were not enemies of Jews. They hate them less than other non-Muslims whom they hate; however, they despise Jews as though they relate to the lowest and most loathsome creature in the world. They call the Jews *wilād al-mayyit*, that is, the sons of dead, despicable creatures, and the possessors of weak hearts [literarily of *rafot-lev*] who do not have a soul to stand up and defend themselves against Arab youngsters, even the ugliest and the most despicable.[64]

Like Sapir, Ben-Yehuda regards Arabs' hostility toward Jews as less fatal than European anti-Semitism, which killed many thousands of Jews in the Russian Empire and eastern Europe, and led to the influx of Jews to Palestine. Muslim Arabs "despise" Jews, he remarks, yet they do not regard them as their nemesis as was the case in Europe. This animosity, from Ben-Yehuda's perspective, stems from the Muslim Arabs' perception of Jews as possessors of weak character, "the sons of the dead" and "possessors of weak hearts"—attitudes that obviously have little to do with the religious beliefs inciting anti-Semitism in Europe.

Notwithstanding their acknowledgment of animosities, Ben-Yehuda and other early European Jewish immigrants tended to minimize Muslim Arabs' hostility as part of their project to attract other Jews in Europe to immigrate to and settle in Palestine. Yet this attitude could also be the expression on the Jews' part of the same spirit of ecumenicalism that, as we noted earlier, characterized late Ottoman Palestine. Some European Jewish immigrants willingly embraced Ottoman citizenship and its prescription of peaceful coexistence among various religious communities. For example, shortly after his arrival in Palestine, Ben-Yehuda presented himself to the local government office to renounce his foreign citizenship in favor of Ottoman citizenship. Ben-Yehuda's Jewish employer in Jerusalem advised him against taking this action, claiming that life as a non-Muslim citizen of the Ottoman Empire would be worse than being a foreign citizen living under the protection of the capitulations. Ben-Yehuda, however, hoped that the embrace of Ottoman citizenship would cleanse his alien status.[65]

Notwithstanding his efforts to become a good Ottoman citizen, Ben-Yehuda's attitudes toward Arabs reflect the clear influence of European Orientalism; he exhibits a sense of superiority that compensates for Arabs' self-perception as the masters of the land, as Ben-Yehuda noted earlier, and their ascription of inferiority to Jews. If Muslim Arabs regarded Jews as "weak souls" who could not stand up for themselves, it was all the more imperative that Jews controvert such notions by defending themselves and asserting their strength. It is in this rivalrous context that in describing how Muslim Arabs suffered from poverty and lack of education, Ben-Yehuda expresses a sense of satisfaction: "I found some comfort in the overall circumstances of the Arabs in the land of Israel whom I saw, which was in general very inferior, in that they were depleted to a state of poverty and complete ignorance." Ben-Yehuda reached that conclusion a few weeks after he arrived in Jaffa and lived in Jerusalem, and learned about the relations between Jews and Arabs from prominent Jewish figures in the city such as Israel Dov Frumkin (1850–1914), the editor of the Hebrew newspaper *ha-ḥavazelet*.[66] The implication is that although apparently abundant in number, and their confidence, joy, and celebratory demeanor that suggests a strong sense of cultural identity and pride, Muslim Arabs were so weakened by poverty and illiteracy that they did not really constitute a threat. In an article published in 1882 in *ha-ḥavazelet*, Ben-Yehuda articulates in some detail how this weakness, specifically the lack of education, was helpful to the Jews:

> The nation in whose midst we dwell . . . is not an enlightened nation. . . . Here too this country is better for us than any other . . . because we want to revive our nation . . . and how can we succeed in this in a country where . . . there is an enlightened nation? In such a country, when the Jews come, they begin to speak the language of the country. . . . [T]heir sons and daughters go to learn in the schools of the nation and will learn its language and imbibe its culture, because it is an enlightened nation. In such a country the Jews will not be able to be a separate nation in spirit and language even if they want to, because an enlightened nation will not let them do so. . . . This is not the case with a non-enlightened nation. In such a nation we can be in the course of time a *bona fide* nation, because in our hands rests the teaching of our language to our sons and daughters, and no one will speak out against this.[67]

Ben-Yehuda argues that in "enlightened nations," the cultural influence is so strong that Jews, as a minority, adopt the language and culture of the majority, diluting Jewish identity, whereas Jews in Palestine would have the opportunity to maintain their distinctiveness—both linguistically and culturally—because the Palestinian Arab population would not exert the same assimilatory pressures. Thus the inferior status of Arabs would not hinder Ben-Yehuda's fulfillment of his national dream.

Relations with Arab Elites

Warning of the dissemination of anti-Jewish sentiments in nineteenth-century Arabic literature, Sapir reproaches his contemporaneous Jews for their idleness in responding: "The hatred towards Israel is rising in the current Arabic literature, penetrating, and bursting into hearts that are not inherently predisposed to it. And the Jews stand by and remain silent." He reminds his readers that Jews' silence in the face of European anti-Semitism should not be repeated in the East: "We left the lands of Europe with our hands upon our heads, and to the lands of the East, we shall come with our hands upon our mouths. We shall block our ears so as not to hear any disgrace spoken of us, but others will hear and come to know us only as a bane, and to see in us a physical and spiritual danger to the land and its possessions." Sapir's portrayal of Jews leaving Europe "with our hands upon our heads" suggests a posture of distress and despair, indicating persecution or a sense of defeat as Jews faced anti-Semitic hostilities on European soil. But he reproaches Jews for denying reality and avoiding conflict in their new land, arguing that the deliberate choice to ignore slander or insult is insufficient. Instead, Sapir calls on his fellow Jews "to foster a sense of belonging, to feel truly at home, not as outsiders, engaging fully with the local languages and cultures of these lands."[68] He urges his fellow Jews, particularly proponents of Zionism, to foster communal relationships with Palestinians and cultivate a true sense of belonging in their ancestral homeland so as to become integral members of society. This call to deeply engage with the local language and culture is a strategic response to—and he hopes a way to circumvent—the threat of growing anti-Semitism: by establishing meaningful connections with Arab elites, who hold significant cultural and political influence in their societies, Jews could play an instrumental role in mitigating the spread of anti-Zionist rhetoric.

The Hebrew writers studied here enjoyed complicated relations with the Arab elite in Palestine and neighboring Arab states during the late Ottoman era. The complexity of these relations is based on the competing loyalties and interests of the parties involved. In their interactions with the Arab elite, Hebrew writers had to negotiate their loyalty to a shared Ottoman homeland alongside their advocacy of the Zionist cause. The essential question for our purposes is how Jews reconciled their support of Zionism with their attempt to seek rapprochement with Arabo-Islamic culture through creating connections with Arab intellectuals.

Isaac Yahuda, a native Jew born in Jerusalem to a family of Iraqi heritage, stood in stark contrast to the European Jewish settlers in late Ottoman Palestine with his extensive as well as robust social and cultural network across the Middle East and North Africa. His profound knowledge of and scholarship in Arabo-Islamic culture not only earned him considerable acclaim but also facilitated meaningful connections with the Arab intelligentsia—a level of integration that many of his European contemporaries struggled to achieve. In his description of Yahuda's personality, historian and scholar of Arabic and Islam Israel Ben-Ze'ev (1899–1980) notes that Yahuda was "a learned and dedicated person who was conversant in different professions, qualities that made him humble and down to earth."[69] These qualities endeared him to the circles of Arab intellectuals such that he became known as "Ibn al-Nadīm al-Yahūdī" (the Jew). The epithet "Ibn al-Nadīm" refers to the medieval Muslim bibliographer and bibliophile from Baghdad best known for his Arabic encyclopedic catalog *Kitāb al-Fihrist* (Index). The comparison honors Yahuda's wide knowledge of Arabo-Islamic literature while recognizing that both scholars were born in Baghdad.[70] The addition of "al-Yahūdī" underscores the acceptance of Yahuda's Jewishness by his non-Jewish interlocutors, ascertains his belonging in the political, social, and cultural context, and makes it a point of pride given his mastery of Arabic and Islamic sciences. Nineteenth-century Jewish writers of Arabic, as literary scholar Lital Levy has explained, selectively underscored or downplayed their Jewishness based on their topic and audience.[71] The emphasis on Yahuda's Jewishness here distinguishes him from the medieval Muslim book collector Ibn al-Nadīm even as it simultaneously bestows on him the approbation of the Muslim community for his meaningful and important work in the preservation of the Arabo-Islamic heritage. Moreover, his Jewishness endows his scholarship on Jewish history and culture with greater authority. Stressing his Jewishness also indicates acceptance of Ottoman Jews as an integral part of the social and cultural fabric in the region as opposed to the foreignness of European Jewish settlers.

Beside his dedication to the advancement of Arabo-Islamic knowledge, Yahuda enjoyed amiable relationships with nahdawi Arab intellectuals that extended from the book trade to intellectual collaboration—relationships that greatly enriched his understanding of Arabo-Islamic civilization. The best articulation of this intellectual intercourse was his editing and publishing of the anthology of Arabic poetry *al-Maḍnūn bihi 'ala ghayr Ahlih* (That which is to be withheld from those unworthy of it), which included a commentary by 'Ubayd-Allah Ibn 'Abd al-Kāfī (d. 1324) on an anthology of Arabic poetry compiled by 'izz al-Dīn 'Abd al-Wahhāb al-Zanjānī (d. 1257).[72] This undertaking, it should be noted, testifies to how deeply Yahuda was involved in the Arab intellectual circles in the late

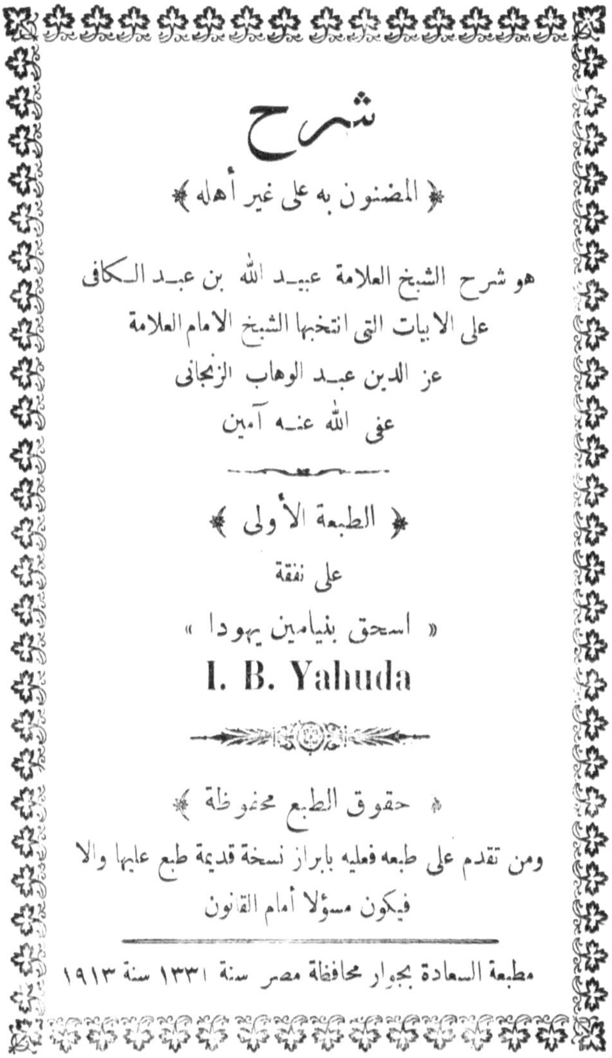
شرح

﴿ المضنون به على غير أهله ﴾

هو شرح الشيخ العلامة عبد الله بن عبد الكافى
على الابيات التى انتخبها الشيخ الامام العلامة
عز الدين عبد الوهاب الزنجانى
عفى الله عنه آمين

﴿ الطبعة الأولى ﴾
على نفقة
« اسحق بنيامين يهودا »
I. B. Yahuda

﴿ حقوق الطبع محفوظة ﴾
ومن تقدم على طبعه فعليه بابراز نسخة قديمة طبع عليها والا
فيكون مسؤلا أمام القانون

مطبعة السعادة بجوار محافظة مصر سنة ١٣٣١ سنة ١٩١٣

FIGURE 1.3. Cover of Isaac Yahuda's *al-Maḍnūn bihi ʿala ghayr Ahlih* (That which is to be withheld from those unworthy of it).

nineteenth and early twentieth centuries. As he mentions in his introduction, the project was based on a manuscript that was only available at al-Maktaba al-Khālidiyya (al-Khālidiyya library) in Jerusalem, and whose founding mission was to produce and transmit Islamic knowledge. Down from Bāb al-Silsila in the Old City, the library was founded in 1899 and contains over twelve hundred manuscripts chiefly in Arabic, alongside selections in Persian and Turkish, with the oldest manuscript hailing from the eleventh century.[73] The fact that a Jewish scholar like Yahuda was granted access to a library known as a rich source for Arabic and Islamic sciences is telling regarding the tenor of relations between Jews and Muslims at this time.

Al-Khālidiyya library exemplifies the fluidity of social and cultural intercommunal relations in late Ottoman Jerusalem that did not distinguish between members of various communities based on their religious identity.[74] Muslims, Jews, and Christians visited, worked at, and borrowed books and manuscripts from the library, which functioned as a shared space for members of the Jerusalemite city irrespective of their religious identity. Just as the West had benefited from the scientific and civilizational achievements of Arabo-Islamic culture in the transition from the "Dark Ages" to the Renaissance, local elites in Jerusalem like Rāghib al-Khālidi (1866–1952) saw the dissemination of Arabic and Islamic sciences through a modern library as necessary to reorient Arab society toward empirically based knowledge rather than tradition and superstition.[75] While it had been an endowed library accessible to elites owned by the al-Khālidi family since the eighteenth century, the Khālidiyya was modernized and reopened in 1900 as the first public library accessible to scholars of any religious background from the city and elsewhere. The modern founders and members of the al-Khālidi family in Jerusalem, according to historian Walīd al-Khālidī, believed that modern Arabs, by emulating their medieval predecessors, could reach the same level of intellectual excellence. To remind modern Arabs of their glorious past, the al-Khālidiaya library was named after Muslim military general Khālid Ibn al-Waliīd (d. 642), who headed the Muslim military campaign on Byzantine Syria between 634 and 638, and is believed to be the great ancestor of the al-Khālidiyya family in Jerusalem.[76] Since its founding in the early twentieth century, the library has attracted the attention of well-known Muslim scholars such as Syrian reformer Ṭāhir al-Jazāirī (1851–1920) and Orientalists such as David Samuel Margoliouth (1858–1940), the author of *Cairo, Jerusalem and Damascus* (1907). In carrying out his project on Arabic poetry, *al-Maḍnūn bihi ʿala ghayr Ahlih*, Yahuda became an active participant in the dissemination and production of Arabo-Islamic knowledge in a way that contributed to the mission of the al-Khālidi family. Yahuda's collaboration with Arab intellectuals is also evident in the editorial work done on the manuscript. In the introduction to the commentary, Yahuda refers to his partnership with Aḥmad Ibn al-Amīn al-Shanqīṭī (1872–1913), one of the distinguished intellectuals of Mauritania and a renowned scholar in Cairo at the time.[77]

It was not only Sephardi and Oriental Jews who advanced relations with Arab intellectuals in late Ottoman Palestine; Ashkenazi Jewish immigrants provided an example of what Levy describes as a "cultural cross-mediation of *nahḍa* and *haskala*" that bridged the two intellectual movements.[78] Ben-Yehuda's interest in Arabs and their culture is evidenced in articles published in his daily newspaper, *ha-Tsevi* (Deer)—a widely circulated Hebrew newspaper published in Jerusalem from 1884 to 1914—to enlighten Hebrew-reading audiences about their neighbors' culture. Under the editorship of Ben-Yehuda, *ha-Tsevi* published columns on Arabs and their culture by several Hebrew writers conversant with Arabo-Islamic culture who were able to consult primary sources in Arabic. Yellin, for instance, wrote columns on Arab legends and stories taken from sources such as the Quran, secular Arabic literature, and Arab folklore.[79] Before World War I, *ha-Tsevi* even featured an Arabic supplement.[80]

In addition to being fascinated by Arab culture, Ben-Yehuda was interested in Arab intellectuals' views on Jews and Zionism. He maintained an intellectual friendship with Rūḥī al-Khālidī (1864–1913), a Palestinian intellectual and public figure whom Ben-Yehuda considered "a respected intellectual colleague" who contributed significantly to Orientalist scholarship.[81] Rūḥī al-Khālidī deepened his secular education in Europe after beginning his studies in Palestine. In 1887, he went to Istanbul's Mekteb-i Mülkiye (Civil Service School) for over six years before moving to Paris, where he had a three-year stint in political science followed by specialized studies in Islamic philosophy and Eastern literature at the École Pratique des Hautes Études (Special School for Higher Studies) under renowned French Orientalists. His academic journey led to a brief yet impactful career teaching Arabic in France, linking his Palestinian heritage with European scholarly traditions.[82] Historian Jonathan Gribetz documents the various conversations that Ben-Yehuda held with the Palestinian Arab intellectual whereby they sought to understand each other and their respective communities.[83] Following the first parliamentary elections after the Young Turk Revolution, Ben-Yehuda interviewed Jerusalem's parliamentary representatives Rūḥī al-Khālidī and Sa'īd al-Ḥusseinī in 1909. In these conversations, as Gribetz has shown elsewhere, Ben-Yehuda asserted his simultaneous loyalty to the Ottoman homeland and commitment to Zionism, while highlighting the values of diversity and cross-cultural friendship.[84] According to Ben-Yehuda, "We live now in a free country, consisting of many groups and nations. Each group and each nation guard its interests and we have to get used to this and accept it, to live in personal friendship with one another, even as the group and national questions separate us."[85] Understanding that each of us is at once an individual and member of a community, race, or religion, Ben-Yehuda points to a way individuals can still maintain personal friendships despite diverging political or religious views. His stance speaks to his acknowledgment that one's communal identity—such as being part of the Zionist movement in his case—does not preclude the possibility of individual relationships based on different criteria like mutual respect, shared interests and values, or personal affinity. This approach allows for practical coexistence in a diverse society by separating personal affections from the political or national agendas that may conflict. Of course, Ben-Yehuda's reconciliatory position is put to the test under conditions of political or religious tension, when separating the personal and communal becomes more problematic. In this regard, his optimism can be seen as an oversimplification of complex personal and national identities.

After both interviewees discussed the future of Jerusalem and the Ottoman homeland, Ben-Yehuda shifted gears to ask the Palestinian delegates to the Ottoman Parliament about Jewish immigration to Palestine. Ben-Yehuda was aware that a debate about Zionism would soon take place in the Parliament, and that the perspectives of the Palestinian representatives would be significant in that discussion and influence delegates from other Arab provinces. Rūḥī al-Khālidī and al-Ḥusseinī essentially reiterated the Ottoman policy on Jewish immigration, stressing that Jews have many positive qualities that render them model residents of the empire, but admonishing them not to concentrate on the single locality of Palestine.[86] They should instead reorient their aspirations, abide by Ottoman policy, and for their own sake as well as the empire's, spread out their settlement in all the provinces of the empire. Ben-Yehuda expressed understanding of their perspectives, but acknowledged that their prescriptions shattered his hopes for Jewish settlement in what he viewed as Jews' ancestral homeland.

Menasche Meirovitch (1860–1949) was another Ashkenazi Jewish immigrant who enjoyed a close relationship with Palestinian Arab elites. Meirovitch immigrated to Palestine from the Russian Empire through Constantinople on the deck of a ship sailing from Alexandria, Egypt, to the shores of Haifa in 1883.[87] Had it not been for his agronomic diploma and a document confirming his intention to pursue agronomic research in Palestine, the Ottoman official at the port would have returned him to Alexandria, as he did with two of Meirovitch's comrades accompanying him on the trip.[88] Considered one of the first Russian Jewish agronomists, Meirovitch sought to make use of his knowledge and training to benefit the Jewish agricultural settlement in Palestine.[89]

Along with dedicating time and effort to educating the Hebrew settlers about agriculture, Meirovitch endeavored to pass on his modern agronomic knowledge to Palestinian Arab farmers by contributing articles to several Arabic newspapers. His essays demonstrate not only his agronomic knowledge but also his familiarity with the life of the peasantry in Palestine. Caught in the middle of a triangle of nationalistic enterprises (Zionism, Ottomanism, and Palestinianism), Meirovitch worked within these competing frameworks to advance, as historians Samuel Dolbee and Shay Hazkani have pointed out, a political imagination based on imperial Ottoman citizenship that cherished partnership between Jews and Arabs.[90]

Following the constitutional reforms resulting from the Young Turk Revolution of 1908 and revival of the suspended Ottoman Constitution of 1876, the Arabic press, as Campos has shown, "went about shaping the revolutionary

Ottoman public sphere."[91] Meirovitch's reputation as the author of articles on the relationship between humans and nature, which appeared in both Hebrew and non-Hebrew newspapers, reached the circles of the liberal Arab intelligentsia, which attempted to recruit him to fill in a gap in the emerging Arab consciousness with respect to the agricultural knowledge and modern technologies needed to enhance the productivity of farmlands. In summer 1911, he was invited to publish articles in the evolving newspaper *Filasṭīn* (Palestine) by ʿIsa al-ʿIsa (1878–1950), a prominent Palestinian Christian voice in late Ottoman Palestine, on the nature of the land and the circumstances of its inhabitants. Born in Jaffa, and educated at Jaffa's Ecole des frères and the American University of Beirut, along with his cousin Yūsef al-ʿIsa (1870–1948), ʿIsa al-ʿIsa founded in 1911 the biweekly newspaper *Filasṭīn*, which would become the most influential publication in Mandatory Palestine. Like other Christian Arab intellectuals such as Yaʿqūb Sarrūf (1852–1927), Fāris Nimr (1856–1951), Najīb Naṣṣār (1865–1947), and Najīb ʿAzūrī (1873–1916), al-ʿIsa viewed Zionism as a major political, economic, and cultural threat to Palestine. His newspaper *Filasṭīn*, then, from its inception, had as its mission warning against and opposing Zionism. Nevertheless, *Filasṭīn* would occasionally publish articles on the accomplishments of Zionism, including the renaissance of the Hebrew language and agricultural achievements of the Jewish settlements.[92] Due to its continuous criticisms of the Ottoman government, the newspaper was shut down several times, and al-ʿIsa himself was eventually exiled to Damascus during the Great War due to his Arab nationalist convictions.[93]

As a strong opponent of Zionism, why would al-ʿIsa invite Meirovitch to contribute articles to his newspaper? The answer is apparent in a meeting between al-ʿIsa and Meirovitch, during which the former commented, "I hear that you contribute articles to several newspapers. Would it be possible for you to participate in my newspaper? You know the nature of the land, the status of its inhabitants . . . etc. It is our duty to work now hand in hand for the sake of the homeland."[94] Meirovitch was perceived as an apolitical Jewish farmer, a "*fallāḥ*" (as the title of the articles he contributed would show), who immigrated to Palestine out of "a mixture of nationalist and religious motivations that had not crystalized into a political form" with the goal of achieving self-realization by the acquisition of land, not intending to form trade unions and political parties.[95] In truth, the fact of Meirovitch's abstinence from the politics of Labor Zionism did not negate the existence of political objectives. As a private agricultural producer, as Liora Halperin has shown, Meirovitch "thrived on the idea that the national collective could succeed only when rooted in private initiative and ownership."[96]

Meirovitch perceived himself as a Hebrew Ottoman (*otoman ʿivri*)—a phrase he used in his writings—and explicitly declared himself an Ottoman subject of the Mosaic persuasion. In the atmosphere of fraternity and equality ushered in

السنة الاولى
العدد ٥٣
جريدة تصدر في يافا مرتين في الاسبوع
ادارة الجريدة
في سوق بسترس
الاعلانات
يتفق عليها مع الادارة
رئيس تحرير الجريدة
يوسف العيسى
فلسطين
LA PALESTINE
قيمة الاشتراك
في يافا : عشرة فرنكات
في الجهات : ثلاثة ريالات مجيدية
المكاتبات
تكون باسم صاحب الجريدة
ومديرها المسؤول
عيسى داود العيسى
السبت

FIGURE 1.4. *Filasṭīn* (Palestine) newspaper, August 5, 1911. Reprinted from the electronic version of the newspaper at Jrayed—Arabic Newspaper Archive of Ottoman and Mandatory Palestine, https://jrayed.org/en/newspapers/home.

by the Young Turk Revolution of uniting the religiously, linguistically, and culturally heterogeneous subjects of the homeland, Meirovitch agreed to work with Palestinian Christian Arabs, and downplayed the warnings of scholars such as Sapir and Ben-Yehuda that Christian Arabs harbored ill feelings toward Jews based on the ideological considerations discussed above.[97] Al-ʿIsa's offer presented Meirovitch with an opportunity to demonstrate his transcendent nationalism, criticism of Labor Zionism, and support for those Arabs whose labor would surely contribute to the common good of Jewish nationalism by supporting private colonies.

Notwithstanding these attractive prospects, Meirovitch initially neither accepted nor rejected the Arab editor's offer to collaborate for the advancement of the welfare of the *moledet* (homeland). Instead, he responded with a contradictory mix of reluctance and eagerness as he asked for clarification regarding what he would and would not write about. In his communications with al-ʿIsa, he made it clear that he would avoid political issues as he was keenly aware of the vehement opposition of the Ottoman authorities to nationalistic aspirations such as political Zionism that threatened the empire.[98] But though he would remain silent on the issue of Zionism, he would promote to the Arab audience Jews' positive contributions, "explain[ing] to them what Jews had contributed over the course of thirty years of labor in the land."[99]

Meirovitch was a supporter of the Ottomanization of European Jewish settlers in Palestine. His views echoed Ben-Yehuda's call in *ha-Tsevi* in January 1909, a few months after the Young Turk Revolution, for Jews in Palestine to revoke their foreign citizenship in favor of Ottoman citizenship in hopes of acquiring legitimacy and political freedom (including the right to participate in elections) in Palestine.[100] This was also the route for Ottoman Jewry to gain power in the Ottoman House of Representatives. Meirovitch was convinced that in return for their loyalty to the constitutional Ottoman authority, Jews would be granted permission to remain in the land. Such was his loyalty to the Ottoman Empire that before the outbreak of the Great War, as a representative of the union of Jewish colonies, he worked to enlist Ottoman Jews in the Turkish Army.[101] In his article "Dallim ve-reḳim anaḥnu" (How vacuous and penurious we are!), published in *ha-'Or* (Light) in 1912, a short time before the Ottoman citizens of Palestine would participate in parliamentary elections for a second time, Meirovitch laments the intellectual backwardness of Hebrew Ottomans (*otomanim 'ivrim*) for their failure to participate in the political life of the country, recalling Ben-Yehuda's call, "Jews, be Ottomans." He also insists on the urgency of Jews' embrace of Arabic language and literature in order to equip themselves to represent their interests in the local press.[102] At the end of the article, Meirovitch encourages Hebrew Ottomans to commence the "serious labor" of learning Arabic and Turkish, along with a greater understanding of Islamic culture, to express their own voices within this cultural milieu:

> It would be unfortunate had we allowed neglect to achieve further victory; for another four years would have passed this time and we would have remained "vacuous and penurious," and perhaps in a worse situation if we had not commenced at that moment our serious work. . . . [W]e should teach in every school the language of the land, and the instruction should be serious. Every time we fail to show concern for our youth, our sons, to become better accustomed to Turkish and Arabic, we remain always silent, and we are unable to wield any influence in the political and social life of the country; we would not take part in it.[103]

Meirovitch understood that the dissemination of Arabic and Turkish literacy was critical for Jews in a land where Arabic was the lingua franca. For one thing, Jews needed to read Arabic to know how they were being portrayed in the Arab press to effectively counter misrepresentations. Likewise, they needed to speak and write Arabic to directly address the Arab masses, thereby undermining the political authority of the Arab elite who incited the Arab population against the nationalistic aspirations of Hebrew Ottomans.[104] Finally, mastery of Turkish was a prerequisite for running for election, and thus would pave the way for future Hebrew Ottomans to serve in the Ottoman Parliament instead of ceding that representation to the likes of Rūḥī al-Khālidī and his comrades who strongly opposed the goals of Zionism.

Meirovitch's advocacy of learning Arabic language and culture to communicate with the Arab population resulted from his own experience with Arabic newspapers as a resource for connecting with the Arabic-reading public. In response to a request from the editor of *Filasṭīn* to publish essays on Palestine's peasant life, Meirovitch began contributing pieces to the nascent Arabic journal on the relationship between humans and nature in Palestine.[105] In a series of articles under the title *Rasā'il fallāḥ* (A fellah's letters), he started publishing under the pseudonym Abū Ibrāhīm (father of Ibrāhīm), after his elder son, Avraham; the use of an epithet (*kunya*) is a common naming tradition in Arabo-Islamic culture that was embraced by contemporary Arab writers in Palestine.[106] In choosing the pseudonym Abū Ibrāhīm for his articles, it seems that Meirovitch was trying to create common cultural ground. By adopting the name Ibrāhīm, the Arabic equivalent of "Abraham," a patriarchal figure revered in Judaism, Christianity, and Islam, Meirovitch established common ground, emphasizing a shared religious heritage and portraying himself as a member of the wider Abrahamic family, which could make his ideas more palatable to Arab Muslim and Christian readers. It was a way for him to root himself into Palestine's common culture. Since the articles contained criticism of the Ottoman authorities' negligent policies toward Arab farmers, anonymity was also a safety measure. Considering the sensitive nature of politics in the region, using a pen name protected his identity, and allowed him to express his views without attracting personal hostility or retribution, particularly if his ideas could be seen as controversial or they criticized the status quo. Furthermore, given the rise of nationalistic movements during that era, including Arab nationalism and Zionism, adopting an Arabic pseudonym could be a subtle political statement signifying Meirovitch's support for Jewish-Arab coexistence or cooperation.

To make his points, Meirovitch created a narrative in which Abū Ibrāhīm is presented as an elder of a certain village who frequently passes back and forth between Arab villages and Jewish colonies, and writes letters to his friend describing the situation in both locales. While representing an Arab peasant himself, Abū Ibrāhīm highlights the troublesome circumstances of the peasant life, including the deteriorating situation of the farmers, burden of taxation, and dangerous medical conditions.[107] In contrast, Abū Ibrāhīm portrays Jewish peasant life in positive terms, characterizing Jews as working not for their own sake but rather for the benefit of Arab villages given the fact that the Arab population utilizes services provided by Jewish physicians and Arabs send their children to Jewish schools in order to learn modern agricultural methods.[108]

Apparently, Meirovitch's articles in the Arabic press under the nom de plume Abū Ibrāhīm became popular enough to attract the attention of other editors, who tried to persuade him to publish in their journals. Among these was Ilya Zakka (1875–1926), the editor of *al-Nafīr* (Clarion), who invited Abū Ibrāhīm to take part in that emerging outlet. Meirovitch readily agreed; he began publishing articles in *al-Nafīr* under the title *Rasā'il Tājir 'Uthmānī* (Letters from an Ottoman merchant), revealing the hard conditions of trade and industry in Palestine, while emphasizing the challenges and obstacles instigated by the authorities.[109]

The radical changes brought about by the Young Turk Revolution were met with jubilation by Jews, Christians, and Muslims alike. Within the atmosphere

رسائل فلاح

٥

حقاً اني جنيت على نفسي بفتحي
باب الكتابة في الجرائد . فقد كنت
مرتاح البال لا يهمني سوى حقلي وغنمي
وابقاري ولا اشعر بتأثير الضريبات
العمومية التي تصيبنا نحن الفلاحين .
كنت عائشاً قرير العين فيما بين مزابل
قريتي لا يهمني من العالم سوى نفسي
وعائلتي فناكل ونشرب بهناء بدون
ان نسأل لماذا وجدنا على الارض
ونموت كما يموت الذباب بدون ان يهتم
بنا احد . كنت سعيداً لما كان عندي
من الاعتقاد بان الفلاح يدعى كباقي بني

ذهابه الحياة .

والان قل ياسيدي من هو المسئول
عن موت هذا الشاب ؟ من يرجع الى
والدين حزينين ولدهما الوحيد ومصدر
عيشتهما ؟ متى اخيراً يفكرون بنا نحن
الفلاحين ويعلمون اننا لا نقدر ان نفهم
مثل هذه الاحتياطات ؟

يقولون انهم قد عينوا بياطرة قانونيين
فاين هؤلاء البياطرة ولماذا لا ياتون الى
قرايانا ويعلموننا ويفهموننا عن لزوم
طمر جثث الحيوانات . لماذا البلديات
او البوليس او من يهمه ذلك لا يرسل
من وقت الى اخر من ينظر كيف هي
حالة معيشتنا ويقدم لنا النصائح
اللازمة . . . .

FIGURE 1.5. Menashe Meirovitch's Arabic letters published under the title *Rasā'il fallāḥ* (A fellah's letters) in the Arabic newspaper *Filasṭīn* (Palestine) on September 23, 1911. At the end of the letter, the author uses the pseudonym Abū Ibrāhīm (the father of Ibrāhīm), after his elder son, Avraham; the use of an epithet (*kunya*) is a common naming tradition in Arab societies. Reprinted from the electronic version of the newspaper at Jrayed—Arabic Newspaper Archive of Ottoman and Mandatory Palestine, https://jrayed.org/en/newspapers/home.

of fellowship and liberty generated by the new regime, there was, as historian Louis Fishman has argued, the opportunity for communal self-definition within this integrative framework. Rather than territorial nationalistic separation, there was acknowledgment of the national aspirations of both Jews and Palestinian Arabs in the context of continuing loyalty to the empire in the postrevolutionary era (1908–14). Ottomanism, as Fishman explains, was for the different religious and ethnic groups "a framework for promoting their identities, languages, and ethno-religious privileges, as well as an empire based on administrative decentralization." For Palestinians, Arabism and Ottomanism coalesced, working in unison to create a Palestinianism with Muslim-Christian allegiance that would contribute to the creation of a full-blown Palestinianism after the Great War.[110]

Within this reality, the Jewish community, with its Sephardic and Ashkenazi constituencies, created a nonseparatist cultural nationalist movement.[111] The opening of an official office for Zionism in Jaffa under the directorship of the economist and father of Zionist settlement Arthur Ruppin (1876–1943) intensified the purchase of lands and promotion of Jewish labor—two issues, as Abigail Jacobson has shown, that greatly disturbed Arab inhabitants of Palestine, and increased tension between Jews and Arabs.[112] This tension played out in the Arabic press. After sensing a turning point in the attitude of the Arab press, particularly *Filasṭīn*, which began giving space to articles that incited the readership against either Jews in general or Jewish settlers, Meirovitch ceased to participate in both journals.[113]

The increased concentration of Zionist activities alarmed members of the Arab elite and raised tension with Jewish settlers like Meirovitch. The success of Rūḥī al-Khālidī in the first parliamentary elections brought him scrutiny from both Arab and Jewish citizens, whose national aspirations differed and even opposed one another given the existence of multiple as well as overlapping identities. Rūḥī al-Khālidī expressed his opposition to the Zionist movement and its aim of forming an independent Jewish nation in Palestine as early as 1909, when he was interviewed by Ben-Yehuda in the daily Hebrew newspaper *ha-Tsevi*.[114] Most significantly, Rūḥī al-Khālidī's public criticism of Zionism and the influx of Jewish immigrants to Palestine gained the attention of Ottoman Jews in Palestine such as Meirovitch, who took issue with Rūḥī al-Khālidī's words in an article in *Ḥivle Teḥiyah*, calling them "hostile sentences and poisonous accusations." Before delving into the details of Rūḥī al-Khālidī's parliamentary speech, Meirovitch extolled the progress and improvements that immigrant Jews had brought to the country through their agricultural labor, whereas elite Arabs such as Rūḥī al-Khālidī and his colleagues had, in his assessment, done nothing for the Ottoman nation:

> There is no need, Ottoman Jews, to debate with our representative, Rūḥī al-Khālidī. We do not have to present an apology for his fabricated allegations; for we, Ottoman Jewry, not only can claim with pride, but also can prove with deeds what we have done on behalf of the welfare of the land. How much have we endured, how much have we produced for the whole nation without distinction! And [by contrast], how much have noble masters such as Rūḥī al-Khālidī and his comrades done for the sake of the welfare of the nation?[115]

With the phrase "for the whole nation without distinction," Meirovitch signifies that Zionist aspirations are not in opposition to Ottoman patriotism but rather a part of the fabric of the empire's progress and prosperity. He emphasizes that Ottoman Jews can "prove with deeds" their contributions to the welfare of the Ottoman land, backing up their claims with practical and positive impacts on the nation.

Agricultural Practices

Meirovitch's focus shifts from defending Zionist contributions against detractors to an exploration of the settlers' integration with the land. In this new context, Palestinian Arabs emerge not as political adversaries, as in the case of al-Khālidī, but instead as unwitting tutors whose agricultural methods and relationship with nature are keenly observed as well as emulated by the Jewish immigrants. This methodical adaptation of Indigenous knowledge is central to the narrative, evidencing a strategy whereby Jewish settlers seek to harmonize their endeavors with the established practices of the local population, thereby inserting themselves into the continuity of the land's agrarian legacy.

In addition to regarding local Arabs as mediators between modern Jews and their ancient ancestors, Jews looked to Palestinian Arabs' agrarian experience for guidance on how to live, feed themselves, and prosper in this new land. We will examine the process whereby Jewish settlers appropriated the Arab population's knowledge of local flora and fauna, attitude toward nature, and agricultural practices, linking their interests to those of local peasants and achieving a symbiosis critical to Meirovitch's national project.

At the outset, it is important to note the sophisticated depiction of the Indigenous population in Meirovitch's work. Intentionally omitting urban Arab elites, he portrays two Palestinian populations, Arab farmers and Bedouins, both of whom are presented as primitive, in contradistinction to civilized Europeans. As previously noted, Jewish settlers like Meirovitch knew that the less politically mobilized rural populations posed less of an obstacle to the Zionist project, which included agricultural settlement and land acquisition. After all, those who held economic and political power—urban elites, political figures, scholars, and merchants—had reason to resist the establishment of Jewish settlements due to concerns that the influx of Jewish immigrants and their financial resources could undermine their own current standing. Meirovitch, who introduced himself as *ben moshavah* (son of a Jewish colony), and whose relationship with the local population revolved around agricultural activities, naturally devoted more attention to Arab peasants than to nomads. As they put roots down in the land, from his perspective, Jewish settlers would live far more harmoniously with the natives of Palestine if they understood their culture and character, and the physical conditions of the land.[116]

Meirovitch's attitude toward the local Arab population echoed the ambivalence within the Bilu movement, of which he was a member.[117] While primitive compared to the civilized West, he maintained, Arabs were not savages. In fact, they could be a resource:

> Arab settlers of the land are not savage robbers and thieves, as they are described by those who reside far away, who say [they] are lions in the street. By nature, the Arab likes serenity and calm and hates quarrel and dispute. By nature, he would form a relationship with the man who deals with him in honesty and straightforwardness, and he would be a sincere servant to him.[118]

Speaking as an authority on the local population, Meirovitch contradicts "those who reside far away," referring to European Jewish writers whose negative portrayals of the Arab population in Palestine were consumed by the majority of potential Jewish immigrants then residing on European soil.

And indeed, Meirovitch's portrayal of the local population was somewhat nuanced. Though he viewed nomads less admiringly than he did peasants, he did not denigrate them or their ways of interacting with their environment, as did European Hebrew writers. For example, he did not represent nomads as a people ravening the landscape, and whose livestock had deforested, overgrazed, or desertified the land. Instead, they were depicted as an integral part of the natural landscape whose presence intensified the romantic connection between modern Jews and ancient Israelites for Meirovitch along with others of his ilk. He admits that the predominantly peaceful Bedouins can occasionally pose a threat to settlements, but analogizes the threat to that of opportunistic thieves or criminals in a European city:

> Regarding wandering Bedouins, they also will not terrorize the settlers of the land.[119] From time to time they might attack visitors and exploit them, but this will occur only very occasionally. Further, in many European cities a human being may not feel entirely safe, and sometimes they are given over to plunder and prey, with none to rescue them, and in particular, we the Jews [are often targets].[120]

Thus Bedouin attacks may happen sporadically and mainly impact transient visitors rather than settled inhabitants, indicating a level of risk, but not an endemic state of violence or threat for those working the land. A Jew who fled Jewish pogroms in Russia addressing potential Jewish settlers, Meirovitch draws an analogy between life in the rural agricultural colonies of Palestine and urban environments in Europe. He notes that even in many European cities, which could be perceived as developed or safer, a person might not feel "entirely safe." These cities, he highlights, sometimes succumb to lawlessness, where plunder and victimization occur without intervention, stressing that Jews are frequently targets of such acts. This comparison serves to relativize the risk posed by Bedouins in Palestine, suggesting that in terms of safety, life in the colonies, despite potential Bedouin threats, is relatively secure when compared to life in European cities, where Jews face their own set of dangers.

Meirovitch's attitude toward Indigenous agricultural practices fluctuates between admiration and contempt. In an article published in 1892 in the journal *Yerushalayim*, for instance, he presents the methods used by Arabs in olive oil production as a model for Hebrew settlers to emulate, and shows how native agricultural practices and by extension other cultural practices could be adopted by the new Hebrew culture. While expressing appreciation for Arabs' agricultural techniques, however (which were similar to those of the ancients), he could not conceal his contempt for the natives' *pashut* (simple/plain) tools and methods of cultivation. He paid particular attention to the uses of the olive, a crop of great economic and cultural importance to both Jewish and Arabo-Islamic traditions, commenting that

> the [olive] oil is processed from the olive trees in the following manner: at the time of the olives' bruising, the farmer will climb up the tree and with a stick in his hand he will beat the branches of the tree. Then, olives fall on the ground and from there they are collected and brought to the olive press.[121]

In this passage, the Arab farmer serves as a model for Jewish settlers to emulate to aid in the self-indigenization process. In fact, the author is offering a portrayal of Jewish ancestral life through an evocative picture of the olive harvest by the local Arab population, which employed simple methods that the author deemed to be used by *ḳadmonim* (the ancients). The reference to holding onto the methods of the ancients indicates both authenticity and primitivity. Authenticity is a notion that has been emphasized in Yahuda's work on the origins of Arabs (*The Antiquities of Arabs*) in the land and the region in general as well as discussed earlier. In referencing the continuation of utilizing instruments and methods of the ancients, Meirovitch attests to the survival of harvest techniques that preceded the Islamic era and were preserved by Arab inhabitants in Palestine.

At the same time, Meirovitch critiques the same simple methods and tools—in this case, the olive presses used by the local Palestinian Arabs—as inefficient. Deriding them as pashut, he signals his European-oriented bias coupled with his assumption of technological and civilizational superiority:

> All olive presses in the land are set up very plainly [pashut], without changing even a little from what existed thousands of years ago. Olive fruits are placed between a pair of grindstones. After they are crushed, they are brought into the press. The oil spouted from the press is the best oil. Then, [the olive fruits are] brought for the second time to the press, and now their oil is surely worse

> than the first. Yet, even after two pressings, the olive press does not have enough power to extract all of the oil, and therefore the olives are boiled in hot water. After that they are brought for the third time to the press. This time the oil is the worst and is not edible. Rather, [it is used] for lamps and the manufacture of soaps. Since approximately 25% of olive oil still remains in the olive waste, it can be extracted with the help of European press machines. Even olive waste is not lost, for it will be sold for the heating oven.[122]

Meirovitch's remark that the crude method of oil extraction has not evolved "even a little from what existed thousands of years ago" implies a static, unprogressive culture untethered from the advancements of modernity.

Meirovitch's ambivalence manifests in the simultaneous recognition of the authenticity and rootedness of Palestinian Arabs' agricultural practices, and condescension toward their resistance to change and modernization. This is highlighted when he points out that a significant amount of oil—25 percent—remains unextracted without the aid of European technology. The juxtaposition of the "best oil" obtained from the first pressing with the inferior oil from subsequent efforts reflects a characteristic mix of appreciation with a paternalistic impulse to introduce improvements. Ultimately, Meirovitch's account reflects a dynamic tension between valuing traditional practices and advocating for progress as defined by European standards.

Elsewhere, Meirovitch suggests a plan to replace the Arabs' outdated oil production methods with modern ones. In his article "Le-Harim Mikhshol me-Derekh 'ami," which he contributed to the Hebrew newspaper *Kenesset Yisrael* in 1887, he wrote:

> The number of olive trees in the entire land of Israel is considered to be ten million. From the overwhelming majority of the olive trees, olive oil is extracted, and a small portion is consumed. The oil is processed from the olives very simply, in the way of the ancients. . . . Initially, olives are crushed with stones, and after that they are placed in a very simple press. The place where the process is carried out is, similar to all Arabs' workplaces, not clean. Therefore, the oil does not look pure, and its taste is bitter, and a great portion of oil stored in the olives is lost, for it will not be processed from the olives in this way.[123]

Meirovitch's observations acknowledge that the Arab farmers follow "the way of the ancients," but as an agronomist he is firmly on the side of economic productivity.

While Meirovitch bemoans the waste and quality issues that characterize these traditional practices, they were evidently efficient enough for the needs of the local population, which had sustained a livelihood for generations through the olive trees' bounty. The fact that the sector continued to provide a source of living for a large number of landholders demonstrates the practical efficacy of these methods. The small producers successfully managed to grow olives, produce olive oil and soap, and generate supplementary income by selling to merchants. The enduring nature of this trade, which extended to the markets and even exportation to regions like Egypt, indicates a level of sophistication and successful integration within the broader economic ecosystem of the time.[124]

Reexamining Meirovitch's observation in light of these facts, it becomes clear that his misgivings about the inadequacy of Arab farmers' practices reveal more about his own vantage point, which is informed by an aspiration for modern industrial techniques that could ostensibly yield better economic returns, than the viability of the practices themselves. It also suggests a Eurocentric bias that undervalues traditional practices in favor of technological innovation, without fully appreciating the existing equilibrium that the traditional practices had achieved in their local context. A few lines later, he complains about the monopoly of Arab farmers and their reluctance to cooperate with the Jews:

> The Arab, *yelid ha-arets* [native of the land], at the sight of someone who needs something that the Arab possesses, is ready to wait a month, or two months, or even three months and it is no question that he would give this matter up by himself. . . . If we placed an oil press house where the olive harvest is bountiful to purchase olive fruits from fellahin to produce oil, the oil press would remain unused, due to the lack of olives. The Arabs would not sell, for they would demand very high prices.[125]

In the same article dealing with the industrial and commercial aspects of Palestine's agricultural production, Meirovitch proposes a form of cooperation between the local population and the Jewish settlers to produce high-quality olive oil in which Jews would rely on the local population to supply them with raw olives since they did not yet own olive groves of their own. In light of the backward extraction methods employed by the natives,

> olive oil is not only good for trade but is also considered one of the prestigious business fields in the land. But experts in this matter indicate that if oil processed by Arabs is refined, we could undoubtedly improve its quality a little bit; nonetheless its quality would not be as high as France's oil. The only reason is that the manner in which oil is extracted from olives is not good. To produce pure oil with real quality, we should improve the process from the beginning; in other words, we should start by pressing the olives with proper tools in an appropriate way.[126]

The driving force behind Meirovitch's concerns regarding the quality of the olive oil was trade, whose success would accrue profit to Jewish settlers in Palestine.

No more than six months following the publication of his article, the first Jewish oil press was founded by Rabbi Yisrael Nimtsuvitz in the city of Lod.[127] That oil press, it should be noted, was later sold to Joseph Fainberg, one of the Ḥovevei Zion (Lovers of Zion) members who maintained a strong relationship with *yeliday ha-arets* (natives of the land) in order to acquire the needed olives.[128] Since Jewish settlers lacked the land to grow olive trees, they had to rely on the local Arab population to supply olives to the new press. Notwithstanding Meirovitch's complaints about the high prices Arab farmers demanded for their olives, the interaction that took place through trade between Muslim farmers and Jewish traders is a telling indicator of the willingness of Arabs to trade with Jews, demonstrating that there was no fear of the Zionist enterprise at that point.[129] Indeed, the local population was willing to provide massive amounts of this essential crop to export to the Western world. Any concerns about the Jewish presence on the land and threats to Palestinians' livelihood were outweighed by the prospect of immediate profits. In Mandate Palestine, however, this would be proven shortsighted as the traditional Palestinian olive production sector faced a significant decline due to the rapid expansion and modernization of olive groves and oil production by Jewish settlers, who were able to produce and market oil products at lower prices than their local Arab counterparts, leading to a sharp decrease in the value and competitiveness of Palestinian-produced olive oil.[130]

Palestinian Arabs: A Model to Emulate, Debate, and Educate

This chapter has described the richly textured tapestry of relations between Jewish settlers and Palestinian Arabs during the waning years of the Ottoman Empire. The complex and multilayered relationship oscillated between admiration and condescension, suspicion and cooperation, reflecting a duality inherent in the Zionist narrative, which simultaneously sought to connect with biblical roots in the context of settler colonialism.

The Bilu members, emblematic of the First Aliyah, embodied the dualistic nature of the settler colonial mentality. On the one hand, they idealized certain Arab traits and practices, and on the other hand, identified with an Orientalist perspective that viewed Palestinian Arabs as culturally static, backward, and in need of "enlightened" guidance. In their quest to establish a Jewish home, the Bilu pioneers revered Hebrew Scriptures, identifying Palestinian Arabs as the biblical Ishmaelites or descendants of Esau—a kinship that paradoxically affirmed their own perceived Jewish superiority as progeny of Isaac and Jacob. Despite these prejudices, Palestinian Arabs were pivotal in shaping Jewish settler identity; their ways of life were seen as living echoes of ancient Israelite forebearers, thus providing a template for the newcomers to culturally and socially acclimatize to their ancestral yet newly rediscovered land. Through this emulation, the Bilu members sought to root themselves in the land by adopting the Indigenous practices that they believed had been preserved since the times of the patriarchs Abraham, Isaac, and Jacob.

As we have seen, Jewish-Arab interactions during this period were marked by a form of hierarchical coexistence, particularly evident in collaborative agricultural enterprises and economic dependencies. Within this framework, Jewish settlers typically assumed the roles of employers and landlords, while Palestinian Arabs were employed as farmers, guards, or produce sellers. Despite the practical aspects of such cooperation, the arrangement faced criticism from members of the Second Aliyah, who introduced an ethos that prioritized Jewish labor, advocating for self-reliance and condemning reliance on Arab workers. This new stance deepened the ideological divide as it challenged the established model of Jewish-Arab relations in favor of Jewish separatism and self-sufficiency within the settler community.

Hebrew writers spanning the Sephardi, Oriental, and Ashkenazi spectrum profoundly influenced the portrayal of Palestinian Arabs in literature, often echoing and intensifying the internal debates as well as contradictions of the Zionist movement. These authors crafted depictions of Arabs as both potential allies and hindrances to Zionist ambitions. Such portrayals simultaneously revealed and at times reluctantly acknowledged the deep-seated connection of Palestinian Arabs to the land, challenging the simplicity of the settler colonial narrative. For instance, Belḳind's observations led him to the contentious belief that Palestinian farmers were descendants of ancient Jews who had converted to Islam in the seventh century to retain their lands. Conversely, Palestinian urbanites typically cast themselves as an endangered elite who opposed Jewish settlers, wary that the burgeoning Jewish immigration along with land acquisitions might undermine their long-standing political and economic dominance.

On the individual level, figures such as Meirovitch and Ben-Yehuda engaged with members of the Palestinian Arab elite in nuanced ways, negotiating the tenets of Zionism with the realities of Ottoman citizenship and their visions for coexistence. During the late Ottoman era, Zionism was understood by many Jews as an expression of a cultural national movement that did not advocate for separation from the Ottoman homeland. The resurrection of modern Hebrew secured the Jewish people's identity, especially while affirming their place in the diverse linguistic, religious, and national landscape of late Ottoman Palestine—a point of pride for Hebrew scholars such as Yellin—in contradistinction to the prevalent linguistic and religious monoculturalism of Europe.

The multiple competing attitudes examined throughout this chapter offer a glimpse into the hearts and minds of Jewish settlers as they navigated the murky waters of their ideological imperatives vis-à-vis the lived realities of Palestine. They were individuals caught between the yearning for what they imagined as their historical homeland, and the recognition of another people's persistent and vibrant presence on that same land. This dynamic, fraught with contention, collaboration, and complexity, deepens our understanding of the historical underpinnings of the modern Israeli-Palestinian conflict.

More than merely recounting historical encounters, this chapter also interrogates the narratives constructed around those encounters. The cognitive dissonance experienced by Jewish settlers—seeing the land as theirs by divine promise yet inhabited by another people deeply attached to it—continues to echo in contemporary debates. As such, the examination of this period is indispensable for grasping the enduring questions surrounding identity, belonging, and entitlement in late Ottoman Palestine.

2

Writing the Landscape, Writing the Homeland

A LANDSCAPE, though produced largely by natural processes, is always imbued with human meaning. Individual and collective identity are influenced by the landscape, and in turn impose significance and purpose on it. Indeed, the interconnectedness of natural landscape and human identity is a given of geohistorical analysis.[1] In the case of European Jews, who claimed they were physically removed from their ancestral landscape, this connection was more imaginative and textual than experiential. Indeed, scholarly consensus posits that European Jews' imagination of the land of Palestine was shaped by the US and European Christians who charted maps of the Holy Land to illustrate biblical events. This reliance on Christian cartography resulted in the incorporation of Christian place-names into the national Hebrew discourse.[2] The Christian discourse, however, was not the only one that informed the Jewish imagination of Palestine's landscape. Obviously, Jewish traditions also informed the Zionist rhetorical formation of the land and enhanced Jews' sense of belonging to it.[3] Scholarship nevertheless has largely overlooked the profound influence of Arabo-Islamic culture on the formation of the Zionist imagination of the same land. This influence is significant for several reasons. First of all, it challenges a narrative that often presents Zionism as solely influenced by European/Christian perspectives. Acknowledging the role of Arabo-Islamic culture offers a more comprehensive and nuanced understanding of the factors shaping Zionist thought as well as the construction of the Hebrew landscape. Second, recognizing the Arabo-Islamic influence highlights the interconnectedness and shared cultural heritage of Jewish and Arab communities in Palestine, and that can contribute to fostering dialogue, reconciliation, and mutual understanding among different groups in the region. Third, acknowledging the Arabo-Islamic influence disrupts the binary perspective on the Jewish-Arab relationship as solely one of conflict or opposition by looking into the practices of constructing Jewish indigeneity. It showcases instances of cultural exchange and hybridity, shared knowledge, and coexistence that have implications, in turn, for challenging stereotypes, promoting cultural diversity, and emphasizing the potential for peaceful coexistence between the two communities.

The linkage between landscape and identity can be constituted either through direct sensoriempirical experience, or textual, pictorial, and musical representations. A materialist approach to landscape privileges the encounter with landscape through the corporeal body, as individuals interact with nature and other individuals within the context of landscape. The other approach assimilates landscape to text. As discussed by cultural geographer James Duncan, "Landscape is one of the central elements in a cultural system, a text."[4] Often, specific vistas, as noted by political geographer John Agnew, "turn into typification of 'a national landscape' as a whole."[5] The collective valorization of specific views and scenery strengthens the connection between a landscape and the people living in it, thus turning it in effect into a national landscape, as in the association between the River Nile and the people of Egypt, the Lebanon Mount and the people of Lebanon, the olive tree and Palestinians, and the sabra (prickly pear cactus) and the Jews of Israel.[6]

The fascination with descriptive geography in the nineteenth and twentieth centuries in the Middle East arose out of contact with the West, where a growing interest in geography in general and that of the East in particular was a product of the search for origins—personal, cultural, and religious.[7] In fact, according to French geographer Paul Claval, at the end of the eighteenth century, the idea prevailed that a people's past is discoverable through the study of their geography; that geography in some sense generates culture. Claval exhibited a notable, albeit typical, ambivalence toward the East; while acknowledging that "civilization took its first steps in the East," he argued for Western supersession, claiming that "progress has been frozen in the centers where it began.... Culture... has moved towards the West."[8] Organizations such as the Palestine Exploration Fund, a British society, and Deutscher Verein zur Erforschung Palästinas (German Association for the Study of Palestine) promoted research into the archaeology and history, customs and culture, topography and geology, of biblical Palestine to further their own objectives, whether the search for their own past or for colonial purposes. Meanwhile, native writers of the region engaged with geographic literature for their own internal purposes, principally to forge a connection between people and their natural landscape.

The emerging intelligentsia of the nahda internalized the European colonial narrative of Arab history, wherein a period of greatness was succeeded by stagnation or decline in the post-Abbasid era. This perspective has become an intrinsic element within Arab historiography, public discourse, and the broader historical imagination.[9] The Arab obsession with *inḥiṭāṭ* (decadence) in the late modern period was coupled with the admiration for the European ascendency that stimulated the desire to import knowledge from the West in order to guide the East to a path of progress.[10] Modern sciences in this regard were given priority in the formation of modern Arab subjectivity, with modern geography garnering particular attention from nahdawi intellectuals who endeavored to enlighten their readers regarding their respective landscapes as a path to modernity. In translating European works of descriptive geography into Arabic, such as Rifāʿa al-Ṭahtāwī's (1801–73) translation of Conrad Malte-Brun's *Précis de la géographie universelle* (Paris, 1810–29), Arab scholars embraced the Enlightenment methodology of objective description, and with it, the Enlightenment spirit of universalism.[11]

The nascent discourse concerning landscape in the modern Middle East during the late nineteenth to mid-twentieth centuries strove to fortify people's connection to their respective landscapes as well as construct a template through which to reassert such a linkage, on the premise that landscape was crucial to the development of territorial identity and cultural consciousness. While recognizing the rich legacy of medieval Arabo-Islamic literature and natural history (geography, botany, and zoology), nahdawi intellectuals contemplated their own landscapes, the Nile in Egypt, and the mountains of Lebanon, in poetry and prose, as though they had never been seen before. The emergent landscape was now more connected with the people surrounding it, not detached from it, but assimilated into it.

The endeavor to construct an overarching sense of "homeland" out of myriad discrete localities was part of the project to forge a national identity, as attested to in the works of several Muslim scholars. 'Ali Mubārak (1823–93), a minister of education under the Khedives Abbas and Ismāʿīl, worked tirelessly on *Al-khiṭaṭ al-tawfiqiyya* (The quarters of Tawfik), a twenty-volume topographical, historical, and biographical encyclopedia published in the 1880s that provided an unprecedented historical record of nineteenth-century Egyptian society, and contributed to the development of a territorially defined Egyptian nationalism.[12] Long before Buṭrus al-Bustānī began publishing his encyclopedia, known in Arabic as *Dā'irt al-Maʿārif* (The dictionary of knowledge), two Beirutis launched their own historical-geographic encyclopedia. Under the title *athar al-'adhār* (Signs of times), Salīm al-Khūrī (1834–75) and Salīm Shihāda (1848–1907) devoted an entire volume to general geography, on the principle that the acquisition of geographic knowledge would organize "the social order" and strengthen the ties of "the human family."[13]

The landscape of Palestine drew the attention and curiosity of both insiders and outsiders. Western Orientalists, be they scholars, travelers, diplomats, or pilgrims, produced an enormous number of works between the mid-nineteenth and early twentieth centuries that depicted both the physical and human landscape of Palestine in exclusively biblical terms. "Both places and peoples," as Kamel Lorenzo has demonstrated, "were depicted as 'shadows' of a far-off past,

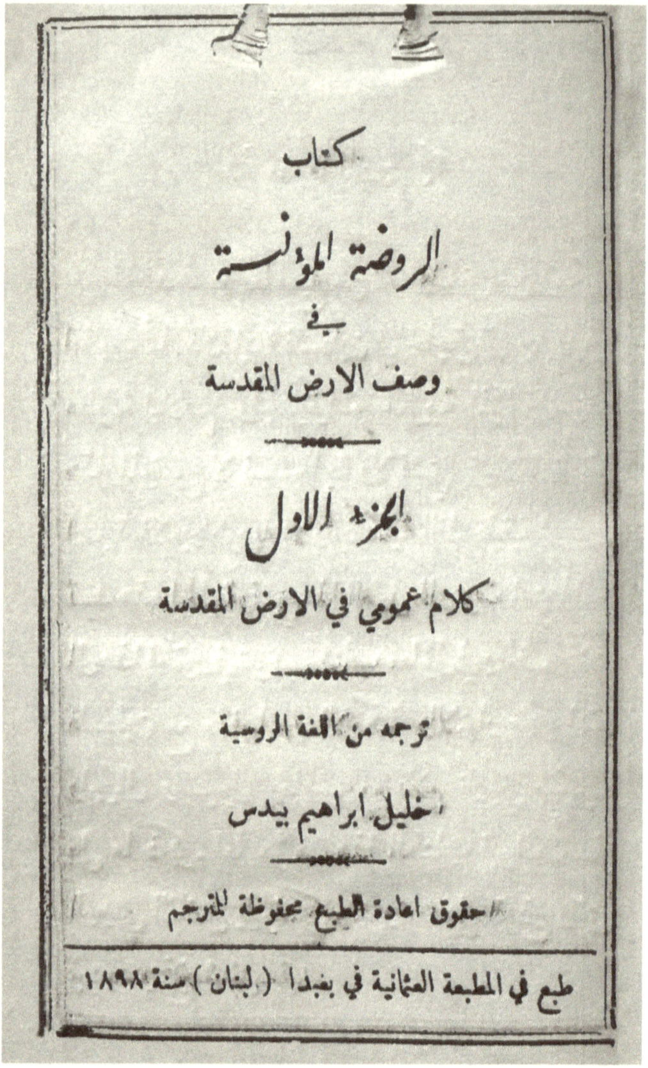
كتاب

الروضة المؤنسة

في

وصف الارض المقدسة

الجزء الاول

كلام عمومي في الارض المقدسة

ترجمه من اللغة الروسية

خليل ابراهيم بيدس

حقوق اعادة الطبع محفوظة للمترجم

طبع في المطبعة العثمانية في بعبدا (لبنان) سنة ١٨٩٨

FIGURE 2.1. Khalīl Baydas's *Kitāb al-rawḍa al-Mu'nisa fī waṣf al-'arḍ al-Muqaddasa* (The book of pleasant gardens in describing the Holy Land). Baydas's work is a translation of an ethnographic geography of Palestine by Russian author Nikolai Aleksander Eloenskii. The book was published in Lebanon in 1896.

'fossils' suspended in time."[14] Nahdawi intellectuals in Palestine turned to Western descriptive geographic works and translated them into Arabic with the aim of making their countries better known to their readers. Khalīl Baydas (1874–1949), a nahdawi intellectual from Nazareth in Palestine, exemplified this impulse. Having been trained at a Russian Orthodox teacher's training seminary in

Nazareth, Baydas translated the ethnographic geography of Palestine by Nikolai Aleksander Eloenskii, published in 1896, into Arabic under the title *Kitāb al-rawḍa al-Mu'nisa fī waṣf al-'arḍ al-Muqaddasa* (The book of pleasant gardens in describing the Holy Land). Eloenskii's account was of interest to Baydas because he believed that disseminating the Russian Orientalist's text would transform the local Palestinians' experience of and relationship to their own landscape as they lacked a comparable work in their own language.[15]

Engagement with Palestine's geography also attracted Jewish figures, both natives and immigrants. For Jews, as for nahdawi intellectuals, the acquisition of geographic knowledge of Palestine was a means of modernizing and consolidating their nativity. Unlike their Arab counterparts, however, Hebrew writers utilized this geographic knowledge as a means of demonstrating and fortifying indigeneity, rooting themselves in the land by knowing it, while contributing to the Hebrew revival movement.

Knowing Palestine in Hebrew

Geography was one component of the construction of a Hebrew cultural infrastructure, which was essential to producing a native Hebrew self-conceptualization, built on Jewish particularism associated with and embodied in the history as well as geography of Palestine and the Orient. In addressing the question of when a settler becomes native, scholar of political philosophy and jurisprudence Raef Zreik reminds us of the peculiarity of Zionism in combining aspects of settler colonialism and nationalism. What sets Zionism apart from other settler colonial movements, as Zreik explains, is the Zionist self-image of a people returning to their ancestral homeland together with the absence of a homeland for settlers to return to.[16] This self-image propelled social and cultural transformations from settler to native once Jews were in Palestine. Concomitant with their dismissal of "the exilic Jew" as a model for the new life, Jewish settlers glorified ancient Hebrews as a model to follow and then looked at the native population, in particular the farmer and the Bedouin, as a concrete living model that appeared to adhere to customs shared by the ancient Hebrews.[17] In addition to identifying contemporary models for Jews to imitate, this cultural project mobilized geographic and botanical knowledge of Palestine as a means to recuperate the nativity of Jews in Palestine.

Late nineteenth-century Palestine witnessed the appearance of a series of works aimed at the advancement of yedi'at ha-arets (as noted earlier, meaning a knowledge of the land) among Hebrew readers. Preceded by an increase in waves of persecution against Jews in Europe and the emergence of the Zionist movement that encouraged Jews to immigrate to late Ottoman Palestine, the objective of these writings, in the words of Naḥum Sokolow (1859–1936), a Zionist leader commonly known as the father of modern Hebrew journalism, was to "bring closer the heart of the people of Israel to the land from which they were exiled."[18]

The modern version of yedi'at ha-arets attracted both native and immigrant Jewish writers, both of whom can be termed "Ottoman Hebrews," to take part in this project as a way of supporting the emerging Zionist movement and the immigration of their kinspeople in faith to Palestine without undermining their loyalty to the Ottoman government. Sephardi and Oriental Jews embraced Ottoman universalism simultaneously with Jewish particularism. And for their part, prominent immigrant Jewish settlers adopted a similar reconciliatory approach in accepting Ottoman citizenship while exhorting their Ashkenazi fellows to live out the principles of Hebrew nationalism.[19]

Hebrew writers' endeavor to embed immigrant Jews in the Palestinian landscape meant they were de facto joining in the nahda discourse connecting the population of each region in Arabic-speaking countries to its landscape. Thus these Hebrew writers can be considered nahdawi Jews due to their participation in and interaction with intellectual projects initiated by nahdawi Arab figures, especially in socializing and politicizing modern sciences, such as geography and botany, to reveal the origins of their people while consolidating those peoples' ties to the land in which they had long been living. Israel Ben-Ze'ev, a contemporary of David Yellin as well as his disciple and admirer, noted how influential the writings of Lebanese and Syrian nahdawi scholars such as Naṣif al-Yazjī (1800–1871), Ibrahīm al-Yazjī (1847–1906), and al-Bustānī (1819–83) were among Yellin and his circle, which included Sephardi and Oriental Jews like the brothers Isaac Yahuda and Abraham Shalom Yahuda as well as Ashkenazi Jewish immigrants like Eliezer Ben-Yehuda.[20]

The efforts of these nahdawi thinkers in the literary and cultural Arab renaissance included the revitalization of literary Arabic, consolidation of Arab identity through affiliative bonding with their physical geography, and modernization of the socioeconomic infrastructure of their society. In the construction of Arab selfhood, al-Bustānī was instrumental in adopting and mediating a paradigm of modernity that was expressed in "the idealized image of the native subject."[21] The modern native subject in al-Bustānī's worldview ushers in "progress" and "civilization." With the support and encouragement of the ruling elite in the Ottoman context, the role of the intellectual, according to al-Bustānī, was to harness Western knowledge and adapt it to awaken Arabs' inherent cultural excellence. Central to nahda discourse in Cairo and Lebanon was the effort to replace oral means of knowledge production with modern modes, such as printed encyclopedias, books, and journals. Al-Ṭahṭāwī found in the Būlāq press in Egypt a powerful instrument to advance his intellectual agenda by publishing several Arabo-Islamic books to raise public awareness of Arabic culture and legacy. Among the earliest books that al-Ṭahṭāwī published was *al-Khiṭaṭ* (The quarters), an urban geography of Cairo by fifteenth-century scholar al-Maqrīzī.[22] Al-Bustānī's encyclopedia *Dā'irat al-ma'ārif* (The dictionary of knowledge) testifies to the importance of print in knowledge production in the nineteenth century as well as the inclusion of various forms of scientific knowledge such as geography, botany, geology, and so on. His encyclopedia innovatively included updated scientific knowledge resulting from exposure to European sources and utilized printed texts for wider dissemination, contrasting them with traditional medieval Arabic texts that relied on manuscripts and had limited circulation.

Baydas's lamentation over the scarcity of Arabic books that could enlighten the Palestinian people about and consolidate their native ties to the physical features of their homeland resonated with the Hebrew scholars in Palestine who expressed similar anxieties. Abraham Moshe Lunts (1854–1918), a learned Jew inextricably linked to the revival of modern Hebrew and dissemination of yedi'at ha-arets among the Jewish communities in Palestine, is among the early Hebrew writers who emphatically remarked on the absence of Hebrew works on the geography of Palestine that would connect the people of Israel to their land of origin, and as such, took it on himself to author and publish such works. In the first volume of the almanac *Yerushalayim* published in 1882, Lunts issues a plea for Jews to be proud of their ancestral land: "We, the people of Israel, even though we were exiled from this desirable land and became wandering among the nations, plundered and looted all the time, we should not be ashamed of our origins when looking back to the cradle of our childhood." His project was to restore the indigeneity of the people of Israel to Palestine by writing on and about the land of their origin in Hebrew. The persecution of Jews in Europe and their immigration to Palestine constituted the pivotal moment to reindigenize Jews and restore them in Palestine: "Even though many eyes are looking today to return and inherit the land, the land that breathes life into the dried bones, now we must spread truthful light on all the manners of the land."[23] It is worth noting that in asserting the nativity of Jews to Palestine, Lunts does not deny the indigeneity of Palestinian Arabs to the same strip of land—an issue that was discussed in chapter 1. In fact, Jews' return to their ancestral homeland and their indigenization hinged on their discovery that the local Palestinian population, both Jews and non-Jews, had preserved as well as sustained the lifestyle and customs of their ancestors.[24]

The policies of the Ottoman government regarding the immigration of Jewish settlers played an important role in both supporting and obstructing the connection between Jews and the human and physical landscape of Palestine. Regulations on Jewish immigration contributed to fostering Jews' connection to the land through settlement while simultaneously disrupting this connection by curbing Jewish immigration to Palestine to protect the territorial coherence of the Ottoman state. For instance, in the almanac *Yerushalayim* in 1887, Lunts praises

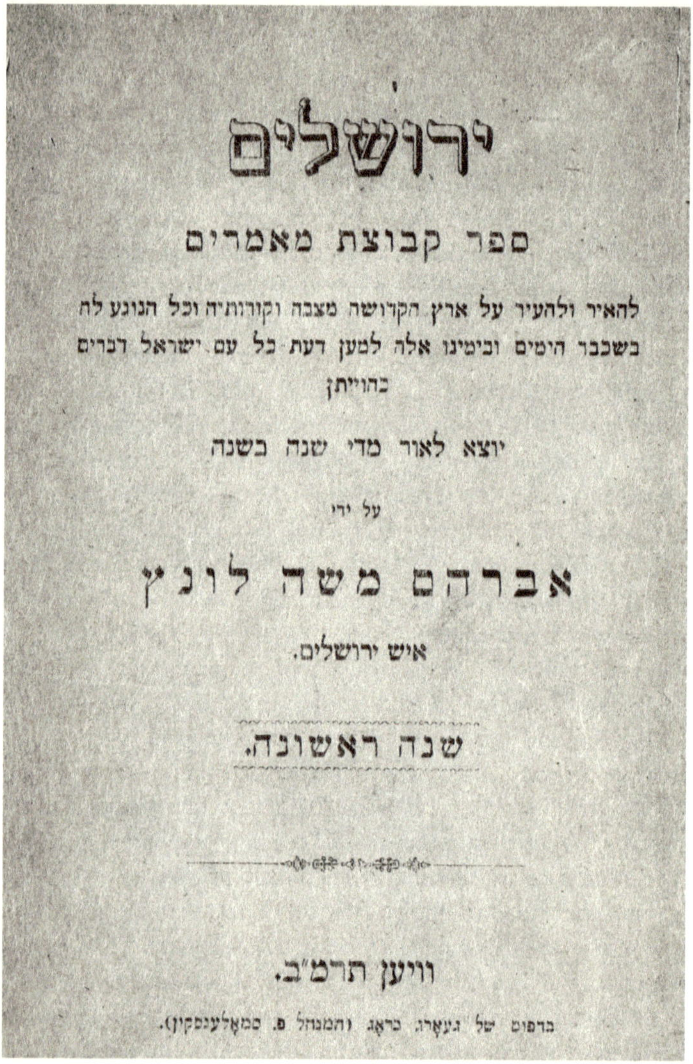
ירושלים

ספר קבוצת מאמרים

להאיר ולהעיר על ארץ הקדושה מצבה וקורותיה וכל הנוגע לה
בשכבר הימים ובימינו אלה למען דעת כל עם ישראל דברים
בהויתן

יוצא לאור מדי שנה בשנה

על ידי

אברהם משה לונץ

איש ירושלים.

שנה ראשונה.

וויען תרמ"ב.

בדפוס של געארג בראג (המנהל פ. סמאלענסקין).

FIGURE 2.2. Cover of Abraham Moshe Lunts's yearbook *Yerushalayim* (Jerusalem). The description of the series reads: "To shed light and provide insight on the Holy Land, its conditions, history, and everything related to it in both the past and the present, so that all the people of Israel may understand these essential matters." The first volume of this yearbook was published in 1881.

the reforms initiated by "our esteemed government" in Jerusalem that include the establishment of a local police council with the inclusion of a Jewish police officer on its force as the authorities attempted to provide security to the residents of the territories under their jurisdiction. He likewise applauds the efforts of the city council to hire a physician to treat patients "without religious discrimination at no cost on their end."[25] These passages highlight the fluidity of the intercommunal boundaries, and testify to interconfessional relations between Jews, Christians, and Muslims.[26] At the same time, when it came to the Ottoman authorities' strict prohibitions on Jewish immigrants fleeing the pogroms in Russia and eastern Europe to seek settlement in Palestine, Lunts respectfully urged the government to consider the economic potential to be gained by accommodating these Jewish immigrants, whose capital and professional skills might benefit Palestine economically.[27]

With the participation of native and immigrant Jewish writers, such as Yellin and Isaac Yahuda, Lunts's journal became influential in the use of modern knowledge forms, notably geography, botany, and ethnography in interpreting biblical and postbiblical sources to assist the indigenization of Jewish settlers returning to what they deemed their ancestral homeland. Lunts's contributions to the dissemination of yediʿat ha-arets went beyond the Hebrew Jerusalemite writers to affect other cultural activists among Jewish immigrants like Ben-Yehuda.

Ben-Yehuda: Reviver of a Language and Land

Ben-Yehuda was not a native of al-Mashriq; he was born in Luzhky, Lithuania, a major center of eastern European Jewry for centuries.[28] His interest in the Muslim world was sparked by nationalist struggles following the Russo-Turkish War of 1877–78, particularly the aspirations of the Bulgarian people for independence from the Ottoman Empire. After his graduation from high school in Daugavpils, Latvia, Ben-Yehuda continued his studies in Paris, then the center of European political and diplomatic life.[29] Though he attended the École de Médecine to become a physician, a profession that would provide social standing, he spent a substantial amount of his time and energy immersed in Jewish culture and politics.

Ben-Yehuda's stay in Paris laid the foundation for his acquaintance with the Muslim world.[30] In Paris, "the great world center of wisdom and learning," as he describes it in a letter to Deborah (whom he married in 1881), he began to quench his thirst to learn about the history of the Jewish people and their presence in the land of their forebearers:

> My immediate object is to reach a certain *niveau* [level] which will enable me to come into intimate contact with the great Jewish personalities of our time to interest them in my plan for the reestablishment of the Jewish people on the soil of our ancestors. I am desirous of learning all that I can about the history of our own people. I hope to find everything in the university called the Sorbonne.[31]

In addition to his political objective of gaining support from eminent French Jews for his nationalist plans, Ben-Yehuda's omnivorous curiosity about his people's history necessarily pulled him into the orbit of Islam and Arabo-Islamic culture.

Ben-Yehuda is well-known for his contributions to the revival of modern Hebrew, yet he is less known for his involvement in Palestine's geography and his efforts to raise the Jewish people's consciousness of the land by writing on yedi'at ha-arets. In 1883, early in the period of Jewish settlement in Palestine, Ben-Yehuda published a geographic book on Palestine titled *Sefer Erets Yisrael: 'Al teva' ha-arets ha-zot* (The book of the land of Israel: On the nature of this land).[32] The work promised to be a comprehensive treatment of Palestine's landscape, with the subtitle, "On the Nature of This Land, Its Seas and Rivers, Its Mountains and Valleys, Its Climate, Its Flora and Fauna, as well as Its Cities and Villages."[33] His intention in composing it was to address émigré Hebrew readers' general lack of knowledge of the land by promoting yedi'at ha-arets. Indeed, he took Hebrew writers to task for demonstrating an interest in the geography of a wide range of lands, with the exception of Palestine:

> Quite a lot of books were composed in Hebrew on the lands of every part of the world near and far; on European kingdoms, be they small or big, on the states of America, be they settled or uninhabited, on the edges of Asia and on the borders of Africa, as well as on far sea islands, save for one land to which Hebrew writers did not pay attention, save for one place in the entire world that was not mighty enough to appeal to them to know to report to their people about.[34]

Nahdawi Arab intellectuals of his time were similarly critical of their people's lack of geographic knowledge pertaining to their own landscapes. Thus both Arabs and Jews were engaged in parallel and overlapping projects to promote their communities' relationship to the land beyond the immediate locality, and bolster their sense of belonging in the homeland.[35]

Sefer Erets Yisrael juxtaposes accounts of insiders' and outsiders' views of Palestine's landscape, and illuminates the ways in which dominant ideologies, held by either local Arabs (be they Muslims, Christians, or even Jews) or Western Orientalists, were communicated through the medium of landscape. The incorporation of knowledge retrieved from these various sources contributed to the emergent modern, Jewish, and Oriental culture. The first sources Ben-Yehuda turns to in composing his work are traditional Jewish ones—that is, the Hebrew Bible and Talmud, which contain references to historical events that took place in the land and some geographic locations. He also makes use of Flavius Josephus's writings, especially *The Jewish War* and *The Antiquities of the Jews*. In addition, he consults Jewish travelogues, especially *Tevo'ot ha-arets* (All the produce of the land) by Josef Schwarz (1804–65), who studied Palestine's landscape, including its fauna and flora, and its inhabitants.[36] But this scant Jewish geographic tradition was insufficient for Ben-Yehuda's purposes.

In the concluding chapters of *Sefer Erets Yisrael*, Ben-Yehuda reflects on the successful completion of his goal: acquainting readers with the landscape of

ספר

ארץ ישראל

על

טבע הארץ הזאת, ימיה ונהריה הריה ועמקיה
וטבע אקלימה, והצמח והחי אשר בה, ועריה
וכפריה.

חברו

אליעזר בן יהודה.

צורת המטבע אשר טבעו הרומאים לזכר גבורתם על ארץ יהודה.
על עצם המטבע שתי המלות יהודה בשבי כתובות רומית.

ירושלם ת"ו

שנת תרמ"ג לפ"ק

נדפס בדפוס ר' יואל משה סאלאמון נ"י

FIGURE 2.3. Eliezer Ben-Yehuda's *Sefer Erets Yisrael: 'Al teva' ha-arets ha-zot* (The book of the land of Israel: On the nature of this land). The book was published in 1883 in Jerusalem. Below the subtitle, it should be noted, is a portrayal of a Roman coin containing two words: Yehuda Be-Shevi ("Judea Capta" in Latin, and "Judea in captivity" in English). These had been minted to commemorate the Roman triumph over Jerusalem. The coin depicts a woman in a scene of mourning seated under a palm tree. Next to the woman stands a Roman soldier in military dress with a spear in one hand and a parazonium in the other, with his right foot on his helmet.

Palestine from the safety of their armchairs. He takes pride in his ability to guide readers through a virtual tour of the Jordanian Desert and Dead Sea, sparing them exposure to potential natural and human threats. Rather than physically visiting these locations, the reader traverses the desert and sea vicariously through the pages of Ben-Yehuda's book: "The scorching heat of the blazing sun did not strike him, nor did the salty waters of the sea harm his flesh. The threats of the Bedouins refrained from causing him harm." Accordingly, Ben-Yehuda urges his readers to fully appreciate Westerners who traveled to Palestine—those individuals who "risked their lives to inform people about its nature."[37] These travelers and their firsthand accounts, which his mastery of German, French, and English rendered accessible, include William McClure Thomson's *The Land and the Book* published in 1859 as a reservoir of his twenty-five-year experience in the Orient.[38] Other travel accounts he consulted include William Francis Lynch's account of his expedition to the Jordan River in 1848, F. De Saulcy's work *Voyage autour de la Mer Morte*, published in 1853, and De Saulcy's two-volume *Voyage en Terre Sainte*, published in 1865.[39] Ben-Yehuda's reading list also encompassed Carl Ritter's *Erdkunde*, a scholarly compendium of geographic knowledge compiled from books available in Western libraries; its first volume was published in 1816.[40]

In addition to his reliance on Western literature and travel narratives, though, Ben-Yehuda utilized geographic knowledge found in either Arabo-Islamic textual sources or the local population. In fact, Ben-Yehuda's interest in Arab geographic knowledge mirrored that of nahda intellectuals who benefited from the same traditional Arabo-Islamic sources. In the nineteenth century, traditional knowledge of the land converged with the modern discipline of European geography to coalesce into the works of nahda writers in Egypt such as ʿAli Mubārak and the Egyptian jurist and writer Muḥammad Amīn Fikrī (1856–99), the author of *Jughrāfīyat Miṣr* (The geography of Egypt), published in 1879.[41] Similarly, Ben-Yehuda incorporates materials drawn from Arabic geographic literature and Arabic lexicons.

Ben-Yehuda's familiarity with Arabo-Islamic culture relies on two main textual sources: literary works by medieval Arab authors and Western travelers' accounts of Palestine.[42] In his dictionary, he demonstrates knowledge of Arabic acquired from reading Arabic lexicons such as *Lisān al-ʿarab* (The language of Arabs) by medieval Arab linguist Ibn Manẓūr (1233–1311/12)—a work so popular that manuscript copies were found in the thousands and in multiple languages. Ibn Manẓūr's lexicon was a fundamental source for al-Bustānī's lexicon *Muḥīṭ al-muḥīṭ* too.[43] Also of great benefit to Ben-Yehuda were the literary and linguistic aspects of Western travelogues to Palestine, such as Carl Brockelmann's multivolume work *Geschichte der arabischen Litterature* (1898–1902) and *Grammatik des arabischen Vulgärdialectes von Aegypten* (1880) by Orientalist Guillaume Spitta-Bey (1853–83), which investigated the grammar of the contemporary Egyptian dialect.[44]

Beyond these textual sources, local populations fluent in Arabic, not only Arabs, but Sephardi and Oriental Jews, served as a rich source for Ben-Yehuda. Among the latter was Yellin, whom Ben-Yehuda mentions in the introduction to his dictionary and with whom he held several discussions over several entries. Their companionship grew closer over the course of Ben-Yehuda's stay in Jerusalem given their mutual social, cultural, and political interests. Their acquaintance began when they were both members of the B'nai B'rith (Children of the Covenant) order in the Jerusalem lodge and teaching faculty at the Alliance Israélite Universelle in Jerusalem. Sephardi members of B'nai B'rith such as Yosef Meyuḥas (1868–1942) and Isaac Yahuda, among the earliest native Jews recruited to join the Jerusalem lodge, were also useful to Ben-Yehuda's project. Another was Avraham Almaliaḥ (1885–1967), who helped Ben-Yehuda in his editorial activities for the newspaper *hashkafah* (Outlook).[45]

Non-Jewish Arab locals were no less central to Ben-Yehuda's geographic enterprise. In his endeavors to help indigenize prospective settler immigrants, Ben-Yehuda utilized the accounts of local Arabs, collected from oral sources through personal interactions, regarding the landscape's aesthetics, history, and cultural meaning. His book references not only the local Palestinian Arab population's topographical terminology but the values, beliefs, and significance they attached to the particularities of the land too. Hence his account frequently cites Arab sources, usually prefaced with phrases such as *le-fi ha-ʿaravim* (according to Arabs . . .), *ha-ʿaravīm ḳorʾīm* (Arabs call . . .), or *ha-ʿaravīm yoshvey ha-arets ḳorʾīm* (Arabs residing in the land call . . .).[46] The consultation with the local Arab population aligns with Ben-Yehuda's perspective on the vitality of the Palestinian Arabic dialect, which incorporates numerous Hebrew words. In *Sefer Erets Yisrael*, however, Ben-Yehuda does not explicitly explain the rationale underlying the practice of seeking knowledge of the landscape from the local population. It is only years later that he articulates this approach. During a 1911 meeting of the Hebrew Language Committee, which he chaired, Ben-Yehuda emphasized the importance of Arabic dialects in enriching Hebrew. He specifically highlighted the significance of the Arabic dialect spoken in Syria and Palestine. This dialect contains many words not found in other varieties, and includes Hebrew terms that do not require the typical letter changes between Arabic and Hebrew. As an illustrative example, Ben-Yehuda cited the Hebrew word *Shetil*, which exists exclusively in the Palestinian dialect as *Shatil* and signifies "seedling."[47]

Ben-Yehuda also turns to folkloric materials to discern the local population's rationale for the coinage of place-names.[48] For instance, when discussing specific place-names in Palestine, whether mountains, rivers, or valleys, he consistently presents the Hebrew name first, followed by its Arabic equivalent. In the exploration of the Transjordan Mountain range, potentially Abarim, traditionally believed to be the location where the Israelites camped on the final leg of their wilderness journey before entering the land of Canaan, Ben-Yehuda references three specific mountains. Regarding these mountains, he employs their Arabic names: ʿagalim (ʿajlon in Arabic), Khafkhafa, and Jabal Hosha (Hosea). Notably, when delving into the etymology of the mountain associated with Hosea, Ben-Yehuda includes an explanation, acknowledging local beliefs that assert that "the prophet Hosea is buried there."[49] In this context, Ben-Yehuda attributes the preservation of site names and conservation of Israelite history in the land to the local Arab population.

The Jewish return to Palestine was accompanied by the reconstruction of the landscape in accordance with the Hebrew Bible. Geographic and botanical knowledge was utilized to introduce interpretations to biblical and postbiblical narratives relevant to Palestine's physical landscape. In connecting the Jewish people to their ancestral homeland, Ben-Yehuda describes the landscape's spatial features vividly in a language couched in the Hebrew Bible, describing Palestine as an *erets ṭovah* (a good land) into which God promised to bring the children of Israel. He quotes from Deuteronomy at the beginning of his work:

> For the Lord your God is bringing you into a good land, a land with streams and springs and fountains issuing from plain and hill; a land of wheat and barley, of vines, figs, and pomegranates, a land of olive trees and honey; a land where you may eat food without stint, where you will lack nothing.[50]

The biblical quotation is echoed in the subtitle of the book and functioned as a vehicle for attaching Jewish individuals to "the good land," Palestine. The term Ben-Yehuda uses here, erets ṭovah, occurs in several places in the Hebrew Bible with reference to the land of Palestine.

Besides deriving Hebrew words from their Arabic cognates, as will be discussed in detail in chapter 3, Ben-Yehuda investigated Arabo-Islamic interpretations of the signification of sites mentioned in the Jewish sources and how these sites were regarded in the cultural system of locals. For example, in a section on the mountains of Palestine, he underscores the significance of Mount Hor in the Jewish sources aided by relevant information from Islamic texts. The Hebrew name of the mountain does not itself indicate the significance of the site for Jews based on the biblical account (Numbers 33:37–39) that Aaron the priest died there. But the same Mount Hor was known among the Arab population of Palestine as Jabal Hārūn (the Mount of Aaron). Ben-Yehuda notes the Muslim reverence for the mountain:

> On one of the summits . . . is a grave that Arabs call Qabr Hārūn (Aaron's Tomb). It is sacred to them, and many of them visit for prayer. The building on the grave is a relatively new building resembling the pattern of Muslims' tombs, and yet the remnants of old pillars are seen in the wall, and these

> contain many Hebrew and Arabic inscriptions, which visitors engraved for their memory at the place of the grave of this eminent saint.[51]

This passage is significant not only for its identification of Mount Hor with *Jabal Hārūn* but also for the way it describes Arab reverence for the burial place of Aaron, as illustrated by the presence of ancient and contemporary architectural features and inscriptions.[52]

When Yehuda first arrives in Jaffa, the local populace that he encountered, whom he described as "dressed in the fashion of the land" and "cheerful, rejoicing, happy, laughing, and reveling," now appear as embedded figures in Palestine's natural landscape.[53] Ben-Yehuda presents a remarkably vivid account of a populated land and its inhabitants' distinct way of life.[54]

Yellin: Ben-Ha-Mizraḥ

A number of Jewish writers joined Lunts's project to disseminate geographic and botanical knowledge of Palestine, with the objective of recuperating the nativity of the Jewish people in the Orient and facilitating their return to what they perceived as their land of origin. Among them, Yellin stands out as a prolific contributor to the shaping of Jewish intellectual life in Palestine. In his writings he reflects on issues central to the Jewish national enterprise, and his views are infused with and guided by his familiarity with the Arabo-Islamic world. In his works, Yellin admits his inclination toward Arabic and Islamic culture, and urges his fellow Jews to show interest in that as well. "For my entire life, I have been a lover of the Arab people (*ohev ha'am ha-'aravi*), occupied with learning their language, reading their literature, and always encouraging my people to study it."[55]

One of Yellin's preoccupations in his writings on late Ottoman Palestine was restoring the connection between Jews and Palestine's landscape.[56] For approximately six years, Lunts's works, in addition to two major Hebrew books, *Sefer Erets Yisrael* (1883) by Ben-Yehuda and *Erets Ḥemdah* (1885) by Hebrew journalist and Zionist leader Naḥum Sokolow, had dominated the discourse on yedi'at ha-arets for Hebrew-reading audiences.[57] In 1889, Yellin authored a book on Palestine's landscape that supplemented those works. Unlike Ben-Yehuda's *Sefer Erets Yisrael*, which endeavored to reach a general Hebrew-reading audience, Yellin's book *Miḳra le-na're Bene Yisrael* (Reading for the youth of the children of Israel) was addressed to Hebrew high school students to increase their awareness of Jewish history in Palestine and the Orient, thereby attaching them to its physical landscape.[58] Yellin followed this with another book, titled *Erets avotenu* (Land of our fathers)—a title that is embedded in the language of nationalism, and that discussed geographic, botanical, and zoological aspects of Palestine. A reviewer of Yellin's *Miḳra* in the Hebrew newspaper *Hamgid* (Preacher)—the first

Hebrew-language and widely circulated newspaper—informs the readers about the new book:

> In the holy land, where a new path has been paved in studies, an urgent necessity has ignited in the hearts of both teachers and students to revitalize the Hebrew language and make it a spoken tongue. There, the demand will heavily burden the teachers to swiftly address the gap in study materials. . . . [W]ithout hesitation, they will be able to enhance this field with our literature. The result of this endeavor is now in front of us, known as "Miḳra for the youth of Israel."[59]

The reviewer values Yellin's *Miḳra* as contributing to the movement of the revival of Hebrew and the return to *erets ha-ḳodesh* (the holy land)—note the connection to the Arabic term *al-arḍ al-Muqaddasa* used by Baydas in his translation of the geographic Russian book discussed earlier—because it serves as a tool for fostering a deeper connection with the Hebrew language and culture. During the early days of the revitalization of Hebrew, there was a strong desire among educators and students to reintroduce Hebrew as a spoken language, and instill a sense of pride and ownership in it, especially among those who lived in Palestine. The reviewer notes that *Miḳra*'s Hebrew language is liberated from the influence of European languages and its immersion in "the spirit of the language of the holy books." The reviewer also indicates another quality of the book, which is its inclusion of essential study material drawn from Jewish sources like the Mishnah along with the sayings of earlier sages that embody the cultural and spiritual heritage of the Hebrew people.[60] Similar to Ben-Yehuda's and Sokolow's works, *Erets avotenu* starts with a geographic description of the land and concludes with the physical history of the Jewish presence in Palestine, including the new Jewish settlement in Erets Yisrael.[61]

Yellin's project parallels al-Bustānī's as a retrieval of collective identity based on affiliation with the land.[62] In the introduction to his *Miḳra*, Yellin acknowledges the existence of other Hebrew books addressed to Jewish youths, but dismisses them for drawing on non-Jewish sources. From his perspective, these other works lack content particular to the Jewish people, and fail to acknowledge the great figures (*anshe mofet l-khol davar ṭov ve-na'aleh*) of Jewish heritage and their achievements.[63] In both books, he takes it on himself to recuperate the Jewish nativity, situating it not only in the history and geography of Palestine but also the broader region. In *Miḳra*, he briefly surveys the history and words of wisdom of *gibbure yisrael* (heroes of Israel) in Palestine and the Orient, such as Mattathias the Hasmonean (died 161 BCE) and Judah Maccabee (died 160 BCE) from the Roman period, the Arab Jewish poet al-Samaw'al Ibn 'Adiya' (died ca. 560), and Moses Maimonides (1135–1204). While critical of other Hebrew texts for drawing from non-Jewish sources, he himself draws on Arabic and Islamic sources in the construction of the nativity of the heroes of Israel to Palestine and the Orient. The destruction of the temple and persecution of the Jewish people at the hands of the Romans led to massive Jewish immigration outside Palestine. Yellin opines that some of these exiled Jews settled in the Arabian Peninsula. As destruction sets the city of Jerusalem in flames and turns its temple into ruins, Yellin paints a picture of Arabia as a bountiful and fertile land with diverse natural resources: "And the land is exceedingly broad and blessed by God, a land of dates, coffee, and rice, with abundant livestock, including numerous horses and camels." Not only is the land bountiful and fertile, but its inhabitants are amicable hosts. As opposed to the cruelty of the Romans, Yellin emphasizes the familial affinity between the Israelites and Arabs as well as their morality: "The people of the land are the Arabs, descendants of Joktan the son of Eber and Ishmael the son of Abraham. These people are generous and hospitable."[64] In fact, if anything, the linkage between the modern native Hebrew and the Orient is stressed in Yellin's cultural project. Yellin is commended in *Hamgid* for the inclusion of Jewish and non-Jewish materials (*ḥiloni*) in his *Miḳra* to educate adults and children about the heroes of the Jewish people in Palestine and the Orient. In undertaking this project, Yellin fails to acknowledge his indebtedness to Arabo-Islamic sources to relate the annals of Jews in Arabia, including the notable Jewish poet al-Samaw'al. Writing in a sacralized Hebrew, Yellin approaches Jewish history from a primarily Jewish-centric perspective, focusing more on Jewish texts, figures, and sources while downplaying the significance of Arabo-Islamic sources. This narrow stance could limit his recognition of the interconnectedness of Jewish and Arabo-Islamic histories in the region, despite underscoring the cultural and social affinity between Jews and Arabs.

Knowledge of Palestine's Arabic toponymy, in Yellin's worldview, was essential for the restoration of Jews' ties to the land. Not only did he incorporate Arabic place-names alongside their Hebrew equivalents, but he saw knowledge of Arabic as essential for restoring the Jewish connection with Palestine. His geographic descriptions include "many placenames according to their Arabic appellation," which he explicitly instructs his readers how to properly read. Like Ben-Yehuda before him, Yellin attributes place-names to his Arab informants with the phrase *yiḳra'u lo ha-'Aravim* (Arabs call it), or a similar phrase, *ve-ha-'Aravim yiḳra'u lo* (and Arabs call it), before associating the Hebrew name with its Arabic counterpart.Elsewhere, Yellin uses the phrase *u-be-'Aravit* (in Arabic) before offering the Arabic equivalent of a certain place-name.[65]

Yellin points out the parallels between Arabic and Hebrew place-names throughout the section devoted to the exploration of the geographic sites as part of his larger project of restoring the Jewish connection to the land. For example, we find this passage in a section describing the mountains of the land:

> To the north of Erets Israel rise the eminent and lofty Lebanon Mountains, which stretch from the northeastern corner to the southwest, divided into two

> sections. The first section is parallel to the [Mediterranean] Sea . . . which Arabs called *al-Libnān*. The second section to the East comprises the Lebanon Mountains facing the East . . . , and Arabs called them *al-Sharqī*, ha-Mizraḥī (the Eastern side). Foreigners call them ante-Lebanon, i.e., before Lebanon. Between [both sections] stretches a large valley known as *Biq'at ha-Levanon*, and Arabs call it *al-Biqā'*. South of the Lebanon Mountains rises Har Ḥermon . . . (in Arabic *Jabal al-Sheikh*) . . . to the south is Mount Tavor (in Arabic *Jabal Ṭūr*) . . . to the south are Mounts Ephraim and Shomron . . . (in Arabic *Jabal Nablus*). Two series of mountains ascend from these points. . . . [T]he first is . . . the mountains of *ha-Gilboa'* (in Arabic, *Jilbūn*) and the second is the mount *ha-Karmel* (in Arabic, *Jabal mār Eliās*). From Jerusalem to the south the Mountains of Yehuda stretch throughout the south of the land of Israel (in Arabic, *Jabal al-Khalīl*).[66]

Yellin's approach facilitates recognition of Hebrew sites since most of the readers the book targeted were well-versed in the Jewish tradition with limited familiarity with late Ottoman Palestine. Second, it guides readers toward recognizing the rootedness of the land in an Eastern culture whose language is embedded in its natural landscape and closely connected with Hebrew. In the reconstruction of a Hebrew map of Palestine, Yellin's efforts envisage a homeland that includes both Jews and Arabs. In his worldview, the Arab inhabitants are 'am ha-arets (the people of the land) and their language is sefat ha-arets (as noted earlier, meaning the language of the land).

Arabo-Islamic Botanical Knowledge and Biblical Interpretation

Central to the construction of Jewish indigeneity, and displaying the connection between Jews and their natural habitat, was the restoration of the botanical knowledge contained in the Hebrew Bible. Crucial to this process was to study the uses and cultural associations of plants among the local population, in addition to consulting Arabo-Islamic botanical texts, both modern and medieval. The incorporation of these materials offered a new reading of the Hebrew Bible in which the botanical world of Palestine became not merely an artifact preserved in textual sources but rather a contemporary, resurrected landscape with real living plants and trees.

Jewish tradition is filled with accounts of plants and trees native to the land of Palestine and adjacent countries, not only for their utilitarian uses, but for their relevance to religious rituals. But since not all the Jewish writers resided in Palestine and its vicinity, certain commentaries on its landscape fell short in terms of accuracy. In late Ottoman Palestine, Hebrew naturalist Menashe Meirovitch stressed the utility of the botanical knowledge to be found dispersed in Arabo-Islamic sources.

Meirovitch's knowledge of Arabic did not go beyond limited phrases in the Palestinian dialect, and surely he did not know literary Arabic.[67] His lack of literary Arabic knowledge, however, did not prevent him from consulting botanical Arabo-Islamic sources that were available in translation. Furthermore, Meirovitch placed primary significance on local peasants' traditional agricultural techniques, which he learned through direct contact with the local farmers with whom he shared his agronomic knowledge.[68] Meirovitch utilized Arabo-Islamic botanical sources in several ways. First, he enriched Hebrew through the incorporation of Arabic botanical nomenclature. Second, he identified biblical and postbiblical botanical references with existing Arabic plant names in hopes of restoring the botanical map of the land in accordance with Jewish sources. Third, he exploited contemporary plant names to provide an interpretation of biblical and postbiblical botanical references to plants in the Holy Land. And finally, he gave an account of the ethnobotanical practices of the Indigenous population.

In his article "Tsimḥe Erets Ha-Tsevi" (The flora of the land of gazelles), Meirovitch associates biblical plant names with the corresponding Arabic plant names in the immediate environment of Palestine—a methodology also used by Meirovitch's predecessors.[69] What distinguished Meirovitch's approach was that he addressed his subject not only as a lexicographer but as a naturalist too. Thanks to his study of the natural history of Palestine, Meirovitch succeeded, to some extent, in identifying biblical plants with extant plants in the region. One such biblically referenced plant discussed in Meirovitch's works is the *atad*. While the atad appears several times in the Hebrew Bible, it is Jotham's parable of trees in Judges that provides the basis for Meirovitch's botanical discussion.[70] What is of interest here is the imagined conversation between the atad and the other trees:

> Then all the trees said to the atad (thorn bush), "You come and reign over us." And the atad said to the trees, "If you are acting honorably in anointing me king over you, come and take shelter in my shade; but if not, may fire issue from the atad and consume the cedars of Lebanon."[71]

Botanically, the atad is recognized as *Ziziphus lotus*, or *Ziziphus spina-christi*.[72] Based on the botanical description of the atad and its place of distribution (which is Shechem—that is, Nablus—according to the biblical parable), Meirovitch identified it with the tree of the *sidr* or *nabaq*, a species that was well-known among the Arab inhabitants of Palestine and revered in Islamic culture:[73]

> The atad is the sidr or nabaq. *Zizyphus lotus, Brutsbeerbaum*. It is a tree that can reach a height of approximately twenty feet. Its branches are numerous, and they spread out to provide a great shade in its environs. Its leaves are short. . . . [I]t grows profusely in the vicinity of Jericho.[74]

In identifying the atad and sidr, Meirovitch consulted Arabic botanical literature while also gathering information from the local population. One of his sources was ʿAbd Allāh Ibn Aḥmad Ibn al-Bayṭār (1197–1248), a medieval Muslim botanist and pharmacologist whose works had been in circulation since the middle of the nineteenth century. Meirovitch consulted Ibn al-Bayṭār's botanical lexicon *Kitāb al-jāmiʿ li-mufradāt al-ʾadwiya wa al-aghdhiya* (The book of compilation of medication and aliment simples)—a work that was translated into German in two volumes by Joseph von Sontheimer (1788–1846) between 1840 and 1842, made available in print in Cairo in 1874, and translated into French by Lucien Leclerc (1816–93) in three volumes between 1877 and 1883. Meirovitch knew French, German, Hebrew, Russian, and Yiddish.[75] The fact that Ibn al-Bayṭār's botanical lexicon was accessible in various Western languages and even in Arabic strengthens the probability that it served Meirovitch as a rich source for collecting, recording, and identifying biblical plants with Arabic ones. We know from his biography, composed by his disciple the Syrian Ibn Abī Uṣaybiʿa (1203–70), that Ibn al-Bayṭār collected plants in Damascus, and his botanical scientific expedition to the East, including Syria and its environs, proved to be an invaluable source. Moreover, the description of the sidr in Ibn al-Bayṭār's *Kitāb al-jāmiʿ* makes the connection between the sidr and nabaq.[76]

Besides consulting medieval Arabic botanical literature, Meirovitch complements his account of the atad and sidr with his observation of the species in its natural Arab habitat, which comes as no surprise given his expertise as an agronomist. In doing so, he refers to the atad's two Arabic names, the sidr and nabaq, with the former referring to the tree and the latter to the tree's edible fruit. The association between the atad and sidr reflects a sense of reverence for that plant in both Jewish and Arabic traditions. In the biblical parable, the atad is revered by other species to the point that it is anointed "the king of the trees." The significance attributed to the atad here is elaborated as Meirovitch turns to Arabo-Islamic culture's treatment of the sidr. To demonstrate the usefulness of "the king of the trees," Meirovitch reflects on the various botanical uses of the sidr by the Indigenous population, and in doing so, incorporates several components of its culture into the emerging Hebrew culture. In his view, the king of the trees is not merely a tree whose numerous branches and hairy leaves supply shade but also a perennial bearing edible fruits with medicinal properties. According to his description,

> Its fruits are circular and small, and their size can reach that of the almond. The [fruits'] color is dark red, and they contain a delicious juice as well as a hard seed. They are commonly known in Arabic as *dūm*. The *dūm* is consumed fresh. In some places in the land, peasants cook it and make some medicines from it.[77]

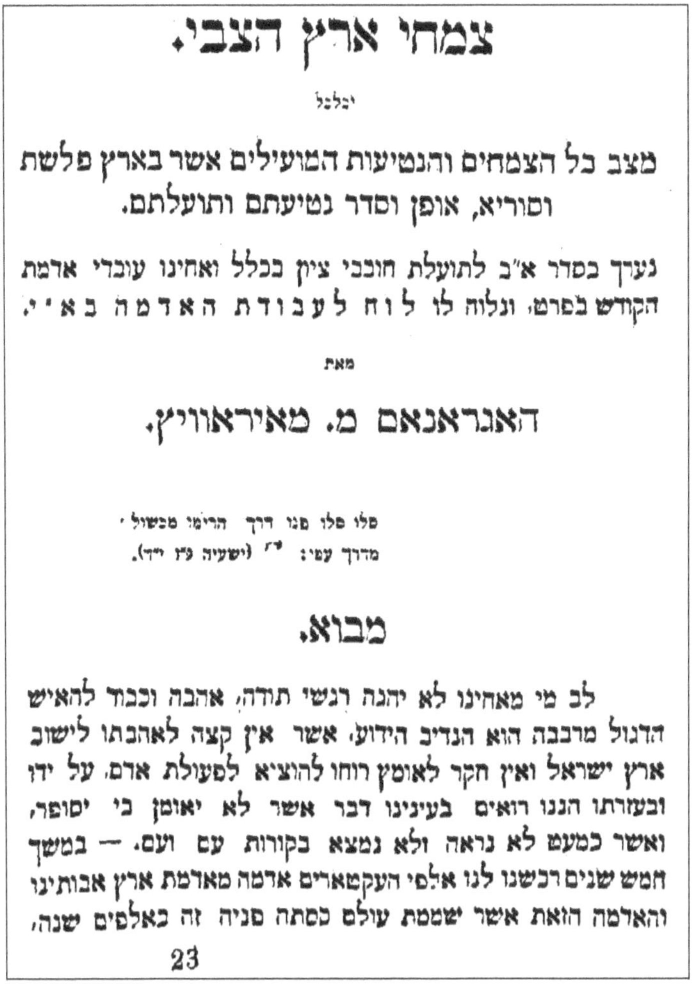

צמחי ארץ הצבי.

יכלכל

מצב כל הצמחים והנטיעות המועילים אשר בארץ פלשת
וסוריא, אופן וסדר נטיעתם ותועלתם.

נערך בסדר א"ב לתועלת חובבי ציון בכלל ואחינו עובדי אדמת
הקודש בפרט, ונלוה לו לוח לעבודת האדמה בא"י.

מאת

האגראנאם מ. מאיראוויץ.

סלו סלו פנו דרך הרימו מכשול
מדרך עמי: ה' (ישעיה פ"ז י"ד).

מבוא.

לב מי מאחינו לא יהגה רגשי תודה, אהבה וכבוד להאיש
הדגול מרבבה הוא הנדיב הידוע, אשר אין קצה לאהבתו לישוב
ארץ ישראל ואין חקר לאומץ רוחו להוציא לפעולת אדם, על ידו
ובעזרתו הננו רואים בעינינו דבר אשר לא יאומן כי יסופר,
ואשר כמעט לא נראה ולא נמצא בקורות עם ועם. — במשך
חמש שנים רכשנו לנו אלפי העקטארים אדמה מאדמת ארץ אבותינו
והאדמה הזאת אשר שממת עולם כסתה פניה זה כאלפים שנה,

23

FIGURE 2.4. The front page of Menashe Meirovitch's series of articles, "Tsimḥe erets ha-tsevi," on the flora of Palestine. The article appeared in the journal *Yerushalayim* (Jerusalem) in 1888. Meirovitch is inspired in this work by the biblical verse, "[GOD] says: Build up, build up a highway! Clear a road! Remove all obstacles from the road of My people!" (Joshua 57:14).

In identifying the atad with the sidr based on the local population's relationship with that tree is part of the larger project of planting Jewish roots in both the human and natural habitat of Palestine.

If botanical uses by the local population prove helpful in identifying the biblical plant known as the king of the trees, they also serve as a window into Palestinian plant lore. Meirovitch reveals how botanical specimens in Palestine exerted an influence on the local population's religious practices, such as the veneration of saints and reverence for trees—a subject that would later catch the attention of Palestinian ethnographer Tawfiq Canaan (1882–1964).[78] In Meirovitch's account, the atad, which is identified as the sidr, becomes a sacred tree within which saints dwell (most likely a wali), and whose destruction is therefore discouraged. In his words,

> Arabs highly respect and venerate the atad [i.e., the sidr tree], and to it they relate several superstitious legends and eccentric stories. One such story recounts that when the atad lives for thirty years, it is believed that the spirit of one of the saints [*ḳedoshim*] dwells within the tree. Therefore, they [Arabs] will humiliate anyone who dares to cut down an old atad, saying that [once the tree is cut down], the housed spirit will be forced to move and live in the world.[79]

Aside from being an agronomist, Meirovitch has claims to be regarded as an ethnographer. He scouted the land, as a botanist as well as a Jewish settler, trying to identify the plants of the Hebrew Bible with the current vegetation of Palestine. In fact, the data he provided regarding Arab veneration of the lotus tree had not been noted in any publication prior to his own, which for its part, devoted significant attention to the topic of sacred trees in Islamic culture, and in particular the reverence for the lotus tree in Greater Syria.[80] For example, in Wolf Wilhelm Baudissin's *Studien zur Semitischen Religionsgeschichte* (1878), where the author discusses trees sacred to Arabs and Hebrews based on scriptural and literary sources, there is no mention of the lotus and its veneration, let alone any attempt to identify it from scriptural accounts.[81]

The Construction of the Jewish Past in Palestine

The Zionist imagination of Palestine was built on the premise of a continuous Jewish presence on the land. To this end, Hebrew writers turned to Arabic and Islamic sources to excavate accounts that accentuated the tangible link between Jews and the physical, cultural, and religious landscape of Palestine. Yellin retrieved and mobilized narratives from Arabic and Islamic sources sketching out the Jewish presence in Palestine, and published them in his earlier works on Jerusalem.

In contrast to other Hebrew writers of Ashkenazi origins, Yellin came from a cosmopolitan background, manifest in his combination of expertise in Arabo-Islamic culture with a sophisticated grasp of European modernity. The diverse world in which he lived is captured by Samuel Klein, Joseph Klausner, and Naḥum Slouschz, prominent Zionist educators in the Jewish communities in Palestine, in their description of Yellin's proficiency in Arabic language and culture:

> Mr. David Yellin is one of a few among our new scholars who [may be called] a son of the Orient [Ben ha-Mizraḥ], Jerusalem-born. In his body . . . and in his spirit, he is a marvelous combination of the Orient and the West. Despite his Western knowledge, the Oriental environment and the Jerusalemite education everlastingly influenced his research. Assuredly, he is one of a few scholars who know Arabic, not only from books, but through life, as a mother tongue. He is, indeed, one of our few Hebrew researchers who knows the Orient: its customs, its natural life. With respect to his relation to religion and literature, not only [did he view them] through books, but also through the fact that his actual life was spent in a Jewish-Arab Oriental environment.[82]

As Ashkenazi Jewish immigrants who appear to consider the Orient and the West two separate worlds, Klein, Klausner, and Slouschz nonetheless acknowledge the fact that these worlds converged in the cosmopolitan environment in which Yellin and other sons of the Orient were raised. The group of Bene ha-Mizraḥ, or Sons of the East, to which Yellin belonged did not see a division between "Eastern" and "Western" but rather were embedded in a shared cultural worldview with their Arab neighbors.

The Bene ha-Mizraḥ were the genesis of a unique hybrid Jewish identity. On his father's side, Yellin was a descendant of an Ashkenazi family that had immigrated to Palestine from Poland in 1834, while his mother was a Baghdadi Jewish immigrant who moved to Jerusalem with her merchant father.[83] Yellin absorbed Arabic language and culture from both his mother, whose native tongue was Arabic, and his father, Yehoshua Yellin (1843–1924), who was a Jerusalem-born leader in the Jewish community in Palestine. In the house of his father-in-law, Shelomo Yeḥezkel (1819–71), a Baghdadi Jew who settled in Jerusalem in 1854, Yehoshua learned Arabic and Oriental customs.[84] Thus David's acquaintance with Islamic culture was an intimate one, acquired through his early personal interactions with his Arab neighbors as well as the customs and traditions of the Iraqi Jewish communities with which his family was well-versed.

Amid the triumphalist celebrations of patriotism in the nineteenth century, Jews from various parts of the Diaspora conceived of their own cognate commemorations, with special attention given to Jewish particularism. In 1891, French Jews, for instance, celebrated the centenary of the legal emancipation through which they had gained civil rights, equality before the law, and social acceptance in France. A year later, in 1892, members of the Jewish community in Izmir, Turkey, commemorated the expulsion of Jews from Spain and their settlement in the Ottoman lands. This spark caught fire among Jews across the Ottoman Empire who began planning a celebration of the fourth centenary of the Jewish arrival in the Ottoman Empire. With the influx of Jewish immigrants to fin de siècle Palestine and Ottoman efforts to curb their numbers, the celebration initiated by Jewish journalists and promoters was not so much a genuine gesture of gratitude as a plea to the Ottoman authorities "to live up to the image Jews had created of the Ottoman government," while reminding them of what they had done to Jewish expellees in the fifteenth and sixteenth centuries.[85]

Partisans of these group commemorations started referring to "four hundred years" of Jewish presence in the Ottoman realms—that is, since the time of Sultan Beyazid II, who issued an edict allowing Jews to settle in the Ottoman territories. This language found expression in two different circles. As a member in the B'nai B'rith association—its Jerusalem lodge having been established in 1888 with a mission to advance ties of fellowship among various Jewish communities, and purchase lands in Jerusalem and its environs to support Jewish immigration—Yellin advocated commemorating the fourth centenary of the Sephardi settlement in Ottoman domains by the founding of a library that would contain the works of great Sephardi authors. He saw this project as aligned with B'nai B'rith's mission of consolidating fraternal ties among various Jewish communities in Palestine, most important between Sephardim and Ashkenazim. In response to Yellin's suggestion, a decision was made in 1892 to found "Midrash Abarbanel" and dedicate the first sources of income to acquire books of "the authors of our brethren in Sepharad."[86]

In his article titled "Yerushalayim li-fnay arba' Me'ot shanah" (Jerusalem four hundred years ago), Yellin calls on his Jewish coreligionists in the Diaspora to come to the holy city. On a tour through the religious, cultural, and social landscape of Jerusalem, he presents the city's sacred history and the sites that had been regarded as holy to the Jewish people before they were recognized by other nations. In his piece, Yellin takes his readers to Mamluk Jerusalem, "Al-Quds Al-Mamlukiyya," when the city was ruled by the Mamluks who preceded the Ottomans in ruling over Palestine. Yellin describes the darkness of Jewish life under the Mamluks, whose oppressive policies coupled with the harsh living conditions in the country discouraged Jews from settling in the land. Though the Jewish population in Mamluk Jerusalem was few in number (he says "around two hundred Jewish families were living in the holy city"), their circumstances were dire. He explains that "the Jews were pressured, oppressed, groaning, and moaning" due to heavy taxes, unjust treatment by their oppressors, and crowded living conditions in the Jewish Quarter in the city.[87]

This bleak picture of Jewish presence in Mamluk Jerusalem contrasts with the more attractive portrayal of Jewish life in Ottoman Jerusalem, whether during the reign of Suleiman the Magnificent, who supported the Jewish settlement in the city, or later after the emergence of the Zionist movement and influx of diasporic Jewish immigrants. Yellin notes that the continuous Jewish presence in the city is to be celebrated, but even more so the return of the Jewish people in modern times to their ancestral homeland with the support and encouragement of

ירושלם לפני ארבע מאות שנה.

לפי דברי סופר קורות ירושלם וחברון השופט (קָצִי) מֻגִ'יר־אלדין־אלחנבלי אשר חי בימים ההם.

מאת

דוד יֶלין.

תקופות שונות עברו על ירושלם עיר קדשנו מיום גלות ישראל מעליה, ופנים חדשות ומראות שונים קִבלה כפעם בפעם. אדריון הרומי עשה לעיר רומית, היא „אליה־קפּתולינה" אשר בהרי יהודה. הילני וקנסטנטין והבאים אחריהם עשוה לעיר נוצרית, ומימי עֻמַר בן אלחַטָּב מלאה חליפות צִיוני האִסְלָם והנצרות; כי גברה יד האסלם מלאה העיר מסגדים ומנורות, וברום יד הנוצרים מלאה העיר כנסיות ופעמונים, ועל כל בית רם ונשא אות הצלב מֻצב מֻצק. ובשוב המֻסלמים לרשתה הפכו כנסיות רבות למסגדים ובתים רבים ערו עד היסוד.

עתה עשה ה' חרשה בארץ, להשיב לעיר הקדש את נדחיה, למלא את ירושלם צאן עמו סגלתו, ובתי־תפלה לאלהי ישראל ובתי־מדרש לתורת קדשו בכל עבר ופנה.

אך לכה נא אתי, ידידי הקורא, ונשובה אל ארבע מאות שנה לפנינו. נבואה בשערי ירושלם ונשוחה ברחובותיה. אך מעטים מאחינו נפגש על דרכנו, כי רק כמאתים משפחה מבני ישראל בעיר הקדושה הזאת, והימים ימי הרעה להישוב, היהודים נלחצים ונדכאים נאנחים ונאנקים מכבד משא מסים ונוגשים, וצפופים המה יושבים בקצה העיר נגבה־ימה ברחוב היהודים.

לא אל ירושלים עיר הקדש לבני ישראל הננו באים, כי אם אל בַּיְתּ־אַלְמַקְדִיש אשר למֻסלמים. מעל מגדליה ישמע קול הקורא: „לַא אִלָהְ אִלָּא אַלָּה וַמֻחַמַּד רַסוּל אַלָּה![1] „בחוצותיה הננו רואים את השיחים[2] במצנפותיהם הירוקות והדַרוִישים[3] בשערותיהם הפרועות, ובכל עבר ופנה מדרשות וזָוִיוֹת[4] לחכמי הקֻרְאָן[5]. והארץ עודנה בידי הממלוכים מלכי מצרים, ושלחו בערי הארץ את נָאִיבִיהם[6] למשל בשמם, וכל דבר רין ישפטו ארבעת השופטים אשר לארבע כתות המסלמים: השופעי, החַנַפִי, המולכי והחַנבַּלי.

---

[1]) אין אלוה רק האלהים ומחמד שליח האלהים. — [2]) שיח (Scheich) בעקרו פרושו זקן ואחרי כן תשאל לכל מלומד. — [3]) נזירים. — [4]) מקלט לנזירים. — [5]) ספר תורת המסלמים. — [6]) ממלאי מקומם. —

FIGURE 2.5. David Yellin's article "Yerushalaym li-fnay arba' Me'ot shanah" (Jerusalem four hundred years ago). The article was published in the Hebrew journal *Ha-Pardes* in 1894.

the Ottoman authorities. In the preface to the aforementioned article, Yellin speaks of the return of the Jews to Jerusalem in a messianic tone, linking its advancement with a divine act. In his words, "God did something new by returning to the Holy City those who were exiled from it, and by filling Jerusalem with His chosen people, houses of worship for the God of Israel, and schools to [study] his Torah in all different areas and corners."[88]

Yellin's article is, in fact, an adaptation of a selection of passages that he borrowed and translated into Hebrew from *Al-'uns al-jalīl bi-tārīkh al-Quds wa-al-Khalīl* (The glorious history of Jerusalem and Hebron) by Jerusalemite judge Mujīr al-Dīn al-Ḥanbalī, who lived in the fifteenth and sixteenth centuries.[89] Yellin's reliance on Mujīr al-Dīn's tome was owed to several factors. For one, drawing on the work of a medieval Muslim author who lived in fifteenth-century Jerusalem during the late Mamluk era lent authenticity to his own account and enabled him to produce a reliable description of the fifteenth-century city, including its magnificent buildings along with its religiously and culturally diverse social life. Second, Mujīr al-Dīn did not rely unquestioningly on literary and documentary sources but instead subjected his materials to scrutiny, which distinguished the book from other works on the virtues of Jerusalem. A third virtue of Mujīr al-Dīn's work, from Yellin's point of view, was that it was highly regarded among both Western Orientalists and Arab scholars. After having influenced nineteenth-century Western scholarship on Jerusalem, the work made its way back to Arab scholars of the nahda. A final motivation for Yellin's reliance was that he and Mujīr al-Dīn shared a perspective on Jerusalem's history. While preserving the Islamic character of Jerusalem, the medieval judge and writer highlighted the continuity of the city's pre-Islamic history. In his view, the Islamic character of Jerusalem was not alien to its earlier history but rather inextricably rooted in the monotheistic traditions of the city.[90] It is no wonder, then, that the work includes a number of references to the Jewish presence in the holy sites of the city, such as the construction of a temple by King Solomon, the son of David.

Moreover, Yellin's purpose in writing about the city mirrors that of the medieval Muslim judge. In the introduction to his work, Mujīr al-Dīn explains the underlying objective of his work: "What inspired me is the fact that most of the towns of Islam have received the attention of the preservers of knowledge, who have recorded what relates to their history. But I am not acquainted with any such work restricted to *bayt al-maqdis* (The Holy House); instead they have scattered mention of matters about it at random in their histories."[91] Mujīr al-Dīn's motive, like that of other works belonging to the literary genre known as *Faḍā'il al Quds*, "the merits of Jerusalem," was to attract people to settle in Jerusalem to safeguard it from possible crusaders. Comprising works published between the eleventh and fifteenth centuries, the merits of Jerusalem literature expound on the religious, historical, and natural merits of Jerusalem, with the aim of raising consciousness of the sacredness and significance of the city among Muslims as well as fortifying their sense of connection to it.[92] Yellin's adaptation of selections from this very genre reiterates and enumerates the virtues of the city not for Muslim readers, as in the case of Mujīr al-Dīn, but instead for a Jewish audience.

Yellin acknowledges Jerusalem as a city of three monotheistic religions, but adopts a tendentious tone, arguing throughout that the sacredness of the city originated with the Jewish people, on which basis they have a particular claim to the city.[93] Yellin, in stressing the originality of Judaism and imitativeness of Islam, is building on the great medieval Jewish thinker Moses Maimonides's views on Islam and its connection to Judaism. Yellin would devote a book in both Hebrew and English to the renowned figure in Jewish thought, discussing his attitude within his historical context. Although Maimonides developed tolerant views on Islam as a monotheistic religion, he was sometimes polemical toward it. To dissuade his Jewish fellows from converting to Islam based on the belief that God had replaced Judaism with Islam and substituted Moses with Muḥammad, Maimonides developed historical and halachic arguments that asserted the originality of Judaism coupled with the derivativeness of Islam.[94] Building on the Maimonidean views, Yellin argues that the sacredness of the city in Islam is in fact an adaptation of its sacrality in Judaism. From his perspective, the original sacred city of the Jewish people after their expulsion at the hands of the Romans in the first century CE became the battlefield between two majestic powers: Christianity and Islam. Once the Jews were expelled, the city became the heart of a persistent competition between the two, each of which aimed to remake the city in the image of its own faith. Hence "when the fortune of Islam goes well, the city becomes filled with mosques and minarets, and when Christians [dominate], it fills with churches and bells."[95] In contrast to the conspicuous presence of Islam and Christianity in Jerusalem, though, the Jewish physical presence in the form of places of worship was somewhat obscure. Rather than in temples and monuments, the Jewish presence in Jerusalem was attested to in the rich Islamic literature that discussed the virtues of the city. Yellin, however, fails to develop a sophisticated view on the sacrality of Jerusalem in Islam and focuses only on its originality in Judaism without applying the same standards to the origins of the sacrality of the city in Jewish thought. In fact, the sacrality of Jerusalem in Jewish thought was an adoption of the sacrality of the city by the Jebusites, who had inhabited the land before David had conquered the city, according to 1 Chronicles 11:4–5, in 1000 CE.[96] Yellin also fails to acknowledge Islam's recognition of the sacrality of the city for Jews and allowance of them to reside in the city after the Romans had banished them from the city in the year 135 CE.[97] In equating Muslims and Christians in venerating Jerusalem as a sacred city, he discounts essential differences between both faiths' approach to the city. For instance, after the destruction of what is believed to be the Second Temple in 70 CE, Christian authorities deliberately prevented Jews from rebuilding the site and kept it in ruins to show that the temple was of importance once, but not anymore as a testament to Jesus's prophecy of the destruction of the temple: "Then, as some spoke of the temple, how it was [a]dorned with beautiful stones and donations, He said, 'These things which you see—the days will come in which not one stone shall be left upon another that shall not be thrown down.'" (Luke 21:5–6). Consequently, the site was claimed by nature and turned into a place where people dumped things. While Muslim authorities identified the site with a former temple, they paid respect to it by changing the character of the site by building a humble mosque amid the ruins of the former temple (638–85), and later during the Umayyad period, constructed an architectural complex known as the Dome of the Rock in 691–92.[98]

Of particular relevance to Yellin's citation of *Al-'uns al-jalīl* is his effort to underscore the Jewish presence in the holy city in order to stir the nationalistic aspirations of the Jewish people and encourage them to renew their relationship with the land. Mujīr al-Dīn's work is a rich source on the connection between Jews and Jerusalem, not only providing accounts of the construction of a "house of God" by David and Solomon but depicting the social life of Jews in the city and their relationships with their Muslim counterparts too.[99] Among the sites Yellin highlights for their noted Jewish presence is al-Ḥaram al-Sharīf (Noble Sanctuary) and its environs. Citing from *Al-'uns al-jalīl*, Yellin emphasizes the Jewish presence in his reference to Solomon's Stables, an underground structure that the medieval Muslim scholar believed had been built by Solomon underneath the Ḥaram. Also, in discussing the Eastern Wall of the sanctuary, Yellin mentions the name of a particular gate, the "Gate of Tribes" (Bāb al-'Asbāṭ), referencing a passage from the Quran (7:161–62) in which the Arabic word *sibṭ* (tribe) is synonymous with the Hebrew word *shevet̩* (tribe).[100]

As noted above, Mujīr al-Dīn and Yellin shared a common goal: to attract their coreligionists to settle in Jerusalem. In his conclusion, acknowledging the harsh conditions and inconveniences visitors to the mountain town might face, Mujīr al-Dīn hopes that their journey will be easy, "but if God bestows his blessing upon the visitor to the holy sites in Jerusalem, he will find in his heart indescribable feelings of comfort and ease and he will forget all the tiredness he suffered in walking to these holy sites."[101] Yellin extends these same good wishes to his Jewish coreligionists. In fact, the article concludes with the following lines: "May God implant feelings of the love of Zion in the hearts of our brethren in the scattered lands so that they will long in their hearts to visit this holy city which had been holy to them before it became holy to other nations."[102] While constructing

חיי אנשי השם.

רבנו משה בן מימון

(רמב"ם).

חייו, ספריו ופעולותיו המדעיות והפילוסופיות.

מאת

דוד ילין.

הוצאת „תושיה".

ווארשא. תרנ"ח.

בדפוס האלטער ואייזענשטאדט, נאלעווקי 7.

РАМБАМЪ.

т. е. Маймонидъ.

Его жизнь, научная и философская дѣятельность.

Соч. Д. Елина.

Изданіе „ТУШІЯ".

ВАРШАВА. 1898.

Тип. М. И. Гальтера и М. Айзенштадта, Наловки 7.

FIGURE 2.6. Cover of David Yellin's book *Rabenu Mosheh Ben Maymun* (Our master Moses Maimonides). The book was published in Warsaw in 1898.

Jerusalem's landscape as a space in which the Jews held precedence, Yellin does not seek to deny or efface the Arab and Muslim past in the city as he passes through the last four hundred years. Instead of an erasure of the Muslim presence, Yellin urges Jews to follow the example of Muslims who left their mark on the city for centuries.

Writing on Holy Sites through Crisis: The Great War

Following the Young Turk Revolution of 1908, a mixture of escalating hostility and rising hopes characterized Jewish-Arab relations, revolving around two major issues: Jewish immigration and property ownership. In the years before World War I, leadership of the World Zionist Organization attested to the increasingly antagonistic attitude of the Palestinian Arab population toward Zionist aims and the transformation of a localized hostility to a national hatred.[103] Ben-Yehuda saw the parliamentary elections following the rise of the Young Turks as a crucial opportunity. He encouraged Jewish settlers to apply for Ottoman citizenship to propose solutions for Jewish immigration to and settlement in Palestine. By subsequently renouncing foreign citizenship, they could gain voting rights, thus influencing the fate of Jewish immigration.[104] These mixed feelings of rising hopes and crystallizing hostilities found expression in the writings of contemporary Hebrew scholars.

In late Ottoman Palestine, several Hebrew writers, as we have seen in the case of Yellin, mobilized narratives from Arabic and Islamic sources to construct Jerusalem as a landscape uniquely sacred to the Jewish people. Without denying the Arab and Islamic past in the country or holy city, they stressed that Arabs' connection to Jerusalem is secondary to as well as derivative of the sacredness of the city in Judaism in a deliberate disregard of Islam's originality and authenticity in transforming the city into a holy site for all followers of monotheistic religions. Furthermore, they demonstrated patriotism toward the Ottoman Empire with the hopes of garnering favor from the authorities with respect to Jewish immigration, just as their ancestors had done with respect to Jewish expellees from Spain in the fifteenth and sixteenth centuries.

Considering the contested narratives surrounding Jerusalem's sacredness, it is necessary to delve into the complexities of European engagement with Palestine, especially during the Victorian era when European powers possessively eyed Palestine in an enterprise they termed a "peaceful crusade"—a phrase that inadvertently reveals their intentions to conquer and dominate.[105] This cultural penetration by the British materialized in their reading of Palestine's landscape against the Bible, which convinced them that the land belonged to the Jewish people. Throughout the nineteenth century and continuing well after the Young Turk Revolution, British archaeologists undertook several excavations in the holy city in their efforts to reveal biblical Jerusalem.[106] In spring 1911, a team of British archaeologists, after acquiring the necessary permission from the Ottoman authorities, undertook an archaeological dig within the compound of the Ḥaram al-Sharīf, which included both the Dome of the Rock and Al-Aqsa Mosque, two of the holiest sites for Muslims. While the Ottoman authorities viewed sponsoring and supervising these archaeological activities as an indication of their modernity, local Muslims perceived them differently. Considering themselves the true guardians of the Ḥaram al-Sharīf, Muslim and Christian Arabs, both educated and illiterate, urban and rural, mobilized in a demonstration against the violation of the sanctity of the holy site. This incident signaled the emergence of a modern Palestinian collective struggle and the formation of a distinctive Palestinian identity.[107]

The peaceful crusade highlighted above agitated Muslim inhabitants' fear of Western encroachment on their city and the desecration of its sacred sites—a fear that was extended to any attempts by Jews to acquire the Western Wall, known in the Jewish tradition as the Wailing Wall and considered a major sacred site, whereas in the Islamic tradition it is known as Ḥāiṭ al-Burāq (Al-Burāq Wall) and considered a sacred site due to its connection to the prophetic Night Journey (henceforth referred to as "the Wall"). While Christian Westerners living in the city grew anxious for their security out of fear that the Muslim population might target them in revenge for what they viewed as a Western violation of the sanctity of their holy site, the Jewish community did not feel its security threatened. Nevertheless, when excavations underneath the holy site compound were undertaken, Muslims' fear of Westerners' encroachment expanded to include the Jewish community whose members were seen as complicit. Throughout the incident of the Ḥaram al-Sharīf in 1911, the Ottoman authorities received complaints from Muslim inhabitants of the Mughrabi Quarter adjacent to the Wall led by Bashīr 'Abdelsalām al-Ḥusseinī, a notable from the al-Ḥusseinī family and the guardian of Abū Madyan al-Ghawth's endowment on which the Mughrabi Quarter was established. In a letter to the Ottoman Mutasarrif Cevdet Bey (1911–12), he requested the removal of benches, chairs, and a divider that Jewish visitors to the site had put in place on the grounds that these seats were a violation of property rights. He justified his request by indicating to the Ottoman governor that Jews have multiple synagogues elsewhere where they can sit and worship freely, whereas they come to the Wall only occasionally and therefore have no need for seating. Moreover, he argued that the seating obstructed the routine movement of Muslim residents in the area, heightening tension. Yet the paramount reason behind requesting the removal of the seats was the Muslims' fear that allowing these accommodations to remain in place might lead to Jews claiming the alley and Wall as their own property.[108] Notably, the complainants represented by Bashīr 'Abdelsalām al-Ḥusseinī did not ask for the suspension of Jewish prayer at the site. Eager to mollify the Muslim population after the Ḥaram al-Sharīf incident, the Ottoman governor prohibited Jewish visitors from placing any sort of accommodation at the Wall.

The invocation of property rights and restrictions connected with such a central institution as al-Waqf, a charitable Islamic endowment under Islamic law involving donating a plot of land or other assets for Muslim or charitable purposes, did not deter Jewish figures from attempting to exert ownership over the Wall given the sacred value Jews ascribe to it. While respecting the prohibitions associated with selling Abū Madyan's waqf, several Jews tried to activate their social and political networks to find a favorable permanent settlement for this issue. In 1914, Yellin, a representative of the Association to Maintain Historical Sites in the Land of Israel, requested that the US ambassador to the Sublime Porte press the Ottoman government to allow the association to purchase the Wall, but to no avail.[109] Two years later, in the midst of the Great War, communications were initiated between Albert Antebi (1873–1919), a Sephardi Jew, Ottoman citizen, and mediator between the Jewish community and Zionist movement, and Cemal Pasha (1872–1922), then a military commander and one of three pashas who ruled over the Ottoman Empire during the Great War. In an exchange of letters between both sides with the involvement of leaders within the Zionist movement and the Jewish community, including Yellin again, the Ottoman commander offered the sale of the Wall and demolition of the Mughrabi Quarter to build a plaza for the Jewish community. Although the proposal was initially kept secret, by mid-1916, the international press had leaked the Ottoman authorities' intent to sell Palestine to the Jews. These developments sufficiently pressured both Antebi and Cemal Pasha to give up the plan.[110]

While Zionists' attempts to claim ownership of the Wall and Mughrabi Quarter continued, several Hebrew writers cited Arabic and Islamic sources to prop up their claims to sacred Jewish sites in Jerusalem and elsewhere in Palestine as part of their ongoing debate with contemporary communal Muslim leaders. During World War I, Israel Horowitz (1880–1918), a rabbi and scholar of the historical geography of Palestine-Israel, published an article titled "Hagadot 'Araviyot" (Arab legends) in Lunts's journal *Luaḥ Erets Yisrael* comprising accounts of four sites in Jerusalem as well as nearby cities considered holy to both Muslims and Jews: the site of the temple (*meḳom ha-miḳdash*), Dome of the Chain (*ḳupat ha-shalshelet*), Rachel's Tomb (*qubat Raḥel*) outside Bethlehem, and the Cave of the Patriarchs (*al-khalīl*) in the heart of the old city of Hebron.[111] The narratives Horowitz weaves together in his text construct the sacredness of these four places for the Jewish people without undermining the Muslims' passion, commitment, and devotion to them. At the same time, however, the author stresses that these sites had been sacred to the Jewish people long before they became holy to Muslims. Indeed, these accounts show that the continued reverence and respect that Muslim leaders accorded these sites originated in their sacredness to the Israelites and their prophets.

The Great War had a significant impact on the daily lives of civilians in Palestine. It created an atmosphere of panic and uncertainty, disrupted the daily patterns of behavior, and propelled the systematic censorship of press and people's private mail.[112] At the same time, it created, as Abigail Jacobson has demonstrated, opportunities for intercommunal relations in the region and Jerusalem, as reflected in the Hebrew works composed during this time.[113] Horowitz's text, for example, instilled in the Hebrew-reading audience an appreciation and respect for the manner in which earlier Muslims treated the sacred landscape. Drawing on works by medieval Muslim authors such as al-Suyūṭī (1445–1505), Yāqūt al-Ḥamawī (1178–1229), Muḥammad al-'Idrīsī (1100–1165), and Nāṣir Khusraw (1004–1088), Horowitz relates such stories as the Prophet Muḥammad's letter to the Roman ruler of Jerusalem commanding him to cleanse the site of the temple, which had become a "garbage can" during the Roman rule of Palestine.[114] Elsewhere, Horowitz gives a short account of the reverence Muslims accorded the patriarchs' sanctuary along with their efforts to make it accommodating to travelers and visitors. Of particular interest to Horowitz was the eleventh-century Persian chronicler Nāṣir Khusraw and his travel report to Jerusalem from the Fatimid period (969–1099). Translating Khusraw's account, Horowitz relates that "it is reported that in early times the sanctuary at Hebron had no door into it, and hence no one could come nearer to the tombs. However, during the Fatimid rule, al-Mahdi commissioned a door into the sanctuary, and he provided tools, carpets, and rugs."[115] While his tone might come across as appreciative, Horowitz musters these stories for a polemic purpose: in the midst of the debate concerning the ownership of the Wall and area next to it, Horowitz exploited medieval sources to contest the claims of contemporary Palestinian Muslims who refused to relinquish their stake in the site.

Jewish Palestine: A Landscape of Texts

"Landscape is the work of the mind," British historian Simon Schama notes, adding, "Its scenery is built up as much from strata of memory as from layers of rock."[116] If "landscape is the work of the mind," then Hebrew intellectuals played an indispensable role in imagining the landscape of Palestine as a home for the Jewish people. The return to the land, a fundamental tenet of Zionist thought, was accompanied by a campaign promoting "knowledge of the land," including its spatial characteristics and their signification. Laying claims to and building ties with the land by way of knowing it entailed the utilization of Arabo-Islamic knowledge that had accumulated over centuries, and was preserved in either medieval literary and historical texts or folkloric accounts with the local population. In their employment of this Arabo-Islamic knowledge, Hebrew writers presented a complex image of the land that encompassed not only the Jewish past but also its Arabo-Islamic past and even present. In so doing, they engraved in a stratum of their readers' consciousness the concept of hierarchical coexistence with the Palestinian Arab population. Calls for integration into the Orient and its culture always concealed a discourse of cultural as well as historical superiority. Likewise, the Palestinian Indigenous experience and narrative were elevated by Hebrew writers since they were instrumental in facilitating Jews' return to the land along with their claims of indigenization (asserting the nativity of Palestinian Jews and turning Jewish settlers into natives).[117] It was in this context that in depicting the entangled lives of Indigenous Palestinians and Jewish settlers, Hebrew writers unapologetically highlighted the Arabness of the landscape, and suggested that this Arabness should neither threaten nor alienate the Jewish community in Palestine.

The intellectual experience of Hebrew writers in Palestine differed in important ways from that of their Jewish counterparts in Europe writing about the land of their imagined forebearers from afar. For the former, Palestine was not an imagined landscape; it was a "real" land in which they settled and continued to live. The actualization of the connection between Jews and their ancestral homeland, as they promulgated it, would happen only by Jews living in the land, learning from Palestinian natives' relationship to the landscape, and emulating the local Palestinians as a model of how their own ancestors had lived and toiled on the same land.

In the Jewish imagination, the Jewish colonization of Palestine for settlers was a fulfillment of a biblical divine promise and reenactment of Israelite patriarchs as agriculturists, but the implementation of this undertaking required assistance from local resources.[118] In their identification of Arabic place-names with Hebrew designations in accordance with Jewish sources, Hebrew authors reconstructed the connection between modern Jews and the ancient Israelite past. The reconstruction of a continuous Jewish presence in the land since ancient times, however, was an objective that could not be attained without drawing on Palestinian natives' folkloric and textual legacies. In an attempt to reconcile the Jewish connection to the territory with the Palestinian presence and heritage, Hebrew writers of late Ottoman Palestine developed a model of parity and cooperation, rather than separation, alienation, or erasure. That model of parity, it should be noted, while not devoid of tension, did not rise to the level of conflict at this historical moment. Nonetheless, a discourse of historical superiority over Arabs with respect to rights to the land surfaced during times of tension and was ironically supported by accounts of Jewish sites found in Arabo-Islamic sources appropriated to advance these Jewish claims.

3

Constructing Jewish Indigeneity through Arabic Language and Literature

THE REVIVAL OF modern Hebrew was linked to the recuperation of Hebrew nativity in Palestine and the Orient coincident with the Jewish return to the "ancestral homeland." The indigenization of Jews in Palestine, fundamental to Zionist thought and settler colonial discourse, as Lorenzo Veracini has indicated, prompted Jewish activists to revive Hebrew, a language that originated, as did they themselves, in Palestine.[1] The renaissance of modern Hebrew, according to David Yellin, one of its early revivalists in late Ottoman Palestine, is constitutive of the Jewish "holy trinity": "the holy Torah, the holy language, and the holy land."[2] Indeed, it is the language that would unite Jews as a nation, connect them to the land, and bind them to the Hebrew Bible. As we saw in the last chapter, Arabic geographic and botanical sources proved instrumental in restoring, enhancing, and revitalizing the ties between Hebrews and the physical landscape of the "ancestral homeland." Likewise, the knowledge of Arabic proved central to the project of reviving Hebrew, the foundation of the new Jewish identity.

The expansion of the Hebrew lexicon to meet the practical needs of modernity depended mainly on the invention of new words. In the nineteenth century, a group of Jewish intellectuals and educators in Jerusalem, including Eliezer Ben-Yehuda, Yellin, Abraham Moshe Lunts, Yehiel Michael Pines, and Eliyahu Sapir, among others, actively embarked on a mission of turning Hebrew from a written into a spoken language and expanding the use of spoken Hebrew in Jewish society in Palestine. In 1889, the Jerusalem-based Jewish intellectuals created the organization Safah Berurah (Pure Language) to establish spoken Hebrew among Jews in late Ottoman Palestine and "uproot from among Jewish residents in the Land of Israel the nonstandard languages, the Ashkenazi and the Sephardi jargon."[3] For the first time, an organization was working in a methodical manner to expand and disseminate conversational Hebrew. The organization functioned until 1891. The above-named scholars constituted the nucleus of the Hebrew Language Committee, which would be founded in 1905. From the late nineteenth to early twentieth centuries, these scholars' activities were disseminated in Hebrew periodicals and journals as well as schools, and through Jewish associations such as B'nai B'rith, where it was proposed that Hebrew replace German as the language in which all meetings should be conducted.[4]

There were competing visions, though, of how to expand modern Hebrew.[5] Hebrew scholars in Palestine believed that the revitalization of modern Hebrew required intimacy with Semitic languages, mainly Arabic, and was embedded in the linguistic and cultural landscape of the Ottoman Empire. In contrast, Hebrew literati in Europe, like Joseph Klausner (1874-1958), regarded both Arabic and Aramaic as archaic and outdated languages that did not meet the practical needs of modern life. Klausner instead proposed to base the revival of the modern Hebrew language and culture on postbiblical literature, advocating for the conservation of ties between Hebrew and European languages.[6] He suggested the invention of new Hebrew words borrowed from European roots to meet the needs of the new generation. This conflict will echo in the writings of Hebrew scholars studied here. Yellin, for his part, dismisses the "obstinate refusal" of writers in the Diaspora to adopt newly coined words deriving from Arabic, pointing to the successful efforts of individuals and linguistic societies in Palestine to integrate such words into modern Hebrew.[7]

Most members of the Hebrew Language Committee were Hebrew writers in Palestine who recognized Arabic's status of their day and its vitality to the Hebrew language.[8] Arabic was viewed as sefat ha-arets, in Yellin and Moshe Smilansky's phrase. Although Ashkenazi Jewish immigrants to early twentieth-century Palestine generally recognized Arabic as "a linguistic force," their use of it was mostly pragmatic in their interaction with Palestinian Arabs or when using it for everyday practical activities.[9] Both Yellin and Smilansky recognized Arabic's significance in a broader sense, as evidenced in their use of the term sefat ha-arets in multiple settings, indicating their understanding of the inextricability of the language from the landscape. Hebrew writers in late Ottoman Palestine felt that knowing Arabic, irrespective of their varied degrees of Arabic literacy, would enhance their connection to the land and their return to a Semitic authenticity.

It was fundamental to the Hebrew intellectuals' cultural project to enlarge the Hebrew lexicon to address specific lacunae, one category of which was words for the natural world. While efforts to modernize Hebrew by coining new words for the exigencies of modern lifestyles and technologies are certainly significant, the focus on connecting Hebrew settlers to the natural world of Palestine also involved linguistic innovation. By emphasizing the connection between Hebrew settlers and the natural world of Palestine, Hebrew revivalists aimed to foster a sense of cultural continuity and belonging among the Jewish immigrants. This connection to the land of their ancestors was central to the creation of a sense of identity and rootedness, particularly for immigrants facing the challenges of displacement and resettlement. Hebrew revivalists had to invent and adapt vocabulary to describe the unique features of the Palestinian landscape, flora, and fauna, thereby expanding the lexicon of modern Hebrew. Analysis of this process of linguistic revival reveals the degree to which Arabic was essential to the enterprise of embedding Jews within the Palestine landscape.

Arabic and the Resurrection of Hebrew Toponymy

In their construction of Palestine as an imagined Hebrew land, Hebrew authors, as scholar of historical geography Gary Fields has indicated, "assign[ed] Jewish attributes to the landscape by immersing it in a Hebrew toponymy." Converting Palestine into a Hebrew land nevertheless hinged on knowing the Arabic toponymy that had dominated Palestine's geographic and botanical map for centuries prior to as well as during the Ottoman era, and continued to exercise control during the Mandate period.[10] Just as Arabic knowledge proved instrumental in the revival of modern Hebrew, so did it enhance Jewish ties to the land by resurrecting a Hebrew toponymy of the Palestine landscape by way of Arabic or Arabicized place-names.

Those who opposed drawing on Arabic in order to renew Hebrew maintained the traditional position that Hebrew was the sacred "mistress" to the secular "maidservant" of Arabic. Consequently, these opponents called for a separatist method that isolated Hebrew from Arabic.[11] Conversely, Ben-Yehuda, in his magnum opus Hebrew dictionary, endeavored not only to resurrect Hebrew but to place both Hebrew and Arabic on equal footing by reasoning that what was missing from Hebrew was retrievable from Arabic, and thus both languages were "almost one" based on their historical and linguistic affinity. In the introduction to his monumental dictionary, Ben-Yehuda explains this view:

> I have regularly compared our language's roots with those of Arabic. I have done this for two reasons: first, the testimony of the animated Arabic debunks doubts about the possibility [of Arabic] to help build [Hebrew] language roots that ceased to be spoken for approximately two millennia. Second, this continuous comparison ingrains in the reader's mind more and more the acknowledgment that both languages are so close in terms of their essence, characteristics, and spirit to the degree they are almost **one language**. This realization will justify and explain the fundamental principle to which I adhered: to pump from Arabic with two full hands to fill what is missing in our language, wherever there is no root in her lexicon from which we can derive the desired word with some satisfaction.[12]

Ben-Yehuda's acknowledgment of the similarities between the two languages as evidence of their being "almost one language" harks back to the shared Semitic legacy between Hebrew and Arabic, and hence merits further examination. In advocating for the recognition of Arabic's utility and significance in the revival of modern Hebrew, he reckons that Arabic preserved the character of proto-Semitic—an opinion upheld by nahdawi Arabs during his time. He went so far as to demand that the Hebrew Language Committee declare that "the majority of the roots of the Arabic vocabulary were once a part of the Hebrew language and that all these roots are not alien to Hebrew, but rather were ours, and had been lost, and now we have found them again."[13]

Ben-Yehuda's approach, however, met with rejection from his European counterparts active in the enterprise of reviving Hebrew who wished to detach Hebrew from its Orientality, and instead tie it to the Mediterranean and Europe. Adopting the Orientalistic views that were an integral part of the European discourse, Hebrew writers based in Europe belittled Arabic and regarded it as an archaic language that, like Hebrew, lacked the means to express modernity and its needs. European Jewish scholars ascribed to the linguistic theory that Hebrew was only distantly related to Arabic within the family of Semitic languages, and based on archaeological excavations, was more closely related to Assyrian and Akkadian languages. Notably, Moshe Leib Lilienblum (1843–1910), a Jewish author and leader in the Zionist movement Ḥovevei Zion (Lovers of Zion), described the efforts of Hebrew scholars in Palestine that depended on Arabic as lacking "the sense of taste needed to coin words in our language in accordance with the spirit of our language and its taste, style, scale, and structure."[14] Hebraist Eliezer Meir Lipschitz (1879–1946), an Ashkenazi member of the Hebrew Language Committee, dismissed the view of reliance on Arabic to enrich and expand the Hebrew lexicon. He also rejected the idea that Arabic is the only living Semitic language and therefore Hebrew should benefit from it. In his view, Arabic in fact lacks what Hebrew needs the most. "What shall we do, especially in what we are missing, Arabic will not be richer than our language. Our poverty lies in cultural visions, in new concepts, and in these, Arabic is not richer than our language."[15] Arabic, in his opinion, continues to be useful in providing interpretations of ancient Hebrew and concepts related to the desert and its life.[16] Lipschitz recognized the historical and cultural connections between Hebrew and Arabic, but he prioritized the development of Hebrew as a distinct language from sources other than Arabic, which lacks "cultural visions" and "new concepts." While he dismisses the idea of relying solely on Arabic roots to enrich contemporary Hebrew vocabulary, he acknowledges the utility of Arabic in certain contexts. Specifically, Lipschitz sees value in Arabic for providing interpretations of ancient Hebrew texts and understanding aspects of primitive lifestyle, particularly those related to desert life. Lipschitz's notion of using Arabic to interpret biblical

Hebrew as well as illuminate the relations between the ancient Israelites and their natural landscape could be useful for the cultural project of reconnecting Jewish immigrants with Palestine's landscape through the enrichment of geographic and botanical Hebrew lexicons with the help of Arabic.

Notwithstanding these sharp differences, Ben-Yehuda received encouragement from Yehuda Leib Gordon (1830–92), the most important Hebrew poet of Haskalah (Jewish Enlightenment movement) in the nineteenth century. Just as Jews in Al-Andalus (Muslim Spain) were open to beneficial influences from the outside world and therefore fluent in Arabic, Gordon believed that Jews should be similarly open to their cultural environment in Palestine. He exhibited a keen awareness of how Arabic could enrich the ancient-modern language. His support was instrumental in establishing a solid foundation for the integration of Arabic into modern Hebrew. In a front-page article published in *Ha-Melitz* (Advocate), the first Hebrew newspaper published in Czarist Russia and the organ of the *Ḥibbat Zion* (Love of Zion) movement—a nineteenth-century nonpolitical proto-Zionist movement that encouraged Jewish immigration from eastern Europe and settlement in Palestine—he explains his stance:

> Scholars residing in the land of our forefathers can expand our language by words borrowed from the Arabic language of the land's inhabitants, words that in their origin and root are common for both sister languages, Hebrew and Arabic. The meaning and the use [of these words] are clearer and more determined [in Arabic], for it is a living language and its meaning stands with it. Undoubtedly, our forefathers were using these words in their time the same way present Arabs do. Therefore, [modern Arabic] will be a trustworthy and living source for the cause of the revivification of [the Hebrew] language. It is a source that scholars living outside the land will not be able to use.[17]

Thus, Gordon sees the enrichment of the Hebrew lexicon through Arabic as essential to the revival of modern Hebrew. While expressing doubts about Hebrew's adaptability for modern communication, he sees reliance on the "trustworthy and living source" of Arabic as a viable as well as organic way to recover the language and "land of our forefathers." First, Arabic was a living language with a long history of use; second, the contemporary Palestinian dialect contained words that, according to Gordon, "our forefathers were using . . . in their time the same way present Arabs do"; and third, the semantic and structural similarities between the two languages facilitated the expansion of Hebrew through a related, rather than linguistically unrelated, language. Arabic, then, would not only help revitalize the ancient-modern Hebrew language but also provide an opportunity for modern Jews to emulate their forebearers who lived on the same soil.

Aside from his dictionary, Ben-Yehuda's views are attested to in works pertaining to Palestine's landscape. His *Sefer Erets Yisrael* reveals the integration of

Arabic terms into the emerging Hebrew geographic literary genre.[18] In the introduction to his geographic monograph, he informs his audience that they will find new words that he "borrowed from the Arabic language, the sister of Hebrew." In his words,

> Here the reader will find in my book . . . new words in our language that I borrowed from the Arabic, the sister to which it bears resemblance, for I thought in this way we would truly succeed in reviving our language and healing it from the *niga'* [plague] of new words that have no *temunah 'ivrit* [Hebrew semblance] or *ruaḥ safah 'ivrit* [Hebrew language spirit], and that are, in the view of many of our writers, similar to the spirit of German and Russian.

Borrowing from Arabic is crucial for the resurgence of Hebrew and will heal it [Hebrew] from the plague of new words, which he sees as alienating the language from both the semblance and spirit of Hebrew.[19] Arabic appears a suitable candidate for safeguarding Hebrew from the alienating influence of the invading Western languages as well as providing it with necessary new words. Those integrated Arabic words are not divorced from their cultural background and so open the door to the inclusion of other cultural constituents of Arabic Palestine, particularly those related to the experience with landscape and its flora and fauna. Hebrew works on Palestine's landscape that utilized whatever was beneficial from the local population to restore the connection between Jews and the land were encouraged by the "Enlightener" (Maskil) Gordon, who comments on this genre, "These books are written in the purity of the holy language, which is expanded by words borrowed from the mouths of the Arab settlers of the land, words that, in their origin and root, are similar in both sister languages, Hebrew and Arabic."[20] In Gordon's assessment, Arabic is vital to *teḥiyyat Yisrael* (the revival of Israel).

The Remaking of the Hebraic Landscape

In the absence of definitive evidence of Ben-Yehuda's first encounter with Arabic, one can only speculate that it was his increasing interest in reviving the modern Hebrew language that whetted the linguist's appetite to study Arabic.[21] In his endeavor to coin new words to increase the lexical stock of the emerging language, he consulted Arabic lexicons, and sought advice from Sephardi and Oriental experts like Yellin, Yosef Meyuḥas, and Isaac Yahuda. If he did not in fact acquire Arabic while in Paris, then his travel to Algeria in 1880, per the recommendation of his doctor after being diagnosed with tuberculosis, might have been conducive to at least some acquaintance with the language. In Algeria, he had the opportunity to listen to the Sephardi Hebrew accent, which was popular in late Ottoman Palestine.[22]

Ben-Yehuda ascribed a good deal of importance to the status of Arabic in Palestine and its potential contribution to his national project. On arriving in the country, he was struck by the linguistic fragmentation among Jews in Jerusalem.[23] At the time, Arabic was one among several languages competing for predominance in Jewish communities. Jerusalemite historian and topographer Yeshayahu Press (1874–1955) describes the linguistic landscape in mid-nineteenth-century Jerusalem this way:

> There was no common language . . . for all the Jews living in Jerusalem. The members of the different communities spoke the languages and dialects they had become accustomed to in their mother countries or in their fathers' homeland. The Sephardim spoke Judeo-Spanish . . . the Musta'rabīn spoke Palestinian Arabic, the Maghrebines (North African Jews) spoke Arabic according to the North African dialect, the Caucasians spoke Georgian, the Crimean Tatar and the Ashkenazim spoke Yiddish in different dialects. Arabic was the language of the street, common to all city dwellers who dealt with work and trade, but when the learned men from the different communities met together, they would speak Hebrew among themselves, with the Sephardic accent.[24]

The variety of languages spoken in Jerusalem among the various Jewish communities posed a significant obstacle to unification. But as we glean from Press's account, Hebrew was already serving as a vehicle of communication across communities: "Therefore, it suited to serve as a *lingua franca* to unite the dissimilar communities, fulfilling an important sociological function."[25] As Press noticed, the dominant accent of Hebrew was the Sephardic accent, which pioneers of the Hebrew language such as Ben-Yehuda and Yellin promoted in late Ottoman Palestine. In a lecture given in 1902 to the settlers of Gedera, most of whom were members of Biluim, Yellin recommended using the Sephardi accent when speaking Hebrew. He justified this recommendation with three reasons: first, Sephardim are the majority of Jews in the country; second, Ashkenazim who settled in Palestine adopted the Sephardi accent to better connect with the Sephardim; and third, Arabs in the country speak Arabic, which is closely related to Hebrew and considered an important sister language.[26] In Yellin's view, adopting the Sephardi Hebrew accent resonates with the sounds of other Semitic languages in the region and creates familiarity with Arabic.

Arabic represented the most significant living Semitic language in Ben-Yehuda's time. Though dominant in the region, Arabic in its spoken form did not serve as a lingua franca among the fragmented Jewish communities in Palestine. Aside from basic conversational words, *sefat ha-reḥov ha-meshutefet* (common street language) in the words of Press, Ben-Yehuda's knowledge of spoken Arabic was limited.[27] Nevertheless, he advocated its use as a primary source for the enrichment of the Hebrew lexicon, which resulted in the assimilation of both linguistic and cultural features of Arabic into Hebrew.[28] In a lecture to members of the Hebrew Language Committee in Jerusalem in 1913–14 on "Sources to Fill the Gap in Our Language," Ben-Yehuda argues for the imperativeness of the use of Arabic to enrich the revived Hebrew. In refuting the claim that Aramaic is closer to Hebrew than any other Semitic language and therefore should be the only source from which modern Hebrew draws its vocabulary, Ben-Yehuda weighed in on the matter with another solution. He excitedly addressed his colleagues thus: "Here, dear sires, I can proudly announce before you that I found it! I found it! I found Arabic roots in tens, in hundreds! I even would not conceal from you the source where I found these treasures. I found them in Arabic lexicons!"[29] That borrowing manifested in Ben-Yehuda's introducing neologisms influenced by Arabic to his newly invented Hebrew words list.[30] The Arabic component in modern Hebrew usage can be classified into several categories: Arabic words that have been integrated into Hebrew, such as *ahlan wa-sahlan*, a saying that conveys the meaning "you have come to a spacious place and to a people like your own and therefore be cheerful"; Arabic phrases like *Allah Karīm* (God is generous); Arabic proverbs like *al-ʿajala min al-shayṭān* (haste is from the devil); expressions like *ʿala ʿinī wa-ʿala rāsī* (on my eyes and my head), expressing a strong willingness to comply with a request or do something for someone; Arabic words whose pronunciation has changed, such as *Dughrī* becoming *Dogri* (straightforward) and *ʿafrīt* becoming *Afrit* (genie); Arabic expressions that have been integrated into Hebrew through their Hebrew translation, such as *Boḳer Or* (*Ṣabāḥ al-Nūr*), which means "good morning," and *Kapparah* (*Kaffara*), which means "atonement or forgiveness"; Arabic words whose roots have an equivalent in Hebrew, such as *Ḥezuḳ* (*h.z.q.*) (to tie or bind something with a rope) and *Kasaḥ* (*k.s.h.*) (to hit hard or make an incursion into a group of people); Hebrew words whose form is shaped according to Arabic words, such as Hebrew words ending with the feminine ending *-yah*, like *Miṭriyah* (umbrella), *Shimshiyah* (parasol), and *ʿiriyyah* (municipality), whose Arabic equivalent with the same meaning is *maṭariyya*, *shamsiyya*, and *balādiyya*, respectively.[31]

Ben-Yehuda's attraction to Arabo-Islamic culture in his construction of Palestine's landscape is evidenced in his identifying place-names found in the Jewish sources with their contemporary Arabic counterparts. In the third chapter in his geographic monograph that deals with rivers, lakes, seas, and streams, he devotes a full section to Lake Tiberius.[32] In his treatment of the lake, Ben-Yehuda consults Arabic sources to establish a link between Yam Kinneret and the contemporary Arabic designation of the same site as Buḥayrat Ṭabariyya. The employment of Arabic is crucial in identifying the lake. After establishing the Hebrew name Yam Kinneret based on a few biblical clues, Ben-Yehuda identifies the lake with buḥayrat Ṭabariyya, the place referred to in the Midrashim as Yama shel Ṭabariyah (the Sea of Tiberius).[33] If the biblical and postbiblical references to Yam Kinneret and Yama shel Ṭabariyah were not as clear to Jewish readers residing outside the Holy Land as they were to those residing in Palestine, the association between the lake's names in the Jewish tradition and the current Palestinian Arab designation for the same site would make the knowledge of the land more vivid and contemporary.

In discussing Yarden, the Hebrew name for the Jordan River, he proposes a reading of the Hebrew name based on the cognate Arabic word *al-'urdun*.[34] Explaining that the word *Yarden* derives from the Hebrew verb *yard*, meaning to descend from a higher place to a lower one, it seems at first glance to offer no association with a body of water, let alone a river.[35] But here Ben-Yehuda turns to the cognate Arabic verb *warad* to clarify the meaning of *Yarden*. In Arabic, he notes, the verb *warad* refers to "the arrival of an animal to a watering-place where it is watered."[36] Here, the Arabic cognate provides significant details that its Hebrew equivalent lacks. Moving further, he proposes that since watering places used to be in the lower areas of a village, coming to a watering place constituted movement from a higher place to a lower one.[37]

When he turns to Midbar Paran (Wilderness of Paran), whose etymology is unclear, he refers to its Arabic name, Bādiyat al-Tīh (Wilderness of Wanderings):

> Arabs call it today Bādiyat al-Tīh—in other words, the wilderness of the wanderings. Jews used to call it the wilderness of Paran. . . . It is the wilderness in which the Israelites wandered for forty years until the generation of the exodus, who suffered under the Egyptians and vanished, and another generation appeared who did not know the house of slavery and the oppressive work that their ancestors did.[38]

Here, he explains the Wilderness of Paran and its significance in Jewish history, but he does so based on the Arabic name Bādiyat al-Tīh (Wilderness of Wanderings), likely drawing on Ibn Yāqūt al-Ḥamawī's *Mu'jam al-Buldān* (The lexicon of lands).[39] Although the Muslim geographer lists a place called fārān in his lexicon, the description he provides for this place would have discouraged Ben-Yehuda from relying on it. Al-Ḥamawī identifies fārān with Mecca, based on the story of Abraham along with the transfer of Ishmael and Hagar mentioned in Genesis 21:21. He says that fārān "is an Arabized Hebrew word. It is one of the names attributed to Mecca that had been mentioned in the Bible."[40] But the Jewish connection to the land would not have been bolstered by a reference to the Wilderness of Paran preserved in Arabo-Islamic culture. A better connection was made through the identification of Paran with the desert of al-Tīh (Wilderness), which would parallel the biblical account in Numbers 10:12 regarding the story of Moses and the children of Israel, who wandered in the wilderness of Paran after their exodus from Egypt. About al-Tīh, al-Ḥamawī says,

> Al-Tīh is the place where Mūsa (Moses) and his people wandered. . . . It is said that the children of Israel reached al-Tīh, their ages ranging between twenty and sixty years. All of them died over the space of forty years, and no one left [al-Tīh] safely of those who arrived to it in the company of Mūsa (Moses), except Yūsha' bin Nūn (Joshua Ben Nun) and Kālib ben Yūfinna (Kaleb ben Yefuneh).[41]

Ben-Yehuda seems to identify Paran with Bādiyat al-Tīh (Wilderness of Wanderings) to attribute to Paran a historical meaning that resonates with the ancient Israelites' experience.

The Expansion of Hebrew through Botanical Names

The association between Jews and Palestine's natural environment was central to early Zionist thought. Trees, as historian Yael Zerubavel notes, became an "icon of national revival, symbolizing the Zionist success in 'striking roots' in the ancient homeland." In her analysis of the Israeli writer Abraham B. Yehushua's *mūl ha-ye'arot* (Facing forests)—a collection of short stories published during the 1960s that focused on the experience of early Jewish guards of the colonies in the forests located far from the Jewish colonies—Zerubavel juxtaposes Jews' and Arabs' encounters with the land. Whereas the Jew is depicted as disconnected from the forest, the Arab man and his daughter, according to her reading, are portrayed as in kinship with the landscape. They are indistinguishable from the trees around them, and when they emerge from the forest, it is described as though they are coming out of its womb.[42] That intimacy between Arabs and their natural environment sparked the Jews' desire to overcome their sense of alienation and craft their own connection with the natural landscape around them by acquiring the necessary knowledge.

Though observed from the viewpoint of the Hebrew authors, the bond between Palestinians and their natural environment naturally predates the Jewish return to Palestine. This bond was made manifest in their popular songs celebrating orange and olive harvests as well as in the form of "holy trees" associated with the tombs of *awliyā'* (saints).[43] With the establishment of the state of Israel, Jaffa oranges held immense significance for post-Nakba Palestinians. They symbolize the Palestinian splendor, pride, and glory that were deeply wounded by the Nakba (catastrophe). The collective memory of Jaffa's oranges is expressed through various mediums, including poetry, prose, cinema, signs, names, and commercial advertising. Hebrew popular songs, on the contrary, replaced Arabic songs and concomitantly distorted collective memory, as historians Mustafa

Kabha and Nahum Karlinsky have shown, in facilitating the forgetfulness of the fact that Palestinian citrus groves had existed even a few years before 1948.[44] Cactus, known in Arabic as *ṣabbār*, assumed dominance in the natural landscape of Palestine, where it was used as a demarcation of land boundaries. The cactus's physical characteristics, as Nasser Abufarha has observed, inculcated senses of resilience and patience in the culture of the local population.[45] The impact of the natural environment on the identity of Palestine's local population caught the attention of Tawfiq Canaan, who was preoccupied with the preservation of the native culture of the local peasant society, which was endangered by forms of modernity. With this goal in mind, Canaan and his circle, as Palestinian sociologist Salim Tamari has explained, began documenting, classifying, and interpreting that endangered peasant culture.[46]

The efforts of the revivers of modern Hebrew in Jerusalem were compounded by the works of Hebrew writers and communal leaders in the Jewish colonies, such as Menashe Meirovitch, who used his knowledge of the botanical world of Palestine and Arabic to link Jews to Palestine's landscape as well as instill a sense of rootedness by enriching the modern Hebrew lexicon with terms and naming techniques from the Arabic language.

Meirovitch was among the Jewish immigrants who settled in late Ottoman Palestine as part of the First Aliyah.[47] The uniqueness of the First Aliyah immigrants, in the assessment of Israeli geographer Ran Aaronsohn, stemmed from their "espousal of new ideas from the realm of nationalism, social reform, and economic planning, which combined with the traditional religious idea of a return to Zion to foster the revival of the Jewish people in their land on a sound, productive basis—that is, primarily an agricultural basis."[48] Agronomists of the First Aliyah, like Meirovitch and Israel Belḳind, both of whom belonged to the Bilu movement, were technocrats who embraced an apolitical entrepreneurial agenda in addition to the biblical agrarian ideals.[49] Meirovitch and Belḳind, for instance, were affiliated with the nonpolitical group of General Zionists or hit'aḥdut ha-'ikarim (Farmers' Federation), one of several nonpartisan "Citizens Circles" organized around professional interests. While abstaining from participation in partisan issues, as historian Liora Halperin has shown, Meirovitch simultaneously, like much of the Palestinian economic elite of the time, believed he was contributing to the nationalist ideals of the Jewish society in Palestine.[50] Meirovitch's interest in Palestine's vegetation, developed when he was in Warsaw some years before he settled in late Ottoman Palestine as an agronomist, was put into the service of the Ottoman authorities as well as the Jewish community.[51]

A member of Ḥovevei Zion (Lovers of Zion), Meirovitch adhered to the biblical ideal of "every man under his vine"—an expression that conveys a sense of peace, prosperity, and security—and viewed the modern Jewish agricultural colonization of Palestine as the foundation for the construction of a nation making the desert bloom, or as he put it, turning the wilderness into the Garden of Eden.[52] He extolled those who worked for and supported settlement in Palestine, such as Edmond de Rothschild (1845–1934), a French Jewish philanthropist and patron of Jewish settlement in Palestine, because they caused him "to see with [his] eyes a thing no one would have believed could happen," and that "has not occurred in the history of any nation." Describing proudly the successes of Jewish settlement in late Ottoman Palestine, he wrote,

> In the last five years, we possessed five thousand hectares of territory in our ancestral land, which wilderness covered for almost two thousand years. Now it has been turned into the Garden of Eden, containing magnificent cities . . . pleasant vineyards, and thousands of industrious hands of our brethren working [the land] with the sweat of their brow.

All of this took place, he noted, "under the auspices of the mighty Turkish government," which, he claimed, would "extend its hand to help whosoever clings tightly to the land." Further, Jewish settlers had received help from Baron Rothschild, whom Meirovitch portrayed as "a generous [man]" who would "support them with his benevolent hand and care for them as a father raising his children."[53] The success achieved by the collaborative efforts of Baron Rothschild and the Jewish farmers proved, according to Meirovitch, that a Jewish nation could be resurrected.

Meirovitch aspired to create a Hebrew culture that articulated a definitive relationship between Jews and Palestine's natural habitat. With his pen, he encouraged Jews to settle in Palestine, and with his hands, he grew grapevines on that very same land and became a landowner. Striking roots in the land necessitated the cultivation of a new national identity in which language would play an integral role. Meirovitch regarded the multilingualism prevalent among Jews in Palestine at the time detrimental to the revival of the Jewish nation. Employing the language of the Bible, he warned against becoming like *dor ha-pelagah* (the generation of the Tower of Babel), and instead advocated for the formation of a national language by which the Jewish nation could be resurrected and unified:

> We should look at our moral circumstances and become worried about the newborn generation that we hope will not take on the likeness of the generation of the Tower of Babel, which did not understand one another, as we were in this state for almost two millennia. Even as we settled in our forefathers' land, one speaks Russian, the other responds in German, the third answers in Romanian, and the fourth replies in French. Ha! If Israel is so scattered, how can she be called a nation [*'am*]? Nonetheless, this obvious shortcoming has been overcome with the aid and munificence of the great baron, who has invested in the education of the dwellers of the settlements, to teach them to converse,

to write, and to read in our ancestral language. [Therefore] we, along with anyone concerned with the resurrection of the nation of Israel, should support that idea, and every one of our brethren should make an effort to establish and encourage it in order to [form] a single language common to all of us, for without this matter we will not build one nation [*goy 'eḥād*] in the land.[54]

If Hebrew was essential to the formation of the national identity along with the immersion in the natural environment, there was a need to enrich the language with necessary botanical terms to sustain Jews' encounter with the nature surrounding them. To promote this knowledge, Meirovitch compiled a book, *Tsemḥe Erets ha-Tsevi* (The vegetation of the land of the gazelle], in which he detailed the flora of Palestine.[55] He expected his book to be an innovative work that would bridge the gulf between the emerging Hebrew scholarly literature and that of other nations, and would lay the foundation for a scientific Hebrew literature on the flora of Palestine:

In general, our literature lacks books and articles that treat scientific matters. In particular, we lack knowledge for working the land, and as a result, also expressions and names. A great many of the new ideas that appear in the literature of all nations are missing in our language. Thus I provide for you, dear readers, my book, which aims at: first, informing on the circumstances of the flora of the land of Israel and Syria, on behalf of our brethren who are concerned with the situation of our forefathers' land in its entirety; and second, benefiting all of our brethren who are working the Holy Land with their hands.[56]

Meirovitch's project was to utilize modern sciences to link the Jewish people to the land of their origins, and borrow terms and concepts from other literatures, specifically Arabo-Islamic culture, to help resurrect the Hebrew language.

Lunts, founder of the literary almanac *Luaḥ Eretz Yisrael* and an active member of the Hebrew Language Committee, was invited by Meirovitch to comment on his work on the plant names in Palestine. Lunts set forth some of the criteria governing nomenclature borrowings from languages other than Hebrew:

The plants whose names we found in rabbinic literature—even though the name of a plant may not fit the character of Hebrew—we named after ones from rabbinic literature. For the plants whose names we found neither in [rabbinic literature] nor in Aramaic, however, we turned to its sister, Arabic. If the name that Arabs used was **authentic** [*meḳori*]—in other words, if the name had not been transformed through Western languages—we would call it by the same name. Also, if the Arabic name had a proper interpretation, we would give the plant a Hebrew name in accordance with the Arabic interpretation. If the Arabic name was not original, however, we would assign the plant the Latin name.[57]

The reconstruction of the natural landscape to align with that which is found in the rabbinic literature is given high priority here. In cases where a plant name is not to be found in the rabbinic repository, there is a need to turn to Arabic. The values of originality and authenticity ascribed to Arabic names and terms gave them priority over European borrowings in accordance with the cultural project of "going native," constructing a native modern Hebrew in harmonious relationship with both the physical and human landscape.

Lunts regards Arabic as a principal and authoritative source for the construction of Palestine's natural environment. Adopting Arabic plant names, though, was contingent on the assumed "authenticity" of those names. As is starkly evident in the quotation above, there was a tendency to emphasize Hebrew's Semitic nature at that early stage of its renaissance by inserting loan words—in this case, names of plants—from other Semitic languages, chiefly Arabic and Aramaic.[58] Lunts noted several roles that Arabic could play in the development of Hebrew appellation for plant names. If the Arabic name was authentic (not an adopted version of a Western name), it must be retained in Hebrew. If the Arabic name had a suitable meaning, a Hebrew name should be designated corresponding to its Arabic significance. If the Arabic name was of Latin origin, the Latin name must be retained. In this case, the Hebrew name must use the original form (sometimes slightly modified) in its Hebrew pronunciation. Although Lunts does not provide examples for these scenarios, the utilization of Arabic as a source for the expansion of Hebrew vocabulary is apparent. Plant names often carry cultural, historical, and symbolic meanings that are retained once the name of a certain plant is adopted into Hebrew. In fact, the hebraization of plant names served as a powerful tool, connecting the plant kingdom in Palestine to the collective memory of Jewish settlers. This process not only facilitated Jewish indigenization and a sense of rootedness but also created a shared cultural space with the Palestinian population.

Hebraizing the Flora of Palestine

The linguistic affinity between Arabic and Hebrew spurred Eliyahu Sapir to turn to the former to assist in the revival of modern Hebrew. His interest in Arabo-Islamic culture was sparked by, among other factors, studying at the Alliance Israélite Universelle school in Jerusalem that attracted Jews of Ashkenazi descent in addition to Palestine-born Jews of Sephardic origins. Sapir, born in Jerusalem to an Ashkenazi family that had settled in the city since the beginning of the nineteenth century, figured prominently among early twentieth-century Hebrew writers. He was the grandson of Jacob Sapir (1822–86), a man of Lithuanian origins who immigrated to Jerusalem in 1832, spoke Arabic fluently, and claimed to have read the Quran and other Muslim books.[59] Jacob was known for his momentous ethnographic travel diary *Even Sapir* (1866, 1874), in which he gave accounts of Jews in Yemen and India.[60] Affected by his connection to his grandfather and living in the mixed city of Jerusalem, the young Sapir felt drawn to explore the Arabo-Islamic world. While pursuing traditional Jewish studies at a rabbinical school in Jerusalem, Sapir began clandestinely visiting the Alliance Israélite Universelle to learn Arabic—an activity that was not approved by his parents. Nissim Behar (1848–1931), founder of modern Hebrew instruction in late Ottoman Palestine and headmaster of the alliance at the time, recognized Sapir's skills, and supported him until he turned out to be one of the philologists in both Hebrew and Arabic in the land. The writer of his obituary describes Sapir as "a literary genius . . . who learned and completed his Arabic studies in a perfect manner until he became one of the few among our [Jewish] brothers who know Arabic language perfectly."[61]

In the assessment of a comparative philologist as Sapir, Arabic was a medium through which Hebrew could overcome its weaknesses and ambiguities—a view that echoed that of Ben-Yehuda and Yellin. In his opinion, modern Hebrew was but a remnant of a language, "preserved in the sacred texts deficient and fragmented."[62] Worse, Hebrew as a remnant language was not even well-defined. Aside from inventing new words and grammatical rules, there was a need to retrieve the language's origins and characteristics, which were, however, lost to time. Sapir sought to restore completeness and clarity to Hebrew through the medium of Arabic:

> To magnify [Hebrew] through these two elements [proficiency and clarity], we should seek mediums that will reveal the ambiguities in our language, and also through which we can realize its deficiencies; [we should] find the obstructed threads and strings, connect its past with our present and fill in the gap between [the two]. These mediums we will find only in a related language, similar and suitable to our own language, which began developing alongside [Hebrew] at the same time and in the same manner, developed over centuries, and remained in its completeness until today, and nonetheless, its natural development has not ceased; it lives in the tongues of its people who speak it, create for it new literature, and enlarge it in accordance with its character and spirit, fashioning it and its sister [languages]. *That language is Arabic.*[63]

Like other Hebrew authors, Sapir noticed the gap between the linguistic signs referring to Palestine in the Hebrew Bible and the actual landscape of Palestine. His work on the flora of Palestine proved useful to the Hebrew Language Committee in bridging that gap.

One of the problems the committee noticed in disseminating Hebrew as a language of instruction in the newly emerging Hebrew schools across Palestine was disagreement over the appropriate name of a certain plant. In 1913, the committee remarked, "The names of the plants and their parts are the cornerstone of the curriculum in our new school in the country, where this subject is given due importance as appropriate for the people living on their land." The committee recognized how fundamental botanical knowledge was not only for Hebrew language development but also for consolidating the lived experience of the Hebrew-learning Jewish population in Palestine and rooting their belonging in its landscape. The human-nature relationship that Jewish teachers tried to establish through the hebraization of Palestine's flora led to division among learners. The committee indicates this disagreement among educators: "The Galilean teachers, the first to seriously engage in this [i.e., the hebraization of Palestine's flora], gave names to plants based on what they found in the Talmud and in the Arabic language. The teachers in Judea [in the south] invented other names for them also based on the Talmud and the Arabic language." In the middle of this division, the committee found it imperative to step in to standardize the language used among Hebrew educators by producing a list of common plants in Hebrew. Regarding the significance of Arabic in the hebraization of Palestine's flora, the committee stated that "only if names for the plants were not found, the committee determined their names according to their Arabic name." In the list the committee provided, for instance, the Hebrew translation *Bekhor aviv* for the Arabic plant *zahr al-Rabīʿ* means "the flower of the spring," with the scientific name primula.[64] Another example is *Dam al-Ghazāl* (gazelle's blood) or *Khāleda* (immortal), whose scientific name is helichrysum. The Hebrew appellation *al-mut/almavet*, which translates as "immortal," is a literal translation of the Arabic name. The incorporation of Arabic in naming Palestine's flora demonstrated Jewish educators' willingness to integrate local perspectives and terminology into their educational materials, illustrating an adaptive, pragmatic approach to language, prioritizing effective communication and local relevance. While adopting Arabic names for plants when Hebrew equivalents were absent, Hebrew educators aimed to assert Jewish connection to the land through the broader project of hebraization to reclaim the land linguistically and culturally, emphasizing Jewish indigeneity in Palestine's diverse linguistic landscape.

While not a botanist by training, Sapir was acquainted with botanical works relevant to Palestine in several Western languages (English, German, and French) as well as Arabic.[65] "In the field of the knowledge of the land of Israel," attests Meir Dizengoff (1861-1936), the mayor of Tel Aviv at the time of Sapir's death, "he [Sapir] was the only one among our brethren settling in the land who [read every] book in that discipline, whether in Hebrew, Arabic, German, French, or in English . . . and consequently he always knew everything new in the field."[66] The Hebrew Language Committee's reference to Hebrew educators drawing on rabbinic literature as well as Dizengoff commending Sapir for his well-versed knowledge in rabbinic literature calls our attention to the centrality of Jewish sources in determining the exact Hebrew appellation of a certain plant. Why was there an obsession with determining the name of a plant in accordance with what is listed in the biblical and postbiblical texts?

We saw in chapter 2 how Hebrew revivalists relied on Jewish sources for place-names, and they exhibited the same preoccupation with linking the flora of Palestine to biblical and rabbinic literature. For these revivalists, the flora of Palestine became a tangible link to their ancient heritage, emphasizing the enduring connection between the land and its people. Moreover, given the religious orientation of early Jewish settlers, one can see in this method the sacralization of Palestine's landscape.[67] By associating local plants with these sacred texts, the revivalists imbued the landscape with divine meaning.

In a series of articles published during 1911 in the Hebrew periodical *Haḥinukh* (Pedagogy) addressing Hebrew teachers in Palestine, Sapir listed plants indigenous to Palestine. The main source on which Sapir drew was *Die Pflanzen Palästinas* (Plants of Palestine), by US botanist John Edward Dinsmore (1862–1951), who for many years took great interest in the botanical world of Palestine, and German Orientalist Gustaf Hermann Dalman (1855–1941), who did extensive fieldwork in Palestine before World War I. Dinsmore and Dalman's work presents a strong case for how crucial Arabo-Islamic knowledge was to Jewish settlers. Sapir appropriated Dinsmore and Dalman's list in coining Hebrew names for Palestine's flora to fill "a big void that is strongly felt in our midst, . . . [which is] the lack of knowledge in terms of the plants of our land."[68] In making this project available in Hebrew, he did not merely function as a translator but also compared Dinsmore and Dalman's list with the terminological usage prevailing among the Arab population.

Die Pflanzen Palästinas was a continuation of and improvement on previous Western studies, such as *Flora Orientalis* by Swiss botanist Edmond Boissier (1810–85) and *Flora of Syria, Palestine, and Sinai* (1896) by George Edward Post (1838–1909), a professor of surgery at the Syrian Protestant College in Beirut who published widely in the areas of natural history, medicine, and theology, mostly in Arabic and occasionally in English. Post's Arabic works, including *mabādi' 'ilm al-nabāt* (Principles of botany) and the Arabic translation of *Flora of Syria*, are considered the earliest scientific reference textbooks in botany, and were circulated widely among Arabic-speaking audiences and cited by Sapir in his Hebrew list.[69]

In writing about Palestine's botanical specimens, Dinsmore and Dalman gave a contemporary account of the uses, cultivation, and distribution of various species in the region, absorbing Arabo-Islamic elements that later found their way into the work of Sapir. *Die Pflanzen Palästinas* lists the Latin names of plants alongside their Arabic names. The credibility of the work was enhanced by the authors' efforts to collect the Arabic names of the plants, which were dispersed

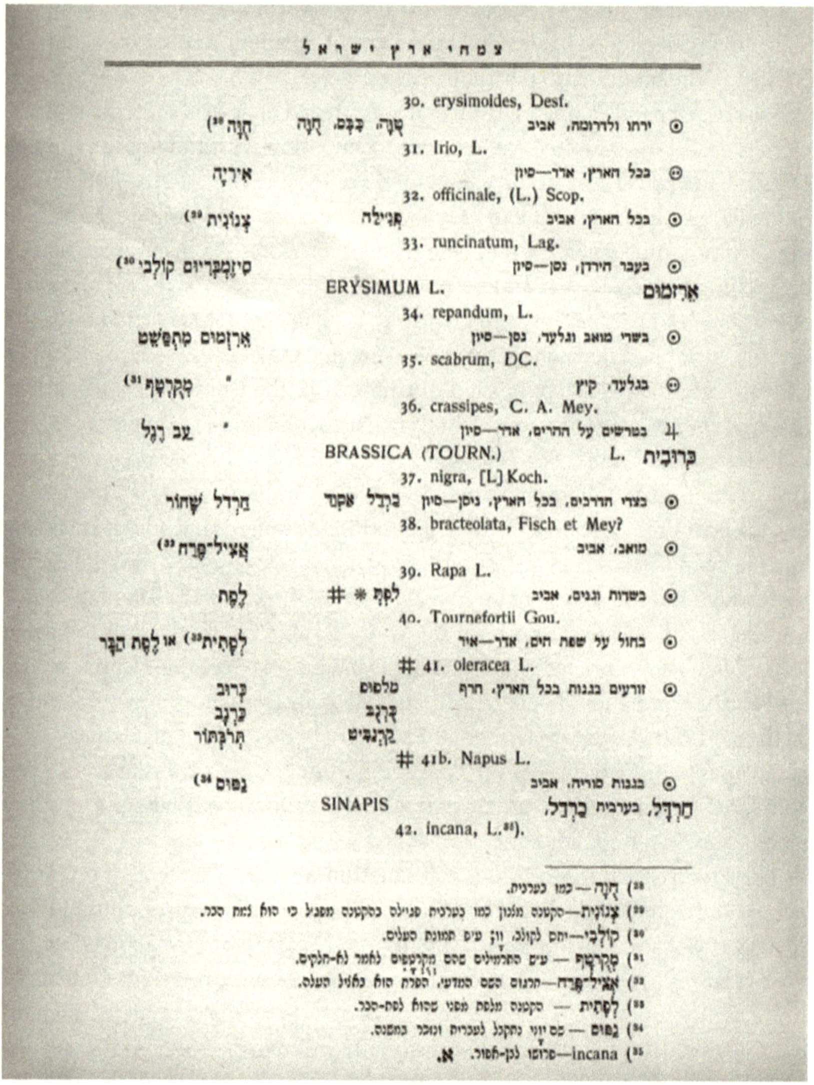

צמחי ארץ ישראל

30. erysimoides, Desf.
⊙ ירתו ולדרומה, אביב — חֻוָּה [28] / חֻוָּה

31. Irio, L.
⊙ בכל הארץ, אדר—סיון — אִירְיָה

32. officinale, (L.) Scop.
⊙ בכל הארץ, אביב — צְנוֹנִית [29]

33. runcinatum, Lag.
⊙ בעבר הירדן, נסן—סיון — סִיזְמְבְּרִיוּם קוֹלְבִּי [30]

ERYSIMUM L. אֶרְזִמוּם

34. repandum, L.
⊙ בשרי מואב וגלעד, נסן—סיון — אֶרְזִמוּם מְתֻפְשָׁט

35. scabrum, DC.
⊙ בגלעד, קיץ — מְקַרְשֵׁף [31]

36. crassipes, C. A. Mey.
♃ בטרשים על ההרים, אדר—סיון — עֲב רֶגֶל

BRASSICA (TOURN.) L. כְּרוּבִית

37. nigra, [L] Koch.
⊙ בצדי הדרכים, בכל הארץ, ניסן—סיון — חַרְדָּל שָׁחוֹר

38. bracteolata, Fisch et Mey?
⊙ מואב, אביב — אֲצִיל־פֶּרַח [32]

39. Rapa L.
⊙ בשדות וגנים, אביב — לֶפֶת * # — לֶפֶת

40. Tournefortii Gou.
⊙ בחול על שפת הים, אדר—איר — לְפָתִית [33] או לֶפֶת הַבָּר

41. oleracea L.
⊙ זורעים בגנות בבכל הארץ, חרף — כְּרוּב / כְּרָנְב / תְּרוּבְתוֹר

41b. Napus L.
⊙ בגנות סוריה, אביב — נָפוּס [34]

SINAPIS חַרְדָּל, בערבית בַּרְדָּל

42. incana, L.[35]).

[28]) חֻוָּה — כמו כערבית.
[29]) צְנוֹנִית—סקטנה מלנון כמו בערבית פגילס כסקטנה מסבל כי הוא נמח הכר.
[30]) קוֹלְבִּי—יחס לקולב, וין; עים תמונת סעלים.
[31]) מְקַרְשֵׁף — עים התרמילים שהם מקרעפים לאמר לא-חלקים.
[32]) אֲצִיל־פֶּרַח—תרגום השם המדעי, הפרח הוא נאציל העלה.
[33]) לְפָתִית — הקטנה מלפת מפני שהוא לפת-הכר.
[34]) נָפוּס — שם יוני נתקבל לעברית ונזכר במשנה.
[35]) incana—פרושו לבן-אפור. א.

FIGURE 3.1. A list of plant names in Palestine appears in Eliyahu Sapir's series of articles "Tsimḥe Erets Yisrael" (Plants of the land of Israel). In the footnotes, Sapir notes the Arabic origins of some of the Hebrew names.

in Arabic lexicons and consulted the local population.[70] Sapir found the plants' Arabic names an invaluable resource to help revive Hebrew.

In his works, Sapir refers to medieval Arab giants who contributed to the cultivation and advancement of medicinal and practical knowledge in their immediate community and beyond. He notes medieval works by Muslim scholars who made use of botanical knowledge for medicinal purposes, such as *al-qānūn fī al-ṭibb* (Canon of medicine) by Ibn Sīna (Avicenna) (980–1037). *Al-qānūn fī al-ṭibb* was rendered into Latin in the twelfth century, and from the fourteenth century onward was considered one of the important books in medical education in both the East and West. The work lost its significance in Europe only with the development of modern science in the seventeenth century.[71] A significant portion of the book consisted of descriptions of hundreds of herbal remedies—a subject that proved essential to Sapir's project.

Another figure important to Sapir's project was the sixteenth-century Arab physician Dāwūd al-ʾAnṭākī (d. 1599), a native of al-Shām (the Levant) whose work drew on his immediate surroundings, thereby reflecting his life experience and community's herbal practices.[72] Al-ʾAnṭākī's works are representative of the heyday of the Shāmī (from greater Syria) medical tradition that reached its peak during the sixteenth century before the decline of the Ottoman Empire.[73] He included in his work *taḏkirat ʾulī al-ʾalbāb wa-al-jāmiʿ lil-ʿajab al-ʿujāb* (A reminder for people of understanding), which described approximately seventy separate medicinal substances representative of those used during the Ottoman period in the al-Shām, whether extracted from plants cultivated domestically or imported by traders.

Sapir was also inspired by the efforts of contemporary Arab intellectuals who sought to expand Arabic's botanical lexicon, as he undertook to produce a corresponding Hebrew botanical work that could stand on equal footing. He did not want Hebrew to go the way of Syriac, whose influence had decreased and whose remaining speakers used it only in religious contexts. To avoid this fate, Hebrew needed to draw on the living language of "Arabic [which] remains rich, whether in its literature or its spoken language, and many plant names are preserved in it; for the Arab people, like the other oriental nations, are experts in plants, and they pass on the names from one generation to another." Sapir exhorted his Hebrew interlocutors to make use of these riches for "we find here for our brethren in the land a wide field from which to collect the names of plants [from the very] tongue of the Arab populace. This work, notably, should be fruitful and useful for the development of our language."[74]

Arabic and Hebrew Cross-Pollination

The borrowings from Arabic we have seen in the work of Sapir and others were taking place against a background of contention whereby many Hebrew literati in Europe opposed resorting to Arabic to renew and expand Hebrew. To justify their position, Jerusalemite Hebrew scholars stressed the shared Semitic sources of both languages, and highlighted the cultural exchange between Jewish and Arab communities that had taken place throughout various historical periods in Palestine.

In an article published in 1911, Sapir, then a member of the Hebrew Language Committee, acknowledged the role of Arabic as a living Semitic language to enrich the resurrected Hebrew. Yet he also emphasized the role of Hebrew and Syriac in the coinage of plant names. Rather than framing the relationship as Hebrew's dependence on Arabic, Sapir promoted the notion of a cross-pollination between Arabic and Hebrew in which both languages interacted with each other and yielded identical botanical nomenclature.[75]

A staunch Hebrew nationalist, Sapir sought to vanquish the feelings of alienation and rootlessness that immigrant Jews brought with them from their countries of origins by instead instilling in them a sense of rootedness along with belonging through the promotion of "knowledge of the land." Sapir went as far as to claim that the Jewish community's very existence in Palestine hinged on knowing its natural environment. The model of Jewish settlement, in the words of Sapir, was not merely about connecting with nature; it was about the *ḳiyūm* (existence) of the Jewish community in the land—an existence that depended on understanding the natural environment. Once that knowledge was inculcated in the minds of individuals, their attachment to the land would no longer be questionable, for they would never imagine their existence in a different land.[76]

A Jerusalemite and native of Palestine, Sapir belonged to a group of Palestinian Jews that included Yellin, Meyuḥas, and Ben-Yehuda, who advocated for the revival of Hebrew and promotion of the Sephardic pronunciation.[77] Sapir recognized the role of teachers in instilling a sense of belonging in the minds and hearts of Jewish youths, and advocated that they acclimate themselves to the land before propagating a similar process of attachment in their disciples. He insisted on the instrumental role teachers could play in shaping the awareness of youths:

> On the shoulders of the teacher in our land lies the obligation to edify the young plant, and help them adjust to this land and its circumstances. [A teacher], however, should first and foremost habituate himself to the new and natural life that is unfolding before our eyes, to know his place and know our land, what it includes, its nature, and its products. [He should be prepared to] train his students and nurture in them that consciousness, so that they will develop a need and ability to become attached to the land and remain in it as citizens.[78]

The argument for cross-pollination between Arabic and Hebrew rested on Sapir's reconstruction of the history of both Semitic languages in Palestine. As he saw it, the two languages interacted with each other, and as a result, certain botanical naming practices crossed from one cultural orbit to the other. Both languages, he further explained, coexisted in Palestine in two major historical periods: first, during the Mishnaic period, approximately 10–220 CE, in which Hebrew was influenced by Arabic, and second, during the Arab conquest of Palestine, in which Arabic was likely influenced by Hebrew.[79]

During the Mishnaic period, the Hebrew language absorbed linguistic elements from both Arabic and Syriac, with the former influence being larger due to the Arab expansion northward. Settling mostly in the southeastern region of Palestine, "Arabs came in close contact with the people of Israel." Since Arabs were peasants and shepherds, "their language was rich [in terms] of the names of plants growing in the land." Due to their joint settlement in the land and their linguistic affinity, Arabs, Syrians, and Hebrews "used similar names for plants of the land . . . to the extent that it would be difficult for us to examine these names and pinpoint their correct origins." Therefore it would not be accurate to claim that a certain people—Sapir used the Hebrew term *'am* (people)—was the originator of a certain plant's name simply because that name was common in one language and forgotten in another:

> The names of plants in these languages [referring to Arabic, Hebrew, and Syriac] often exhibit similarities, with many being shared across languages with minor differences in form and pronunciation. A glance at plant names mentioned in the Bible, such as Remon, Tenah, Ḥitta, She'orah, Pul, Batzel, Avatiaḥ, Ketsaḥ, and Shoshan, reveals these similarities, with slight variations observed in Arabic, especially in the spoken language used in our land today.[80]

While Sapir focuses here on the overlap between these languages, there are also minor differences in form and pronunciation between the Arabic and Hebrew versions of these names. Sapir gave the Hebrew plant names found in the Bible as a way of making his point without listing their Arabic equivalent, as though the Hebrew reader could easily discern the same names in Arabic: *remon/rummān* (pomegranate), *tenah/tīn* (fig), *ḥitta/ḥinṭa* (wheat), *she'orah/sha'īr* (barely), *pul/fūl* (fava beans), *batzel/baṣal* (onions), *avatiaḥ/baṭīkh* (watermelon), *ketsaḥ/qazḥa* (nigella or black cumin), and *Shoshan/Sawsan* (lily).

If the name of a certain plant was common in Arabic, whether written or oral, but was not mentioned at all in Hebrew, that might not actually indicate a Arabic origin for the plant's name. In fact, according to Sapir's theory, the name might have been circulated in spoken Hebrew, but forgotten over the course of time due to the vicissitudes of the Hebrew language over the centuries. Sapir concluded,

> Who knows whether many of the names common at the moment in the language of the Arab multitude in the land were not ours, and when we annex them to our language we in fact do not imitate or take nurture from others; rather we are restoring our loss and we through them take nurture from our own.[81]

Sapir provided an example of a number of plants whose form remains in Jewish sources, yet their meanings/significance are lost. He noted that "there are plant names whose significance have long been forgotten in our literature, yet they are

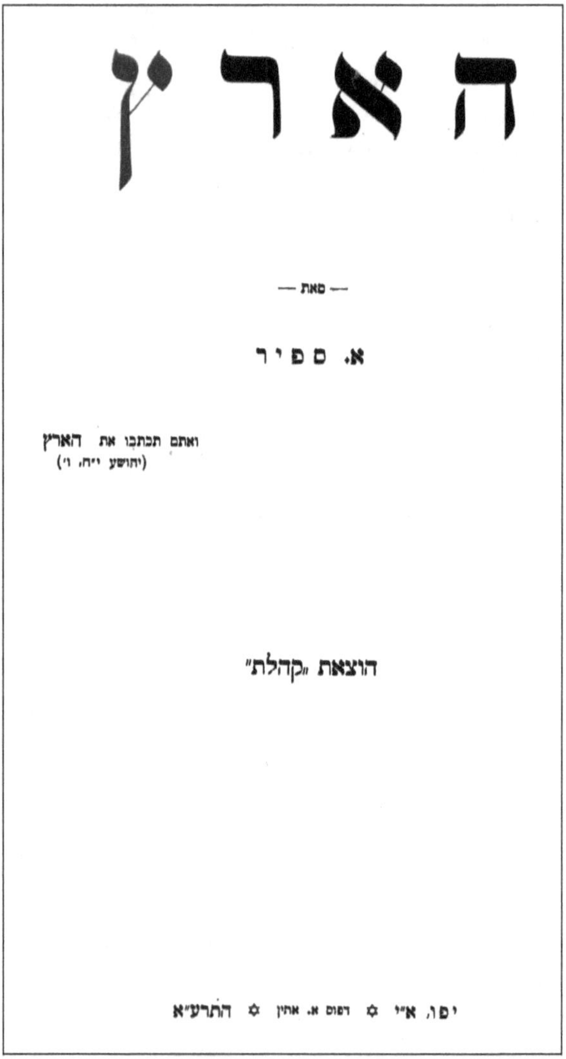

הארץ

— מאת —

א. ספיר

ואתם תכתבו את הארץ
(יהושע י״ח, ו׳)

הוצאת „קהלת"

יפו, א״י ✡ דפוס א. אתין ✡ התרע״א

FIGURE 3.2. Eliyahu Sapir's geographic book *Ha-arets* (The land) published in 1911 in Jaffa. The author seems driven by the biblical verse written on the book cover, "When you have written down the description of the land" (Joshua 18:6), to record the geographic description of Palestine.

common among the Arab masses in our land until today." Sapir referred to the plant maror (bitter herb), whose meaning was not known during the time of the Jerusalemite Talmud. The maror is usually eaten at the Pesach Seder in accordance with the biblical commandment, "They shall eat the flesh that same night; they shall eat it roasted over the fire, with unleavened bread and with bitter herbs"

(Exodus 12:8). He indicated that the significance of this plant is retrieved from the observation of the ethnobotanical practices of Palestine's farmers, who identify this plant as *mirār* or *murrār* (bitter herb).[82]

The other historical period in which Jews and Arabs came into contact was during the Arab conquest of Palestine in 634 CE when Arab conquerors came under the influence of the local Jewish culture, which dominated during the Roman rule of Palestine, regardless of the Romans' efforts to propagate their language and Hellenic culture. Despite the Arabs' tireless attempts to Arabize and Islamize Palestine, the natives did not forget "the names they created for the trees and particularly the plants, which were attached to the land as one body." In fact, according to Sapir,

> The people of the land influenced the new language and transmitted to the foreign people their names of the land's plants. Nonetheless, with the passage of time, a sort of confusion occurred with regard to these names, and we could not investigate and learn the source of these names and with which language they were initially created.[83]

The Semitic origins of both Arabic and Hebrew, in addition to the cultural similarity of two nomadic cultures, yielded similar approaches to naming plants. These shared features resulted in the production of names that were either identical or differed only slightly in pronunciation.

Arabic Instruction in Ashkenazi Schools

Prior to the end of the nineteenth century, Jewish communities in late Ottoman Palestine were divided into Sephardim and Ashkenazim. Despite their shared religious beliefs, the two communities remained socially and culturally distinct, and congruent with this separation, maintained separate school systems. While the Sephardic community was economically independent and successful, the Ashkenazi community was dependent on donations from Jewish communities in Europe.[84] While literary Arabic was included in the Sephardi schools and colloquial Arabic gained more of a presence with the arrival of Arabic-speaking Jews to Palestine, the Arabic language was entirely absent from Ashkenazi religious schools, where it was considered a non-Jewish and secular subject unfit for their curriculum.[85]

Despite Ashkenazi Jews' insularity regarding Arabic, concerns about the representation of their community before the Ottoman authorities eventually led them to study Arabic and Islamic culture. As Israeli geographer Yehoshua Ben-Arieh has noted, the most important source of income for Ashkenazim living in Jerusalem during the nineteenth and twentieth centuries was the charitable donations (*ḥaluḳah*) flowing to these communities from their Western countries of origin.[86] Their ties to Europe increased their social and cultural separation from the Sephardi community, and resulted in their lack of efficient leadership. Therefore the Ḥakham Bashi (chief rabbi), who belonged to the Sephardic community, represented the Ashkenazi Jews before the Ottoman authorities.[87] As its presence in the city grew, the Ashkenazi community wished to represent itself instead of relying on the office of the Ḥakham Bashi.[88] But that was impossible without mastering what both Ashkenazi and Sephardi Jewish writers referred to as sefat ha-arets, not to mention the Turkish language as well. Consequently, despite minimal interest in the language itself and fearing distraction from their immersion in religious studies, Ashkenazi leaders were forced to introduce the study of Arabic to facilitate communication with the governing body.

The study of Arabic also became necessary for an entirely separate reason from that outlined above: the Ashkenazi community was obligated to appease European Jewish philanthropists, who imposed their progressive visions on Ashkenazi communities. A manifest example is Moses Montefiore (1784–1885), a British financier, who pushed for the incorporation of Arabic instruction into the curriculum of Jewish schools.[89] Learning the language was crucial to the process of urbanization going on outside the walls of the Old City, which entailed communicating with local municipalities to purchase land and fulfill the required procedures. Montefiore was concerned about the living conditions of Jerusalemite Jewry—in particular Ashkenazi Jewry, who lacked organization and relied on *ḥaluḳah* a great deal more than other Jewish communities—and regarded education and work as the means to achieve self-sufficiency.[90] In an 1875 visit to the Old City, including its Jewish educational institutions, he championed the idea of introducing Arabic instruction to students at Jewish schools such as 'Ets Haim of the Ḥirbah, where Yosef Yo'el Rivlin (1889–1971) would study many years later "at the hands of God-reverent mentors (*melamedim yir'e eluḳim*)."[91] Ultimately, Montefiore threatened to suspend distribution of his charitable funds to the Jews of Jerusalem if they did not agree to implement his vision.[92] In light of their heavy reliance on the funds of the octogenarian philanthropist, both to sustain the needy and carry out a building plan to address overcrowding within the Old City, Jewish leaders had no alternative but to agree.

The comprehensive reforms initiated by the Ottoman authorities in the mid-nineteenth century enhanced the social, cultural, and economic conditions in late Ottoman Palestine, and made learning Arabic requisite to upward economic mobility. The improvement in the infrastructure and security measures stimulated the influx of tourists, pilgrims, and traders to the country, and aided in the integration of Palestine's economy into the world economy. By 1914, Haifa and Jaffa had become the most important port cities, and played a major role in the economic growth of the country through trade export to Europe starting in the mid-nineteenth century.[93] The political and economic changes introduced by the Ottoman state attracted civilians to major cities like Jaffa, Haifa, and Jerusalem. With the modernization of several cities in late Ottoman Palestine, many governmental jobs became available in urban communities. Tremendous opportunities were newly available to those who, irrespective of their faith, achieved certain levels of proficiency in Arabic and a knowledge of Islam. More broadly, life in Jerusalem and Jaffa encouraged a sense of competition, which motivated youths to find a place in the government. The Tanzimat of the Ottoman Empire promised non-Muslim communities' equitable treatment and fair representation within the ruling regime. Palestinian Jews of Ashkenazi descent had the opportunity to follow the same career path as ambitious Arabs.[94] It was certainly true that an influential family background would help a young applicant find a job, but a young Jew from an obscure background could rise to a career in public service if they gained the requisite command of Arabic and Turkish, in addition to Western languages.[95]

No less significant than the interest of Ashkenazi Jews of the Old Yishuv in Arabic is that of Ashkenazi Jewish immigrants who arrived in Palestine in 1882 with Zionist motives. The Biluim immigration to and settlement in Palestine, mainly propelled by the anti-Jewish pogroms in Russia, was a manifestation of the productivization ethos prevalent among eastern European Jews. This ideology deemed occupational transformation vital to the economic development, moral regeneration, and social integration of Jewry.[96] Their interest in Arabic, then, was part of a project of self-renewal that required discarding diasporic characteristics and occupations, and instead undertaking agricultural activities through transactions with various segments of the Palestinian Arab population, whether farmers, Bedouins, or even city dwellers.[97] Belḳind was a Bilu member and a Jewish educator who would later promulgate Arabic instruction in the Jewish settlements.[98] The examination of Belḳind's attitudes toward Arabic provides us with a window into the ways in which Biluim approached Arabic and appropriated it into their national project.

Like Meirovitch, Belḳind's knowledge of spoken Arabic evolved over time through practical communication with local Arab communities, and perhaps through self-study guided by the similarities between Arabic and Hebrew.[99] It is noteworthy that neither he nor other Bilu members spoke Arabic on their arrival in Jaffa. For instance, when seeking to rent an apartment from an Arab Christian, he had to resort to his familiarity with French and German.[100] After acquiring Arabic proficiency, Belḳind, along with other Bilu members, used Arabic at social events or in business dealings with Arabs.[101]

Belḳind's experience in restoring the Jewish linkage to the land did not involve direct agricultural labor on his part. Unlike his comrades who suffered harsh labor conditions in Miḳveh Yisrael, an agricultural colony associated with the Alliance Israélite Universelle, under the strict supervision of ʿAbd al-ʿAzīz, the head of the

Arab village Yāzūr, east of Jaffa, Belḳind ran the organizational and administrative work of the Bilium movement as a supervisor as well as a director of farming and gardening in Miḳveh Yisrael.[102] In this capacity, he came in contact with Arab workers and farmers in Rishon Le-Zion and Gedera, a Jewish settlement established in 1884 under the management of the Rothschild administration. Along with other Bilu members in Gedera, he interacted with the settlement's nearby rural Arab population. Irrespective of the tensions experienced on both sides of this relationship, the encounter between Jewish settlers and rural Arabs provided an opportunity for the former to learn about their neighbors' culture and language, and even mimic their lifestyle.[103] In other words, the daily interactions engendered by the demands of agricultural life forced Belḳind and his comrades to learn about Arabs' customs and their behaviors as well as their perceptions of the Jewish settlers.

But Belḳind's interest in Arabic went beyond its utility in practical communication. In addition to enriching the Hebrew lexicon, he believed that introducing Arabic in the educational system in the Jewish settlements was vital to instill nativism in the emerging Jewish generation. The organized efforts of asefat hamorim (Teachers' Association) between 1892 and 1896 yielded a plan for the creation of an educational system for the Jewish youths in the Jewish settlements of the First Aliyah. The ultimate motive for these organized efforts was to educate a new generation of Hebrew farmers in the agrarian ideals laid down by the immigrant parents. It was hoped that the emerging generation would live up to the ideals of the love of land and labor, and materialize the ethos of the new person: an educated Jewish farmer and national Hebrew.[104] The introduction of Arabic instruction in schools in the Jewish settlements of the First Aliyah contributed to the fulfillment of that cause.

Belḳind's educational theory valorized bridging the gap between the theoretical and practical to prepare young people for life.[105] In articulating his educational views, Belḳind was implicitly criticizing the educational models that prevailed at the end of the nineteenth century: the Alliance Israélite Universelle, Jewish school in Rishon Le-Zion, and Miḳveh Yisrael. Dissatisfied with Miḳveh Yisrael as a pioneer Jewish agricultural school, he longed to build his own school that would merge agricultural and Hebrew language learning.[106] Teaching Arabic to Hebrew children, he insisted, was essential for their educational development as well as their navigation of everyday life after their school years. Appointed in 1889 as the principal of the first Hebrew school for Jewish children in Jaffa, he hired instructors to teach both Turkish and Arabic. Some years later, at a teachers' conference in 1893, Belḳind expressed the view that the teaching of foreign languages, specifically Arabic and French, with the latter being the dominant foreign language in the Ottoman state and the Middle East at large, should be expanded at Jewish schools in Palestinian towns. This was a different approach from that of the agricultural colonies (moshavoth). His eye was on the job market in more urban areas, where there was a higher demand for foreign languages than in rural areas, and he was insistent that education should prepare Jewish students for profitable careers and successful lives.[107]

To better understand the broader intellectual and ideological landscape within which Belḳind operated, it is worth noting that Belḳind's focus on practical education was contrary to the priorities of political Zionism that centered around diplomatic and political maneuvering. Belḳind did not see eye to eye with the political Zionist leadership. He critiqued Theodor Herzl's book *Der Judenstaat: Ver-such einer modernen Lösung der Judenfrage* (The Jewish state: An endeavor for a modern solution to the Jewish question) (1896) as largely theorizing about the Jewish problem instead of proposing practical means to the desired end. Belḳind also believed that Herzl was unfit for the mission he had taken on himself: to find a solution to the Jewish question through diplomacy. Herzl thought that he could convince the Ottoman sultan to give the Jewish people Palestine in return for Zionists or Jews regulating the finances of the entire Ottoman state.[108] From Belḳind's perspective, Abdul Ḥamid II's complete rejection of Herzl's proposal simply proved Herzl's inadequacy for the task he set himself.[109] As an exponent of practical Zionism, Belḳind prioritized establishing facts on the ground without pursuing diplomatic or political means, as evidenced in the Bilu society's plan to settle in Palestine by 1882 and go forward with working the land in the absence of any political agreement.[110]

Ironically, Belḳind's practical approach to education also brought him under fire from the Ha-Po'el ha-Tza'ir (Young Worker) movement, which was similarly devoted to a belief in the value of labor and development of agricultural settlements to establish a Jewish presence in Palestine. The Young Worker's group, however, differed significantly in its exclusively Jewish approach to labor and land. As members of the Second Aliyah, the Young Worker group believed that Jewish conquest of the land would take place through the capitalist development of the Jewish community in Palestine through Jewish labor.[111]

Belḳind's aspiration to establish an agricultural school came to fruition with the building of Ḳiryat Sefer in 1907 on fifty dunams (acres) of the Ben Shemen estate for the orphans who survived the Kishinev pogroms in 1903—orphans he himself had brought from Ukraine to Palestine. Belḳind planned to train the orphans to become skilled farmers, but a few years later he ran out of funds and the school collapsed.[112] Belḳind's inability to keep the school running exposed him to criticism by members of the Young Worker who accused Belḳind of various kinds of mismanagement, including his collaboration with Arabs. The newspaper *Ha-Po'el Ha-Tza'ir* attacked him for leasing part of the land to a wealthy Arab and hiring Arab farmers to work the land on behalf of the students who were supposed to work the land themselves.[113]

Arabic Prose and the Retrieval of Hebrew Nativity

Thus far, the discussion has concentrated on the ways in which Hebrew writers in urban cultural centers in Palestine, such as Jerusalem and Jaffa, and the Jewish agricultural colonies turned to Arabic as a source for the revitalization of modern Hebrew. As we have seen, Arabic was instrumental in the coinage of new words to help expand the resurrected Hebrew language, especially in areas where the connection between modern Hebrew and its natural habitat were centralized. During this process, however, as shown earlier, Hebrew writers in Palestine met with rejection and ridicule from Hebrew literati residing in Europe for resorting to Arabic, rather than to European languages, as a source for the enrichment of modern Hebrew. Figures such as Hebrew poet Ḥaim Naḥman Bialiḳ (1873–1934), Hebrew essayist and thinker Ahad ha-ʿAm (1856–1927), and others claimed that only Hebrew literati have the agency to develop new words drawn from Jewish culture and European sources.[114] To dispel such doubts, Hebrew scholars in Palestine made efforts to demonstrate to their critics in Europe that their project was not merely to coin new words detached from cultural and spatial context but instead to embed the language in its immediate context, and moreover, continue the achievements of earlier outstanding figures of Jewish culture who originated in the Orient. By distancing their cultural enterprise from European circles, Hebrew writers in Palestine drew themselves closer to the geocultural landscape of the Orient, whether in their interaction with premedieval and medieval Arabic and Islamic texts, or their contemporary nahda Arab intellectuals.

In response to charges from their European counterparts that their borrowings from Arabic were nonliterary, Hebrew writers turned to Arabic literary texts produced since the pre-Islamic era with the intention of molding modern Hebrew to its Oriental environment. This turn paralleled a similar tendency of nahdawi Arab intellectuals who exploited the same materials in their quest to rejuvenate modern Arabic. One of the Hebrew writers' strategies was to identify Jewish figures of the past whose greatness was attested to by contemporary Arabs as well as Arab literary eminences who were also renowned for their personal embodiment of universal human values such as nobility, hospitability, and bravery. In addition, the translation of Arabic literary texts into Hebrew, with the intentional employment of biblical Hebrew, aimed to fulfill two objectives: first, to revive biblical Hebrew as a usable language for modern Jews, just as nahdawi Arabs were doing with classical Arabic, and second, to root Jews in the cultural sphere of the Orient.

Jewish scholars' turn to Arabic literature was in part spurred by their European counterparts' investment in and engagement with the cultural legacy of

Andalusian Jews. Al-Andalus, or Islamic Spain, has been celebrated in popular culture and scholarship as an "extraordinary period of dynamic social interaction, cultural ferment, creativity, and transfer among the Muslims, Christians, and Jews of the medieval Iberian Peninsula."[115] Ashkenazi Jews found in Andalusian heritage a rich source for the renewal and development of Jewish culture in modern times. Members of the reform movement, Wissenschaft des Judentums, which aimed at the restoration of Judaism as both a cultural and historical entity through scientific research, turned to Andalusian heritage to justify the affiliation of Jews with European culture. At the core of these Jewish intellectuals' scheme, as historiographical studies on the Wissenschaft have shown, is the view that Jewish modernity is intrinsically bound to Western culture and Europe.[116] European Jewish intellectuals, as historian Amnon Raz-Krakotzkin has explained, severed medieval Hebrew heritage from its Oriental origins, including Arabic language and literature, to align it with Western culture.[117] As opposed to connecting the Sephardic legacy to the modernization processes in Europe, Hebrew intellectuals in cultural centers in Palestine, particularly in Jerusalem (and elsewhere, like Hong Kong in the case of Baghdadi Shaul Abdallah Yosef (1849–1906), as Yuval Evri and Almog Behar have demonstrated), pulled the Jewish cultural legacy to the East on the premise that the best way to comprehend the Jewish cultural treasures from Al-Andalus was to situate them in their immediate cultural and social environment by means of returning to their earlier source: Arabic poetry in the pre-Islamic era.[118]

Ben-Yehuda and Yellin were both part of the movement to encourage young Jews of the time to identify with the cultural landscape around them, linguistically and otherwise. They collaboratively authored the monograph *miḳra le-yilde bene Yisrael* (Reading to the children of the people of Israel), which tries to instill a sense of the Orientality of Palestine's cultural sphere in Jewish youths. In doing so, they use works from wisdom literature, a literary genre that "inherited and generated vast numbers of concise, encapsulating aphorisms and moralising or cautionary maxims, which were adaptable to multiple occasions and accordingly acquired a very wide circulation."[119] The adaptable nature of these maxims has encouraged authors to include examples from parables such as "Mishle shuʿalim" (Parables of foxes) to help integrate children into the Oriental culture. Ben-Yehuda and Yellin are careful to couch their discussion of Palestine's cultural landscape in a biblical Hebrew that preserved the land's Orientalness in both form and content. For instance, the adoption of a parabolic style as a pedagogical method delivered Oriental values to the youths in a medium that was endemic to the peoples of the Orient—both Arabs and Jews.[120]

One section of *Miḳra le-yelde bene Yisrael* is devoted to parables of foxes, a common literary theme in classical Arabic literature. The following anecdote is emblematic of those Ben-Yehuda and Yellin chose to pass on to the Hebrew youths of their day:

> One day the lion became sick, and all the jungle's animals came to visit him, except for the fox, whom the wolf falsely accused. The fox knew what the wolf had said. On his arrival, the lion said to him, What detained you from visiting, O you the father of valiance [lit. *avi-ḥayil*]? Then he [the fox] said, I was wandering the land looking for a medicine for your sickness, and the physicians said to me, "If the lion drinks the blood of the father of prey [lit. *avi ṭeref*], he will recover." When the wolf arrived before the lion, the latter struck the wolf's leg with his paw, wounding him. The wolf escaped from the lion, but with blood on his leg. When the fox met him, he said, Why are your shoes red? Have you sat in the company of kings, careless of what came out of your mouth and defaming your brother?[121]

The origins of this parabolic fable can be found in a number of classical Arabic literary texts, and the fable is repeated with minor variations in several works. Perhaps the earliest versions are found in a section of *Kitāb al-adhkiyā'* (The book of intelligent people) by Abū al-Faraj Ibn al-Jawzī (1116–1201), *al-baṣā'ir wa-al-dhakhā'ir* (Insights and treasures) by Abū Ḥayyān al-Tawḥīdī (923–1023), and *Ḥayāt al-ḥayawān* (Life of animals) by al-Damīrī (1341–1405).[122] Each of these bestows on these animals, familiar to Arabs, the quality of human intelligence. A similar motif is found in *Mishle shu'alim* by Berechiah ben Natronai.[123]

Reviving Lost Hebrew Virtues through Arabic Poetry

In his magnum opus *Ṭabaqāt Fuḥūl al-Shu'arā'* (Classes of champion poets), Muḥammad Ibn Sallām al-Jumaḥī (756–845/46), an Arab scholar who lived in ninth-century Baghdad, noted that pre-Islamic Arabic poetry embodied "the reservoir of . . . [Arabs'] knowledge and the peak of their wisdom." Moreover, al-Jumaḥī attributes to 'Umar Ibn al-Khaṭṭāb (d. 644), the second Muslim caliph, the view that Arabic poetry functioned as "the science of a people who could not produce more sound science in its likeness."[124] The medieval Arab scholar's assessment was, in short, that the most significant achievement of Arab culture was its poetry. That poetry guided Arabs in pre- and post-Islamic times, and continued to resonate throughout the nineteenth century, which witnessed the Arab intellectual renaissance (*al-Nahḍa al-'Arabiyya*).[125]

Like nahdawi Arabs who sought inspiration from the literary past in the search for the modern Arab self, Hebrew scholars of late nineteenth-century Palestine viewed Arabic literature as a means to revive the culture of the ancient Israelites. Jewish scholars in Palestine proffered a connection between their audience and their forebearers by drawing on accounts of Arab heroes and nobles whose values as well as customs resembled to a great extent, they speculated, those of the Israelite patriarchs, and whose literary expressions would thus clarify the poetic world of the Hebrew Bible.

Hebrew writers' construction of Jewish identity, as drawn from the Arabic poetical corpus, focused on three points that underlie the current discussion. First, these writers searched for an ideal Jewish self who is in harmonious relationship with the cultural landscape of the Orient, and embodies the moral virtues associated with ancient Israelites, as ascertained from Arabic poetical literature. Second, they interpreted medieval Hebrew poetry through a mastery of Arabic literature in contradistinction with their European counterparts, who looked to Andalusian heritage to contextualize their identity within Western culture. Finally, they employed comparative philology in their translation of selected Arabic poetic texts to advance a proper understanding of the Hebrew Bible while at the same time establishing roots in the cultural world of the East. Taken together, these three points elucidate Hebrew scholars' engagement with classical Arabic poetry and its implications for budding Jewish culture in late nineteenth-century Palestine.

Classical Arabic poetry contains depictions of certain aspects of pre-Islamic Arab society, specifically the valorization of certain moral qualities, the adherence to which was not common in a community vulnerable to existential threats, whether from nature or humans. Those Arab characters who exemplified bravery, generosity, and loyalty were venerated, and their names and qualities memorialized in their odes (*qaṣīda*).[126] Hebrew scholars in Palestine believed that ancient Israelites had shared these moral virtues with their Arab neighbors. The reconstruction of the New Jew, whose presence in Palestine symbolized the continuation of their ancestors, therefore depended on invoking the distinctive character traits of the Jewish patriarchs that are portrayed in historical accounts, particularly in biblical and postbiblical sources.

More Faithful than al-Samaw'al Ibn 'Adiya'

In addressing the Jewish youths in his work *Mikra le-na're bene Yisrael* (1889), Yellin instructs them about great figures who rose to prominence throughout Jewish history, and left a lasting impact on both Jews and non-Jews. Among these great figures he chronicles in brief the annals of al-Samaw'al Ibn 'Adiya' of the sixth century.[127] The historical and literary al-Samaw'al is commonly introduced in Arabic sources as al-Samaw'al Ibn 'Adiya' al-Yahūdī (the Jew), whereas heroic Arab figures are identified by their tribal blood. It might appear that underlining his Jewishness singled him out from the surrounding society in which he lived. In fact, as it emerges from Yellin's brief account, the lives of al-Samaw'al and his father

'Adiya' were so embedded in the socioeconomic and cultural life of neighboring Arabs that the two became indistinguishable from one another. The historical and literary al-Samaw'al, as Hasan El-Shamy has pointed out, is represented in Arabic sources as being as noble and hospitable as any other prominent Arab figures, like 'Antar Ibn Shaddād or Imru' al-Qays.[128] Indeed, the Jewish poet is portrayed in Yellin's account through a heroic lens that both magnifies his good reputation among Arabs and reflects those unique qualities for which only a handful of Arab figures were themselves memorialized. The first indication of his esteemed economic and social status among Arabian tribes is his acquisition of a fortress that had no equal among his Arab contemporaries. Known as al-ablaq al-fard (Piebald the Unique), the family's fortress was said to be situated on the road between Hejaz and Syria. Due to its strategic location and impressive size, the fortress was represented as a rest destination for the Arab merchants whom both al-Samaw'al and his father before him treated with hospitality. In Yellin's narrative, which stresses the Jewishness of al-Samaw'al, the wealth and goodwill of both 'Adiya' and his son accumulated were seen as gifts from God. After the death of 'Adiya', according to Yellin, al-Samaw'al became a chieftain, and the Arab residents of the Thayma' praised his name and sought refuge in his fortress in light of his courageousness and fidelity to God. Yellin also emphasizes al-Samaw'al's poetic achievements, noting that his poems continued to be remembered and circulated by Arabs throughout the ages even to his own day.[129]

Arabic sources also preserve accounts of al-Samaw'al's loyalty and fidelity in proverbial phrases such as *awfā min al-Samaw'al* (more faithful than al-Samaw'al) and *fi wafā' al-Samaw'al* (in the likeness of al-Samaw'al's fidelity). The celebration of al-Samaw'al and faithfulness or fidelity in Arabic sources indicates his standing as equal to notable Arab figures celebrated for those same virtues.

Al-Samaw'al's fame, based on Arabic sources and Yellin's adopted account, is attributed to an event that brought together two eminent figures of the time: Al-Samaw'al Ibn 'Adiya' along with the notable Arab poet and chieftain Imru' al-Qays. According to reports by Ibn al-Athīr (1160–1233) in his history text *al-Kāmil fī al-Tārīkh* and Abū al-Faraj al-Iṣfahānī (897–967) in his literary work *al-Aghānī* (The songs), on whose writings Yellin relies, Imru' al-Qays was traveling north with his entourage to seek the assistance of the Byzantine Caesar in war with another tribe. On their way to Syria, Imru' al-Qays entrusted al-Samaw'al with some of his shields, weapons, and money as well as his daughter Hind. When Imru' al-Qays's adversary al-Mundhir learned that Imru' al-Qays's belongings and daughter were in al-Samaw'al's fortress, he requested Ibn 'Adiya' to deliver these possessions to him. When al-Samaw'al refused to do so, al-Mundhir sent an army to siege the fortress, but the troops could not overcome it due to its fortification. In the meantime, al-Samaw'al's son was captured by al-Mundhir's army, which threatened to slaughter him if al-Samaw'al did not hand over Imru' al-Qays's possessions. The father chose to sacrifice his son to fulfill his promise of protection to Imru' al-Qays.[130] Yellin writes proudly, "Our brother won fame for himself among Arabs and all Arabic literary sources (adab) that treat exemplary men of virtue pay respect to **the Jew** who witnessed the death of his son without breaking his word."[131] The greatness of al-Samaw'al, Yellin remarks elsewhere, is not only embodied in his transactions with his neighbors the Arab but in his poetry too. Yellin notes that al-Samaw'al's most famous poem, *al-lamiyyat: inna al-kirām qalūl* (The nobles are few), survives due to the efforts of Arabs to preserve and disseminate it throughout the ages as ranking among the best of their poetry *ḥamāsa*, a reference to an anthology of selected verses of bravery.

Al-Samaw'al's ode itself reflects the intertwinement of Jews in the cultural life in Arabia and the adoption by Jews of the prevalent Arabic poetic forms. These verses additionally take the readers to the time of al-Samaw'al and allow the audience a glimpse into the heroic life of the Jewish people on the Arabian Peninsula. *Al-lamiyya*, as Yellin notes, reveals the circumstances of the children of Israel during their civilizational pinnacle in Arabia. Even though they were few in number, Yellin asserts, they "were outstanding and distinguished whether youth or old. . . . [T]hey were heroes on the battlefield and the death did not frighten them."[132]

Yellin's emphasis on the history of neighborly relations between Arabs and Jews had pointed relevance to the political issues that preoccupied Jewish society in Palestine at the time. While discussing the case of al-Samaw'al, Yellin points to the social value accorded to the protection of neighbors and refugees in Arabic culture, which bore directly on one of the pressing issues of Yellin's time: Jewish immigrants and refugees fleeing oppression and persecution in Europe to seek permanent settlement in Palestine. As a large number of Russian Jews settled in Palestine while maintaining their foreign passports and avoiding taxes as noncitizens, Ottoman authorities perceived these acts as a threat to their vision of multiethnic and multireligious coexistence in the Ottoman state, based on which Ottomans had allowed refugees and immigrants to settle in the empire since 1857 regardless of their religion, race, and ethnicity. Despite the restrictions on Jewish immigration, the Jewish population doubled in the two decades from 1881 onward.[133] The increase of Jewish immigrants in towns in the 1880s and their willingness to purchase land at any price, as Neville Mandel has shown, alarmed the Arab urban community, prompting demonstrations in protest.[134] Thus Yellin's invocation of the Arab virtues of hospitality and neighborly protection, according to their cherished legacy, had a contemporary relevance.[135] Moreover, by relating the story of the sacrifice made by al-Samaw'al ("our brother" and "the Jew") on behalf of an Arab, Yellin aims an implicit criticism at Palestinian Arabs who fail to imitate their ancestors' code of ethics in this regard as well as an implicit exhortation to them to return the favor.

The Most Hospitable of Arabs: Ḥātim al-Ṭāʾī / Ḥātim of Ṭayyʾ

As viewed through the prism of Arabic literature, Abraham Shalom Yahuda was another scholar of Judaic cultural roots in the Orient. In the introduction to his essay "Nedive ve-gibure ʿArav" (Arab noblemen and heroes), Yahuda relates,

> The Hebrew reader will rejoice to know the lifestyle of the Arab, his customs, and his regulations. [The Arab] was so similar to our fathers, when they lived safely on their lands, in terms of his customs, his way of life, his generosity feeding the hungry, providing from the best he had to anyone who experienced misfortune, defending his neighbor faithfully and whosoever sought his protection. With his cleverness and might, he destroyed the leader of his nemeses.[136]

The qualities of the ideal Arab that Yahuda excavates from classical Arabic literature throw light on the conceptualization of the ideal Jew, repeating the pattern of reflection, refraction, mirroring, and opposition that continually enmesh the two peoples.

First, though, we must ask, Who was "the Arab" to whom Yahuda refers in the aforementioned remark? Clearly, he is referring to ancient Arabs. But do these characteristics apply to contemporary Arabs as well from his standpoint? Or is he drawing a distinction between the Arabs of his time and ancient Arabs? In fact, Yahuda does make a clear distinction from the outset of his discussion between contemporary Arabs and their relevance to the model he wants his present-day Jews to resemble. With the exception of Yemeni Arabs, he sees the Arabs of his time as corrupt and lacking the moral qualities he invokes. Yahuda therefore suggests that his readers pull from the example of pre-Islamic Arabs, who characteristically possessed the moral virtues that he desires to promote among his Jewish audience. In a footnote, he deromanticizes contemporary Arabs, arguing that

> almost all of the customs that we will be discussing in this regard were dominant among Arabs before Muḥammad, and [these Arabs] we shall explore—not contemporary Arabs—for a significant amount of ancient Arabs' customs had already vanished. Some of these customs, however, remain with Arabs who dwell in Yemen, for they have not changed their path yet.[137]

It is thus major Arab figures who lived in the pre-Islamic Arabia whose example should be a model for the ideal Arab as well as the ideal Jew—an ideal abstracted from the on-the-ground reality of the Arabs encountered by Jewish settlers.

Among pre-Islamic Arab poets, Yahuda chooses to highlight two widely known figures: Ḥātim of Ṭayyʾ and ʿAntar Ibn Shaddād. These "two eminent figures," in his words, "exceed all Arab noblemen and heroes in terms of generosity and bravery."[138] Yet it is not these figures in and of themselves so much as the ideals represented through them that he admires. In these characters, Yahuda sees

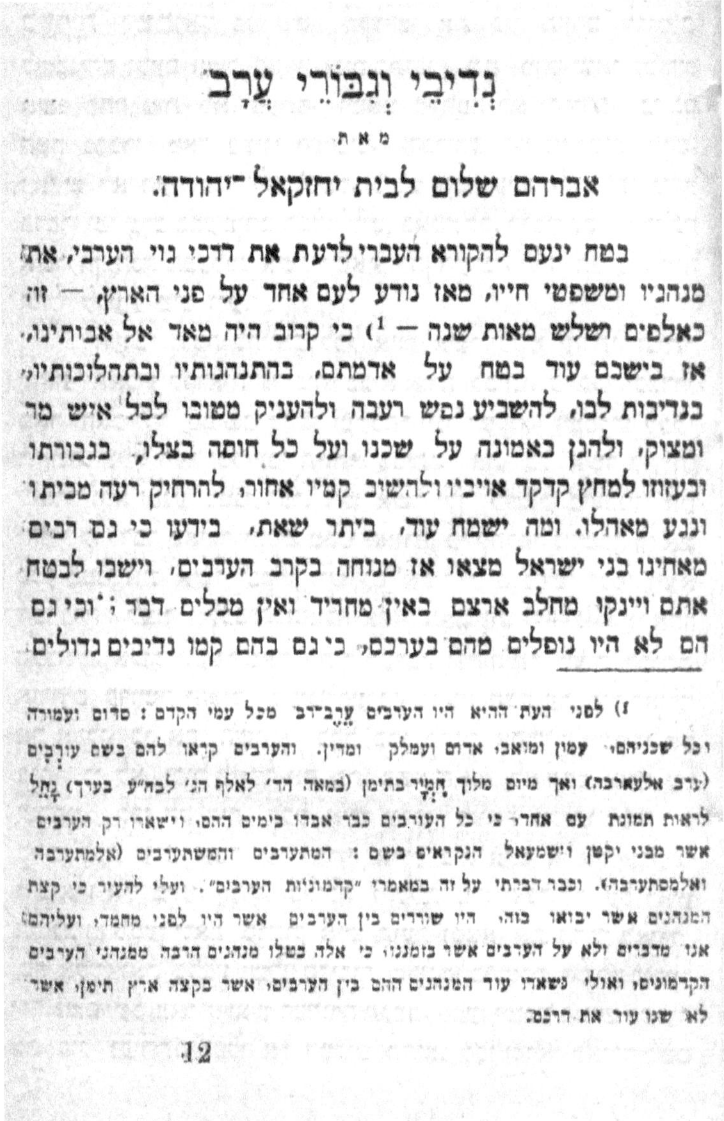

נדיבי וגבורי ערב

מאת

אברהם שלום לבית יחזקאל־יהודה.

בטח ינעם להקורא העברי לדעת את דרכי גוי הערבי, את מנהגיו ומשפטי חייו, מאז נודע לעם אחד על פני הארץ, — זה כאלפים ושלש מאות שנה — [1]) כי קרוב היה מאד אל אבותינו, אז בישבם עוד בטח על אדמתם, בהתנהגותיו ובתהלוכותיו, בנדיבות לבו, להשביע נפש רעבה ולהעניק מטובו לכל איש מר ומצוק, ולהגן באמונה על שכנו ועל כל חוסה בצלו, בגבורתו ובעזוזו למחץ קדקד אויביו ולהשיב קמיו אחור, להרחיק רעה מביתו ונגע מאהלו. ומה ישמח עוד, ביתר שאת, בידעו כי גם רבים מאחינו בני ישראל מצאו אז מנוחה בקרב הערבים, וישבו לבטח אתם ויינקו מחלב ארצם באין מחריד ואין מכלים דבר; וכי גם הם לא היו נופלים מהם בערכם, כי גם בהם קמו נדיבים גדולים.

1) לפני העת ההיא היו הערבים עֲרֵב־רב מכל עמי הקדם: סדום ועמורה וכל שכניהם, עמון ומואב, אדום ועמלק ומדין. והערבים קראו להם בשם עורבים (ערב אלעארבה) ואך מיום מלוך חמיר בתימן (במאה הד׳ לאלף הג׳ לבה״ע בערך) נחל לראות תמונת עם אחד, כי כל העורבים כבר אבדו בימים ההם, וישארו רק הערבים אשר מבני יקטן וישמעאל הנקראים בשם: המתערבים והמשתערבים (אלמתערבה ואלמסתערבה). וכבר דברתי על זה במאמרי "קדמוניות הערבים". ועלי להעיר כי קצת המנהגים אשר יבואו בזה, היו שורדים בין הערבים אשר היו לפני מחמד, ועליהם אנו מדברים ולא על הערבים אשר בזמננו, כי אלה בטלו מנהגים הרבה ממנהגי הערבים הקדמונים, ואולי נשארו עוד המנהגים ההם בין הערבים, אשר בקצה ארץ תימן, אשר לא שנו עוד את דרכם.

12

FIGURE 3.3. The front page of Abraham Shalom Yahuda's essay "Nedive ve-gibure ʿArav" (Arab noblemen and heroes).

bravery, hospitality, and loyalty—virtues that past Israelites had internalized, their offspring now lack, and they must strive to recapture as they restore their connection with the land of their ancestors. Yahuda looked to pre-Islamic rather than Islamic culture as a repository of lost Arab virtues because he believed it was unaffected by the theological and ideological differences that emerged with the advent of Islam. Moreover, the ethical values of the Israelites were aligned with those of pre-Islamic Arabia. Yahuda writes nostalgically of a time in which "many of the Israelites found comfort in the middle of Arabs with whom they lived safely and drank from the milk of their land without nothing [to] humiliate or frighten them."[139] Yahuda's engagement with modern Jewish culture and the retrieval of the lost characteristics in pre-Islamic Arabic poetry suggest that his project of Jewish nationalism is one of recovery rather than invention.

The first figure Yahuda explores in his article on noble and brave men among Arabs is Ḥātim of Ṭayy'—known in Arabic as Ḥātim al-Ṭā'ī. Among Arabs, the name Ḥātim of Ṭayy' is synonymous with hospitality, generosity, and selflessness. His reputation for generosity spread among Arabs of his time, who commemorate him in proverbs such as *akram min Ḥātim* (more generous than Ḥātim!). In Islamicate *adab* (literature), the figure of Ḥātim is synonymous with wise sayings and legendary deeds. Here, nineteenth-century Hebrew literature is by no means an exception. In Yahuda's portrayal, Ḥātim's altruism and liberality are represented as much as in any literary work in the Islamic world at the time. Aside from the dissemination of humanistic values, however, the figure of Ḥātim al-Ṭā'ī here invokes *hakhnasat 'orḥīm* (hospitality), one of the ethical qualities believed to be possessed by Israelite patriarchs, particularly in the example of Abraham.[140]

It is worth highlighting that in his portrayal of Ḥātim al-Ṭā'ī, Yahuda frequently cites examples from primary sources for his Hebrew readership from the poet's corpus. Referring to the abundance of literary accounts that relate the deeds and actions of Ḥātim, Yahuda admits that his survey will be limited to sketching only some "features of his generosity and the favors he did for many people."[141]

To best exemplify Arab hospitality as embodied in pre-Islamic Arabic poetry, Yahuda translates two poems attributed to Ḥātim of Ṭayy' into Hebrew. One illustrates Yahuda's perspective on aspects of Ḥātim's personality. When Ḥātim of Ṭayy' demonstrated his generosity to others by spending an excessive amount of his wealth, Nūwār, one of his two wives, who was terribly anxious about her son's inheritance, scoffed at him for his profligate spending. In response to his wife's severe critique, which is voiced in several poems, Ḥātim is reported to have said:

> Enough Nūwār with blaming me!
> And do not say about vanishing money: stop spending!
> When the miser dies, his wickedness remains after him
> And he bequeaths his wealth to him who wished his death.
> Yet when the gracious one passes away, his name remains forever
> And his master and his glory mourn him.[142]

It is in the generosity of this nobleman that Yahuda sees the most authentic characteristics that shaped the personality of Arabs and Israelites before the advent of Islam.

ʿAntar Ibn Shaddād

If Ḥātim al-Ṭāʾī exemplifies the quality of generosity, ʿAntar Ibn Shaddād is an Arab knight and poet who embodies bravery. Born a half-caste slave to a prominent Arab father and a Black African slave mother, ʿAntar won his freedom and ended life as a respected member of the northern Arabian tribe of ʿAbs.[143]

Yahuda regarded ʿAntar as a role model for Arabs, "a man in whom all the characteristic mores to which an Arab yearns are gathered."[144] But ʿAntar's life, as portrayed in popular literature, also enriched the folk literature of the Jewish communities in the Orient, especially that in Iraq.[145] Given his Iraqi origins, we should view Yahuda's interest in the poetry and character of ʿAntar as a continuation of an attitude that considered the figure of ʿAntar as the highest representative of the Oriental character. In addition to his ideal character, ʿAntar was one of the greatest writers of heroic poetry. Yahuda argues that his poetry stands on equal footing with that of the great ancients such as Homer, Virgil, and Torquato Tasso. Indeed, Yahuda seems to imply the superiority of ʿAntar over his Western counterparts because ʿAntar's work is not only a literary achievement but also records his deeds and heroic acts.[146]

But in addition to his significance as a representative of Oriental ideals, applicable to Arabs and Jews alike, ʿAntar is read in a Zionist context, where he exemplifies heroic characteristics that are to guide the New Jew: "How glorious are the deeds of this unbelievable hero, and how amazing his cleverness that he demonstrated in the battle against his enemies." ʿAntar himself is an authentic source, not only for his poetry, but for the way he embodied the noble ideas he wrote about. To stress this, Yahuda explains, "We can understand his strong feelings and his courageous heart and spirit from his poems. Despite strong ideas infused in them, [his] poems are easy and pleasant, and they awaken bravery and courageousness in the weak heart."[147] Yahuda instrumentalizes ʿAntar's poetry as a means to inspire his readers to reclaim for themselves the character traits that once lived in the heart of the ancient Arab. In his words,

> Thus the Hebrew reader will be delighted to hear the history of this mighty hero wrapped in a cloak of bravery, cleverness, and generosity, and read and sing his poem, which comprises the character traits of the Arab: poetry, cleverness, and love. These dominated the nature of the Arab from the day of his birth until his death.[148]

Addressing his thoughts to "the Hebrew reader," Yahuda encourages a view of integration in the Orient that revolves around building the Jew's consciousness of the characteristic qualities of ʿAntar. In so doing, Yahuda not only instructs the reader in the virtues embodied in ʿAntar's poetry but explicitly links the concepts of "poetry, cleverness, and love" to the ancient Arab as well. To emphasize the pivotal role the model of ʿAntar played throughout Arab history and the impact it has left on the consciousness of Arabs, Yahuda finally explains that "Arabs devoted a great chapter in the history of their wars where they relate his story and the courageous deeds that he performed."[149]

Classical Arabic Poetry in the Context of Hebrew Identity Formation

In a controversial monograph on classical Arabic literature, originally published in 1914, Ṭaha Ḥussein, the Egyptian intellectual known as the doyen of Arabic literature, denounces the methodologies embraced by his contemporary scholars in their study of Arabic literature. Ḥussein stipulates that to study classical Arabic literature, both prose and poetry, in an innovative and enriching way, researchers should study the Bible to gain access to the cross-cultural context of the region where Arabic and Hebrew texts were produced. Ḥussein asks,

> Is there a way that Arabic literature can be studied appropriately without studying the material and the semantic relations between Arabic and Semitic languages? And is there a way to study Arabic literature without comprehending the Torah and Gospels? Do you believe there is someone among scholars of literature in Egypt who has read the Hebrew Bible or one who has read the Gospels?[150]

There is a Jewish parallel to Ḥussein's critique. Earlier, in late nineteenth-century Palestine, a few Jewish individuals interested in the revival of modern Hebrew came to the realization that studying classical Arabic literature was essential. These Jewish individuals included Yahuda and eastern European poet Saul Tschernichovsky (1875–1943).

In response to Yahuda's article on Arab poetry, Tschernichovsky wonders, in a letter to Yahuda, how Jewish writers could have failed to absorb that literature and its ethos into Jewish life. He speculates that if such absorption had occurred, it would have changed Jewish consciousness in an unprecedented way:

> When I received *Luaḥ Erets Yisrael* from Lunts, I enjoyed reading the article on "Nedive ve-gibure ʿArav" (Arab noblemen and heroes). Several times I related to our friend Mr. Klausner that our writers had not done well in that they turned a blind eye to our brethren, the Arabs. The lack of respect—respect in and of itself—elevated hospitality, love of homeland, longing for liberty, and spirit of war, which are natural signs of a living nation—they were lost from us [at the hands of our] exilers and oppressors, who forced us to become an ordinary nation [goy] trading with the people of the earth. They

> [the positive qualities] remained . . . with our brethren the Arabs, from whom they arise and stand out in their poetry. Had they been translated into our language, had they found a way into our literature, they would have influenced us; because of their strong spirit, which was not made of fright—the spirit that longs for liberty—they would have helped us release the chain of despicable slavery and the shackles of subservient fear that are absorbed in our midst, and they would have fed us from the breasts of our slave mothers until a time came when our desire intensified to live the life of a nation with the entirety of the meaning of the word.[151]

Of all the unique features that characterized classical Arabic poetry, certain prevailing themes attracted the attention of the young poet. Amid the rise of Jewish nationalistic aspiration, Tschernichovsky was preoccupied with concepts such as revolution, liberty, and "the spirit of war." Fascinated by the thematic style of *Jāhilī* poetry that venerated bravery and the protection of the needy, Tschernichovsky lamented the fact that this poetry had not been transmitted into the Jewish consciousness. Its revolutionary ethos, he thought, would have freed the Jewish nation from its misery. From this lament, we can see that Arab poetical literature offered a means to recover that which had once been attributed to Jews, but had been lost with exile and remained now only among the Arabs.

Young Tschernichovsky's opinion on Arabic literature was aligned with Yahuda's enterprise of constructing Jewish self-consciousness. Pre-Islamic Arabic literary texts constituted a reservoir of ethical values that he imagined having once been the possession of Jews as well as Arabs. Furthermore, in his view, the discovery of the Jewish past was contingent on the study of Arabic as well as Hebrew literature:

> I want to finish in support of your opinion that our writers should pay attention to Arabic poetry and literature, for there is much to be learned in understanding our ancient poetry in the Hebrew Bible and penetrating the spirit of Hebrew poetry in Spain.[152]

The Role of Arabic in Interpreting the Hebrew Bible

Like his older brother, Isaac Yahuda, Abraham Shalom Yahuda also served as a bridge between the East and West through providing the Oriental context for Jewish history and culture. His background, intellectual formation, scholarly interests, and political engagements instilled in him the desire to play a role in connecting two different cultures, and consequently placed him at the intersection of "multiple and at times conflicting scholarly and ideological movements, including *Wissenschaft des Judentums*, Sephardim, Zionism and imperial affinity."[153] What mattered most among Abraham's variegated intersectionalities were his endeavors as a reviver of modern Hebrew, builder of Hebrew culture, and conduit between Jews and Arabs.

Isaac mentored his younger brother during Abraham's formative years, no doubt contributing to Abraham's perspective on the cross-pollination between Arabic and Hebrew culture. In September 1894, a year before embarking on his academic journey to Germany, Abraham published a series of articles on "The Value of Arabic" (to'elet lashon 'Aravit) in *Ha-Melits* (Mediator).[154] These articles convey his goal of a rapprochement between Arabic and Hebrew, and the essential role of Arabic in understanding biblical passages and Hebrew words—a view that suited the self-proclaimed mediatory mission of *Melits*.[155]

Under the name Abraham Shalom Le-Beit Yeḥezḳiel, Yahuda published three articles in *Melits* discussing Hebrew words whose roots and denotation are similar to those of Arabic.[156] In a footnote at the beginning of the article, Yahuda reveals his intention before his audience: "My aim is not to demonstrate to my beloved readers how Arabic can benefit Hebrew; this point has already been well-established. Rather, my intention is to offer an interpretation of specific words that share a similar connotation in Arabic."[157] For instance, he questions the association between the Hebrew word *tseriaḥ* (tower) in its noun form and the Arabic equivalent *ṣarḥ* (tower), suggesting instead that *tseriaḥ* should be understood in relation to the Arabic word *ḍarīḥ* (grave), asserting a new understanding of *tserihim* [in I Samuel 13:6] to mean "graves" or "tombs," cognate with the Arabic *ḍarīḥ*, which bears the same denotation.[158] To support his argument, he cites a verse by the most famous of all medieval Hebrew poets, Yehuda Halevi:

וחטא הורים שכנוה כגרים *** וקנו שם למתיהם צריחים

And sinful that fathers lived there [Jerusalem] as strangers
Who would buy graves to [bury] their dead there.[159]

Invoking a work by the best-known medieval Hebrew poet harks back to a time when Hebrew and Arabic culture were integrated, producing the unique Andalusian culture. This trope would play a prominent role in Yahuda's intellectual project in his scholarly writings as well as his vision of cultivating relations between Jews and Arabs in Palestine in modern times.[160] Although the language of medieval Hebrew poetry was connected to the Jews, the role accorded to poetry originated not in Jewish culture but rather in the Arabian Desert, where the ability to compose poetry spontaneously had long been valued and celebrated.[161] The practice of turning to pre-Islamic Arabic poetry in exploring the origins of Jewish forebearers found resonance in Yahuda's works.

Comprehension of the Hebrew Bible was another path to recovering lost Jewish culture, and the mastery of classical Arabic poetry was instrumental to that purpose. Addressing the Hebrew writers of his time, literary scholar Shmuel Moreh pointed out that they "should pay attention to Arabic poetry and literature, for there is a lot to be learned for understanding our ancient poetry in the Hebrew Bible."[162] Moreh's remark aligned with the understanding of earlier Sephardi and Oriental Jews who realized the usefulness of Arabic poetry for connecting with the Jewish literary legacy, whether in Al-Andalus or the Hebrew Bible.

Based on the view that both languages are of Semitic origin and share similar lexicons, Yahuda worked on the etymology of Hebrew words, and equated them with Arabic words and concepts drawn from extrabiblical textual sources. The application of comparative philology to Hebrew and Arabic for the interpretation of the Hebrew Bible was not a new method. In fact, it goes back to the medieval period, when Arabic, its language and literature, penetrated Jewish intellectual life, which flourished in the tenth century with the appearance of Saʿadyah Gaon's (882–942) translation of the Hebrew Bible.[163] Nonetheless, Yahuda was innovative in his application of a comparative philological methodology in two ways. First, instead of applying this method to Arabic irrespective of time and place, he confined himself to the Arabic of the pre-Islamic Arabia. With the contention that only pre-Islamic Arab tribal society shared essential features with the Israelite society, he sought illumination of biblical sources and noted the values shared by both sides.

Yahuda's methodology aligned with his Zionist promotion of a return to Jewish origins. The Arabic words Yahuda selected, it should be stressed, were restricted to an elucidation of the text's original intent rather than the text's present meaning. In his view, the original meaning of the text was a legitimate, even necessary concern. His theory of the use of comparative philology was embedded in his belief in the idea of the return to origins instead of the need to appropriate the Jewish legacy for the present. To this end, the Arabic language served as a legitimate device to elucidate the meaning of the Bible for the Jewish forebearers.

One example will illustrate Yahuda's interpretative methods. In sketching the character of ʿAntar—based on his poems and accounts found in the Arabic sources—and his refusal by his tribe to treat him equally due to his hybrid identity (a Black man born to an Arab master and Abyssinian slave woman), Yahuda comments, "ʿAntar increasingly proved to his tribe's fellows and Mālek [the father of his lover ʿAbla] their stubbornness, and he found it difficult to speak against them and threaten them to riot if they continued to harden their heart against him."[164] In describing ʿAntar's threatening his tribe's fellows to rampage them if they did not accept him, Yahuda uses the Hebrew word *vayʿudem* (he threatened them), which is extracted from the denotation of the Arabic word *wa“ad*. Yahuda looked to ʿAntar's response as a basis for interpreting Psalms 119:61 within the social and cultural framework of pre-Islamic Arabia.

חֶבְלֵי רְשָׁעִים עִוְּדֻנִי תּוֹרָתְךָ לֹא שָׁכָחְתִּי׃

> Though the bonds of the wicked are coiled round me,
> I have not neglected Your teaching.[165]

Yahuda points out that the Hebrew word *ʿiwudūnī* in the cited biblical verse is better understood with the help of Arabic. The Arabic word *waʿad* and its *fa“ala* derivative—in other words, its second form that is built by doubling (adding *shadda*) the middle radical of the first form—can illuminate the meaning of the Hebrew word *ʿud*. In his view, the Arabic verb *wa“ad* means to threaten and should be embraced for the interpretation of the Hebrew *ʿ-w-d*. In light of his suggestion, Psalms 119:61 should be read, "Though the bonds of the wicked threaten me, I have not neglected your teaching."

Revitalizing Hebrew, Reshaping the New Jew, through Arabic Language, Prose, and Poetry

The Jewish community renewed its ties with what it perceived as the ancestral landscape in late Ottoman Palestine simultaneously with the renewal of Hebrew as the national language. The return to the land of the forebearers entailed reconfiguring Jews' relations to the Orient in general. While Hebrew literati in Europe were preoccupied with the construction of a cultural model in harmony with the West, and in explicit contradistinction to the Orient, a group of Jewish intellectuals conversant with Arabo-Islamic culture in Palestine was headed in the opposite direction, seeking common ground with Oriental communities and their customs, traditions, and norms, and looking for the Jewish past within Arab culture.

Encounters with the natural world of Palestine exposed the limited resources of Hebrew in connecting modern speakers with their natural habitat. In this regard, the Arabic geographic and botanical lexicon proved valuable in expanding the resurrected Hebrew language. Seeing Arabic as a Semitic sibling of Hebrew, Jewish writers in Palestine returned to it to retrieve lost words, characteristics, and styles to restore them to Hebrew. Moreover, in Sapir's view, the Semitic sibling language functioned as a rich source in the revitalization of Hebrew by supplying geographic place-names and plant names to help render Hebrew a living, practical language. By introducing a bilingual list comprising Arabic and Hebrew place-names and plant names, Hebrew scholars effectively accorded an equal status to both languages.

The enrichment of Hebrew by means of turning to Arabic was accompanied by the indigenization of modern Hebrew through Arabic literary sources. Beyond the mere insertion of Arabic words into Hebrew, Hebrew writers turned to classical Arabic poetry as part of the construction of a Jewish identity that integrated the cultural norms of the Orient rather than those of the West and consolidated an Oriental character in the enterprise of the New Jew. That Oriental character, however, was presented from the perspective of a return to origins. To emphasize the "return to the origins" constituent in the emerging Hebrew culture, Hebrew writers advocated the acquisition of knowledge of classical Arabic literature. This view culminated in, first, the appropriation and transference of Arab cultural values such as faithfulness, bravery, and generosity to the ideal Jew.

The engagement with Arabic literature was key to the internal dynamics between Jewish scholars in Palestine and their counterparts in Europe. The Andalusian Jewish legacy was used to justify the affiliation of Jews to European culture and society as well as affiliate Jewish modernity with the West. In contradistinction, Hebrew scholars in Palestine advocated immersion in the Arabic heritage as a fundamental way to reclaim their shared ancient culture with pre-Islamic Arabs and revitalize the Jewish nation in Palestine.

The return to the Hebrew Bible along with the adoption of biblical Hebrew signaled the purity and indigeneity of the cultural enterprise Hebrew scholars were forging in Palestine. From the perspective of the Hebrew naturalists, Jewish settlers lacked living, contemporary interactions with the land, as evidenced by incomprehensible references in the Hebrew Bible and other Jewish sources. The association between the flora of Palestine as depicted in the Jewish tradition and the actual natural landscape as seen through Arabo-Islamic botanical materials aided Jewish settlers in strengthening their ties to the land of Palestine while deepening their sense of belonging.

The return to the Hebrew Bible was linked to the exploration of its textual and historical context. Studying, translating, and interpreting ancient Arabic poetry was ultimately a means for Hebrew scholars to connect with the Hebrew Bible and biblical Hebrew, given that they viewed the Hebrew Bible and ancient Arabic literature as culturally and linguistically cognate.

PART II

The Construction of a National Home in Mandate Palestine, 1917–48

THE ISSUANCE OF THE Balfour Declaration disrupted the ecumenical framework that had supported the model of peaceful coexistence established among members of the three religious communities in Palestine during the late Ottoman era.[1] The Balfour Declaration, issued on November 2, 1917, in the form of a letter from the British foreign secretary, Arthur Balfour, stated that Great Britain viewed "with favor the establishment in Palestine of a national home for the Jewish people" while referring to Arab inhabitants of Palestine not as an ethnic community with national rights to the land but rather as "non-Jewish communities in Palestine" whose rights are confined only to civil and religious rights, which the British government pledged not to prejudice. Under the condition of increasing tension between two communities, Hebrew scholars and educators continued to draw on Arabo-Islamic culture not only through individual efforts but also institutional activities backed by Zionist organizations. Even though in late Ottoman Palestine Jews' acquisition of Arabo-Islamic knowledge was a demonstration of loyalty to the shared homeland while recuperating Jewish indigeneity in the region and harboring Orientalistic attitudes toward the Palestinian Arab population, in Mandate Palestine that same knowledge became strategic and instrumentalized, providing information of the social and religious differences within Palestinian society, and arming them in their polemics with Palestinian Arab nationalists.

Zionists both abroad and in the Yishuv hailed the declaration as imperial support for the establishment of a national home for the Jewish people in the land that they considered their ancestral homeland in accordance with the Bible. In early April 1918, the Zionist Commission was established to advise the British authorities in Palestine on matters relevant to the implementation of the declaration. In the Yishuv, voices mounted calling for the construction of an exclusive Jewish community, with little or no involvement with the local Palestinian Arab population.[2] Aaron Aaronsohn (1876–1919), a Palestinian Jew and agronomist, is reported to have written in 1917 following the issuance of the declaration that

> we have strictly avoided Arab infiltration in our villages, and we are glad of it. From national, cultural, educational, technical and mere hygienic points of view this policy has to be strictly adhered to.[3]

Socialist Zionists (also known as Labor Zionists) justified the exclusion of Arabs from working in the Jewish colonies as corrective to their exploitation and use as cheap labor by the First Aliyah landowners. Under the slogan "the conquest of labor," Labor Zionists saw fit to realize the goals of Zionism through the conquest of all jobs in Palestine by Jews. The monopolization of the labor market for Jewish settlers, at first all manual labor and subsequently all skilled jobs, showed a desire for the exclusion of the Palestinian workers from the new society in the making.[4] Notwithstanding the effort to marginalize the Arab population and growing exclusivism, Arabs and their culture remained central to the Zionist enterprise to advance claims of Palestine that turned from having been a shared homeland to a national home for the Jewish people with minimum consideration of the native Arab population. Indeed, the same issues that concerned Zionist educators and scholars before the Great War—land, language, and people—remained relevant in the wake of the issuance of the Balfour Declaration, and Arabo-Islamic sources continued to be consulted and appropriated to address them.

The accumulation of Jewish land in Palestine, accompanied by the hebraization of the landscape, was of utmost priority for Zionists in Mandate Palestine, including efforts by Jewish scholars well-versed in Arabo-Islamic culture who aided in the advancement of this scheme. Land acquisition was pivotal for the implementation of the Balfour Declaration by creating facts on the ground that would pave the way for the establishment of a national home in Palestine. Historian Kenneth Stein enumerates five reasons underlying the success of Jewish land acquisition under the British Mandate in Palestine: first, the vulnerability of the inherited Ottoman land laws to manipulation; second, the social and political fragmentation of Palestinian society, which prevented the formation of real opposition to Zionists' land acquisitions; third, the susceptibility of the postwar economically enfeebled Palestinian society to the orchestrated Zionist proposals to purchase land; fourth, the British embrace of laws and regulations from the Ottoman era, and their self-positioning as the exclusive arbitrator in enforcing these regulations; and finally, the British imperial backing allowed Zionists to organize and institutionalize their efforts.[5]

Jewish scholars fluent in Arabic and knowledgeable about Arabo-Islamic culture were instrumental in mediating between Arab landlords and Zionist organizations in the Mandate period. Furthermore, they played a role in the communication and dissemination of the Zionist message as a show of strength to leaders of the Palestinian nationalist movement to intimidate them into compromise.[6] In addition, they served in Zionist organizations by rendering Arabic place-names into Hebrew in a project to hebraize the landscape.

In Mandate Palestine, British officials replaced the Ottoman cosmopolitanism that embraced the multitude of languages spoken within the country with a policy of monolingualism. British administrators endorsed, as Suzanne Schneider has shown, the "educational separation of communities along linguistic lines" as a political and pedagogical necessity.[7] Both the Zionist and Palestinian national movements endorsed this policy, viewing monolingualism as useful to separatist national enterprises. Each community would teach and learn in its respective language, Hebrew or Arabic. For their part, Palestinian nationalists welcomed the elevation of Arabic as the language of instruction in their public schools. Indeed, Palestinian educators and political leaders had long promoted the use of Arabic as an administrative and educational linguistic force in Ottoman regions where Arabs constituted the majority. In fact, one of the clearest departures from the Ottoman system of schooling, as Hilary Kalisman has noted, was substituting Arabic for Turkish as the language of instruction in Palestine.[8] Furthermore, Palestinian educators decried the negative influence missionary Christian schools had on local children who were taught in foreign languages.

Among Zionists, multilingualism was deeply associated with *galutiyut* (diasporic existence) and therefore perceived as jeopardizing the Jewish national project of striking roots in the ancestral homeland. Indeed, as Liora Halperin has demonstrated, Jewish settlers in Mandate Palestine were alarmed by foreign languages in their homeland because of their concern about the weakness of Hebrew in the Yishuv. Arabic, however, unlike other "foreign" languages, was not alien. It was the language of the land, sefat ha-arets, as several Hebrew educators had called it in the late Ottoman era, and was, according to Halperin, the linguistic "bedrock upon which the Yishuv was built and into which it penetrated as Jews built the foundations for a Hebrew society on an Arab landscape," as is explored in chapter 3 of this book. Thus in the Mandate era, as Halperin has argued, "separation from Arabic did not entail uninterest in or ignorance of Arabic." Jews encountered Arabic in various settings, including deploying Arabic in Jewish-Arab contacts in Tel Aviv, offering Arabic courses to kibbutz dwellers and other agricultural communities in rural regions, using Arabic in Zionist Arabic-language newspapers to shape Arab public opinion, and deploying Arabic-speaking Sephardi and Oriental Jews to gather intelligence about the local community.[9] Arabic proved useful in these settings to serve the Yishuv, but Jews' interest in Arabic was not limited to these situations. Jewish educators used Arabic for the enrichment of modern Hebrew and the expansion of its lexicon. In fact, that was one of the goals of Jewish educators' interest in Arabic in Mandate Palestine according to Israel Ben-Ze'ev, the supervisor of Arabic studies in the Jewish National Assembly in Mandate Palestine. Responding to a series of articles in the Hebrew newspaper *Ha-Boker* (Morning) during the early years of the state of Israel that lamented the devotion of time and energy to teaching Arabic in Jewish schools, Ben-Ze'ev stressed the linguistic and cultural value of Arabic along with its paramount usefulness for the enrichment of Hebrew.[10] Arabic was also central to understanding the legacy of Sephardi and Oriental Jews as well as their representation in pre-Islamic and medieval Arabic literature.

Even as separatist tendencies intensified, Jews continued to interact with Arabs within and outside Palestine in various ways due to the sociospatial entwinement in which both communities lived in the twilight of the Ottoman Empire. When Bilād al-Shām (Greater Syria) came under the control of European powers, as historian Cyrus Schayegh has explained, there was not a stark disruption from the late Ottoman world. First of all, the infrastructure from the Ottoman era that survived the war continued to function to connect the region. Second, the protracted process of regional integration under the Ottoman Empire accumulated a strength that neither the nationalist movements of the 1920s nor the European imperial administration could erase. On the contrary, the French and British recognized that reality, and adapted to it by making major policy decisions accordingly.[11]

The above factors enabled, and even mandated, interconnection between Jews and Arabs in post-Ottoman Greater Syria and other neighboring countries, like Egypt and Iraq, and made the Yishuv part and parcel of the region. While the Balfour Declaration boosted Zionists' aspirations for the establishment of a national home in Palestine, they understood, as Schayegh has remarked, that they were an integral part of the region-wide structures.[12] A pervasive uncertainty about the boundaries of the national home echoed in the imagination of Jewish authors. Rabbi Binyamin, a prolific Hebrew writer, religious Zionist, and founder of Brith Shalom (Covenant of Peace), for instance, suggested in a 1930 proposal the integration of Jews in an Arab federation that would sprawl from Iraq to Palestine.[13] Members of Brith Shalom, established in Jerusalem in 1925, promoted peaceful coexistence in Palestine via a binational Arab-Jewish state in which both communities would share equal political rights.[14]

Zionists found it imperative to work with Palestinians from different social and religious backgrounds to advance the objectives of the imperial pledge. Zionist leaders, explains Hillel Cohen, adopted several strategies with respect to the local Palestinian population. First, they supported opposition forces within the Arab society to create alternative leadership. Second, they sought to deepen the divisions within the Arab society between Bedouins and settled populations, on the one hand, and Christians and Muslims, on the other hand. Third, they sponsored Arabic writers and newspapers to advocate for Zionism and Jewish immigration to Palestine.[15] Finally, they refused to acknowledge the authenticity of the Arab nationalist movement in Palestine—a refusal that was shared by both Ashkenazi and Sephardi Oriental Jews.

Representatives of the Zionist movement traversed the region to persuade the Arab public of the benefits of the Zionist movement to the Orient and proclaim their indigeneity to Palestine and the Orient in general. We will see that throughout the British era, Arab intellectuals and public figures from neighboring Arab countries became involved in the situation between Jews and Arabs in Palestine, only to find themselves every time in a divisive situation where they were hailed by one party and criticized by another. Ahmad Zaki Pasha (1867-1934), a well-known Arab intellectual and former secretary in the Egyptian government, addressed a letter in 1922 to Dr. David Eder, who served as the Zionist executive in Palestine, in which he congratulated the latter about the issuance of the Balfour Declaration, and expressed his wish for collaboration between Jews and the people of the Orient. That letter, published in the *Jewish Chronicles*, a London-based newspaper, under a controversial title "An Arab's Support of Zionism," provoked Palestinian writers to question the connection between Zaki Pasha and Zionism.[16] In a similar incident, Iraqi poet and writer Maʿrūf al-Ruṣāfī (1875–1945) visited Jerusalem in 1921 and attended a lecture by Abraham Shalom Yahuda on the coexistence between Jews and Arabs in the al-Andalus that envisioned a similar scenario in Palestine. Out of admiration, respect, and hope, the Iraqi poet composed a poem in which he praised Herbert Samuel, the Jewish high commissioner, and paid respect to Yahuda, at the time a professor at Madrid University. That panegyric poem was viewed by the Palestinian newspaper as an endorsement of the Zionist movement against Palestinians.[17]

And where did Sephardi and Oriental Jews stand in relation to Arabs in British Palestine? How did their attitude toward the native Arab population differ from that of Ashkenazi Jews? It must first be recognized that the top priority of Sephardi and Oriental Jews during the British era was to recover their own political centrality after having been pushed to the periphery in the wake of the collapse of the Ottoman Empire and the emergence of the imperial British rule in the country. Ethnic divisions within the Jewish community were not, Abraham Haim has observed, a top priority of the Yishuv. More pressing were ideological differences and political disagreements surrounding foreign relations, security, the Arab question, and the construction of infrastructure. With the increase of the Jewish immigration from European countries during the 1930s and 1940s, Sephardi and Oriental Jews were pushed to the sidelines, outnumbered by new immigrants.[18]

Hence it was anxieties about their own marginalization under the Ashkenazi leadership of the Zionist movement that informed the engagement of Sephardi and Oriental Jews with the Arab question. As the leaders of political Zionism became closer to and influential with the British authorities, displacing the Sephardi and Oriental Jewish leaders who had enjoyed a privileged status with the Ottomans, one of the strategies the Sephardi and Oriental Jews adopted to compensate for this loss of prestige was to assert their relevance to the Zionist enterprise by emphasizing the significance of Arabs as well as their culture to the future of Zionism in Palestine.

In their efforts to convince Arab intellectuals in Palestine and neighboring countries to accept a Zionist state, Jewish scholars adopted a discourse that highlighted their indigeneity to the land: Jews are not coming to Palestine; rather they are returning to the land of their forebearers. In the Arabic-language Jewish newspapers that appeared in al-Mashriq in the interwar period and extended to the mid-twentieth century, Jewish writers underscored, as Lital Levy has noticed, a shared identity as *yahūd al-sharq* (Eastern Jews) or *yahūd al-ʿarab* (Arab Jews). In advocating for the Zionist enterprise, Jewish writers found in the role of Jews in Arabo-Islamic civilization, to use Levy's phrasing, a "usable past."[19] Sephardi and Oriental Jews in Mandate Palestine took advantage of this usable past to both persuade, on the one hand, the Arab community of their Arabness or Easternness, and on the other, the Ashkenazi of their role as a bridge between the two communities. Reviving and promulgating the Jewish past in the East also advanced the notion of indigeneity—an idea that Ashkenazi Jews frequently stressed in their discourse.

If the Balfour Declaration was a victorious achievement for Zionists, it was otherwise for Arabs in Palestine. The declaration was known in the Palestinian newspaper as *al-waʿd al-mashʾūm* (the sinister pledge) that sliced Palestine off the Bilād al-Shām region (Greater Syria), granted it to the Zionist movement, and aimed at converting the minority status of Jews in Palestine into a majority one.[20] The issuance of the Balfour Declaration, as Ussama Makdisi has indicated, replaced a system of religious communities with a sectarian national system. Jews of the Yishuv went from being a religious community under the Ottomans to a national community under the British. This solidified a preexistent religious affiliation between Christian and Muslim Arabs as opposed to Jews. A bold example in this regard is the establishment of MCAs in response to the issuance of the Balfour Declaration and in objection to the declaration goal of establishing a national home for Jews in Palestine. The main uniting theme among various local MCAs was their opposition to Zionism and its supportive British policy. Their rejection of Zionism was based on refuting claims made by Zionists about their indigeneity and immemorial ties with the land, and affirming the long and uninterrupted historical connection between Palestinians and their land as well as their numerical advantage over Jews.[21] For MCA members and other members of the Palestinian society beyond them, the Balfour Declaration was a gift from those who do not possess to those who do not deserve. Palestinian nationalists and opponents to Zionism were incredulous as to how a foreign power could claim ownership over Palestine to begin with, and then how it could grant Jews a national home in a land where their number did not exceed one-tenth of the entire Arab population.

We have seen how Sephardi and Oriental Jews viewed their relationship with Arabs, but how did Arab nationalists in Palestine view Sephardi and Oriental Jews? The religiously based alliance between local Muslims and Christians in the Mandate era that emerged in response to the issuance of the Balfour Declaration was not anti-Jewish in principle. That association in part aimed at resisting divisive efforts orchestrated by either the British officials or Zionists who plotted to distinguish between Muslim and Christian Arabs to create a state of fragmentation and disunity, as indicated earlier, among the rising national movement. Palestinian nationalists, indeed, distinguished in their ideology between Indigenous Jews who had been living in Palestine along with Muslims and Christians for centuries, and foreign Zionists who arrived from Western countries with nationalist ideas that undermined the centuries-long amicable and neighborly relations between Jews, Muslims, and Christians. In her reading of an editorial published in the Jerusalemite newspaper *al-Quds al-Sharīf* in July 1920, Abigail Jacobson notes the distinction made between local Jews, referred to as "Arab Jews," who had been living among Arabs for centuries, and were honored and well treated considering their weak status as outnumbered and powerless, and Zionists, described as *ghurabā'* (foreigners or aliens) who put forward baseless claims on Palestine as their ancestral homeland while ignoring the prior history of the Canaanites, portrayed in the editorial as the ancestors of Palestinians who had resided in the country long before the Israelites.[22] The editorial asserts the inconceivability of coexistence between Zionists and local Palestinians given their different language and lifestyle.

From the perspective of Arab Palestinians, the distinction between native Jews and foreign Zionists was contingent on the former community's rejection of Zionism as a form of settler colonialism. But by the Mandate period, the only Jews who rejected Zionism were the extreme Orthodox, who did so for religious reasons, and some Sephardim who feared the loss of their leadership status in Jerusalem to secular immigrant European Jews who mocked their tradition.[23]

Just as Zionists attempted to persuade Arab Palestinians of the desirability of their project, so did Arab Palestinians attempt to dissuade Sephardi and Oriental Jews from joining it. That strategy is demonstrated in the recruitment letters Palestinian nationalists published in local newspapers to sway local Jews away from supporting the Zionist enterprise. For two years between 1922 and 1923,

Jamāl al-Ḥusseinī, a member in the Arab Executive Committee, repeatedly appealed to native Jews to nullify the Balfour Declaration, abandon the false dream of Zionism, and join the Palestinian national movement to reestablish lost friendship and eliminate animosity.[24] Despite al-Ḥusseinī's efforts, native Sephardi and Oriental Jews showed no objection to the issuance of the Balfour Declaration, although unlike their European counterparts, they attempted to maintain neighborly relations with Arabs in the region.[25]As we evaluate and assess Jewish-Arab relations in Mandatory Palestine, we must attend to the influence that British policy exerted on both communities. The British policy in Palestine institutionalized the dual society paradigm with the introduction of a dual administrative structure that offered Jews and Arab separate and unequal civil, economic, social, and political positions.[26] That Mandatory separation, to use Schneider's phrase, manifested itself in the ways in which Jews adapted Arabo-Islamic culture for polemic discourse while advancing Hebrew culture in Mandatory Palestine. Arabic sources were used to ascertain Jewish indigeneity and bolster Jewish claims to Palestine as a national home for the Jewish people. Obviously, these rhetorical strategies were strengthened and legitimized by a British policy that demonstrably favored Jewish over Arab interests.

At first glance, it seems that the British policy in Palestine was filled with contradictions. The same land, Palestine, appeared to be twice promised: as a national home for both Jews and Arabs. "I'll be frank with you," said Lloyd George, prime minister of Great Britain, "During the World War they gave the Arabs and the Jews conflicting assurances. We sold the same horse twice."[27] British politicians such as George and Balfour, as Bernard Regan has shown, based their choices about the future of the Middle East on Christian messianic prophecies in the Book of Revelation along with a belief that the return of Jews to Palestine was a prerequisite to the coming of the Apocalypse.[28] In short, the issuance of the Balfour Declaration created a binational reality that extended from 1918 until 1948 and was the main reason for the tension that rose between the two communities during this era.

4

The Ethnonationalization of the Palestine Landscape

IN PREVIOUS CHAPTERS, we have seen the efforts of Jewish scholars in late Ottoman Palestine to underscore the religious, racial, cultural, and linguistic similarities between Jews and Arabs. Israel Belḳind marks a pivot point toward a different relationship to the Arab Palestinian population in the Mandate period by arguing for Jewish particularity and the cultural superiority of Jewish settlers. In their ancestral homeland, Belḳind argues, Jews must now produce a Judaism based on their particularity, speak Hebrew, and establish their own social and cultural Hebrew institutions.[1] Palestine as a multireligious and multilinguistic landscape that allowed for the existence as well as growth of unparalleled cultural and religious diversity will rapidly be consigned to a faded memory, as Belḳind and others of his ilk attribute the achievements of Jews solely to their own perseverance along with the genius of the pioneers who turned parts of forsaken Palestine, a land abandoned for fifteen centuries, into an oasis in the midst of the desert.[2]

During the celebratory period following the issuance of the Balfour Declaration, Belḳind wrote about the future of Jews in Palestine against the background of his native Belarus. He reminds his readers of the history of persecution and misery of Jews in Russia, which compelled him, along with other young Russian Jews, to found the Bilu movement and emigrate to late Ottoman Palestine without looking back. For the last thirty-five years, he notes, not a single day passed without news of the imposition of new restrictions on Jews in Russia, such as their expulsion from cities and villages, professions, and educational institutions, and frequent massacres—circumstances that ultimately led to the immigration of two million Jews. He maintains that while Jews founded centers among Western communities around the globe, even in South Africa and Australia, they failed to establish a geographic home for Judaism. Approaching the topic from an Orientalist point of view, he omits from mention the great number of Jews who found refuge in Middle Eastern and North African countries in the nineteenth century.

Given that "Western communities" exert such a strong cultural influence that immigrant Jews are absorbed into the mainstream, lose their original culture, and "assume the prevalent shape and form" of the host culture, the only antidote to the ongoing deterioration of Jewish identity is to found a Jewish national home in Palestine where Jews would build their own social and cultural institutions, and hence preserve their distinct identity. In order to achieve this national home, a physical as well as spiritual refuge, Palestine "must first become colonized; first there must be established an agricultural laborers' class." Since most potential Jewish settlers were urbanites who worked as either merchants or professionals, they would have to study agriculture on their settlement in Palestine. Belḳind then proceeds to articulate the importance of knowledge of the land as a condition for building a center for Jews in their ancestral homeland:

> The agriculturalist must be able to do every part of his work. He must be able to plow, to sow, to harvest, etc. He must know how to plant all kinds of fruit-trees and vegetables and how to take care of them. He must know how to rear the cattle which help him in his work or supply him with milk, and how to attend to his fowls, bees, and silkworms. He must know how to use to the fullest every part of his land, the nature around him, every moment of his time. He must also be handy with the axe and the hammer and other tools, so as not to have to call upon the artisan at every emergency.[3]

In practice, the agricultural model that took root within the Jewish settlement in Palestine during the late nineteenth century, as Ran Aaronsohn has shown, emulated the practices of the local Arab population—hardly a revolutionary model.[4] Since the Jewish settlers had never engaged in agricultural work, they would need to prepare themselves for working the land: Jews must study agriculture just as a physician studies medicine and an engineer studies engineering. Arabo-Islamic materials were principal resources in the cultivation, naming, uses, and taxonomy of Palestine's flora and fauna, and the acquisition of "knowledge of the land."

Belḳind boasted to Jews in the Diaspora of the Zionist achievements in Palestine: the consolidation of the Jewish national identity, revival of Hebrew, and establishment of social and cultural institutions in the ancestral land. Even though Jewish settlers constituted a minority in Mandatory Palestine, Belḳind expresses pride in their accomplishments, which he emphasizes were achieved independently "in their own country" without any assistance, implicitly erasing the influence of the Arabs in Palestine.[5] Hailing largely from impoverished villages in eastern Europe, Jewish settlers lacked not only experience but also the means to afford modern technology so they relied on Palestinian peasants as their source of agricultural knowledge and practice. In almost all settlements, Jewish settlers hired local peasants to work the land for them while Jewish settlers supervised. Settlers of the first wave of immigration preferred employing local Palestinian peasants to Jewish workers, prioritizing pragmatism over ideology. The number of Hebrew laborers was initially unable to keep up with the demands of increasingly large parcels of agricultural land, and hiring a local Palestinian peasant was more affordable than hiring members of the second wave of immigration who demanded higher wages, even though, as inexperienced workers, they were less productive.

A case in point is that of Michel Pines, who purchased a tract of village land for the Bilu group from the French consul in Jaffa Poliovierre. In 1896, he asked permission from the leaders of the colony to employ young men from the recently established Yishuv Erets Ha-Ḳodesh (Settlement of the Holy Land) association in Jerusalem, which was founded with the aim of settling members of the Old Yishuv and training them to work as laborers in the settlements. Dov Ariel Leibovitz, who was then the secretary of the Jewish settlement of Gedera, objected that the wage for an Arab was 5 to 6.5 kurus per day, which would not support a Jewish worker. Moreover, Leibovitz pointed out, Jewish workers were inexperienced, lacked agricultural knowledge, and were unaccustomed to hard labor. Nevertheless, Pines was allowed to employ three young men as a trial on the condition that the Bilu group only pay their wages, and they "would not bear the burden of their livelihood [food and clothes], travel from and to the city, sickness, no acceptance of their complaining about the labor or making mistakes.... Do not suspect me of malice and great cruelty, for surely like me you will understand, that only a worker who can withstand conditions like these will be able to achieve the good goal."[6] Despite their ideological goal of training Jewish workers to work the land, hiring Jewish urbanites was both financially challenging and practically risky given their lack of experience. It is also suggested that potential Jewish workers considered physical labor beneath them and akin to slave labor. Leibovitz prioritized practicality over ideology, expressing a nuanced view that wrestles with the desire to support Jewish workers while recognizing the economic and cultural realities that make employing local Palestinian peasants more appealing as well as more feasible for the Jewish settlement of Gedera. For our purposes, however, a key reason Leibovitz cited for preferring Palestinian peasants over inexperienced Hebrew workers was the former's expertise in local soil, climate conditions, and crop selection. The colonists began to embrace traditional methods, such as the rain-fed cultivation of cereal crops like wheat and barley as well as potatoes and typical Mediterranean fruit varieties, including grapes, olives, and figs, all grown without the aid of irrigation. As some scholars have noted, this adaptation happened across all the agricultural communities, despite the fact that the individuals in each community operated on their own and seldom interacted with one another.[7]

Despite adapting Arabs' agricultural methods and yielding to local expertise, settlers felt themselves impervious to assimilation into Arab society based on the theory that whenever immigrant Jews possess a "higher culture" than that in which they are embedded—denoting a combination of cultural sophistication and intellectual advancement—they will maintain their distinct identity while benefiting their host society, as in the case of Jews' exile in Babylon, where they preserved their distinct identity because of their superior status. In Spain and Germany, Jews were in danger of losing their national identity because they were embedded in a "higher culture," but when persecution drove them eastward to Poland, Belḳind asserts that they retained their cultural identity because the Polish natives were of inferior cultural status.[8] Consequently, fears of assimilation, Belḳind stresses, dissipate in Palestine irrespective of the numerical disadvantage of Jews over the Arab majority. Belḳind here echoes Aziza Khazzoom's argument about Jews' embrace of the East/West dichotomy as a paradigm of self-evaluation and assessment of others.[9] Jews are less advantaged when they settle in Western communities, and are vulnerable to losing their history and identity in their attempt to produce a Judaism attentive to their new society's ideals and values—for instance, sending their children to public schools, abandoning Hebrew in favor of the majority language, and celebrating Sunday instead of Saturday as their holy day.[10] On the other hand, when Jewish ancestors settled in Poland, they brought with them a cultural heritage that they considered more advanced than that of the native population. This "higher culture" enabled them to retain their national identity despite living among a different cultural group.

Belḳind's legacy revolves around more than simply his educational philosophy in instructing Jewish settlers to study agriculture in order to root themselves in its soil.[11] He weaves his knowledge of Palestine's landscape, which he acquired through intercommunal relations with the native Palestinian population, Arabs as well as Sephardi and Oriental Jews, into a series of works detailing the topography of the land.[12] The first of his published works was a book on the geography of contemporary Palestine. In preparing to commemorate the first full decade of the foundation of *Ḥibbat Zion* (Love of Zion), a committee suggested contributing a geographic survey of the land of Palestine, entrusting Belḳind with the undertaking given his innovative works and experience. Although Belḳind was pleased with the idea since it was brought up at a time when he was "dreaming of composing an educational book on the geography of the land," things did not go as smoothly as he had hoped. Belḳind wanted to publish the book in Hebrew, while the members of the committee in Odessa expected it to be in Russian. After some negotiation, they agreed to publish the book in both languages, but it appeared first in Russian in 1902.[13] Because it was popular, the book was published in several subsequent editions.[14] Due to increased publishing expenses in the wake of World War I, the Hebrew edition was put on hold for more than twenty years and included only one of the previously published two volumes, with the title *Erets Yisrael shel zemanenu* (The land of Israel in our time).[15] Similar in structure to the works of Eliezer

Ben-Yehuda and David Yellin discussed previously, *Erets Yisrael shel zemanenu* provides a descriptive account of Palestine's physical features.

Despite similarities in content to previous Hebrew geographic texts, *Erets Yisrael shel zemanenu* offers its readers a visual depiction of the land to further yediʿat ha-arets. Yet the images portray Palestine's natural landscape in a way that is directly influenced by the biblical imagery of a land flowing with milk and honey, a trope that dominated English literature on Palestine in the nineteenth and twentieth centuries. While it may have aimed to bridge reality and imagination, this representation owes more to the biblical tradition than to reality.[16] Belḳind deploys imagery of glorious mountains, abundant water sources, and beautiful trees to simulate the biblical imagination of the land.

While these images depict an inhabited land—there are Arab horse riders and Arab townspeople—the people in these visual representations are part of the physical landscape, unremarked upon. In their stead, he gives attention to identifying natural sites in accordance with the biblical map of the land. Natives here are represented as inanimate landscape features, like mountains, rivers, and lakes. His lack of interest in the contemporary population of Palestine is exemplified in his use of outdated images that most likely date back centuries, which suits his conception of a landscape that has not changed since time immemorial, as denoted in the biblical citations under the images.[17]

To indigenize Jewish settlers in Palestine, existing Arab villages and towns were used to identify Jewish settlements from previous historical periods, and at the same time assist the process of Hebrew place-naming. Belḳind finds it instrumental to take advantage of Arabo-Islamic culture in both naming the emergent Jewish settlements and identifying the landscape of Palestine with that of the Hebrew Bible. This strategy was followed in late Ottoman Palestine, gaining momentum in the British era with institutional and imperial support. It is worth mention that Belḳind was among the founders of the previously noted settlement of Gedera, a Jewish settlement established in 1884 on land that had been purchased by Miḳveh Yisrael. The settlement came under the management of Baron Rothschild's administration after a failed attempt by the young Russian Jewish immigrants to manage Gedera in accordance with collectivist principles.[18] The selection of that particular location for the Bilu settlement is in part inspired by the nearby Palestinian village called Qaṭra ("drop" in Arabic).[19] This strategy of choosing an inhabited Arab location for a new Jewish settlement will become a fundamental principle guiding the establishment and nomenclature of sites in Palestine through the activities of the Naming Committee of the Jewish National Fund, as will be discussed below. Scholars have explained that Qaṭra, the Arab village that had been settled since the early Islamic period according to early Christian writings, is identified with the biblical place-name Gedor or Gidirtha.[20] The identification of a previous Jewish settlement is thus made possible through the existing Palestinian settlement that is seen as

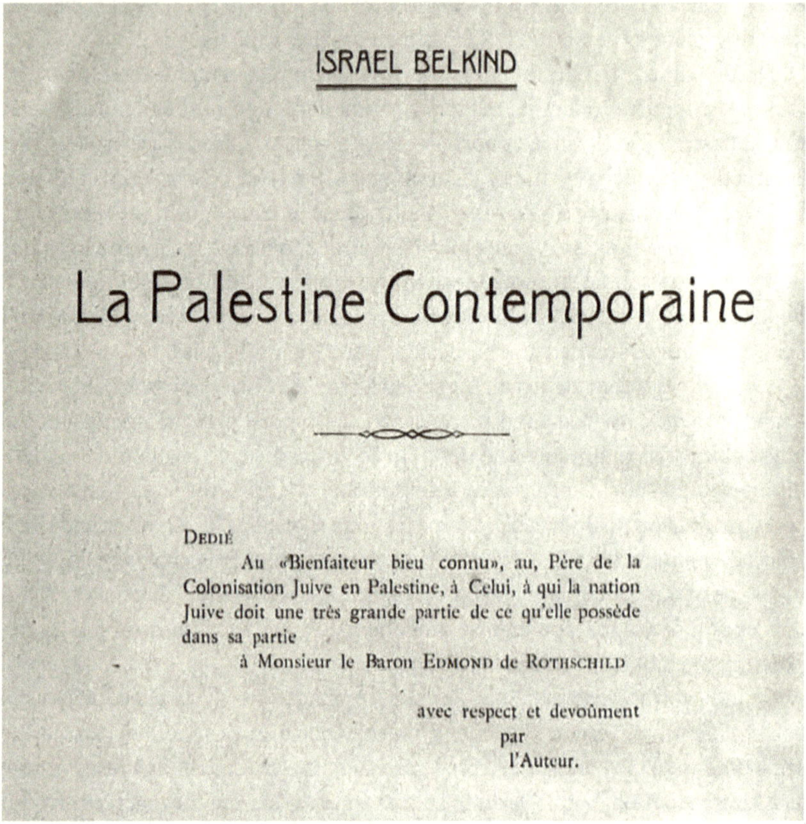
ISRAEL BELKIND

La Palestine Contemporaine

DEDIÉ

Au «Bienfaiteur bieu connu», au, Père de la Colonisation Juive en Palestine, à Celui, à qui la nation Juive doit une très grande partie de ce qu'elle possède dans sa partie

à Monsieur le Baron EDMOND de ROTHSCHILD

avec respect et devoûment
par
l'Auteur.

FIGURE 4.1. Cover of Israel Belḳind's *Erets Yisrael shel zemanenu* (The land of Israel in our time), published in British Palestine in 1928. Belḳind dedicates the book to French Jewish philanthropist Baron Edmond de Rothschild, whom he refers to as the father of modern Hebrew settlement and someone to whom the people of Israel owe a great portion of what they have in their land.

strengthening the assumption of Bilu members of an ancient Jewish settlement.[21] Not only did Palestinian villages provide labor for farming and guarding but even more important, they supplied geographic legitimacy, rootedness in the land, and connection with Jewish heritage.

The Judaization of the Homeland

The Balfour Declaration sparked celebration among those seeking the restoration of Jewish indigeneity on the land of their forebearers until the unsettling analogy between the British conquest of Palestine and the medieval Crusades, replete with British general Edmund Allenby's victory march through the walled city of Jerusalem in 1917, turned Jewish hopes and aspirations into anxieties. Jews were soon to realize that the imperial pledge mainly served the religious and political objectives of the British rather than those of the Jews who hoped for the unconditional delivery of Palestine territory. That is attested to in the attention the British officials gave to the Muslim, rather than Jewish, sensibilities at the time of the conquest of Jerusalem.[22] While the British were motivated to cast the conquest of Jerusalem as a religious victory in which they played the part of modern crusaders who could accomplish what the medieval English king Richard the Lionheart could not achieve during the time of Saladin in the late twelfth century, they were simultaneously anxious not to displease the majority Muslim subjects in the British colonies. A few weeks before the conquest of Jerusalem, the News Department of the Foreign Office issued a statement that shows how sensitive British intelligence was to the response of people in the Muslim world:

> The attention of the press is again drawn to the undesirability of publishing any article, paragraph, or picture suggesting that military operations against Turkey are in any sense a Holy War, a modern crusade, or have anything whatever to do with religious questions. The British Empire is set to contain a hundred million of Mohammedan subjects of the King and it is obviously mischievous to suggest that our quarrel with Turkey is one between Islam and Christianity.[23]

From this note we see that British intelligence avoided the perception of the conquest of Jerusalem as a manifestation of a holy confrontation between Christianity and Islam in order not to trigger the wrath of millions of Muslim subjects living in the British colonies. Nevertheless, when General Allenby entered Jerusalem in December 1917, he was portrayed as the heir of Godfry of Bouillon, who had captured Jerusalem from the Muslims in 1099. Media and newspapers defined the occupation of the city as the most memorable event in the history of Christendom, presenting the similarities between Allenby and Godfry. Both were Christians, both shared a common fate as Christian conquerors of the city, and both had to face the rising tensions between different communities after the conquest.[24]

The religious symbolism of Palestine for Christian European authors stirred correlative religious sentiments among Hebrew authors who believed that they, not the British, were the authentic heirs of the Holy Land. The Balfour Declaration reflected Balfour's "romantic classical-biblical vision of the civilizational benefits of a cultured Jewish homeland."[25] Israel Horowitz rhetorically asks that if religion had motivated Western politicians' and scholars' interest in the Holy Land, shouldn't the religion of the people of Israel exert an even more powerful attraction? He continues, "We, who have closer relations to this land, are standing aside with crossed hands while the fulfillment of our obligations is carried out by foreigners [*nokhrim*]. . . . What a tremendous shame!"[26] Horowitz decries

Jews' apathy, as they stand idly by, watching non-Jews, both scholars and politicians, fulfill Jews' "obligation" to learn about and connect with their own land.

The vast corpus of literature concerning Palestine produced by Christian Western writers since the mid-nineteenth century loomed large for Horowitz, both as inspiration and threat. "Wise men of the European nations instigated wonders in this profession," he says, adding, "[We now find] copious and large volumes concerned with the land of Israel. What a wonderful work! And what an excellent order!" In his admiration of Western authors, he makes the point that their connection to Palestine is only based on religion: "We should not forget that only religious traditions draw them to this ancient Land." Theirs is not a nationalist interest because "these researchers are citizens in their lands," unlike the Zionist endeavor, which asserts a singular bond between the Jewish people and Palestine as the exclusive national homeland for Jews.[27]

Hebrew writers consulted European works for the identification of biblical places and natural sites. In the Hebrew works, the biblical places and natural sites in Palestine were dissociated from Christian thought, and brought closer to the Jewish consciousness. European geographic and archaeological activities from the mid-nineteenth to the first half of the twentieth centuries, as historian Nur Masalha has noted, were instrumental for the indigenization of European Jewish immigrants in Palestine and "the nationalization of the Hebrew Bible."[28] In composing *Erets Yisrael shel zemanenu*, Belḳind utilized only information from those who resided in the land and experienced it firsthand. The sources on which Belḳind drew include Jewish ones such as the Hebrew Bible, Talmud, and works of Flavius Josephus.[29] But he also relied on literature and travel accounts by Westerners who lived in Palestine, shunning those works that derived their information from other sources or whose authors had never been to the land of Palestine. Of the former, Belḳind cites Max Blanckenhorn's *Naturwissenschaftliche Studien am Toten Meer und im Jordantal* (1908), Gabriel Charmes's *Voyage en Palestine: Impressions et souvenirs* (1891), William Hepworth Dixon's *The Holy Land* (1869), Gaston Maspero's *Histoire ancienne des peuples de l'Orient* (1875), Karl Baedeker's *Palestine et Syrie: Manuel du voyageur* (1893), and finally, a map of Palestine on a scale of 1:700,000 produced by German scholars Hans Fischer and Hermann Guthe and titled *Neue Handkarte von Palästina* (1890).[30]

The Identification of Historic Settlement: Institutional Activities

In late Ottoman Palestine, efforts to identify historic Jewish settlements and sites in accordance with the Bible as well as with the use of Arabo-Islamic knowledge contributed to Jews' sense of belonging to a shared multiethnic and multireligious homeland. In Mandate Palestine, however, these attempts were institutionalized to serve the establishment of a national home for Jews in the land. Throughout the Mandate period, Jewish writers experienced in and familiar with Arabo-Islamic culture dedicated themselves and their knowledge to help materialize this national objective. Experts in Arabo-Islamic culture among Jews in the Yishuv who were previously Ottoman Hebrews (especially Sephardi and Oriental Jews such as Yosef Meyuḥas, Abraham Elmaleḥ (1885–1967), and Yellin, and Ashkenazi Jews like Zev Vilnai (1900–1988)) became members of Jewish institutions founded in the Mandate, such as Va'adat ha-shemot shel ḳaḳal (Naming Committee of the Jewish National Fund) and ha-ḥivrah le-ḥaḳirat erets yisrael ve-'atiḳoteyha (Association for the Exploration of the Land of Israel and Its Antiquities), whose mission it was to retrieve the Jewish past and ascertain Jewish connection to the land in the present.

The Naming Committee set out to prove the indigeneity of Jews in Mandatory Palestine by revealing historic Jewish sites in the country and giving their names to new settlements. The committee included members knowledgeable about the history and geography of Palestine, among whom were three Jerusalemite Jews well-versed in Arabic and Islamic culture: Meyuḥas, Elmaleḥ, and Yeshayahu Press.

The main principle that initially guided the Naming Committee in naming new Jewish settlements in Mandatory Palestine was to redeem the names of historic Jewish settlements from generational amnesia by establishing new settlements on the legacy of the old ones. If a new settlement, however, was not built on a site previously settled by Jews, the committee directed that efforts should be made to search for the nearest Arab site within a 3 kilometer (1.86 miles) radius and an investigation should be carried out to ascertain whether the Arabic name of that village was originally a Hebrew name that had been subsequently Arabized.[31]

The Naming Committee's choice to name a new Galilean settlement Beit She'arim (House of Gates) was influenced by a mix of historical documentation and the geographic location of a nearby Arab village. On March 18, 1928, members of the Naming Committee discussed the proper name to give to the settlement meant to accommodate Jewish settlers from Yugoslavia in southern Galilee. This land, acquired in 1926 and originally belonging to the Lebanese Sursock family, was sold to the Jewish National Fund and the American Zion Commonwealth. A debate arose between committee members about the most suitable name for the new settlement. Some members suggested naming the settlement Beit She'arim, adhering to the name's traditional roots found in Jewish texts such as the Talmud, Midrash, and works of Josephus. Joseph Klausner, though, challenged the correlation between the town "Besara" in Josephus's autobiography and the proposed site, as the nearby hill's Jewish necropolis was not definitive proof of an ancient Jewish settlement. Klausner favored a different name that did not depend on this uncertain connection. Yet Meyuḥas favored "the redemption of the historic name" instead of inventing a new name for the new Jewish settlement. Meyuḥas took his clue as to the accuracy of the geographic location of the site not from the Jewish texts only but also from an Arab village nearby named Jidda, whose inhabitants numbered over three hundred in 1925 and decreased to less than a hundred by 1931, a few years after it was sold to a Zionist organization. He contended that this justified the assumption that there once had been a Jewish settlement at that site in an ancient period.[32] In addition to Jidda, Meyuḥas found evidence of a historic Jewish presence in the southern Galilee town of Sheikh Burayk, which he abstained from referring to explicitly and instead referred to it as an existing town. Meyuḥas subtly used the town of Sheikh Burayk as a geographic and historical reference to indicate the Jewish site, though he downplayed the town's own history in favor of its utility in pinpointing the settlement's location. With the support of Press, who apparently sided with Meyuḥas, Klausner was convinced, and the majority of the committee members decided to call the newly established settlement of Yugoslavian settlers Beit She'arim as opposed to giving it another name. We see here that the identification between Sheikh Burayk and the historic Beit She'arim was established by members of the Naming Committee, like Meyuḥas and Press, based on the presence of an Arab town on the top of the hill almost a decade before the archaeological excavations that had been carried out by Benjamin Mazar, who discovered a Greek epigram that carries "Besara," the Greek name of the place.[33]

In addition to the institutional work on the hebraization of Jewish settlement in the land, individual Hebrew writers worked outside these institutions guided by the same principles highlighted above. If the priority of the Naming Committee was to limit its naming activities to those settlements built on lands purchased by the Jewish national funds, other Jewish individuals directed their efforts and energy to redeem the landscape from amnesia by taking clues from nearby Arab towns and villages in assigning Hebrew names to settlements.

Arabs and Popular Culture as a Source for Knowledge of the Land

Horowitz's dissemination of yedi'at ha-arets as a means for the restoration of Jewish connection to the land echoes Ben-Yehuda's earlier call to his fellow scholars to write about Palestine's physical features for a Hebrew-reading audience.[34] He noticed in his own time a lack of interest in learning about the land among his contemporary Jewish audience as well as the absence of a comprehensive work containing detailed accounts of the Palestine landscape. "Even though [nowhere land in the world . . . comprises such noble memories as our ancestors' land]," Horowitz remarked, "our literature does not contain even a single comprehensive book encompassing all the knowledge related to the study of the land." Astounded that a land so rich with history could lack a text that related its significance and importance, he urged the compilation of a work that would gather its "natural geography, the quality of the outcome of its soil, the study of its antiquities and the characters of its places in the past and present, and its history in general and in detail."[35] Horowitz stated,

> We want to know everything relevant to us in the land, from the past and present, in full detail. Since we want to live in peace and honesty with all of our neighbors who settle in the land, we want to know everything relevant to them. Everything, even the simplest in its value and the slightest of all, we should treasure and preserve. The work is so magnificent. We need to recruit the best of our forces. Every wise force in the land should bring us benefit and blessing. The work of the study of the land should fall entirely in the hands of Jews for the Jews. We should conquer *mada' ha-arets* [knowledge of the land]. And with respect to that, we should reach the situation where nations seek knowledge from us [literally from our mouths]![36]

If Jewish settlers saw in the conquest of the land a means for its redemption, in the worldview of Horowitz that redemption is only conceivable through his conception of the conquest of *mada' ha-arets*. Horowitz here identifies two interrelated categories of knowledge for his comprehensive enterprise. The first category correlates with the land and encompasses its circumstances throughout the ages, including the time when Palestine came under the rule of Islam. The pursuit of this type of knowledge had the objective of constituting historical continuity in support of the Zionist ideological claim that Jews' ties to the land had never ceased to exist despite being a minority in the land or distanced from it. Horowitz seeks to transform it into a Jewish land by "knowing it," through studying, exploring, and describing it for the Hebrew audience. This project also had the purpose of shaping the New Jew in accordance with Palestine's landscape, where the Israelite patriarchs were believed to have lived, and whose ways of connecting with the land were passed on and preserved in the lifestyle of Palestinian Arabs that must be redeemed along with the land.

The second type of knowledge relates to the land's inhabitants. His view suggests that the local population constitutes an integral part of the landscape. From the Zionist perspective, Jewish continuity is established by the revival of Hebrew place-names retrieved from biblical and postbiblical sources.[37] According to Horowitz, that continuity is strengthened further by collecting the toponymic data possessed by the local population. In keeping with this, he proposes to learn the customs and traditions of the locals in detail, including their ways of

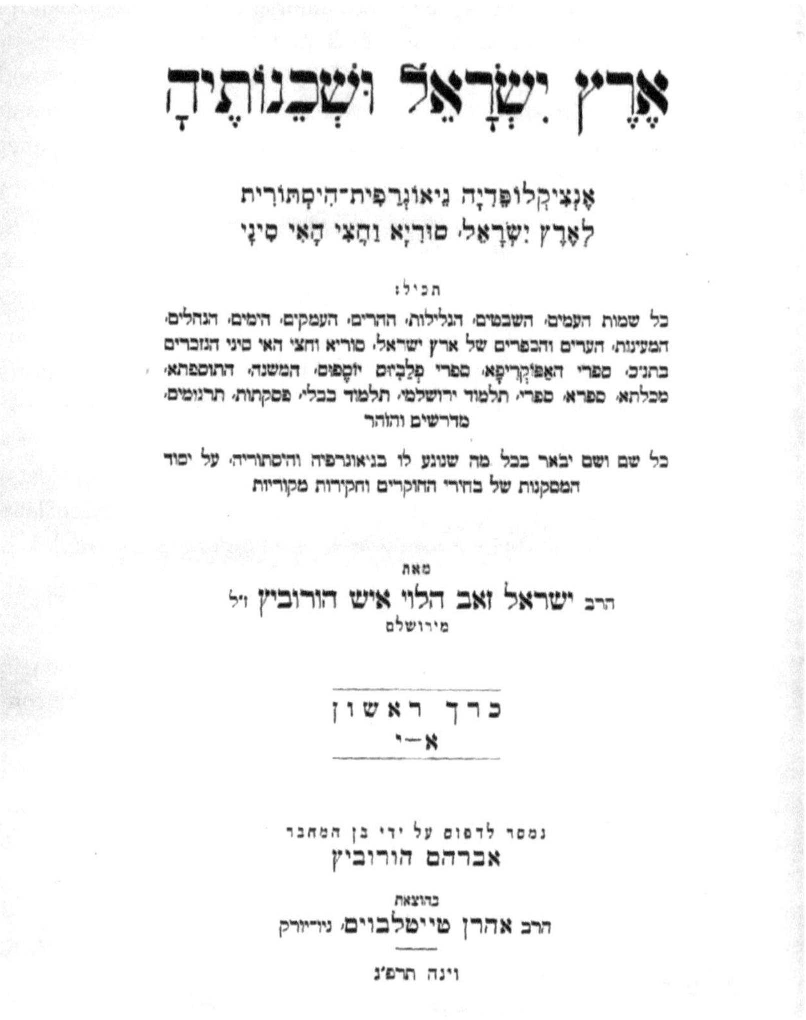

ארץ ישראל ושכנותיה

אנציקלופדיה גיאוגרפית־היסתורית
לארץ ישראל, סוריא וחצי האי סיני

תכיל:

כל שמות העמים, השבטים, הגלילות, ההרים, העמקים, הימים, הנהלים, המעינות, הערים והכפרים של ארץ ישראל, סוריא וחצי האי סיני הנזכרים בתנ"כ, ספרי האפוקריפא, ספרי פלביוס יוספוס, המשנה, התוספתא, מכלתא, ספרא, ספרי, תלמוד ירושלמי, תלמוד בבלי, פסקתות, תרגומים, מדרשים והזהר

כל שם ושם יבאר בכל מה שנוגע לו בגיאוגרפיה והיסתוריה, על יסוד המסקנות של בחירי החוקרים וחקירות מקוריות

מאת
הרב ישראל זאב הלוי איש הורוביץ ז"ל
מירושלם

כרך ראשון
א—י

נמסר לדפוס על ידי בן המחבר
אברהם הורוביץ

בהוצאת
הרב אהרן טייטלבוים, ניו־יורק

וינה תרפ"ג

FIGURE 4.2. The cover of Israel Wolf Horowitz's encyclopedic work *Erets Yisrael u-shekhenoteha* (The land of Israel and its adjacent countries). The book was published posthumously in Vienna in 1923 at the expense of Abraham Horowitz, the author's son, and was reviewed by a number of Western Orientalists abroad.

connecting with the land. While his account attests to the existence of people in the land with their distinct way of life, it also implies that those people are as static and unchangeable as the land they dwell in. Although he employs binary language in this epigraph, differentiating between Jews ("us") and the dwellers of the land, he describes the land's Arab residents as "neighbors" since some lived next to Jews, sharing the same land, while others lived in neighboring territories. *Erets Yisrael u-shekhenoteha* (The land of Israel and its adjacent countries), the encyclopedic work for which Horowitz is best known and most highly regarded, lays out the implementation of the requisites Horowitz stipulated in his programmatic essay on *ḥaḳīrat ha-arets* (study of the land). Horowitz's magnum opus was praised by his contemporaries as "a tremendous program," for the sake of the completion of which the author and his family literally went hungry during the Great War.[38] Horowitz compiled a comprehensive geographic and historical work that would include "the names of all the nations, tribes, districts, mountains, valleys, seas and lakes, rivers, springs, towns and villages" of Palestine and its adjacent countries. That meant that any geographic or historical name that appeared in the literature of Jewish religious and secular authorities would receive treatment, along with explanations of their "geographic and historical relations, according to . . . the most eminent authorities [and] the author." *Erets Yisrael u-shekhenoteha* thus combines ancient and recent data to craft a work attesting to the continuous Jewish history in the land. The textual sources on which the author draws are both Jewish and non-Jewish. As for the former, Horowitz lists in the front page of his work "the Bible, the Apocrypha, the writings of Flavius Josephus, the Mishna, Tosefta, Mechilta, Sifra," and various others as his point of departure in reconstructing a geographic and historical account of the land along with its environs.[39] As for the latter, Arab geographers and their works are referenced throughout the first volume of the encyclopedia.[40]

Erets Yisrael u-shekhenoteha evidences Horowitz's acquisition of Arabic—both spoken and written—and his comprehension of the culture of the land's residents in a manner that gives his work manifest weight. The introduction, though written by his son Abraham, explains his view of *yediʿah ʿaravit* (Arabic knowledge), and anticipates a multilingual reader who knows both Arabic and Hebrew. Abraham apologizes to the reader for not listing place-names in Arabic alphabetical form due to "technical reasons" that prevented him from using Arabic letters and vowels when he provided clarification on the Arabic transcription.[41] It is possible that his father might have followed Eliyahu Sapir's practice in his innovative work *Ha-arets* (The land) of listing Arabic place-names in Arabic letters along with their Hebrew names. Instead, Abraham includes a list of common keywords found in Arabic place-names that will help the reader identify Hebrew place-names with their Arabic equivalents to maintain a better understanding of the Palestine landscape and its connection to the land of the forebearers. The keywords are mostly in the form of prefixes to the multitude of Arabic place-names, such as *ʾab* (father of), *ʾom* (mother of), *bāb* (gate/door), *bīr* (well), *nahr* (river), and *nabī* (prophet). The keyword list is accompanied by a Hebrew translation, and not all the words share the same roots in Hebrew and Arabic.[42] Could it be that the depiction of locations and natural resources in Jewish literature, along

—) הארץ (—

	השם העתיק והעברי	השם הערבי *)	ערך המקום וקורותיו	מראה מקום	הערות
1		אַבְדָר ابدر	כפר בגלעד. (ארביד)		
2		אַבּוּ דִיס ابوديس	כפר אצל ירושלם. אנשיו ידועים למורי דרך להתַּיָרים. (ירושלם)		
3		אַבּוּ מַשְׁעַל ابومشعل	כפר קטן מצפון ירושלם. (ירושלם)		
4		אַבּוּ עֻבֵּיְדָה ابوعبيدة	כפר בהר הגלעד. (ארביד)		
5		אַבּוּ זְרֵיק ابوزريق	כפר של דרוזים בחורן. (חורן)		
6		אַבּוּ קַשׁ ابوقش	כפר קטן מצפון ירושלם. (ירושלם)		
7		אַבּוּ שׁוּשָׁה ابوشوشا			ראה גזר
8		אִבְטַע ابطع	כפר בחורן. (חורן)		
9	אַבִּילָה לְזָנְיָה	סוּק וָדִי בַּרָדָא سوق وادي بردى	חבל ארץ אצל דמשק אצל נהר ברדא. קליגולא וקלודיוס נתנו זה לאגריפא. היום כפר מצפון דמשק. תחנת מסה״ב בירות-דמשק. (דמשק)	קדמוניות יט 1.5	
10	אַבִּילָה	כַּפְר אַבִּיל كفرابيل	נודעת במלחמת אנטיוכוס עם סקפוס. היתה אחת מערי הדיקפולים. כעת חרבות יפות בגלעד. (ארביד)	קדמוניות יב 3.3 מלחמות ד׳ 6.7	
11	אָבֵל או אוּבְלִין	עַבְּלִין عبلين	עיר בגליל. ישבו בה יהודים רבים אחרי החרבן. היום כפר אצל צפורי. (נצרת)	תוספתא שביעית ז ערובין פז פסחים עב	נקרא ג״כ אבל-ערב
12	אָבֵל בֵּית מַעֲכָה	אַבִּל אַלְקַמְח ابل القمح	יואב צר עליה ברדפו אחרי שבע בן בכרי. כפר ידוע בימי הערבים. היום כפר גדול אצל מטלה. (גידידה)	שמואל ב, כ, טו קדמוניות ח 4.12	יוסיפוס קרא לה Abellana
13	אָבֵל הַשִּׁטִּים	כַּפְרֵין كفرين	עיר לפנים בעבר לירדן. תחנת בני׳. היום כפר ממזרח ים-המלח. (כרך)	במדבר לג, מט	
14	אָבֵל מְחוֹלָה	עֵין חִלְוֶה عين خلوه	עיר אלישע. כעת חרבה מדרום בית שאן.	מלכים א, יט, טז	
15	אָבֵל כְּרָמִים	בֵּית אַל־כַּרְם بيت الكرم	לפנים עיר. בה הכה יפתח את בני עמון. כעת חרבה בצפון כרך. (כרך)	שופטים יא, לב	
16	אָבֵל מַיִם	אַבִּל אַסַּקִי ابل الساقي	עיר בנפתלי. כפר בצפון גידידה. (גידידה)	דה״י ב, טז, ד	
17	אֶבֶן הָעֵזֶר	דֵּיר אַבָּן دير ابان	במלחמת פלשתים הגיחו עליה ארון האלהים. תחנת מסה״ב יפו-ירושלם. (יפו)	שמו״א ד, א ה, א	נקראת גם אבל הגדולה. שמו״א, ו׳ יח

*) עיד הקריאה הנכונה עיין במבוא הספר.

— 1 —

FIGURE 4.3. A list of Arabic place-names along with their Hebrew equivalents and their references in the Hebrew Bible in Eliyahu Sapir's *Ha-arets* (The land).

with the linking of Hebrew place-names to present Arabic localities, was intended to overshadow the latter in favor of the former?

For Horowitz, the model of an emerging Jewish settlement did not necessarily entail the eradication of the current population, whom he referred to several times as "the inhabitants" of the land, while also warning his audience about Arabs' deceitful nature and how difficult it was to get "the truth of their mouths." He advocated for the exploitation of Arabic knowledge as fundamental to the restoration of the Jewish past in the land. But the aims of the systematic allocation of places within the land and its adjacent countries were twofold, as he explains in his programmatic essay on *ḥaḳīrat ha-arets*. First, he wanted the Jewish newcomers to live in peace with their neighbors in the land:

> Everything is essential to know. We must know everything related to us in the land in the past and present, [in] minute detail. Since we want to live in peace and [prosperity] with all of our neighbors who [settle] the land, we want to know everything related to them. Everything, even the simplest, we should collect and preserve.[43]

Here, the pursuit of knowledge about the land would advance, in accordance with his vision, a future of peaceful and fruitful coexistence between Jews and the Arab population.[44] In his eyes, collecting and preserving all the details related to the Jews' neighbors in the land and the areas surrounding it would promote understanding, not from the Arab side, but from the Jewish one.

The second aim of the acquisition of Arabic knowledge was to trace the origins, customs, and habits of the biblical patriarchs through a segment of the native population, which could serve as a mediator. More precisely, to make possible the Zionist return to history, Horowitz suggested collecting information about the lifestyle of Arab farmers, the fellahin.

> Our [Jewish] farmers are very qualified to collect mass information regarding the fellahin's way of life in the land and their spiritual, economic, and social circumstances. From this gathered [information] we could extract a double benefit: first, we could understand the lifestyle of our ancestors, which is treasured in our ancient literature, and second, to know how to organize our future settlement in the land.[45]

Arab farmers in Ottoman Palestine made up 80 percent of the total population, and encountering them was inevitable. Therefore they occupied an important place in the Jewish imagination of themselves and their homeland as "mediators making possible the Zionist return to history."[46] As rightly claimed by sociologist Gil Eyal and attested to in the cited passage from Horowitz, the New Jews saw themselves reflected in the fellahin—a mirror image of their ancient selves, harking back to biblical times. The lifestyle of modern fellahin could connect the modern

Jewish settlers of Palestine with their biblical roots in the land of Palestine.[47] No less significant than connecting the New Jews to their patriarchs' past, Arab farmers' way of life could guide Jewish settlers' future in establishing agricultural settlements in Palestine while benefiting from locals' experience with the land.

In addition to the agricultural practices of the local population, their popular culture, including practices, beliefs, and oral anecdotes and folklore, was significant in reinscribing the Palestinian landscape with Hebrew place-names. In *Erets Yisrael shel zemanenu*, the association of Arabic nomenclature for places and natural sites (e.g., mountains, lakes, and water sources) with their Hebrew equivalents occupied a significant place. As Belḳind reconstructs the physical landscape of Palestine, he identifies natural sites with their contemporary, not historical, appellations according to "the Arab settlers of the land," employing this phrase frequently as evidence of the validity of the information. Hence Hare Yerushaliym (Jerusalem's mountains) were identified with Jabal al-Quds, Hare Ḥebron (Hebron's mountains) were associated with Jabal al-Khalīl, and Mount Ḥermon was Jabal al-Sheikh or Jabal al-Thalj.[48]

Contrary to the efforts of Belḳind and his ilk, members of the Naming Committee in the statehood era epitomized the official Zionist efforts to restore and disseminate what they deemed the original Hebrew names found in biblical and postbiblical sources as place-names in Palestine. In their efforts, committee members attributed a pivotal role to place-names in advancing their ideological and nationalist goals, emphasizing the Jewish connection to Palestine and fostering that link with Jews in the Diaspora.[49] In the process, Arabic place-names, while initially being of great consequence in the restoration of Hebrew place-names and thus that historical linkage, came to be considered, according to Amer Dahamsheh, a hindrance to the representation of Palestine as the exclusive homeland for the nationally defined Jewish people. Once the Arab connection was no longer useful to the Zionist enterprise, Arabic place-names and the history of their toponymy were intentionally effaced to distance these places from the Arab perception as well as draw them closer to the emergent Hebrew national consciousness. That tendency, as Dahamsheh has noted, evolved into "hostility and arrogance" at the hands of committee members, like Press and Vilnai, in the statehood era. In the new era, Arabic names symbolized "the illegitimate landscape whose story threatens the integration in the space of Zionism and disrupts the historical continuity of the Jewish culture in the land."[50]

The Arabic map of Palestine, unlike the Zionist-constructed map of Palestine, took shape, as the Israeli historian and political scientist Meron Benvenisti has demonstrated, through "an evolutionary process" integrating the "Arab geographical heritage" that long preceded the Muslims' arrival in the seventh century.[51] In his works, Belḳind sought the origins of natural sites by turning to the oral traditions of Arab inhabitants. What stands out in his work *Erets Yisrael* is the desire to explain the underlying connotations of Arabic place-names instead of using them as identifiers for Hebrew place-names obscured in Jewish sources. He describes the underlying wisdom of Arabic naming of several sites and identifies these places with their biblical equivalents. About the name Jabal al-Sheikh, he writes,

> Due to its great importance, it [Har-Ḥermon / Jabal al-Sheikh] is also known by several names: Senir, Seryon, Siaon, and perhaps also Amana. In Arabic, it is called Jabal al-Sheikh, which is to be translated into Hebrew as an elder among the mountains (*sheikh* denotes the head of the tribe or chief of the village among Arabs). Because it [the Mount] is covered with snow most of the year, it resembles the gray hair covering the head of an old man.[52]

Similarly, he embarks on a discussion of the various names for the Jezreel Valley in biblical references and their origins.[53] To him, the valley appears to be inhabited by Arabs who established a "town" at some point and called it Zirʿīn.[54] Belḳind also points out that the western side of the valley is called Megiddo, after a large city there, which was called Legio during the period of Roman rule. Then Belḳind explains that when Arabs inhabited the place (without providing specific dates for the settlement), they adopted the Roman name with a slight modification: it is now known as al-Lajūn.[55] In contemporary times, however, the Jezreel Valley has come to be known as Marj Ibn ʿĀmer (actually, Marj banī ʿĀmer), after a Bedouin tribe that settled on the site.[56]

The deployment of Arabic place-names in *Erets Yisrael shel zemanenu* includes not only places whose Hebrew names are known but also place-names whose Hebrew counterparts are unknown. Perhaps due to the limited nature of the sources, Belḳind could not successfully associate the names in this category with Hebrew appellations, or it is possible that these sites were established by Arab dwellers in places that had not been inhabited before the Arab settlement. In surveying the mountains of Transjordan, the author includes a long list of Arabic place-names without any associations with Hebrew. This inclination to refer to Arabic place-names alone appears several times throughout his work.[57] One example will suffice:

> Except for this mountain [Tal al-Sheikha], it is necessary to mention Tal Abū-Nida, whose height is 1,257 meters, Tal-al-Aḥmad, 1,238 meters, Tal-Abū-Yusūf, 1,029 meters, Tal Abū-Ḥanzīr, 1,164 meters, Hāmī-Korṣū, 1,198 meters, Tal al-ʿAkāsha, 1,060 meters, Tal Farsh, 946 meters, and others.[58]

Listing Arabic site names without assigning Hebrew names to them appeared in both the original 1902 edition of *Erets Yisrael shel zemanenu* and the Hebrew edition of 1928. In accordance with Arabic nomenclature, Belḳind provided an explanation of the Hebrew construction of the Palestine landscape, portraying it as a land inhabited by Arabs, and consequently undermining a view of the land as desolate and empty. That he maintained the same method despite the expansion of Jewish settlements and achievement of political gains—that is, the Balfour Declaration—suggests that his vision of coexistence with Arab inhabitants did not vanish with the disappearance of Ottoman rule but rather continued during the British Mandate and is in line with the British policy of dual society: an Arab one side by side with a Jewish one.

Legends found in Arabic sources were of use to Hebrew writers in establishing the linkage between Jews and Palestine. Horowitz's *Erets Yisrael* contains a substantial number of Arab legends connected to place-names within Palestine and its adjacent countries, whose heroes are figures believed by the Hebrew-reading audience to be "Jewish." In one place, for instance, while detailing the "magnificent" stone buildings in Baalbek, Horowitz pinpoints a certain building believed to have been constructed by Solomon in honor of the Queen of Sheba. In another place, also related to Solomon, Horowitz cites an Arab legend about the burial place of the king. According to that legend, a projecting rock in the middle of the lake of Tiberias is the tomb of Solomon.[59] What should be noted here is that even though the cited Arab legends may have originated in Jewish sources, Horowitz refrains from intervening in the narrative. Neither does he point out the sources from which the Arab legends sprang nor the transformation these legends underwent to offer evidence of the importance of Palestine in Islamic civilization. Horowitz's approach, as he mentioned earlier in his programmatic essay on *ḥaḳīrat ha-arets*, aims at the advancement of Islamic knowledge of the land without intervention on the part of the author. But there is more to it than that. The mere fact that he translated these textual accounts into Hebrew, making them accessible to a Hebrew-reading audience, was motivated by his aim to preserve Jewish manifestations within Arabo-Islamic culture. In so doing, Horowitz conveyed a sense of the deep-rootedness of the Jewish presence within Arabo-Islamic culture and continuation of the Jewish presence in the past.

Contesting Sacred Spaces

With the fall of Ottoman Palestine, the British Mandate nurtured sectarianism between Jews, Muslims, and Christians in the country—a viewpoint attested to by Wāṣif Jawhariyyeh, who lived in Jerusalem during the Ottoman and Mandate historical periods as well as identified with the Orthodox Christian faith.[60] Hebrew writers' adaptation of Arabo-Islamic materials took on a polemical tone in writings published in the second decade of the British rule in Palestine under the influence of the political and historical circumstances. The optimistic atmosphere at the sixteenth Zionist Congress convened in Zurich, Switzerland, stimulated by the developing economy and growing Jewish immigration, soon dissipated due to the disturbances of 1929, when a conflict over the religious rights of Jews to pray at the Wall intensified between Jews and Arabs.

For both Jews and Arabs, the Wall—known as such in the Jewish tradition—or al-Burāq Wall in the Islamic tradition—symbolized religious and national significance that intensified during and in the aftermath of riots in 1929, when the long-standing dispute about access to the Wall escalated into violence, triggering a countrywide outbreak of bloody clashes that engaged the British officials as arbitrators.[61] In the Islamic tradition, the Wall's sacredness derives from the belief that Prophet Muḥammad tethered to the Wall the flying steed he rode in his night journey from Mecca to Jerusalem, and from there, his ascension to heaven, commonly known as *al-isrā' wa al-mi'rāj* (The night journey and ascension). Scholars have argued that the identity of the Palestinian people consolidated around defending the sacred sites in Jerusalem, particularly Al-Aqsa Mosque and the Wall—a commitment that goes back to the twelfth and thirteenth centuries during the Ayyubid era.[62] Religious Jews and secular Zionists were divided about the significance of the Wall. Religious Jews believed that the Wall was the holiest site for the Jewish people as the remnant of the Second Temple built around 516 BCE, rebuilt and renovated by Herod the Great (72–74 BCE) and destroyed by the Romans in 70 CE (of which, as archaeologist Jodi Magness has indicated, no archaeological remains have yet been found); some even believed, contrary to the view long held by archaeologists, that the Wall itself dates to the First Temple, built by David and Solomon.[63] Since then, Jews in the Diaspora have regarded the site as a place of mourning toward which they direct their prayer wherever they physically are in the world.[64] Since the Middle Ages, Jews have prayed at the Wall thanks to the accommodations of Muslim rulers who allowed them to get closer to the Wall instead of directing their prayer from the Mount of Olives.[65] For their part, secular Zionists regarded the Wall as a national and historical symbol, a testament to the ancient roots of the Jewish people detached from Judaism's messianic roots and adapted instead to Western notions of the nation-state.[66] In his trip to late Ottoman Jerusalem to attend an audience with the German kaiser, Theodor Herzl's visit to the city was not uplifting. He was dismayed by the filth and squalor around the Wall, and hoped to "clear out everything that is not something sacred, set up workers' homes outside the city, empty the nests of filth and tear them down." He also aspired to replace these homes with a new urban plan: "I would build around the Holy Places a comfortable, airy new city with proper sanitation."[67]

The events of 1929, as Israeli historian Hillel Cohen argues, brought about a radical change in the relations between the two communities that shaped their conception of each other for decades to come. The events surrounding the Wall in 1929, observes Cohen, marked the start of "a journey to the roots of Jewish life in the Land of Israel, of the long-time Arab experience in Palestine, and the causes of violence and bloodshed between the two."[68] The creation of a historic narrative of Jews' connection to Palestine, as I have shown in the first part of this book, began in the late Ottoman era with a vision of a shared homeland and Ottoman Hebrews as citizens in an ecumenical society.[69] As demonstrated in the first three chapters, Ottoman Hebrews in this ecumenical society absorbed a significant amount of Orientalist fantasy regarding what "coexistence" should entail as they started to anchor their national claims to the land. In Mandatory Palestine, although Hebrew scholars continued to use Arabo-Islamic sources, the discourse intensified claims of Jewish ownership of sacred sites, overshadowing Arab claims to those same sites. Hence a shadow fell on the relations between Jews and Arabs within intellectual circles on both sides.

The Wall riots illuminated the role that Sephardi and Oriental Jews played during the British era as intermediaries between Ashkenazi Zionists and Palestinian nationalists as well as revealing the political, social, and cultural pressures this group experienced from both communities. During the riots, Sephardi and Oriental Jews suffered the most loss of life among the Jewish communities that lived in Jerusalem. This turn of events, as Cohen remarks, provided the Zionist establishment with an impetus to bring "the established Jewish communities in Palestine and the new Zionist community together under a single political roof."[70] Assaults on local Sephardi and Oriental Jews by Arab Palestinians, on the one hand, and their recruitment by the Zionist establishment, on the other hand, led local Jews eventually to throw in their lot with Zionists. As Abigail Jacobson and Moshe Naor have shown, Sephardi and Oriental Jews collaborated with the newly established Zionist entities to "examine ways of advancing rapprochement between Jews and Arabs in Palestine."[71] Their support of and collaboration with Zionist bodies, such as the United Bureau of the Jewish Agency and the National Council, the Arab Bureau of the Political Department of the Jewish Agency, and the Arab Department of the Histadrut (the workers' union), provoked criticism and recurring calls from Palestinian Arab spokespeople to abandon Zionism, denounce the Balfour Declaration, and return to the national struggle of the Palestinian national movement.[72] Palestinians' differentiation between European Jews and local Jews, as Cohen points out, started to wane in the aftermath of the 1929 riots when the nationalist common ground between the two communities began to overshadow their ethnic differences.[73] Indeed, these new Zionist entities persuaded local Jews to subordinate their own knowledge of Arabo-Islamic culture to the Ashkenazi Zionist decision-makers, who nevertheless saw fit to remove notable Sephardi and Oriental figures from leadership positions because of suspicions that they would side with Arabs.

When the disturbances occurred, Yellin had already been overseas for almost a year. While abroad, he was working on his research, participating in the sixteenth Zionist Congress, and carrying on business related to the newly established Hebrew University, taking part in other activities linked to the Jewish National Council (Va'ad Le'umi), of which he was then president, and collecting donations for *beit ha-midrash* (Teachers' School).[74] In a letter to Yehuda Magness (1877–1948), then the chancellor of the Hebrew University, after hearing of the turbulence at home, Yellin expressed his fear that "such revolution (*mahpekhah*) could uproot our labor in the land," pointing out that "the news published in the newspapers could anger [even] he who has nerves made out of iron."[75]

As a Jerusalemite Jew, Yellin was not immune from the suspicions directed toward Sephardi and Oriental Jewish communities at large. Indeed, Yellin was ousted from the presidency of the National Council, a position the Oriental and Sephardi community had relentlessly fought with Ashkenazi Zionists to obtain, as Abraham Haim has demonstrated.[76] The assembly of representatives found Yellin's leadership insufficiently tough toward the British and Arabs, and decided to hand the presidency over to Russian Jewish hydraulic engineer and political activist Pinḥas Rutenberg (1879–1942). Rutenberg was portrayed as *'ish ḥazaḳ* (a strongman) in contrast to Yellin, who was depicted as a lenient Arabophile. This change in position signaled a shift away from the Ottoman era leadership of local Jews to a new Ashkenazi leadership attentive to the needs and challenges of the Mandate period. Yellin's ousting from the presidency of the council was a huge blow to him as well as the Sephardi and Oriental communities.[77] Yellin's leadership of the council was a powerful marker that a Jerusalemite was the rightful representative of native Jews (*bene ha-arets*) in the land.[78] By the same token, his ouster from that position signaled the marginalization of Sephardi and Oriental Jews as a whole. The marginalization of local Jews went along with a shift in the National Council's policy toward Arabs from the dovish approach it had adopted since 1921 to a more hawkish line.[79]

While the changes discussed above adversely affected the leadership status of Jewish natives of Palestine, it also turned them into useful individuals in the service of Zionist institutions advancing claims to Palestine's sacred landscape by undermining the assertions of Muslim Arabs. The riots of 1929 landed members of the Sephardi and Oriental communities squarely in the middle of long-running religious and national disputes between Muslims and Jews over access to the Wall in Jerusalem. Several Sephardi and Oriental Jews asserted Jewish rights over the Wall based on textual evidence from medieval Arabic works commonly known as *faḍā'il al-Quds* (Virtues of Jerusalem)—literary works devoted to praise of the city that emerged in the eleventh century, composed by Jerusalemite Muslim scholars. *Faḍā'il al-Quds* accentuated the Islamic character of the city, ascribing to it the same sacred status as Mecca and Medina, given the long-standing perception of Jerusalem as the first of two prayer directions and the Noble Sanctuary as the third-holiest site in Islam. Over various historical periods, the Virtues of Jerusalem texts served as fundraising tools for the maintenance of the holy sites within Jerusalem.[80] During periods of strain, particularly after the 1929 Wall riots, certain historical accounts that medieval Muslim scholars had once borrowed from Jewish traditions (*Isra'iliyyāt*) were repurposed by Jewish writers. These authors reinterpreted the narratives in a way that supported Zionist claims to the key religious sites in Jerusalem, a city with a significant place in Islamic reverence. When modern Muslim scholars realized that these accounts were being used to advance Zionist ideology, they challenged the authenticity of the Jewish versions of these stories. They also encouraged their communities to dismiss and forget these accounts by emphasizing their Jewish origins, arguing that such narratives were not an integral part of Islamic thought and history.[81]

Isaac Yahuda and Yellin were chief among the Sephardi and Oriental Hebrew writers who dwelled on Arabo-Islamic texts from the literary genre of the Virtues of Jerusalem. Shortly after the disturbances, Yahuda published a comprehensive article on the Wall in the Hebrew journal *Me'asef Zion*, whose first issue was published in Mandate Palestine in 1925 to share research on the history of Jewish settlement in Palestine. The editorial board of the journal, which included Simḥa Assaf, Samuel Klein, and Ben-Zion Dinur, proudly connected their mission to that of the Jerusalemite Abraham Moshe Lunts, "who dedicated himself to study the land and the firm linkage between the inheritance of the land and its construction as well as the study of its history and its features." The editorial board indicated its interest in the inclusion of a section on "ethnographic and folkloric materials that contribute to the comprehension of visions of the national 'being' and its ways of expression."[82]

The appearance of Yahuda's article on the Wall fit perfectly into the program of the journal to include ethnographic and folkloric materials pertinent to "the land of Israel." Yahuda's view on the subject differed from Romantic Orientalism, which primarily sought to present the Arab world's point of view and customs through a lens of fascination as well as exoticization. In contrast, Yahuda's approach, as echoed by other Sephardi and Oriental Jews such as Yellin, Abraham Yahuda, and Meyuḥas, differed significantly. Their rhetoric aimed to highlight the importance of a cultural and moral renaissance rooted in the heritage and ethical principles of Middle Eastern societies. While Romantic Orientalism often treated the Middle Eastern cultures as subjects of curiosity, Yahuda and his contemporaries advocated for a genuine revival that respected as well as drew from the region's own traditions and values.[83] Yahuda underscored the historical connection between the Jewish people and the Wall by identifying the current Wall with the First Temple built by David and Solomon in accordance with Jewish tradition.[84] He supported this claim with textual accounts from Jewish sources along with Arabo-Islamic accounts that verify the accuracy of those Jewish texts.

Yahuda refers to a story from the Midrash Eikhah Rabba concerning an encounter between Rabbi Yoḥanan ben Zakai and Vespasian, who was a Roman

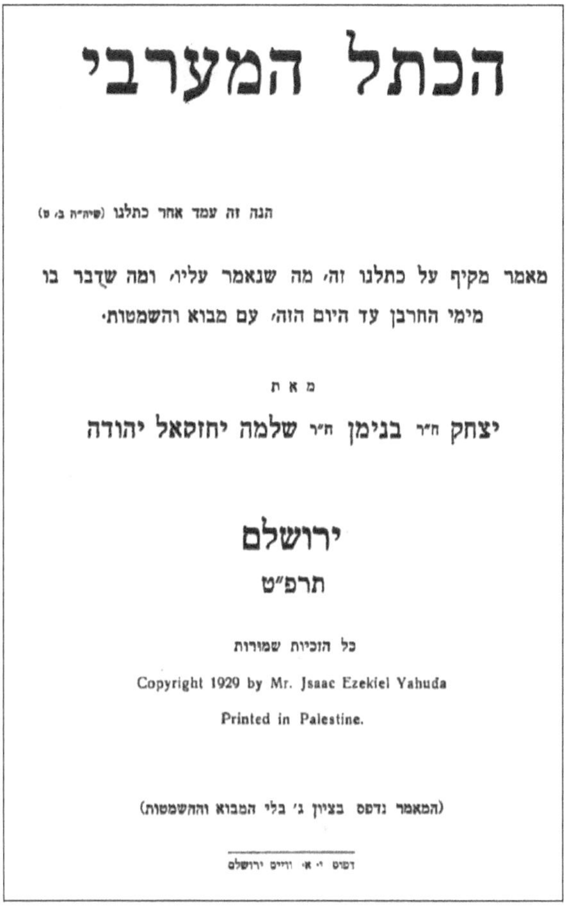

הכתל המערבי

הנה זה עמד אחר כתלנו (שיה״ש ב׳ ט)

מאמר מקיף על כתלנו זה׳ מה שנאמר עליו׳ ומה שדבר בו
מימי החרבן עד היום הזה׳ עם מבוא והשמטות·

מ א ת

יצחק ח״ר בנימן ח״ר שלמה יחזקאל יהודה

ירושלם
תרפ״ט

כל הזכיות שמורות

Copyright 1929 by Mr. Jsaac Ezekiel Yahuda

Printed in Palestine.

(המאמר נדפס בציון ג׳ בלי המבוא וההשמטות)

דפוס י׳ א׳ ווייס ירושלם

FIGURE 4.4. The cover of Isaac Yahuda's book *Ha-Kotel ha-Ma'aravi* (The Western Wall), published in Jerusalem in 1929.

general at the time, but would later become emperor of Rome. During their initial meeting, Rabbi Yoḥanan ben Zakai greeted Vespasian as "king," although Vespasian protested, claiming he was not a king yet. When Vespasian did indeed rise to become emperor, however, he remembered the rabbi's seemingly prophetic greeting and offered a reward. In this account, Rabbi Yoḥanan ben Zakai, recognizing the impending threat to Jerusalem posed by the Roman authorities, requested that Vespasian spare the city from destruction. Unfortunately, Vespasian denied this request. The rabbi then made a more modest plea: to spare the city's western gate, which faced toward the city of Lod. He reasoned that this would allow the city's inhabitants to flee and find safety, as anyone who could travel for four hours from this gate would be saved during the Roman assault.[85] The Midrash narrative further introduces Pangar, identified within the story as one of the four Roman governors assigned a quarter of Jerusalem to destroy after its conquest. Pangar's portion included the western gate. Yet according to the Midrashic tradition, a divine decree protected this gate from destruction because the Divine Presence (Shekhinah) was believed to dwell in the west. When Pangar was questioned by Vespasian about his decision not to destroy the gate, he argued that leaving it intact would provide a powerful visual of Vespasian's might while sparing the gate, only enhancing the emperor's image by demonstrating his ability to conquer and yet show clemency where he willed.[86] Yahuda supports the belief depicted in the Midrash that the western side of Jerusalem was spared from destruction due to the divine presence in that area, attributing religious and perhaps mystical significance to the survival of the western gate amid the Roman devastation of the city.

To identify the location of the western gate, Yahuda resorted to Arabo-Islamic sources and in particular to that literary genre of *faḍā'il al-Quds*, one of the recurring tropes of which is the city's unique role in the eschatology of the Day of Resurrection. A prophetic Ḥadith teaches that at the end of days, Jesus will come to Jerusalem to confront *al-dajjāl* (the false messiah) and stop his plans. Jesus will meet him at the Lod gate (*bāb Ludd*), where the Antichrist will melt like salt in water when he looks on his face. Yahuda connects ben Zakai's plea to the Roman emperor to spare the western gate that points toward Lod, with the Lod gate mentioned in the prophetic Ḥadith. According to Yahuda, the intended gate here is the Jaffa gate, which the Arabs call *bāb al-Khalīl*.[87] By citing this Ḥadith, Yahuda is calling his Hebrew readers' attention to the Muslim belief in the survival of the Wall since it was linked with events that will take place at the end of days, which also affirms the Midrashic claim that the survival of the site was in the first place a divine decree.

The British Commission of Inquiry was formed to investigate the reasons for the events surrounding the Wall. It heard evidence for several weeks, from 120 witnesses in public testimony and 20 behind closed doors. Yellin was among the witnesses on the Jewish side.

Yellin's appearance before the al-Burāq Commission, as it was called in the Arabic press, where he sided with the Zionist claims on the Wall, received attention in the Arabic newspapers. In their reports, he was given the designation *khawāja*, a form used for a foreigner in Arabic, even though Yellin was born in Jerusalem. When Yellin's testimony was published in Arabic by a press in Jerusalem run by Nissim Malūl, a Palestinian native, the latter was also referred to as khawaja.[88] Addressing both Yellin and Malūl as foreigners echoes Cohen's point that the 1929 riots radically altered local Palestinians' perception of the differences between local Jews, whom they used to call *abnā' al-balad* (natives),

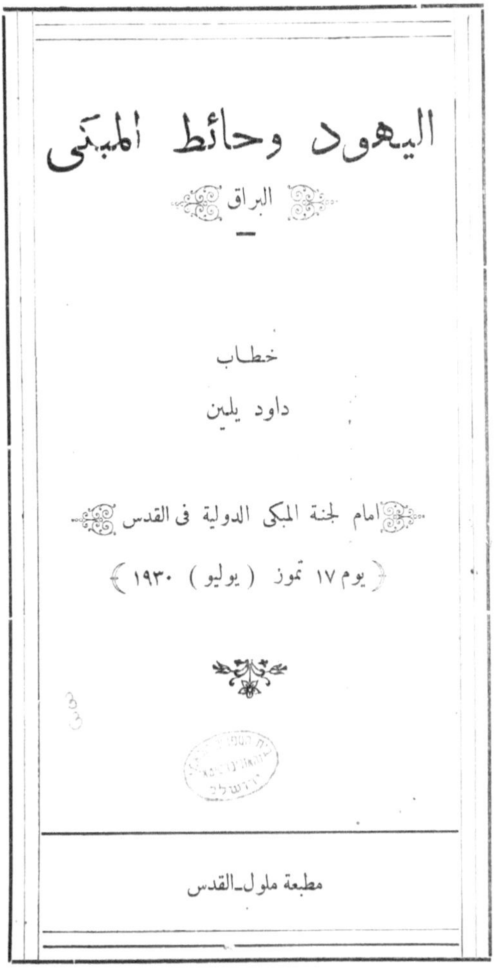

اليهود وحائط المبكى

البراق

خطاب

داود يلين

امام لجنة المبكى الدولية فى القدس

يوم ١٧ تموز (يوليو) ١٩٣٠

مطبعة ملول ـ القدس

FIGURE 4.5. David Yellin's testimony to the British Commission of Inquiry published by Nissim Malūl's press in Jerusalem in Arabic in 1930. To be able to convey his speech to an Arabic-reading audience, Yellin uses in the title both the Jewish and Islamic appellation of the site known in Arabic as, respectively, *hā'iṭ al-burāq* / *Kotel ha-bekhi* or *Kotel ha-dema'ot* (the Wailing Wall or Wall of Tears).

al-Waṭaniyyin (national Jews), or *al-Yahūd al-'Arab* (Arab Jews), and Ashkenazi Jews, whom they had always called *al-ghurabā'* (foreigners/strangers).

In his appearance before the commission, Yellin emphasized his indigeneity in Palestine and his Arabo-Islamic knowledge to establish himself as an authoritative voice supporting the Jewish claims in this quarrel between Jews and Muslims:

> I was born here and have lived among the notable Muslims and learned their language and literature. I continue to give lectures at the Hebrew University on the influence of their poetry on the Andalusian Hebrew poetry.

He also underscores, throughout the testimony, the commonalities between Judaism and Islam in his appeal to the sympathies of Muslim and Arab audiences. His speech highlights how Jews and Muslims worship the same God, whom he refers to as *ilāhunā* (our God), and venerate the same prophets such as Abraham, Isaac, and Jacob. The invocation of Abraham here reflects his understanding of Abraham in both Judaism and Islam as one person in agreement with the Maimonidean view. He indicates that the Muslims' veneration of the Temple Mount / al-Ḥaram al-Sharīf (the Noble Sanctuary) is in fact rooted in the Hebrew Bible, and suggests the inclusiveness of the Jewish faith to welcome non-Jews to Jewish sites. Yellin cites a biblical passage (First Kings 8:41–43) that relates a prayer of Solomon to God to hear the prayers of foreigners who visit his house, which in Yellin's understanding is the Temple Mount. Yellin levied a strong critique against the Arab community, referring to it as "that great nation" for its perceived misdirection of efforts. He contended that Palestinian Arabs were preoccupied with minor religious debates, such as whether to allow a partition at the Wall for gender-separated prayer, or the installation of seats for the infirm and elderly, rather than channeling their energies into more significant endeavors like unearthing the historical layers beneath the Temple Mount. Yellin openly called for Palestinian Arabs to fund archaeological digs at the site known to Muslims as al-Ḥaram al-Sharīf. His insistence on Arab-sponsored excavations in this holy area, however, was seen as an affront to the national and religious sentiments of both the Muslim and Arab communities. Such demands were perceived to further Zionist interests, seeking to establish historical claims to al-Ḥaram al-Sharīf by attempting to demonstrate that the Al-Aqsa Mosque stands atop the remnants of the ancient Jewish temple. Hence Yellin's propositions were viewed as an effort to bolster Zionist territorial claims at the expense of Arab and Muslim historical as well as cultural ties to the site.[89]

Yellin draws on Islamic sources to undermine the conventional Muslim interpretation of the sacredness of the Wall, a site that was considered holy because of its association with Prophet Muḥammad's tethering his flying steed there before embarking on his ascension to heaven. Listing the opinions of renowned medieval Muslim scholars, Yellin claims that they were not unanimous in identifying the location of the place where al-Burāq was tied up and in fact suggested different locations, including Solomon's Stables and the eastern side of the al-Ḥaram al-Sharīf, close to the Golden Gate and not the Wall.[90]

The accumulating Arab fears and anxieties regarding Zionists eyeing the al-Ḥaram al-Sharīf to take it over as part of their scheme to restore evidence of earlier Jewish presence would have been exacerbated by Yellin's calls to Arabs to busy themselves with the excavation of the remnants of the al-Ḥaram al-Sharīf, urging them to dig up the roots of the Jewish temple. Thus at the end of his speech before the commission, Yellin acknowledges those fears and appears to be at pains to dissipate them. As a representative of several Jewish organizations, including the Jewish Agency and Knesset Yisrael, he offers verbal assurances and promises that neither the Jewish Agency nor the Jewish people have an interest in taking over the al-Ḥaram al-Sharīf area. He emphasizes that Jews harbor no intention regarding the al-Ḥaram al-Sharīf, nor do they plan to turn the Wall into a temple, nor do they intend to weaken the terms of *al-waqf* (Muslim endowment) in the Mughrabi neighborhood where the Wall is located. All Jews want, he argues, is to continue praying at their holiest site as they had been doing for centuries, "to pray before our God with dignity and without interruption."[91] But here Yellin's assertion becomes disingenuous regarding Arabs' well-founded anxieties about the intention of Zionists. In fact, the fears of the local Arabs about being dispossessed of the Wall and the adjacent area are based on actual previous attempts by different Jewish figures to acquire the site. Indeed, Yellin himself was involved in an unsuccessful attempt before the outbreak of the Great War to purchase the Wall and the adjacent neighborhood that Yellin described as filled with "filthy houses that belong to al-Waqf."[92] And this effort followed earlier ones by Jewish philanthropists to acquire the holy site from the Ottoman authorities and local leaders.[93]

In 1930, Yellin's testimony before the British Commission of Inquiry was published in Arabic with the help of Malūl, a native of Safed and early supporter of the Zionist movement. In British Palestine, Malūl, by virtue of his Arabic proficiency and knowledge of Arab culture, was active in several Zionist organizations, such as the United Bureau of the Jewish Agency and the National Council, and managed Zionist-sponsored Arabic newspapers in an effort, as Jacobson and Naor have shown, to "bridge the growing gap between Jews and Arabs on the basis of direct links and contacts, based specifically on a common language, Arabic, and on shared culture and historical ties."[94] But in bridging this gap between Jews and Arabs along with creating a direct link with an Arab audience, Malūl circumvented Arab leaders and tried to gain unmediated influence over Palestinian public opinion, especially to convince them of the benefits of Zionism and the legitimate rights of the Jewish people to the land of Palestine.[95] The publication of an eloquent Arabic translation of Yellin's speech before the commission is manifest evidence of Malūl's dual objectives: to tarnish the reputation of Palestinian nationalists and promote the Zionist position regarding Palestine to the local population. This distinction between Palestinian nationalists and the majority of the Palestinian population, which had no stakes in politics, was acknowledged in earlier discussions in 1921 between leaders of the National Council, such as Yellin and Meyuḥas, and editors of Hebrew newspapers, like Malūl and Asher Sapir, who aimed at communicating their Zionist plans in Palestine to the majority Palestinian public instead of Palestinian nationalists.[96] Yellin's testimony portrays Palestinian leaders and Arab public figures from neighboring countries as *muḥariḍūn* and *muhayijūn* (instigators and agitators, respectively) who seek to incite violence between Jews and Arabs by turning a purely religious matter concerning worship into a worldwide religious campaign with the objective of demonizing the Zionist movement while mobilizing the Muslim world to support Palestinians.[97] Those "instigators and agitators" included Palestinian nationalists like Hajj Amin al-Ḥusseinī (1895–1974), to whom Yellin refers only as the person in charge of the Supreme Muslim Council without mentioning him by name; Jamāl al-Ḥusseinī, then the secretary to the Executive Committee of the Palestine Arab Congress; and those from outside Palestine who supported the Palestinian national movement and rejected Zionism, such as Egyptian Sufi Muḥammad al-Ghunemī al-Taftāzānī.

While opposing contemporary Muslim scholars who rejected his conclusions regarding the *marbaṭ al-burāq* (the location of the flying steed), Yellin cites the works of another contemporary Arab scholar who studied the history and architecture of holy Muslim sites in Jerusalem. Unlike other contemporary scholars whose testimony before the commission Yellin dismissed as compromised either by national and political agendas, or by their incompetence and ignorance, Ahmad Zaki Pasha acquired a unique position.[98] During the 1920s, the Egyptian state adopted a position on the Palestine question congruent with British policy, and maintained a strictly neutral attitude toward Palestine and Zionism, even inviting Zionist delegates to celebrate the coronation of the Egyptian king.[99] Accordingly, the Egyptian government recognized the British Mandate over Palestine in 1926 and raised no objection to the implementation of the Balfour Declaration with regard to a Jewish national home in Palestine.

As a former secretary of the Egyptian government, Zaki Pasha in 1922 congratulated the Palestine Zionist Executive for the recognition of the British Mandate by the League of Nations. In writing to Dr. David Eder, the secretary general of the Zionist Executive, Zaki Pasha is reported to have praised the victory of Zionism and the support it received from the British government represented by the Balfour Declaration. According to a report in the *Jewish Chronicle* (September 1922), Zaki Pasha interpreted the success of the Balfour Declaration as "a turning point for the fulfillment of an ideal which is so dear to me: the revival of the Orient."[100] Zaki Pasha concluded his letter by expressing his hope for the survival of the Zionist movement, which "will hold high the torch which will illumine a path for the East to noble and peaceful ideals."[101] Zaki Pasha's perception of Zionism and its ideals at the time emanate from the objectives of Jam'iyyat al-Rābiṭa al-Sharqiyya (Association of the Eastern Bond), which was established in 1922 to "elevate the Eastern nations by the means of science . . . and by strengthening the bonds between those nations, by reviving the civilization of the East and bringing it back to its virtues while absorbing the achievements of Western civilization that do not clash with the Eastern spirit." The mission of the Association of the Eastern Bond was "to disseminate Eastern knowledge and literature . . . and consolidate the ties of acquaintance and solidarity between Eastern nations irrespective of their different races or religions."[102] At this point, as Zaki Pasha saw it, Zionist aspirations coalesced with those of the association in terms of aiming to revive the Jews as an Eastern people. Given this perspective, association members were careful not to confuse sympathy for the Palestinian cause with their neutrality with respect to Zionism and Egyptian Jewry.[103]

Nevertheless, the attempts of Palestinian Arabs to pressure members of the association to support their cause ultimately bore fruit when they succeeded in soliciting the support of Zaki Pasha. The congratulatory letter Zaki Pasha sent to Eder made waves among Palestinian nationalists, who in two consecutive editorials published in the newspaper *Filasṭīn* (Palestine), demanded clarification from Zaki Pasha as to his stance toward Zionism.[104] At first, Zaki Pasha abstained from direct involvement and delegated his response to intermediaries like Sheikh 'Ali Surūr al-Zankalūnī (1872–1940), a member of the association of the Eastern Bond and a renowned scholar at al-Azhar. Ultimately, delegates of the Palestinian Committee including 'Isa al-'isa, the owner of *Filasṭīn* newspaper, accompanied by well-known writer Nissim Ṣibi'a, traveled to Cairo to meet with Sheikh al-'Urūba in his house in Giza, at which meeting Zaki Pasha was himself present. In the meeting, the details of which were published in a report in *Filasṭīn*, Zaki Pasha emphasized his steadfast support of the Palestinian cause, reminding his guests that he serves only the Arab cause and nothing else. He then explained that his positive approach toward Zionism stemmed from his perception of that movement as an integrative nonseparatist one, based on what he had learned from Eder, who denied that the Zionist movement aspired to obtain exclusive rights to or achieve sovereignty over Palestine and Arabs. Rather, Zionists desired peaceful cooperation with Arabs and the people of the East. Moreover, according to Eder, Zionist immigration should be subject to regulation, and Zionist settlers should abide by the rules of Palestine as their homeland.[105]

Zaki Pasha exemplifies the way Egyptian public intellectuals were subject to pressure from both sides. Both Zionists and Palestinian nationalists put forward their case in hopes of his support. Pointedly, after hearing Zaki Pasha's view of Zionism, the Palestinian delegates demonstrated that Eder had in fact betrayed him; Eder and other Zionist figures had made public statements contradicting their claims to desire amicable relations between Jews and Arabs. To support their argument, the delegates proceeded to share with their host the report of the Haycraft Commission of Inquiry that had investigated the Jaffa disturbances of 1921:

> Dr. Eder was a most enlightening witness. He was quite unaggressive in manner and free from any desire to push forward opinions that might be offensive to the Arabs. But when questioned on certain vital matters, he was perfectly frank in expressing his view of the Zionist ideal. He gave no quarter to the view of the national home as put forward by the secretary of state and the high commissioner. In his opinion, there can only be one national home in Palestine, and that a Jewish one, and no equality in the partnership between Jews and Arabs, but a Jewish predominance as soon as the numbers of that race are sufficiently increased. He declined to admit the word "dominion," but chose "predominance." As acting chair of the Zionist Commission, Dr. Eder presumably expresses in all points the official Zionist creed, if such there be, and his statements are therefore most important. There is no sophistry about Dr. Eder; he was quite clear that the Jews should, and the Arabs should not, have the right to bear arms, and he stated his belief that this discrimination would tend to improve Arab-Jewish relations.[106]

On hearing this evidence, Zaki Pasha became furious and put the report aside, saying, "I have been betrayed, and a believer can be betrayed."[107]

Against this context, Zaki Pasha promised to assure that the Palestine cause flew under the radar of the Egyptians. In 1924, he published an article stressing the territorial continuity and integrity of the Arab world. He sees Palestine as an integral part of Greater Syria (al-Shām), and in turn al-Shām as an indispensable part of "that blessed territory that expands from the Taurus Mountains in southern Turkey to El-Arish in northern Sinai and from the banks of the Euphrates to the shores of the Mediterranean." But the reality, as he admits, shows the fragmentation of Greater Syria, which he attributes to the intervention of Western powers in the region. He thinks that the imposition of the French and British Mandate as well as the division of Greater Syria into several states—Syria, Iraq, Jordan, Palestine, and Lebanon—leads to the construction of "small meaningless states" whose fates are their inevitable demise for "it contradicts nature," which is manifested in territorial continuity. While he is critical of Western intervention along with the imposing of the French and British Mandate, he also perceives them as "a vigorous earthquake that had returned to us [members of the umma] the feelings of solidarity to push against the aggression of strangers, those feelings that we had inherited from our ancestors." In his statements, Zaki Pasha insists on the unity of the Arab nation and denounces the vile scheme of Western intervention, but abstains from specifically addressing Palestine except in a secondary way. Palestine in his view is only "a branch in the lofty tree al-Shām" and thus does not constitute by itself an independent entity. In fact, the establishment of the British Mandate in Palestine, in his mind, is but an instrument "to cut the veins of that lofty tree [al-Sham] and dissect its body by dividing it into small states."[108]

Zaki Pasha was peculiarly suited to testify before the Shaw Commission (officially, the Commission on the Palestine Disturbances of August 1929) given his scholarship on the history and architecture of Islamic monuments in Jerusalem. In 1924, he had published his encyclopedic work *Masālik al-ʾabṣār fī mamālik al-ʾamṣār* (Voyages of eyes) by fourteenth-century Egyptian geographer Ibn Faḍl-Allah al-ʿUmarī. *Masālik al-ʾabṣār* contains a chapter on Jerusalem and its holiness for Muslims with meticulous descriptions of Muslim holy sites, such as the Dome of the Rock, the Wall, the Dome of Chains, Solomon's Stables, and other places. Indeed, Yellin cites Zaki Pasha in his testimony before the commission to support his claims to the Wall being the only remnant of Solomon's Temple. Zaki Pasha, commonly known as *al-baḥḥātha* (the eminent researcher) in reference to his scholarly rigor and dedication, brought his expertise in Islamic and Arab history to bear in his testimony. His unwavering support for Arab nationalism and belief in Palestine's centrality in the Islamic Umma made him a superb candidate to communicate the concerns of the Palestinians as well as counter the testimony of Jewish individuals such as Yellin and others regarding Muslims' claims to the Wall as a sacred site. Under the title "Sheikh of Arabism and the Holy Burāq," the Jerusalem-based newspaper *Mir'āt al-Sharq* (Mirror of the East) praised the efforts of "the master of Arabism" to muster, over the course of fifteen days of testimony, documents and historical accounts "to prove that the Holy Burāq (i.e., the al-Burāq Wall, which is the Western Wall) is an integral part of the Al-Aqsa Mosque."[109] Such was his effectiveness as a witness that during his stay in Jerusalem to give his testimony, Zaki Pasha received multiple letters and requests from various Islamic organizations to represent them before the commission

Yellin's publication of his speech before the commission in which he quotes Zaki Pasha to support his argument that the Wall is not the location of al-Burāq motivated Zaki Pasha to prepare a treatise in response, which was published by the Jerusalem-based press *Dār al-ʾaytām al-Islāmiyya* (Islamic orphanage), sponsored by the Islamic Supreme Council. As a pillar of the Association of the Eastern Bond who firmly believed in the renaissance of the nations of the East, including native Jews, Zaki Pasha seemed hopeful that Yellin, the Jerusalemite and scholar, would change his mind about his position once he read Zaki Pasha's treatise. First Zaki Pasha acknowledges Yellin's esteemed place in the Jewish society in Palestine and notes that he, "among the defenders of the Jews before the international commission, is one of the finest rabbis and greatest scholars." Then he draws attention to his linguistic skills: "He masters Arabic as much as Hebrew in addition to his knowledge of English and French." Finally, Zaki Pasha attests to his scholarly status in the Yishuv: "He is well-versed in the history of medieval Hebrew literature, a discipline that he alone teaches at the Hebrew University." In addition to referencing Yellin's erudition, Zaki acknowledges the amicable

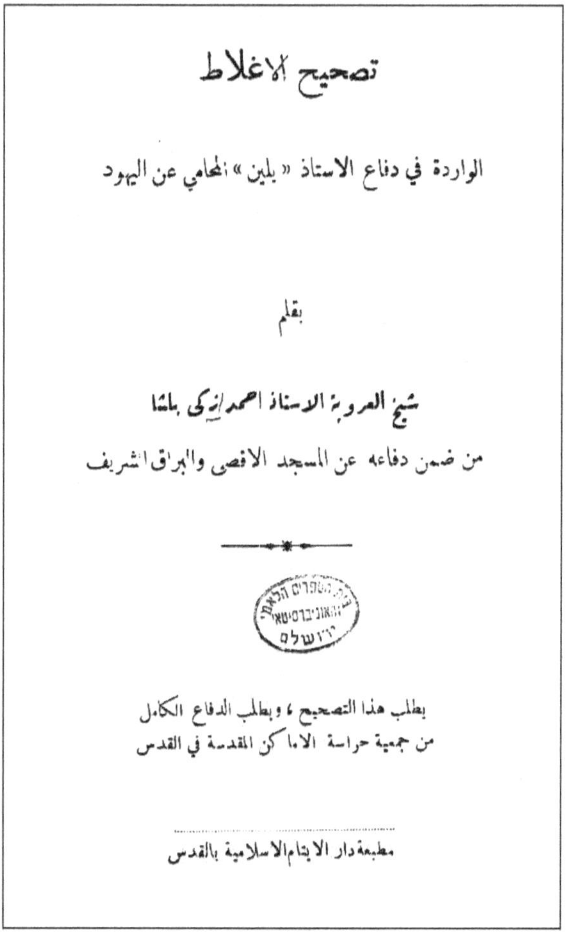

تصحيح الاغلاط

الواردة في دفاع الاستاذ « يلين » المحامي عن اليهود

بقلم

شيخ العروبة الاستاذ احمد زكي باشا

من ضمن دفاعه عن المسجد الاقصى والبراق الشريف

يطلب هذا التصحيح ، ويطلب الدفاع الكامل
من جمعية حراسة الاماكن المقدسة في القدس

مطبعة دار الايتام الاسلامية بالقدس

FIGURE 4.6. Ahmad Zaki Pasha's *Taṣḥīḥ al-Aghlaṭ al-Wārida fī Difāʿ al-Ustādh Yalīn al-Muḥāmī ʿan al-Yahūd* (Correcting errors occurred in the defense of Mr. Yellin the defender of Jews). In this book, Zaki addresses what he deemed to be false statements brought in Yellin's testimony before the British Commission of Inquiry in 1929. Zaki Pasha's book was published in Jerusalem by Dār al-Aytām al-Islāmiyya in 1930.

relations shared between them as Yellin was among the Jerusalemite Jews who frequented Cairo. Zaki says, "That is my old friend, the knowledgeable Dāwūd Yellīn, the possessor of leadership and power, and the one whose word is well received by his Jewish people."[110]

Zaki Pasha then expresses his disappointment with Yellin's decision to deviate from Arabism and throw in his lot with the Zionist movement. He accuses

Yellin of subordinating his Arabo-Islamic knowledge to advance the Zionist scheme to take over the Al-Aqsa Mosque by claiming Jewish rights and privileges to the Wall. According to Zaki Pasha, Yellin makes his case by twisting the authorial intention of medieval Muslim scholars to prove that *marbaṭ* al-Burāq—again, the place where Prophet Muḥammad hitched his flying steed—was not commonly identified with the southern part of the Wall but instead located elsewhere, such as Solomon's Stables or the Eastern Wall of al-Ḥaram al-Sharīf. Juxtaposing Yellin's published defense with the medieval works in question, Zaki Pasha shows that Yellin twists the cited sentences from *ṣīghaa iḥtimaliyya* (speculative or probable form) in which authors use the passive voice *yuqāl 'ann* (it is said, or it is told) into *ṣīghat jazm* (the assertive/affirmative form).[111]

Zaki Pasha's refutation of Yellin's testimony was not meant to alienate the latter. On the contrary, Zaki Pasha had faith that Yellin would change his mind once he realized that he had misinterpreted the texts, for Yellin had always followed the truth.[112] But Yellin did not change his mind. Indeed, he reached out to David Tidhar, a retired police officer who was living in Egypt in 1931, and asked him to disseminate his Arabic speech in popular newspapers in Cairo, which Tidhar managed to do in the British-sponsored daily newspaper *'al-Muqaṭṭam.*

Commemorating Jewish Heroes from Arab Lands

The narrative of Jewish claims to holy sites in Jerusalem, as articulated by Yellin, is steeped in a complex interplay between asserting Jewish ties to these places while simultaneously engaging with Arabo-Islamic scholarship. Yellin, a figure deeply rooted in Arabic studies and the regional intellectual milieu, attempted to fortify the historical connection between Judaism and Jerusalem using Arab-Islamic sources. His endeavors were part of a larger Zionist effort to establish Jewish historical and religious claims, specifically seeking to validate the Wall's significance to Jewish heritage. In stark contrast, the activities of the Jewish National Fund's Naming Committee demonstrated a different approach to anchoring Jewish presence in the land. This committee, charged with assigning Hebrew names to places in Palestine, often eschewed the rich tapestry of Eastern Jewry's historical and cultural contributions. By adopting new, sometimes Western-sounding names, there was an overlooked opportunity to reflect the deep legacy of Eastern Jews, who had significantly influenced Jewish thought and tradition. Such hebraization practices, while focused on knitting a distinct Jewish identity into the landscape, inadvertently neglected to honor the profound connections Sephardi and Oriental Jews had with both the land and broader Oriental context of Jewish heritage.

The efforts of the Jewish National Fund's Naming Committee to hebraize Arabic place-names or designate new names for settlements provoked criticism from Jewish scholars who saw this as disconnecting the Yishuv from its social and cultural context. One such scholar was Israel Ben-Ze'ev, a local Jew of Ashkenazi descent who had mastered both colloquial and standard Arabic in Jerusalem before pursuing his doctoral studies in 1922 in Arabo-Islamic culture at the Egyptian University in Cairo, where he studied under Ṭaha Ḥussein and Muṣṭafa Abd al-Rāzeq, and integrated into the local milieu of nahda intellectuals. Ben-Ze'ev's cultural projects in Palestine from 1938 onward, including an Arabic library, a research institute on Jews in Arabo-Islamic texts, and others relied greatly on his experience in Egyptian academia and integration into the nahdawi intellectual circles in the interwar period.[113]

In his post as a professor at the Egyptian University and an active member in several associations such as d'Études Historiques Juives d'Egypte, Ben-Ze'ev promulgated the integration of the Yishuv in the native culture and history of the Orient. In line with his ideals, Ben-Ze'ev criticized the Jewish National Fund's Naming Committee for failing to commemorate Jewish heroes who had lived and thrived in the Arab lands, and whose works are widely acknowledged and celebrated in Arab circles in Palestine as well as neighboring states, complaining that the Zionist movement had amnesia regarding Jewish contributions to Arab society in the pre-Islamic period.

The Naming Committee gave Jewish settlements erected on sites that had never been settled by Hebrews new rather than historical names. The committee followed nomenclature guidelines that commemorated a special Zionist or national event, or a figure who contributed to the Hebrew settlement, Jewish people (mostly western), or Zionist movement.[114] In 1937, during the heyday of the Arab Revolt, Ben-Ze'ev took issue with the Westernization of Hebrew settlements in Palestine on the grounds that such names displaced the Yishuv from its geographic place in the East. Specifically, he criticized Jewish institutions in Palestine for their obliviousness to the great Jewish figures who had played a central role in the Jewish and Islamic history in the past, and whose memory should be honored. Effacing the memory of these Jewish figures, in Ben-Ze'ev's perspective, was "a painful and a tortuous question." In an open letter he published in *Ha-arets* in 1937 during the time of the Arab Revolt, he observed,

> I would like to express my opinion about a painful question that has been torturing me for many years. In the land of Israel that is coming to revival, in the last few years, hundreds of streets were constructed in towns and villages that were named after towering figures of Israel who left their everlasting fingerprint on the history of the people of Israel. Oddly, throughout the land of Israel not a single street was named after one of Israel's heroes who emerged among Jews in the Arab lands. Have you not heard about what the Jewish king, Yosef Dhu Nuwās, had done for the Jewish Yemen? Have you not heard about

the well-known Jewish poet al-Samaw'al Ibn 'Adiyya' who sang a song of freedom and heroism for Israel in Arab lands?[115]

Obviously, certain members of the committee were not ignorant of these figures. Meyuḥas, for instance, had earlier contributed an article on the proverbial legacy of al-Samaw'al Ibn 'Adiya' and his poetry.[116] Likewise, Elmaleḥ surely knew about these historic figures. But these two members were a minority within the committee, whose decisions about place-naming were determined by the Ashkenazi majority. Apparently, both were overshadowed by the majority, which may have appreciated their knowledge of Arabic and Islam, but limited their influence in the decision-making process.

The Collapse of the Ecumenical Frame and the Evolving Landscape of Jewish Palestine

This chapter has focused on forms of interaction between Hebrew writers along with the natural environment and sacred sites in Mandatory Palestine through the exploration of texts on place-names and sites in the country. The continuation of the construction of Hebrew cultural imaginings of the homeland in the Mandate era involved the continual invocation of the concept and motto "knowledge of the land," a principle that had guided Hebrew writers in late Ottoman Palestine in restoring and enhancing Jews' ties with the land.

Whereas in late Ottoman Palestine, "knowledge of the land" consolidated Jews' ties to a shared homeland, an ecumenical society in late Ottoman Palestine where Jews, Christians, and Muslims lived together free from extreme sectarianism, the Balfour Declaration in the post-Ottoman era intensified competing national aspirations and kindled sectarian sentiments. As the Zionist movement turned fully political and became more viable, Hebrew scholars affiliated with Zionism mobilized Arabo-Islamic knowledge to promote the construction of the Jewish national home in Palestine while also minimizing or marginalizing the ways in which the local Arab population had identified with as well as enriched its habitat.

The events concerning the Western or Burāq Wall in 1929 brought to the surface competing claims and interpretations of specific sites in Palestine. In these confrontational episodes, Sephardic and Oriental Jews found themselves between the hammer and the anvil. On the one hand, their familiarity with Arabic and Arabo-Islamic culture made them valuable resources for the Ashkenazi Zionist leadership in its project of restoring the Jewish connection to Palestine and consolidating claims of indigeneity. On the other hand, that same familiarity with Arab culture made the local Jews attractive allies to Palestinian nationalists, who attempted to draw them closer to their national cause and urged them to abandon their ties with Zionism. As tensions erupted in Palestine, however, local Jews threw their lot in with the Jewish national movement. Consequently, Palestinians ceased to distinguish between local and foreign Jews. Yellin's testimony before the Shaw Commission on behalf of the Jewish Agency cemented this division.

The practice of naming places in Palestine after prominent Zionist figures along with milestones in Western Jewish culture and history was indicative of the direction in which Jewish institutions were taking the Yishuv—namely, away from its geographic location. Such practices, though, sparked dissatisfaction among local Jews who warned that severing the ties with the East completely would culminate in disconnecting Jews from a rich and valuable period in their history. Ben-Ze'ev warned against this tendency too, and advocated for the revival of the names of great Jewish figures who lived in the East and contributed to its culture as well as history by so naming certain streets in Jewish neighborhoods in Mandatory Palestine.

5

The Hebrew Construction of an Arabo-Islamic Literary Past

HEBREW SCHOLARS STUDIED, translated, explored, and exploited Arabic literature as a means to undergird their foundational objective to construct a Jewish nativity in Palestine and the region. Their engagement with Arabic literature was part of a broader effort to reinforce the narrative of return to and reconnection with the Orient, which was central to Zionism's core tenet of Jewish indigeneity in Palestine in accordance with Zionists' reading of the Bible. The return to Palestine was not confined to settlement of the land; it also involved utilization of the culture found in that land. This involved reclaiming Jews' identity as part of the Orient, central to which was the rich Arabic literary legacy. That legacy functioned as a repository of stories that among other things, attest to the long Jewish presence in the region. The engagement with Arabic literature, including Arabic proverbs and *The Arabian Nights* in the Mandate period, then, served as a strategic avenue for Hebrew writers to assert a sense of Jewish nativity and authenticity by drawing on textual evidence from the very cultural milieu they sought to associate with.

This chapter examines two Jewish writers who viewed themselves as an indispensable part of the Orient, and drew on Arabic texts, including folkloric materials and fictional literature, to reconstruct the literary and historical past of the Jewish people in the East. At the center of their discussions lay fundamental issues that preoccupied Jewish circles in Palestine: first, familiarity with Arab social, cultural, and religious characteristics to inform strategies for coexistence or confrontation; second, claims to historical rights to Palestine through the retrieval of native Jews' presence in folkloric Arabic materials; third, the construction of the New Jew rooted in Oriental culture and framed as the natural successor to the land; and finally, an understanding of the Hebrew Bible gleaned from the broader social and cultural context of the Orient.

This chapter looks at the engagement of Jerusalemite writers Isaac Yahuda and Yosef Yo'el Rivlin with Arabic literature, as embodied in translations, critical analysis, collections, and commentaries published by Hebrew publishing houses and circulated in Mandate Palestine. Both authors were abreast of the local intellectual and cultural developments, and their efforts to revive Hebrew culture paralleled those of the revivers of Arabo-Islamic heritage (*turāth*) as part of the Arab Renaissance movement in major cultural centers in the region, including Cairo, Beirut, and Baghdad. In those cultural centers, book collectors and scholars harmonized activities in the literary revival movement *ḥarakat iḥyā' al-'ādāb al-'arabiyya*, championed in the first quarter of the twentieth century by the efforts of Ahmad Zaki Pasha and Ahmad Taymūr, among others.[1]

Yahuda settled in Cairo in 1906, and established himself as a dealer in Arabic, Hebrew, and Persian books, with a plan to create a European-model membership library.[2] During his years in Cairo, from 1906 to 1919/20, he successfully developed social and cultural connections with major nahdawi authors and publishers, and took part in the preservation of turāth through the publication of *al-Madhnūn bihi 'alā Ghayr Ahlihi* (1913–15).[3] Yahuda demonstrated, in the eulogizing words of a contemporary, Isaac Ben-Zvi, president of the Jewish National Council, the "unique skill" of being able to draw from "the depth of being of the neighbors, the Bedouin tribes, the farmers, and the city dwellers, the shared tradition of the Semites and Hebrews to extract the hidden light in them to illustrate ambiguities in the Bible." Furthermore, Ben-Zvi notes that Yahuda personally embodied the indigeneity of Jewish ancestors in Baghdad and the East. Yahuda himself is described as a Jew who "could trace his descent from a line of Rabbis who lived in Palestine since the Babylonian period."[4] Lamenting the diasporic Ashkenazi Jews' lack of Oriental social and cultural values, he champions Yahuda as a model to emulate, through whom Jewish immigrants could recuperate their Indigenous character.[5] Ben-Zvi here instrumentalizes Yahuda's identity by using him as a symbol of what Ashkenazi Jews should strive for. His invocation of Yahuda's identity and practices are not being valued for their own sake but rather as tools for the political or ideological aims of the Zionist movement, particularly in its efforts to establish a cohesive national identity that resonates with claims to the land.

Yo'el Rivlin was born in Jerusalem, where he became culturally and socially connected to the circle of Sephardi and Oriental intelligentsia, including figures such as Isaac Yahuda, his brother Abraham Yahuda, David Yellin, and Yosef Meyuḥas.[6] He became conversant in Arabic through contact with Arab families in Jerusalem such as the al-Ḥusseinīs and al-Khālidīs, with whom he developed personal relationships and became "close . . . from internal attraction." He consolidated his knowledge through friendships with Arab students, such as Ḥilmī al-Ḥusseinī, who taught him Arabic in exchange for Hebrew.[7] Additionally, studying with Arab students who were enrolled in predominantly Jewish schools helped Rivlin become more familiar with Arabo-Islamic culture. Rātib al-Khālidī, for instance, studied at the non-Zionist Hilfsverein der deutschen Juden or Beit ha-Sefer shel Ezrah (Ezrah School).[8] The inclusion of both non-Jewish and Jewish students from various backgrounds was a point of pride at this school, whose principal, Ephraim Cohen, celebrated its plurality. Indeed, when guests visited, Cohen would proudly introduce three students as "the best of the best": Rātib al-Khālidī, Elyahu Elyashar, and Rivlin—an Arab, a Sephardi, and an Ashkenazi Jew.[9]

Another institution that contributed to the dissemination of Arabic and Islamic knowledge in twentieth-century Palestine was the *madrasa*, which was designed to teach advanced studies in Islamic sciences and Arabic language.[10] Rivlin's experience in Jerusalem grounded his familiarity with Islam and its culture beyond the sort of practical knowledge that could be gained from daily life alone. In his adolescence, Rivlin joined the Islamic school Rawḍat al-maʿārif (Garden of Knowledge), where he remained a student for about a year, acquiring the foundation of his knowledge of Arabic and Islam.[11] Rivlin received kind treatment from the head of the school, Sheikh Muḥammad al-Ṣāliḥ (1867–1940), a man "with [a] patriarchal personality," who treated him in the "spirit of fatherhood."[12] Founded in 1906 by a number of leading Palestinian elites—al-Ṣāliḥ, Ḥasan Abū al-Suʿūd (1897–1957), Muḥammad Isḥāq Darwīsh (1896–1974), and ʿAbd al-Laṭīf al-Ḥusseinī—Rawḍat al-maʿārif emerged as a school specifically concerned with the dissemination of Arabic and Islamic studies in Jerusalem.[13] Rivlin's enchantment with Arabo-Islamic culture led him to continue his studies at the University of Frankfurt in Germany. After finishing his studies, Rivlin became first a research assistant and then a professor at the Hebrew University.

The discussion in this chapter will reveal how both writers' works contributed to the Zionist discourse that mirrored that of Arab nahda circles. As mentioned above, that discourse was concerned with the construction of the New Jew by way of reclaiming the old Jew—which involved utilizing Arabic literary texts to recover moral virtues to which Jewish ancestors once adhered and that survived only in the character of Jews who remained in the Orient as well as in their Arab neighbors, but were lost in exile, according to Ben-Zvi.[14] First, we will examine Arab popular culture and various Hebrew engagements with it by exploring Yahuda's involvement with Arabic proverbs along with the retrieval of the Jewish place within those cultural materials. Second, this chapter will analyze Yo'el Rivlin's Hebrew translation of the *Nights.*

Arabic Proverbs as Cross-Cultural Discourse

Proverbs reflect the social and cultural life of a given society, and reveal the characteristic structures of its thought.[15] The literary beauty and universality of proverbs, as Andalusian anthologist Ibn ʿAbd Rabbih (860–940) notes in *Al-ʿiqd al-farīd* (The unique necklace), lies in their brevity. In his words,

> Proverbs are the embellishment of speech, the gem of utterance, and the jewel of meaning, which Arabs selected and non-Arabs advanced. Over the course of time, all languages have uttered them. They are longer lasting than poetry and the most noble form of rhetoric. There is nothing so widely disseminated as they, nor so universally spread.[16]

For Abū 'Ubayd (d. 838), a medieval Arab paroemiographer, three characteristics define *mathal* (proverbs) in Arabic: metaphoric expression (*tashbīh*), succinctness or brevity (*ījāz al-Lafẓ*), and wide familiarity (*sā'ir*).[17] Many centuries later, Abū 'Ubayd's definition would be adopted by Yahuda in his collection of Arabic proverbs, *Mishle 'Arav* (Proverbia Arabica).[18]

Arabic proverbs attracted the attention of premodern European Orientalists following the publication of *Adagiorum chiliades* (Thousands of proverbs) by Dutch theologian Erasmus Roterodamus (1466–1536). European interest in this literary genre grew steadily after the first translation of a paroemiography of Arabic proverbs at the end of the sixteenth century. Recognizing the value of proverbs as a window into a culture, European Orientalists systematically collected and encouraged their students to learn them.[19] The European interest in Arab folklore was a manifestation of the Romantic interest in folk culture "as a bygone way of life that had been disturbed by the industrial revolution."[20]

Fin de siècle Arab nahdawis found Arabic proverbs a vital repository for their culture that they deemed fundamental in the context of nation building as part of the construction of a literary and historical past. Egyptian intellectuals and political leaders from the 1870s onward, as historian James Jankowski observes, formulated and disseminated a "vivid sense of the historical as well as the contemporary uniqueness of the land and the people of Egypt." Jankowski posits that the primary aim of early Egyptian nationalist intellectuals was to highlight "the historical, the geographical, and political distinctiveness of Egypt and its inhabitants."[21] Interestingly, the introductions to works on Arabic proverbs produced during this period often adopt and adapt European concepts of homeland and patriotism. In *Kitāb Amthāl al-mutakallimīn min 'awām al-miṣriyyīn* (A book of sayings of the Egyptian common people) by linguist Maḥmūd 'Umar al-Bājūrī, published in Cairo in 1889, the author advances the idea that nations' diversity and distinctive customs as well as mannerisms are expressed in common sayings:

> Since every people (*qawm*) has customs and manners with which they comply, and states to which they adhere, and from which they will not deviate; and while all people have been tempted by patriotic (*waṭaniyya*) customs and traditions until they rush to them without forethought, the essential evidence for these customs is what people employ in terms of parables.[22]

This quotation echoes the discourse of Egyptian nationalist intellectuals who advocated for the creation of distinctive Arab provinces comparable to the states of the European continent. The employment of *waṭaniyya* (patriotism) builds on Rifāʿa al-Ṭahtāwī's idea that "the earth was comprised of countries with their special characteristics, and that inhabitants of each country had a peculiar relationship to and a special love for it."[23] These Arabic proverbs provide evidence for the distinctiveness of Egyptians in terms of their customs and mannerisms.

Another example of Arab intellectual interest in proverbs, although with an emphasis on the development and variations of Arabic, is found in the work of Lebanese scholar Naʿūm Shuqayr (d. 1922). In *Amthāl al-ʿawām fī Miṣr wa-al-Sūdān wa-al-Shām* (1894) (On the proverbs of the masses in Egypt, Sudan, and Sham), Shuqayr says,

> Proverbs are the most important element that should be known about the literature of (*al-qawm*) a people, for they function as a mirror that reflects their manners and customs, as well as [functioning as] a just witness for the state of their language. Therefore I have decided to include a collection of modern proverbs in my book.[24]

Thus beyond their value as a source for understanding the social and moral life of the people of the Arab provinces, Arabic proverbs attest to the state of the Arabic language.

While Arab intellectuals looked to proverbs to articulate the distinctiveness of the inhabitants of Arab provinces, Yahuda believed that Arabic proverbs were the literary expression of a wider Oriental Weltanschauung. Believing that Easterners shared common ground beneath their complex differences, Yahuda published his crowning achievement, the collection of Arabic proverbs *Mishle ʿArav*, in 1932.[25] As a Jew and product of Oriental culture, Yahuda possessed a dual identity without internal contradiction. He maintained this hybrid identity by fusing Jewish culture with the cultural world of the Orient. His interest in Oriental paroemiography sprang from his identification with the Oriental culture of the geographic territory known today as the Middle East and North Africa as well as its inhabitants, irrespective of their ethnicity and religious affiliation. His collection of proverbs represents an endeavor to cross the boundaries between Jews and Arabs, and Hebrew and Arabic. Similar to other works published by native Jews in Morocco with the mission to shield the eroded Eastern identity from the process of Westernization, Yahuda's project can be viewed as one mirroring these projects.[26]

Yahuda's connection with the Orient stemmed from his familial and historical ties to those regions. His ancestors hailed from Baghdad and settled in Jerusalem in the mid-nineteenth century; they contributed to that city's urbanization and the vibrancy of its spiritual life through his grandfather's establishment of a

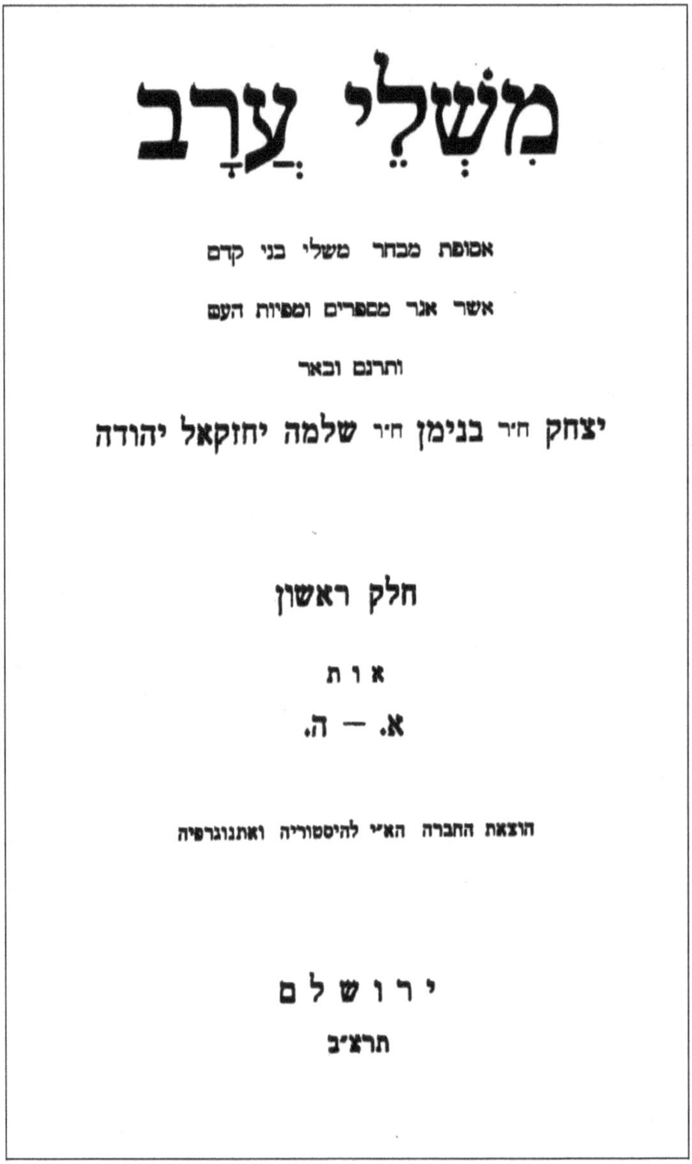

משלי ערב

אסופת מבחר משלי בני קדם

אשר אגר מספרים ומפיות העם

ותרגם ובאר

יצחק ח״ר בנימן ח״ר שלמה יחזקאל יהודה

חלק ראשון

אות

א. — ה.

הוצאת החברה הא״י להיסטוריה ואתנוגרפיה

ירושלם

תרצ״ב

FIGURE 5.1. The book cover of Isaac Yahuda's *Mishle 'Arav* (Proverbia Arabica), published in 1932 in Jerusalem.

yeshiva at his own expense. Yahuda himself was born and raised in Jerusalem, and identified himself as al-Maqdisī (the Jerusalemite) in some of his works.[27] In his forties, he settled in Cairo and remained proud of this connection, as evidenced by his retention of a Cairo address on his letterhead even after he left Cairo for Jerusalem. His wife, Vaida, with whom he had eight children, was the daughter of a Moroccan Jew who settled in Jerusalem in the nineteenth century.[28]

Yahuda embraced the idea that the advent of Islam and spread of Arabs in the Orient did not necessarily eclipse or replace the previous cultural, social, and intellectual currents that had already shaped the identity of the people of the region. Moreover, the presence of a significant Jewish population throughout the Orient at that time, which had become variously integrated into local subnational groups, suggests that Yahuda found an amplified significance in the study of folklore. His interest reflects a dual concern: to understand how Jewish communities maintained their identity amid the broader Arabo-Islamic culture and explore how they contributed to the cultural tapestry of the Orient. His crossing of Jewish and Arab cultural boundaries, while remaining in the Orient, manifests in various ways. First, we see it in his employment of Arabic proverbs as a medium of communication between the people of the Orient, but second, in the adaptation of a number of proverbs for the purpose of enriching biblical interpretation. Finally, Arabic proverbs reveal how Jews were viewed by the region's other inhabitants.

Mishle 'Arav and the Orient

Yahuda's interest in the cultural and social practices of native Jewish communities within Arabo-Islamic culture was influenced in part by his examination of both Jewish and Arabo-Islamic ethnographic and folkloric sources that depicted the relationships between different religious and cultural groups in the East. Unlike the Romantic Orientalism that presented Arab culture and customs through the prism of otherness, Yahuda's rhetoric, which was shared by other Sephardi and Oriental Jews, such as Yellin, Abraham Yahuda, and Meyuḥas, called for a cultural and moral reawakening based on the shared values and culture of the East.[29]

The rich repository of proverbs that Yahuda collected from both oral and literary sources renders *Mishle 'Arav* a window into the multifaceted intercommunal life of the people of the Orient—*bene ḳedem* (people of the East), to use his phrase. Nevertheless, the majority of the Arabic proverbs are presented as providing insights into specifically Arab social and cultural life:

> The proverbs are the wisdom of the [Arab] people and an expression of their taste, their character, and their customs; they are the essence of their perspective and the nature of their spirit, and the judgment of their morals; they are the torches that illuminate into the chambers of their soul and the cords of

> their heart. Through them, we learn to know the history of the people and their moral standing on the ladder of civilization. They clearly show us the inner life of the people, which is unknown to us even though we live among them and walk with them every day. As the saying goes: "Proverbs are the illumination of speech."[30]

Despite his hybrid identity, Yahuda addresses the Hebrew reader employing the dichotomy of "us," the Jews, versus "them," the Arabs, when emphasizing the importance of Arabs' proverbial lore. Undoubtedly, the national tension escalated between Jews and Arabs in Mandate Palestine, particularly after the Wall disturbances of 1929 had widened the rift between the two communities and created a sense of otherness. After the event, certain Sephardi and Oriental Jewish intellectuals, such as Yahuda and Yellin, published works that drew on Arabo-Islamic sources to consolidate Jewish claims to the Wall, a site deemed sacred by both Jews and Muslims.[31] According to Yahuda, the Arab other should not be dismissed or ignored. Rather, the Arab's mind and psyche should be studied in hopes of establishing a bridge between the two communities. Yahuda posits that proverbs are a concentrated form of collective wisdom that encapsulates the values, aesthetics, and behavioral norms of a people. Hence by studying these, one gains insight into what the Arab community esteems along with how it perceives itself and the world. Proverbs yield access to "the inner life of the people, which is unknown to us even though we live among them and walk with them every day"—but we should keep in mind that such access can be used strategically to gain knowledge that could facilitate both engagement with and potential control over the local population. This can be associated with the broader settler colonial goal of consolidating power within the colonized space, with its inherent power dynamics and complexities in British Palestine, where the Yishuv was more resourceful and more supported by the British authorities than Arab society.

In bringing together proverbs by Muslims, Christians, and Jews, *Mishle 'Arav* resembles medieval works on proverbs such as *al-Tamthīl wa-al-muḥāḍara* (The book of exemplification and discussion) by linguist and literato Abū Manṣūr Ismā'īl al-Tha'labī (961–1038), whose works attracted the attention of Orientalists and scholars in the nahda movement, and were published and edited in both the West and East. A significant parallel between the two works is their comprehensive nature, collecting proverbs that crossed social, cultural, and religious boundaries of the nations of the East. Al-Tha'labī notes in his introduction that he collects proverbs (*tamthīl*) from a wide range of sources, including the Quran, Torah, Gospels, and Psalms as well as sayings of prophets, kings, sages, philosophers, scholars, poets, common people, and people of various professions.[32] This comprehensive approach is also evident in Yehuda's complete title: *Mishle 'Arav: asufat mivḥar mishle bene ḳedem* (Proverbia Arabica: A collection of the sons of the Orient's proverbs). The phrase *bene ḳedem* is important here. For someone like Yahuda, who was well-versed in the study of the Jewish tradition, the phrase alludes to the biblical reference to Job: *wayhi ha'ish ha-hu gadol mi-kol bene ḳedem* (That man was wealthier than anyone in the East) (Job 1:3). The character Job, found in the writings (*ketubim*) in the Hebrew Bible, is part of the wisdom literature of the ancient East. Though he is not an Israelite, Job belongs to a broader ancient Near Eastern tradition. With connection to the Orient, *Mishle 'Arav* comprises Arabic proverbs employed and circulating among the various peoples of the Orient, including Jews, Christians, and Muslims. The use of *bene ḳedem* along with the inclusion of sayings by the peoples of the Orient translated into Hebrew and accompanied by Hebrew commentary is part of the construction of a Jewish character who belongs organically to the Orient. The proverbs served to situate the Jewish people firmly among the peoples of the Orient and acculturate them to the East. In so doing, the proverbs assist the project of Jewish self-indigenization after millennia of exile, according to the Zionist claim.

Yahuda's collection of proverbs played a role in the Jewish nation-building process, which echoed to an extent that which was simultaneously taking place among nahda Arab intellectuals. The Arabic proverbs collected from various locales constitute a repository of practices, traditions, and customs of the people of the Orient, including Jews, and a resource for the reconstruction of the Jewish character. The paroemiography testifies to Yahuda's conversance with Judeo-Islamic sources, particularly his intimacy with Arabic and Hebrew, as evidenced in the countless commentaries he provides in addition to the variety of sources he uses, which range from oral to written sources, premodern to contemporary.[33] His commentaries illustrate the degree to which both cultures were intertwined such that each contributed to the clarification of the other.

What adds value to the work is its impact on the intellectual sphere of the Hebrew-reading Jewish community in Palestine. *Mishle 'Arav*, which began publication in 1899 in several Hebrew journals and newspapers, influenced a substantial number of Jewish scholars, who employed these proverbs in their literary works, as noted by Israel Ben-Ze'ev.[34] *Mishle 'Arav* appears to have been a lifelong project. In the introduction to his work, Yahuda writes,

> At first, I collected these [Arabic] proverbs to memorize them, for I was fond of proverbs ever since I was young. Every time I heard a beautiful proverb, I would record it. After I began reading books of proverbs, I would record these proverbs that I enjoyed. By so doing, I collected many aphorisms. When I decided to compile a book, however, I added others to them.[35]

Although he was born and grew up in Jerusalem, Yahuda frequently traveled in the Oriental world, collecting, trading, and selling rare books and manuscripts.[36] He also enjoyed friendly relationships with Iraqi Jews given his ancestry and was involved in the Babylonian Jewish community in Palestine. These social and cultural relations enriched his knowledge of Arabic, with its various dialects and cultural forms, as evidenced in *Mishle ʿArav*.

Arabic Proverbial Lore and Biblical Interpretation

Yahuda contends that the interpretation of the Hebrew Bible is enhanced by a knowledge of Oriental customs and traditions. It is this knowledge that enabled him to offer insights into certain knotty controversies in biblical exegesis—a contribution that distinguished him among other Hebrew writers.[37] The rise of Hebrew journalism provided Yahuda with a means to disseminate his interventions in controversial readings of the Hebrew Bible. Under the title "Binah ba-Miḳra" (Understanding the Hebrew Bible), he published several essays in the Jerusalemite journal *Yerushalayim*, whose dictum, as it appears in the secondary German title on the first page, was the advancement of scientific knowledge of Palestine, present and past. Yahuda's discussion of the biblical character Esther in one essay instantiates the ways in which he draws on multilingual and multicultural sources to interpret verses from the Hebrew Bible. In the biblical verse "Hadassah is Esther" (Esther 2:7), many commentators have concluded that Hadassah, a type of plant, is the translation of Esther. Yahuda, however, questions this connection, noting, "Until this very day it has not become clear as how Esther is the translation of Hadassah, which only indicates a star in Persian."[38] Thus he points to Arabic as a more likely source. While he agrees with medieval commentator Rabbi Yehuda Ben Kalamonyos (d. 1199) in his assertion that Esther is a translation of Hadassah, he suggests the reference is to greenness as a sign of beauty. Based on his comparative analysis, Yahuda posits that Esther is in fact a combination of two words: the Arabic word *ʾaās*, which refers to myrtle, and the Persian suffix *tar*, which denotes exaggeration in Persian. To ascertain his theory, he reiterates that in ancient days several Arabic words penetrated Persian, including the word *ʾaās* (myrtle), referring to that particular flora. He claims that at the time, Persian people might have called the flora by its Arabic appellation *ʾaās*. In order to indicate that this myrtle is the apex of all myrtles, they would annex the exaggeration suffix *tar* to indicate the most beautiful myrtle of all. Therefore *Esther*, in his view, is a reference to the most beautiful myrtle among myrtles.[39] Aside from clarifying the etymology of the name Esther based on his knowledge of Arabic and Persian, Yahuda looks to Arabic poetry for a wider context and broader explanation.

Yahuda turns to classical Arabic poetry to clarify the meaning of Esther's name, observing how the trope of a white face represents female beauty in classical Arabic poetry. In some instances, Arab poets would evoke the color of an ostrich's egg to indicate the beauty of a woman's face as not completely white but instead "white mingled with yellowness." Ascribing to a woman's face the color of an ostrich's egg is found in the work of one of the pre-Islamic Arab poets. In the suspended ode of Imru' al-Qays, the Arab poet praises his beloved as follows:

كبكر مقاناة البياض بصفرة *** غذاها نمير الماء غير المحلل

Ka-bikri muqānāti al-bayāḍi bi-ṣufraten *** ghadhaha namīru al-mā' ghayur al-muḥallali

[She is] like the first egg of the ostrich—its whiteness mingled with yellow—nurtured on water pure and unsullied by many peddlers.[40]

Yahuda found the ostrich egg's color evoked by Imru' al-Qays similar to the blossom of myrtle that refers to the first Arabic part in Esther's name. He concluded that if that color symbolized female beauty in Arab poetry, the same color might have been evoked to indicate Esther's beauty.[41] While Imru' al-Qays invoked the ostrich's egg to indicate the color of his beloved's face, the society in which the biblical character Esther existed invoked the myrtle blossom for the same purpose, both symbols drawn from the natural landscape shared by Jews and Arabs.

Yahuda's translation choices in rendering Imru' al-Qays's poetic verse, especially regarding color, are of interest. Yahuda renders the abovementioned poetic verse as follows:

כלבנת ביצת בת-היענה בירקרק מעורבה *** מים זכים וצלולים כלכלוה

ke-livnat betsat bat ha-ya'anah be-yarakrak me'oravah
mayim zakim u-tselulim kilkulah

[She is] like the paleness of an ostrich egg nurtured on water pure and unsullied by many peddlers

Imru' al-Qays describes the beauty of his beloved as "whiteness mingled with yellow," but here Yahuda translates this phrase as "the paleness of an ostrich egg," where pale complexion is intended to contrast with dark, sunburned, or rough skin. The confusion here stems from his inclination to reconcile the Talmudic description attributed to Esther by Rabbi Yehoshua ben Korḥa, who said, "Esther yeraḳroḳet haytah" (Esther was greenish) (Megillah 13a), the color of myrtle, with the ostrich egg as a symbolic evocation of a woman's beauty. Following his translation of the verse, he explains that "the face of the beloved is white, but leans a bit towards the *yarḳon* (greenish/pale) of ostrich's egg, whose whiteness is mingled with *yeraḳon*."[42] Choosing *yeraḳraḳ* in his rendering is significant in many ways. First, he does not ignore the Talmudic description of Esther and therefore adopts the color *yeraḳraḳ*. He clarifies, though, that this color is not greenish per se but instead pale, which is close to yellow, as in the biblical passage, "Why have all faces turned pale [*yeraḳon*]?" (Jeremiah 30:6). While it may denote illness or fear elsewhere, here paleness indicates Esther's endowment of beauty like that of Imru' al-Qays's beloved.

If Arabic proverbs illuminate the meaning and origins of phrases in the Hebrew Bible, they can also function as a vehicle to show the interrelatedness of Jewish and Arab cultures, as Yahuda demonstrates throughout his proverb collection by drawing comparisons between the two cultures. If proverbs, in general, represent everyday life, expressing a common underlying wisdom, they speak of the parallel development in Jewish and Arab societies too. In *Mishle 'Arav*, Yahuda points to several Arabic proverbs whose underlying wisdom resembles parallel sayings in extrabiblical Jewish sources.

This group of proverbs occupies a great portion of *Mishle 'Arav*. An example is proverb 46, which says, *Rāsīn fī 'amāmah mā yākūn* (Two heads cannot fit in a single turban), referring to the difficulty of two parties sharing one thing. This Arabic proverbial saying, Yahuda argues, illuminates the Talmudic saying *Efshar le-shney melakhim shi-yishtamshu be-keter 'eḥad?* (Can two kings use one crown?). Before learning about the Arabic analog, S. D. Goitein, a well-known historian of Jewish history in Muslim lands and renowned scholar of the Cairo Geniza, understood the Jewish saying as "one kingdom cannot oppose another in terms of governing."[43] But his understanding of the proverb changed after he learned about the Arabic proverbial saying, which attests to Yahuda's unique erudition in two kings cannot simultaneously rule over the same kingdom.[44] In other words, the underlying wisdom of the Hebrew proverb became clearer only in the context of this Arabic saying, within the cultural sphere of the Orient, where Jews and Arabs shared similar daily life experiences. Another example is found in proverb 711, *Al-bīr al-fārigh mā yitmilī min al-nāda* (An empty well is not filled by dew), which might convey the concept that significant problems or needs cannot be resolved with solutions that are too minor or insubstantial. To put it another way, it suggests that serious issues require substantial efforts or resources, and relying on minimal or inadequate measures will not suffice to address the situation at hand. This proverb clarifies the Talmudic phrase *'En ha-bor mitmale me-ḥolyato* (A pit cannot be filled by its own earth), which has been understood, especially in Ashkenazi circles, in the literal sense as "a pit cannot be filled from its own digging."[45] The Arabic proverb here directs our attention from sand to water. According to the Arabic saying, a well cannot be filled from dew droplets that appear on the stones surrounding a well but rather from water flowing into it from surrounding underground water sources. Commenting on the analogy between the Talmudic saying and the Arabic proverb, Goitein remarked that "this meaning had never been grasped by anyone before reading the [Arabic proverb]."[46]

Arabic Proverbs as a Mirror of Intercommunal Life in the Orient

Like others who grew up in the Orient, Yahuda memorized proverbs for his own self-edification.[47] His knowledge of proverbs not only enriched his vocabulary but also served a practical purpose as a means of communication. Al-Bājūrī points out that knowledge of a people's proverbs can bring the learned closer to the people they study: "He who knows the customs of a certain people and their manners is able to live with them and get along with them, giving from what he possesses and taking from what they have; thus they benefit from him and he benefits from them."[48] Hence the mastery of proverbs could, for instance, help someone in the Orient to settle a dispute between quarreling parties. It was a means of communication among the people of the Orient, irrespective of their ethnicity or religious affiliation.

A portion of Yahuda's selection of proverbs treats the intercommunal life between Jews and Arabs. This selection relates not only to how Jews and Arabs lived together but to how they perceived each other too. For example, one encounters several proverbial sayings about the pluralistic social and ethnic lives of the followers of the three Abrahamic faiths. Proverb 2568 indicates *Al-Qahwa min ghayr dukhān mithl al-Yahūdī min ghayr hakhām, wa-al-Nuṣrānī min ghayr muṭrān, wa-al-Muslim min ghayr Imām.* ([Drinking] coffee without smoking is like a Jew without a Rabbi, a Christian without a priest, and a Muslim without an Imam).[49] Analogizing the practice, common among people of the region, of pairing the pleasures of coffee and cigarettes with the religious pairings indicates the universality of both. That is, Muslims, Jews, and Christians are alike in finding coffee and cigarettes inseparable; so too are they alike in their devotion to their religious leaders. The proverb recognizes the divisions among the three groups, as Christians look to priests, Jews to rabbis, and Muslims to imams, but it simultaneously emphasizes the common ground of closeness to their spiritual leaders and respect for their traditions. In effect, it treats their differences as a ground of shared values.

Other proverbs in Yahuda's collection further illustrate how these communities value shared traditions while maintaining their distinct differences. In Egypt, for instance, people used to mourn the death of the deceased by hiring a professional female mourner. Proverb 76 captures the difference between the actual bereaved and the professional mourner, and is significant for its ability to contextualize the social life of the people of the Orient: *Lays al-nā'iḥa al-musta'jara mithl al-thaklā* (The hired female mourner is unlike the bereaved [the one who lost her beloved]), which can mean that one should always be suspicious of those who pretend to feel deeply or loudly proclaim such feeling.[50] Yahuda's clarification offers background on the shared custom. He states, "In the Oriental land, in particular in Egypt, also in the midst of the Jews, it is a custom to invite [female] mourners to mourn over the deceased as it was a custom for us."[51] Yahuda's observation of local customs during his stay in Egypt equipped him to see how proverbs might also serve to illuminate the laws of bereavement, *avelut*, in the section on *mo'ed ḳatan* in the Talmud, with respect to mourning.[52]

In addition to the previous proverbs, Yahuda's rendering of other ones gives ethnic and social context to Oriental life while attesting to his familiarity with Arabo-Islamic culture, which he demonstrates in his engagement with subject matters that concern both Jews and Arabs. For instance, Yahuda presents proverbs related to beards in various Oriental cultures. Proverb 88, for example, says, *Mā ṭala'at liḥya illa wa naqaṣ min al-'aql wa ma zāda fī al-liḥya biqadr ma naqaṣ fī al-'aql* (No beard grew long, but that wisdom decreased, and whatever was added to the beard was taken from wisdom). This proverb suggests that a man's appearance is secondary to his intelligence, and people should not judge others based on their appearance; an increase in the length of a beard is inversely proportional to wisdom or intelligence, such that the longer the beard, the less sense a person might have. Yahuda devotes a lengthy discussion to the significance of the beard among Jews and Christians, and then cites a Hebrew proverb that makes the same point as the Arabic one, criticizing the common perception of a beard as indicative of intelligence and wisdom. The Hebrew proverb goes, *Keres ve-Zaḳen, Ḥatsi rabban* (A belly and beard, half a rabbi).[53] This saying humorously implies that a person who possesses both a prominent belly and beard might be perceived as wise, as these features were traditionally associated with individuals who are well-fed (suggesting prosperity) and aged (suggesting experience and knowledge)—traits that are stereotypically linked to rabbis or wise people who grow a belly due to their dedication and lack of physical exercise. The proverb speaks to the human tendency to judge wisdom or scholarly status by appearances. While playfully suggesting that having a belly and beard might make one look important or respectable, it simultaneously undercuts such judgments, humorously asserting that outward appearances contribute only superficially to genuine knowledge or authority.

Portrayal of the Jews

Mishle 'Arav is replete with portrayals of Jews from medieval to modern times. In compiling his collection of Arabic proverbs, Yahuda paid particular attention to those that revealed Arab perceptions of Jews. According to him, "I did not record all the proverbs that I heard . . . but I recorded proverbs about Jews, due to the urgent need to know what *ha-goyim* [the nations] say and think about us."[54] In documenting and publishing these Arabic proverbs on Jewish representation, Yahuda aims at revealing the ways in which the Jew is perceived in the Arab's mind. Whether the proverbs themselves originated in premodern or modern times, it is their use and dissemination during the Mandate period that is of interest here. As British support for the Zionist project to establish a national home in Palestine agitated Palestinian nationalists and created unprecedented tension between the two sides, it became crucial for members of the Yishuv to understand how the local population perceived the Jews. A substantial number of these proverbs had already been published in the works of intellectuals of the Arab renaissance, such as Taymūr, Shuqayr, Muḥammad Ibn Abī Shanab, Yusūf Toma al-Bustānī, and others. In the following, I will attempt to reconstruct the major features of Arab portrayals of Jews.

Throughout his annotated comments, the author underscores the continuation of several ideas about Jews from the Middle Ages to modern times. Of the qualities associated with the Jews in the proverbs, trickery and deception stand out. The Moroccan proverb 375 identifies various qualities with women from different ethnic communities. While it associates cleanliness with Turkish women, eagerness with Byzantine women, and beauty with Georgian women, it specifically associates trickery with Jewish women: *Illi yiḥib al-ḥīla yakhod yahūdiyya* (He who desires trickery, should marry with a Jewish woman). Meanwhile, the proverb lauds Arab women, saying, *Illī yiḥib al-jūd wa al-karam yakhud imra'ā 'arabiyya* (He who desires generosity and nobility should marry an Arab woman). In the commentary, the Jew is portrayed as someone who plots and schemes for their own self-interest. The Jew's deceptive character is said to persist even if they convert to Islam, which points to a quasi-ethnic categorization.[55] This saying reflects stereotypical cultural characterizations of women from different ethnic backgrounds, framing them within the context of marital preferences. Such generalizations are obviously overly simplistic and not representative of individuals but rather speak to traditional perceptions that may have been widespread at the time the proverb was popularized. This type of proverb is more reflective of historical societal attitudes and gender stereotypes than of contemporary views. Nevertheless, Yahuda remains silent on the matter, allowing these stereotypes to stay with his reader. In the absence of contextualization or nuanced understanding, this proverb is left to reinforce the stereotype to which it alludes.

Proverb 891 identifies the yellow color with the Jew: *Azraq ḥadīdī wa aṣfar yahūdī, illi mawlāh yiwwalī qaṭṭa' lī yadī* (As blue as iron and as yellow as a Jew; he whose patron wins will cut off my hand).[56] Arabs customarily believe that if a horse has yellow or blue tinges to the whites of its eyes, it is unlikely to win on the battlefield, as expressed in the second part of the saying: "If they win, then you can cut off my hand." What is of interest here is the link between yellowness and the Jew. According to Yahuda, this proverb originates in the era that followed the regulations of Caliph al-Mutawakkil (859 CE), who ordered that the "people of the book" be made to wear honey-colored turbans.[57]

As we have seen above, Yahuda includes in his collection a set of proverbs that contain negative representations of Jews. His silence about these stereotypical representations of Jews conveys the underlying message that if Jews want to live in the East, they must get acquainted with the reality of how they are perceived in the Oriental culture. More importantly, however, from the Zionist perspective, the representations themselves prove the indigeneity of Jews to the region. In this way, the proverbs refute local Palestinian nationalists' denial of the indigeneity of Jewish settlers and their assertion of the Jewish settlers' alienness given their European origins. Indeed, such stereotypical tropes infused in the folkloric legacy serve as manifest evidence of the indigeneity of Jews in the region. It is crucial to note, though, that Yahuda's method overlooks the distinction Palestinian nationalists had made between native Jews vis-à-vis European Jewish settlers who hailed from Western countries and were backed by British imperialism.

In fact, prominent Palestinian leaders throughout the 1920s and 1930s made a distinction between native Palestinian Jews and Zionist settlers. Musa Kāẓim al-Ḥusseinī, who served as the president of the Palestine Arab Congress, along with other leaders like Jamāl al-Ḥusseinī, embraced the view that Palestinian Jews, or "native Jews," were an integral part of Palestinian society, and should not be conflated with the ideological and colonial aspirations of the Zionist movement. As early as March 1921, Musa Kāẓim al-Ḥusseinī conveyed this perspective to Winston Churchill, then secretary of state for the colonies, during Churchill's visit to Jerusalem. Al-Ḥusseinī articulated a clear opposition not to Jews per se but instead to the political project of Zionism, which aimed to transform Palestine into a Jewish homeland. He clarified that Arabs did not hold prejudice against Jews for their religious identity and emphasized that Jews had enjoyed full rights of citizenship before the war. The Arab executive's demands at the time included the abolition of the concept of Palestine as a "national home for the Jews" and the establishment of a national government that would represent all of the prewar Palestinian population, including Jews. Throughout the 1920s and 1930s, this rhetoric continued. On February 26, 1922, Jamāl al-Ḥusseinī published an article in the newspaper *al-Ṣabāḥ* (Morning) urging the local Jews to align with their Arab-Palestinian compatriots, asserting that they shared the same rights and responsibilities in their motherland of Palestine. He spoke against Zionism's persecution of local Jews and invited them to join the fight against the Balfour Declaration.[58]

Jewish Proverbs

As the title *Mishle 'Arav: asufat mivḥar mishle bene ḳedem* indicates, the proverbs are not confined to a certain ethnic group or religious community but instead include sayings attributed to various peoples of the Orient. In the introduction to his collection, Yahuda addresses the circulation of Hebrew proverbs among Arabs and vice versa:

> There are Arabic proverbs that resemble Hebrew proverbs. In some instances, a Hebrew proverb has been adopted into Arabic with its content and style intact. In other cases, the content of an Arabic proverb is akin to that of a Hebrew one not because it was directly translated but because the same spirit imbued them, leading to the creation of proverbs similar to ours, though with distinct style and phrasing.[59]

Yahuda's comments can be understood as referring to the universal nature of certain themes in human life that transcend language and culture, but they also speak to the specific similarities between Jewish and Arabic culture.

The selection of shared proverbs varies, depending on whether they were originally written in Arabic, Hebrew, or a mixture of the two. An example of the first group, which includes sayings of Hebrew origin, but that circulated among Jews in Arabic, is 755, *Illī yiḍāyiq al-sā'a, al-sā'a tiḍayqw* (He who stresses about the hour, the hour will stress him).[60] The author indicates that this proverb is common among Iraqi Jews and originates in the Talmud, such as the version *Ha-doḥeḳ 'et ha-sha'ah, ha-sha'ah doḥeḳeto* (He who pushes his hour will be pushed by his hour), in which the proverb cautions that if a person attempts to rush or control life instead of yielding to the natural flow of events, they will face resistance or negative consequences.[61] Yahuda also claims that another group of Arabic proverbs derived from Jewish heritage, including *Al-quṭ mā kanshī fi al-bāl/al-ḥisāb* (The cat was not taken into consideration), referring to an avoidable misfortune.[62] Furthermore, some proverbs include both Hebrew and Arabic in their wording. An example is 467: *Bi-ḥayat al-rābī jāzat* (By the life of the rabbi, it passed).[63] It is said of a Jew who begged for a lenient legal ruling by the rabbi.[64] Another illustration is 476, which states, *Awwal yūm 'oreyaḥ, tini yūm boreaḥ, talit yūm la ṭa'am wa-la rīḥa* (On the first day he should be a guest, on the second he should depart [or flee], but on the third he [should leave] neither taste nor smell).[65] This aphorism is used by Iraqi Jews to admonish a guest not to overstay their welcome, lest they burden their host. As Yahuda indicates in his commentary, this saying resonates with the Jewish tradition regarding the period of *hakhnasat orḥim* (hospitality), which is a commandment.[66]

The Nights

Thus far we have examined Yahuda's *Mishle 'Arav* not just as the Hebrew translation of a collection of proverbs but rather as part of a cultural effort to root Jews within Oriental culture. In addition to proverbs, Hebrew writers in Palestine were interested in works belonging to what Arab and Muslim scholars called *al-turāth al-sha'bī* (folkloric heritage) or *al-adab al-sha'bī* (folkloric literature), a literary genre that includes the *Nights*, among other tales.[67] The nahdawis recognized the importance of these tales to the construction of a national identity as they expressed the worldview of the common people across different historical periods and various geographic locations.[68] Despite the various ethnic origins of the tales, through their telling and retelling, as Arabist Muhsin Mahdi has observed, they were "modified to conform to the general life and customs of the Arab society that adapted them and to the particular conditions of that society at a particular time."[69] The tales turned into an Arab cultural touchstone that utilized a Persian frame tale and made its way into a popular tradition to become part of the collective societal unconscious.[70] The tales of the *Nights* emerged from a rich folkloric repository that testifies to the plurality and diversity of cultures as well as nations in the East, and the indigeneity of Jews within that plurality. Indeed, the *Nights* reveal the interconnectedness of Jewish and Arabo-Islamic cultures as many of the tales contain textual materials from *al-israeliliyyat* (Israelite lore), including biblical and extrabiblical sources as well as featuring Jewish characters (even prompting some Orientalist scholars to assume a Jewish author), providing a window into the Jewish way of life within the Oriental cultural realm.[71] Native Jews (*bene ha-arets*), whether of Oriental or Ashkenazi origin, such as Yellin, the Yahuda brothers, and Rabbi Benyamin, among others, who opposed separatism as the optimal solution for the relations between Jews and Arabs, and instead promoted cultural rapprochement, found the cross-cultural content of the *Nights* a rich resource.[72]

Alf Laylah wa-Laylah in Jewish Vernacular

The Hebrew rendition of the *Nights*, by Yo'el Rivlin, can be read as a collection of tales about the marvels and wonders of the medieval Islamicate world, of which many non-Arab nations were an integral part, but Rivlin's contemporary Jewish audience read his Hebrew rendering otherwise. The Hebrew *Nights* did not merely introduce the culture of the Arab other to the Jewish audience, despite that having been one of his objectives.[73] Rather, it went beyond that to contribute to the construction of Jewish consciousness at the time of the revival of modern Hebrew. Rivlin's rendition served as a prism through which his audience would view the major issues that preoccupied the advocates of the emergent Jewish culture in Palestine. His engagement with the *Nights* contributed to the formation of the New Jew by promoting notions such as the Jewish "renaissance" and "return" to the Orient, Jewish self-conceptualization, the boundaries between self and the other, the reconstruction of the Jewish past, and the enrichment of the modern Hebrew language and its literature.

Placing the *Nights* in the context of nationalism and Orientalism illustrates the relationship between Jews and the Orient in a variety of ways. Fascination with the *Nights* among Ashkenazi Jews living in Europe paralleled the general popularity of the collection in the West. The text was rendered into Yiddish in 1718, only a year after the publication of Antoine Galland's (1646–1715) French translation that contributed to the popularization and exoticization of the Orient in the West.[74] Later, German Jewish Orientalist Gustav Weil's translation of the *Nights* from an original Arabic manuscript into German between 1839 and 1842 was widely read.[75]

In contrast to this relatively late reception of the *Nights* by Jews living in the West, Jewish communities in the Orient had been familiar with the tales virtually ever since they first found a curious audience and listening ear. Documentary evidence from the Cairo Geniza from around 1150 indicates that Jewish audiences had been familiar with *Alf Laylah wa-Laylah* since the Middle Ages.[76] They would have encountered the *ḥikāyāt* (tales) found in the *Nights* from listening to the stories of the *al-Ḥakawātī* (storyteller) who would travel around the region with countless stories derived from Arabic folklore, or through family members who retold the tales either for entertainment or to impart life lessons. Oriental Jewish engagement with the *Nights* in modern times was part and parcel of having been nurtured on Arabo-Islamic cultural heritage. Moreover, the tales integrate and adapt Jewish folklore, reflecting the intertwined social and cultural life of Jews and non-Jews in the Orient. Although Oriental Jews had been familiar with the genre through oral transmission by listening to ḥikāyāt, their involvement took a different form in modern times. With the advancement of publishing and growing literacy, Jewish individuals transcribed a selection from the *Nights* into Judeo-Arabic (Arabic written in Hebrew script). The collection of the *Nights*, along with other popular Arabic literary works such as *Kalīla wa-Dimna* and *ʿAntar Ibn Shaddād*, as historian Yitsḥaḳ Avishur has indicated, was one of the sources that enriched Jewish folktales from the eighteenth century onward.[77]

Despite their acquaintance with the content of the ḥikāyāt found in the *Nights*, at least from listening to the stories of the al-Ḥakawātī or through family members, the involvement of Jewish communities in the Oriental world was intensified in modern times by European Orientalists' concern with *Alf Laylah wa-Laylah.* An example of this can be found in the cooperation between a Tunisian Jew and several European Orientalists. To earn his livelihood, the Tunisian Jew Mordechai Ibn al-Najjār (d. ca. 1841)—known also as Murād al-Najjār—developed relationships with European Orientalists in which he shared not only his knowledge of Arabic and Berber but also provided manuscripts to Orientalists who demonstrated curiosity about and interest in the Orient. In his publication of the Arabic manuscript of the *Nights*, Christian Maximilian Habicht (1775–1839) refers to a native teacher of Arabic with whom he lived in Paris and who was transcribing manuscripts of the *Nights.* Ibn al-Najjār had, in fact, supplied Habicht with a complete manuscript of the *Nights*, laying the foundation for Habicht's German translation *Tausend und eine Nacht*, which appeared in 1825. It is interesting to note, apropos to the connection of Oriental Jews to the collection under discussion, that Ibn al-Najjār had two daughters named Ḥalīma and Morjāna, two common names in the stories of the *Nights*. It is hard to determine whether he named his daughters after the figures who appear in the stories or if the names of the figures merely reflect the commonness of these two names in Oriental society.[78]

Oriental Jews' engagement with the *Nights* is a manifestation of their identification with the Oriental culture embedded in the stories' collection. Although the stories appeared as part of an Arab cultural tradition, at least in terms of the language in which they were circulated, Jews in the Orient identified themselves with this world and had long been as familiar with the tales as Arabs were. A sense of familiarity with the tales and their content is found in the preface to the introduction of a Judeo-Arabic transcription that was published in 1886 in Bombay by an unknown author:

> As it is known to you, the tales [of *A Thousand and One Nights*] are of the finest entertainment to man, and therefore one finds joy in listening to them and reading them. They [the tales] entertain people, prevent sorrow, and rid them of worries and problems if [they are] particularly significant stories from which one draws manners and good behavior and directing his human morality. When one sees the subject of each story and how it takes place as well as the causes behind it and when he reflects and investigates, he will gain benefits and will be wise and intelligent and will overcome any situation. The book known as *Alf Laylah wa-Laylah* is one of the oldest Arabic books that has been published widely and has been translated into a number of languages such as English, French, and others. I have transcribed it here in Hebrew letters out of consideration here for those who do not recognize Arabic letters. I have also provided explanations for every difficult word . . . in case one might not understand.[79]

Making the collection accessible to a Judeo-Arabic reading audience had several objectives: providing amusement and entertainment, teaching lessons from history, offering exposure to a literary genre that would turn out to be universal given the Western translations of the work, and supplying materials for ethical lessons such as acquiring good manners and correcting misbehavior. What is notable for our purposes is the degree to which the translator identified himself with the content of the *Nights*, notwithstanding his Jewishness, attesting to the assimilation of Jews into a cosmopolitan Oriental cultural heritage.

The *Nights* as World Literature

A primary motivation for rendering the *Nights* into Hebrew was the elevated status the tales had assumed as one of the most widely celebrated works of world literature, or *sifrut 'olamit* in Rivlin's words.[80] But who canonized the tales and bestowed on them such a central status, and for what purpose? In medieval Arabic literature, the *Nights* were peripheral. Historians and bibliographers such as al-Masʿūdī and Ibn al-Nadīm, respectively, pointed out the legendary and entertaining nature of the tales in passing without devoting significant space to a discussion of the collection. From their perspective, these fairy tales were meant to help people pass time and entertain themselves without carrying serious literary or moral merits.[81] Aḥmad Ḥasan al-Zayyāt, a prominent intellectual in Egypt and Arab countries in the 1930s, explains in a lecture to his audience that the *Nights* occupied a marginalized status among elite medieval literary scholars since it represents the lifestyles and customs of the common people. Consequently, literary scholars either ignored or expressed contempt for the collection, with some even dubbing it *ghath bārid* (meager and feeble) in comparison to "the aristocratic literature" that "depicts the delicacy of imagination and the beauty of the craft."[82] Thus in the eyes of medieval scholars in the Arabo-Islamic world, the tales were fit for entertainment purposes only and unworthy of literary attention—an attitude that was passed down to modern Arab scholars.[83] Western Orientalists, in contrast, devoted time and energy to organizing, translating, editing, and disseminating the tales in every possible European language. Al-Zayyāt remarks that only when Arab scholars heard from Europeans that "in our literature there is a hidden treasure of this sort that has left a remarkable impact on their literature," did they begin paying attention to the *Nights*. Hence under the influence of European Orientalists, modern Arab scholars started reading, publishing, and documenting Arab folkloric literature.[84] In short, the repositioning of the *Nights* from the periphery to the center of Arabic culture came at the hands of Westerners. Arab scholars contemporaneous with Rivlin acknowledged the scholarly efforts of Orientalists who breathed life into the folkloric tales, rendering them more popular, albeit in the West at first. Al-Musawi has observed that through appropriated translation, the *Nights* has regained a compelling presence that no one, not even its detractors, can ignore. "In this migration," he further adds, "it is transmuted into something else without losing its basic nucleus and properties. As a European legacy, it reminds readers, adaptors, manipulators, scholars, and everyone else that it is a transplant."[85] That legacy started with the work of Galland, who popularized the text when he translated it from an Aleppian Arabic manuscript into French in the early eighteenth century, and continued further through scholarship on the *Nights* by other Orientalists, such as French Orientalist and linguist Silvestre de Sacy, who argued in two articles on the *Nights* published in 1817 that the tales were not the product of a single author.[86]

Thus it is that after becoming "a European legacy," the *Nights* aroused both Arab and Jewish scholars' interest. Nevertheless, that European interest in the *Nights* went hand in hand with certain racial and colonialist biases—namely, the claim that the tales were Aryan in origin (Persian or Indian), in accordance with the theory of Aryan racial superiority over the Semites found in the works of Friedrich von Schlegel and Joseph von Hammer-Purgstall. Other Orientalists, such as French Semitic scholar Ernst Renan, averred that the copious creative imagination evidenced in the *Nights*, replete with supernatural creatures and fantastic worlds, contradicted the severely monotheistic Semitic spirit. These claims of the tales' supposed Aryan origins surprised both nahdawis and contemporary scholars.[87] In his critical edition of the *Nights*, Mushin Mahdi expresses his surprise at Schlegel's and von Hammer-Purgstall's views:

> How did they come to think that a collection of stories presumably originating in ancient India could survive transmission from one culture to another, from one language to another, and from one storyteller to another and yet remain identifiable in eighteenth-century Paris or Cairo as belonging to a particular ancient nation?[88]

In his brief introduction to the *Nights*, Rivlin refers readers to his Hebrew translation of his mentor Josef Horovitz's German study of the origins on the tales.[89] Horovitz's study then can be presumed to reflect the views and opinions that guided Rivlin in his project. In his study, Horovitz concludes that the stories of the *Nights* represent Arabic "Entertainment Literature," which included various forms of folktales. He refers to the various origins of some of the stories—Indian, Persian, Egyptian, Baghdadi, and even Greek—but notes that "all the stories, including those that came from afar, are imbued with the spirit of Islam, just as they found a place in all the lands where the Arabic language is spoken."[90] In this light, Rivlin's translation can be perceived as an endorsement of the Semitic imagination and creative force against Renan, Schlegel, and other scholars who argued for the Aryan origins of the *Nights*. The translation of the *Nights* was one among many literary projects that proclaimed the rootedness of the New Jew in the Orient, of which Jews, as evidenced in the tales, had always been part and parcel.

The invocation, by Hebrew writers such as Rabbi Binyamin and Rivlin, among others, of the Semitic origin shared by Jews and Arabs as two ethnicities of the same racial origin was meant to lay the foundation for common ground between Jews and Arabs in Palestine as well as the neighboring Arab states.[91] The *Nights* can be seen as a cultural enterprise that could restore the Semitic origins of the Jewish people and their racial affinities with other Semite nations, the Arabs.[92]

Reading the *Nights* in Hebrew and Striking Roots in the Orient

In their construction of the New Jew, some Hebrew writers aspired to build a Jewish character whose moral qualities were in harmony with the values of the "authentic" Oriental cultural world.[93] One of the internal tensions inherent in the

Jewish national movement, as historian Arieh Bruce Saposnik has pointed out, was the question of whether it was essentially Occidental or Oriental.[94] While some thinkers argued for the Western foundations of the emergent culture, others defended its Oriental roots by emphasizing the origins of Jewishness.[95] As Saposnik has demonstrated elsewhere, the Jewish fascination with the Orient in the nineteenth century later served as "one of the wellsprings for the emergence of Zionism as part of the European interest in the Orient and things Oriental."[96]

The *Nights* collection, as British historian Robert Erwin has noted, in addition to folktales and fairy tales, includes "heroic epics, wisdom literature, fables, cosmological fantasy, pornography, scatological jokes, mystical devotional tales, chronicles of low life, rhetorical debates and masses of poetry."[97] These literary genres were wrapped in an Oriental garment that drew the interest of leading Jewish intellectuals seeking immersion in the Orient. Thus the Hebrew rendering of the *Nights* served the cause of Jewish nationalism by allowing Hebrew readers to internalize and familiarize themselves with cultural artifacts that would facilitate their integration into the Orient and the recuperation of Jewish indigeneity.

The strong desire among Jewish nationalists to restore the *ha-mizraḥaniyut* (Easternness/Orientality) of the Jewish nation led to an enchantment with the Orient such as is found in the works of Jewish poet Yitsḥaḳ Katzenelson (1886–1944), who translated selections from the *Nights* into Hebrew in a work titled *Elef ve-Laylah Eḥad: agadot mizraḥiyot la-ne'urim* (A thousand and one nights: Oriental legends for youths), in which he stresses the Orientalness of the collection.[98] Another influential figure was Ḥaim Naḥman Bialiḳ (1873–1934), who in the aftermath of the disturbances of 1929 over sovereignty of the Western/al-Burāq Wall, stressed the right of the Jews to return to *Erets Yisrael* (the land of Israel) because it is the only place of refuge for them, while pointing to the return to the land as a return to *ha-mizraḥ* (the East):

> There is no deliverance for Israel apart from Erets Yisrael. The situation of the children of Israel in the entire world has become terrifying and eventually will become worse. There is no shelter nor rescue without Erets Yisrael. From the time the children of Israel left Erets Yisrael, they began returning to it. This is the path of Israel's wanderings: it begins in Erets Yisrael and ends there! We wandered from ha-mizraḥ to the South, from the South to the North, and from the North back to ha-mizraḥ: For we are now returning to Erets Yisrael.[99]

In his capacity as an editor at the Odessa-based publishing house ha-turgman (Translator), Bialiḳ invited Yellin to translate a selection from the *Nights* into Hebrew.[100] The publishing house had a noble mission: the dissemination of universally acclaimed literary works. Ha-turgman was established with the aim of enriching Jewish pedagogical literature by making non-Jewish literary works accessible by means of "excellent Hebrew translation."[101] The works chosen carried a universal imprint. According to a statement by the publishing house attached to each translation, the selected works had to have been recognized by *ha-'amim ha-mitkademim* (advanced nations) as classics appropriate for youths. In addition to a Hebrew translation of Mark Twain's 1876 novel *The Adventures of Tom Sawyer* by Hebrew essayist and expert pedagogue Israel Chaim Tawiow (1858–1920) in 1910, and *Don Quixote* by Bialik, Yellin's translation of the *Nights* appeared with an announcement of the forthcoming publication of *Sepertkum*, Ze'ev Jabotinsky's Hebrew rendering of the Italian novel *Spartacus*, which had originally been published by Raffaello Giovagnoli in 1874.

The first Hebrew translation in the era of Jewish nationalism, which emphasized the return to the Orient, was a selection from the collection by Yellin under the title *Sipure Elef Laylah va-Laylah* (The thousand and one nights) in 1912. For Jewish readers, the tales were more than mere entertainment; they reinvigorated the return to origins. The concept of returning is found in the works of the pedagogue Yellin, according to whose version of Zionism the Yishuv was to grow as an organic community on its ancestral land.[102] And to grow organically, the Jewish community in Palestine must adapt itself to its circumstances, absorbing cultural artifacts from the surrounding Arabo-Islamic culture, as discussed in previous chapters.

Growing up in Jerusalem, the young Yellin would hear stories from his Iraqi maternal grandmother that originated in Oriental popular literature and were circulated among Iraqi Jewry.[103] The repertoire of folktales preserved in her memory included stories from *Alf Laylah wa-Laylah*, which stirred the young Yellin's imagination.[104] This enchantment would keep Yellin preoccupied with the *Nights*, spending time and energy working on a translation from the collection even while he was exiled to Damascus during World War I.[105]

Yellin's earliest contribution involving the *Nights* was his Hebrew translation of sixteen stories with the intention of attracting Hebrew readers to the cultural world of the Orient. Aside from the literary style, which is exemplary of Oriental culture, Yellin invited readers to draw moral lessons from the tales. For instance, in "The Story of the Ox and the Donkey," included in Yellin's collection, the reader learns to avoid miscalculations and think carefully before advising someone.[106] Yellin's approach, in fact, resonates with the objective of the collections' anonymous original compiler as stated in the preface to the collection:

> This book, which I have called *The Thousand and One Nights*, abounds also with splendid biographies that teach the reader to detect deception and protect himself from it as well as delight and divert him whenever he is burdened with the cares of life and the ills of this world.[107]

One of the most important ways Yellin assimilated Oriental culture in his selections was by adopting storytelling as the medium to convey moral lessons.

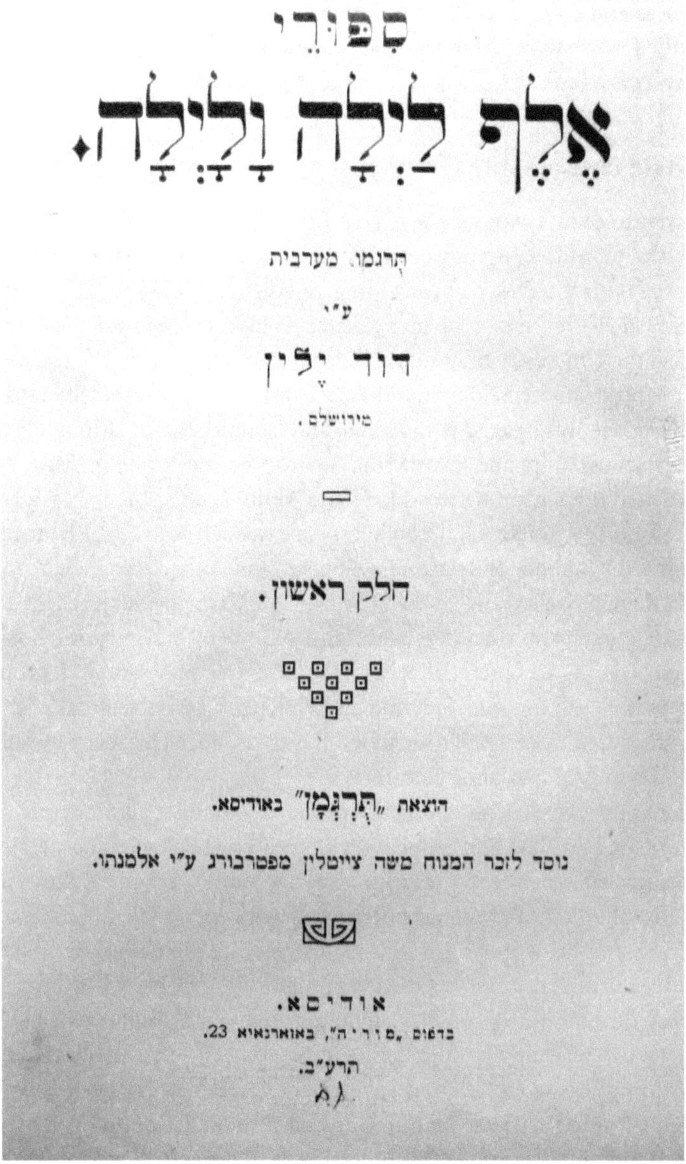
ספורי

אלף לילה ולילה.

תרגמו מערבית

ע"י

דוד ילין

מירושלם.

חלק ראשון.

הוצאת „תרגמן" באודיסא.

נוסד לזכר המנוח משה צייטלין מפטרבורג ע"י אלמנתו.

אודיסא.

בדפוס „מוריה", באורנאיא 23.

תרע"ב.

FIGURE 5.2. The cover of David Yellin's *Sipure Elef Laylah va-Laylah* (The thousand and one nights), published in Odessa in 1912. It contains the first modern Hebrew translation of several tales from *The Nights*.

Moreover, he adapted and adjusted the stories to resonate with both the readers' Jewishness and cultural world of their newly adopted home. The genre of storytelling, it is worth mentioning, was already familiar to readers of the Hebrew Bible, who would thus feel at home in the world of the *Nights*.

The Jerusalemite Orientalist and the *Nights* in Hebrew

In contrast to Yellin's work on the *Nights*, Rivlin's enterprise was comprehensive; his translation of the *Nights* went beyond drawing moral lessons and seeking resonance with the Oriental world to give voice to ideological concerns that preoccupied Hebrew nation builders.[108] During his career as a student of Oriental Studies at the University of Frankfurt, starting in 1924, and in the teaching and academic positions he held in Mandatory Palestine after his return in 1927, Rivlin became deeply engaged with Arabic and Islamic studies through learning, teaching, scholarship, and translation. Against the watershed of critical events that widened the schism between Jews and Arabs, such as the 1929 Wall disturbances and 1936 Arab Revolt, Rivlin's response was self-restraint. Rivlin admired Jabotinsky, the founder of Revisionist Zionism, and appreciated his core message as set forth in his well-known essay "The Iron Wall," which advocated for a strong Jewish state to ensure the safety and rights of Jews in their historic homeland before considering accommodation with the local Arab population.[109] As opposed to Jabotinsky's call for confrontation and violence against Arabs after the Wall events of 1929, however, Rivlin's reaction was to produce Hebrew translations of major texts in Arabo-Islamic culture.[110]

Unlike other Jerusalemite writers who never obtained an academic degree, such as Yellin, Meyuḥas, and Yahuda, Rivlin combined European academic training in Arabic and Islamic studies with his Jerusalemite nativity. Rivlin's German Orientalist philological training endowed his work with a scientific character. In fact, Rivlin and his works were viewed favorably by scholars at ha-makhon limude ha-mizraḥ (Institute of Oriental Studies) at the Hebrew University on his candidacy for a position in Arabic literature.[111] Rivlin's suitability in the hegemony of the field of Arabic and Islamic studies in Mandatory Palestine allowed the dissemination of his works among a wider audience that valued the work of a European-trained scholar. Rivlin's German Orientalist philological training equipped him to provide a faithful translation of the source without any intervention on his part—an approach he adopted not only in the *Nights* (1947) but also in the preceding projects, such as the translation of the prophetic biography of Ibn Hisham (1932) and the Quran (1936).[112]

While his Palestinian nativity did not initially play a decisive role in his hiring at the Hebrew University—though retrospectively, some scholars at the institution would allude to his nativity on their failure to recruit a reputable Muslim scholar to teach Arabic at the nascent Institute of Oriental Studies—Rivlin self-consciously identified himself with the Orient and emphasized this connection on several occasions. One of his contemporaries described him as someone "who viewed himself as an integral part of the same environment known by the name 'Orient.'" Even though he was the descendant of an Ashkenazi family that immigrated to Palestine at the beginning of the nineteenth century, Rivlin, according to the same observer, objected to those who identified him as Ashkenazi, saying, "How am I different from the rest of the people of the Orient who immigrated and settled here many generations ago?"[113]

Rivlin was intellectually and socially associated with "the Jerusalemite circle," a group of elite, mostly native Jewish writers, such as Yellin, Meyuḥas, and the Yahuda brothers, among others. With members of this group, Rivlin shared a commitment to the revival of the "Semitic bond" between Jews and Arabs.[114] His selective translation and annotation of the poetry of the Arab poet 'Antar Ibn Shaddād, published in 1916 against the background of the Great War, connected him with another Jerusalemite writer, Abraham Yahuda, who published an article on Ibn Shaddād's poetry.[115] A manifest reference to the intellectual and social bond Rivlin shared with native Jewish writers is found in the dedication of his translation to Yellin, whom he considered his mentor.[116] Further confirmation of his social affiliation with native Jews is his marriage to Rachel, the daughter of Isaac Yahuda, in 1922.[117] Yahuda, who had connections with many Orientalists, wrote to Carl Heinrich Becker (1876–1933), the renowned German Orientalist, to thank him for facilitating his new son-in-law's admission into the department of Oriental studies at the University of Frankfurt.[118] When Rivlin's translation of the Quran saw the light in 1936, he dedicated it to his wife, Rachel (1904–35), who had passed away a year before the work was accomplished.[119] Due to Rachel's upbringing and education, she was able to provide constructive critique and valuable assistance in his translation endeavors. Alongside her expertise in European languages such as German and French, she possessed a strong command of Arabic and Hebrew. These two languages played a crucial role in her exceptional proficiency in studying the Bible and Jewish literature in Spain. Rachel's linguistic and literary abilities were instrumental in supporting Rivlin's projects related to the Quran, a biography of Muḥammad, and Reynold Nicholson's *A Literary History of the Arabs*.[120] Rivlin's nativity in Palestine as well as his active role in the Hebrew revival movement, as a member of the Hebrew Language Committee from 1929 until his death in 1971, equipped him to serve as a mediator between the culture of the Orient and that of the West.[121] From the perspective of David Siton, an Oriental and Sephardi critic and writer, Rivlin "longed to bring to the other [the Jewish other who did not originate in the Orient] the characteristics of the Orient, without damaging our original Hebrew spirit, however."[122]

Rivlin's engagement with the *Nights* can be seen through the prism of his role as a mediator between the Orient and the West. His self-perception as a native "motivated him to dedicate himself to the holy work (*melakhah ḳedushah*) of translating priceless treasures from Arabic language and literature into Hebrew."[123] Yet note the caveat "without damaging the Hebrew spirit, however." The dissemination of Arabic knowledge among the Hebrew readership had to be carried out cautiously to maintain the uniqueness of Jewish identity through the preservation of *ha-ruaḥ ha-'ivrit ha-meḳurit* (the original Hebrew spirit) so as to prevent its being swallowed by Arabo-Islamic culture. It is out of this fear of assimilation that Rivlin's ambivalence toward Orientalness arises: while he is proud of his connection with the Orient and is perceived as a son of the Orient (*ben ha-Mizraḥ*), he always maintains a distance from the Oriental culture. Thus while he invites his Jewish audience to root themselves in the Orient, he strongly urges them to preserve their distinctiveness. In other words, although the emergent Jewish culture must retrieve its lost Oriental character, it must concomitantly be distinct from the Arab version of Oriental culture.

The German scholarly interest in the *Nights* paved the way for Rivlin to produce his own scholarly translation of the collection guided by the Orientalist philological method and motivated by his self-perception as a mediator between two worlds: the East and West. His earliest publication of the collection of narratives took the form of stand-alone volumes based on certain tales from the *Nights* and served to test their reception among the Jewish community in Palestine. Members of the Oriental and Sephardi communities were among the first critics and reviewers to discuss the new enterprise as well as introduce it to the wider reading community.[124] The newspaper *Hed ha-Mizraḥ*, the organ of the Oriental and Sephardi communities in Mandatory Palestine, announced the publication in 1943 of the Hebrew translation of individual tales: "ha-Melekh Yonan ve-ha-Rofe Royan" (The king Yonan and the physician Royan) and "ha-Galav me-Baghdad" (The barber from Baghdad) by Jerusalemite publisher Or La-'Am with illustrations.[125] A wider Hebrew readership encountered the tales with the publication of the first volume in 1947 by the Ḳiryat Sefer publishing house, the bibliographic quarterly of the Jewish national and university library.[126] This volume was reviewed in the liberal newspaper *Ha-arets*, under the title "Tirgum Ḥadash shel agadot 'Arav" (A new translation of Arab legends), in which the reviewer notes the continuous Hebrew engagement with these tales, as evidenced by Yellin's translation discussed earlier. Unlike Yellin's strict translation, which adhered to biblical Hebrew, Rivlin weaves a more flexible literary Hebrew style from various sources including the Bible, Midrash, Al-Andalusian literature, and works of reputable Jerusalemite authors.[127]

The Jewish Past Encoded in the *Nights*

The *Nights* is replete with reflections on the self and the other, the alien and the familiar. In fact, the *Nights* emerges as a source of not only Jewish presence in the Orient but also Jewish integration into the culture of the East. Although the historical validity of the collection is doubtful, Jewish readers would have found in the tales several clues about their Oriental past from the perspective of the Arab other.

The *Nights* is rich in names, themes, and ethical lessons that resonate with parallels in Jewish sources. These parallels, while they cultivate affinity with the Arab other as an Oriental neighbor, buttressed Jewish nationalists' claims of Jewish presence in Oriental culture too. In the *Nights'* tales, readers confront Jewish figures playing either central or secondary roles, including, for example, Solomon, David, Asaf, Burakhiya, Daniel, and Buluḳiya.[128] For instance, from *Alf Laylah wa-Laylah*, one can draw a lesson about faithfulness and the abuse of power from the story of the virtuous and devout Jewish woman who was threatened by two powerful elders who told her she must lie with them or they would accuse her of fornication. When the woman refused to surrender to their lust, they accused her of adultery and summoned people to stone her. To save her, God sent down a blasting fire on the elders and consumed them on the intercession of the prophet Daniel, who revealed to the masses the wickedness and lies of the two elders. This tale, as literary scholar William Brinner has indicated, seems to be a reworking of the story of Susanna and the Elders found in the Apocrypha.[129]

The representation of Jews in the tales is not univocal; the portrayals are diverse and do not adhere to a homogeneous stereotype, instead rendering a complex and nuanced picture of how the Jew was perceived by the population of the Orient and Jews perceived themselves. Throughout the tales, one learns about Jews who faced adversity, but were eventually saved because of their faithfulness and piety.[130] Alongside positive projections of the spirituality of several Jewish characters, attributes such as beauty and intelligence are highly praised, as in the story of Masrūr and Zayn al-Mawāṣif, which furnishes us with a vivid picture of intercommunal life in the Orient. Masrūr, a Christian merchant, fell in love with Zayn al-Mawāṣif, an exceedingly beautiful Jewess who was married to a Jewish merchant. Living among a Muslim majority, neither Jews nor Christians were identifiable by their external appearance or dress. The heroine in the *ḥikāya* is depicted as possessing a combination of intelligence, compassion, beauty, and cunning. The moment Masrūr looked at her, he said, in Richard Burton's translation, "She were the rondure of the lune and the full moon shining boon she had eyes kohl'd with nature's dye and joined eyebrows, a mouth as it were Solomon's seal and lips and teeth bright with pearls and coral's light." The moment

FIGURE 5.3. The cover of Yosef Yo'el Rivlin's book *Elef Laylah va-Laylah* (One thousand and one nights), the first comprehensive Hebrew translation of the entire Arabic collection based on the *al-Bulāqiyya* version. The first volume was published in 1947. At the advice of Islamic art historian Leo Ary Mayer (1895–1959), Rivlin incorporated aspects from Islamic art to better reflect the content of the tales.

he saw her, Masrūr was "amazed at the sweetness of her speech, the coquetry of her glances and the straightness of her shape."[131] Moreover, she is portrayed as a woman of wit who could defeat the successful merchant Masrūr in a chess game to claim his fortune, but instead returns his wealth to him.

"The Story Told by the Jewish Physician" illustrates another role a Jew played in Oriental society as a source of trust. The story is told in the first voice by a Jewish physician living in Damascus under Mamluk rule. Due to his talent in the art of medicine, the Jewish doctor is invited to the abode of the governor to treat a young sick man. After successfully treating the mysterious patient, the governor conferred on the Jewish doctor a dress of honor and appointed him the superintendent of the hospital of Damascus. After concluding his mission, the patient opened his heart to the Jewish physician, sharing with him personal matters. The Jewish doctor speaks about himself as a secret keeper. He is not only being entrusted with his patients' lives but also with keeping their status a secret.[132]

Elsewhere we encounter negative portrayals of Jewish characters, as in the story of Dalila the Wily, her daughter Zainab, and Ezra the Jew, a sorcerer who set impossible conditions to marry off his daughter, Qamar. Entranced by Zainab, ʿAli El-Zeibaq vowed to secure Qamar's luxurious gold bridal attire crafted by Ezra. Despite the formidable challenge issued by Ezra, who transformed failed thieves into animals, ʿAli stubbornly pursued the golden treasures to adorn Zainab, but ultimately fell victim to Ezra's magic, ending up as a mule.[133] Nonetheless, it should be noted that the affiliation with magic, as Robert Irwin has shown, was attributed also to the Maghribi—whether to be Arab or Berber Muslims from North Africa.[134] Conceptualized as an attempt to achieve control over people, magic and those who practiced it were perceived negatively, whether Jew or non-Jew.

The *Nights* as a Guide to the Arab

Amid the ideological currents of the era, Rivlin appears to have embraced the perspective that Arabs should be integrated into the future Jewish national home. While he recognized the vital importance of the Jews' return to Palestine, he also believed in reconnecting with the Semitic heritage that Jews shared with Arabs in the past, and emphasized the need for this connection to endure and evolve in the future.[135] Rivlin believed that the establishment of a Jewish homeland should be pursued in a way that respected the rights and aspirations of the Arab population, and sought to build bridges of understanding and cooperation between the two communities. Striking roots in the Orient, then, entailed gaining and maintaining familiarity with the Arabs who constituted the demographic majority in Palestine as well as its neighboring states. Rivlin subscribed to Jabotinsky's politics opposing the partition of Palestine, anticipated a Jewish majority overtaking Arabs, and prepared for military confrontation with Arabs in

Palestine.[136] Jabotinsky had already predicted, in his famous "Iron Wall" article from 1923, a future confrontation with Arabs. His logic was that Zionists should not expect Palestine's Arabs to willingly accept efforts to establish a Jewish majority in the land without resistance given that "every colonial initiative naturally encounters indigenous resistance." But that does not mean that Arabs should not live within the Zionist state. On the contrary, Zionists would be able to secure agreement with Arabs to live together in one state only after Arabs' resistance was broken militarily. The Jabotinskian view adhered to the universal principle of giving each national minority collective rights, stemming from the concern that expelling "the Arabs from the Jewish state might serve as . . . an 'instructive precedent' for all those who threaten the existence of Jewish collectives in the diaspora."[137]

A conversation between Rivlin and Christian and Muslim Palestinian acquaintances at the peak of World War II is instructive here. Discussing the advancement of German troops in al-'Alamin in western Egypt, the Christian and Muslim Arab families told Rivlin and his wife not to worry about their safety when the Germans arrive in Palestine to thwart the British, for Arabs would protect them. Rivlin, with a bitter smile responded, "You have no chance of seeing the Germans victorious. Once the war is over, the British will allow us to establish a state. Immediately after the war, we will establish the Jewish state, and in this state, we will not protect you because you will be citizens of Israel."[138] In other words and in agreement with Jabotinsky's views, peaceful coexistence with the minority is only possible when Jews attain majoritarian status.[139] Arabs, according to Rivlin's political vision, will not be expelled from the future Jewish state, yet they are expected to resist the Jewish national project. Eventually both nations will live in a Jewish sovereign state with Arabs granted their collective rights as a national minority.

When the *Nights* turned into a European legacy, it became a reference for philological, literary, and ethnographic studies that sought, among other things, to recuperate the origins of Arabs along with their literary styles, customs, and manners.[140] Horovitz, a German Jewish Orientalist and the director of the Institute of Oriental Studies from 1926 until his death in 1931, published a study in 1925 on the *Nights*, which Rivlin translated into Hebrew to make it accessible to Hebrew readers in Palestine and abroad. Writing about the *Nights* as a resource for contemporary social studies, Horovitz observes,

> The lives of the people continue to this day in those Arab regions, far from European influence, just as they are revealed to us in the realistic descriptions of *One Thousand and One Nights*. And those ideas and influences that were woven into the hearts of the heroes of *One Thousand and One Nights* still live and exist to this day in the hearts of the people, unchanged.[141]

This testimony by Horovitz to the ethnographic value of the *Nights* rendered Rivlin's enterprise valuable beyond its literary merit. From the perspective of Rivlin, the collection of tales encompasses "wisdom of the entire Orient from India to Persia including various Arab lands," and constitutes an "unrivaled mirror that reflects the entire life of the Arab, his world of thinking, the life of the body, the spirit, and the soul."[142]

Rivlin's rendition of the *Nights* also served his own professional objectives in demonstrating his bona fides as an adherent of the German Orientalist school as well as his authority on contemporary Arab society, as per Horovitz's statement.[143] Moreover, Rivlin could claim to have made a significant contribution to the growth of Arabic literary sources in Hebrew, putting Hebrew on par with the Western languages into which the collection had long been translated, beginning with the first French translation by Galland.[144]

Rivlin's work lies at the intersection of storytelling and ethnography. In approaching the tales as an ethnographic site, without sacrificing the text's literary characteristics, Rivlin justifies his translation project by highlighting the valuable insights that can be gained about Arab culture and society from the *Nights*. This objective is evidenced in the introduction to the *Nights*, in which Rivlin declares that by virtue of his translation, the Hebrew-reading audience will gain intimate insight into the inhabitants of the region:

> [In the tales' collection] we meet the Arab in his house to the secret of the secrets, in the street and the market. We learn how to understand his manners and many of his religious affairs, his way of thinking, his ethics, his mockery. . . . It is possible to say that anyone who wants to know Arabs should seek the book of *Elef Laylah va-Laylah*, which no guide is better than it for learning about the Arab.[145]

Guided by Horovitz's conclusion that even though the *Nights* contains a variety of stories of different origins—Indian, Persian, Egyptian, and even Greek—the tales as a whole are "imbued with the spirit of Islam, just as they found a place in all the lands where the Arabic language is spoken."[146] Rivlin contends that the tales provide a rich and layered portrayal of Arab life that captures the intricate dynamics of both private and public spheres as well as the diverse religious practices, ways of thinking, and social customs. By translating these tales and sharing them with a broader audience, Rivlin aims to dismantle prevalent stereotypes and promote a deeper, more nuanced appreciation of Arab culture.[147] Nevertheless, I would call the reader's attention to the ways in which the *Nights* may inadvertently perpetuate certain Eurocentric perspectives that have historically shaped Western perceptions of the Arab world. While Rivlin's work aims to present a varied and authentic image, the broader context of its reception creates the potential for these stories to reinforce exoticized views, rooted in a colonialist discourse. Acknowledging this tension allows for a more critical engagement with Rivlin's translation and its role in shaping the understanding of Arab culture within a global context.

We have been investigating how the tales reflected Arab life to non-Arabs, as entertainment and ethnographic information, but for Arabs themselves the *Nights* served principally as a source of social and moral admonition by means of storytelling. For Arab readers and listeners, the tales encompassed lessons from the past that guided behavior in the present. According to the introduction to the Arabic version of the *Nights*—that is, the *al-Bulāqiyya* version that Rivlin used to render his translation—the main objective of the tales is to admonish, and the main takeaway for readers and listeners is, in Rivlin's words, to "be admonished" and "restrained" in their behavior. In the Hebrew *Nights*, after translating the opening statement in a manner consistent with most of medieval Arabic literature, including praising God and the Prophet Muḥammad, Rivlin renders the following passage:

> To proceed—the lives of former generations are a lesson to posterity; that a man may review the remarkable events which have happened to others and be admonished; and may consider the history of people of preceding ages, and of all that has befallen them, and be restrained. Extolled be the perfection of Him who hath thus ordained the history of former generations to be a lesson to those which follow. Such are the tales of a Thousand and One Nights, with their romantic stories and their fables.[148]

In addition to assuming the accuracy of the stories contained within, the original anonymous compiler of the collection deems them worthy of historical consideration and reviewing "the remarkable events which have happened to others . . . to be admonished." Thus Hebrew readers could extract from the tales insights into the lessons Arab society deemed most critical to teach over many generations.

The European approach to the *Nights* as an ethnographic site from which they could deduce a vivid picture of an Arab society that had not changed from the thirteenth century onward was central to the consecutive editions of the tales. Galland, the first Orientalist to disseminate the tales in the West, considered the *Nights* to display "not only the consummate art of storytelling, but also an adequate representation of Eastern—meaning Arab—customs and manners."[149] Galland's successors continued on the same path, and competed among themselves as to who was the most equipped and skilled to represent the social, cultural, and religious life of the Arab. British translator and lexicographer Edward William Lane, in demonstrating the supremacy of his edition over that of Galland's, cites his firsthand knowledge of Arabic, the support he received from Arab philologists, and his five years of experience living in Egypt—factors that set him apart from other philologists of his time.[150] Even as these Orientalists competed with each other in depicting the East, however, they were in fact revealing more about themselves as Europeans and about European society than about the Arab other. While Galland, Lane, and Burton effectively conceal themselves behind what Edward Said viewed as "a creative presence," letting the tales speak for themselves, their intended audience was European, not Oriental.[151]

Nonetheless, European interest in the *Nights* ultimately redounded to the East to influence Arab self-perception. The perception of the *Nights* as providing insight into Arab society penetrated the circles of modern Arab intellectuals, who related to the tales as a historic and social document. In January 1932, al-Zayyāt, a scholar and literary luminary based in Egypt, delivered a two-lecture series in Baghdad on "Tārīkh ḥayāt Alf Layla wa Layla" (The life history of one thousand and one nights), which covered the Eastern and Western engagement with the tales from medieval to modern times.[152] Al-Zayyāt called on Arab scholars to investigate the *Nights* to ascertain its Arabness along with its relevance to the social, cultural, and religious life of Arab societies to challenge Orientalists' attribution of the tales to Aryan sources. Lamenting the lack of studies among Arab scholars on the origins of the *Nights* amid Western denial of the Semitic sources of the tales, he insists that the tales are a document of Arab social and cultural life:

> [The *Nights*] documents, throughout the centuries, the evolution of our society. It vividly portrays our diverse morals and characters. It has published in the East and the West the brilliance of our civilization, and the flourishing of our culture, and the beauty of our traditions. It has bridged the historical gaps that have ignored the people and the literature that have [been] looked down on [by] the general public.[153]

Hence in al-Zayyāt's view, the renewed interest in the *Nights* makes up for its marginalization at the hands of Arab elites, and bridges historical and literary gaps in Arab history and literature while providing insights into aspects of society that have been neglected.

Yet in stressing the positive ramifications of the rediscovery and dissemination of the *Nights*, al-Zayyāt overlooks the limitation of this enterprise in accurately representing Arab society and its culture. The claim that the *Nights* represents Arab society throughout the ages radically oversimplifies the diversity and complexities of that society, and fails to recognize that the tales are not representative of the entire society but rather the particular time and location in which a particular storyteller creates as well as tells their story. Moreover, al-Zayyāt follows in the footsteps of Western Orientalists in claiming that the *Nights* portrays the diverse morals and characters of Arab society, which may be seen as idealized or romanticized.[154] In fact, the stories do not accurately reflect the full range of morals and characters within Arabian society, and they can be said to enrich the imagination more than they reflect reality.

Modern Arab scholars contemporaneous with Rivlin criticized the prevalent Orientalist perception of the *Nights* as an abundant ethnographic document that reveals and makes accessible the Arab's universe, without considering the limitations, prejudices, and exaggerations of the text. They warned against simplistic wholesale acceptance of what is found in the narratives without applying critical insights to its content. The deficiencies of the tales as a faithful ethnographic source can be traced to several factors. First, Orientalists had established that the narratives that comprise the *Nights* were attributed to several storytellers and compilers from different historical periods. Second, the collection of the tales' settings points to different and distinct regions within the Arab world, especially Egypt and Baghdad. The Arabs of Palestine, those to whom Rivlin meant to draw attention, are barely represented in the *Nights*. Third, the stories not only point to social and cultural settings in an Arabo-Islamic environment but also encompass narratives from other Oriental nations.[155] With these notes in mind, the tales emerge as limited in depicting "the entire life of the Arab, his world of thinking, the life of the body, the spirit, and the soul," as Rivlin promised his readers, and the absence of critical insights in the treatment of these stories would create stereotypes of Arabs rather than introduce a realistic portrayal of their social, cultural, and religious life.[156]

The Enhancement of Modern Hebrew

For Rivlin, the *Nights* represented an opportunity to enhance both the general status of the Hebrew language, by making it one of the languages into which the *Nights* was translated, and enrich the lexicon of the language itself. Therefore Rivlin's rendition can be seen as an effort simultaneously to elevate the status of the resurgent Hebrew language by putting it on the map of world literature and situate himself as well as his community within the dominant Oriental culture of Palestine.[157] The linguistic contribution of Rivlin's translation was certainly among his own priorities as he was a major force in the revival of modern Hebrew. He himself taught Hebrew at several schools in Jerusalem between the years 1910 and 1914, and in 1917 volunteered to teach Hebrew to children whose families had been expelled from Jaffa and Tel Aviv in the wake of World War I. While in Damascus, Rivlin took charge of the Hebrew school established by *ha-histadrut ha-tsiyonit* (Zionist Organization). In Mandatory Palestine, Rivlin took part in several Jewish educational and cultural organizations, such as the organization of Erets Yisrael Hebrew teachers, the Hebrew University, and the Academy for Hebrew Language.[158]

Shortly before the outbreak of World War I, the Jewish community in Palestine witnessed the outbreak of the Language War (*Milḥemet ha-safot*), an internal dispute among the Yishuv that pitted Hebrew against the growing influence of German. At the center of the controversy was the decision of the Curatorium at the Technion, intended to be the first Jewish high-level technological institute in the country, to make German—instead of Hebrew—the main language of instruction.[159] At the heart of this heated war of words was the need to enlarge and enrich the Hebrew lexicon. The memoirs of members of the Hebrew Language Committee (*va'ad ha-lashon*) show that one of the pressing issues the members discussed was how to supplement the incomplete lexicon of the emergent Hebrew language.[160]

The usefulness of Arabic as an instrumental linguistic source for modern Hebrew appears as a motif in the writings of Jewish intellectuals even before the outbreak of the Language War, and it continued to play this pivotal role after the war was settled in 1914 and later in 1922, when the Mandate government recognized Hebrew as an official language alongside Arabic and English.[161] The instrumentality of Arabic for the revitalization of Hebrew can be seen in the way the Oriental nature of Hebrew was being underscored by Hebrew scholars and advocates, stressing the art of Oriental storytelling, using the Hebrew equivalent of Arabic expressions and idioms, and rendering rhymed verses from Arabic into Hebrew utilizing the Hebrew legacy from Muslim Spain.

The Hebrew rendering of *One Thousand and One Nights*, for instance, would enable Hebrew readers to realize the indigeneity of their national language in the Orient, with the text serving as a return to origins. According to David Siton, an Oriental and Sephardi critic and writer,

> Those who want to know the spirit of our language should turn to the tales of *One Thousand and One Nights*. How rich the phrases (*nivey ha-lashon*) are and how vivacious they are! As though the Hebrew language was returned to its origins [lit. to the rock whence she was hewn] (*tsur maḥtsavtah*).

In essence, according to Siton, Rivlin's translation from the Arabic literary corpus was considered "a great service for the Hebrew language and its literature."[162] Moreover, it suggests that by immersing oneself in the collection of tales, one can gain a deeper understanding of the essence and character of Hebrew. According to a certain reviewer in the newspaper *Hed ha-Mizraḥ* (Echo of the East), the collection of tales is full of "idioms and complete concepts that have become the common parlance in Arabic-speaking countries [that] found their proper expression in Hebrew translation." Rivlin's project, according to the reviewer, effectively conveys idioms and complete concepts originating from Arabic-speaking countries in Hebrew, thanks to his success in finding the appropriate equivalents or expressions in Hebrew to capture the original meaning and cultural nuances.[163]

Rivlin's Hebrew rendering was a literary manifestation of the return to the origins as he translated the *Nights'* Arabic verses into Hebrew using the patterns of medieval Hebrew poetry. In his article on the manifestations of the Orient in

Bialiḳ's literary pieces, Rivlin points out Bialiḳ's effort to highlight the significance of the Sephardic Jewish poetry for the national project that aimed at the return to the ancestral land. According to Rivlin,

> The duty of the time, which should not be wasted, is to uproot the Sephardic poetry from the individual property of the research and to transfer into mass property of the generation's literature and to feel the bringing together and the structure of such literature and to build a layer above layer on what is built and already standing.[164]

Rivlin thus urges Hebrew writers to lift Sephardic Jewish poetry out of the realm of dry academic study and share it with the masses—a mission he had in common with Yellin. In their Hebrew rendering of the Arabic verses throughout the *Nights*, both writers took it on themselves to maintain the medieval flavor that was emblematic of the Andalusian register in terms of adherence to the rhyme (*qāfiya*)—although both dismiss quantitative meter in their Hebrew translation.

Rivlin's treatment of the Arabic verse of the *Nights* differed from Yellin's with respect to fidelity to the text as opposed to essential accuracy. For example, in the story of 'Umar al-Nu'mān and his children, there is a scene in which Sharkān, the king's older son, is overcome with drowsiness while riding his horse. He awakens to find himself in a place surrounded by trees, flowers, herbs, and birds expressing joy and gladness in their diverse tongues. The narrator describes this marvelous natural scene with this short poem:

ما تحسن الأرض إلا عند زهرتها *** والماء من فوقها يجري بإرسال
صنع الإله العظيم الشأن مقتدرا *** معطي العطايا ومعطي كل مفضال[165]

Most beautiful is a land in budding bloom,
As water courses through it consistently.
It is the creation of the all great and gracious God,
The giver of all gifts, the giver to every generous person.

In rendering these same two verses into Hebrew, Yellin strives to capture the essence of this poem, substituting the portrayal of the nature embedded in the scene in the Arabic version, which may have been inspired by a similar image from the Quran (16:65), with images of nature drawn from the Hebrew Bible (Song of Songs 1:12). Yellin also renders the verses in a rhymed poem that although it resembles the style of Andalusian Hebrew poetry, differs in terms of employing quantitative meters. Here is how Yellin translates the verses:

נתנו ריח יחדיו הנרדים,
צץ וצומח פרדס המגדים
ועצי חמדה נטו בין צללים,
משמאל קדה מימין אהלים.[166]

Together spikenards send forth their scents.
The garden of delightful fruits has budded and blossomed.
Pleasant trees incline among shadows.
On the left is cassia and on the right aloe.

Yellin's liberal rendering of the Arabic verses stems from his approach to translating poetry by abstaining from "word-for-word" translation while paying close attention to the meaning of the original. In allowing himself a considerable measure of freedom with the Arabic text, Yellin followed the advice given by medieval poet Moses Ibn Ezra (1055-1135) in his treatise on the poetic art, *Kitāb al-muḥādhara wa al-muḏākara* (The book of discussion and remembrance): "And if you plan to bring a matter from Arabic into Hebrew, grasp the spirit and intention of the work, but do not transpose it word for word, for not all languages are alike. . . . And if it does not turn out as you had hoped, rid yourself of it entirely, for sometimes silence is better than speech, and the speaker who pleases will please with his silence too, though the opposite is not true."[167] Yellin's translation of the two verses embraces the principles highlighted by the poet and philosopher Ibn Ezra. Whereas the original Arabic poem hints at a divine presence interwoven with the natural world, Yellin strips away the direct religious undertones, yet retains the spirit of the sacred texts by employing biblical Hebrew to convey the essence of the Arabic narrative. This linguistic choice not only enriches the Hebrew version with a nuanced layer of cultural and historical significance but also forges a link with the biblical tradition, ensuring that the story, even in its translated form, maintains a profound connection to the religious and literary heritage of the Hebrew language.

In contrast, Rivlin preserves the original Arabic poem and does his best to translate the verses into Hebrew without great alteration. In rendering the same verses, he writes,

לֹא תִיף הָאָרֶץ בִּלְתִּי אִם בִּפְרָחֶיהָ,
וְהַמַּיִם מֵעַל לָהּ יִזְרְמוּ שְׁלוּחֶיהָ.
מַעֲשֵׂה אֱלֹהִים אַדִּיר עָשָׂה וַיַּעַרְכֶהָ,
נוֹתֵן כָּל מַתָּת, וְכָל טוֹבָה הוּא יַעֲנִיקֶהָ.[168]

The land is beautiful only with its flowers
And the water above it flows its delivery
It is the creation of a mighty God who created it and laid it out
The giver of all gifts and the provider of every act of kindness

As we see, in his translation of the two couplets, Rivlin strove for a "word-for-word" approach, demonstrating fidelity to the surface of the original and doing his best to translate both verses into a rhymed poem that looks similar to the two Arabic verses. Unlike Yellin, who aspired to Judaize the Arabic text, Rivlin assimilated the Arabic verse into Hebrew without substituting passages and images from the Hebrew Bible for those from the Quran.

Unlike Western translations of the *Nights* that dismissed the Arabic verse in the collection as being of low quality, Hebrew translations of *One Thousand and One Nights*, both the partial rendering by Yellin or complete translation by Rivlin, preserved the Arabic verse and used it as a medium to address national concerns relevant to the Jewish connection to the Orient, albeit through different approaches. With partial adherence to the Andalusian register, in terms of employing biblical Hebrew and rhymes without employing quantitative meters, both Yellin and Rivlin viewed Arabic poetry as a means by which they could enrich the modern Hebrew language along with its literature by diffusing Oriental phrases and scenes.

The Path Home through Proverbs and Folktales

The work of Hebrew writers such as Yahuda and Rivlin on Arabic folkloric literature, from proverbs to common tales to wisdom literature, constituted a significant contribution to the intellectual life of the Jewish community in Palestine. Their exploration followed in the footsteps of Western Orientalists, who viewed this literature as an ethnographic treasure trove, providing profound insights into the social, cultural, and religious aspects of the Orient, particularly the Arab world. Simultaneously, they engaged in dialogue with contemporary Arab scholars, who were also influenced by Orientalists' curiosity in their cultural heritage, recognizing the wealth of popular literary narratives as a means of rejuvenation, fostering authenticity, reestablishing a vibrant connection with ancestral roots, and reaffirming their cultural identity. What sets the works of Hebrew authors apart, while being informed and influenced by the activities of both Orientalists and native Arab scholars of nahda, is that their scholarly endeavors were driven by national and cultural aspirations linked to the advancement of a Jewish national home in Palestine, as founded in the Balfour Declaration. These aspirations included shaping the New Jew in alignment with the spirit of the Semites and people of the Orient, reclaiming Jewish heritage through literary sources, utilizing Arabic language as well as Arab customs and manners as a means to comprehend the Bible within its Oriental context, and ultimately enriching the Hebrew language through the utilization of Arabic.

Underlying much Hebrew scholarship was a deep-seated anxiety about the legitimacy of Jewish indigeneity in the Orient. In contrast to *bene ha-arets*—Sephardi and Oriental and Ashkenazi Jews who perceived themselves as natives to Palestine—who felt at home within the cultural world of the Orient, Jewish immigrants struggled with feelings of exoticism, foreignness, and rootlessness. They were familiar neither with the land nor the people, nor the Oriental cultural world. Yahuda's and Rivlin's investigations of Arabic proverbs and the tales of the *Nights*, respectively, would contribute to the reconstruction of the New Jew rooted in the Orient. Unlike works that concentrated on the collection of proverbs of certain ethnic, religious, or national communities, Yahuda's *Mishle 'Arav* comprised proverbs in use among all communities of the Orient, regardless of their religious affiliation and social class. Seemingly, the author recorded any maxim or popular saying he chanced to hear or learn throughout his voyages and the life he lived in the Orient. Consequently, his work *Mishle 'Arav* opens a window into the rich amalgam of cultures present in the Orient.

Similarly, by presenting a vivid and multifaceted image of the Orient through the already familiar medium of storytelling, the *Nights* offered a bridge of understanding for Jewish immigrants who were new to the land, its people, and its cultural nuances. If the *Nights* served Jewish returnees as a gateway to the Oriental culture in which they found themselves, these tales also created stereotypes and prejudices about Arabs in the midst of whom Jewish immigrants aspired to dwell. In general, the tales provided them with glimpses into the customs, traditions, and ways of life in the region, allowing them to become acquainted with the cultural tapestry of the Orient. While this familiarity nurtured a sense of connection and belonging, it constructed false perceptions of the Orient too, since the tales record the life of Arabs from the thirteenth to the sixteenth centuries, with less relevance to nineteenth- and twentieth-century Palestinian Arabs.

Folkloric materials offer valuable insights into the diverse life circumstances of Arabs as well as the other nations of the Orient. These narratives not only offer a vivid portrayal of Arab life but also serve as a repository of unwritten historical accounts derived from the tribal traditions and customs of various Eastern nations mentioned in the Bible, especially the Israelites. By delving into these folkloric materials, Hebrew scholars were able to uncover hidden layers of ancient history and gain a deeper understanding of the cultural milieu in which biblical events unfolded. Yahuda's study of Arabic proverbial lore paved a path to greater understanding of both the proverbial texts found in the Bible and certain ambiguous expressions and idioms therein.[169]

Finally, the translation of Arabic proverbs as well as folkloric tales and fables into Hebrew enriched the Hebrew language with expressions and concepts prevalent among the Arabic-speaking masses. With regard to vocabulary expansion, the infusion of Arabic vocabulary into the resurgent Hebrew provided Hebrew speakers with a broader linguistic palette. Hebrew scholars facilitating social and cultural understanding through their translation projects would present Hebrew readers with deeper insights into the cultural nuances, traditions, and values of the Arab world. This understanding fostered greater cultural appreciation and empathy, promoted cross-cultural dialogue, and enhanced social interactions between Hebrew and Arabic speakers. By translating expressions and concepts from Arabic to Hebrew, Hebrew speakers were exposed to new ways of thinking and understanding the world. This exposure would both broaden their cognitive horizons and stimulate creativity as well as innovation within the Hebrew language and culture.

Conclusion

ON MAY 15, 1948, when the British left Palestine, it was a very different place from that which they conquered on December 11, 1917. On their arrival in the post-Ottoman Shām, the area lacked an official name, defined boundaries, and a cohesive structure. The Mandate played a significant role in establishing the name "Palestine," making Jerusalem its capital, determining its borders, and building its structure. Operating in a politically tumultuous environment, the administration faced challenges that hindered the success of development initiatives, despite the demand for such projects. The impact of Britain's imperial history along with the activities, laws, and institutions implemented during the Mandate era as well as the eventual partition of Palestine left a lasting legacy.[1]

The proposal for the division of Palestine aimed to accommodate British interests and advance the goals of Jewish Zionists, while detrimentally impacting Palestinian Arabs. The approval of the partition of Palestine in 1947 led to a war between Jews and Arabs that started first with a civil war, and then developed into a war between Israel and neighboring Arab states. The outcome of the war, known in Israeli collective memory as the War of Independence and in Palestinian collective memory as the Nakba (catastrophe), yielded the birth of the Jewish state on 78 percent of the territory of the former Mandatory Palestine and the refugeedom of about 720,000 of the 1.3 million Palestinians.[2]

The birth of the state of Israel marked a transformation point with regard to the central themes of this book: land, people, and language. As part of the formation of the state, the dominant Arab map of historic Palestine was erased to be replaced with a Hebrew map to emphasize Jewish proprietorship of the land. Palestinians, meanwhile, were dispossessed of their land and displaced—a trauma that resulted in the erasure of Arab geographic memory, as Meron Benvenisti has indicated.[3] The establishment of Israel also led to the denial of Palestinian rights along with the ongoing struggle for self-determination and recognition as a distinct people. The change in the geographic and human landscape occurred in tandem with the changing linguistic power dynamics whereby Hebrew was promoted as the primary language and given official status while Arabic was relegated to the second rank as an official language, although in practice far lower.

Not all of the Zionist scholars and educators studied in this book witnessed these crucial transformations. Those who lived through the decisive war and witnessed the genesis of the Palestinian Nakba, dispossession of Palestinians' lands and intellectual properties (such as public and private libraries), and weakening status of Arabic, however, were faced with a new reality. In this context, I propose in this space to look at how the Jewish intellectuals studied here—Yeshayahu Press and Yosef Yo'el Rivlin, who dedicated their lives and careers to engaging with Arabo-Islamic culture and lived during the Ottoman and British Palestine eras as well as welcomed the Balfour Declaration—responded to these radical changes. Through the exploration of the book's central themes—land, language, and people—we will conclude that after the founding of the Israeli state, these intellectuals demonstrated their unwavering support for the Jewish state while simultaneously promulgating understanding and appreciation of Arabs and their culture, so long as they remained in a minority status. In other words, they mobilized their knowledge of Arab culture to better control the Arab minorities living in their midst without feeling compelled to deal with them as equal partners.

The Status of the Land

The construction of Jewish indigeneity through physical return to Palestine since the late Ottoman era was accompanied by the recovery of the region's historic geography in accordance with Jewish sources. Zionist educators and scholars soon discovered, though, that Jewish sources were insufficient to restore the connection between the land and the Jewish people. To rectify this lacuna, they utilized the rich body of geographic and botanical Arabo-Islamic knowledge (based on both textual materials and oral narratives by the local population) in their pursuit of connection with a temporally distant as well as unfamiliar landscape whose physical and natural features in Jewish sources were ambiguous at best. Their endeavor to hebraize the names of places in Palestine began during the late Ottoman era, and their mission evolved with the advancement of the Zionist movement in establishing a presence in the land.

In the Ottoman period, Zionist educators and scholars found geographic and botanical knowledge from Arabo-Islamic sources instrumental to their cultural project to hebraize urban and rural communities, seas and mountains, rivers and lakes, flora and fauna, in line with references found in Jewish texts, as discussed in depth in chapter 2. Notably, the hebraization process at this early stage did not lead to the marginalization of the Arabic signifier of a certain place, or a certain zoological or botanical species. Rather, during this period the landscape bore a dual identity, both Hebrew and Arabic. Arabic remained the language spoken by the majority in Mandate Palestine, and functioned to signify, identify, and communicate regarding a certain place or a geographic entity. With the elevation of the status of Hebrew into an official language in British Palestine and the emergence of Jewish institutions with the mission to carry through the Balfour Declaration, the efforts and activities of the hebraization of the landscape drifted away from fostering fraternity as in the Ottoman period to promote the construction of a Jewish national home in the land, as explored in chapter 4.[4] With the birth of Israel, Zionist scholars and educators joined institutionalized efforts orchestrated by the newly formed government to create the Hebrew map for the Jewish state to completely replace the cultural and geographic Arabic map.

The institutionalized activities surrounding the creation of a Hebrew map began with the formation of the Governmental Naming Committee (*va'adat ha-shemot ha-mimshaltit*) (GNC) in March 1951.[5] The committee drew its authority from the fact that its decisions were "binding on state institutions" and became official with their publication by the government.[6] Moreover, the close connection between the GNC and Prime Minister David Ben-Gurion also rendered the committee's decisions authoritative.[7] Members of the newly formed committee had previous experience in determining Hebrew names for Jewish settlements in Mandate Palestine, as some of its members, such as Press, had been active in the Jewish National Fund's Naming Committee, which had been in operation since 1925, as noted in chapter 4.[8]

Palestine's Arabic map had not come into existence as a result of an administrative committee or to assert claims of ownership over the land. Rather, it was crystallized in an "evolutionary process, layer upon layer, from one generation to another" throughout a period of about fourteen hundred years. The names of places and natural sites had been preserved in Arabo-Islamic geographic texts since the ninth century. This literature continued to grow from the period of the Crusades through the Ottoman era. By the end of the nineteenth century, the Palestine Exploration Fund, a British association established to study the East, including Palestine, published about nine thousand Arabic names, nearly 10 percent of which had Aramaic, Hebrew, or Greek origins.[9] GNC members utilized their Arabo-Islamic geographic knowledge of the Palestine landscape in their deliberations for the construction of the Hebrew map and creation of Hebrew place-names, which would ultimately give Hebrew exclusive rights over the landscape and lead to the complete erasure of Arabic place-names. At the time of the formation of the state of Israel, thousands of human and natural sites were known only by their Arabic names—a fact that perturbed members of the naming committee, who wished to eliminate all traces of "foreignness" from the map of Palestine.[10] The irony, then, is that the GNC's members not only used their Arabo-Islamic knowledge to create the Hebrew map but to erase it too. Members knowledgeable about the Palestine landscape employed this information in restoring what they contended were the original Hebrew names instead of preserving the Arabo-Islamic past of a certain place. They deemed "historical" only those sites they succeeded in identifying with the Jewish past, with little interest in or consideration of other pasts.

In 1951, Press published the second edition of his work on the geography of Israel/Palestine bearing the title *Erets-Yisrael: Entsiḳlopedyah topografit-hisṭorit* (The land of Israel: Topographical-historical encyclopedia). Published two years after the birth of Israel, interestingly, the author chose to describe the land he studied geographically and historically as "Erets Yisrael" (the land of Israel), and "Palestine" as the corresponding English equivalent—a name used during the Mandate era to refer to historical Palestine. Tracing the development of the topographical and geographic landscape in Palestine along with the influence of historical circumstances on its toponymy, Press begins with the ancient period, proceeding to the period of the Second Temple and Arab conquest. After this long history of Palestine, during which the names of the land changed under different rulers, Press concludes his survey with a section on the modern times, which he describes as *be-shov banim le-gevolam* (with children returning to their borders). This new historical phase starts with "the immigration of the new Jewish Yishuv pioneers to the land to settle in it and make its desert bloom *'le-hafrot et shem-emoteha'*" (to make the desert bloom). "Since [their arrival] in 1870," Press continues, "they established settlements in lands which had been desolated for centuries, in sandy deserts, in the middle of swamps, and on the top of dry rocks on mountains." Under the Zionist motto "to make the desert bloom," the coinage of names for these settlements clearly expressed an exclusively immigrant vision.[11]

Despite efforts to exclude prior histories, Arabo-Islamic sources were unavoidably instrumental in the Jewish reacquaintance with the land. Press's encyclopedia is replete with facts drawn from Arabo-Islamic references, be they medieval Arabic and Islamic texts, or folkloric materials collected and maintained among the local Arab population, which express the cultural distinctiveness of those residing on the land. The author himself does not shy away from admitting his dependence on these sources. Indeed, Press acknowledges the prominence among his sources of medieval Arab-Muslim geographers and historiographers' writings on Palestine. What makes them stand out, he acknowledges, is the geographers' reliable and detailed description of the land, its various population centers, and the ways in which the region's inhabitants aligned themselves, both spiritually and economically, to the demands and fruits of the land itself.[12] Press exploited the vivid picture of the land derived from Arabic sources to acquaint the Jews with the land and its past.[13]

A native of Jerusalem and an educator, Press had a profound knowledge of Arabo-Islamic sources, as his encyclopedia entries demonstrate. Like David Yellin and the Yahuda brothers, Press was *ben ha-Mizraḥ* (a son of the Orient), acquainted with Islamic culture on a day-to-day basis. In the early years of the Israeli statehood, he took his familiarization with Islamic knowledge in the direction of the consolidation of statehood. In the preface to his encyclopedia, he reveals to his readership the authorial intention underlying the composition of the work on which he had spent, in his words, "countless years." He states that "the exile of Judah and Israel caused the hearts of *ha-'am* (the people) to forget most of the names that had been spoken without hesitation by the mouths of our ancestors residing peacefully in the land—everyone sitting under his grapevine or fig tree." The collective forgetting of the Hebrew toponymy was the consequence of exile. The reemergence of the Jewish people in Palestine meant the recovery and reinstatement of the Hebrew map at the cost of the local Arab population's connection with the same land. "As we [the Jews] lay the foundation for our political and national life in the land once again," Press remarks, "we are obligated to renew our olden days and 'Judaize' the land's map."[14] As a member of the naming committee with deep-seated Arabo-Islamic knowledge, Press took on himself the mission of replacing Arabic place-names with Hebrew ones—a role he had played ever since he had been an active member of the Jewish National Fund's Naming Committee established in 1925.[15]

What is the place of Arabic in the hebraization process? GNC members found Arabic place-names essential for the recuperation of what they claimed to be the ancient Hebrew map. Even if they did not know the original Hebrew name and could not justify it historically, they contended that the original Hebrew names were somehow concealed in the dominant Arabic name. Arabic place-names, then, were regarded as a potential bearer of Hebrew origins. The mission of the committee was to revive the historical Hebrew names and determine their location based on toponymic references found in biblical and Mishnaic sources. The revival of the ancient Hebrew map was crucial for validating the Jewish connection with the ancient homeland and to support the historic Jewish right to the land.[16] For example, in May 1952, GNC members deliberated and discussed their policy toward unsettled historic sites whose Arabic names were identical to their Hebrew historic names. Even though the names were identical, GNC members agreed to prioritize the Hebrew name by transliterating the Hebrew pronunciation into Arabic, such as Tel 'Arad, Tel Lakhish, Tel Afek, and Tel Erubut. If the places used to be inhabited by Arabs and became populated by Jews, the Arabic names were to be replaced with Hebrew names accompanied by the Arabic transliteration of their new Hebrew appellation. Some of the places to which they agreed to apply this new rule included Betzet to replace al-Basa, Ben-'Ami instead of al-Nahr, Ḳeren Yesha' instead of Abū Shūsha, and Ono rather than Kafr 'Ana.[17]

Ultimately, the process of restoring Hebrew toponymy rendered Arabic foreign and alien to the map.[18] Compelling the Arab population to pronounce the hebraized names of familiar places rendered those places alien and foreign. At the same time, because of the GNC members' belief that Arabic place-names concealed original Hebrew place-names, Arabic was essential to their efforts to identify ancient Jewish settlements. When the majority of the committee members decided to assign Hebrew names to certain locations associated with Jewish history that were now predominantly inhabited by Arabs, they agreed to transliterate the Hebrew name into Arabic. As part of this process, apparently to meet the practical needs of the Arab communities in these places, it was decided to place the Arabic names of these places in brackets on maps. Examples of this are the conversion of Shafa 'Amr (an Arab city in the north of Israel and east of Haifa that was used by Saladin between 1190 and 1191 as a military base for attacks on the Crusaders in Acre) into Shefar'am, and al-Buqei'a (a Druze-Arab town in northern Israel) into Peḳi'in.[19] Not all of the committee members agreed to placing the original Arabic name in brackets and instead suggested placing the transliterated Hebrew name in brackets.[20] While signaling the Hebrew imprint on and ownership of the place, this method was less sensitive to the needs of the dominant Arab population living in the place. The inhabitants of the village al-Bassa (a Palestinian village in Acre) would find their home had acquired a new Hebrew name, Betst, which surely created confusion and solidified their alien status on a land that used to be the land of their ancestors.

The linguistic affinity between Arabic and Hebrew ironically functioned in the new order to create not familiarity but disorientation. Arabic, as a second official language and the mother tongue of one-fifth of the nascent Jewish state's population, was used as a signifier of place-names, but that did not mean the assertion of the Arabic landscape of Palestine as both Jews and Arabs had come to know it during the thirty years of the Mandate. Rather, Arabic was utilized to contribute further to the erasure of the Arabic landscape through the meticulous process of the transcription of the newly designated Hebrew place-names (which in many cases were in fact hebraizations of Arabic place-names) into Arabic with the use of the Hebrew appellation. Instead of maintaining the original Arabic place-names, the members of the GNC effaced any cultural and historic significance a certain place had with the Arab population in favor of marking its connection to Jewish historic memory or Jewish history, be it ancient, medieval, or contemporary.

The Status of Arabs in the Early Years of the Jewish State

In the Mandate period, both Arabs and Jews were colonial subjects of the British Empire. Prominent Zionist leaders, however, succeeded in mobilizing the support of British policymakers to sponsor Jewish national aspirations as opposed to the interests of the Arab population, which comprised about 70 percent of the total population in 1922 and owned nearly 90 percent of the country's privately owned land at the time.[21] With the termination of the British Mandate in May 1948, the settler colonial yoke did not come to an end, however. With the establishment of the state of Israel, a settler colonial regime remained in place and took a heavy toll on one-fifth of the entire Palestinian population living in the Jewish state. Around 150,000 Palestinians became subjugated to colonial practices of control and domination in the nascent Jewish state. Palestinians who remained in the country became "a trapped minority" caught in between "the incongruent demarcation lines of state control and ethnocultural belonging." On the one hand, they were integrated into the Jewish state as that state's citizens, at least according to the Declaration of Independence. Designated Arab Israelis, they were made citizens of the state by the Israeli Citizenship Law of 1952, while being considered a "dangerous population."[22] In the newly established state, Jewish leaders adopted separatist political aspirations that maintained a separate Jewish state distinct from the Palestinian Arab population and privileged Jewish subjects. From 1948 to 1966, Palestinians in Israel came under the rule of a military regime, and those Palestinian Knesset members who voiced criticism against that rule were suppressed by other Knesset members as well as chastised as impudent and ungrateful toward a Jewish nation that was benevolent enough to keep them in its midst. That military rule yielded more than only displacement, exclusion, and repression. The Israeli Citizenship Law of 1952 was formulated not primarily to grant citizenship rights to the Jewish majority but rather to counteract "the unanticipated determination" of Palestinians to either remain in or return to their ancestral homeland. Palestinians were not merely neglected or marginalized but instead actively "recruited into the state's public culture in order to reassure Jewish labor leaders, school principals, commanders, and civil servants that they had internalized their defeat and that they were grateful for it as well."[23]

With the establishment of the state of Israel, the Palestinian minority was placed under military rule (1948–66) not just to control, suppress, and marginalize them but also to segregate them from the public culture. In the wake of the 1948 war, leaders of the Jewish state, mainly affiliated with Labor Zionism, allowed no space for public debate on the expulsion of 750,000 Arabs from their homes.[24] S. Yizhar, in his powerful novella *Khirbet Khizeh* (the name of a fictional Palestinian village), was the only Jewish writer to deal openly with the expulsion of Palestinians from their land by the Israeli Army.[25] The novella, published in 1949, about four months after the war's dust had settled and two months before the official conclusion of it, was one of the few works of fiction on the 1948 war that was incorporated into the scholastic canon of Hebrew literature.[26]

Although Zionist educators and scholars remained silent about the Nakba and the displacement of 750,000 Palestinians from their homes, they did not erase Arabs' history from their memory. As a way of accommodating their new realities, after they had lived in proximity to Arabs, Zionist veterans in the first two decades of Israeli statehood remembered the First Aliyah settlers as those who enjoyed intimate relationships with Arabs.[27] Likewise, Jewish educators and scholars who had lived in proximity to Arabs during late Ottoman and Mandate Palestine invoked memories of close relations with Arabs, after finding themselves severed from interaction with them. In the early years of statehood, Zionist educators selectively invoked narratives of past harmonious relations with Arabs in service of specific ideological positions. One of these was the promulgation of the idea that animosity toward Arabs is not built into or inseparable from the Zionist settlement project. Another was the notion that Palestinian national leaders were solely responsible for the fate of Palestinians, both within Israel and in other territories.

Rivlin, whom we have discussed in connection with his translation of the *Nights* in chapter 5, provides an interesting case with respect to selective Zionist settler memory. In 1950, he published a series of three articles under the title "Beit Hashem be-me'arbolet" (The Hashemite dynasty in a whirlpool) in the newspaper *Hed ha-Mizraḥ*, the mouthpiece of the Sephardi and Oriental communities in Mandate Palestine and Israel. Though his expertise lay in classical Arabic literature and Islam, Rivlin offered his thoughts on contemporary issues that concerned the residents of the nascent Jewish state in relation to the Hashemite kingdom that had annexed the West Bank and Jerusalem as the outcome of the 1948 war. As the title of the articles suggests, Rivlin treated the history of the Hashemites in the Middle East from the time of Sharif Hussein of Mecca to that of King Abdullah I of Jordan. Building on Rivlin's exploration of the interplay between the nascent Jewish state and its neighbors, particularly the Hashemite kingdom, one can see a more intricate picture of the geopolitical landscape in which Zionism operated. It is in this context that we can appreciate the unique nature of the Zionist project.

Zionism as a settler colonial movement differed from other European colonial ventures by lacking a supporting colonial metropole. Early Zionist leaders believed that the realization of the Jewish aspiration in Palestine would not materialize without the backing of an imperial power, namely the British. Positioning the Zionist movement within imperial power served the enterprise in two ways. First, by aligning the movement with British imperialism, Zionist leaders ensured a power position necessary to pursue their colonization enterprise. Second, positioning itself within the imperial power allowed the Zionist movement to assert itself as an extension of Western geopolitical interests in the region.[28]

Rivlin's recollection of the British policy toward Jews reflects the internal debates within Revisionist Zionism regarding the British in the last decade of the Mandate. During the stressful events of the Arab Revolt of 1936, Revisionist Zionists debated among themselves the relations with the British. Their disagreement yielded two opposing positions toward the British Mandate: moderates wanted to secure the support of Britain for the Zionist project, whereas the radicals wanted to break away from the British and abolish the Mandate altogether.[29] Supporters of Avraham (Yair) Stern, who were involved in Etzel (a right-wing paramilitary group that adopted the Revisionist Zionism ideology of political violence to achieve Jewish sovereignty on both banks of the Jordanian River), argued that the traditional political Zionism led by Ze'ev Jabotinsky was ineffective, and they believed in the termination of the British Mandate over Palestine. Menaḥem Begin, a prominent figure in Etzel, was already advocating for an end to the Mandate in 1938. The fact that the majority of younger members in the Revisionist movement shared this viewpoint indicates their support for Begin rather than Jabotinsky. While acknowledging that Yellin was his "mentor," Rivlin criticized Yellin and his ilk for, in Rivlin's words, "minimizing our national aspirations," whereas younger-generation Zionists like himself "in [their] conversations with Arabs and their leaders in various occasions could not obscure the Jewish aspirations, starting from mass Jewish immigration to the land of Israel and the realization of autonomous rule."[30]

Whereas Zionist leaders, even moderates like Jabotinsky within the Revisionist movement, regarded the British as the bedrock of the Zionist enterprise, Rivlin belonged in the radical camp, which advocated for the removal of the British Mandate from Palestine.[31] Rivlin denied any positive impact the British had on the Jewish settlement, and took to task the British policy toward both Jews and Arabs, both inside and outside Palestine. Instead, he promulgated the heroic aspect of Zionism, particularly Revisionist Zionism, which claimed the entire credit for pushing the British outside Palestine. Rivlin argued that British policy in Mandate Palestine favored Arabs over Jews. He claimed that the British support of Palestinian nationalists whom he described as "fanatics," such as Hajj Amin al-Ḥusseinī and 'Aref al-'Aref (1891–1973), who were favored by Herbert Samuel, an English Jew who had been the high commissioner of Palestine from 1921 to 1925, was a manifestation of its policy to keep the Zionists at bay. Rivlin overlooked the British policy of divide and rule, which encouraged divisions among Palestinians to diminish their collective strength.

Another manifestation of the British policy favoring Arabs over Jews is the establishment in 1921 of Transjordan, which was intended to control the Jewish state on the western bank of the Jordanian River. Rivlin believed that the Jewish state should include the two banks of the river, aligning with his biblically derived understanding of its borders. He described the Hashemite kingdom as a British scarecrow, established to keep Jews in check. Frustrated with the British Mandate policy, Rivlin proposed to Samuel the appointment of a moderate Arab ruler who would support a Jewish national home and recognize Jewish rights to the eastern bank of the river.

Capitalizing on his personal accounts and the connections he had forged with Arab politicians, Rivlin related a meeting he had with Ali Riḍa Pasha al-Rikābī (1864–1943), the previous prime minister of Syria under King Faisal, sometime between 1920 and 1921. Rivlin clarified that al-Rikābī, as a seasoned politician, was aware that the British would establish another "vassal" state in the region aside from Iraq to serve two objectives: as a "shield against the strengthening of the Jewish national movement in the land of Israel" and to counter the French influence on the Arabs in Syria.[32]

Al-Rikābī did not mind becoming the ruler of this "vassal" state on behalf of the British. According to Rivlin, al-Rikābī invited him to explain his objectives, asking him to prepare a memorandum on the matter and submit it to Samuel, the high commissioner in Jerusalem. Rivlin saw this conversation and proposal as an opportunity to seek further clarifications from the veteran politician about his stance on Jewish immigration to as well as settlement in East Jordan—a territory that Rivlin considered an integral part of the Jewish national homeland. Then al-Rikābī explained that he would welcome Jewish settlement in East Jordan as long as it contributed to the prosperity of the land. He made it clear, however, that this support did not extend to the possibility of Jewish autonomous rule or the annexation of East Jordan to the future Jewish state in Palestine. Al-Rikābī simply welcomed Jewish immigration and settlement in the anticipated Arab sovereign state. Although al-Rikābī attested to the difficulties and challenges associated with this prospect, he still considered it with one condition, which he relayed to Rivlin.

Concerned about tensions between Jewish settlers and Arabs in Palestine, and worried about possible clashes with the local population in Transjordan, al-Rikābī proposed to allow the immigration of only Jews from "the Orient" and not from "the West." The ambitious Arab leader preferred to establish settlements for Jews from the East for several reasons, which received appreciation from Rivlin's side. First, their settlement would not trigger public opinion in Transjordan against them given "the shared lifestyle between the Jews of the Orient and Arabs, which would benefit both of them tremendously." Al-Rikābī also indicated that those Jewish immigrants would serve as a liaison in the future between Eastern and Western Jews, and would create a natural and vital link between Jews and Arabs. Rivlin indicated to his readers that he forwarded this memorandum to Samuel and received "a thank you note" from the secretary of the High Commissioner in Palestine, yet this memorandum yielded no results, so he expressed his disappointment in British policymakers.[33] He then concluded his account by observing that the British had preferred to give this position to Prince Abdullah Ibn al-Hussein, who became the first ruler of Jordan in 1921.

Throughout three newspaper articles, Rivlin portrayed the Palestinian minority as "a dangerous population," troublemakers, power seekers, and conspirators who sought to undermine the relations between Jews and Arabs, even outside Palestine. Rivlin invoked several accounts surrounding Palestinian figures whom he described as *nos'e degel ha-ḳana'ut ha-le'umit* (advocates of nationalist fanaticism) who were empowered by British policymakers during the Mandate to counteract Zionism despite their objection to the British policy altogether. He consistently criticized the British officials' attitude toward Jews and blamed them for empowering those Palestinians, whom they made "a pawn to intimidate Jews."[34]

Rivlin singled out those who were active in the Palestinian movement during the Mandate era, such as 'Abd al-Qāder al-Muẓafar (1880–1949) and 'Aref al-'Aref, leading members of al-Nādī al-'Arabī (Arab Club), a Palestinian political club dedicated to staging anti-Zionist activities and distributing anti-Zionist statements in 1919 in Syria.[35] Then Rivlin mentioned Sālim 'Abd al-Raḥmān, who founded the Arab Union newspaper (*al-'itiḥād al-'Arabī*) in 1925 in Tulkarm and became the director of ṣundūq al-Umma al-'Arabī (Arab Nation Fund), a fund to purchase lands in Mandate Palestine to settle dispossessed Palestinian farmers whose lands had been purchased by Jewish organizations such as the Jewish National Fund to settle Jewish immigrants.[36]

Rivlin portrayed Palestinian nationalists' struggle against British colonialism and Zionism as motivated not by collective Palestinian interest but instead by the personal gains of the Palestinian elite. Despite denouncing Palestinians' position on Zionism, Rivlin did not negate their indigeneity, referring to them as Arabs from "the land of Israel," which can be translated as Israeli Arabs. While asserting their indigeneity—a concept central to this book—he depicted their national struggle as inauthentic and contrived. This view is in line with the dominant perspective among Zionist leaders, who considered Arabs in Palestine as individuals rather than a people with a unique identity distinct from other Arab nations in the surrounding states.

The failure of Palestinian nationalists, from Rivlin's perspective, was due to their "fanatic" views, which not only damaged relations between Arabs and Jews in Palestine but also strained the Palestinians' relations with neighboring Arab states. He attributed to them the radicalization of moderate Arab leaders, who demonstrated sympathy toward the just cause of the Zionist movement. He looks back on Faisal's positive attitude toward Zionism and his vision of the revival of the Umayyad Arab caliphate, which according to Rivlin's recollection, included "the restoration of Jews in the land of Israel [Palestine]." "The national home," according to Rivlin's understanding of Faisal's vision, was "an absolute autonomous rule for Jews in the land of Israel," and even the idea of a "Jewish state" was not alien to Faisal's thought. Why would Faisal support the Jewish national enterprise? According to Rivlin, Faisal's sympathy toward Zionism was based on his recognition of the racial affinity between Jews and Arabs; his interest in

Jewish assets throughout the world, which "Zionist lobbyists . . . had beautified and elevated in his eyes," and his fascination with Jewish achievements in both science and politics. All of these considerations made possible the establishment of a caliphate under the rule of the Hashemite dynasty with the inclusion of "a Jewish national home" in one form or another.[37]

During his reign over Syria, Faisal maintained continued communication with Zionism in Palestine either directly or indirectly in order to secure his vision against his Arab opponents and the French. Yet Rivlin criticized Faisal's vision as "naive" for believing "in the power of Jewish influence over the world's politics, and particularly their influence over the British policy."[38] At the time, leading Palestinian members in the Arab Club, whom Rivlin mentioned earlier, sought to dissuade Faisal from cooperating with Zionists, arguing that such alliances would not secure his throne or British support against French ambitions in Syria.[39] Rivlin claimed these efforts by Palestinian nationalists to undermine Faisal's collaboration with Zionists also worsened relations between local Jews and Arabs in Syria. Leaders of the Syrian Jewish community lodged official complaints to the king about Palestinian provocations against Zionists, which they claimed disrupted peace and stability in Syria. In response, Faisal reportedly reassured Musa Eliyahu Totaḥ, the head of the Syrian Jewish community, that "he who sprays you with water, I will spray them back with blood."[40] Rivlin questioned the sincerity of this statement, and whether it was a reflection of Faisal's genuine feelings toward Jews or his naivete regarding the British policy toward Jews under the Mandate. This skepticism underscored Rivlin's broader critique of Faisal's approach and the challenges posed by Palestinian nationalists to Zionist aspirations in the region.

The war and the creation of the state of Israel disrupted the delicate balance within the field of Jewish Arabists. Some experts saw these events as opportunities to enhance their position, while others felt the need to defend themselves as Arabophiles. Their actions were driven by their relative position within the field and the perceived opportunities that emerged rather than a specific political ideology.[41] For his part, Rivlin's series of articles on the Hashemites cemented his status as an expert on Arab affairs. He emphasized his firsthand experience to supplement his Orientalist expertise. For example, he recounted having seen Sharif Hussein of Mecca when he came to Jerusalem during World War I, accompanied by either Jamal Pasha or Anwar Pasha at the time. He then spoke about Faisal's inauguration ceremony in Damascus, which he attended. He described the custom of *bay'a* (pledging allegiance) in which representatives of all communities pass before the king and shake hands with him in a demonstration of loyalty. Rivlin stressed his scholarly role as an Orientalist during the inauguration ceremony, presenting himself as someone whose interest was strictly anthropological and ethnographic. He clarified that his participation in certain traditions and customs of the subjects he studied was not personal but instead solely for the purpose of gathering, analyzing, and constructing firsthand knowledge—a practice highly valued among Orientalists of the time. In his words, "I was initially driven to this honor, only out of the desire to observe with my own eyes and to participate in this act, which a lot of 'Orientalists' were longing to out of love of the profession."[42] Thirty years after attending Faisal's inauguration ceremony to the throne of Syria in 1920, Rivlin reframed events to demonstrate his adherence to scientific methods in studying and learning about the Arab community in Syria. His participation in the ceremony was but an experiment to learn firsthand about the Arab customs and traditions he only learned about from the pages of *One Thousand and One Nights.*

The Status of Arabic

This book has dealt at length with the ways that Hebrew writers in late Ottoman and British Palestine interacted with Arabic in their construction of Jewish indigeneity. The 1948 war changed the way these same writers perceived the very same language and its function in the new political order. The plurilingualism that had prevailed in late Ottoman Palestine had allowed Hebrew to flourish.[43] The British Mandate further strengthened the status of Hebrew in 1922 by making it an official language on par with Arabic and English.[44] The British officials did not impose English instruction on either Arabs or Jews, leaving the way open for each community to teach its own language.[45]

With the establishment of the state of Israel, ideological Hebrew monolingualism suppressed other languages. Hebrew was instrumental in the integration of successive non-Hebrew-speaking Jewish immigrants who brought with them a plethora of foreign languages that were replaced with Hebrew. Several factors contributed to the rapid dissemination of Hebrew among immigrants: the young age of immigrants, linguistic affinity (especially among Arabic-speaking Jewish immigrants), and formal Hebrew education.[46] Furthermore, the Israeli Citizenship Law of 1952 required knowledge of Hebrew as a condition for naturalization.[47]

During the statehood era, Arabic was theoretically granted official status, though it was considered secondary to Hebrew. The Declaration of Independence gave Palestinians in Israel the right to maintain their ethnic and cultural identity: "The State of Israel will uphold the full social and political equality of all its citizens . . . [and it] will guarantee the freedom of religions, conscience, language, education and culture." Additionally, currency, legal documents, and government forms in Israel were issued in both Hebrew and Arabic. The Knesset (Israeli Parliament) passed laws published in both languages, even though Arabic was commonly used in the law courts. Palestinian Knesset members were allowed to address the House in Arabic, and an official interpreter was employed to assist with translation between Arabic and Hebrew during their speeches.[48] That official status bestowed on Arabic, however, triggered opposition among Revisionist Zionist circles, which claimed that the Arab population in Israel constituted only a small minority, about one-fifth, of Israel's total population, and therefore it was unreasonable and unprecedented to elevate Arabic to the status of an official language. The Revisionists agreed to give the Arab minority the right to publish books in Arabic and teach the language in their schools, but insisted that they must learn the language of the majority. Among these extremists, officializing Arabic meant acknowledging that they did not have sole sovereignty of the land. It signaled that Jews were not *ha-adonim ha-yeḥidim 'al erets ha-avot* (the only masters on the ancestral homeland) but instead *kovshe ha-arets* (conquerors of the land).[49] A few years later, in 1952, right-wing opposition parties proposed to make Hebrew the sole official language of the state and called for the abolition of the official status of Arabic. These proposals, though, were ultimately rejected by the majority of the Knesset.[50]

Any state views language policy as a crucial exercise of power. So why did the Labor government of Israel grant Arabic official status in the first place? First, the founders of the state were continuing the British Mandate policy regarding official languages, with the exception of eliminating English as an official language in the country.[51] Second, some scholars have argued that by granting Arabic official status, the nascent state fended off criticism from the international community regarding minority rights, forcing the government to honor the principles laid out in the Declaration of Independence. For its part, the Arabic-speaking population was unwilling to relinquish its mother tongue in favor of embracing Hebrew as the sole language in the country.[52] The position of Arabic as an "official-non-official" language in Israel allowed Israeli official institutions and the majority of Israeli Jews to maintain an image of a democratic country that honors minority rights, with the liberal connotations and international approbation that brings, without necessarily becoming a more egalitarian and inclusive society. The official status of Arabic is not evident in higher education, public institutions, or diplomatic sectors.[53] The status of Arabic inside Israel diminished as it ceased to be the dominant language and was denied many of the privileges that normally accompany official status.[54]

The fate of Arabic became closely tied to that of Palestinians in Israel—a minority population considered suspicious and potentially a threat, and thus placed under a military regime. Ironically, the main reason for doubting Palestinians' loyalty to the Jewish state was their mother tongue, which emotionally, historically, and culturally linked them not only to Palestinians in Gaza, East Jerusalem, and the West Bank but also to the broader Arab world. Arabic became an important language for the Palestinian minority living in Israel, though it played hardly any role in the national public sphere.[55]

In the 1940s, the divisive political atmosphere led to reduced interactions between Jews and Arabs in Mandate Palestine. And in the wake of 1948, the two societies became more divided than ever before. Due to the ongoing conflict, many Israeli Jews believed that Palestinians outside Israel supported the Arab enemy who fought against the Jewish state and aspired to prevent its birth. At the same time, Palestinians within Israel were seen as a potential threat from within, or a "fifth column." This perception hindered integration efforts among students and teachers of Arabic, and discouraged the study of the language. Yet there were Jewish scholars, such as Ben-Ze'ev, who resisted the marginalization of the Arabic language and promoted the study of the language in Israel. These scholars were, in part, motivated by security concerns and indeed promoted Arabic instruction in Jewish institutions on security grounds. Nevertheless, some scholars who genuinely wished to promote Arabic language and culture within Israel were forced to defend these endeavors against majority prejudice, and as such, were relegated to the sidelines for their efforts.[56] Unable to elevate Arabic to an equal footing with Hebrew, they found themselves confined to integrating Palestinian citizens into the nascent state rather than disseminating Arabic studies among Israeli Jews.

Despite the separation between Israeli Jews and Palestinians in the Jewish state, occasional events were sponsored by the state to project an image of Israel as a democratic country that cared about its minority, which at the time was under military rule due to the public perception of Palestinians as a "dangerous population." These events received coverage in the Hebrew newspapers, and were framed as cultural and social meeting points between Israeli Jews and Palestinians. The second pedagogical conference for Arab teachers convened in Nazareth in August 1950 and was one such event that purported to represent the "winning strategy of the Jewish state" to promote Arabic language learning. The Hebrew newspaper *Davar*, the official newspaper of the Histadrut—Israel's largest workers' union, presented the two-week conference as a successful event not only from an educational and cultural perspective but from a public and political point of view too. The conference was attended by 350 teachers, including Muslims and Christians, along with approximately 50 Jewish teachers of Arabic in Hebrew schools. Government representatives also participated in the event. The conference, according to the newspaper report, represented an "excellent opportunity for social and cultural rapprochement between Jewish intellectual circles and the Arab audience in Israel." At the center of this media coverage was Ben-Ze'ev, who was represented as the mastermind of this Arabic teachers' conference given his governmental position as the supervisor of Arabic language in the Ministry of Education.[57]

On the eve of World War II, Ben-Ze'ev resettled in British Palestine. In 1940, he became the first supervisor of Arabic studies in the Jewish education system within the *Va'ad ha-Le'umi* (National Assembly). Ben-Ze'ev continued to supervise Arabic within the Ministry of Education until 1964.[58] The media reports warmly celebrated Ben-Ze'ev as a prominent scholar who "delved into the treasure houses of Arab culture and the wisdom of the Orient," and in turn used his expertise to "organize, supervise, and train in the field of education in the state of Israel with love, force, and enthusiasm." His efforts resulted in a respectful welcome among his colleagues in both Jewish and Arab circles, according to the newspaper. Several pictures were published of him with prominent Palestinian public figures, such as Yusef Fahum, the acting mayor of Nazareth, and Sheikh Ṭāher al-Ṭabarī, the sole *qadi* (Islamic jurist) and Supreme Muslim Council member from the Mandate period who remained in Israel after 1948, and was appointed as the qadi of Nazareth in 1950.[59] Ben-Ze'ev's "harmonious fusion of spiritual richness and practical ability," according to *Davar*'s reporter, manifested in his relentless efforts to promote cultural rapprochement between Jews and Arabs by focusing on Jewish figures who rose to prominence in the medieval Islamic world as well as by campaigning for the promotion of Arabic studies within his capacity as a supervisor in the Ministry of Education.[60]

Ben-Ze'ev was among the speakers at the annual conference. Lecturing in Arabic was not unusual for Ben-Ze'ev, who taught Judaism at the Egyptian University (today Cairo University) and Semitic languages at Dār al-ʿulūm School (House of Sciences) throughout the 1930s.[61] In particular, his lecture on Moses Maimonides attracted the attention of *Davar*'s reporter:

> It is difficult to describe the strong impression made by Dr. Y. Ben-Ze'ev's public lecture on Maimonides, and the influence of reciprocity between Hebrew and Arabic philosophy. Hundreds of Arabs, both men and women, Christians and Muslims, filled the auditorium and listened attentively to the beautiful lecture, which captivated everyone with its content and the flowing, rich Arabic language. After the lecture, some of the attendees responded with applause and comments that demonstrated a serious attitude toward the discussed topic, and an effort to adapt to objective thinking and mutual tolerance—an uncommon phenomenon in the atmosphere of Nazareth and its spiritual environment until today.

The fact that both Christians and Muslims attended a lecture on a historical Jewish figure by a Jewish scholar shows a shared interest in exploring the philosophical connections between Hebrew and Arabic traditions. The lecture also fostered a sense of mutual understanding and respect, as evidenced by the reactions of the attendees. This indicates a willingness to bridge cultural and religious divides through open-mindedness and tolerance—an objective that Ben-Ze'ev strove to realize as he stated in a brief interview with the reporter after the lecture that "these conferences contribute to rapprochement with Arabs in Israel, and the dissipation of feelings of bitterness and alienation." Ben-Ze'ev's lecture served as a catalyst for dialogue and intellectual exchange between the Hebrew and Arabic philosophical traditions, fostering a more inclusive and harmonious environment in Nazareth. At the time, the city was under military rule, and its inhabitants were not allowed to travel beyond its boundaries without a permit from the military governor. Indeed, the reporter reminded readers of the fact that Palestinian citizens of Israel, as a "dangerous population," remain under military rule, and noted that among the speakers at that pedagogical conference were representatives of the military government. On the other hand, the lecture was an orchestrated triumph for state officials, including Ben-Ze'ev, offering an opportunity to portray "the moral and civilizational power of the Israeli government," according to *Davar*'s reporter.[62] The fact that this annual conference for Palestinian teachers of Arabic took place in a predominantly Arab town indicates the status of Arabic as an "official language" only among Palestinians, with little impact in Jewish circles.

Within his capacity as a supervisor of Arabic studies within the Ministry of Education, Ben-Ze'ev relentlessly promoted the study of Arabic (the Palestinian dialect and literary Arabic) in the Jewish school system. He justified his proposal to teach Jewish students Arabic by contending that it was useful to Israelis to be able to understand contemporary Arab media and the Arab people's way of life.[63] Thus the argument for teaching Hebrew and Jewish history to Arabs in Nazareth was to integrate them within the larger Jewish culture, while the argument for teaching Arabic to Jews was that it facilitated observing, surveilling, and controlling them. The "rapprochement" and "dissipation of alienation" he referred to were on the part of Palestinians in Israel, not on the part of Israeli Jews.

Despite his assertion that teaching Arabic to Israeli Jews was in their interests and that of the state of Israel, hostile views against Arabs and Palestinians doomed Ben-Ze'ev's attempts to failure. The arc of intercommunal relations can be observed in Barukh Ben-Yahuda's succession of Ben-Ze'ev as head of the Department of Education in 1947. In 1944, Ben-Yehuda published a textbook on the history of Zionism in which he rejected the concept of racial affinities and amicable relations between Jews and Arabs in Palestine, claiming that "the true destruction of [the land of] Israel was caused by the Arab rule of the country. All [of] their years of rule were one chain of perpetual wars between kings, rulers and tribes who demolished the country and emptied it [of its Jewish inhabitants]."[64] This framing of Arab history in Palestine displaces nostalgia for the Ottoman Empire with a monolithic, exclusivist national narrative.[65] Indeed, this Orientalist portrayal of Arabs as violent and barbaric is contrasted with the presentation of the state of Israel as bringing civilization and morality to Palestinians.[66]

Literary Triumph, Not Occupation

The prevailing derogation of the Arab population did not deter some Jewish scholars from utilizing Arabo-Islamic culture to further benefit the national project in the newly born state. They continued to dwell on Arabic culture's rich legacy and appropriate aspects of it to nurture the Jewish settler colonial enterprise. As remarked earlier, while Zionist scholars embarked on their enterprise to create a Hebrew map, Arabic place-names continued to play a central role in the retrieval of the original Hebrew name of a given site. The great service Arabic could render to future scholars propelled Press, a member of the GNC, to oppose the eradication of the Arabic place-names of abandoned Palestinian villages. Press was concerned not with the preservation of the Arabic place-names per se or the documentation of Palestinian landownership but rather the conservation of the historical and geographic memory to enable the identification of previous Hebrew place-names that might be concealed in the Arabic names.[67] Thus Arabic toponyms could function as a geographic memory device to aid the indigenization of the Jewish people in Palestine.

As we have shown throughout this book, most Jewish writers were not interested in Arabic in and of itself but instead for its utility in the revival of Hebrew and as a tool to instill a sense of indigeneity (by associating Jews with Semites and stressing their roots in the region). While subject to military rule in the early years of Israeli statehood and relegated to a second-class status, Palestinians were recruited in the public sphere to demonstrate their internalization of their defeat and their gratitude to the Jewish people for allowing them to remain in their midst.[68] Similarly, the Arabic language, even while relegated to secondary status, was recruited in the public sphere to demonstrate the linguistic and literary richness of Hebrew.

Hebrew scholars' continuous efforts to recruit Arabic for the advancement of national objectives is attested to in a review of the fourth volume of Rivlin's Hebrew rendition of the *Nights*, which came out in 1950. Writing under the pseudonym of M. Ḥen in the weekly newspaper *Hed ha-Mizraḥ*, the reviewer refrains from discussing the content of the narratives, assuming their familiarity to readers, and devotes his review to Rivlin's Hebrew translational style and the contribution his translation adds to the Hebrew language.

At the outset, the critic regards Rivlin's work as performing a service to the Arabic language: "Arabic finds in Rivlin a gracious translator" whose Hebrew rendition "gives an impression of an original work with wonderful stylistic integrity." Rivlin is portrayed as a remarkable translator for mastering both Arabic and Hebrew as well as preserving the original aura of the *Nights*. But of course Hebrew benefited from Rivlin's translation more than Arabic. The Hebrew translation of that volume of the *Nights*, according to the reviewer, presents an "unparalleled expression of the Eastern experience," not only because of Rivlin's translational integrity, but most importantly, because of his ability to render the aphorisms of the *Nights* in Hebrew as "finely crafted as the most exquisite gold pieces of our language"—that is, Hebrew.[69]

The reviewer noted that "the aphoristic expressions [of the tales] contain a glimpse of the spirit of Pirke Avot" (Ethics of the Fathers)—one of the Mishnah tractates that contains a collection of ethical, moral, and philosophical maxims—and for that these newly coined expressions deserve "a place in the anthology of Arabic and Eastern proverbs." The incorporation of Mishnaic Hebrew, as the critic noticed, in translating the *Nights*, emphasizes the Semitic origins of Hebrew and asserts its linguistic affinity with Arabic.[70] The reviewer indicated that hundreds of maxims "are integrated like gems."[71]

The reviewer cited a few examples of how Rivlin masterfully translated some of the most common Arabic expressions into Hebrew to reflect the Eastern experience. It should be noted that the reviewer does not cite the original Arabic, either in Arabic letters or transliteration. What mattered was the dissemination of the Hebrew language through the translation of a text that reflected the Eastern experience along with the promotion of expressions that would emphasize the Semitic roots of Hebrew and its belonging in the region's linguistic landscape to negate any claims of its alien status.

Among the expressions the critic listed without giving the Arabic equivalent are deeply ingrained phrases in the religious and cultural context of Arabo-Islamic culture: *Elohim ho ha-gadol* (God is Great / Allah Akbar), *ein ḥail ve-ein ḳoaḥ ila le-eilohim* (There is no strength or power but in, or by means of, *God/lā ḥawla wa lā quwata illā billah*), and *shama'ti u-mitzvato 'imala* (His wish is my command / *sam'an wa ṭā'aṭan / 'amrak muṭā' / shubeik lubeik*).

The reviewer devoted no space to the merits of the original Arabic, which is relegated to the status of a mediator connecting readers to the Semitic past. What is important was the potential of Arabic aphorisms, through the skills of Rivlin, to underscore the Eastern experience by rendering Arabic expressions into Hebrew. Just as Arabic place-names were appropriated to create Hebrew place-names in the national effort to craft a Hebrew map, the *Thousand and One Nights* was appropriated to connect Jews with Orientality. At this triumphant time, when Israel had achieved its independence and defeated Arab armies in the 1948 war, the reviewer drew an analogy between the Israeli military victory and the literary achievement of Rivlin. The reviewer provocatively described Rivlin's translation as a *kibbush* (conquest), a term usually employed to assert Jewish claims over Palestine as the ancestral homeland. The critic insinuatingly characterized Rivlin's translation as "not only an occupation but also a literary victory."[72] Moreover, the reviewer suggested that the Arab should be grateful for this occupation and victory, highlighting Rivlin's work as a significant contribution to Arabic. Still, the reviewer acknowledged that the primary objective of Rivlin's translation was not to connect Jews with contemporary Arabs—who were living in oppressed conditions at the time—but rather to link Jews with their own past. This was despite the fact that a masterpiece of Arab culture, the *Nights*, was being published in Hebrew.

This book contributes to the growing literature on Jewish individuals and groups that crossed the social, cultural, and religious boundaries to connect with other religious and ethnic communities in late nineteenth- and twentieth-century Palestine. In studying Jewish-Arab relational history, this book uses Arabo-Islamic knowledge accumulated and practiced by Jewish individuals to better understand settler-native relations as Zionism took root and evolved in Palestine, encompassing both settler colonial and national elements. It proposes that a settler-native and settler-colonist analytic framework is useful for understanding Jews' relationship to Arabic and Islamic culture as well as wider Jewish-Muslim relations in Palestine from the Ottoman era to the early years of the state of Israel by providing a narrative that moves beyond conventional simplistic binary conceptions. Analysis of the Hebrew literary corpus, our central subject, reveals several ways in which the adoption of this framework produces a more nuanced understanding of Jewish-Arab relations in Palestine. These include the dual self-perception of Jewish settlers as both settlers trying to establish roots in Palestine through colonization and nationalists aspiring to return back to the land of their ancestors. The framework also sheds light on the complex relationships between settlers and natives, emergence of diverse interaction between the two communities beyond simple conflict or coexistence, appropriation of native cultural elements for self-construction, and variety of Jewish approaches to producing and circulating Arabo-Islamic knowledge to strengthen Jewish ties to the land.

The book examines the connections between Islam and Jewish culture in Palestine within the context of settler-native relations, and explores how Jewish scholars embraced aspects of Arabo-Islamic culture to strengthen Jewish ties to the land and the region. The scholars aimed to construct a sense of Jewish indigeneity, portraying themselves not as refugees settling in Palestine but instead as exiled Jews returning to their ancestral homeland. The narrative is reframed from a simple perpetrator-victim dichotomy to that of settler-native interactions, emphasizing the settlers' strategic use of Arabo-Islamic knowledge to solidify their ties to the land and its native inhabitants. Such an approach uncovers the rich engagement of Hebrew scholars with the local Arab culture, challenging the prevailing view of these scholars as disinterested or even antagonistic toward Arabo-Islamic traditions. In tracing the development of Hebrew texts integrated with Arabo-Islamic sources—from texts to oral traditions—the study aligns with the chronology of Jewish settlement expansion in Palestine, from the initial wave of Jewish settlers to the eventual founding of a Jewish state within its historical borders.

In tandem with perceiving themselves as returnees to the ancestral homeland, Jewish settlers to late Ottoman Palestine viewed themselves as settlers and colonizers using the Hebrew term *kovesh* to refer to themselves and their community as settlement or colony *yishuv*, and their project as *hityashvut* (colonization). They also viewed the native population in Palestine through a lens that affirmed their own sense of nativity. Bilu member Israel Belḳind, for example, viewed Palestine's Arabs as *yoshve ha-arets* (inhabitants of the land), and *ʿam ha-arets* (people of the land)—language that almost all of the figures studied in this book had used to refer to both themselves and the Palestinian population.[73] Assessing Zionist immigrants to Palestine as settlers, and not merely refugees or returnees, aids in examining their motivations to engage with Arabo-Islamic culture as part of an effort to establish cultural legitimacy, rootedness, and a claim to the land through appreciation, adaptation, and sometimes appropriation of native traditions as well as knowledge.

The settler-native framework highlights a range of interactions between the settler community and Indigenous population. With the typical definition of the first group as consisting of those who had come to stay, the analysis has shown that this interaction was not solely adversarial but also characterized by cultural exchanges, intellectual curiosity, and mutual influences. This framework could help us pinpoint the historical circumstances that led to the evolution of a certain form of interaction along with the shift toward another as Jewish settlers grow in numbers and their activities spread in Palestine.

In addition to shedding light on the variegated forms of human and cultural interactions, Hebrew writers' engagement with Arabo-Islamic culture is a significant factor in understanding how the Jewish settlers' identity in Palestine was crafted. This appropriation of local knowledge can be seen as a strategic part of forming a new "native" identity, or a New Jew as we have seen, for the Jewish settlers, in contrast to their often European backgrounds. Through the invocation of historic and literary figures, Hebrew writers epitomized the ideal New Jew as one who embodied Oriental virtues such as nobility, courage, and hospitality—values that were welcomed and esteemed in the Arab context.

The settler-native analytic framework necessitates an exploration of the hybridization that takes place in colonial settings, where settlers selectively adopt aspects of the native culture. This approach provides a deeper understanding of the complex dynamics between Jewish settlers and the Palestinian native population, highlighting moments of coexistence and collaboration as well as conflict and resistance. Moreover, the framework redefines the narrative of settlement by critically reexamining the foundational narratives used to justify colonization. It reveals how these narratives were not only shaped by historical and political motives but also by the strategic integration of Arabo-Islamic elements, which helped reinforce a sense of entitlement to the land. This nuanced analysis offers a more comprehensive understanding of the settler colonial process and its lasting impact on Israeli-Palestinian relations.

NOTES

Introduction

1. Rashid Khalidi, *Palestinian Identity: The Construction of Modern National Consciousness* (New York: Columbia University Press, 1997), 145–46.

2. In adopting this approach, I build on the method in Suzanne L. Marchand, *German Orientalism in the Age of Empire: Religion, Race, and Scholarship* (Washington, DC: Cambridge University Press, 2009).

3. Abigail Jacobson and Moshe Naor, *Oriental Neighbors: Middle Eastern Jews and Arabs in Mandatory Palestine* (Waltham, MA: Brandeis University Press, 2016), 16.

4. Jacobson and Naor, *Oriental Neighbors*, 16.

5. Yuval Evri and Hagar Kotef, "When Does a Native Become a Settler? (with Apologies to Zreik and Mamdani)," *Constellations* 29, no. 1 (2020): 4.

6. According to an anonymous writer in *Ḥaqīqat al-'amr*, he resembled a tree "with its roots in this land [Palestine] and its branches extending to Jewish and Arab circles." "Dāwūd Yellīn fī al-khāmisa wa al-sab'īn," *Ḥaqīqat al-'Amr*, March 29, 1939. The newspaper *Ḥaqīqat al-'Amr* was the organ of the Palestine Labor League and published by the Arab Department of the Histadrut. For more details, see Jacobson and Naor, *Oriental Neighbors*, 91–92.

7. The English translation is found in Franz Rosenzweig, *Ninety-Two Poems and Hymns of Yehuda Halevi* (Albany: SUNY Press, 2012), 272. On the 1921 Jaffa riots, see Tom Segev, *One Palestine Complete: Jews and Arabs under the British Mandate* (New York: Henry Holt and Company, 2000), 173–201.

8. While Jews celebrated Balfour Day as a national holiday, Arabs had commemorated that day as a tragedy since 1918. See Tamir Sorek, *Palestinian Commemoration in Israel: Calendars, Monuments, and Martyrs* (Stanford, CA: Stanford University Press, 2015), 24–25.

9. Yellin's letter to the secretary of the Mandate government is found here: https://benyehuda.org/read/22662, accessed June 28, 2021. *Al-Ṣabāḥ* began to be published in 1921 under the editorship of Kamil al-Budayri and Yusuf Yasin, both members in Jerusalem's *al-Nādī al-'Arabī* (the Arab Club). See Yehoshua Porath, *The Emergence of the Palestinian-Arab National Movement, 1918–1929* (London: Frank Cass, 1974), 1:291.

10. The letter Yellin wrote was not published in the Palestinian newspaper and therefore he instead published it in Hebrew in the Hebrew journal *Ha-arets* in December 1921 to explain his position. See David Yellin, "Mikhtav Mr. David Yellin el 'orekh ha-Ṣābaḥ," *Ha-arets* (Jerusalem), December 4, 1921, 3. For an overview on the institution of Majlis 'Umūmī (Provincial Council) and other administrative entities, see Gudrun Krämer, *A History of Palestine: From the Ottoman Conquest to the Founding of the State of Israel*, trans. Graham Harman and

Gudrun Krämer (Princeton, NJ: Princeton University Press, 2008), 72–74. See also Yuval Ben-Bassat, *Late Ottoman Palestine: The Period of Young Turk Rule* (London: I. B. Tauris, 2011), 23, 78n60.

11. Louis A. Fishman, *Jews and Palestinians in the Late Ottoman Era, 1908–1914: Claiming the Homeland* (Edinburgh: Edinburgh University Press, 2020), 85.

12. Yael Zerubavel, *Desert in the Promised Land* (Stanford, CA: Stanford University Press, 2018), 56.

13. Itamar Even-Zohar, "The Emergence of a Native Hebrew Culture in Palestine, 1882–1948," *Poetics Today* 11, no. 1 (1990): 180–81.

14. Moshe Behar and Zvi Ben-Dor Benite, *Modern Middle Eastern Jewish Thought: Writings on Identity, Politics, and Culture, 1893–1958* (Waltham, MA: Brandeis University Press, 2013), 65–69.

15. Yitsḥaḳ Bezalel, *Noladetem Tsiyonim: ha-Sefaradim be-Erets-Yisrael ba-Tsiyonut uva-Tehiyah ha-'ivrit ba-Teḳufah ha-'Otmanit* [You were born Zionists: The Sephardim in Eretz Israel in Zionism and the Hebrew revival during the Ottoman period] (Jerusalem: Yad Yitsḥaḳ ben-Tsevi: Mekhon Ben-Tsevi le-ḥeḳer ḳehilot Yisra'el ba-mizraḥ, 2007), 406.

16. Michelle U. Campos, *Ottoman Brothers: Muslims, Christians, and Jews in Early Twentieth-Century Palestine* (Stanford, CA: Stanford University Press, 2010).

17. Jacobson and Naor, *Oriental Neighbors*, 26–27.

18. For a discussion on the role of Al-Bustānī in the nahda movement, see Stephen Sheehi, *Foundations of Modern Arab Identity* (Gainesville: University Press of Florida, 2004), 19–20.

19. Alan Dowty, *Arabs and Jews in Ottoman Palestine: Two Worlds Collide* (Bloomington: Indiana University Press, 2021), 25; Campos, *Ottoman Brothers*, 60–61.

20. Even-Zohar, "The Emergence of a Native Hebrew Culture in Palestine," 179.

21. Anthony Smith, "'The Land and Its People': Reflections on Artistic Identification in an Age of Nations and Nationalism," *Nations and Nationalism* 19, no. 1 (2013): 90.

22. Harvey E. Goldberg, "The Oriental and the Orientalist: The Meeting of Mordecai Ha-Cohen and Naḥum Slouschz," *Jewish Culture and History* 7, no. 3 (2004): 2.

23. Ivan Davidson Kalmar and Derek Jonathan Penslar, eds., *Orientalism and the Jews* (Hanover, NH: University Press of New England, 2005), xiii.

24. John M. Efron, "Orientalism and the Jewish Historical Gaze," in *Orientalism and the Jews*, ed. Ivan Davidson Kalmar and Derek Jonathan Penslar (Hanover, NH: University Press of New England, 2005), 81.

25. Gil Eyal, *The Disenchantment of the Orient: Expertise in Arab Affairs and the Israeli State* (Stanford, CA: Stanford University Press, 2006), 35. Cf. Yaron Peleg, *Orientalism and the Hebrew Imagination* (Ithaca, NY: Cornell University Press, 2005), 18–19.

26. On the use of settler colonialism as an interpretative paradigm for the Palestine-Israel conflict, see Rachel Busbridge, "Israel-Palestine and the Settler Colonial 'Turn': From Interpretation to Decolonization," *Theory, Culture & Society* 35, no. 1 (2018): 91–115.

27. Patrick Wolfe, "Settler Colonialism and the Elimination of the Native," *Journal of Genocide Research* 8, no. 4 (2006): 387.

28. Baruch Kimmerling, *Zionism and Territory: The Socio-Territorial Dimensions of Zionist Politics* (Berkeley: Institute of International Studies, University of California, 1983), 8.

29. Gershon Shafir, *Land, Labor and the Origins of the Israeli-Palestinian Conflict, 1882–1914* (Berkeley: University of California Press, 1996), 18.

30. Lorenzo Veracini, *Israel and Settler Society* (London: Pluto Press, 2006), 19–20.

31. Rachel Z. Feldman and Ian McGonigle, *Settler-Indigeneity in the West Bank* (Montreal: McGill-Queen's University Press, 2023), 12–13.

32. Areej Sabbagh-Khoury, *Colonizing Palestine: The Zionist Left and the Making of the Palestinian Nakba* (Stanford, CA: Stanford University Press, 2023), 86.

33. Meron Benvenisti, *Sacred Landscape: The Buried History of the Holy Land since 1948*, trans. Maxine Kaufman-Lacusta (Berkeley: University of California Press, 2000).

34. Rana Barakat, "Writing/Righting Palestine Studies: Settler Colonialism, Indigenous Sovereignty and Resisting the Ghost(s) of History," *Settler Colonial Studies* 8, no. 3 (2018): 353. Cf. Busbridge, "Israel-Palestine and the Settler Colonial 'Turn,'" 109.

Part I: Shared Homeland

1. Yehudah Shenhav, *Ha-tsiyonut ve-ha-imperyot* [Zionism and empires] (Jerusalem: Hotsa'at ha-Ḳibuts ha-me'uḥad, 2015), 14.

2. Jonathan Marc Gribetz, "Arab–Zionist Conversations in Late Ottoman Jerusalem: Sa'id al-Husayni, Ruhi al-Khalidi and Eliezer Ben-Yehuda," in *Ordinary Jerusalem, 1840–1940: Opening New Archives, Revisiting a Global City*, ed. Angelos Dalachanis and Vincent Lemire (Leiden: Brill, 2018), 313.

3. On the role that Palestinian Jews like Yellin played in the purchase of lands for Jewish settlers, see Michelle U. Campos, "Between 'Beloved Ottomania' and 'The Land of Israel': The Struggle over Ottomanism and Zionism among Palestine's Sephardi Jews, 1908–13," *International Journal of Middle East Studies* 37, no. 4 (2005): 462.

4. On the Sephardi and Oriental Jews' position on the Balfour Declaration, see Hillel Cohen and Yuval Evri, "Moledet meshutefet ou beit le'umi: bene ha-arets, hatsaharat Balfour ve he-she'elah ha-'Aravit" [Shared homeland or Jewish national home: Sephardi natives of the land, Balfour Declaration, and the Arab question], *Te'oriah u-veḳoret* 49 (2017): 293. For more on Palestinian Arabs' distinction between native and settler Jews, and representing the former group as opposing the Balfour Declaration, see Abigail Jacobson and Moshe Naor, *Oriental Neighbors: Middle Eastern Jews and Arabs in Mandatory Palestine* (Waltham, MA: Brandeis University Press, 2016), 23.

5. Michael Provence, *The Last Ottoman Generation and the Making of the Modern Middle East* (Cambridge: Cambridge University Press, 2017), 4.

6. Isaac Benjamin S. E. Yahuda, *Ha-Kotel ha-Ma'aravi: ma'amar maḳif 'al kotlenu zeh, ma she ne'emar 'alav, u-mah she dubar bo, mi-yeme ha-ḥurban 'ad ha-yom hazeh 'im mavo ve-hashmatot* [The Western Wall: A comprehensive essay on our wall] (Jerusalem: Y. A. Weiss, 1929), i.

7. Wāṣif Jawhariyyeh, *The Storyteller of Jerusalem: The Life and Times of Wasif Jawhariyyeh, 1904–1948*, ed. Salīm Tamārī and Issam Nassar, trans. Nada Elzeer (Northampton, MA: Olive Branch Press, 2014), 145–46.

8. Michelle U. Campos, *Ottoman Brothers: Muslims, Christians, and Jews in Early Twentieth-Century Palestine* (Stanford, CA: Stanford University Press, 2010), 6–7.

9. Ussama Makdisi, *Age of Coexistence: The Ecumenical Frame and the Making of the Modern Arab World* (Berkeley: University of California Press, 2019), 7, 10.

10. Jonathan Marc Gribetz, *Defining Neighbors: Religion, Race, and the Early Zionist-Arab Encounter* (Princeton, NJ: Princeton University Press, 2014).

11. Makdisi, *Age of Coexistence*, 28–29.

12. Arieh Bruce Saposnik, *Becoming Hebrew: The Creation of a Jewish National Culture in Ottoman Palestine* (New York: Oxford University Press, 2008), 25–26; Makdisi, *Age of Coexistence*, 30.

13. Makdisi, *Age of Coexistence*, 32–33.

14. On coexistence on a daily basis between Jews and Arabs in late Ottoman Palestine, see Menachem Klein, *Lives in Common: Arabs and Jews in Jerusalem, Jaffa and Hebron*, trans. Haim Watzman (London: Hurst & Company, 2014).

15. Jawhariyyeh, *The Storyteller of Jerusalem*, 56–138.

16. Makdisi, *Age of Coexistence* 100.

17. Provence, *The Last Ottoman Generation and the Making of the Modern Middle East*, 6.

18. Makdisi, *Age of Coexistence*, 98–99.

19. Muṣṭafa Kāmil, *Kitāb al-mas'ala al-sharqiyya* [The book of the Eastern question] (Cairo: Maṭba'at al-Ādāb, 1898), 8.

20. Yoni Furas, "We the Semites: Reading Ancient History in Mandate Palestine," *Contemporary Levant* 5, no. 1 (2020): 34–37.

21. Orit Bashkin, "On Noble and Inherited Virtues: Discussions of the Semitic Race in the Levant and Egypt, 1876–1918," *Humanities* 10, no. 3 (2021): 1–20.

22. On Makāryus and Zaydān embracing race thinking, see Gribetz, *Defining Neighbors*, 139–43.

23. Hanan Harif, *Anashim aḥim anaḥnu: Ha-peniyah mizraḥah ba-hagut ha-tsiyonit* [For we be Brethren: The turn to the East in Zionist thought] (Jerusalem: Merkaz Zalman Shazar le-ḥeḳer toldot ha-'am ha-Yehudi, 2019), 40–43.

24. Gil Z. Hochberg, "'Remembering Semitism' or 'On the Prospect of Re-Membering the Semites,'" *ReOrient* 1, no. 2 (2016): 203.

25. On the realization that anti-Semitism targeted both Jews and Arabs in the late nineteenth century, see Harif, *Anashim aḥim anaḥnu*, 46.

26. Orit Bashkin, "The Colonized Semites and the Infectious Disease: Theorizing and Narrativizing Anti-Semitism in the Levant, 1870–1914," *Critical Inquiry* 47, no. 2 (2021): 198.

27. For more on the newspaper's handling of the Beilis affair and the publication of a series of articles refuting conspiratorial theories against Jews, see Emanuel Beška, "'The Disgrace of the Twentieth Century': The Beilis Affair in *Filastin* Newspaper," *Jerusalem Quarterly File* 66 (2016): 99–108.

28. For recent scholarship on the subject, see Iair G. Or, *Bor'im signon le-dor: ha-emunot ve-ha-ide'ologyot shel metakhnene ha-lashon ha-'ivrit be-Erets Yisrael* [Creating a style for a generation: The beliefs and ideologies of Hebrew language planners] (Tel Aviv: Hidkel, 2016); Eran Buchaltzev, "'Ivri, 'Ivrit ve-'Ivriut—va'ad ha-lashon ha-'Ivrit ve-ha-tode'ah ha-le'umit ha-yehudit ba-shanim 1905–1941" (PhD diss., Ben-Gurion University, 2016).

29. Joshua Blau, *The Renaissance of Modern Hebrew and Modern Standard Arabic: Parallels and Differences in the Revival of Two Semitic Languages* (Berkeley: University of California Press, 1981), 18:18.

30. Stephen Sheehi, *Foundations of Modern Arab Identity* (Gainesville: University Press of Florida, 2004), 18.

31. Rana Issa, "The Arabic Language and Syro-Lebanese National Identity Searching in Buṭrus al-Bustānī's Muḥīṭ al-Muḥīṭ," *Journal of Semitic Studies* 62, no. 2 (2017): 465–84.

Chapter 1: Ambivalent Encounters

1. For an analysis of Moses Smilansky's novel *Ḥawaja Nazar*, see Shai Ginsburg, *Rhetoric and Nation: The Formation of Hebrew National Culture, 1880–1990* (Syracuse, NY: Syracuse University Press, 2014), 95. Cf. Ehud Ben-Ezer, *Be-moledet ha-ga'agu'im ha-menugadim: Ha-'Aravi ba-sifrut ha-'ivrit: mivḥar sipurim* [In the homeland of conflicting yearnings: The Arab in Israeli fiction: An anthology] (Tel Aviv: Agudat ha-sofrim ha-'ivrim, 1992), 17–23.

2. Gil Eyal, *The Disenchantment of the Orient: Expertise in Arab Affairs and the Israeli State* (Stanford, CA: Stanford University Press, 2006), 157.

3. On their political plans drafted in their manifesto, see Bilu, "Manifesto," in *Israel in the Middle East: Documents and Readings on Society, Politics, and Foreign Relations, Pre-1948 to the Present*, ed. Itamar Rabinovich and Jehuda Reinharz (Waltham, MA: Brandeis University Press, 1882), 11.

4. Liora Halperin, *The Oldest Guard: Forging the Zionist Settler Past* (Stanford, CA: Stanford University Press, 2021), 69–70.

5. Yosef Salmon, *Religion and Zionism: First Encounters* (Jerusalem: Hebrew University Magnes Press, 2002), 88.

6. This letter is cited in Shulamit Laskov, *Ha-Biluyim* [The Biluim], ed. Reuven Eshel (Jerusalem: Ha-Sifriyah ha-Tsiyonit, 1979), 33.

7. Muhammad Y. Muslih, *The Origins of Palestinian Nationalism* (New York: Columbia University Press, 1988), 70–78.

8. I should define here my employment of the concept "hierarchical coexistence" versus Halperin's use of the same concept in her work. She uses the term "hierarchical coexistence" in the labor and economic context to describe a discourse among First Aliyah private landowners who were commemorating their past relations with the local population. In this context, I use it to capture the historical relations between Jewish settlers of the First Aliyah and Palestinian farmers. My definition of the concept is that in multiethnic contexts where ideological, political, or religious differences are prominent, "coexistence" captures the ongoing effort to maintain peace and mutual respect amid underlying tensions. It suggests a scenario wherein groups or individuals may not necessarily agree or align with each other on every aspect, but have found a way to navigate their differences and live together without resorting to violence or overt hostility. Halperin, *The Oldest Guard*, 95.

9. Gershon Shafir, *Land, Labor and the Origins of the Israeli-Palestinian Conflict, 1882–1914* (Berkeley: University of California Press, 1996), 200.

10. Penimi, "Bifnim ha-arets," *Ha-Po'el Ha-Tza'ir* (Jerusalem), July 29, 1909.

11. Cited in Ran Aaronsohn, "The Beginnings of Modern Jewish Agriculture in Palestine: 'Indigenous' versus 'Imported,'" *Agricultural History* 69, no. 3 (1995): 444.

12. Aaronsohn, "The Beginnings of Modern Jewish Agriculture in Palestine."

13. Raef Zreik, "When Does a Settler Become a Native? (with Apologies to Mamdani)," *Constellations* 23, no. 3 (2016): 358.

14. Yochai Oppenheimer, *Me'ever lagader: ytsug ha-'Aravim ba-sipuret ha-'ivrit v-ha-yisraelit, 1906–2005* [Barriers: The representation of the Arab in Hebrew and Israeli fiction, 1906–2005] (Tel Aviv: 'Am 'oved, 2008).

15. Aziza Khazzoom, "The Great Chain of Orientalism: Jewish Identity, Stigma Management, and Ethnic Exclusion in Israel," *American Sociological Review* 68, no. 4 (2003): 481–510.

16. I differ from Alan Dowty regarding his attribution of the phrase "our brother Ishmael" in the Bilu manifesto to the Muslim Turks and not to the local Arab inhabitants in Palestine. In my view, it was common among early Zionists, especially regarding a nationalistically conscious group such as the Biluim, to work on two fronts. First, they sought political settlement for their national project through reaching out to and opening channels with the Ottoman authorities. Second, they attempt to persuade the local Arabs of the benefits of their project to head off resistance. For more on his reading, see Alan Dowty, *Arabs and Jews in Ottoman Palestine: Two Worlds Collide* (Bloomington: Indiana University Press, 2021), 78–79.

17. Rashid Khalidi, *The Hundred Years' War on Palestine: A History of Settler Colonialism and Resistance, 1917–2017* (New York: Metropolitan Books, 2020), 4–5.

18. Walter Laqueur and Barry M. Rubin, *The Israel-Arab Reader: A Documentary History of the Middle East Conflict*, 7th ed. (New York: Penguin Books, 2008), 4.

19. Carol Bakhos, *Ishmael on the Border: Rabbinic Portryals of the First Arab* (Albany: SUNY Press, 2006), 14.

20. Derek Jonathan Penslar, "Zionism, Colonialism and Postcolonialism," *Journal of Israeli History* 20, no. 2–3 (June 1, 2001): 86.

21. Derek Jonathan Penslar, *Zionism and Technocracy: The Engineering of Jewish Settlement in Palestine, 1870–1918* (Bloomington: Indiana University Press, 1991), 18.

22. Penslar, *Zionism and Technocracy*, 22–23.

23. On their political plans drafted in their manifesto, see Bilu, "Manifesto"; Dowty, *Arabs and Jews in Ottoman Palestine*, 78–79.

24. Abraham Shalom Yahuda, *Ḳadmoniyot ha-'aravim: bi-yeme ha-ba'arut asher li-fene Muḥammad* [The antiquities of the Arabs] (Jerusalem, 1894).

25. Yahuda, *Ḳadmoniyot ha-'aravim*, iii.

26. For a critique on the origins of Arabs from Arabo-Islamic sources, see Jan Retso, *The Arabs in Antiquity: Their History from the Assyrians to the Umayyads* (London: Routledge, 2013), 24–62.

27. Reuven Firestone, "The 'Other' Ishmael in Islamic Scripture and Tradition," in *The Politics of the Ancestors: Exegetical and Historical Perspectives on Genesis 12–36*, ed. Mark G. Brett, Jakob Wöhrle, and Friederike Neumann (Tübingen: Mohr Siebeck, 2018), 420.

28. S. D. Goitein, *Jews and Arabs: Their Contact through the Ages* (New York: Schocken Books, 1964), 21–23.

29. Israel Eph'al, "'Ishmael' and 'Arab(s)': A Transformation of Ethnological Terms," *Journal of Near Eastern Studies* 35, no. 4 (1976): 231. On the kinship between Jews and Arabs as cousins based on Midrashim, see Bakhos, *Ishmael on the Border*, 67–79.

30. For a reference to his description of Arabs as cousins, see David Yellin, *Kitve David Yellin: yerushalayim shel temol* [The writings of David Yellin: The Jerusalem of yesterday (letters from Jerusalem to "Hamelitz," 1896–1904)], ed. Benyamin Rivlin (Jerusalem: Ha-Va'ad

le-Hotsa'at Kitve Dayid Yellin, Hotsa'at Rubin Mass, 1972), 1:114–15. For his reference to the significance of Arabic, see Yellin, *Kitve David Yellin*, 1:93.

31. As noted earlier, he made a curative trip to Algeria in 1880, and married his first wife, Debora, in Cairo on his way to Jerusalem in 1881. For a reference to his acquaintance with Arabic during his stay there, see Jack Fellman, *The Revival of a Classical Tongue: Eliezer Ben Yehuda and the Modern Hebrew Language* (The Hague: Mouton, 1973), 23.

32. For more details, see the connotation of the adjectival phrase *magor* in Eliezer Ben-Yehuda, *Milon ha-lashon ha-'ivrit ha-yeshanah ve-ha-ḥadashah: ha-mavo' ha-gadol* [A complete dictionary of ancient and modern Hebrew: Prolegomena] (Tel Aviv: Sefer, 1948).

33. Eliezer Ben-Yehuda, *Kol kitve Eliezer Ben-Yehuda* [Collected works of Eliezer Ben-Yehuda] (Jerusalem: Ha-Ma'arav, 1941), xxvi, 26.

34. Ben-Yehuda, *Kol kitve Eliezer Ben-Yehuda*, 26.

35. Eliezer Ben-Yehuda, *Kol kitve Eliezer Ben-Yehuda* [Collected works of Eliezer Ben-Yehuda] (Jerusalem: Ha-Ma'arav, 1941), xxvi, 26.

36. For a detailed study of the biblical portrayal of Ishmael and Esau along with their pairing in rabbinic literature, see Bakhos, *Ishmael on the Border*, 54–64.

37. Ben-Yehuda, *Kol kitve Eliezer Ben-Yehuda*, 26.

38. His involvement in ethnographic research led him to advance a far-reaching theory on the origins of Palestine's Arab population that would echo in the future Canaanite movement in Israel. See Laskov, *Ha-Biluyim*, 392–93. Belḳind did not publish his work at the time. The earliest publication on the subject is Israel Belḳind, "Motsa ha-'Aravim she-be-Erets Yisrael" [The origins of Arabs in the land of Israel], *Ha-Schiloach* 38 (1921): 438–45.

39. The theory was the focus of a question and answer in the column "Aḥenu ha-'Aravi, Ḥidon" [Our Arab brother, a mystery] in the daily Hebrew newspaper *Maariv*, August 9, 1985.

40. Lasḳov, *Ha-Biluyim*, 389.

41. Shmuel Almog, "Ha-adamah le-'ovdeha ve-giur ha-pallaḥim," in *Umah ve-toldoteha*, ed. Samuel Ettinger (Jerusalem: Mirkaz Zalman Shazar, 1984), 171. On Belḳind's views on the origins of Palestinian Arabs as Hebrews, see Belḳind, "Motsa ha-'Aravim she-be-Erets Yisrael."

42. Belḳind, "Motsa ha-'Aravim she-be-Erets Yisrael," 438.

43. Israel Belḳind, *Ha-'Aravim asher be-Erets Yisrael* [The Arabs in the land of Israel], ed. David Ben-Gurion (Tel-Aviv: Ḥermon, 1969), 26.

44. In his letter, Yusūf Ḍiyā al-Dīn recognizes the Jewish tragedy in Europe and shows sympathy for Jews' dreadful circumstances, yet advises Herzl against engineering mass Jewish immigration to Palestine, saying that it would be "pure folly" for Zionists to plan to take over Palestine, a country that was an integral part of the Ottoman Empire and inhabited by others. Khalidi, *The Hundred Years' War on Palestine*, 6; Julia Phillips Cohen, *Sephardi Lives: A Documentary History, 1700–1950* (Stanford, CA: Stanford University Press, 2014), 222–24.

45. Louis A. Fishman, *Jews and Palestinians in the Late Ottoman Era, 1908–1914: Claiming the Homeland* (Edinburgh: Edinburgh University Press, 2020), 70–71.

46. Shafir, *Land, Labor and the Origins of the Israeli-Palestinian Conflict*, 200–202. On the various meanings of heroism and victimhood attributed to this incident in the Zionist newspapers from the time of the accident to subsequent years, see Liora R. Halperin, "Petah Tikva, 1886: Gender, Anonymity, and the Making of Zionist Memory," *Jewish Social Studies* 23, no. 1 (2017): 1–28.

47. Yuval Ben-Bassat, "Bedouin Petitions from Late Ottoman Palestine: Evaluating the Effects of Sedentarization," *Journal of the Economic and Social History of the Orient* 58, no. 1–2 (2015): 150–51.

48. Dowty, *Arabs and Jews in Ottoman Palestine*, 93.

49. Muslih, *The Origins of Palestinian Nationalism*, 72.

50. Dowty, *Arabs and Jews in Ottoman Palestine*, 93.

51. Neville J. Mandel, *The Arabs and Zionism before World War I* (Berkeley: University of California Press, 1976), 32–33.

52. Studies that discuss Nahḍawī Arab intellectuals' interest in Jewish matters include Lisa Lital Levy, "Jewish Writers in the Arab East: Literature, History, and the Politics of Enlightenment, 1863–1914" (PhD diss., University of California at Berkeley, 2007); Jonathan Marc Gribetz, *Defining Neighbors: Religion, Race, and the Early Zionist-Arab Encounter* (Princeton, NJ: Princeton University Press, 2014).

53. Orit Bashkin, "The Fruit of the Arts and the Mob: Global Minorities during the Dreyfus Affair," *Comparative Studies of South Asia, Africa and the Middle East* 41, no. 3 (2021): 404–12.

54. Orit Bashkin, "The Colonized Semites and the Infectious Disease: Theorizing and Narrativizing Anti-Semitism in the Levant, 1870–1914," *Critical Inquiry* 47, no. 2 (2021): 193–94.

55. Ussama Makdisi, *Age of Coexistence: The Ecumenical Frame and the Making of the Modern Arab World* (Berkeley: University of California Press, 2019), 7.

56. Eliyahu Sapir, "Ha-sin'ah le-Yisrael ba-sifrut ha-'Aravit" [Israel hatred in Arabic literature], *Ha-Schiloah* 6 (1899): 222–32.

57. Sapir, "Ha-sin'ah le-Yisrael ba-sifrut ha-'Aravit."

58. Mandel, *The Arabs and Zionism before World War I*, 39.

59. Walter Lacquer, *The History of Zionism* (New York: Holt, Rinehart, and Winston, 2003), 212.

60. Sapir, "Ha-sin'ah le-Yisrael ba-sifrut ha-'Aravit," 222.

61. Sapir here reiterates the views of nineteenth-century German Jewish historians who approached the history of Jewish-Christian relations as a history of Jewish suffering. Meanwhile, historians such as Heinrich Graetz contended that Islam had been good to the Jews and the contemplation of Jewish life under the rule of Islam provided comfort to a traumatized Jewish historian who had to write about Christian persecution.

62. Sapir, "Ha-sin'ah le-Yisrael ba-sifrut ha-'Aravit," 226–27.

63. Sapir, "Ha-sin'ah le-Yisrael ba-sifrut ha-'Aravit," 232.

64. Ben-Yehuda, *Kol kitve Eliezer Ben-Yehuda*, 37. There is an inclination to assume that Ben-Yehuda borrowed the phrase *qalbuh khafīf* (his heart is weak), which was circulating in the Oriental dialect and used to refer to a "coward," as opposed to a clever person.

65. Dowty, *Arabs and Jews in Ottoman Palestine*, 97, 101.

66. Ben-Yehuda, *Kol kitve Eliezer Ben-Yehuda*, 37.

67. Cited in Fellman, *The Revival of a Classical Tongue*, 43–44.

68. Sapir, "Ha-sin'ah le-Yisrael ba-sifrut ha-'Aravit," 232.

69. Israel Ben-Ze'ev, "R' Yitsḥaḳ Yahuda: 'Ishiyuto ve-Tilmudo" [R' Yitsḥaḳ Yahuda: His personality and teachings], *Moznaim* 3 (1941): 71.

70. This account is found in Ben-Ze'ev, "R' Yitsḥaḳ Yahuda." Ibn Al-Nadīm (d. 995 or 998) lived in Iraq and took part in the court circle of Abū al-Qāsim 'Īsa b. 'Alī b. al-Jarrāḥ (d. 1001). He is the first and most famous bibliographer, for he tried in his work *Kitāb al-Fihrist* to mirror everything that was known in the Islamic world through written texts. For more details on Ibn al-Nadīm, see Bruna Soravia, "Arabic Bibliographies," in *Encyclopaedia of Islam*, ed. Kate Fleet et al. (Third ed., 2015).

71. Lital Levy, "The Nahḍa and the Haskala: A Comparative Reading of 'Revival' and 'Reform,'" *Middle Eastern Literatures* 16, no. 3 (2013): 308.

72. Al-Zinjānī, a distinguished scholar of Arabic language and literature, collected the Arabic poetry for *al-Maḍnūn bihi 'ala ghayr Ahlih*. A century later, al-'Ubaydī published a *sharḥ* (commentary) on the collection. Perhaps the Iraqi origins of Yahuda and al-Zanjānī, who passed away in Baghdad, motivated the latter to edit his work. For more details on the work, see 'Ubayd Allāh Ibn 'abd Al-Kāfī al-'Ubaydī, *Sharḥ al-maḍnūn bi-hi 'alā ghayr ahlih: huwa sharḥ al-Sheikh al-'allāmah 'Ubayd Allāh ibn 'Abd al-Kāfī 'alā al-abyāt allatī intakhabahā al-Sheikh al-imām al-'allāmah 'Izz al-Dīn 'Abd al-Wahhāb al-Zanjānī* [That which is to be withheld from those unworthy of it], Isaac Yahuda (Cairo: Maṭba'at al-Sa'āda, 1913–15).

73. Khalidi, *The Hundred Years' War on Palestine*, 1–2.

74. Salīm Tamārī, "Wasif Jawhariyyeh, Popular Music, and Early Modernity in Jerusalem," in *Palestine, Israel, and the Politics of Popular Culture*, ed. Rebecca L. Stein and Ted Swedenburg (Durham, NC: Duke University Press, 2005); Menachem Klein, *Lives in Common: Arabs and Jews in Jerusalem, Jaffa and Hebron*, trans. Haim Watzman (London: Hurst & Company, 2014).

75. On the development of the circulation and production of texts among Palestinians in the early twentieth century, see Ami Ayalon, *Reading Palestine: Printing and Literacy, 1900–1948* (Austin: University of Texas Press, 2004), 43–44. On the development of the al-Khālidiyya library, see Walīd al-Khālidī, *Al-maktaba al-Khālidiyya fī al-Quds, 1720–2001* [The Khalidi library in Jerusalem, 1720–2001] (Beirut, 2002), 30.

76. al-Khālidī, *Al-maktaba al-Khālidiyya fī al-Quds*, 30.

77. 'Ubayd Allāh Ibn 'abd Al-Kāfī al-'Ubaydī, *Sharḥ al-maḍnūn bi-hi 'alā ghayr ahlih: huwa sharḥ al-Sheikh al-'allāmah 'Ubayd Allāh ibn 'Abd al-Kāfī 'alā al-abyāt allatī intakhabahā al-Sheikh al-imām al-'allāmah 'Izz al-Dīn 'Abd al-Wahhāb al-Zanjānī* [That which is to be withheld from those unworthy of it], ed. Isaac Yahuda (Cairo: Maṭba'at al-Sa'āda, 1913–15), i.

78. Levy, "The Nahḍa and the Haskala," 309.

79. David Yellin, "Hagadot ve-sipurim," *Ha-Tsvi* (Jerusalem), 1884.

80. Levy, "The Nahḍa and the Haskala," 309.

81. Gribetz, *Defining Neighbors*, 39.

82. Gribetz, "Arab–Zionist Conversations in Late Ottoman Jerusalem," 312–13.

83. Gribetz, *Defining Neighbors*, 39.

84. Gribetz, "Arab–Zionist Conversations in Late Ottoman Jerusalem," 315.

85. Cited in Gribetz, "Arab–Zionist Conversations in Late Ottoman Jerusalem," 315.

86. Gribetz, "Arab–Zionist Conversations in Late Ottoman Jerusalem," 316–17.

87. Yehuda Slutsky, "Menashe Meirovitch," in *Ha-'Entsayklopedyah ha-'Ivrit; Kelalit, Yehudit ve-Eretsyisraelit* (1970).

88. Menashe Meirovitch, *Ḥevle teḥiyah: kovets ma'amarim nivḥarim bi-she'elot ha-yishuv ha-'ivri be-Erets Yisrael mili-fene 50 shanah ṿe-'ad perots milḥemet ha-'olam* [Pains of

rejuvenation], ed. Yitshak Avinery (Tel Aviv: Ḥevrat Misḥar ṿe-Ta'asiyah, 1931), 8. Meirovitch and two other Bilu members sought to enter Jaffa using English passports issued during their short stay in Alexandria at the time of the British seizure. For more details on this story, see Menashe Meirovitch, *Mi-zikhronotav shel aḥaron ha-Biluyim* [From the memoirs of the last of Bilu members] (Jerusalem: Ha-ḳeren ha-ḳayemet le-yisrael, 1946), 26–28.

89. Meirovitch, in the words of Moshe Smilansky, was "one of the first Russian Jewish agronomists." See Moshe Smilansky and Aryeh Samsonov, *Ha-dorkhim ba-gat: gefen ve-yayin be-Yisrael* [Walkers on wine press: Grapevine and wine in Israel] (1957), 74–75; Yossi Ben-Artzi, "Changes in the Agricultural Sector of the Moshavot, 1882–1914," in *Ottoman Palestine, 1800–1914: Studies in Economic and Social History*, ed. Gilber Gad G. (Leiden: Brill, 1990), 157.

90. Samuel Dolbee and Shay Hazkani, "Unlikely Identities: Abu Ibrahim and the Politics of Possibility in Late Ottoman Palestine," *Jerusalem Quarterly*, no. 63 (2015): 26–27.

91. For more details on the Arabs' response to the Young Turk Revolution, see Tawfiq Barru, *Al-'Arab wa-al-Turk fī al-'Ahd al-Dustūrī al-'Uthmānī, 1908–1914* [Arabs and Turks in the Ottoman constitutional era, 1908–1914] (Damascus: Ma'had al-Dirāsāt al-'Arabiyya, 1960), 75–95; Campos, *Ottoman Brothers*, 138.

92. Yehoshua Porath, *The Emergence of the Palestinian-Arab National Movement, 1918–1929* (London: Frank Cass, 1974), 1:29.

93. Laura Robson, *Colonialism and Christianity in Mandate Palestine* (Austin: University of Texas Press, 2011), 34–35.

94. Menashe Meirovitch, *Me-ha-shevil el ha-derekh: kovets ma'amarim u-mikhtavim bi-she'elot ha-yishuv ha-'ivri be-Erets Yisrael* [From the trail to the road: A collection of essays and letters regarding the Hebrew settlement in the land of Israel] (Tel Aviv: Be-hotsa'at ḥevrat shṭibel ṿe-ḥever yedide ha-meḥaber, 1936), 61.

95. Penslar, *Zionism and Technocracy*, 22.

96. Halperin, *The Oldest Guard*, 22.

97. Campos, *Ottoman Brothers*, 138.

98. For a discussion on postrevolutionary Ottoman officials' acceptance of cultural Zionism in contrast to their strong rejection of political Zionism, see Campos, *Ottoman Brothers*.

99. Meirovitch, *Me-ha-shevil el ha-derekh*, 61.

100. Eliezer Ben-Yehuda, "Yehudim, Heyu 'otomanim," *Ha-Tsevi*, January 11, 1909.

101. Yaakov Markovitzki, *Be-khaf ha-kela' shel ha-ne'emanuyot: Bene ha-yishuv ba-tsava ha-Turḳi, 1908–1918* [Conflicts of loyalties: The enlistment of Palestinian Jews in the Turkish Army] (Ramat Ef'al: Ha-Merkaz le-Toldot Koaḥ ha-Magen ha-Haganah 'al shem Yisra'el Gelili, 1995), 29.

102. The piece was republished along with his other articles in Meirovitch, *Ḥevle teḥiyah*.

103. Meirovitch, *Ḥevle teḥiyah*, 110–14.

104. To be elected as a deputy in the postrevolutionary Ottoman Parliament, the candidate had to be at least thirty years of age and know the Turkish language. For more details, see M. Şükrü Hanioğlu, *A Brief History of the Late Ottoman Empire* (Princeton, NJ: Princeton University Press, 2008), 151.

105. Meirovitch, *Ḥivle teḥiyah*.

106. Meirovitch's choice of pen name appears to have been influenced by his grief over the death of Avraham (1884–1930), who passed away at the age of fifty. That his deep sadness

resulted from burying his son before his time is expressed in the Hebrew phrase "'al shem beni Avraham she-met be-ibu." For context, see Menashe Meirovitch, *Me-Bilu 'ad ya'pilū: 'al shishim ve-ḥamesh shenot he'avḳūt 'aliyah, binyan, vi-yetsirah* [Sixty-five years of struggle with immigration, building, and creation], ed. Yitsḥaḳ Sela' (Rishon Le-Ẓion: Hotsa'at ha-Teḥiyah, 1946), 132. His sorrow is expressed in the dedication of one of his works to both sons, the elder Avraham and the younger Ya'ḳov. See Meirovitch, *Me-ha-shevil el ha-derekh.*

107. Meirovitch, *Me-ha-shevil el ha-derekh*, 62. For an example of his Arabic writings, see Abu Ibrahim, "Rasā'il Fallāḥ (5)," *Filasṭīn* (Jaffa), 23 Tammuz / July 1911, 2–3.

108. Meirovitch, *Me-ha-shevil el ha-derekh.*

109. Meirovitch, *Me-ha-shevil el ha-derekh.*

110. Fishman, *Jews and Palestinians in the Late Ottoman Era*, 57, 56.

111. Fishman, *Jews and Palestinians in the Late Ottoman Era*, 58.

112. Abigail Jacobson, "Sephardim, Ashkenazim and the 'Arab Question' in Pre-First World War Palestine: A Reading of Three Zionist Newspapers," *Middle Eastern Studies* 39, no. 2 (2003): 109.

113. Meirovitch, *Me-ha-shevil el ha-derekh.*

114. For a meticulous discussion regarding Rūḥī al-Khālidī's writings on Zionism and how he conceived of Jews and Judaism, see a chapter on Rūḥī al-Khālidī's still unpublished book on Zionism, composed in late Ottoman Palestine, in Gribetz, *Defining Neighbors*, 39–92.

115. Meirovitch, *Ḥivle teḥiyah.*

116. Meirovitch, *Ḥivle teḥiyah.*

117. Yonatan Mendel, *The Creation of Israeli Arabic: Political and Security Considerations in the Making of Arabic Language Studies in Israel* (Hampshire: Palgrave Macmillan, 2014), 21–22.

118. Meirovitch, *Ḥivle teḥiyah.*

119. The phrase the author uses is a biblical one; see Ezekiel 32:32.

120. Meirovitch, *Ḥivle teḥiyah.* The author uses biblical phrases, found in 2 Kings 21:14 and Isaiah 42:22.

121. Menashe Meirovitch, "Tsimḥe erets ha-tsevi" [The flora of the land of gazelles], *Yerushalayim* 4 (1892): 126.

122. Meirovitch, "Tsimḥe erets ha-tsevi," 126.

123. The article "Le-Harim Mikhshol me-Derekh 'ami" is republished with a brief introduction by Yiẓhak Avinery in Meirovitch, *Ḥivle teḥiyah.*

124. Nahla Zu'bi, "The Development of Capitalism in Palestine: The Expropriation of the Palestinian Direct Producers," *Journal of Palestine Studies* 13, no. 4 (1984): 105–6.

125. Meirovitch, *Ḥivle teḥiyah.*

126. Meirovitch, *Ḥivle teḥiyah.* The word "proper" could also be translated as "modern" since the Hebrew is *metukan.*

127. Meirovitch, *Ḥivle teḥiyah.*

128. David Idelovitch, *Sefer ha-Mishar va-Haroshet ha-Ma'aseh be-Erets Yisrael* [The book of trade and industrial factories in the land of Israel] (Warsaw: Bi-defus Boymriter ve-Gonshor, 1890), 4.

129. Meirovitch, *Ḥevle teḥiyah.*

130. Zu'bi, "The Development of Capitalism in Palestine," 104.

Chapter 2: Writing the Landscape

1. James Stuart Duncan Jr., "Landscape Taste as a Symbol of Group Identity: A Westchester County Village," *Geographical Review* 63, no. 3 (1973): 334–55. Also, for a discussion on the impact of the interface between identity and landscape in the field of humanities along with the prolific literature that relationship has generated, see Shelley Egoz, "Landscape and Identity: Beyond a Geography of One Place," in *The Routledge Companion to Landscape Studies*, ed. Peter Howard et al. (London: Routledge, 2013), 273–74.

2. Shai Ginsburg, *Rhetoric and Nation: The Formation of Hebrew National Culture, 1880–1990* (Syracuse, NY: Syracuse University Press, 2014), 118.

3. Yael Zerubavel, *Recovered Roots: Collective Memory and the Making of Israeli National Tradition* (Chicago: University of Chicago Press, 1995), 13.

4. James S. Duncan, *The City as Text: The Politics of Landscape Interpretation in the Kandyan Kingdom* (Cambridge: Cambridge University Press, 2005), 17.

5. John Agnew, "European Landscape and Identity," in *Modern Europe: Place, Culture, Identity*, ed. Brian Graham (London: Hodder Education Publishers, 1998), 213–14.

6. Oz Almog, *The Sabra: The Creation of the New Jew* (Berkeley: University of California Press, 2000), 4.

7. For a discussion on the impact of Western geographic literature on nahda scholars, see Jurjī Zaydān, *Tārīkh 'Adāb al-lugha al-'Arabiyya* [A history of Arabic literature], ed. Shawqī Dhayf (Cairo: Dār Al-Hilāl, 1950), 4:255.

8. Cited in Colette Zytnicki, The 'Oriental Jews' of the Maghreb: Reinventing the North African Jewish Past in the Colonial Era," in *Colonialism and the Jews*, ed. Ethan B. Katz, Lisa Moses Leff, and Maud S. Mandel (Bloomington: Indiana University Press, 2017), 52n39.

9. Syrinx von Hees, *Inḥiṭāṭ—The Decline Paradigm: Its Influence and Persistence in the Writing of Arab Cultural History* (Würzburg: Ergon, 2017).

10. David Fieni, "French Decadence, Arab Awakenings: Figures of Decay in the Arab Nahda," *Boundary* 39, no. 2 (2012): 145.

11. Laura Péaud, "Relire la géographie de Conrad Malte-Brun," *Annales de géographie* 701, no. 1 (2015): 110. See also, for example, Rifā'a Rāfi' al-Ṭahṭawī, *Al-Kanz al-Mukhtār fī iktishāf al-'arāḍī w-al-biḥār* [The fine treasure in the discovery of land and sea] (1833). For a discussion on Ṭahṭawī's interventions into the dissemination of geographic knowledge among Arabic readership, see Peter Hill, *Utopia and Civilisation in the Arab Nahda* (Cambridge: Cambridge University Press, 2020), 139–43.

12. Michael J. Reimer, "Contradiction and Consciousness in 'Ali Mubarak's Description of al-Azhar," *International Journal of Middle East Studies* 29, no. 1 (1997): 53; Darrell Dykstra, "Pyramids, Prophets, and Progress: Ancient Egypt in the Writings of 'Alī Mubārak," *Journal of the American Oriental Society* 114, no. 1 (1994): 54–65.

13. Salīm Gabriel Al-Khūry and Salīm Michael Shihāda, *Kitāb 'āthār al-adhār: Al-qism al-Jughrāfī* [The book of the signs of times] (Beirut: Al-Maṭba'a al-sūriyya, 1875), 1. For a survey on other nahdawi figures who engaged in geography, see Zaydān, *Tārīkh 'Adab al-lugha al-'Arabiyya*, 4:277.

14. Lorenzo Kamel, "The Impact of 'Biblical Orientalism' in Late Nineteenth- and Early Twentieth-Century Palestine," *New Middle Eastern Studies* 4 (2014): 1.

15. See the introduction to his work: Khalīl Baydas, *Kitāb al-Rawḍa al-Mu'nisa fī waṣf al-'arḍ al-Muqaddasa* [The book of pleasant gardens in describing the Holy Land] (Abda [Lubnan]: Al-Maṭba'a al-Uthmāniyya, 1898), 2. For an English translation of Baydas's translational intention, see Scoville Spencer, "Translating Orientalism into the Arabic 'Nahda,'" *Alif: Journal of Comparative Poetics* 38 (January 1, 2018): 17.

16. Raef Zreik, "When Does a Settler Become a Native? (with Apologies to Mamdani)," *Constellations* 23, no. 3 (2016): 359.

17. Yael Zerubavel, "Memory, the Rebirth of the Native, and the 'Hebrew Bedouin' Identity," *Social Research* 75, no. 1 (2008): 318; Yael Zerubavel, *Desert in the Promised Land* (Stanford, CA: Stanford University Press, 2018), 40.

18. Naḥum Sokolow, *Erets Ḥemdah: Kolel Yedi'at Gelilot Erets ha-Ḳodesh 'al pi Gedole ha-Tayarim u-vo-gam Tamtsit Sefer ha-Masa' shel ha-Sar ha-Angli Laurence Oliphant* [A desirable land] (Warsaw: Bi-defus Yitsḥaḳ Goldman, 1885), iii. Sokolow's *Erets Ḥemdah* is beyond the historical scope of this project for a host of reasons. First, even though the author mastered several languages, almost all of them were Western, except for Hebrew, the only Oriental language he knew well. Second, *Erets Ḥemdah* was published in Warsaw to reach out to a Hebrew-reading audience outside Palestine. Third, the author did not pay any attention to the significance of Arabic language and culture, or proper investigation of the geographic aspect of the land. Fourth, other than several visits to Palestine starting from just prior to the outbreak of World War I, Sokolow himself never settled in the land of Palestine, and his role in the advancement of the Zionist cause took place solely in the West. See his biography: Getzel Kressel, "Sokolow, Nahum," in *Encyclopaedia Judaica*, ed. Michael Berenbaum and Fred Skolnik (Detroit: Macmillan Reference USA, 2007), 747–49. Fifth, many of the sources on which Sokolow draws are either Western-oriented works or belong to travelogue literature such as Laurence Oliphant's (1829–88) *The Land of Gilad*, in which he relates the places and experiences he encountered in his travels in Palestine. Sokolow translated this work into Hebrew and annexed a summary to the end of his *Erets Ḥemdah*. For more details, see his reasons for drawing on *The Land of Gilad* in Sokolow, *Erets Ḥemdah*, iii. Members of the Bilu movement are a notable example of the Palestinophiles who did not want for either political arrangement or messianic deliverance to Palestine. See Alan Dowty, *Arabs and Jews in Ottoman Palestine: Two Worlds Collide* (Bloomington: Indiana University Press, 2021), 98–99.

19. Michelle U. Campos, *Ottoman Brothers: Muslims, Christians, and Jews in Early Twentieth-Century Palestine* (Stanford, CA: Stanford University Press, 2010), 204.

20. Aviv Derri, "The Construction of 'Native' Jews in Late Mandate Palestine: An Ongoing Nahda as a Political Project," *International Journal of Middle East Studies* 53 (2021): 260; Israel Ben-Ze'ev, "Darko el ha-lashon ha-'aravit," *Davar*, March 24, 1939.

21. Stephen Sheehi, *Foundations of Modern Arab Identity* (Gainesville: University Press of Florida, 2004), 62.

22. Ahmed El Shamsy, *Rediscovering the Islamic Classics: How Editors and Print Culture Transformed an Intellectual Tradition* (Princeton, NJ: Princeton University Press, 2020), 78.

23. Abraham Moshe Lunts, "Mavo" [Introduction], *Yerushalayim* 1 (1882).

24. Amos Noy, *'Edim o mumḥim: Yehudim maskilim bene Yerushalayim ve-ha-mizraḥ bi-teḥilat ha-me'ah ha-'isrim* [Experts or witnesses: Jewish intelligentsia from Jerusalem and the Levant in the beginning of the 20th century] (Tel Aviv: Resling, 2017), 53–54.

25. Abraham Moshe Lunts, "Matsav ha-arets bekhlal" [The general state of the land]. *Yerushalayim* 2 (1887): 168–69.

26. This integration is also affirmed by Salim Tamari in his reading of the diaries of the Christian Jerusalemite Wāṣif Jawhariyyeh. See Salīm Tamārī, "Wasif Jawhariyyeh, Popular Music, and Early Modernity in Jerusalem," in *Palestine, Israel, and the Politics of Popular Culture*, ed. Rebecca L. Stein and Ted Swedenburg (Durham, NC: Duke University Press, 2005), 28–29.

27. Lunts, "Matsav ha-arets bekhlal," 181.

28. Eliezer Ben-Yehuda, *A Dream Come True*, trans. T. Muraoka, ed. George Mandel (Boulder, CO: Westview Press, 1993), 1.

29. Robert St. John, *Tongue of the Prophets: The Life Story of Eliezer Ben Yehuda* (New York: Doubleday and Company Inc., 1952), 36.

30. Yoseph Lang, a biographer of Ben-Yehuda, speculates that the latter's visit to Paris started in fall 1877 or at the latest January 1878. For a reference, see Yoseph Lang, *Daber 'ivrit!: Haye Eliezer Ben-Yehuda* [Speak Hebrew! The life of Eliezer Ben-Yehuda], vol. 1 (Jerusalem: Yad Yitsḥaḳ Ben-Tsevi, 2008).

31. John, *Tongue of the Prophets*, 36, 37. For more details on Ben-Yehuda's dedication to political science for the advancement of his political plan aimed at the revival of the Jewish people on the land of Palestine, see Ben-Yehuda's own account of his objectives: Eliezer Ben-Yehuda, *Milon ha-lashon ha-'ivrit ha-yeshanah ve-ha-ḥadashah: ha-mavo' ha-gadol* [A complete dictionary of ancient and modern Hebrew: Prolegomena] (Tel Aviv: Sefer, 1948).

32. For a bibliographic guide to the Hebrew literature on Palestine, including Ben-Yehuda's works, see Getzel Kressel, *Erets Yisrael ve-toldoteha: madrikh bibliografi, ha-sifrut ha-'ivrit 'al Erets Yisrael* [The land of Israel and its history: A bibliographic guide] (Tel Aviv: Makhon Mazkeret, 1980), 57. For a discussion on Hebrew geographic literature on Palestine that contained general geographic descriptions of the land during the Ottoman rule with the aim of capturing the attention of Hebrew readers, see Yehoshua Ben-Arieh, "Le-'ofiha shel ha-sifrut ha-geografit ha-'ivrit 'al Erets Yisrael ba-me'ah ha-tesha' 'esreh 'ad milḥemet ha-'olam ha-rishonah" [The character of Hebrew geographic literature about Erets-Israel during the nineteenth century and until World War I], *Eretz-Israel: Archaeological, Historical and Geographical Studies* 22 (1991): 38–39. For a discussion on *Sefer Erets Yisrael*, see Lang, *Daber 'ivrit!*. A brief description of Ben-Yehuda's geographic work might be useful for understanding the topics that concerned him about the land of Palestine. The book consists of seven chapters: the first discusses the names, borders, location, and size of the land; the second, the view of the land from on high; the third details the various springs flowing into the land; the fourth, the mountains; the fifth looks at the valleys and its wilderness; the sixth considers the climate of the land; and the seventh tells of the features of the land and its appearance. There is also an addendum. For more details, see the introduction in Eliezer Ben-Yehuda, *Sefer Erets Yisrael: 'al ṭeva' ha-arets ha-zot* [The land of Israel's book: On the nature of this land] (Jerusalem: Joel Moses Solomon, 1883).

33. The subtitle appears on the front page of the book. Below that subtitle, it should be noted, is a portrayal of a Roman coin containing two words: Yehuda Be-Shevi ("Judea Capta" in Latin, and "Judea in captivity" in English). These had been minted to commemorate the Roman triumph over Jerusalem. The coin depicts a woman in a scene of mourning seated under

a palm tree. Next to the woman stands a Roman soldier in military dress with spear in one hand and a parazonium in the other, with his right foot on his helmet.

34. Ben-Yehuda, *Sefer Erets Yisrael*, 1.

35. It might be significant to compare the rise of the geographic literary genre in the Arab world and among Hebrew writers during the nineteenth century. For a brief history on geographic literary works by Arab writers, see Zaydān, *Tārīkh ʾAdab al-lugha al-ʿArabiyya*, 4:254–67.

36. The work, as Lunts had noted, was published for the first time in Jerusalem in 1845 in Rashi script. See Joseph Schwarz, *Tevoʾot ha-arets* [All the produce of the land], ed. Abraham Moshe Lunts (Jerusalem: Abraham Moshe Lunts, 1880). For a discussion on Schwarz's book, see Kressel, *Erets Yisrael ve-toldoteha*. Despite the fact that *Tevoʾot ha-arets* by Schwarz is the earliest geographic work on Palestine in modern times, the book lies beyond the historical scope of the current analysis. In addition, the author does not use Arabo-Islamic sources in *Tevoʾot ha-arets*, but rather his sources are mostly Jewish and Western.

37. Ben-Yehuda, *Sefer Erets Yisrael*, 91.

38. See Ben-Yehuda's reference to *The Land and the Book* in Ben-Yehuda, *Sefer Erets Yisrael*, 35.

39. Ben-Yehuda refers to Lynch's voyage on the Jordan River and Dead Sea in Ben-Yehuda, *Sefer Erets Yisrael*.

40. For a discussion on Ritter's contribution to the geographic knowledge of Palestine and its adjacent lands, see Yehoshua Ben-Arieh, *The Rediscovery of the Holy Land in the Nineteenth Century* (Detroit: Wayne State University Press, 1979), 145–52. For a discussion on Ritter's voluminous work and its significance to future nonphilological studies on the Orient, see Suzanne L. Marchand, *German Orientalism in the Age of Empire: Religion, Race, and Scholarship* (Washington, DC: Cambridge University Press, 2009), 141–43. And for Ben-Yehuda's reference to *Erdkunde*, see Ben-Yehuda, *Sefer Erets Yisrael*, 39.

41. Yoav Di-Capua, *Gatekeepers of the Arab Past: Historians and History Writing in Twentieth-Century Egypt* (Berkeley: University of California Press, 2009), 48–49.

42. In a meeting with members of the Hebrew Language Committee (Vaʿad ha-Lashon ha-ʿIvrit), Ben-Yehuda highlighted the linguistic wealth of Arabic lexicons, which extensively incorporate hundreds of Hebrew words. He encouraged members of the committee to explore these sources as a means of coining new Hebrew terms to address the requirements of the revitalized language. See Eliezer Ben-Yehuda, "Mekorot le-male he-ḥaser bi-leshonenu" [Sources to fill the gap in our language], *Zikhronot vaʿad ha-lashon ha-ʿivrit* 4 (1914): 9–10.

43. Rana Issa, "The Arabic Language and Syro-Lebanese National Identity Searching in Buṭrus al-Bustānī's Muḥīṭ al-Muḥīṭ," *Journal of Semitic Studies* 62, no. 2 (2017): 473.

44. For a reference to Ben-Yehuda's exposure to these works, see Moshe Piamenta, "Hashpaʿat ha-ʿAravit ʿal ḥidushe Ben-Yehuda," *Leshonenu la-ʿam* 12 (1961): 151.

45. For a reference to Almaliaḥ's collaboration with Ben-Yehuda, see Yitsḥaḳ Bezalel, "Ha-Levantim ha-reshonim" [The first Levantines in the Ottoman period in Eretz Israel—Their Zionist identity and attitude towards Arab identity], *Peʿamim* 125–127 (2011): 84. The name of the newspaper was intended to mirror two European newspapers of the time: the *London Observer* and *Paris Observateur*.

46. Ben-Yehuda, *Sefer Erets Yisrael*, 6, 9, 10, 11, 78.

47. Abraham Shalom Yahuda, "To'elet leshonot 'Arav le-havanat ha-Miḳra" [The value of Arabic dialects to understanding the Hebrew Bible], *Zikhronot Va'ad ha-Lashon* 6 (1911): 22–23.

48. The use of geographic knowledge drawn from Arabo-Islamic sources to retrieve the Jewish names of certain places in Palestine will be discussed in detail in chapter 3.

49. Ben-Yehuda, *Sefer Erets Yisrael*, 28.

50. Deuteronomy 8:7–9. Unless otherwise noted, I use the Jewish Publication Society for translations of biblical texts into English.

51. Ben-Yehuda, *Sefer Erets Yisrael*, 30.

52. Compare the sacredness of Aaron's tomb for the Muslim population in the account of medieval Muslim geographers Yaqūt al-Ḥamawī and al-Mas'ūdī in Guy Le Strange, *Palestine under the Moslems: A Description of Syria and the Holy Land from A. D. 650 to 1500* (London: Committee of the Palestine Exploration Fund, 1890), 73–74.

53. Eliezer Ben-Yehuda, *Kol kitve Eliezer Ben-Yehuda* [Collected works of Eliezer Ben-Yehuda] (Jerusalem: Ha-Ma'arav, 1941), 26.

54. For a brief discussion on Ben-Yehuda's views on Muslim Arab society in Palestine, see Yosef Gorny, *Zionism and the Arabs: 1882–1948, a Study of Ideology* (Oxford: Clarendon Press, 1987), 18, 53. The reconstruction of accounts of the Arab population from *Sefer Erets Yisrael* provides a lens through which one may explore the development of Ben-Yehuda's views on Jewish integration within the Ottoman government—views that he would vocalize at several points in his life, including a call to the nonnative Jewish community in Palestine to renounce its foreign citizenship and join the parliamentary election of the Turkish government.

55. David Yellin, "Mikhtav Mr. David Yellin el 'orekh ha-Ṣābaḥ," *Ha-arets* (Jerusalem), December 4, 1921, 3.

56. For a partial list of Yellin's Hebrew writings on the land of Palestine, see Kressel, *Erets Yisrael ve-toldoteha*, 38, 107.

57. Ben-Arieh, "Le-' ofiha shel ha-sifrut ha-geografit ha-'ivrit 'al Erets Yisrael ba-me'ah ha-tesha' 'esreh 'ad milḥemet ha-'olam ha-rishonah," 39.

58. The book has a French title, *Livre de lecture et demorale pour la jeunesse israélite suive de la géographie de la terre sainte*. See David Yellin, *Miḳra le-na're bene Yisrael* [Reading for the youth of the children of Israel] (Jerusalem, 1889), book cover.

59. "Yedi'at Sefarim: Miḳra le-yelde bene Yisrael," *Ha-Magid*, June 13, 1889.

60. "Yedi'at Sefarim."

61. At the bottom of the table of the contents made by Yellin, he indicates his reliance on Arabic literature while addressing the parables of foxes. Yellin, *Miḳra le-na're bene Yisrael*, 159–64.

62. Sheehi, *Foundations of Modern Arab Identity*, 62.

63. See introduction in Yellin, *Miḳra le-na're bene Yisrael*.

64. Yellin, *Miḳra le-na're bene Yisrael*, 11.

65. Yellin, *Miḳra le-na're bene Yisrael*, 121, 123, 4, 5, 6, 7, 8.

66. Yellin, *Miḳra le-na're bene Yisrael*, 123.

67. Samuel Dolbee and Shay Hazkani, "Unlikely Identities: Abu Ibrahim and the Politics of Possibility in Late Ottoman Palestine," *Jerusalem Quarterly*, no. 63 (2015): 25.

68. Consider Yellin's testimony according to Liora Halperin, *The Oldest Guard: Forging the Zionist Settler Past* (Stanford, CA: Stanford University Press, 2021), 99–100.

69. See, for example, some of the plants in Francis Brown et al., *A Hebrew and English Lexicon of the Old Testament: With an Appendix Containing the Biblical Aramaic* (Peabody, MA: Houghton Mifflin, 1907).

70. With his massive knowledge of Jewish scripture and literature, Lunts refers to three biblical passages where the Hebrew plant name atad appears: first in Genesis 50:10, second in Judges 9:14–15, and third in Psalms 58:10. See Menashe Meirovitch, "Tsimḥe erets ha-tsevi: yikhlol matsav kol ha-tsemaḥim ve-ha-neṭi'ot ha-mo'ilim asher be-erets Paleshet ve-suryah, ofen ve-seder neṭi'atam ve-to'eletam" [The flora of the land of gazelles], *Yerushalayim* 3 (1888): 183–84n1.

71. Judges 9:14–15. According to the Jewish Publication Society's English translation of the Bible, the atad is a thorn bush, which is a barren shrub whose fruit is inedible. For an interpretation of Jotham's parable, including a short definition of atad, see Adele Berlin, Marc Zvi Brettler, and Michael A. Fishbane, *The Jewish Study Bible: Jewish Publication Society Tanakh Translation* (Oxford: Oxford University Press, 2004), 531–52.

72. For a survey on the ethnobotany of *Ziziphus spina-christi* in the Middle East relating to various aspects (historical, religious, philological, and others) among the followers of the Abrahamic faiths, see Amots Dafni, Shay Levy, and Efraim Lev, "The Ethnobotany of Christ's Thorn Jujube (Ziziphus Spina-Christi) in Israel," *Journal of Ethnobiology and Ethnomedicine* 1 (2005): 8. *Ziziphus lotus* is Meirovitch's exact translation. See Meirovitch, "Tsimḥe erets ha-tsevi."

73. Suffice it to say here that the name of the plant sidr is mentioned in Islamic scripture, both in the Quran and the Hadith tradition.

74. Meirovitch, "Tsimḥe erets ha-tsevi," 183–84.

75. Dolbee and Hazkani, "Unlikely Identities," 25.

76. For further details, see 'Abd Allāh ibn Aḥmad Ibn al-Bayṭār, *Kitāb al-jāmi' li-mufradāt al-'adwiya wa al-aghdhiya* [The book of compilation of medication and aliment simples] (Beirut: Dar al-Kutub al-'ilmiyya, 1992), 3:6–7.

77. Meirovitch, "Tsimḥe erets ha-tsevi," 183–84. Meirovitch's definition of the sidr here is analogous to the botanical depiction by Ibn al-Bayṭār. See, for comparison, Ibn al-Bayṭār, *Kitāb al-jāmi' li-mufradāt al-'adwiya wa al-aghdhiya*, 3:6–7.

78. See, for example, Canaan's article from 1928 on the influence of the botanical world on Palestinian society and culture, recently republished as Canaan Tawfiq, "Plant-Lore in Palestinian Superstition," *Jerusalem Quarterly* 24 (2005): 57–64.

79. Meirovitch, "Tsimḥe erets ha-tsevi," 183–84.

80. Even books published subsequent to Meirovitch's works did not include such information, although they addressed the topic of sacred trees, among which was the lotus (or the sidr tree). See, for example, the discussion in Ignác Goldziher, *Muslim Studies*, trans. C. R. Barber and Samuel Miklos Stern, ed. Samuel Miklos Stern (London: Geo. Allen & Unwin, 1971), 2:316–18.

81. For more details, see Baudissin's discussion on trees sacred to Arabs, under his section "Heilige Bäume bei den Arabern," in Wolf Wilhelm Baudissin, *Studien zur Semitischen Religionsgeschichte* (Leipzig: Verlag von Fr. Wilh. Grunow, 1878), 2:221–22. See also his exploration of the ancient Hebrew veneration of certain trees based on Jewish literature in Baudissin, *Studien zur Semitischen Religionsgeschichte*.

82. Samuel Klein, Joseph Klausner, and Naḥum Slouschz, "Le-Yuvalo shel mar David Yellin" [The jubilee of Mr. David Yellin], *Bulletin of the Jewish Palestine Exploration Society* 1, no. 2 (1933): 3.

83. Avraham Ḥayim Elḥanani, "David Yellin 'ish Yerushalaiym," in *Mi-Dan ve-'ad Beer Sheva': Pirkey Hayav shel David Yellin*, ed. David Yellin and Avraham Hayim Elḥanani (Jerusalem: Ha-Va'ad le-Hotsaat Kitve Yellin, Hotsaat Rubin Mass, 1973), 6.

84. For a brief biography of Yehoshua Yellin, see Elḥanani, "David Yellin 'ish Yerushalaiym," 6. See also Abraham Yaari's introduction to Yehoshua's travel from Jerusalem to Transjordan, the eastern side of the Jordanian river, in Abraham Yaari, *Masa'ot Erets-Yisrael* [Voyages to the land of Israel] (Ramat Gan: Hotsa'at Masadah, 1976), 610–12. For a biography of Yellin's family, see Yehuda Slutsky and Benzion Dinur, "Yellin," in *Encyclopaedia Judaica*, ed. Michael Berenbaum and Fred Skolnik (Detroit: Macmillan Reference USA, 2007), 300–301.

85. Julia Phillips Cohen, *Becoming Ottomans: Sephardi Jews and Imperial Citizenship in the Modern Era* (New York: Oxford University Press, 2014), 46–47, 50.

86. Nathan Efrati, "Ha-Protokolim shel lishkat B'nai B'rith Yerushalayim, 1888–1919" [The Jerusalem lodge of B'nai B'rith, 1888–1919], *Cathedra: For the History of Eretz Israel and Its Yishuv* 50 (1988): 150.

87. David Yellin, "Yerushalayim li-fnay arba' Me'ot Shanah" [Jerusalem four hundred years ago], *Ha-Pardes* 2 (1894): 157.

88. Yellin, "Yerushalayim li-fnay arba' Me'ot shanah," 157.

89. Yellin made reference in the subtitle of his article to the fact that he would rely on the account of Mujīr al-Dīn al-Ḥanbalī. Yellin, "Yerushalayim li-fnay arba' Me'ot shanah," 157.

90. Donald P. Little, "Mujīr al-Dīn al-'Ulaymī's Vision of Jerusalem in the Ninth/Fifteenth Century," *Journal of the American Oriental Society* 115, no. 2 (1995): 237.

91. Cited in Little, "Mujīr al-Dīn al-'Ulaymī's Vision of Jerusalem in the Ninth/Fifteenth Century," 239.

92. Emanuel Sivan, "The Beginnings of the 'Faḍā'il al Quds' Literature," *Der Islam; Zeitschrift für Geschichte und Kultur des Islamischen Orients* 48 (1972): 100–101.

93. In the Mandate era, particularly during the 1929 Western Wall events, another Jerusalemite Jew, Isaac Yahuda, emphasized the sacredness of Jerusalem in the Jewish tradition and its penetration into the Islamic tradition. See that discussion in chapter 4.

94. Yellin published the Hebrew version first: David Yellin, *Rabenu Mosheh Ben Maymun* [Our master Moses Maimonides] (Warsaw: Toshyah, 1898); David Yellin and Israel Abrahams, *Maimonides* (Philadelphia: Jewish Publication Society of America Philadelphia, 1903), 37. For a discussion on Maimonides's views on Islam, see Daniel Boušek, "Polemics in the Age of Religious Persecutions: Maimonides' Attitude towards Islam," *Asian and African Studies* 20, no. 1 (2011): 46–85.

95. Yellin, "Yerushalayim li-fnay arba' Me'ot shanah," 157.

96. Karen Armstrong, "The Holiness of Jerusalem: Asset or Burden?," *Journal of Palestine Studies* 27, no. 3 (1998): 18.

97. Michael Zank, *Jerusalem: A Brief History* (Hoboken, NJ: Wiley-Blackwell, 2018), 186.

98. Andreas Kaplony, "635/638–1099: The Mosque of Jerusalem (Masjid Bayt al-Maqdis)," in *Where Heaven and Earth Meet: Jerusalem's Sacred Esplanade*, ed. Oleg Grabar and Benjamin Z. Kedar (Jerusalem: Yad Ben-Zvi Press, 2009), 103.

99. For an example of the relationship between Muslims and Jews in the fifteenth century during the lifetime of Mujīr al-Dīn, see his account on the question of the Jewish synagogue and its rebuilding in Mujīr al-Dīn al-Ḥanbalī, *Al-ʿuns al-jalīl bi-tārīkh al-Quds wa-al-Khalīl* [The glorious history of Jerusalem and Hebron] (Amman: Maktabat Dandis, 1993), 2:432–37. In *al-ʿuns al-jalīl*, Mujīr al-Dīn sets apart several sections that treat issues that Hebrew thinkers of the time, like Yellin, found relevant to constructing their past and emphasizing the Jewish presence in the city of Jerusalem. See, for instance, Mujīr al-Dīn's account of the Wall of Solomon; presumably the reference meant the wall commonly recognized nowadays among Christians and Jews as either the "Western Wall" or "Wailing Wall," and among Muslims as the "Burāq Wall." Al-Ḥanbalī, *Al-ʿuns al-jalīl bi-tārīkh al-Quds wa-al-Khalīl*, 142.

100. Yellin, "Yerushalayim li-fnay arbaʿ Me'ot shanah," 160–61.

101. Cited in Yellin, "Yerushalayim li-fnay arbaʿ Me'ot shanah," 172.

102. Yellin, "Yerushalayim li-fnay arbaʿ Me'ot shanah," 172.

103. Gershon Shafir, "Settler Citizenship in the Jewish Colonization of Palestine," in *Settler Colonialism in the Twentieth Century: Projects, Practices, Legacies*, ed. Caroline Elkins and Susan Pedersen (London: Routledge, 2005), 51.

104. Jonathan Marc Gribetz, "Arab–Zionist Conversations in Late Ottoman Jerusalem: Saʿid al-Husayni, Ruhi al-Khalidi and Eliezer Ben-Yehuda," in *Ordinary Jerusalem, 1840–1940: Opening New Archives, Revisiting a Global City*, ed. Angelos Dalachanis and Vincent Lemire (Leiden: Brill, 2018), 314.

105. "Peaceful crusade" was espoused by evangelical Protestants during the Victorian period to "rescue" the Holy Land from what they perceived as the deplorable fate of the city under the rule of the Ottoman Turks. This peaceful campaign was led by travelers, missionaries, archaeologists, diplomats, and others. See Gabriel Polley, *Palestine in the Victorian Age: Colonial Encounters in the Holy Land* (London: I. B. Tauris, 2022).

106. Karen Armstrong, *A History of Jerusalem: One City, Three Faiths* (London: Harper Perennial, 2005), 360.

107. Louis A. Fishman, *Jews and Palestinians in the Late Ottoman Era, 1908–1914: Claiming the Homeland* (Edinburgh: Edinburgh University Press, 2020), 126.

108. This incident is reported at length in Avraham Moshe Lunts, *Kotel ha-maʿaravi shel har bet Elohenu: mehuto, tekhunato, ve-zikhronotav* [The Western Wall of our God's Temple Mount: Its essence, features, and memories] (Jerusalem, 1912), 51–60.

109. Menachem Klein, *Lives in Common: Arabs and Jews in Jerusalem, Jaffa and Hebron*, trans. Haim Watzman (London: Hurst & Company, 2014), 34.

110. On the failed attempt to sell the Western Wall in 1916, see Roberto Mazza, "The Deal of the Century? The Attempted Sale of the Western Wall by Cemal Pasha in 1916," *Middle East Studies* 57, no. 5 (2021): 696–711.

111. For a detailed account of the stories, see Israel Wolf Horowitz, "Hagadot ʿAraviyot: ʿal davar ha-meḳomot ha-ḳedushim be-Erets Yisrael" [Arab legends: On the holy places in the land of Israel], *Luaḥ Erets Yisrael* 20–21 (1915–16): 236–44. It is interesting to point out that the journal commemorated the seventy-first birthday of Sultan Muhammad V, who reigned from 1909 to 1918 after the Young Turk Revolution.

112. On the impact of the Great War on Palestine, see Salim Tamari, *Year of the Locust: A Soldier's Diary and the Erasure of Palestine's Ottoman Past* (Berkeley: University of California Press, 2015), 3–12.

113. Abigail Jacobson, "A City Living through Crisis: Jerusalem during World War I," *British Journal of Middle Eastern Studies* 36, no. 1 (2009): 73–92.

114. Horowitz, "Hagadot 'Araviyot," 236.

115. See the story in Horowitz, "Hagadot 'Araviyot," 241. Cf. a further detailed account with English translation: Le Strange, *Palestine under the Moslems*, 315.

116. Simon Schama, *Landscape and Memory* (New York: Alfred A. Knopf, 1995), 7.

117. To ascertain this point, see Rana Barakat, "Writing/Righting Palestine Studies: Settler Colonialism, Indigenous Sovereignty and Resisting the Ghost(s) of History," *Settler Colonial Studies* 8, no. 3 (2018): 349–63.

118. Anita Shapira, *Land and Power: The Zionist Resort to Force, 1881–1948* (New York: Oxford University Press, 1992), 274.

Chapter 3: Constructing Jewish Indigeneity

1. Lorenzo Veracini, "The Other Shift: Settler Colonialism, Israel, and the Occupation," *Journal of Palestine Studies* 42, no. 2 (2013): 35.

2. David Yellin, "The Renaissance of the Hebrew Language in Palestine," in *Zionist Work in Palestine*, ed. Israel Cohen (New York: Judaean Publishing Company, 1912), 144.

3. On the history of safah berurah (Pure Language), its members, and vision, see Eran Buchaltzev, "'Ivri, 'Ivrit ve-'Ivriut," 36–40.

4. Buchaltzev, "'Ivri, 'Ivrit ve-'Ivriut," 23.

5. Buchaltzev, "'Ivri, 'Ivrit ve-'Ivriut," 23–24.

6. Buchaltzev, "'Ivri, 'Ivrit ve-'Ivriut," 25.

7. Yellin, "The Renaissance of the Hebrew Language in Palestine," 154.

8. Eliezer Meir Lipschitz, who preferred the use of Aramaic over Arabic to expand the Hebrew lexicon, noted that in his response to Ben-Yehuda's proposal to draw on Arabic lexicons to fill in the gap in modern Hebrew in Eliezer Ben-Yehuda, "Mekorot le-male he-ḥaser bi-leshonenu" [Sources to fill the gap in our language], *Zikhronot va'ad ha-lashon ha-'ivrit* 4 (1914): 16.

9. Liora R. Halperin, *Babel in Zion: Jews, Nationalism, and Language Diversity in Palestine, 1920–1948* (New Haven, CT: Yale University Press, 2014), 142–43.

10. Gary Fields, *Enclosure: Palestinian Landscapes in a Historical Mirror* (Oakland: University of California Press, 2017), 221–22.

11. For a discussion on the opposition to comparisons between Arabic and Hebrew in the Middle Ages, see James Barr, *Comparative Philology and the Text of the Old Testament: With Additions and Corrections* (Winona Lake, IN: Eisenbrauns, 1987), 14.

12. On Ben-Yehuda's language policy in the introduction to his dictionary, see Moshe Piamenta, "Hashpa'at ha-'Aravit 'al ḥidushe Ben-Yehuda," *Leshonenu la-'am* 12 (1961): 150–58; Eliezer Ben-Yehuda, *Milon ha-lashon ha-'ivrit ha-yeshanah ve-ha-ḥadashah: ha-mavo' ha-gadol* [A complete dictionary of ancient and modern Hebrew: Prolegomena] (Tel Aviv: Sefer, 1948), cited in Piamenta, "Hashpa'at ha-'Aravit 'al ḥidushe Ben-Yehuda," 150.

13. Joshua Blau, *The Renaissance of Modern Hebrew and Modern Standard Arabic: Parallels and Differences in the Revival of Two Semitic Languages* (Berkeley: University of California Press, 1981), 18:18, 33.

14. Cited in Buchaltzev, "'Ivri, 'Ivrit ve-'Ivriut," 64–65.

15. Cited in Ben-Yehuda, "Meḳorot le-male he-ḥaser bi-leshonenu," 21.

16. In putting forward this perspective, he refers to the works of Abraham Shalom Yahuda in specifying what studies he had in mind. Ben-Yehuda, "Meḳorot le-male he-ḥaser bi-leshonenu," 21.

17. Judah Leib Gordon, "'Inyane De-yoma," *Ha-Melits* 1883. Cf. the introduction in Eliezer Ben-Yehuda, *Sefer Erets Yisrael: 'al ṭeva' ha-arets ha-zot* [The land of Israel's book: On the nature of this land] (Jerusalem: Joel Moses Solomon, 1883).

18. Ben-Yehuda's nationalistic enterprise lay on three foundations: the revival of the Jewish people, restoration of the Jewish connection to the ancestral patrimony, and revival of Hebrew.

19. Ben-Yehuda, *Sefer Erets Yisrael*, introduction.

20. Gordon, "'Inyane De-yoma."

21. Jonathan Marc Gribetz, *Defining Neighbors: Religion, Race, and the Early Zionist-Arab Encounter* (Princeton, NJ: Princeton University Press, 2014), 188.

22. Jeff Halper, *Between Redemption and Revival: The Jewish Yishuv of Jerusalem in the Nineteenth Century* (Boulder, CO: Westview Press, 1991), 169.

23. Jack Fellman, *The Revival of a Classical Tongue: Eliezer Ben Yehuda and the Modern Hebrew Language* (The Hague: Mouton, 1973), 28.

24. Yeshayahu Press, *Me'ah shanah be-Yerushalaiym: me-zikhronot 'ish Yerushalaiym* [A hundred years of Jerusalem: Memories of a Jerusalemite man] (Jerusalem: Rubin Mass, 1964), 29. I benefited from Fellman's English translation of the aforementioned passage, which he cites in his sketch of the cultural circumstances of the various Jewish communities in Jerusalem at the time that Ben-Yehuda arrived in the city. See Fellman, *The Revival of a Classical Tongue*, 28.

25. Moshe Bar-Asher, "Some Observations on the Revival of Hebrew," *Jewish Studies* 32 (1992), 29.

26. David Yellin, *Ha-mivṭa ve-ha-ketiv be-'Ivrit: hartsa'ah ba-asefah ha-kelalit ha-shenit le-agudat ha-morim be-Erets Yisrael she-hayetah be-moshavat Gederah be-Elul 664* [The accent and writing in Hebrew] (Jerusalem: Lunts, 1904).

27. Press, *Me'ah shanah be-Yerushalaiym*. Writing in December 1908 in the wake of the Young Turk Revolution, Ben-Yehuda described an encounter with Turkish officials, which he published in *Ha-Tsevi*. During the interrogation by the Turkish officials, Ben-Yehuda recalled that at this time, his knowledge of Arabic was limited, and his interrogation was facilitated by Yellin as translator. See Ben-Yehuda's own account in Eliezer Ben-Yehuda, "Ḥanukah," *Ha-Tsevi* (Jerusalem), December 18, 1908. See also Yoseph Lang, *Daber 'ivrit!: Haye Eliezer Ben-Yehuda* [Speak Hebrew! The life of Eliezer Ben-Yehuda], vol. 1 (Jerusalem: Yad Yitsḥaḳ Ben-Tsevi, 2008).

28. Arabic was not the only language Ben-Yehuda considered as a cultural and linguistic reference for the revival of modern Hebrew. In fact, it was one among several tongues from which Ben-Yehuda borrowed to meet the internal features of Hebrew. See Bar-Asher, "Some Observations on the Revival of Hebrew."

29. Ben-Yehuda, "Meḳorot le-male he-ḥaser bi-leshonenu," 8.

30. For a discussion on the influence of Arabic on Ben-Yehuda's dictionary, see Yitsḥaḳ Avishor, "Ha-markiv ha-'aravi ba-lashon ha-'Ivrit bat zemanenu u-ve-sifrutah m-Eliezer

Ben-Yehuda 'ad Netivah Ben-Yehuda (ve-Dan Ben-Amuz)" [The Arabic component in modern Hebrew language and literature], *Ha-'Ivrit ve-aḥyoteha: ketav 'et le-ḥeḳer ha-lashon ha-'Ivrit ve-ziḳatah la-leshonot ha-Shemiyot veli-leshonot ha-Yehudim* 2–3 (2002–3): 9–50.

31. Avishor, "Ha-markiv ha-'aravi ba-lashon ha-'Ivrit bat zemanenu u-ve-sifrutah m-Eliezer Ben-Yehuda 'ad Netivah Ben-Yehuda (ve-Dan Ben-Amuz)," 9–10.

32. Before discussing the Arabic name of the lake, Ben-Yehuda lists two names also used by Jews to refer to it, along with an explanation of their etymology. The first name, according to the Jews, was Kinneret, and then he cites three biblical verses from Numbers and Joshua. The origin of the name, in Ben-Yehuda's view, is simple. The name Kinneret originated from the Hebrew word *kinnor* (harp) in relation to the shape of the lake. The second name that Jews called the lake was the Sea of Ginosar. See Ben-Yehuda, *Sefer Erets yisrael*, 9–10.

33. Ben-Yehuda, *Sefer Erets Yisrael*, 9–10.

34. It should be noted that in identifying the word *Yarden* with the names used by the Arab population to refer to the same river, he cites two other names. "The Arabs' name is al-sharī'ah, that is, a place of beverage, and in order to differentiate between it and another river that is called also al-sharī'a, Arabs call the Jordan [River] sharī'at al-kabīr, and there are others who call it al-Urdun." Ben-Yehuda, *Sefer Erets Yisrael*, 16.

35. See his clarification of the meaning of *Yarden* in Ben-Yehuda, *Sefer Erets Yisrael*, 16–17.

36. For a comparative discussion on the verbs *yarad* and *warad*, see Eliezer Ben-Yehuda, "Yarad," in *Milon ha-Lashon ha-'Ivrit ha-Yeshanah ve-ha-Ḥadashah* (New York: International News Company, 1914), 2145–50.

37. Ben-Yehuda, *Sefer Erets Yisrael*, 16–17.

38. Ben-Yehuda, *Sefer Erets Yisrael*, 43.

39. *Mu'jam al-Buldān* was published in six volumes by Heinrich Ferdinand Wüstenfeld (1808–99) in Leipzig between 1866 and 1873. Ben-Yehuda is likely to have known it well, and drawn on it in restoring the Hebrew map of Palestine and its neighboring countries.

40. Ibn Yāqūt al-Ḥamawī, *Mu'jam al-Buldān* [Dictionary of countries], (Beirut: Dār Ṣādir, 1977), 2:225.

41. al-Ḥamawī, *Mu'jam al-Buldān*, 2:69.

42. Yael Zerubavel, "The Forest as a National Icon: Literature, Politics, and the Archaeology of Memory," *Israel Studies* 1, no. 1 (1996): 60, 72.

43. Carol B. Bardenstein, "Trees, Forests, and the Shaping of Palestinian and Israeli Collective Memory," in *Acts of Memory: Cultural Recall in the Present*, ed. Mieke Bal, Jonathan Crewe, and Leo Spitzer (Hanover, NH: Dartmouth College Press, 1999), 149.

44. Mustafa Kabha and Nahum Karlinsky, *The Lost Orchard: The Palestinian-Arab Citrus Industry, 1850–1950* (Syracuse, NY: Syracuse University Press, 2021), 127–28, 146–49.

45. Nasser Abufarha, "Land of Symbols: Cactus, Poppies, Orange and Olive Trees in Palestine," *Identities: Global Studies in Culture and Power* 15, no. 3 (2008): 347–38.

46. Salim Tamari, *Mountain against the Sea: Essays on Palestinian Society and Culture* (Berkeley: University of California Press, 2009), 97–98.

47. "Menashe Meirovitch: aḥaron ha-biluyim ben 85," *Ha-mashkif*, June 13, 1945.

48. Ran Aaronsohn, "The Beginnings of Modern Jewish Agriculture in Palestine: 'Indigenous' versus 'Imported,'" *Agricultural History* 69, no. 3 (1995): 438–53.

49. Derek Jonathan Penslar, *Zionism and Technocracy: The Engineering of Jewish Settlement in Palestine, 1870–1918* (Bloomington: Indiana University Press, 1991), 20.

50. Liora Halperin, *The Oldest Guard: Forging the Zionist Settler Past* (Stanford, CA: Stanford University Press, 2021), 22.

51. For an indication as to his reputation as an agronomist, see Menashe Meirovitch, *'Etsah ve-tushiyah, o, hatsa'ah 'al devar maṭa' keramim ve-gidul gefanim be-Erets Yisrael* [Help and initiative: An offer about planting vineyards in Erets Yisrael] (Warsaw: Hayyim Kelter, 1885), preface. According to Aaronsohn, Meirovitch was the only agronomist by profession. See Ran Aaronsohn, "Vines and Wineries in the Jewish Colonies: Introducing Modern Viticulture into Nineteenth-Century Palestine," *Journal of Israeli History* 14, no. 1 (1993): 34.

52. Penslar, *Zionism and Technocracy*, 20.

53. Menashe Meirovitch, "Tsimḥe erets ha-tsevi: yikhlol matsav kol ha-tsemaḥim ve-ha-neṭi'ot ha-mo'ilim asher be-erets Paleshet ve-suryah, ofen ve-seder neṭi'atam ve-to'eletam" [The flora of the land of gazelles], *Yerushalayim* 3 (1888): 177–78.

54. Meirovitch, "Tsimḥe erets ha-tsevi."

55. It should be noted that *Tsemḥe Erets ha-Tsevi* was published in two separate articles in the nineteenth-century Jerusalemite Hebrew journal *Yerushalayim*, edited by Abraham Moshe Lunts.

56. Meirovitch, "Tsimḥe erets ha-tsevi."

57. The emphasis is found in the original text. Lunts outlines his view on the utilization of Arabic plant names in a footnote in Meirovitch, "Tsimḥe erets ha-tsevi," 179.

58. It might be of interest to investigate the emphasis on modern Hebrew's Semitic character, as opposed to its non-Semitic features, by revivers of the language. Some scholars during the late 1960s, for instance, suggested that the modern Hebrew language as practiced in Israel had lost many, if not all, of its Semitic character. For more details, see Haiim B. Rosén, *A Textbook of Israeli Hebrew: With an Introduction to the Classical Language* (Chicago: University of Chicago Press, 1966). In another work, some authors rejected the Semitic nature of modern Hebrew, attributing it to Slavic language with a stress on the heavy influence of Russian. See Paul Wexler, *The Schizoid Nature of Modern Hebrew: A Slavic Language in Search of a Semitic Past*, 4 vols. (Wiesbaden: O. Harrassowitz, 1990).

59. Richard G. Marks, "Hinduism, Torah, and Travel: Jacob Sapir in India," *Shofar* 30, no. 2 (2012): 28.

60. In 1858, Jacob was sent by one of the Jewish communities in Jerusalem to India to collect funds from wealthy Indian Jews. On his return, he published a two-volume work in 1866 and 1874 on his travels to Yemen and India titled *Even Sapir*. In this book, he relates the annals of Jewish communities in distant places. He also dedicates a lot of his account to discuss his observations of non-Jewish communities, including Indian culture, customs, and traditions. Jacob expresses explicitly his disapproval of Hindu worship, portraying it as a form of *'avoda zarah* (idiolatry). While historian Simon Dubnow criticizes Jacob's work as naive as well as uninformed about history and geography, Yosef Yo'el Rivlin commends Sapir as a man of sharp observation who draws his knowledge from the ecosystem of the Gaon of Vilna. For more on Jacob's work, see Marks, "Hinduism, Torah, and Travel," 28, 33, 43.

61. "Eliyahu Sapir Halevi Einennu," *Ḥerut* (Jerusalem), September 4, 1911.

62. Eliyahu Sapir, *Ḳovets mi-kitve Eliyahu Sapir* [A collection of Eliyahu Sapir's writings] (Jaffa: Hotsa'at ḥevrat Anglo-Palestinah, 1913), 88–89.

63. He initially publicized his view in Eliyahu Sapir, "Harḥavat sefatenu ve-ha-'Aravit" [The enlargement of Hebrew and the issue of Arabic], *Haschiloah: Litterarisch-wissenschaftliche Monatsschrift* 4 (1898): 328–35. The article was reproduced posthumously in Sapir, *Ḳovets mi-kitve Eliyahu Sapir*, 89–90 (emphasis in the original).

64. Va'ad ha-Lashon, "'Avodat va'ad ha-lashon" [Works of the language committee], *Zikhronot va'ad ha-lashon ha-'ivrit* 3 (1913): introduction, list A.

65. In his acquisition of foreign languages at the turn of the twentieth century, Sapir faced challenges from traditional Jewish leaders in Jerusalem who imposed a boycott on modern schools. See Sapir, *Ḳovets mi-kitve Eliyahu Sapir*, 10–11.

66. Meir Dizengoff, "Eliyahu Ben Benjamin Ze'ev Hallevi Sapir Zal," *Ha-ḥinukh* 2, no. 2 (1911): 75.

67. Baruch Kimmerling, *The Invention and Decline of Israeliness: Society, Culture and Military* (Berkeley: University of California Press, 2001), 193.

68. Eliyahu Sapir, "Tsimḥe Erets Yisrael" [Plants of the land of Israel], *Ha-ḥinukh: 'Itun Pedagugi la-Morim ve-la-Horim* 1, no. 4–5 (1911): 343.

69. Sapir, "Tsimḥe Erets Yisrael," 346.

70. Sapir, "Tsimḥe Erets Yisrael."

71. Raphaela Veit, "Greek Roots, Arab Authoring, Latin Overlay: Reflections on the Sources for Avicenna's Canon," in *Vehicles of Transmission, Translation, and Transformation in Medieval Textual Culture*, ed. Rovbert Wisnovsky et al. (Turnhout, Belgium: Brepols Publishers, 2011), 355.

72. Sapir, "Tsimḥe Erets Yisrael."

73. Efraim Lev, "Reconstructed *materia medica* of the Medieval and Ottoman al-Sham," *Journal of Ethnopharmacology* 80, no. 2–3 (May 2002): 177.

74. Sapir, "Tsimḥe Erets Yisrael," 346.

75. For his discussion on the multiplicity of the names of plants, see Sapir, "Tsimḥe Erets Yisrael."

76. Sapir, "Tsimḥe Erets Yisrael," 345, 347.

77. Yaffa Szekely, "Deyoḳno shel ha-Moreh ha-'Ivri be-Moshavot ha-'aliyah ha-reshonah 1881–1904" [The character of the teachers in the First Aliya colonies, 1881–1904], *Cathedra: For the History of Eretz Israel and Its Yishuv* 84 (1997): 147.

78. Sapir, "Tsimḥe Erets Yisrael," 347.

79. Sapir, "Tsimḥe Erets Yisrael."

80. Sapir, "Tsimḥe Erets Yisrael," 349.

81. Sapir, "Tsimḥe Erets Yisrael," 349.

82. Sapir, "Tsimḥe Erets Yisrael," 349.

83. Sapir, "Tsimḥe Erets Yisrael," 349.

84. Yonatan Mendel, *The Creation of Israeli Arabic: Political and Security Considerations in the Making of Arabic Language Studies in Israel* (Hampshire: Palgrave Macmillan, 2014), 16–17. For more details on the Sephardic encounter with modernity in Ottoman and Mandate Jerusalem, see Nathan Efrati, *Ha-'edah ha-Sephardit be-Yerushalayim: 1840–1917* [The Sephardic community in Jerusalem during the years 1840–1917] (Jerusalem: Bialiḳ Institute, 1999); Joseph B. Glass and Ruth Kark, *Sephardi Entrepreneurs in Jerusalem: The Valero Family 1800–1948* (Jerusalem: Gefen Publishing House, 2007).

85. On Sephardi and Ashkenazi Jewries' approach to the inclusion or exclusion of Arabic in their educational school systems, see Mendel, *The Creation of Israeli Arabic*, 17–18.

86. Yehoshua Ben-Arieh, *'ir bi-rei teḳufah: Yerushalayim ba-me'ah ha-tesha' 'esreh, ha-'ir ha-'atiḳah* [A city reflected in its times: Jerusalem in the nineteenth century, the Old City] (Jerusalem: Yad Yitsḥaḳ Ben-Tsevi, 1977), 54.

87. For more details on the history of the institution of the Hakham Bashi and its features, see Efrati, *Ha-'edah ha-Sephardit be-Yerushalayim*, 11–14.

88. Ben-Arieh, *'ir bi-rei teḳufah*, 335.

89. In addition to Montefiore, Rothschild made significant contributions to the advancement of Arabic learning in the Yishuv. For further details, see Ran Aaronsohn, *Rothschild and Early Jewish Colonization in Palestine* (Lanham, MD: Rowman & Littlefield, 2000), 149–51.

90. In a meeting with another Jewish philanthropist, Montefiore suggested that giving charity to the Jewish communities in Jerusalem should be at the top of the list of charitable priorities. This perspective echoes the traditional attitude preferring Jerusalemite Jewry to Jewish communities of the philanthropists' home countries. See Abigail Green, *Moses Montefiore: Jewish Liberator and Imperial Hero* (Cambridge, MA: Harvard University Press, 2012), 322–23.

91. Yosef Yo'el Rivlin, "Hora'at ha-Safah ha-'Aravit be-Batey ha-Sefer ha-Yehudim be-Erets Yisrael," in *Sedeh Ilan 2: Sefer Zikaron le-Aryeh Ilan* (Jerusalem, 1967), 128.

92. For details on the account of Montefiore and his discussion with local rabbis in Jerusalem about learning Arabic, see Rivlin, "Hora'at ha-Safah ha-'Aravit be-Batey ha-Sefer ha-Yehudim be-Erets Yisrael," 128.

93. Gudrun Krämer, *A History of Palestine: From the Ottoman Conquest to the Founding of the State of Israel*, trans. Graham Harman and Gudrun Krämer (Princeton, NJ: Princeton University Press, 2008), 86–89.

94. Compare, for instance, Rivlin's career with that of Wāṣif Jawhariyyeh, an Orthodox Christian who lived during the same years in Jerusalem. For a study on the transition of Jerusalem into modernity through the life of Jawhariyyeh, see Salim Tamari, "Jerusalem's Ottoman Modernity: The Times and Lives of Wasif Jawhariyyeh," *Jerusalem Quarterly File* 9 (2000): 27. A parallel career path is found in Yellin's life. The motivation to teach young Yellin Arabic and Islamic studies was to allow him to compete with non-Jewish, Arabic-speaking Jerusalemite communities—that is, Muslims and Christians—to find a position within the government. For more details on this attitude, see David Yellin, *Mi-Dan ve-'ad Be'er Sheva'* [From Dan to Beer Sheva], ed. Avraham Ḥayim Elḥanani (Jerusalem: Ha-Vaad li-Hotsaat Kitve David Yellin, 1973).

95. Because of his language skill, I should note, Rivlin would be conscripted into the Ottoman Army on the eve of the outbreak of the World War I.

96. Penslar, *Zionism and Technocracy*, 18.

97. On the symbolic meanings of learning Arabic, see Oz Almog, *The Sabra: The Creation of the New Jew* (Berkeley: University of California Press, 2000), chapter 5.

98. This group adopted the name of their movement, Bilu, from the Hebrew initials from Isaiah 2:5 הָכְלְנוּ וְכָל בְּקֶעֵי תֵּיב" "O House of Jacob! Come, let us walk."

99. On the discussion about the limited nature of Arabic literacy among Palestine's Zionists and anxiety evoked among Zionist leaders, see Gribetz, *Defining Neighbors*, 187–88; Almog, *The Sabra*, 198–99.

100. On the life conditions of the pioneer members of the Biluim movement after their arrival in Palestine, see Shulamit Laskov, *Ha-Biluyim* [The Biluim], ed. Reuven Eshel (Jerusalem: Ha-Sifriyah ha-Tsiyonit, 1979), 91.

101. Haim Hissin, *A Palestinian Diary: Memoirs of a Bilu Pioneer 1882–1887*, trans. Francis Miller (New York: Herzl Press, 1976), 64–65. For details about Belkind's account with his Arab creditors, see Israel Belkind, *Bi-netiv ha-Biluyim: Zikhronot* [In the path of Biluyim: Memoirs of Israel Belkind], ed. Ran Aharonson (Tel Aviv: Misrad ha-biṭaḥon, 1983), 49–50.

102. Joseph Shapiro, *Me'ah Shanah Miḳveh-Yisrael: 630–730, 1870–1970* [A century of Miḳveh-Yisrael] (Tel-Aviv: Tarbut ve-ḥinukh, 1970), 174. According to the organizational features of the movement, two of the members were *sheliḥim* (emissaries) who abstained from cultivating the land, asking for privileges from other members even though they neither worked nor earned money. That kind of leadership incited opposition among other members, who decided on their own to leave Miḳveh Yisrael. For further details, see Laskov, *Ha-Biluyim*, 96–97.

103. For an overview of the encounter between the Biluim's members and Arabs, see Yosef Gorny, *Zionism and the Arabs: 1882–1948, a Study of Ideology* (Oxford: Clarendon Press, 1987), 13. For a nuanced study on the relationship between Jewish settlements and their proximate Arab population, see Yuval Ben-Bassat, "Proto-Zionist–Arab Encounters in Late Nineteenth-Century Palestine: Socioregional Dimensions," *Journal of Palestine Studies* 38, no. 2 (2009): 42–63.

104. Szekely, "Deyoḳno shel ha-Moreh ha-'Ivri be-Moshavot ha-'aliyah ha-reshonah 1881–1904," 143.

105. For further details on Belkind's educational activities in Palestine, see Ben-Zion Keren, *Israel Belkind: Educator and Dreamer* (Jerusalem: Institute of Contemporary Jewry, Hebrew University of Jerusalem, 1980), 37.

106. Laskov, *Ha-Biluyim*, 389.

107. Keren, *Israel Belkind*, 35, 37.

108. Derek Penslar, *Theodor Herzl: The Charismatic Leader* (New Haven, CT: Yale University Press, 2020), 90.

109. Laskov, *Ha-Biluyim*, 396.

110. Alan Dowty, *Arabs and Jews in Ottoman Palestine: Two Worlds Collide* (Bloomington: Indiana University Press, 2021), 99–100.

111. Penslar, *Zionism and Technocracy*, 33.

112. Laskov, *Ha-Biluyim*, 390.

113. Penimi, "Bifnim ha-arets," *Ha-Po'el Ha-Tza'ir* (Jerusalem), July 29, 1909.

114. Buchaltzev, "'Ivri, 'Ivrit ve-'Ivriut," 23–24.

115. Ross Brann, *Al-Andalus, Sefarad, and the Tropes of Exceptionalism* (Philadelphia: University of Pennsylvania Press, 2021), 1–3.

116. On the use of Sephardic legacy to provide solutions and answers to Jews in Europe, see Ismar Schorsch, "The Myth of Sephardic Supremacy," *Leo Baeck Institute Year Book* 34, no. 1 (1989): 47–66; Ross Brann and Adam Sutcliffe, eds., *Renewing the Past, Reconfiguring Jewish Culture: From al-Andalus to the Haskalah* (Philadelphia: University of Pennsylvania Press, 2004).

117. Amnon Raz-Krakotzkin, "Orientalism, Jewish Studies, and the Israeli Society: Several Observations," *Jama'ah* 3, no. 1 (1999): 34–61.

118. Yuval Evri and Almog Behar, “Between East and West: Controversies over the Modernization of Hebrew Culture in the Works of Shaul Abdallah Yosef and Ariel Bension,” *Journal of Modern Jewish Studies* 16, no. 2 (May 4, 2017): 295–311.

119. Louise Marlow, “Among Kings and Sages: Greek and Indian Wisdom in an Arabic Mirror for Princes,” *Arabica* 60, no. 1–2 (2013): 1–57.

120. Although neither author provides the exact sources from which they drew their materials, they refer to Arabic literary texts in general as one of their inspirations. For more details, see Eliezer Ben-Yehuda and David Yellin, *Miḳra le-yilde bene Yisrael kolel reshit limudim, sipure ha-Talmud ve-ha-Midrashim u-mishle shoʻalim* [Lecture to the children of the people of Israel including the beginning of learning, Talmudic and Midrashic stories, and fox fables] (Jerusalem: Kol yisrael ḥaverim, 1887), 42.

121. For the Hebrew account of the anecdote, see Ben-Yehuda and Yellin, *Miḳra le-yilde bene Yisrael kolel reshit limudim, sipure ha-Talmud ve-ha-Midrashim u-mishle shoʻalim*, 35.

122. Abū al-Faraj al-Jawzī, *Kitāb al-adhkiyā'* [The book of intelligent people] (Cairo: Al-Ghazali, n.d.), 241; Abū Ḥayyān al-Tawḥīdī, *al-baṣā'ir wa-al-dhakhā'ir* [Insights and treasures] (Beirut: Dār Ṣādir, 1988), 9:117; al-Damīrī, *Ḥayāt al-ḥayawān* [Life of animals] (Beirut: Dār al-Kutub al-ʻIlmiyyah, 2003), 1:257.

123. Berekhiah ben Natronai, *Mishle shuʻalim* [Fox fables] (Jerusalem: Hirsch Zuckermann, 1919), fable number 77. Cf. parable 85 in the English translation: Berechiah ben Natronai, *Fables of a Jewish Aesop* [Mishle shuʻalim], trans. Moses Hadas (New York: Columbia University Press, 1967), 154–56.

124. Muḥammad Ibn Sallām al-Jumaḥī, *Ṭabaqāt Fuḥūl al-Shuʻarā'* [Classes of champion poets], ed. Maḥmūd Muḥammad Shākir (Cairo, 1974), 1:24.

125. For the importance of classical Arabic poetry and its influence on Arab culture, see Shawqi Dhayf, *Tārīkh al-'Adab al-'Arabī: Al-Shiʻr al-Jāhilī* [History of Arabic literature: Pre-Islamic era] (Cairo: Dār al-Maʻārif, 1960), 138–82.

126. For more details with examples from classical Arabic poetry, see Dhayf, *Tārīkh al-'Adab al-'Arabī: Al-Shiʻr al-Jāhilī*, 68–69.

127. David Yellin, *Miḳra le-naʻre bene Yisrael* [Reading for the youth of the children of Israel] (Jerusalem, 1889).

128. Hasan El-Shamy, “Qâla al-Samaw'al ibn Âdiyâ al-Yahudiyy (the Jew, Al-Samaw'al Son-of Âdiya Said: . . .)” Conscientiousness and Fidelity as Heroic Qualities in Arab Traditions (the Jewish Example),” *Folk Culture* 5, no. 16 (2012): 4.

129. Yellin, *Miḳra le-naʻre bene Yisrael*, 19.

130. El-Shamy, “Qâla al-Samaw'al ibn Âdiyâ al-Yahudiyy (the Jew, Al-Samaw'al Son-of Âdiya Said: . . .),” 6.

131. The article was published initially as David Yellin, “Melitsat Yisrael ʻal adamat Yishmaʻel” [The oratory of Israel on the soil of Ishmael], *Yerushalayim* (1891): 37–48. I cite here another edition: David Yellin, “Melitsat Yisrael ʻal adamat Yishmaʻel,” in *Kitve David Yellin: leḥeḳer ha-shirah ha-ʻIvrit be-Sefarad*, ed. A. M. Habermann (Jerusalem: Committee for Republication of David Yellin's Writings, 1975), 3–9 (emphasis in the original).

132. Yellin, “Melitsat Yisrael ʻal adamat Yishmaʻel,” 8–9.

133. Başak Kale, “Transforming an Empire: The Ottoman Empire's Immigration and Settlement Policies in the Nineteenth and Early Twentieth Centuries,” *Middle Eastern Studies* 50, no. 2 (2014): 261.

134. Neville J. Mandel, *The Arabs and Zionism before World War I* (Berkeley: University of California Press, 1976), 38–40.

135. Yellin, "Melitsat Yisrael 'al adamat Yishma'el," 8–9.

136. Abraham Shalom Yahuda, "Nedive ve-gibure 'Arav" [Arab noblemen and heroes], *Luaḥ Erets Yisrael* 2 (1896): 89.

137. Yahuda, "Nedive ve-gibure 'Arav," 89. This article was republished in his collection *'Ever ve-'Arav*. See: A. S. Yahuda, "Nedive ve-gibure 'Arav," in *'Ever ve-'Arav*, ed. A. S. Yahuda (New York: Shlusinger Bros., 1946), 173.

138. Yahuda, "Nedive ve-gibure 'Arav," 89.

139. Yahuda, "Nedive ve-gibure 'Arav," 89–90.

140. For a discussion on hospitality in Judaism and specifically as embodied in the deeds of Abraham, see Ronald L. Eisenberg, *Jewish Traditions: A JPS Guide* (Philadelphia: Jewish Publication Society, 2008), 539.

141. Yahuda, "Nedive ve-gibure 'Arav," 93.

142. See the Hebrew poem in Yahuda, "Nedive ve-gibure 'Arav," 96.

143. On the life of 'Antar, see Dhayf, *Tārīkh al-'Adab al-'Arabī*, 369.

144. Yahuda, "Nedive ve-gibure 'Arav," 119.

145. Yitsḥaḳ Avishur, *Ha-sipur ha-'amami shel yehudey 'Iraq* [The folktales of the Jews of Iraq] (Haifa: University of Haifa, 1992), 1:15.

146. Yahuda, "Nedive ve-gibure 'Arav," 119. Interestingly, Yahuda omits this comparison from the later edition of this article, which he republished in his collection *'Ever ve-'Arav*. Cf. Yahuda, "Nedive ve-gibure 'Arav," 191.

147. Yahuda, "Nedive ve-gibure 'Arav," 97.

148. Yahuda, "Nedive ve-gibure 'Arav," 97.

149. Yahuda, "Nedive ve-gibure 'Arav," 97.

150. Ṭaha Ḥussein, *Fī al- 'Adab al-Jāhilī* [On classical Arabic literature], 3rd ed. (1914; repr., Cairo: Lajnat al-Ta'līf wa-al-Nashr, 1933), 12.

151. Yahuda, "Nedive ve-gibure 'Arav," 270.

152. See A. S. Yahuda, "Ḥalifat mikhtavim 'im Tschernichovsky 'al ha-shirah ha-'Aravit," in *'Erev ve-'Arav: 'osef miḥḳarim u-ma'amarim, shirat ha-'Aravim, zikhronot u-reshamim*, ed. A. S. Yahuda (New York: Shulsinger Bros., 1946), 269–79. Why did someone like Tschernichovsky fail to digest Arabic poetry? He shunned Arabic poetry because of the difficulties involved in the study of Arabic language and literature, and mostly preferred to compose Hebrew verse. Medieval Jews from Spain encountered similar difficulties, according to Joshua Blau, composing Arabic poetry. A prerequisite for composing Arabic poetry was the study of Arabic syntax, morphology, literature, and rhetoric, which medieval Jews were not interested in. Joshua Blau's view is quoted in Shmuel Moreh, "Oriental Literature," in *Encyclopaedia Judaica* (Jerusalem: Keter Publishing, 1973), 472.

153. Michal Rose Friedman, "Orientalism between Empires: Abraham Shalom Yahuda at the Intersection of Sepharad, Zionism, and Imperialism," *Jewish Quarterly Review* 109, no. 3 (2019): 437.

154. Abraham Shalom Le-Beit Yehezkiel, "To'elet lashon 'Aravit," *Ha-Melits* (Petersburg) September 11, 1894.

155. Eli Lederhendler, *The Road to Modern Jewish Politics: Political Tradition and Political Reconstruction in the Jewish Community of Tsarist Russia* (New York: Oxford University Press, 1989), 125.

156. The articles were published on September 11, 14, and 16, 1894.

157. Yehezkiel, "To'elet lashon 'Aravit."

158. Abraham Shalom Le-Beit Yehezkiel, "To'elet lashon 'Aravit," *Ha-Melits* (Petersburg), September 14, 1894, 7.

159. In translating Halevi's Hebrew verse, I consulted the English translation in Franz Rosenzweig, *Ninety-Two Poems and Hymns of Yehuda Halevi* (Albany: SUNY Press, 2012), 236. Yet I decided to translate the verse in a manner that articulates the meaning Yahuda intended in his discussion when making a reference to the Arabic word *ḍarīḥ*.

160. For a discussion about the place of the Andalusian legacy in Yahuda's intellectual project, see Almog Behar and Yuval Evri, "From Saadia to Yahuda: Reviving Arab Jewish Intellectual Models in a Time of Partition," *Jewish Quarterly Review* 109, no. 3 (2019): 461.

161. For a discussion about the role of Arabic poetry in public life as a means of publicity and its impact on medieval Hebrew poetry, see Raymond P. Scheindlin, "Merchants and Intellectuals, Rabbis and Poets: Judeo-Arabic Culture in the Golden Age of Islam," in *Cultures of the Jews*, ed. David Biale (New York: Schocken Books, 2002), 361.

162. Moreh, "Oriental Literature," 462.

163. For a discussion on the influence of Sa'adyah Gaon's Arabic translation of the Hebrew Bible on Arabic-speaking Jewish communities, see Yitsḥaḳ Avishur, "Ha-'ibudim shel tirgum Rav Sa'adya Gaon la-Tanakh ba-Mizraḥ" [The adaptations of R. Saadya Gaon's Bible translation in the East], *Sefunot: Studies and Sources on the History of the Jewish Communities in the East* 54 (1991): 181–202. See also Aaron Maman, *Comparative Semitic Philology in the Middle Ages: From Sa'adiah Gaon to Ibn Barūn (10th–12th c.)* (Leiden: Brill, 2004); Moreh, "Oriental Literature," 472.

164. Yahuda, "Nedive ve-gibure 'Arav," 106–7.

165. https://www.sefaria.org/Psalms.119.61?lang=bi&with=all&lang2=en.

Part II: Construction of a National Home

1. Ussama Makdisi, *Age of Coexistence: The Ecumenical Frame and the Making of the Modern Arab World* (Berkeley: University of California Press, 2019), 168.

2. Neil Caplan, *Palestine Jewry and the Arab Question, 1917–1925* (London: Routledge, 2015), 16.

3. Cited in Caplan, *Palestine Jewry and the Arab Question*, 14.

4. Gershon Shafir, "Zionism and Colonialism: A Comparative Approach," in *The Israel/Palestine Question*, ed. Ilan Pappé (London: Routledge, 1999), 88.

5. Kenneth W. Stein, *The Land Question in Palestine, 1917–1939* (Chapel Hill: University of North Carolina Press, 1984), 212.

6. Hillel Cohen, *Army of Shadows: Palestinian Collaboration with Zionism, 1917–1948*, trans. Haim Watzman (Berkeley: University of California Press, 2008), 28.

7. Suzanne Schneider, "Monolingualism and Education in Mandate Palestine," *Jerusalem Quarterly File* 52 (2013): 69.

8. Hilary Falb Kalisman, *Teachers as State-Builders: Education and the Making of the Modern Middle East* (Princeton, NJ: Princeton University Press, 2022), 67.

9. Liora R. Halperin, *Babel in Zion: Jews, Nationalism, and Language Diversity in Palestine, 1920–1948* (New Haven, CT: Yale University Press, 2014), 143, 144.

10. Yonatan Mendel, *The Creation of Israeli Arabic: Political and Security Considerations in the Making of Arabic Language Studies in Israel* (Hampshire: Palgrave Macmillan, 2014), 50.

11. Cyrus Schayegh, *The Middle East and the Making of the Modern World* (Cambridge, MA: Harvard University Press, 2017), 138–39.

12. Schayegh, *The Middle East and the Making of the Modern World*, 152.

13. Avi-Ram Tzoreff, "Beyond the Boundaries of 'The Land of the Deer': R. Binyamin between Jewish and Arab Geographies, and the Critique of the Zionist-Colonial Connection," *Jerusalem Quarterly* 82 (2020): 130–53.

14. Adi Gordon, *Brit Shalom ve-ha-Tsiyonit ha-Dole'omiyut: Ha-She'elah ha-'Aravit kishe'elah Yehudit* [Brith Shalom and the binational Zionism: The Arab question as a Jewish question] (2008), 7.

15. Cohen, *Army of Shadows*, 18.

16. "An Arab Support of Zionism," *Jewish Chronicle* (London), September 22, 1922, 50–52; 'Isa al-'isa, "Aḥmad Zakī Pashā wa al-Ṣuhyūniyya," *Filasṭīn* (Jaffa), October 6, 1922.

17. Safa Khulusi, "Ma'ruf al-Rusafi in Jerusalem," *Jerusalem Quarterly* 22–23 (2005).

18. Abraham Haim, *Yiḥud ve-hishtalvut: Hanhagat ha-Sefaradim bi-Yerushalayim bi-tekufat ha-shilṭon ha-Briṭi, 678–708 (1917–1948)* [Particularity and integration: The Sephardi leadership in Jerusalem under British rule, 1917–1948] (Jerusalem: Carmel, 2000), 215–16.

19. Lital Levy, "Historicizing the Concept of Arab Jews in the 'Mashriq,'" *Jewish Quarterly Review* 98, no. 4 (2008): 467–68.

20. In his diary, Jawhariyyeh described the Balfour Declaration using the same combination *al-wa'd al-Mash'um*. Wāṣif Jawhariyyeh, *The Storyteller of Jerusalem: The Life and Times of Wasif Jawhariyyeh, 1904–1948*, ed. Salīm Tamārī and Issam Nassar, trans. Nada Elzeer (Northampton, MA: Olive Branch Press, 2014), 10.

21. Abigail Jacobson, *From Empire to Empire: Jerusalem between Ottoman and British Rule* (Syracuse, NY: Syracuse University Press, 2011), 155.

22. Jacobson, *From Empire to Empire*, 112–13. For the editorial, see "Ila al-Yahūd al-'Arab wa al-Ṣahyūnyyin," *Al-Quds al-Sharif* (Al-Quds), July 8, 1920.

23. Jacobson, *From Empire to Empire*, 158; Yehoshua Porath, *The Emergence of the Palestinian-Arab National Movement, 1918–1929* (London: Frank Cass, 1974), 1:61–62.

24. Abigail Jacobson and Moshe Naor, *Oriental Neighbors: Middle Eastern Jews and Arabs in Mandatory Palestine* (Waltham, MA: Brandeis University Press, 2016), 22.

25. Hillel Cohen and Yuval Evri, "Moledet meshutefet ou beit le'umi: bene ha-arets, hatsaharat Balfour ve he-she'elah ha-'Aravit" [Shared homeland or Jewish national home: Sephardi natives of the land, Balfour Declaration, and the Arab question], *Te'oriah u-veḳoret* 49 (2017): 293.

26. Lauren Banko, *The Invention of Palestinian Citizenship, 1918–1947* (Edinburgh: Edinburgh University Press, 2016), 26.

27. Cited in Elie Kedourie, *In the Anglo-Arab Labyrinth: The McMahon-Husayn Correspondence and its Interpretations, 1914–1939* (Cambridge: Cambridge University Press, 1976), 265.

28. Bernard Regan, *The Balfour Declaration: Empire, the Mandate and Resistance in Palestine* (London: Verso, 2017), 55–58.

Chapter 4: Ethnonationalization of the Landscape

1. Israel Belḳind, *Our National Work in Palestine* (New York: Pinski-Massel Press, 1918), 17.

2. Ussama Makdisi, *Age of Coexistence: The Ecumenical Frame and the Making of the Modern Arab World* (Berkeley: University of California Press, 2019), 164–65. It is worth mentioning that despite the limited achievements of the Bilu members, the glorification of their works and rebranding of them as pioneers is attributed to Labor Zionists, who "had become disappointed in their conservative predecessors and employers and found in Bilu an alternative model that fit their notion of Jewish settler pioneering." See Liora Halperin, *The Oldest Guard: Forging the Zionist Settler Past* (Stanford, CA: Stanford University Press, 2021), 45.

3. Belḳind, *Our National Work in Palestine*, 7, 9, 15, 21.

4. Ran Aaronsohn, "The Beginnings of Modern Jewish Agriculture in Palestine: 'Indigenous' versus 'Imported,'" *Agricultural History* 69, no. 3 (1995): 451.

5. Belḳind, *Our National Work in Palestine*, 18.

6. Shulamit Lasḳov, *Ha-Biluyim* [The Biluim], ed. Reuven Eshel (Jerusalem: Ha-Sifriyah ha-Tsiyonit, 1979), 337.

7. Aaronsohn, "The Beginnings of Modern Jewish Agriculture in Palestine," 444.

8. Belḳind, *Our National Work in Palestine*, 9.

9. Aziza Khazzoom, "The Great Chain of Orientalism: Jewish Identity, Stigma Management, and Ethnic Exclusion in Israel," *American Sociological Review* 68, no. 4 (2003): 484.

10. Belḳind, *Our National Work in Palestine*, 9.

11. In the first chapter, we discuss his promotion of Arabic instruction at Hebrew schools.

12. In his diary, Haim Hissin, one of the Bilu members, highlights how Jewish settlers who did not have previous agricultural knowledge learned from the local farmers when, for example, to plow the land and what crops to grow in various seasons. Haim Hissin, *A Palestinian Diary: Memoirs of a Bilu Pioneer 1882–1887*, trans. Francis Miller (New York: Herzl Press, 1976), 198–99.

13. Belḳind relates in some detail the reasons for publishing the work in Russian and not in Hebrew in Israel Belḳind, *Erets Yisrael shel zemanenu* [Contemporary Palestine] (Tel Aviv: Hotsaat ha-Mmeir, 1928), vii.

14. Getzel Kressel, *Erets Yisrael ve-toldoteha: madrikh bibliografi, ha-sifrut ha-'ivrit 'al Erets Yisrael* [The land of Israel and its history: A bibliographic guide] (Tel Aviv: Makhon Mazkeret, 1980), 57. For a discussion on Belḳind's work, see Yehoshua Ben-Arieh, "Le-'ofiha shel ha-sifrut ha-geografit ha-'ivrit 'al Erets Yisrael ba-me'ah ha-tesha' 'esreh 'ad milhemet ha-'olam ha-rishonah" [The character of Hebrew geographic literature about Erets-Israel during the nineteenth century and until World War I], *Eretz-Israel: Archaeological, Historical and Geographical Studies* 22 (1991): 40.

15. For more details regarding the difficulties Belḳind experienced while trying to publish the book in Hebrew, see Belḳind, *Erets Yisrael shel zemanenu*, vii–viii.

16. Eitan Bar-Yosef, *The Holy Land in English Culture 1799–1917: Palestine and the Question of Orientalism* (Oxford: Oxford University Press, 2005), 10–11.

17. The illustrations are scattered over the pages of the book for clarification purposes. They are found on several pages. See Belḳind, *Erets Yisrael shel zemanenu*, 18, 55, 62, 66, 73, 74, 81, 83, 91, 93–97, 99, 102–5, 107, 108, 114, 125, 127–29, 133, 137, 141–44, 146–60, and 162–63.

18. Halperin, *The Oldest Guard*, 44.

19. Nur Masalha, "Settler-Colonialism, Memoricide and Indigenous Toponymic Memory: The Appropriation of Palestinian Place Names by the Israeli State," *Journal of Holy Land and Palestine Studies* 14, no. 1 (2015): 14.

20. Moshe Fischer, Itamar Taxel, and David Amit, "Rural Settlement in the Vicinity of Yavneh in the Byzantine Period: A Religio-Archaeological Perspective," *Bulletin of the American Schools of Oriental Research* 350 (2008): 28.

21. Hissin, *A Palestinian Diary*, 161.

22. Bar-Yosef, *The Holy Land in English Culture 1799–1917*, 247, 261. Zionists were disappointed by the declaration's wording because it merely promised the construction of a national home for Jews in Palestine, and did not honor their demands that their "historic rights" to Palestine be explicitly stated and that Palestine be acknowledged as the national home for Jews without any consideration to the current "inhabitants in the land." Ahad ha-'Am wrote on this in *She'efotenu*, vol. 1.

23. Cited in Roberto Mazza, *Jerusalem: From the Ottomans to the British* (London: Tauris Academic Studies, 2009), 123.

24. Mazza, *Jerusalem*, 123.

25. Jonathan Parry, *Promised Lands: The British and the Ottoman Middle East* (Princeton, NJ: Princeton University Press, 2022), 401.

26. Israel Wolf Horowitz, *Sefer meḥḳere erets avotenu* [The book of the study of our ancestral land] (Jerusalem: Bi-defus ha-ahim Lipshitts, 1909–10), 4.

27. Horowitz, *Sefer meḥḳere erets avotenu*, 4.

28. Masalha, "Settler-Colonialism, Memoricide and Indigenous Toponymic Memory," 2.

29. For a reference to *The Jewish War* by Josephus, see Belḳind, *Erets Yisrael shel zemanenu*, 72.

30. Belḳind, *Erets Yisrael shel zemanenu*, 50, 77, 88, 120. Fischer and Guthe's map of Palestine is referred to several times in the book; see Belḳind, *Erets Yisrael shel zemanenu*, 10, 63.

31. Yossi Katz, "'Aliyah ve-hityashvut: Va'adat ha-shemot shel ḲḲ"l u-ḳevi'at shemot ha-yishuvim ha-yehudim be-teḳufat ha-mandeṭ" [Immigration and settlement: The Jewish National Fund Committee and naming Jewish settlements in the Mandate period], *'iyunim bi-teḳumat yisrael: me'asef li-ve'ayot ha-tsiyonut, ha-yishuv u-medinat yisrael* 9 (1999): 286.

32. "Doḥot va'adat ha-Shemot shel ḲḲ"L Lashanim 1925 ve-'ad 1950," 18. Compare what Mostafa al-Dabbagh wrote about Jidda in *Biladuna Filastin*, 7:150–51.

33. Moshe Sharon, *Corpus Inscriptionum Arabicarum Palaestinae* (Leiden: Brill, 2004), 3:xxxvii.

34. Eliezer Ben-Yehuda, *Sefer Erets Yisrael: 'al ṭeva' ha-arets ha-zot* [The land of Israel's book: On the nature of this land] (Jerusalem: Joel Moses Solomon, 1883), introduction.

35. Horowitz, *Sefer meḥḳere erets avotenu*, 4.

36. Israel Wolf Horowitz, *Erets Yisrael u-shekhenoteha: Entsiḳlopedyah ge'ografit-hisṭorit le-Erets Yisrael, Suriyah va-ḥatsi ha-'i Sinai* [Palestine and the adjacent countries: A geographic and historical encyclopedia of Palestine, Syria and the Sinai Peninsula], ed. Aaron Teitelbaum (Vienna: Abraham Horowitz, 1923), 1:xii.

37. Yossi Katz, "Identity, Nationalism, and Placenames: Zionist Efforts to Preserve the Original Local Hebrew Names in Official Publications of the Mandate Government of Palestine," *Names* 43, no. 2 (1995): 104.

38. Horowitz's encyclopedic work was reviewed in the *Zeitschrift des Deutschen Palästina-Vereins* by Samuel Krauss, who would become the first professor to be appointed at the Hebrew University in the field of yedi'at ha-arets, shortly after its publication. See Samuel Krauss, review of *Erets Yisrael u-shekhenoteha: Entsiḳlopedyah ge'ografit-hisṭorit le-Erets Yisrael, Suriyah ya-ḥatsi ha-'i Sinai, Zeitschrift des Deutschen Palästina-Vereins (1878–1945)* 46, no. 3–4 (1923): 228–31. Also, the publication of the first volume is listed in Leop Fonck, "Elenchus Bibliographicus," *Biblica* 4, no. 4 (1923): 67. Furthermore, Abraham Horowitz, the son of the author, noted in the introduction that the work received praises from some of "the eminent *hakhame yisrael*," who recognized the book and thought it would generate studies of "the Holy Land." See Horowitz, *Erets Yisrael u-shekhenoteha*, 1:vii.

39. For a list of the Jewish sources, see the front page of Horowitz, *Erets Yisrael u-shekhenoteha]*, 1:1.

40. In the introduction, Abraham Horowitz explains that the author composed the articles in the encyclopedia up to the last letter of the Hebrew alphabet. Still, although his father prepared the articles for publication, up to letter *kaf*, Israel Wolf's sudden death at the age of thirty-eight prevented the publication of the prepared volumes. In view of the conquest of Jerusalem by the British, as Abraham notes, the article on Jerusalem would be published as a separate volume. See Horowitz, *Erets Yisrael u-shekhenoteha*, 1:v–vi.

41. Horowitz, *Erets Yisrael u-shekhenoteha*, 1:vi.

42. For a review of the list and the suggested Hebrew translations, see Horowitz, *Erets Yisrael u-shekhenoteha*, 1:viii.

43. Horowitz, *Erets Yisrael u-shekhenoteha*, 1:viii.

44. The late Ottoman Palestine of 1900 had a total population of around six hundred thousand. Muslim Arabs constituted about 75 percent of that, compared to 10 percent Christian Arabs and 15 percent Jewish communities. For some evaluation of Palestine's demographic figures up to the end of the Ottoman rule, see Alexander Schölch, *Palestine in Transformation, 1856–1882: Studies in Social, Economic, and Political Development* (Washington, DC: Institute for Palestine Studies, 1993), 46–170. For an account of the Jewish communities of late Ottoman Palestine, see Yeshayahu Press, "Ha-yishuv ha-Yehudi bi-Yerushalayim ba-me'ah ha-tesha' 'isreh" [The Jewish settlement in Jerusalem in the nineteenth century], *Report (World Congress of Jewish Studies)* 1 (1947): 427–33.

45. Horowitz, *Erets Yisrael u-shekhenoteha*, 1:xii.

46. Beshara Doumani, *Rediscovering Palestine: Merchants and Peasants in Jabal Nablus, 1700–1900* (Berkeley: University of California Press, 1995), 27.

47. Gil Eyal, *The Disenchantment of the Orient: Expertise in Arab Affairs and the Israeli State* (Stanford, CA: Stanford University Press, 2006), 53–54.

48. Belḳind, *Erets Yisrael shel zemanenu*, 33, 37, 56–57.

49. Katz, "Identity, Nationalism, and Placenames," 105.

50. Amer Dahamsheh, *Maḳom la-dor bo ve-shem lo: Ḳeri'ah sifrutit ve-tarbutit ba-shemot ha-'Aravim shel ha-arets* [A local habitation and a name: A literary and cultural reading of the Arabic geographic names of the land] (Beersheba: Dvir, 2017), 52, 54.

51. Meron Benvenisti, *Sacred Landscape: The Buried History of the Holy Land since 1948*, trans. Maxine Kaufman-Lacusta (Berkeley: University of California Press, 2000), 47–48. See, for instance, an article on earlier Arab settlement in Safad: Ze'ev Vilnai, "'Araviye Tsafa u-sefatam" [Arabs of Safa and their language], *Mizraḥ u-Ma'arav* 3, no. 7 (1929).

52. Israel Belḳind, *Erets Yisrael* (New York: Hotsaat ha-Mmeir, 1919), 19. Somewhere else, Belḳind explains the Arabic word *al-Sheikh*; see Belḳind, *Erets Yisrael shel zemanenu*, 56.

53. Belḳind refers to Joshua 17:16 and Hosea 1:5. See Belḳind, *Erets Yisrael shel zemanenu*, 21.

54. Belḳind, *Erets Yisrael shel zemanenu*, 21. According to Muṣṭafa Murād al-Dabbāgh, Zirʿīn was an Arab village with a population of 1,420 before 1948. See Muṣṭafa Murād al-Dabbāgh, *Bilādunā Filasṭīn* [Our land Palestine] (Kafr Qara: Dār al-Huda, 1991), 1:213.

55. In his encyclopedia, al-Dabbāgh refers to such a village, drawing the attention to medieval Muslim scholar Mujīr al-Dīn al-Ḥanbalī's description of al-Lajūn as "a town on the borders of Palestine in the mountains. It has flowing water, and is spacious, and pure." For more details, see al-Dabbāgh, *Bilādunā Filasṭīn*, 1:212.

56. Belḳind, *Erets Yisrael shel zemanenu*, 21. According to al-Dabbāgh, Banī ʿĀmer was a tribe of Banī Kalb that settled the valley during the early Islamic settlement in Palestine. For more details, see al-Dabbāgh, *Bilādunā Filasṭīn*, 1:50–52.

57. For another list of valleys inhabited by the Arab population, see Belḳind, *Erets Yisrael shel zemanenu*, 29.

58. Belḳind, *Erets Yisrael shel zemanenu*, 58. To elaborate on the meaning of the mountain's nomenclature, he provides a footnote explaining that the Sheikha is a feminine name derived from al-Sheikh. In his opinion, the reason why the mountain takes a feminine name is its closeness to Mount al-Sheikh and the former's lower height compared with the latter, so it took the names al-Sheikha as though it were the wife of al-Sheikh. See Belḳind, *Erets Yisrael shel zemanenu*, 58.

59. Horowitz, *Erets Yisrael u-shekhenoteha*, 1:296, 1:67.

60. Makdisi, *Age of Coexistence*, 178; Wāṣif Jawhariyyeh, *The Storyteller of Jerusalem: The Life and Times of Wasif Jawhariyyeh, 1904–1948*, ed. Salīm Tamārī and Issam Nassar, trans. Nada Elzeer (Northampton, MA: Olive Branch Press, 2014), 140.

61. As arbitrators, the British formed an investigatory commission in 1930 chaired by Walter Shaw, a retired chief justice of the Straits Settlements, and produced a 211-page report. See Penny Sinanoglou, *Partitioning Palestine: British Policymaking at the End of Empire* (Chicago: University of Chicago Press, 2019), 28.

62. Hillel Cohen, "The Temple Mount / Al-Aqsa in Zionist and Palestinian National Consciousness: A Comparative View," *Israel Studies Review* 32, no. 1 (2017): 2.

63. Jodi Magness, *Jerusalem through the Ages: From Its Beginnings to the Crusades* (New York: Oxford University Press, 2024), 214, 320–22.

64. Kobi Cohen-Hattab and Doron Bar, *The Western Wall: The Dispute over Israel's Holiest Jewish Site, 1967–2000* (Leiden: Brill, 2020), 17.

65. Hillel Cohen, *Year Zero of the Arab-Israeli Conflict*, trans. Haim Watzman (Waltham, MA: Brandeis University Press, 2015), 70.

66. Cohen, "The Temple Mount / Al-Aqsa in Zionist and Palestinian National Consciousness," 14.

67. Cited in Derek Penslar, *Theodor Herzl: The Charismatic Leader* (New Haven, CT: Yale University Press, 2020), 146.

68. Cohen, *Year Zero of the Arab-Israeli Conflict*, xi–xvi.

69. Makdisi, *Age of Coexistence*, 19.

70. Cohen, *Year Zero of the Arab-Israeli Conflict*, 52–53.

71. Abigail Jacobson and Moshe Naor, *Oriental Neighbors: Middle Eastern Jews and Arabs in Mandatory Palestine* (Waltham, MA: Brandeis University Press, 2016), 54.

72. Hillel Cohen and Yuval Evri, "Moledet meshutefet ou beit le'umi: bene ha-arets, hatsaharat Balfour ve he-she'elah ha-'Aravit" [Shared homeland or Jewish national home: Sephardi natives of the land, Balfour Declaration, and the Arab question], *Te'oriah u-veḳoret* 49 (2017): 293.

73. Cohen, *Year Zero of the Arab-Israeli Conflict*, 53.

74. Ofra Meitlis, *Be-derekh ha-emtsa': David Yellin—sipur ḥayim* [On the middle path: David Yellin—a life story] (Tel Aviv: Tel Aviv University Press, 2015), 314.

75. Cited in Meitlis, *Be-derekh ha-emtsa'*, 313.

76. Abraham Haim, *Yiḥud ve-hishtalvut: Hanhagat ha-Sefaradim bi-Yerushalayim bi-tekufat ha-shilṭon ha-Briṭi, 678–708 (1917–1948)* [Particularity and integration: The Sephardi leadership in Jerusalem under British rule, 1917–1948] (Jerusalem: Carmel, 2000), 215–17.

77. See this description in Eli Sheltiel, *Pinhas Rutenberg: 'alyato u-nefilato shel "ish hazak" be-erets yisrael, 1879–1942* [Pinhas Rutenberg: The rise and fall of a strongman in the land of Israel, 1879–1942] (Tel Aviv: 'am 'oved, 1990).

78. Meitlis, *Be-derekh ha-emtsa'*, 316.

79. Nahamah Knar, "Nitsige ha-sefardim ve-yehude ha-mizraḥ ba-asifat ha-nivḥarim ha-reshonah shel ha-yishuv ha-yehudi be-erets yisrael ve-ha-va'ad ha-le'umi" (MA thesis, Hebrew University, 2004), 68.

80. Itzhak Hasson, "The Muslim View of Jerusalem, the Qur'an and Hadith," in *The History of Jerusalem: The Early Muslim Period, 638–1099*, ed. Joshua Prawer and Haggai Ben-Shammai (Jerusalem: Yad Izhak Ben-Zevi, 1996), 365–66.

81. Aḥmad Zakī Pasha, "Al-ṣakhra al-muqaddasa fī al-masjid al-ḥarām" [The sacred rock in Al-Aqsa Mosque], *Al-Ma'rifa al-Miṣriyya* 2 (1931): 170–72.

82. Simḥa Assaf, Samuel Klein, and Ben-Zion Dinur, "Me-et ha-Ma'rekhet" [From the editor], *Zion: Me'asef ha-ḥevra ha-Erets Yisraelit le-hisṭoryah ve-etnografyah* 1 (1925): i–ii.

83. Amos Noy, *'Edim o mumḥim: Yehudim maskilim bene Yerushalayim ve-ha-mizraḥ bi-teḥilat ha-me'ah ha-'isrim* [Experts or witnesses: Jewish intelligentsia from Jerusalem and the Levant in the beginning of the 20th century] (Tel Aviv: Resling, 2017), 90.

84. Isaac Yahuda, "Kotel ha-Ma'aravi" [The Western Wall], *Zion: Me'asef ha-ḥevra ha-Erets-Yisraelit le-hisṭoryah ve-etnografyah* 3 (1929): 95.

85. Yahuda, "Kotel ha-Ma'aravi," 99.

86. https://www.sefaria.org/Eikhah_Rabbah.1.31?vhe=Midrash_Rabbah_--_TE&lang=bi.

87. Yahuda, "Kotel ha-Ma'aravi," 100.

88. "Khiṭāb al-Khawaja Yalīn 'Amām Lajnat al-Burāq," *Al-Ṣirāṭ al-Mustaqīm*, August 14, 1930.

89. David Yellin, *Al-Yahūd wa-Ḥā'iṭ al-Mabka (al-Burāq)* [Jews and the Wailing Wall (al-Buraq)] (Al-Quds: Maṭba'at Malūl, 1930), 24, 8, 12.

90. Yellin, *Al-Yahūd wa-Ḥā'iṭ al-Mabka (al-Burāq)*, 12.

91. Yellin, *Al-Yahūd wa-Ḥā'iṭ al-Mabka (al-Burāq)*, 24.

92. Roberto Mazza, "The Deal of the Century? The Attempted Sale of the Western Wall by Cemal Pasha in 1916," *Middle East Studies* 57, no. 5 (2021): 698.

93. For earlier Jewish attempts to purchase the Western Wall, see Cohen, *Year Zero of the Arab-Israeli Conflict*, 70–71.

94. Jacobson and Naor, *Oriental Neighbors*, 89.

95. Liora R. Halperin, *Babel in Zion: Jews, Nationalism, and Language Diversity in Palestine, 1920–1948* (New Haven, CT: Yale University Press, 2014), 164–67.

96. Knar, "Nitsige ha-sefardim ve-yehude ha-mizraḥ ba-asifat ha-nivḥarim ha-reshonah shel ha-yishuv ha-yehudi be-Erets Yisrael ve-ha-va'ad ha-le'umi," 68–69.

97. Yellin, *Al-Yahūd wa-Ḥā'iṭ al-Mabka (al-Burāq)*, 11.

98. Yellin, *Al-Yahūd wa-Ḥā'iṭ al-Mabka (al-Burāq)*, 11.

99. Thomas Mayer, *Egypt and the Palestine Question, 1936–1945* (Berlin: K. Schwarz Verlag, 1983), 10–11; James Jankowski, "Egyptian Responses to the Palestine Problem in the Interwar Period," *International Journal of Middle East Studies* 12, no. 1 (1980): 1–38.

100. Cited in Mayer, *Egypt and the Palestine Question*, 11.

101. "An Arab Support of Zionism," *Jewish Chronicle* (London), September 22, 1922, 50–52.

102. "Jam'iyyat al-Rābiṭa al-Sharqiyya" [Association of the Eastern Bond], *Al-Hilal* 6 (March 1, 1922): 569.

103. Mayer, *Egypt and the Palestine Question*, 13.

104. 'Isa al-'isa, "Aḥmad Zakī Pashā wa al-Ṣuhyūniyya," *Filasṭīn* (Jaffa), October 6, 1922; 'Isa al-'isa, "Aḥmad Zakī Pashā wa al-Ṣuhyūniyya," *Filasṭīn* (Jaffa), October 31, 1922.

105. Nissim Ṣib'a, "Aḥmad Zakī Pasha wa al-ṣuhyūniyya," *Filasṭīn* (Jaffa), November 7, 1922.

106. Ṣib'a, "Aḥmad Zakī Pasha wa al-ṣuhyūniyya." Compare the Arabic translation with the original English here: Sir Thomas Haycraft, H. C. Luke, and Stubbs, *Palestine. Disturbances in May, 1921. Reports of the Comission of Inquiry with Correspondence Relating Thereto Presented to Parliament by Command of His Majesty, October 1921* (London: His Majesty's Stationery Office, 1921), 57.

107. Ṣib'a, "Aḥmad Zakī Pasha wa al-ṣuhyūniyya."

108. Anwar al-Jundi, *Aḥmad Zakī al-Mulaqqab be-Sheikh al-'urūba: ḥayatuh, Ara'uh, Atharuh* [Aḥmad Zakī called by sheikh of Arabism: His life, his opinions, and his legacy] (Cairo: Al-Mu'assasa al-Miṣriyya al-'āma, 1964), 246, 247.

109. *Mir'āt al-Sharq*, July 8, 1930.

110. Aḥmad Zakī Pasha, *Taṣḥīḥ al-Aghlaṭ al-Wārida fī Difā' al-Ustādh Yalīn al-Muḥāmī 'an al-Yahūd* [Correcting errors occurred in the defense of Mr. Yellin the defender of Jews] (Al-Quds: Dār al-Aytām al-Islāmiyya, 1930), 3.

111. Zakī Pasha, *Taṣḥīḥ al-Aghlaṭ al-Wārida fī Difā' al-Ustādh Yalīn al-Muḥāmī 'an al-Yahūd*, 10.

112. Zakī Pash, *Taṣḥīḥ al-Aghlaṭ al-Wārida fī Difā' al-Ustādh Yalīn al-Muḥāmī 'an al-Yahūd*.

113. Aviv Derri, "The Construction of 'Native' Jews in Late Mandate Palestine: An Ongoing Nahda as a Political Project," *International Journal of Middle East Studies* 53 (2021): 254, 256.

114. Katz, "'Aliyah ve-hityashvut," 289.

115. Israel Ben-Ze'ev, "Mikhtav Galuy" [Open letter], *Ha-arets*, July 1937, 4.

116. Yosef Meyuhas, "Mishle moreshet yildey 'Arav," *Do'ar ha-Yom*, September 13, 1935.

Chapter 5: Arabo-Islamic Literary Past

1. Mahmūd Muḥammad al-Ṭanāhī, *Madkhal 'lā tārīkh nashr al-tūrāth al-'arabī* [An introduction to the publication of the Arab heritage] (Cairo: Al-Khānjī, 1984), 81.

2. Abraham Shalom Yahuda to Morris Jastrow, March 27, 1906, file 1248a, ASYA, NLI. In a letter from 1919, Isaac Yahuda lists various reasons that prevented him from making progress in this enterprise. See Isaac Yahuda to A. S. Yahuda, November 26, 1919, file 3145, Abraham Shalom Yahuda Archives, National Library of Israel.

3. Israel Ben-Ze'ev, "R' Yitsḥaḳ Yahuda: 'Ishiyuto ve-Tilmudo" [R' Yitsḥaḳ Yahuda: His personality and teachings], *Moznaim* 3 (1941): 71–77.

4. "Obituary: Rabbi Yitzhak Yahuda," *Palestine Post*, March 25, 1941.

5. Isaac Ben-Zvi, "Le-zekher rav Isaac Eziekiel Yahuda Z"L," *Davar*, March 26, 1942.

6. Rivlin was Isaac's son-in-law, having married Yahuda's daughter Raḥel in March 1922. For the wedding invitation, see *Do'ar ha-Yom*, March 29, 1922.

7. Yosef Yo'el Rivlin, "Be-dameseḳ," *Hed ha-Mizraḥ*, December 23, 1949, 8.

8. For a study of the foundation of Hilfsverein der deutschen Juden and its relationship with Zionism, see Isaiah Friedman, "Ḥivrat 'ezra, misrad ha-ḥuts ha-Germani, ve-ha-pulmos 'im ha-tsiyunim, 1901–1918" [The "Hilfsverein der deutschen Juden," the German foreign ministry and the controversy with the Zionists, 1901–1918], *Cathedra*, no. 20 (1981): 97–122.

9. Rivlin, "Be-dameseḳ," 8.

10. Ami Ayalon, *Reading Palestine: Printing and Literacy, 1900–1948* (Austin: University of Texas Press, 2004), 20.

11. For more on the biography of Rivlin, see Moshe Kohen, "First a Jerusalemite," *Jerusalem Post*, September 26, 1969.

12. Rivlin, "Be-dameseḳ," 8.

13. For more on the founders of Rawḍat al-ma'ārif college and its educational programs, including some useful information about the school even though it dates to the period of Mandatory Palestine, see Kolliyat Rawḍat al-Ma'ārif al-Waṭaniyya, *Barnamij Kolliyat Rawdat al-Ma'arif al-Waṭaniyya* [The program of Rawḍat al-ma'ārif college] (Al-Quds: Maṭba'at Dār al- 'Aytām al-Islāmiyya, 1930).

14. Ben-Zvi, "Le-zekher rav Isaac Eziekiel Yahuda Z"L."

15. For discussion on the significance as well as social and cultural value of a proverb, see Rudolf Sellheim, *Kitāb al- 'Amthāl al-'Arabiyya al-Qadīma* [The book of old Arabic proverbs], trans. Ramaḍān 'Abd al-Tawwāb (Beirut: Mu'assasat al-Risāla, 1971), 13–14. Cf. R. Sellheim et al., "Mathal," in *Encyclopaedia of Islam*, ed. Th. Bianquis P. Bearman et al. (Leiden: Brill, 2012), doi.org/10.1163/1573-3912_islam_COM_0707.

16. For the definition of the concept of *mathal*, see Ibn 'Abd Rabbih, *Al-'iqd al-farīd* [The unique necklace] (Beirut: Dār al-Kutub al-'ilmiyya, 1981), 3:3.

17. Sellheim, *Kitāb al- 'Amthāl al-'Arabiyya al-Qadīma.*

18. Yahuda defines *mathal* (proverb) in Isaac Yahuda, *Mishle 'Arav: asufat mivḥar mishle bene ḳedem* [Proverbia Arabica: A collection of the sons of the Orient's proverbs], ed. Isaac Benjamin S. E. Yahuda (Jerusalem: Ha-ḥivrah ha-Erets Yisraelit le-hisṭorya ve-ithnographia, 1932), 1:7.

19. For a concise history of the European scholarship on Arabic proverbs, see Rudolf Sellheim, *Die Klassisch-Arabischen Sprichwörtersammlungen: Insbesondere die des Abu 'Ubaid* (The Hague: Mouton, 1954), introduction. Cf. the Arabic translation in Sellheim, *Kitāb al-'Amthāl al-'Arabiyya al-Qadīma*, 3–20.

20. Inea Bushnaq, "The Role of Folklore in Nation Building," trans. Sharif Kanaana, in *Folk Heritage of Palestine*, ed. George K. Rishmawi, Aziz Khalil, and Daifallah Othman (Tayibeh, Triangle, Israel: Research Center for Arab Heritage, 1994), 172.

21. James Jankowski, "Egypt and Early Arab Nationalism, 1908–1922," in *The Origins of Arab Nationalism*, ed. Rashid Khalidi et al. (New York: Columbia University Press, 1991), 244–45.

22. Maḥmūd ʿUmar al-Bājūrī, *Kitāb Amthāl al-mutakallimīn min ʿawām al-miṣriyyin* [A book of Egyptian common people sayings] (Cairo: Al-Maṭbaʿa al-Sharafiyya, 1889), 1.

23. For discussion on al-Ṭahṭāwī's ideas on Egyptian nationalism, see C. Ernest Dawn, "The Origins of Arab Nationalism," in *The Origins of Arab Nationalism*, ed. Rashid Khalidi et al. (New York: Columbia University Press, 1991), 4–5.

24. For more details regarding the parameters that determined the popularity of Arabic proverbs, see Naʿūm Shuqayr, *Amthāl al-ʿawām fī Miṣr wa al-Sūdān wa al-Shām* [Proverbs of the common people in Egypt, Sudan, and al-Sham], ed. Muhammad Ibrahim Abu Salim (Beirut: Dār al-Jīl, 1995), 18.

25. Today, *Mishle ʿArav* is published in three volumes. The author, however, published only two volumes in his lifetime: the first in 1932, and the second in 1934. The third volume was published posthumously in 1990, sixty years from the time when the readers of the work first awaited its publication. The publication of the third volume, it should be noted, was based on a manuscript that the author left before he passed away.

26. Colette Zytnicki, "The 'Oriental Jews' of the Maghreb: Reinventing the North African Jewish Past in the Colonial Era," in *Colonialism and the Jews*, ed. Ethan B. Katz, Lisa Moses Leff, and Maud S. Mandel (Bloomington: Indiana University Press, 2017), 38.

27. See, for instance, his signature at the end of the introduction to ʿUbayd Allāh Ibn ʿabd Al-Kāfī al-ʿUbaydī, *Sharḥ al-maḍnūn bi-hi ʿalā ghayr ahlih: huwa sharḥ al-Sheikh al-ʿallāmah ʿUbayd Allāh ibn ʿAbd al-Kāfī ʿalā al-abyāt allatī intakhabahā al-Sheikh al-imām al-ʿallāmah ʿIzz al-Dīn ʿAbd al-Wahhāb al-Zanjānī* [That which is to be withheld from those unworthy of it], Isaac Yahuda (Cairo: Maṭbaʿat al-Saʿāda, 1913–15).

28. Ben-Ze'ev, "R' Yitsḥaḳ Yahuda."

29. Amos Noy, *ʿEdim o mumḥim: Yehudim maskilim bene Yerushalayim ve-ha-mizraḥ bi-teḥilat ha-me'ah ha-ʿisrim* [Experts or witnesses: Jewish intelligentsia from Jerusalem and the Levant in the beginning of the 20th century] (Tel Aviv: Resling, 2017), 53–54.

30. Yahuda, *Mishle ʿArav*, 1:12.

31. We have discussed the impact of these events on the Arabo-Islamic knowledge patterns produced and utilized by Jewish figures in chapter 4.

32. Abū Manṣūr Ismāʿīl al-Thaʿlabī, *Al-Tamthīl wa al-muhāḍara* [The book of exemplification and discussion], ed. Tabʿa Jadīda and ʿAbd Al-Fattaḥ Muḥammad Al-Ḥilw (Tunis: Al-dār al-ʿarabiyya lil-kitāb, 1983), 14–24, 5.

33. Although the author promised to reveal the sources of his work in the third volume of the work, which was not published before his death in 1941, the third volume made no mention as to the sources. In the introduction to the first volume, however, he refers to a collection of proverbs from the Jewish scholar Abu Nissim, whose collection Yahuda included in his work. Still, he attributes a great deal of the proverbs to his life experience as a native of the Orient. From the reviews of some scholars, we can retrieve the principal sources that Yahuda relied on to furnish his work. In his review, S. D. Goitein directs attention to Georg Wilhelm

Freytag's voluminous work on Arabic proverbs and makes the case that the author must have relied on it. Also, Robert Attal, in his "Bibliographie raisonnée des proverbes Arabes et Judéo-Arabes du Maghreb," argues that the majority of *Mishle 'Arav* originates in proverbs that were circulated in North Africa, including Algeria, Tunisia, and Morocco, where the majority of Jews in modern times were settling. Furthermore, he links Yahuda's work to that of Ben Cheneb, whose comprehensive collection contained 3,124 Arabic proverbs. For more discussion on the sources of the work, see S. D. Goitein, "Mishle 'Arav," *Moznaim* (1932): 12–14; Robert Attal, "Bibliographie raisonnée des proverbes Arabes et Judéo-Arabes du Maghreb," *Studies in Bibliography and Booklore* 17 (1989): 43–54.

34. It would have been more useful had Ben-Ze'ev mentioned the names of these Jewish individuals who benefited from Yahuda's writings on Arabic proverbs. Unfortunately, his remark is general in this regard. Yet it gives us a sense of how Yahuda was influential in the Jewish circles of his time. See Ben-Ze'ev, "R' Yitsḥaḳ Yahuda," 76.

35. See Yahuda, *Mishle 'Arav*, 1:7.

36. On his travel to Egypt and embarking on book trading, see Ben-Ze'ev, "R' Yitsḥaḳ Yahuda," 73–74; Yitsḥaḳ Avishor, "Mishle 'Arav: le-hashlamat mif'alo shel Yitsḥaḳ Benjamin Yahuda" [Proverbia Arabica: To complete Isaac Benjamin Yahuda's project], *Pe'amim* 54 (1993): 143.

37. Ben-Zvi, "Le-zekher rav Isaac Eziekiel Yahuda Z"L."

38. Isaac Yahuda, "Binah ba-Miḳra" [Understanding the Hebrew Bible], *Yerushalayim* 6, no. 3 (1903): 261.

39. To review Yahuda's explanation and proposed commentary on the etymology of the name Esther, see Yahuda, "Binah ba-Miḳra," 261.

40. For the English translation, see Arthur John Arberry, ed. and trans., *The Seven Odes: The First Chapter in Arabic Literature* (London: Macmillan, 1957), 63.

41. To compare Yahuda's Hebrew translation with the original verse, see Imru' al-Qays's ode with several suggested commentaries on the discussed poetic verse in Al-Zawzanī, *Sharḥ al-Mu'allaqāt al-'Ashr* [A commentary on ten suspended odes] (Beirut: Dār Maktabat al-Hay'āh Lilṭibā'ah wa-al-Nashr, 1983), 50–51.

42. Yahuda, "Binah ba-Miḳra," 262.

43. The Cairo Geniza refers to a collection of Jewish manuscript fragments that were found in the Geniza, or storage room, of the Ben Ezra Synagogue in Fustat, presently Old Cairo, Egypt.

44. For a review of Goitein's discussion on how the comparative method advanced his understanding of several Jewish proverbs, see his review of *Mishle 'Arav* in Goitein, "Mishle 'Arav."

45. Goitein, "Mishle 'Arav." I benefited from the English translation available at http://www.sefaria.org/Berakhot?lang=bi, accessed October 16, 2019.

46. Goitein, "Mishle 'Arav," 14.

47. About his personal motivation to learn Arabic proverbs as a means of communication, see Yahuda, *Mishle 'Arav*, 1:1.

48. Al-Bājūrī, *Kitāb Amthāl al-mutakallimīn min 'awām al-miṣriyyin*, 3.

49. Isaac Yahuda, *Mishle 'Arav*, 3:28–39. Similar to the content of this proverb, the saying 1353 indicates the ways in which the followers of the three Abrahamic faiths celebrate their holy days. See Yahuda, *Mishle 'Arav*, 2:10–11.

50. The proverb is found in Yahuda, *Mishle 'Arav*, 1:19.

51. Yahuda, *Mishle 'Arav*, 1:19.

52. For a concise sketch of mourning in the Jewish tradition, see Ronald L. Eisenberg, *Jewish Traditions: A JPS Guide* (Philadelphia: Jewish Publication Society, 2008), 91.

53. Yahuda, *Mishle 'Arav*, 1:21–23.

54. Yahuda, *Mishle 'Arav*, 1:21–33.

55. Yahuda, *Mishle 'Arav: asufat mivḥar mishle bene ḳedem*, 1:87.

56. Yahuda, *Mishle 'Arav*, 1:21–23.

57. For more details about the regulations that al-Mutawakkil imposed on the people of the book, see Yahuda, *Mishle 'Arav*, 1:87.

58. Yuval Evri and Hillel Cohen, "Between Shared Homeland to National Homeland: The Balfour Declaration from a Native Sephardic Perspective," in *The Arab and Jewish Questions: Geographies of Engagement in Palestine and Beyond*, ed. Bashir Bashir and Leila Farsakh (New York: Columbia University Press, 2020), 148–50.

59. Yahuda, *Mishle 'Arav: asufat mivḥar mishle bene ḳedem*, 1:10.

60. Yahuda, *Mishle 'Arav*, 1:87.

61. In the English translation of tractate (Berakoth 64:71), it is suggested, "Whoever tries to force his [good] fortune will be dogged by [ill] fortune." For the English translation, see Yahuda, *Mishle 'Arav*, 1:87.

62. Yahuda, *Mishle 'Arav*, 1:87. This saying is based on an anecdote about a Jew who traveled to Morocco knowing about the dangers that would face him on his journey, with the promise of demonstrating patience. In walking on one of the city streets, however, it is said that a Muslim threw the dead body of a cat at him. Losing all the patience he had shown since his arrival to the city, the Jew responded to his humiliation by striking the Muslim in exchange. In response, Muslims came to help their fellow Muslim, attacking the local Jewish community en masse. After things were settled, local Jews blamed the Jewish traveler for stirring the Muslim population against them. Troubled by the Muslim's attack with a dead cat, the stranger Jew said that he knew about all the troubles that would await him in Morocco and had learned about them so that he could avoid them. Yet the scenario of being attacked by a dead cat was not among the issues that he expected to face and therefore he said, *Al-quṭ ma kanshī fī al-bāl/al-ḥisāb* (The cat was not taken into consideration). For the account of this anecdote, see Yahuda, *Mishle 'Arav*, 1:87.

63. Yahuda, *Mishle 'Arav*, 1:193.

64. It is based on an anecdote circulated in the countryside of Morocco. For a detailed account of the anecdote, see Yahuda, *Mishle 'Arav*, 1:213.

65. Yahuda, *Mishle 'Arav*, 1:87.

66. For a review of the commentary, see Yahuda, *Mishle 'Arav*, 1:87. A similar proverb is 1067, *'Ish fi ḥidush al-dunya bidaha ḳerush* (There is nothing new, the world needs money).

67. Fū'ād Ḥasanein 'Ali, at the time a professor in the School of Literature at Fuad the First University (later Cairo University), uses the possessive pronoun to claim ownership of folkloric tales, mainly the *Nights*, against the context of anti-Semitic sentiments that denied Arab people, and the Semites in general, the creative force to generate as imaginative tales as found in the *Nights* and instead asserted the Aryan origins of the tales. See Fū'ād Ḥasanein 'Ali, *Qaṣaṣuna al-sha'bī* [Our folkloric tales] (Cairo: Dār al-Fikr al-'Arabi, 1947), 155–56. In the preface to Suhair al-Qalamāwī's study on the *Nights*, which is based on her dissertation, Ṭaha

Ḥussein attributes the tales to *al-Adab al-Shaʿbi.* See Suhair al-Qalamāwī, *Alf Layla wa-Layla* [A thousand and one nights] (Misr: Dār al-Maʿārif, 1943), 2.

68. See, for instance, Aḥmad Ḥasan al-Zayyāt's lecture on the *Nights* in Aḥmad Ḥasan al-Zayyāt, *Fī ʹuṣūl al-adab: Muḥāḍarāt wa-Maqālāt fī al-Adab al-ʿArabī* [On the principles of Arabic literature: Lectures and essays on Arabic literature] (Maṭbaʿat Lajnat al-Taʾlif, wa-al-Tarjama, wa-al-Nashr, 1935). For a brief discussion of the *Nights*, their origins, their indication of the abundant imagination of the Arab and Semite people in general, their reflection of the social, cultural, religious, and political life of Arabs among other Oriental nations, and their impact on Western thought, see Jurji Zaydān, *Tārīkh ʹAdab al-lugha al-ʿArabiyya* [A history of Arabic literature], ed. Shawqī Dhayf (Cairo: Dār Al-Hilāl, 1950), 2:298. See also the example of Alfred Farağ and his utilization of the *Nights* to construct new theatrical devices that enhanced the quality of the plays as well as connected the audience with their rich heritage in Daniela Potenza, "Alfred Farağ's Arabian Nights: Ongoing Experimentation in Arabic Theatre," in *The Thousand and One Nights: Sources and Transformations in Literature, Art, and Science*, ed. Ibrahim Akel and William Granara (Leiden: Brill, 2020), 213.

69. Muhsin Mahdi, *The Arabian Nights* (New York: W. W. Norton and Company, 2010), xi.

70. Muhsin al-Musawi, *The Arabian Nights in Contemporary World Cultures: Global Commodification, Translation, and the Culture Industry* (New York: Columbia University Press, 2021), 50–51. Cf. The argument in al-Qalamāwī, *Alf Layla wa-Layla*, 163–77.

71. On Victor Chauvin's view of the Jewishness of its author, see al-Qalamāwī, *Alf Layla wa-Layla*, 17. For a negation of the Jewishness of the author of stories that contain Jewish figures, see Enno Littmann, "Alf Laila wa-Laila," in *The Encyclopedia of Islam: New Edition*, ed. H. A. R. Gibb et al. (Leiden: Brill, 1960), 364. According to Fūʾād Ḥasanein, the Jewish materials found in the collection became the legacy of the Arabo-Islamic civilization, or Islamicate in the sense of Marshal Hudgenson—inherited tales and stories of Arabs and other Semitic nations, such as the Babylonians, Aramaites, and Israelites as evident in the *Nights*. See ʿAli, *Qaṣaṣuna al-shaʿbī*, 153.

72. A recent study on the *Nights* has focused on the discourse about the tales' collection in the field of modern Hebrew literature, and demonstrated how the tales solidified the binaries between realism and fantasy as well as East and West. See Avi-Ram Tzoreff, "Reading the Arabian Nights in Modern Hebrew Literature: Judaism, Arabness and the City," *Philological Encounters* 5, no. 2 (2020): 223–53.

73. Yosef Yoʾel Rivlin, *Elef Laylah va-Laylah* [One thousand and one nights], vol. 1 (Jerusalem: Ḳeryat Sefer, 1947), introduction.

74. Haim Lieberman, "Tirgum Yidi bilti Yaduʿ shel Sefer Elef Laylah va-Laylah," [An unknown Yiddish translation of "A thousand and one nights"], *Alei Sefer: Studies in Bibliography and in the History of the Printed and the Digital Hebrew Book* (1977): 156. For more details on the influence of Galland's *Mille et une nuits* on European culture from the eighteenth century onward, see Saree Makdisi and Felicity Nussbaum, *The Arabian Nights in Historical Context: Between East and West* (Oxford: Oxford University Press, 2008), 25–50.

75. For a discussion on Weil's translation into German from the original Arabic, see Ruchama Johnston-Bloom, "Oriental Studies and Jewish Questions: German-Jewish Encounters with Muhammad, the Qurʾan, and Islamic Modernities" (PhD diss., University of Chicago, 2013), 88.

76. Goitein points out the originality of the title given to the collection *Alf Laylah wa-Laylah* based on documentary evidence from the Cairo Geniza around 1150. A reference to *Alf Laylah wa-Laylah* appears in a notebook owned by a Jewish bookseller in a notation that the title *Alf Laylah wa-Laylah* had been lent to one called Majd al-ʿazīzī. This evidence indicates medieval Jewish communities' familiarity with the *Nights*. For more details, see S. D. Goitein, "The Oldest Documentary Evidence for the Title Alf Laila Wa-Laila," *Journal of the American Oriental Society* 78, no. 4 (1958): 301–2.

77. For a discussion on Arabo-Islamic sources of the Jewish folktale among Oriental Jews, see Yitsḥaḳ Avishur, *Ha-sipur ha-ʿamami shel Yehudey ʿIraq* [The folktales of the Jews of Iraq] (Haifa: University of Haifa, 1992), 1:19–20. For a discussion on the subsequent processes of translation and the adaptation of stories from Arabo-Islamic sources, including by individual Jews in modern times, see Avishur, *Ha-sipur ha-ʿamami shel Yehudey ʿIraq*, 1:15. For an example of Jewish adaptation of stories from the *Nights*, see in particular the analysis of the following stories: "Nūr al-Dīn," identified with one of the *Nights*' stories in Avishur, *Ha-sipur ha-ʿamami shel Yehudey ʿIraq*, 2:404–16; and the story of "the Kurdish man and what occurred to him" in Avishur, *Ha-sipur ha-ʿamami shel Yehudey ʿIraq*, 1:288–95.

78. On Murād al-Najjār and his biography, see Mohammed Kenbib, "Naggiar, Mardochee (Mordechai Ibn al-Najjar), in *Encyclopedia of Jews in the Islamic World*, ed. Norman A. Stillman (Leiden: Brill, 2010), doi:https://doi.org/10.1163/1878-9781_ejiw_SIM_000385.

79. The introduction to the Judeo-Arabic version is found in Yitsḥaḳ Avishur, "Sifrut ve-ʿitonut ba-ʿAravit Yehudit shel Yehudey Bavel bi-defusey Hodo" [Iraqi Jewish Judeo-Arabic literature and newspapers published in India], *Peʿamim* 52 (1992): 108–9. I learned about this reference from Lisa Lital Levy, "Jewish Writers in the Arab East: Literature, History, and the Politics of Enlightenment, 1863–1914" (PhD diss., University of California at Berkeley, 2007), 293.

80. Rivlin, *Elef Laylah va-Laylah*, vol. 1, introduction.

81. For more on that, see al-Zayyāt, *Fī ʹuṣūl al-adab*, 56–57. Cf. Zaydān, *Tārīkh ʹAdab al-lugha al-ʿArabiyya*, 2:298–99. In her review of al-Zayyāt and Zaydān's discussion on the *Nights*, al-Qalamāwī criticizes the former as less rigorous scientific research on the *Nights* and whose purpose was to only provide listeners with a general idea about the tales, while she views the latter as general and brief. After reviewing the limited interest that Orientals "al-Sharqiyyūn," whether in the medieval or modern times, have shown in the *Nights*, she concludes that Oriental scholars have not adequately studied the collection of tales. See al-Qalamāwī, *Alf Layla wa-Layla*, 4–5.

82. al-Zayyāt, *Fī ʾuṣūl al-adab*, 53.

83. Josef Horovitz, "The Origins of the Arabian Nights," *Islamic Culture* 1, no. 1 (1927): 56.

84. al-Zayyāt, *Fī ʾuṣūl al-adab*, 53, 54.

85. al-Musawi, *The Arabian Nights in Contemporary World Cultures*, 50–51.

86. Josef Horovitz, "Elef Laylah va-Laylah" [One thousand and one nights], *Ha-Teḳufah* 23 (1925); al-Zayyāt, *Fī ʾuṣūl al-adab*; al-Qalamāwī, *Alf Layla wa-Layla*.

87. Fūʾād Ḥasanein addresses this unfounded view on the Aryan origins of the *Nights* and instead emphasizes its Semitic origins in ʿAli, *Qaṣaṣuna al-shaʿbī*, 155–56. He explains that it is natural to find Persian, Indian, and Egyptian elements in the *Nights*. Yet that does not mean the tales are Aryan in origin; they exhibit features shared by various nations. Even if a certain element of the tales originated in either a Persian or Indian environment, the Islamic mentality

had appropriated them and turned them into a new form. His views are in line with those expressed in Horovitz, "The Origins of the Arabian Nights."

88. Muhsin Mahdi, *The Thousand and One Nights* (Leiden: Brill, 1995), 1.

89. Rivlin, *Elef Laylah va-Laylah*, vol. 1, introduction.

90. Horovitz, "Elef Laylah va-Laylah," 294.

91. On Hebrew works on Muḥammad and the utilization of the Semite trope, see Mostafa Hussein, "Muhammad in Zion: On the Hebrew Perceptions of the Prophet of Islam," *Journal of Religious Minorities under Muslim Rule* 1 (2023): 1–38.

92. Josef Joel Rivlin, ed., *Al-ḳuran* [The Quran] (Tel Aviv: Devir, 1936), preface.

93. For a discussion on the various conceptualizations of the New Jew within Zionist circles, see Yitsḥaḳ Conforti, "'The New Jew' in the Zionist Movement: Ideology and Historiography," *Australian Journal of Jewish Studies* 25 (2011): 89–103.

94. Arieh Bruce Saposnik, *Becoming Hebrew: The Creation of a Jewish National Culture in Ottoman Palestine* (New York: Oxford University Press, 2008), 146.

95. For further details on the concept of the New Jew in the Yishuv, see Anita Shapira, "The Fashioning of the 'New Jew' in the Yishuv Society," in *Major Changes within the Jewish People in the Wake of the Holocaust*, ed. Yisrael Gutman and Avital Saf (Jerusalem: Yad Vashem, 1996), 427–41.

96. Arieh Bruce Saposnik, "Europe and Its Orients in Zionist Culture before the First World War," *Historical Journal* 49, no. 4 (2006): 1105.

97. Robert Irwin, *The Arabian Nights: A Companion* (London: I. B. Tauris, 2004), 2.

98. Yitsḥaḳ Katzenelson, *Elef ve-Laylah Eḥad: agadot mizraḥiyot la-ne'urim* [A thousand and one nights: Oriental legends for youths] (Varshah: Gitlin, 1921).

99. This quotation is found in Ḥaim Naḥman Bialiḳ, "Erets Yisrael," (1930), http://benyehuda.org/bialik/dvarim_shebeal_peh33.html. This statement came to my attention through reading a partial English translation, from which I benefited while translating this quotation, in Sami Shalom Chetrit, "Revisiting Bialik: A Radical Mizrahi Reading of the Jewish National Poet," *Comparative Literature* 62, no. 1 (2010): 11.

100. Ha-turgman was established in Odessa in 1911 through the initiative of Ze'ev Jabotinsky with the aim of translating selections from world literature into Hebrew for Jewish youths. Funding for the establishment of the publishing house was provided by Moshe Zeitlin's widow, whom Jabotinsky described as a woman who was neither a Zionist nor supporter of the revival of the modern Hebrew language. Bialiḳ was among the directors of the publishing house. It seems that the collection of the *Nights* received the attention of significant Zionist figures. In a letter to Bialiḳ, Jabotinsky makes a few suggestions with respect to the font size of the book and vocalization of some words. For more, see Ze'ev Jabotinsky to Ḥaim Naḥman Bialiḳ, correspondence, March 1, 1912.

101. This statement is found on the cover of David Yellin, *Sipure Elef Laylah va-Laylah* [The thousand and one nights], vol. 1 (Odessa: Turgman, 1912).

102. Benzion Dinur, *Bene Dori: Tsiyonim ve-ḳavim li-demuyot ḥa-khamim u-meḥankhim, anshe tsibur ve-'omdim be-sha'ar* [People of my generation: Notes and lines about scholars and educators, public figures, and gatekeepers] (Tel-Aviv: Masadah, 1962), 89.

103. As part of the popular literature, *Alf Laylah wa-Laylah* enriched the Jewish folk literature among the Oriental Jewish communities in general and Iraqi Jewry in particular. For a

discussion on the *Nights* as a source for enriching Jewish folk literature in modern times, see Yitsḥaḳ Avishur, "Ha-yitsirah ha-sifrutit ba-safah ha-'aravit-yehudit," in *Ḳehilot Yisrael ba-mizraḥ ba-me'ot ha-tesha' 'esreh ve-ha-'isrim: 'Iraq*, ed. Ḥaim Sadoun (Jerusalem: Misrad ha-ḥinukh, Makhon Ben Zvi, 2002), 87–100.

104. David Yellin, *Mi-Dan ve-'ad Be'er Sheva'* [From Dan to Beer Sheva], ed. Avraham Ḥayim Elḥanani (Jerusalem: Ha-Vaad li-Hotsaat Kitve David Yellin, 1973), 13.

105. See Shalom Kassan, *David Yellin: Ha-Meḥanekh ve-ha-Manhig* [David Yellin: Leader and educator] (Jerusalem: Publications of Binai Brith in Israel, 1980), 121.

106. Yellin, *Sipure Elef Laylah va-Laylah*, 1:1–5.

107. Cited in Husain Haddawy, *The Arabian Nights* (New York: W. W. Norton and Company, 1995).

108. For a discussion on Rivlin's project of rendering *Alf Layla wa-Layla* into Hebrew, see Mostafa Hussein, "Arabian Nights, Hebrew Nights: On the Influence of Alf Laylah wa-Laylah on Jewish Culture in Palestine/Israel," *Journal of Levantine Studies* 8, no. 2 (2018): 125.

109. Dory Manor, "Aba sheli hayah Mizraḥ u-Ma'rav bo-zemanit: Siḥah 'im ha-Nasi Reuven (Rubi) Rivlin" ["My father was both East and West simultaneously": A conversation with president Reuven (Ruby) Rivlin], *Ho: Literary Magazine* 16 (2018): 18.

110. Cohen, *Year Zero of the Arab-Israeli Conflict*, 88.

111. Aviv Derri, "The Construction of 'Native' Jews in Late Mandate Palestine: An Ongoing Nahda as a Political Project," *International Journal of Middle East Studies* 53 (2021): 260; Amit Levy, "Conflicting German Orientalism: Zionist Arabists and Arab scholars, 1926–1938," *British Journal of Middle Eastern Studies* (2022): 10.

112. For more on his translation of the prophetic biography and its comparison to other Hebrew works, see Hussein, "Muhammad in Zion."

113. "Le-'inyaney ha-Sha'ah," *Hed ha-Mizraḥ*, December 23, 1949.

114. Hanan Harif, "Islam in Zion? Yosef Yo'el Rivlin's Translation of the *Qur'an* and Its Place within the New Hebrew Culture," *Naharaim* 10, no. 1 (2016): 43–44.

115. Abraham Shalom Yahuda, "Nedive ve-gibure 'Arav" [Arab noblemen and heroes], *Luaḥ Erets Yisrael* 2 (1896): 89–119. For a similar argument, see Mostafa Hussein, "The Integration of Arabo-Islamic Culture into the Emergent Hebrew Culture of Late Ottoman Palestine," *Jewish Quarterly Review* 109, no. 3 (2019): 464–69.

116. Yosef Yo'el Rivlin, *Mi-shire 'Antar: tirgum me-'Aravit ve-hi'arot* [From Antar's poetry: Translations from Arabic and comments] (Jerusalem: Avraham Moshe Lunts, 1916).

117. *Do'ar ha-Yom*, March 29, 1922.

118. Isaac Yahuda to Carl Heinrich Becker, December 19, 1922, Geheimes Staatsarchiv Preußischer Kulturbesitz.

119. Rivlin, *Al-ḳuran*.

120. "Yerushalayim: Raḥel Rivlin le-Beit Yahuda Z"L," in *Do'ar ha-Yom*, January 28, 1935.

121. https://hebrew-academy.org.il/2016/05/01/יוסף-יואל-ריבלין/, accessed May 17, 2023.

122. David Siton, "'Al tirgumav me-'Aravit," *Hed ha-Mizraḥ* (Jerusalem), December 23, 1949, 6.

123. Siton, "'Al tirgumav me-'Aravit," 6.

124. Although the first volume of Rivlin's translation appeared in 1947, his engagement with the collection dates to 1925, when he translated Horovitz's article on the *Nights* into Hebrew. For his translation, see Horovitz, "Elef Laylah va-Laylah."

125. "Elef laylah va-laylah be-tirgum 'ivri ḥadash," *Hed ha-Mizraḥ*, April 19, 1943.

126. *Ḳiryat Sefer: Rivaʻon l-bibliografyah shel beit ha-sefarim ha-leʼumi ve-ha- ʻuniversitaʼi be-Yerushalayim* [Kiryat Sefer: Bibliographic quarterly of the Jewish national and university library] (Jerusalem: Hebrew University Press Association, 1947–48), 24:95.

127. "Tirgum Ḥadash shel agadot ʻArav," *Ha-arets*, July 18, 1947.

128. Littmann, "Alf Laila wa-Laila," 362.

129. William M. Brinner, "The Image of the Jew as *Other* in Medieval Arabic Texts," *Israel Oriental Studies* 14 (1994): 233. See the story here: http://www.usccb.org/bible/daniel/13/, accessed October 17, 2019.

130. See, for instance, the story of nights 453 and 454 in *Alf Laylah wa-Laylah* [A thousand and one nights], vol. 1 (Cairo: Saʻīd ʻAli al-Khuṣūṣī, 1935).

131. See the English translation in Richard Francis Burton and Leonard Charles Smithers, *The Book of the Thousand Nights and a Night* (New York: H. S. Nichols and Company, 1894), 8:206.

132. Rivlin, *Elef Laylah va-Laylah*, 2:313–24.

133. *Alf Laylah wa-Laylah*, 1:240–44.

134. Irwin, *The Arabian Nights*, 201.

135. Ruth Roded, "A Voice in the Wilderness? Rivlin's 1932 Hebrew Life of Muhammad," *Middle East Critique* 18, no. 1 (2009): 53–54.

136. For a reference to Rivlin's tendency toward the right-wing Revisionist movement, see Harif, "Islam in Zion?," 42. Rubi Rivlin, Yosef Rivlin's son, referred to his father's joining the ranks of Revisionist Zionism after he had discovered that his wife and daughter joined the ranks of the paramilitary organization Irgun headed by Jabotinsky. See Gil Samsonov, *Netanyahu and Likud's Leaders: The Israeli Princes*, trans. Kaeren Fish (Abingdon, UK: Routledge, 2020), 34. Although Rivlin was distant from the political orientation of the Labor Party, by the time of 1942 after the declaration of the Biltmore program, the preparation for a violent confrontation with the Arabs was advocated by mainstream Zionism. See Anita Shapira, *Israel: A History* (Waltham, MA: Brandeis University Press, 2012), 89.

137. Dimitri Shumsky, *Beyond the Nation-State: The Zionist Political Imagination from Pinsker to Ben-Gurion* (New Haven, CT: Yale University Press, 2018), 153, 167.

138. Cited in Manor, "Aba sheli hayah Mizraḥ u-Maʻrav bo-zemanit," 17.

139. Shumsky, *Beyond the Nation-State*, 154.

140. Anne Duggan has argued that Galland's version, which set the precedent for future versions, has presented the collection of tales as both a work of fiction that represented an imaginary space and an ethnographic document that portrayed a real and geographic space. Cited in al-Musawi, *The Arabian Nights in Contemporary World Cultures*, 273–74.

141. Horovitz, "Elef Laylah va-Laylah," 294.

142. Rivlin, *Elef Laylah va-Laylah*, 1:8.

143. Horovitz, "Elef Laylah va-Laylah," 294.

144. Littmann, "Alf Laila wa-Laila."

145. Rivlin, *Elef Laylah va-Laylah*, 1:8.

146. Horovitz, "Elef Laylah va-Laylah," 294.

147. Rivlin, *Elef Laylah va-Laylah*, 1:8.

148. For the Hebrew translation, see Rivlin, *Elef Laylah va-Laylah*, 1:10–11. The English translation is cited from Edward William Lane, *The Arabian Nights' Entertainments* (Boston: Little, Brown and Company, 1853), 1–2.

149. al-Musawi, *The Arabian Nights in Contemporary World Cultures*, 261.

150. al-Musawi, *The Arabian Nights in Contemporary World Cultures*, 258.

151. Edward W. Said, *Orientalism* (New York: Vintage Books, 1978), 164.

152. al-Zayyāt, *Fī ʹuṣūl al-adab*, 41. On the role of al-Zayyāt in the intellectual life of Egypt, and his objection to the rise of Nazism and Fascism, see Israel Gershoni, "Demon and Infidel: Egyptian Intellectuals Confronting Hitler and Nazism during World War II," in *Nazism, the Holocaust, and the Middle East*, ed. Francis R. Nicosia and Bogac A. Ergene (New York: Bergham, 2018), 77–105.

153. al-Zayyāt, *Fī ʾuṣūl al-adab*, 54.

154. al-Qalamāwī, *Alf Layla wa-Layla*, 3–4.

155. al-Qalamāwī, *Alf Layla wa-Layla*, 294–95.

156. Rivlin, *Elef Laylah va-Laylah*, 1:8.

157. Rivlin, *Elef Laylah va-Laylah*, vol. 1.

158. For further details on his Zionist activities, see Benjamin Rivlin, "Rivlin, Joseph Joel," in *Encyclopaedia Judaica*, ed. Michael Berenbaum and Fred Skolnik (Jerusalem: Keter Publishing, 2007), 17:351.

159. Margalit Sheila, "Milḥemet ha-Safot Ke-Tenuʻa ʻamamit" [The language war as a popular movement], *Katedrah* 74 (1994): 87.

160. On the place of Arabic as a treasure house for the revival of modern Hebrew, see Iair G. Or, *Bor'im signon le-dor: ha-emunot ve-ha-ide'ologyot shel metakhnene ha-lashon ha-ʻivrit be-Erets Yisrael* [Creating a style for a generation: The beliefs and ideologies of Hebrew language planners] (Tel Aviv: Hidkel, 2016), 129ff.

161. Gary Fields, *Enclosure: Palestinian Landscapes in a Historical Mirror* (Oakland: University of California Press, 2017), 217.

162. Siton, "ʻAl tirgumav me-ʻAravit," 6.

163. "Elef laylah va-laylah be-tirgum ʻivri ḥadash."

164. Yosef Yo'el Rivlin, "Ha-mizraḥ be-yetsirotav shel Ḥaim Naḥman Bialiḳ," *Hed ha-Mizraḥ*, July 14, 1944.

165. *Alf Laylah wa-Laylah*, 1:166.

166. David Yellin, *Ha-Melekh ʻUmar al-Noʻman u-vanav: Me-sipure Elef laylah va-laylah* [The king ʻUmar al-Nuʻman and his sons: From the tales of one thousand and one nights] (Tel Aviv: Devir, 1937), 2:7.

167. For a discussion on various approaches adopted by medieval Hebrew translators of Arabic poetry, see Peter Cole, *The Dream of the Poem: Hebrew Poetry from Muslim and Christian Spain, 950–1492* (Princeton, NJ: Princeton University Press, 2007), 15.

168. Rivlin, *Elef Laylah va-Laylah*, https://benyehuda.org/read/265 accessed April 18, 2025.

169. Yahuda, *Mishle ʻArav*, 1:193.

Conclusion

1. Roza El-Eini, *Mandated Landscape: British Imperial Rule in Palestine 1929–1948* (London: Routledge, 2004), 454.

2. Rashid Khalidi, *The Hundred Years' War on Palestine: A History of Settler Colonialism and Resistance, 1917–2017* (New York: Metropolitan Books, 2020), 58.

3. Meron Benvenisti, *Sacred Landscape: The Buried History of the Holy Land since 1948*, trans. Maxine Kaufman-Lacusta (Berkeley: University of California Press, 2000).

4. Maoz Azaryahu and Arnon Golan, "(Re)naming the Landscape: The Formation of the Hebrew Map of Israel 1949–1960," *Journal of Historical Geography* 27, no. 2 (2001): 183.

5. Scholars have used various English translations of the Hebrew names given to this committee, including the Governmental Names Commission (Azaryahu and Golan, "(Re)naming the Landscape"); Government Names Committee (Noga Kadman, *Erased from Space and Consciousness: Israel and the Depopulated Palestinian Villages of 1948*, trans. Dimi Reider [Bloomington: Indiana University Press, 2015]); and Governmental Naming Committee (Benvenisti, *Sacred Landscape*). In the absence of an official English translation of the committee by the committee members themselves, I will adhere to Benvenisti's translation.

6. Benvenisti, *Sacred Landscape*, 24.

7. Azaryahu and Golan, "(Re)naming the Landscape," 185.

8. Benvenisti, *Sacred Landscape*, 26.

9. Meron Benvenisti, "Ha-mappah ha-'ivrit" [The Hebrew map], *Te'oryah oveḳoret* 11 (1997): 25, 26.

10. Kadman, *Erased from Space and Consciousness*, 92–93.

11. Yeshayahu Press, *Erets-Yisrael: Entsiḳlopedyah topografit-hisṭorit* [The land of Israel: Topographical-historical encyclopedia], 2nd ed. (Jerusalem: Hots'at R. Mas, 1951), 69–75.

12. Press, *Erets-Yisrael*, 63–64.

13. For a list of Jewish individuals and institutions that funded the project, see Press, *Erets-Yisrael*, introduction.

14. Press, *Erets-Yisrael*, 63–64.

15. For his role in the naming committee, see Benvenisti, *Sacred Landscape*, 25, 51.

16. Kadman, *Erased from Space and Consciousness*, 94.

17. Complete reports, GNC, meeting no. 28, July 13, 1952, Israel State Archives, GL-22171/3.

18. Azaryahu and Golan, "(Re)naming the Landscape," 186.

19. Andrew Petersen et al., *A Gazetteer of Buildings in Muslim Palestine: Part 1* (Jerusalem: Council for British Research in the Levant, 2001), 276–77; complete reports, GNC. Cf. Kadman, *Erased from Space and Consciousness*, 95.

20. Complete reports, GNC.

21. Amos Nadan, *The Palestinian Peasant Economy under the Mandate: A Story of Colonial Bungling* (Cambridge, MA: Harvard University Press, 2006); Laura Robson, *Colonialism and Christianity in Mandate Palestine* (Austin: University of Texas Press, 2011); Rashid Khalidi, *The Iron Cage: The Story of the Palestinian Struggle for Statehood* (Boston: Beacon Press, 2007), 1–8.

22. Adriana Kemp, "'Dangerous Populations': State Territoriality and the Constitution of National Minorities," in *Boundaries and Belonging: States and Societies in the Struggle to Shape Identities and Local Practices*, ed. Joel S. Migdal (Cambridge: Cambridge University Press, 2004), 74.

23. Shira Robinson, *Citizen Strangers: Palestinians and the Birth of Israel's Liberal Settler State* (Stanford, CA: Stanford University Press, 2013), 8–9.

24. Anita Shapira, *Land and Power: The Zionist Resort to Force, 1881–1948* (New York: Oxford University Press, 1992), 357.

25. The name of the fictional Palestinian village is also spelled Ḥirbet Ḥizeh or Ḥirbet Ḥizah. The novella narrates the experience of young Israeli soldiers who received orders to evacuate Palestinian villagers after the end of the 1948 war. The narrator is a young Israeli soldier who struggles between fitting in with his comrades or submitting to his conscience. He eventually chooses to join the other soldiers and leaves the resolution of his remorse for a later time.

26. Anita Shapira, "Hirbet Hizah: Between Remembrance and Forgetting," *Jewish Social Studies* 7, no. 1 (2000).

27. For a discussion on the invocation of an Arab past (their absence and presence) in the First Aliyah's commemorative discourses, see Liora Halperin, *The Oldest Guard: Forging the Zionist Settler Past* (Stanford, CA: Stanford University Press, 2021), 28, 151–53.

28. Tariq Dana and Ali Jarbawi, "A Century of Settler Colonialism in Palestine," *Brown Journal of World Affairs* 24, no. 1 (2017): 200.

29. Ofira Gruweis-Kovalsky, "The Revisionist Movement and the British Mandate for Palestine," *Israel Studies* 26, no. 3 (2021): 187.

30. Yosef Rivlin, "Beit Hashem be-me'arbolet," *Hed ha-Mizraḥ*, June 2, 1950.

31. Reuven Rivlin, the former Israeli president and Yosef Rivlin's son, relates that his father signed up for the Irgun (or Etzel), a Zionist paramilitary organization, during the Mandate along with his wife and daughter. See Gil Samsonov, *Netanyahu and Likud's Leaders: The Israeli Princes*, trans. Kaeren Fish (Abingdon, UK: Routledge, 2020), 34.

32. Rivlin, "Beit Hashem be-me'arbolet."

33. Rivlin, "Beit Hashem be-me'arbolet."

34. Yosef Rivlin, "Beit Hashem bi-me'arbolet," *Had ha-Mizraḥ*, February 3, 1950.

35. Muslih, *The Origins of Palestinian Nationalism*, 122. After the Nakba, 'Aref al-'Aref left his hometown of Jaffa and settled in Jordan.

36. Rivlin, "Beit Hashem bi-me'arbolet."

37. Rivlin, "Beit Hashem bi-me'arbolet."

38. Rivlin, "Beit Hashem bi-me'arbolet."

39. Muslih, *The Origins of Palestinian Nationalism*, 122.

40. Cited in Rivlin, "Beit Hashem bi-me'arbolet."

41. Gil Eyal, *The Disenchantment of the Orient: Expertise in Arab Affairs and the Israeli State* (Stanford, CA: Stanford University Press, 2006), 97.

42. Rivlin, "Beit Hashem bi-me'arbolet."

43. Muhammad Amara, "The Place of Arabic in Israel," *International Journal of the Sociology of Language* (2002): 57.

44. Jacob M. Landau, "Hebrew and Arabic in the State of Israel: Political Aspects of the Language Issue," *International Journal of the Sociology of Language* 67 (1987): 119.

45. Suzanne Schneider, *Mandatory Separation: Religion, Education, and Mass Politics in Palestine* (Stanford, CA: Stanford University Press, 2018).

46. Bernard Spolsky and Elana Goldberg Shohamy, *The Languages of Israel: Policy, Ideology, and Practice* (Clevedon, UK: Multilingual Matters, 1999), 18, 19.

47. Landau, "Hebrew and Arabic in the Ṣtate of Israel," 119.

48. Immanuel Koplewitz, "Arabic in Israel: The Sociolinguistic Situation of Israel's Arab Minority," *International Journal of the Sociology of Language* 1992, no. 98 (1992): 32.

49. "Lo tihenah shtey leshonot rishmiyot ba-Medinah," *Ha-Mashkif*, September 10, 1948.

50. On further attempts by right-wing parties to denigrate the official status of Arabic, see Koplewitz, "Arabic in Israel," 33.

51. Ayelet Harel-Shalev, "Arabic as a Minority Language in Israel: A Comparative Perspective," *Adalah's Newsletter* 14 (2005): 4.

52. Amara, "The Place of Arabic in Israel," 60.

53. Yonatan Mendel, *The Creation of Israeli Arabic: Political and Security Considerations in the Making of Arabic Language Studies in Israel* (Hampshire: Palgrave Macmillan, 2014), 44–45.

54. Koplewitz, "Arabic in Israel," 33.

55. Amara, "The Place of Arabic in Israel," 55, 57–58.

56. On the linkage between Arabic instruction and security considerations, see Mendel, *The Creation of Israeli Arabic*, 45–46.

57. Z. Ben-David, "Kinus Morim be-Nasseret," *Davar*, August 18, 1950.

58. Aviv Derri, "The Construction of 'Native' Jews in Late Mandate Palestine: An Ongoing Nahda as a Political Project," *International Journal of Middle East Studies* 53 (2021): 256.

59. Ben-David, "Kinus Morim be-Nasseret." Sheikh al-Ṭabarī was a scholar, writer, respected qadi, and the primary Muslim leader in the early years of the state. He aimed to establish a meaningful leadership role for qadis in Israel while also advocating for autonomous religious institutions that would be accepted and respected by the public they served. His efforts, however, led to conflicts with Joshua Palmon, the first adviser to the prime minister on Arab affairs, who imposed strict political restrictions on the qadi position, effectively silencing al-Ṭabarī. See Alisa Rubin Peled, *Debating Islam in the Jewish State: The Development of Policy toward Islamic Institutions in Israel* (Albany: SUNY Press, 2001), 151.

60. Ben-David, "Kinus Morim be-Nasseret."

61. Derri, "The Construction of 'Native' Jews in Late Mandate Palestine," 258.

62. Ben-David, "Kinus Morim be-Nasseret."

63. Mendel, *The Creation of Israeli Arabic*, 48.

64. Cited in Yoni Furas, *Educating Palestine: Teaching and Learning History under the Mandate* (New York: Oxford University Press, 2020), 142.

65. Furas, *Educating Palestine*, 142.

66. Ben-David, "Kinus Morim be-Nasseret."

67. Kadman, *Erased from Space and Consciousness*, 97–98.

68. Robinson, *Citizen Strangers*, 8–9.

69. M. Ḥen, "Besdeh Sefer: Elef Laylah va-Laylah," *Hed ha-Mizraḥ*, May 26, 1950.

70. On the use of biblical and Mishnaic Hebrew in modern Hebrew to stress its Semitic roots, see Paul Wexler, *The Schizoid Nature of Modern Hebrew: A Slavic Language in Search of a Semitic Past* (Wiesbaden: Otto Harrassowitz, 1990), 4:10–11.

71. Ḥen, "Besdeh Sefer: Elef Laylah va-Laylah."

72. Ḥen, "Besdeh Sefer: Elef Laylah va-Laylah."

73. Israel Belḳind, *Bi-netiv ha-Biluyim: Zikhronot* [In the path of Biluyim: Memoirs of Israel Belḳind], ed. Ran Aharonson (Tel Aviv: Misrad ha-biṭaḥon, 1983), 51, 143, 58.

REFERENCES

Aaronsohn, Ran. "The Beginnings of Modern Jewish Agriculture in Palestine: 'Indigenous' versus 'Imported.'" *Agricultural History* 69, no. 3 (1995): 438–53.

———. *Rothschild and Early Jewish Colonization in Palestine.* Lanham, MD: Rowman & Littlefield, 2000.

———. "Vines and Wineries in the Jewish Colonies: Introducing Modern Viticulture into Nineteenth-Century Palestine." *Journal of Israeli History* 14, no. 1 (1993): 31–51.

Abufarha, Nasser. "Land of Symbols: Cactus, Poppies, Orange and Olive Trees in Palestine." *Identities: Global Studies in Culture and Power* 15, no. 3 (2008): 343–68.

Agnew, John. "European Landscape and Identity." In *Modern Europe: Place, Culture, Identity*, edited by Brian Graham (London: Hodder Education Publishers, 1998), 213–35.

al-Bājūrī, Maḥmūd 'Umar. *Kitāb Amthāl al-Mutakallimīn min 'awām al-miṣriyyin* [A book of Egyptian common people sayings]. Cairo: Al-Maṭba'ah al-Sharafiyya, 1889.

al-Bayṭār, 'Abd Allāh ibn Aḥmad Ibn. *Kitāb al-jāmi' li-mufradāt al-'adwiya wa al-aghdhiya* [The book of compilation of medication and aliment simples]. Vol. 3. Beirut: Dar al-Kutub al-'ilmiyya, 1992.

al-Dabbāgh, Muṣṭafa Murād. *Bilādunā Filasṭīn* [Our land Palestine]. Vol. 1. Kafr Qara: Dār al-Huda, 1991.

al-Damīrī. *Ḥayāt al-ḥayawān* [Life of animals]. Vol. 1. Beirut: Dār al-Kutub al-'Ilmiyya, 2003.

Alf Laylah wa-Laylah [A thousand and one nights]. Vol. 1. Cairo: Sa'īd 'Ali al-Khuṣūṣī, 1935.

al-Ḥamawī, Ibn Yāqūt. *Mu'jam Al-Buldān* [Dictionary of countries]. Vol. 2. Beirut: Dār Ṣādir, 1977.

al-Ḥanbalī, Mujīr al-Dīn. *Al-'uns al-jalīl bi-tārīkh al-Quds wa-al-Khalīl* [The glorious history of Jerusalem and Hebron]. Vol. 2. Amman: Maktabat Dandis, 1993.

'Ali, Fu'ād Ḥasānein. *Qaṣaṣuna al-sha'bī* [Our folkloric tales]. Cairo: Dār al-Fikr al-'Arabī, 1947.

al-'isa, 'Isa. "Aḥmad Zakī Pashā wa al-Ṣuhyūniyya." *Filasṭīn* (Jaffa), October 6, 1922.

———. "Aḥmad Zakī Pashā wa al-Ṣuhyūniyya." *Filasṭīn* (Jaffa), October 31, 1922.

al-Jawzī, Abū al-Faraj. *Kitāb al-adhkiyā'* [The book of intelligent people]. Cairo: Al-Ghazālī, n.d.

al-Jumaḥī, Muḥammad Ibn Sallām. *Ṭabaqāt Fuḥūl al-Shu'arā'* [Classes of champion poets]. Edited by Maḥmūd Muḥammad Shākir. Vol. 1. Cairo, 1974.

al-Jundī, Anwar. *Aḥmad Zakī al-Mulaqqab be-Sheikh al-'urūba: ḥayatuh, Ara'uh, Atharuh* [Ahmad Zaki called by sheikh of Arabism: His life, his opinions, and his legacy]. Cairo: Al-Mu'assasa al-Miṣriyya al-'āma, 1964.

al-Khālidī, Walīd. *Al-maktaba al-Khālidiyya fī al-Quds, 1720–2001* [The Khalidi library in Jerusalem, 1720–2001]. Beirut, 2002.

Al-Khūry, Salīm Gabriel, and Salīm Michael Shihada. *Kitāb ʾāthār al-adhār: Al-qism al-Jughrāfī* [The book of the signs of times]. Beirut: Al-Maṭba'a al-sūriyya, 1875.

Almog, Oz. *The Sabra: The Creation of the New Jew.* Berkeley: University of California Press, 2000.

Almog, Shmuel. "Ha-adamah le-ʿovdeha ve-giur ha-pallaḥim." In *Umah ve-toldoteha*, edited by Samuel Ettinger. Jerusalem: Mirkaz Zalman Shazar, 1984.

al-Musawi, Muhsin. *The Arabian Nights in Contemporary World Cultures: Global Commodification, Translation, and the Culture Industry.* New York: Columbia University Press, 2021.

al-Qalamāwī, Suhair. *Alf Layla wa-Layla* [A thousand and one nights]. Miṣr: Dār al-Maʿārif, 1943.

al-Ṭanāhī, Maḥmūd Muḥammad. *Madkhal 'ilā tārīkh nashr al-tūrāth al-ʿArabī* [An introduction to the publication of the Arab heritage]. Cairo: Al-Khānjī, 1984.

al-Tawḥīdī, Abū Ḥayyān. *al-baṣā'ir wa-al-dhakhā'ir* [Insights and treasures]. Vol. 9. Beirut: Dār Ṣādir, 1988.

al-Thaʿlabī, Abū Manṣūr Ismāʿīl. *Al-Tamthīl wa al-muḥāḍara* [The book of exemplification and discussion]. Edited by ʿAbd Al-Fattāḥ Muḥammad Al-Ḥilw. Tūnis: Al-dār al-ʿarabiyya lil-kitāb, 1983.

al-ʿUbaydī, ʿUbayd Allāh Ibn ʿabd Al-Kāfī. *Sharḥ al-maḍnūn bi-hi ʿalā ghayr ahlih: huwa sharḥ al-Sheikh al-ʿallāmah ʿUbayd Allāh ibn ʿAbd al-Kāfī ʿalā al-abyāt allatī intakhabahā al-Sheikh al-imām al-ʿallāmah ʿIzz al-Dīn ʿAbd al-Wahhāb al-Zanjānī* [That which is to be withheld from those unworthy of it]. Edited by Isaac Yahuda. Cairo: Maṭbaʿat al-Saʿāda, 1913–15.

al-Waṭaniyya, Kolliyat Rawḍat al-Maʿārif. *Barnamij Kolliyat Rawḍat al-Maʿārif al-Waṭaniyya* [The program of Rawḍat al-maʿārif college]. Al-Quds: Maṭbaʿat Dār al-ʾAytām al-Islāmiyya, 1930.

Al-Zawzanī. *Sharḥ al-Muʿallaqāt al-ʿAshr* [A commentary on ten suspended odes]. Beirut: Dār Maktabat al-Hay'ā Lilṭibāʿa wa-al-Nashr, 1983.

al-Zayyāt, Aḥmad Ḥasan. *Fī 'uṣūl al-adab: Muḥāḍarāt wa-Maqālāt fī al-Adab al-ʿArabī* [On the principles of Arabic literature: Lectures and essays on Arabic literature]. Cairo: Maṭbaʿat Lajnat al-Ta'līf, wa-al-Tarjama, wa-al-Nashr, 1935.

Amara, Muhammad. "The Place of Arabic in Israel." *International Journal of the Sociology of Language* (2002): 53–68.

"An Arab Support of Zionism." *Jewish Chronicle* (London), September 22, 1922, 50–52.

Arberry, Arthur John, ed. and trans. *The Seven Odes: The First Chapter in Arabic Literature.* London: Macmillan, 1957.

Armstrong, Karen. *A History of Jerusalem: One City, Three Faiths.* London: Harper Perennial, 2005.

———. "The Holiness of Jerusalem: Asset or Burden?" *Journal of Palestine Studies* 27, no. 3 (1998): 5–19.

Assaf, Simḥa, Samuel Klein, and Ben-Zion Dinur. "Me-et ha-Maʿrekhet" [From the editor]. *Zion: Meʾasef ha-ḥevra ha-Erets Yisraelit le-hisṭoryah ve-etnografyah* 1 (1925): i–ii.

Attal, Robert. "Bibliographie raisonnée des proverbes Arabes et Judéo-Arabes du Maghreb." *Studies in Bibliography and Booklore* 17 (1989): 43–54.

Avishor, Yitsḥaḳ. "Ha-ʿibudim shel tirgum Rav Saʿadya Gaon la-Tanakh ba-Mizraḥ" [The adaptations of R. Saadya Gaon's Bible translation in the East]. *Sefunot: Studies and Sources on the History of the Jewish Communities in the East* 54 (1991): 181–202.

———. "Ha-markiv ha-'aravi ba-lashon ha-'Ivrit bat zemanenu u-ve-sifrutah m-Eliezer Ben-Yehuda 'ad Netivah Ben-Yehuda (ve-Dan Ben-Amuz)" [The Arabic component in modern Hebrew language and literature.]. *Ha-'Ivrit ve-aḥyoteha: ketav 'et le-ḥeḳer ha-lashon ha-'Ivrit ve-ziḳatah la-leshonot ha-Shemiyot veli-leshonot ha-Yehudim* 2–3 (2002–3): 9–50.

———. *Ha-sipur ha-'amami shel Yehudey 'Iraq* [The folktales of the Jews of Iraq]. 2 vols. Haifa: University of Haifa, 1992.

———. "Ha-yitsirah ha-sifrutit ba-safah ha-'aravit-yehudit." In *Ḳehilot Yisrael ba-mizraḥ ba-me'ot ha-tesha' 'esreh ve-ha-'isrim: 'Iraq*, edited by Haim Sadoun, 87–100. Jerusalem: Misrad ha-ḥinukh, Makhon Ben Zvi, 2002.

———. "Mishle 'Arav: le-hashlamat mif'alo shel Yitsḥak Benjamin Yahuda" [Proverbia Arabica: To complete Isaac Benjamin Yahuda's project]. *Pe'amim* 54 (1993): 143–48.

———. "Sifrut ve-'itonut ba-'Aravit Yehudit shel Yehudey Bavel bi-defusey Hodo" [Iraqi Jewish Judeo-Arabic Literature and Newspapers Published in India]. *Pe'amim* 52 (1992): 108–9.

Ayalon, Ami. *Reading Palestine: Printing and Literacy, 1900–1948.* Austin: University of Texas Press, 2004.

Azaryahu, Maoz, and Arnon Golan. "(Re)naming the Landscape: The Formation of the Hebrew Map of Israel 1949–1960." *Journal of Historical Geography* 27, no. 2 (2001): 178–95.

Bakhos, Carol. *Ishmael on the Border: Rabbinic Portryals of the First Arab.* Albany: SUNY Press, 2006.

Banko, Lauren. *The Invention of Palestinian Citizenship, 1918–1947.* Edinburgh: Edinburgh University Press, 2016.

Barakat, Rana. "Writing/Righting Palestine Studies: Settler Colonialism, Indigenous Sovereignty and Resisting the Ghost(s) of History." *Settler Colonial Studies* 8, no. 3 (2018): 349–63.

Bar-Asher, Moshe. "Some Observations on the Revival of Hebrew." *Jewish Studies* 32 (1992): 25–34.

Bardenstein, Carol B. "Trees, Forests, and the Shaping of Palestinian and Israeli Collective Memory." In *Acts of Memory: Cultural Recall in the Present*, edited by Mieke Bal, Jonathan Crewe, and Leo Spitzer, 148–68. Hanover, NH: Dartmouth College Press, 1999.

Barr, James. *Comparative Philology and the Text of the Old Testament: With Additions and Corrections.* Winona Lake, IN: Eisenbrauns, 1987.

Barru, Tawfiq. *Al-'Arab Wa-Al-Turk Fī Al-'Ahd Al-Dustūrī Al-'Uthmānī, 1908–1914* [Arabs and Turks in the Ottoman constitutional era, 1908–1914]. Damascus: Ma'had al-Dirāsāt al-'Arabiyya, 1960.

Bar-Yosef, Eitan. *The Holy Land in English Culture 1799–1917: Palestine and the Question of Orientalism.* Oxford: Oxford University Press, 2005.

Bashkin, Orit. "The Colonized Semites and the Infectious Disease: Theorizing and Narrativizing Anti-Semitism in the Levant, 1870–1914." *Critical Inquiry* 47, no. 2 (2021): 189–217.

———. "The Fruit of the Arts and the Mob: Global Minorities during the Dreyfus Affair." *Comparative Studies of South Asia, Africa and the Middle East* 41, no. 3 (2021): 404–12.

———. "On Noble and Inherited Virtues: Discussions of the Semitic Race in the Levant and Egypt, 1876–1918." *Humanities* 10, no. 3 (2021): 1–120.

Baudissin, Wolf Wilhelm. *Studien zur Semitischen Religionsgeschichte.* Vol. 2. Leipzig: Verlag von Fr. Wilh. Grunow, 1878.

Baydas, Khalīl. *Kitāb al-Rawḍa al-Mu'nisa fī waṣf al-'arḍ al-Muqaddasa* [The book of pleasant gardens in describing the Holy Land]. Ba'abda: Al-Maṭba'a al-Uthmāniyya, 1898.

Behar, Almog, and Yuval Evri. "From Saadia to Yahuda: Reviving Arab Jewish Intellectual Models in a Time of Partition." *Jewish Quarterly Review* 109, no. 3 (2019): 458–63.

Behar, Moshe, and Zvi Ben-Dor Benite. *Modern Middle Eastern Jewish Thought: Writings on Identity, Politics, and Culture, 1893–1958*. Waltham, MA: Brandeis University Press, 2013.

Belḳind, Israel. *Bi-netiv ha-Biluyim: Zikhronot* [In the path of Biluyim: Memoirs of Israel Belḳind]. Edited by Ran Aharonson. Tel Aviv: Misrad ha-biṭaḥon, 1983.

———. *Erets Yisrael*. New York: Hotsaat ha-Mmeir, 1919.

———. *Erets Yisrael shel zemanenu* [Contemporary Palestine]. Tel Aviv: Hotsaat ha-Mmeir, 1928.

———. *Ha-'Aravim asher be-erets Yisrael* [The Arabs in the land of Israel]. Edited by David Ben-Gurion. Tel-Aviv: Ḥermon, 1969.

———. "Motsa ha-'Aravim she-be-erets Yisrael" [The origins of Arabs in the land of Israel]. *Ha-Schiloach* 38 (1921): 438–45.

———. *Our National Work in Palestine*. New York: Pinski-Massel Press, 1918.

Ben-Arieh, Yehoshua. *'Ir bi-rei teḳufah: Yerushalayim ba-me'ah ha-tesha' 'esreh, ha-'ir ha-'atiḳah* [A city reflected in its times: Jerusalem in the nineteenth century, the Old City]. Jerusalem: Yad Yitshak Ben-Tsevi, 1977.

———. "Le-'ofiha shel ha-sifrut ha-geografit ha-'ivrit 'al Erets Yisrael ba-me'ah ha-tesha' 'esreh 'ad milḥemet ha-'olam ha-rishonah" [The character of Hebrew geographic literature about Erets-Israel during the nineteenth century and until World War I]. *Eretz-Israel: Archaeological, Historical and Geographical Studies* 22 (1991): 36–44.

———. *The Rediscovery of the Holy Land in the Nineteenth Century*. Detroit: Wayne State University Press, 1979.

Ben-Artzi, Yossi. "Changes in the Agricultural Sector of the Moshavot, 1882–1914." In *Ottoman Palestine, 1800–1914: Studies in Economic and Social History*, edited by Gilber Gad G., 131–58. Leiden: Brill, 1990.

Ben-Bassat, Yuval. "Bedouin Petitions from Late Ottoman Palestine: Evaluating the Effects of Sedentarization." *Journal of the Economic and Social History of the Orient* 58, no. 1–2 (2015): 135–62.

———. *Late Ottoman Palestine: The Period of Young Turk Rule*. London: I. B. Tauris, 2011.

———. "Proto-Zionist–Arab Encounters in Late Nineteenth-Century Palestine: Socioregional Dimensions." *Journal of Palestine Studies* 38, no. 2 (2009): 42–63.

Ben-David, Z. "Kinus Morim be-Nasseret." *Davar*, August 18, 1950.

Ben-Ezer, Ehud. *Be-moledet ha-ga'agu'im ha-menugadim: Ha-'Aravi ba-sifrut ha-'ivrit: mivḥar sipurim* [In the homeland of conflicting yearnings: The Arab in Israeli fiction: An anthology]. Tel Aviv: Agudat ha-sofrim ha-'ivrim, 1992.

Ben-Yehuda, Eliezer. *A Dream Come True*. Translated by T. Muraoka. Edited by George Mandel. Boulder, CO: Westview Press, 1993.

———. "Ḥanukah." *Ha-Tsevi* (Jerusalem), December 18, 1908, 1–2.

———. *Kol kitve Eliezer Ben-Yehuda* [Collected works of Eliezer Ben-Yehuda]. Jerusalem: Ha-Ma'arav, 1941.

———. "Meḳorot le-male he-ḥaser bi-leshonenu" [Sources to fill the gap in our language]. *Zikhronot va'ad ha-lashon ha-'ivrit* 4 (1914): 3–16.

———. *Milon ha-lashon ha-ʿivrit ha-yeshanah ve-ha-ḥadashah: ha-mavoʾ ha-gadol* [A complete dictionary of ancient and modern Hebrew: Prolegomena]. 17 vols. 1908–27; repr., Tel Aviv: Sefer, 1948.

———. *Sefer Erets Yisrael: ʿal ṭevaʿ ha-arets ha-zot* [The land of Israel's book: On the nature of this land]. Jerusalem: Joel Moses Solomon, 1883.

———. "Yarad." In *Milon ha-Lashon ha-ʿIvrit ha-Yeshanah ve-ha-Ḥadashah*, 2145–50. vol 4. New York: International News Company, 1914.

———. "Yehudim, Heyu ʿOtomanim." *Ha-Tsevi*, January 11, 1909.

Ben-Yehuda, Eliezer, and David Yellin. *Miḳra le-yilde bene Yisrael kolel reshit limudim, sipure ha-Talmud ve-ha-Midrashim u-mishle shoʿalim* [Lecture to the children of the people of Israel including the beginning of learning, Talmudic and Midrashic stories, and fox fables]. Jerusalem: Kol yisrael ḥaverim, 1887.

Ben-Ze'ev, Israel. "Darko el ha-lashon ha-ʿaravit." *Davar*, March 24, 1939.

——— "Mikhtav Galuy" [Open letter]. *Ha-arets*, July 1937, 4.

———. "R' Yitsḥaḳ Yahuda: 'Ishiyuto Ve-Tilmudo" [R' Yitsḥaḳ Yahuda: His personality and teachings]. *Moznaim* 3 (1941): 71–77.

Ben-Zvi, Isaac. "Le-zekher rav Isaac Eziekiel Yahuda Z"L." *Davar*, March 26, 1942.

Benvenisti, Meron. "Ha-mappah ha-ʿivrit" [The Hebrew map]. *Te'oryah oveḳoret* 11 (1997): 7–29.

———. *Sacred Landscape: The Buried History of the Holy Land since 1948*. Translated by Maxine Kaufman-Lacusta. Berkeley: University of California Press, 2000.

Berlin, Adele, Marc Zvi Brettler, and Michael A. Fishbane. *The Jewish Study Bible: Jewish Publication Society Tanakh Translation*. Oxford: Oxford University Press, 2004.

Beška, Emanuel. "'The Disgrace of the Twentieth Century': The Beilis Affair in *Filastin* Newspaper." *Jerusalem Quarterly File* 66 (2016): 99–108.

Bezalel, Yitsḥaḳ. "Ha-Levantim ha-reshonim." *Pe'amim* 125–127 (2011): 75–95.

———. *Noladetem Tsiyonim: ha-Sefaradim be-Erets-Yisra'el ba-Tsiyonut uva-Teḥiyah ha-ʿivrit ba-Teḳufah ha-ʿOtmanit* [You were born Zionists: The Sephardim in Eretz Israel in Zionism and the Hebrew revival during the Ottoman period]. Jerusalem: Yad Yitsḥaḳ ben-Tsevi: Mekhon Ben-Tsevi le-ḥeḳer ḳehilot Yisra'el ba-mizraḥ, 2007.

Bialiḳ, Ḥaim Naḥman. "Erets Yisrael." 1930. http://benyehuda.org/bialik/dvarim_shebeal_peh33.html.

Bilu. "Manifesto." In *Israel in the Middle East: Documents and Readings on Society, Politics, and Foreign Relations, Pre-1948 to the Present*, edited by Itamar Rabinovich and Jehuda Reinharz, 10–11. 1882; repr., Waltham, MA: Brandeis University Press, 2008.

Blau, Joshua. *The Renaissance of Modern Hebrew and Modern Standard Arabic: Parallels and Differences in the Revival of Two Semitic Languages*. Vol. 18. Berkeley: University of California Press, 1981.

Boušek, Daniel. "Polemics in the Age of Religious Persecutions: Maimonides' Attitude towards Islam." *Asian and African Studies* 20, no. 1 (2011): 46–85.

Brann, Ross. *Al-Andalus, Sefarad, and the Tropes of Exceptionalism*. Philadelphia: University of Pennsylvania Press, 2021.

Brann, Ross, and Adam Sutcliffe, eds. *Renewing the Past, Reconfiguring Jewish Culture: From Al-Andalus to the Haskalah*. Philadelphia: University of Pennsylvania Press, 2004.

Brinner, William M. "The Image of the Jew as *Other* in Medieval Arabic Texts." *Israel Oriental Studies* 14 (1994): 227–40.

Brown, Francis, Samuel Rolles Driver, Charles Augustus Briggs, Edward Robinson, and James Strong. *A Hebrew and English Lexicon of the Old Testament: With an Appendix Containing the Biblical Aramaic*. Peabody, MA: Houghton Mifflin, 1907.

Buchaltzev, Eran. "'Ivri, 'Ivrit ve-'Ivriut—va'ad ha-lashon ha-'Ivrit ve-ha-tode'ah ha-le'umit ha-yehudit ba-shanim 1905–1941." PhD diss., Ben-Gurion University, 2016.

Burton, Richard Francis, and Leonard Charles Smithers. *The Book of the Thousand Nights and a Night*. Vol. 8. New York: H. S. Nichols and Company, 1894.

Busbridge, Rachel. "Israel-Palestine and the Settler Colonial 'Turn': From Interpretation to Decolonization." *Theory, Culture & Society* 35, no. 1 (2018): 91–115.

Bushnaq, Inea. "The Role of Folklore in Nation Building." Translated by Sharif Kanaana. In *Folk Heritage of Palestine*, edited by George K. Rishmawi, Aziz Khalil, and Daifallah Othman, 166–77. Tayibeh, Triangle, Israel: Research Center for Arab Heritage, 1994.

Campos, Michelle U. "Between 'Beloved Ottomania' and 'The Land of Israel': The Struggle over Ottomanism and Zionism among Palestine's Sephardi Jews, 1908–13." *International Journal of Middle East Studies* 37, no. 4 (2005): 461–83.

———. *Ottoman Brothers: Muslims, Christians, and Jews in Early Twentieth-Century Palestine*. Stanford, CA: Stanford University Press, 2010.

Caplan, Neil. *Palestine Jewry and the Arab Question, 1917–1925*. London: Routledge, 2015.

Chetrit, Sami Shalom. "Revisiting Bialik: A Radical Mizrahi Reading of the Jewish National Poet." *Comparative Literature* 62, no. 1 (2010): 1–21.

Cohen, Hillel. *Army of Shadows: Palestinian Collaboration with Zionism, 1917–1948*. Translated by Haim Watzman. Berkeley: University of California Press, 2008.

———. "The Temple Mount / Al-Aqsa in Zionist and Palestinian National Consciousness: A Comparative View." *Israel Studies Review* 32, no. 1 (2017): 1–19.

———. *Year Zero of the Arab-Israeli Conflict*. Translated by Haim Watzman. Waltham, MA: Brandeis University Press, 2015.

Cohen, Hillel, and Yuval Evri. "Moledet meshutefet ou beit le'umi: bene ha- arets, hatsaharat Balfour ve he-she'elah ha-'Aravit" [Shared homeland or Jewish national home: Sephardi natives of the land, Balfour Declaration, and the Arab question]. *Te'oriah u-veḳoret* 49 (2017): 291–304.

Cohen, Julia Phillips. *Becoming Ottomans: Sephardi Jews and Imperial Citizenship in the Modern Era*. New York: Oxford University Press, 2014.

———. *Sephardi Lives: A Documentary History, 1700–1950*. Stanford, CA: Stanford University Press, 2014.

Cohen-Hattab, Kobi, and Doron Bar. *The Western Wall: The Dispute over Israel's Holiest Jewish Site, 1967–2000*. Leiden: Brill, 2020.

Cole, Peter. *The Dream of the Poem: Hebrew Poetry from Muslim and Christian Spain, 950–1492*. Princeton, NJ: Princeton University Press, 2007.

Conforti, Yitzhak. "'The New Jew' in the Zionist Movement: Ideology and Historiography." *Australian Journal of Jewish Studies* 25 (2011): 89–103.

Dafni, Amots, Shay Levy, and Efraim Lev. "The Ethnobotany of Christ's Thorn Jujube (Ziziphus Spina-Christi) in Israel." *Journal of Ethnobiology and Ethnomedicine* 1 (2005): 8.

Dahamsheh, Amer. *Maḳom la-dor bo ve-shem lo: Ḳeri'ah sifrutit ve-tarbutit ba-shemot ha-'Aravim shel ha-arets* [A local habitation and a name: A literary and cultural reading of the Arabic geographic names of the land]. Beersheba: Dvir, 2017.

Dana, Tariq, and Ali Jarbawi. "A Century of Settler Colonialism in Palestine." *Brown Journal of World Affairs* 24, no. 1 (2017): 197–220.

Dawn, C. Ernest. "The Origins of Arab Nationalism." In *The Origins of Arab Nationalism*, edited by Rashid Khalidi, Lisa Anderson, Muhammad Muslih, and Reeva S. Simon, 3–30. New York: Columbia University Press, 1991.

"Dāwūd Yellīn fī al-khāmisa wa al-sabʿīn." *Ḥaqīqat al-ʾAmr*, March 29, 1939.

Derri, Aviv. "The Construction of 'Native' Jews in Late Mandate Palestine: An Ongoing Nahda as a Political Project." *International Journal of Middle East Studies* 53 (2021): 253–71.

Dhayf, Shawqī. *Tārīkh al-ʾAdab al-ʿArabī: Al-Shiʿr al-Jāhilī* [History of Arabic literature: Pre-Islamic era]. Cairo: Dār al-Maʿārif, 1960.

Di-Capua, Yoav. *Gatekeepers of the Arab Past: Historians and History Writing in Twentieth-Century Egypt*. Berkeley: University of California Press, 2009.

Dinur, Benzion. *Bene Dori: Tsiyonim ve-ḳavim li-demuyot ḥa-khamim u-meḥankhim, anshe tsibur ve-ʿomdim be-shaʿar* [People of my generation: Notes and lines about scholars and educators, public figures, and gatekeepers]. Tel-Aviv: Masadah, 1962.

Dizengoff, Meir. "Eliyahu Ben Benjamin Ze'ev Hallevi Sapir Zal." *Ha-ḥinukh* 2, no. 2 (1911): 73–78.

Dolbee, Samuel, and Shay Hazkani. "Unlikely Identities: Abu Ibrahim and the Politics of Possibility in Late Ottoman Palestine." *Jerusalem Quarterly*, no. 63 (2015): 24–39.

Doumani, Beshara. *Rediscovering Palestine: Merchants and Peasants in Jabal Nablus, 1700–1900*. Berkeley: University of California Press, 1995.

Dowty, Alan. *Arabs and Jews in Ottoman Palestine: Two Worlds Collide*. Bloomington: Indiana University Press, 2021.

Duncan, James S. *The City as Text: The Politics of Landscape Interpretation in the Kandyan Kingdom*. Cambridge: Cambridge University Press, 2005.

———. "Landscape Taste as a Symbol of Group Identity: A Westchester County Village." *Geographical Review* 63, no. 3 (1973): 334–55.

Dykstra, Darrell. "Pyramids, Prophets, and Progress: Ancient Egypt in the Writings of ʿAlī Mubārak." *Journal of the American Oriental Society* 114, no. 1 (1994): 54–65.

Efrati, Nathan. *Ha-ʿedah ha-Sephardit be-Yerushalayim: 1840–1917* [The Sephardic community in Jerusalem during the years 1840–1917]. Jerusalem: Bialik Institute, 1999.

———. "Ha-Protokolim Shel Lishkat B'nai B'rith Yerushalayim, 1888–1919" [The Jerusalem lodge of B'nai B'rith, 1888–1919]. *Cathedra: For the History of Eretz Israel and Its Yishuv* 50 (1988): 140–66.

Efron, John M. "Orientalism and the Jewish Historical Gaze." In *Orientalism and the Jews*, edited by Ivan Davidson Kalmar and Derek Jonathan Penslar, 80–93. Hanover, NH: University Press of New England, 2005.

Egoz, Shelley. "Landscape and Identity: Beyond a Geography of One Place." In *The Routledge Companion to Landscape Studies*, edited by Peter Howard, Ian Thompson, Emma Waterson, and Mick Atha, 290–303. London: Routledge, 2013.

Eisenberg, Ronald L. *Jewish Traditions: A JPS Guide*. Philadelphia: Jewish Publication Society, 2008.

"Elef laylah va-laylah be-tirgum ʿivri ḥadash." *Hed ha-Mizraḥ*, April 19, 1943.

El-Eini, Roza. *Mandated Landscape: British Imperial Rule in Palestine 1929–1948*. London: Routledge, 2004.

Elḥanani, Avraham Hayim. "David Yellin 'ish Yerushalaiym." In *Mi-Dan ve-'ad Beer Sheva': Pirkey Hayav shel David Yellin*, edited by David Yellin and Avraham Ḥayim Elḥanani, 3–102. Jerusalem: Ha-Va'ad le-Hotsaat Kitve Yellin, Hotsaat Rubin Mass, 1973.

"Eliyahu Sapir Halevi Einennu." *Ḥerut* (Jerusalem), September 4, 1911.

El-Shamsy, Ahmed. *Rediscovering the Islamic Classics: How Editors and Print Culture Transformed an Intellectual Tradition.* Princeton, NJ: Princeton University Press, 2020.

El-Shamy, Hasan. "Qâla al-Samaw'al ibn Âdiyâ al-Yahudiyy (the Jew, Al-Samaw'al Son-of Âdiya Said: . . .): Conscientiousness and Fidelity as Heroic Qualities in Arab Traditions (the Jewish Example)." *Folk Culture* 5, no. 16 (2012): 6–23.

Eph'al, Israel. "'Ishmael' and 'Arab(s)': A Transformation of Ethnological Terms." *Journal of Near Eastern Studies* 35, no. 4 (1976): 225–35.

Even-Zohar, Itamar. "The Emergence of a Native Hebrew Culture in Palestine, 1882–1948." *Poetics Today* 11, no. 1 (1990): 175–91.

Evri, Yuval, and Almog Behar. "Between East and West: Controversies over the Modernization of Hebrew Culture in the Works of Shaul Abdallah Yosef and Ariel Bension." *Journal of Modern Jewish Studies* 16, no. 2 (May 4, 2017): 295–311

Evri, Yuval, and Hillel Cohen. "Between Shared Homeland to National Homeland: The Balfour Declaration from a Native Sephardic Perspective." In *The Arab and Jewish Questions: Geographies of Engagement in Palestine and Beyond*, edited by Bashir Bashir and Leila Farsakh, 148–72. New York: Columbia University Press, 2020.

Evri, Yuval, and Hagar Kotef. "When Does a Native Become a Settler? (with Apologies to Zreik and Mamdani)." *Constellations* 29, no. 1 (2020): 3–18.

Eyal, Gil. *The Disenchantment of the Orient: Expertise in Arab Affairs and the Israeli State.* Stanford, CA: Stanford University Press, 2006.

Feldman, Rachel Z., and Ian McGonigle. *Settler-Indigeneity in the West Bank.* Montreal: McGill-Queen's University Press, 2023.

Fellman, Jack. *The Revival of a Classical Tongue: Eliezer Ben Yehuda and the Modern Hebrew Language.* The Hague: Mouton, 1973.

Fields, Gary. *Enclosure: Palestinian Landscapes in a Historical Mirror.* Oakland: University of California Press, 2017.

Fieni, David. "French Decadence, Arab Awakenings: Figures of Decay in the Arab Nahda." *Boundary* 39, no. 2 (2012): 143–60.

Firestone, Reuven. "The 'Other' Ishmael in Islamic Scripture and Tradition." In *The Politics of the Ancestors: Exegetical and Historical Perspectives on Genesis 12–36*, edited by Mark G. Brett, Jakob Wöhrle, and Friederike Neumann, 419–32. Tübingen: Mohr Siebeck, 2018.

Fischer, Moshe, Itamar Taxel, and David Amit. "Rural Settlement in the Vicinity of Yavneh in the Byzantine Period: A Religio-Archaeological Perspective." *Bulletin of the American Schools of Oriental Research* 350 (2008): 7–35.

Fishman, Louis A. *Jews and Palestinians in the Late Ottoman Era, 1908–1914: Claiming the Homeland.* Edinburgh: Edinburgh University Press, 2020.

Fonck, Leop. "Elenchus Bibliographicus." *Biblica* 4, no. 4 (1923): 65–104.

Friedman, Isaiah. "Ḥivrat 'ezra, misrad ha-ḥuts ha-Germani, ve-ha-pulmos 'im ha-tsiyonim, 1901–1918" [The "Hilfsverein der deutschen Juden," the German foreign ministry and the controversy with the Zionists, 1901–1918]. *Cathedra*, no. 20 (1981): 97–122.

Friedman, Michal Rose. "Orientalism between Empires: Abraham Shalom Yahuda at the Intersection of Sepharad, Zionism, and Imperialism." *Jewish Quarterly Review* 109, no. 3 (2019): 435–51.

Furas, Yoni. *Educating Palestine: Teaching and Learning History under the Mandate.* New York: Oxford University Press, 2020.

———. "We the Semites: Reading Ancient History in Mandate Palestine." *Contemporary Levant* 5, no. 1 (2020): 33–43.

Gershoni, Israel. "Demon and Infidel: Egyptian Intellectuals Confronting Hitler and Nazism during World War II." In *Nazism, the Holocaust, and the Middle East,* edited by Francis R. Nicosia and Bogac A. Ergene, 77–105. New York: Bergham, 2018.

Ginsburg, Shai. *Rhetoric and Nation: The Formation of Hebrew National Culture, 1880–1990.* Syracuse, NY: Syracuse University Press, 2014.

Glass, Joseph B., and Ruth Kark. *Sephardi Entrepreneurs in Jerusalem: The Valero Family 1800–1948.* Jerusalem: Gefen Publishing House, 2007.

Goitein, S. D. *Jews and Arabs: Their Contact through the Ages.* New York: Schocken Books, 1964.

———. "Mishle 'Arav." *Moznaim* (1932): 12–14.

———. "The Oldest Documentary Evidence for the Title Alf Laila Wa-Laila," *Journal of the American Oriental Society* 78, no. 4 (1958): 301–2.

Goldberg, Harvey E. "The Oriental and the Orientalist: The Meeting of Mordecai Ha-Cohen and Naḥum Slouschz." *Jewish Culture and History* 7, no. 3 (2004): 1–30.

Goldziher, Ignác. *Muslim Studies.* Translated by C. R. Barber and Samuel Miklos Stern. Edited by Samuel Miklos Stern. Vol. 2. London: Geo. Allen & Unwin, 1971.

Gordon, Adi. *Brit Shalom ve-ha-Tsiyonit ha-Dole'omiyut: Ha-She'elah Ha-'Aravit kishe'elah Yehudit* [Brith Shalom and the binational Zionism: The Arab question as a Jewish question]. 2008.

Gordon, Judah Leib. "'Inyane De-yoma." *Ha-Melits,* 1883, 1–2.

Gorny, Yosef. *Zionism and the Arabs: 1882–1948, a Study of Ideology.* Oxford: Clarendon Press, 1987.

Green, Abigail. *Moses Montefiore: Jewish Liberator and Imperial Hero.* Cambridge, MA: Harvard University Press, 2012.

Gribetz, Jonathan Marc. "Arab–Zionist Conversations in Late Ottoman Jerusalem: Sa'id Al-Husayni, Ruhi Al-Khalidi and Eliezer Ben-Yehuda." In *Ordinary Jerusalem, 1840–1940: Opening New Archives, Revisiting a Global City,* edited by Angelos Dalachanis and Vincent Lemire, 305–29. Leiden: Brill, 2018.

———. *Defining Neighbors: Religion, Race, and the Early Zionist-Arab Encounter.* Princeton, NJ: Princeton University Press, 2014.

Gruweis-Kovalsky, Ofira. "The Revisionist Movement and the British Mandate for Palestine." *Israel Studies* 26, no. 3 (2021): 179–95.

Haddawy, Husain. *The Arabian Nights.* New York: W. W. Norton and Company, 1995.

Haim, Abraham. *Yiḥud ve-hishtalvut: Hanhagat ha-Sefaradim bi-Yerushalayim bi-teḳufat ha-shilṭon ha-Briṭi, 678–708 (1917–1948)* [Particularity and integration: The Sephardi leadership in Jerusalem under British rule, 1917–1948]. Jerusalem: Carmel, 2000.

ha-Lashon, Va'ad. "'Avodat va'ad ha-lashon" [Works of the language committee]. *Zikhronot va'ad ha-lashon ha-'ivrit* 3 (1913).

Halper, Jeff. *Between Redemption and Revival: The Jewish Yishuv of Jerusalem in the Nineteenth Century*. Boulder, CO: Westview Press, 1991.

Halperin, Liora R. *Babel in Zion: Jews, Nationalism, and Language Diversity in Palestine, 1920–1948*. New Haven, CT: Yale University Press, 2014.

———. *The Oldest Guard: Forging the Zionist Settler Past*. Stanford, CA: Stanford University Press, 2021.

———. "Petah Tikva, 1886: Gender, Anonymity, and the Making of Zionist Memory." *Jewish Social Studies* 23, no. 1 (2017): 1–28.

Hanioğlu, M. Şükrü. *A Brief History of the Late Ottoman Empire*. Princeton, NJ: Princeton University Press, 2008.

Harel-Shalev, Ayelet. "Arabic as a Minority Language in Israel: A Comparative Perspective." *Adalah's Newsletter* 14 (2005): 1–10.

Harif, Hanan. *Anashim aḥim anaḥnu: Ha-peniyah mizraḥah ba-hagut ha-tsiyonit*. [For we be brethren: The turn to the East in Zionist thought]. Jerusalem: Merkaz Zalman Shazar le-ḥeḳer toldot ha-'am ha-Yehudi, 2019.

———. "Islam in Zion? Yosef Yo'el Rivlin's Translation of the *Qur'an* and Its Place within the New Hebrew Culture." *Naharaim* 10, no. 1 (2016): 39–55.

Hasson, Itzhak. "The Muslim View of Jerusalem, the Qur'an and Hadith." In *The History of Jerusalem: The Early Muslim Period, 638–1099*, edited by Joshua Prawer and Haggai Ben-Shammai, 349–85. Jerusalem: Yad Izhak Ben-Zvi, 1996.

Haycraft, Sir Thomas, H. C. Luke, and Stubbs. *Palestine. Disturbances in May, 1921. Reports of the commission of Inquiry with Correspondence Relating Thereto Presented to Parliament by Command of His Majesty, October 1921*. London: His Majesty's Stationery Office, 1921.

Hees, Syrinx von. *Inḥiṭāṭ—The Decline Paradigm: Its Influence and Persistence in the Writing of Arab Cultural History*. Würzburg: Ergon, 2017.

Ḥen, M. "Besdeh Sefer: Elef Laylah va-Laylah." *Hed ha-Mizraḥ*, May 26, 1950.

Hill, Peter. *Utopia and Civilisation in the Arab Nahda*. Cambridge: Cambridge University Press, 2020.

Hissin, Haim. *A Palestinian Diary: Memoirs of a Bilu Pioneer 1882–1887*. Translated by Francis Miller. New York: Herzl Press, 1976.

Hochberg, Gil Z. "'Remembering Semitism' or 'On the Prospect of Re-Membering the Semites.'" *ReOrient* 1, no. 2 (2016): 192–223.

Horovitz, Josef. "Elef Laylah va-Laylah" [One thousand and one nights]. *Ha-Teḳufah* 23 (1925).

———. "The Origins of the Arabian Nights." *Islamic Culture* 1, no. 1 (1927): 36–57.

Horowitz, Israel Wolf. *Erets Yisrael u-shekhenoteha: Entsiḳlopedyah ge'ografit-hisṭorit le-Erets Yisrael, Suriyah ṿa-ḥatsi ha-'i Sinai* [Palestine and the adjacent countries: A geographic and historical encyclopedia of Palestine, Syria and the Sinai Peninsula]. Edited by Aaron Teitelbaum. Vol. 1. Vienna: Abraham Horowitz, 1923.

———. "Hagadot 'Araviyot: 'al davar ha-meḳomot ha-ḳedushim be-Erets Yisrael." *Luaḥ Erets Yisrael* 20–21 (1915–16): 236–44.

———. *Sefer meḥḳere erets avotenu* [The book of the study of our ancestral land]. Jerusalem: Bi-defus ha-aḥim Lipshitts, 1909–10.

Hussein, Mostafa. "Arabian Nights, Hebrew Nights: On the Influence of Alf Laylah wa-Laylah on Jewish Culture in Palestine/Israel." *Journal of Levantine Studies* 8, no. 2 (2018): 125.

———. "The Integration of Arabo-Islamic Culture into the Emergent Hebrew Culture of Late Ottoman Palestine." *Jewish Quarterly Review* 109, no. 3 (2019): 464–69.

———. "Muhammad in Zion: On the Hebrew Perceptions of the Prophet of Islam." *Journal of Religious Minorities under Muslim Rule* 1 (2023): 1–38.

Ḥussein, Ṭaha. *Fī al- 'Adab al-Jāhilī* [On classical Arabic literature]. 3rd ed. Cairo: Lajnat al-Ta'līf wa-al-Nashr, 1933. Originally published in 1914.

Ibrahim, Abu. "Rasā'il Fallāḥ (5)." *Filasṭīn* (Jaffa), 23 Tammuz / July 1911, 2–3.

Idelovitch, David. *Sefer ha-Mishar va-Haroshet ha-Ma'aseh be-Erets Yisrael* [The book of trade and industrial factories in the land of Israel]. Warsaw: Bi-defus Boymriter ve-Gonshor, 1890.

"Ila al-Yahūd al-'Arab wa al-Ṣahyūnyyin." *Al-Quds al-Sharif* (Al-Quds), July 8, 1920.

Irwin, Robert. *The Arabian Nights: A Companion*. London: I. B. Tauris, 2004.

Issa, Rana. "The Arabic Language and Syro-Lebanese National Identity Searching in Buṭrus Al-Bustānī's Muḥīṭ Al-Muḥīṭ." *Journal of Semitic Studies* 62, no. 2 (2017): 465–84.

Jacobson, Abigail. "A City Living through Crisis: Jerusalem during World War I." *British Journal of Middle Eastern Studies* 36, no. 1 (2009): 73–92.

———. *From Empire to Empire: Jerusalem between Ottoman and British Rule*. Syracuse, NY: Syracuse University Press, 2011.

———. "Sephardim, Ashkenazim and the 'Arab Question' in Pre-First World War Palestine: A Reading of Three Zionist Newspapers." *Middle Eastern Studies* 39, no. 2 (2003): 105–30.

Jacobson, Abigail, and Moshe Naor. *Oriental Neighbors: Middle Eastern Jews and Arabs in Mandatory Palestine*. Waltham, MA: Brandeis University Press, 2016.

"Jam'iyyat al-Rābiṭa al-Sharqiyya." *Al-Hilal* 6 (March 1, 1922): 569–70.

Jankowski, James. "Egypt and Early Arab Nationalism, 1908–1922." In *The Origins of Arab Nationalism*, edited by Rashid Khalidi, Lisa Anderson, Muhammad Muslim, and Reeva S. Simon, 243–70. New York: Columbia University Press, 1991.

———. "Egyptian Responses to the Palestine Problem in the Interwar Period." *International Journal of Middle East Studies* 12, no. 1 (1980): 1–38.

Jawhariyyeh, Wāṣif. *The Storyteller of Jerusalem: The Life and Times of Wasif Jawhariyyeh, 1904–1948*. Edited by Salīm Tamārī and Issam Nassar. Translated by Nada Elzeer. Northampton, MA: Olive Branch Press, 2014.

John, Robert St. *Tongue of the Prophets: The Life Story of Eliezer Ben Yehuda*. New York: Doubleday and Company Inc., 1952.

Johnston-Bloom, Ruchama. "Oriental Studies and Jewish Questions: German-Jewish Encounters with Muhammad, the Qur'an, and Islamic Modernities." PhD diss., University of Chicago, 2013.

Kabha, Mustafa, and Nahum Karlinsky. *The Lost Orchard: The Palestinian-Arab Citrus Industry, 1850–1950*. Syracuse, NY: Syracuse University Press, 2021.

Kadman, Noga. *Erased from Space and Consciousness: Israel and the Depopulated Palestinian Villages of 1948*. Translated by Dimi Reider. Bloomington: Indiana University Press, 2015.

Kale, Başak. "Transforming an Empire: The Ottoman Empire's Immigration and Settlement Policies in the Nineteenth and Early Twentieth Centuries." *Middle Eastern Studies* 50, no. 2 (2014): 252–71.

Kalisman, Hilary Falb. *Teachers as State-Builders: Education and the Making of the Modern Middle East*. Princeton, NJ: Princeton University Press, 2022.

Kalmar, Ivan Davidson, and Derek Jonathan Penslar, eds. *Orientalism and the Jews*. Hanover, NH: University Press of New England, 2005.

Kamel, Lorenzo. "The Impact of 'Biblical Orientalism' in Late Nineteenth- and Early Twentieth-Century Palestine." *New Middle Eastern Studies* 4 (2014): 1–15.

Kāmil, Muṣṭafa. *Kitāb al-mas'ala al-sharqiyya* [The book of the Eastern question]. Cairo: Maṭba'at al-Ādāb, 1898.

Kaplony, Andreas. "635/638–1099: The Mosque of Jerusalem (Masjid Bayt al-Maqdis)." In *Where Heaven and Earth Meet: Jerusalem's Sacred Esplanade*, edited by Oleg Grabar and Benjamin Z. Kedar, 100–131. Jerusalem: Yad Ben-Zvi Press, 2009.

Kassan, Shalom. *David Yellin: Ha-Mehanekh ve-ha-Manhig* [David Yellin: Leader and educator]. Jerusalem: Publications of Binai Brith in Israel, 1980.

Katz, Yossi. "'Aliyah ve-hityashvut: Va'adat ha-shemot shel ḲḲ"l u-ḳevi'at shemot ha-yishuvim ha-yehudim be-teḳufat ha-mandeṭ" [Immigration and settlement: The Jewish National Fund Committee and naming Jewish settlements in the Mandate period]. *'iyunim bi-teḳumat yisrael: me'asef li-ve'ayot ha-tsiyonut, ha-yishuv u-medinat yisrael* 9 (1999): 280–315.

———. "Identity, Nationalism, and Placenames: Zionist Efforts to Preserve the Original Local Hebrew Names in Official Publications of the Mandate Government of Palestine." *Names* 43, no. 2 (1995): 103–18.

Katzenelson, Itzhak. *Elef ve-Laylah Eḥad: agadot Mmizraḥiyot la-ne'urim* [A thousand and one nights: Oriental legends for youths]. Varshah: Gitlin, 1921.

Kedourie, Elie. *In the Anglo-Arab Labyrinth: The Mcmahon-Husayn Correspondence and Its Interpretations, 1914–1939*. Cambridge: Cambridge University Press, 1976.

Kemp, Adriana. "'Dangerous Populations': State Territoriality and the Constitution of National Minorities." In *Boundaries and Belonging: States and Societies in the Struggle to Shape Identities and Local Practices*, edited by Joel S. Migdal, 73–98. Cambridge: Cambridge University Press, 2004.

Keren, Ben-Zion. *Israel Belkind: Educator and Dreamer*. Jerusalem: Institute of Contemporary Jewry, Hebrew University of Jerusalem, 1980.

Khalidi, Rashid. *The Hundred Years' War on Palestine: A History of Settler Colonialism and Resistance, 1917–2017*. New York: Metropolitan Books, 2020.

———. *The Iron Cage: The Story of the Palestinian Struggle for Statehood*. Boston: Beacon Press, 2007.

Khazzoom, Aziza. "The Great Chain of Orientalism: Jewish Identity, Stigma Management, and Ethnic Exclusion in Israel." *American Sociological Review* 68, no. 4 (2003): 481–510.

"Khiṭāb al-Khawaja Yalīn 'Amām Lajnat al-Burāq." *Al-Ṣirāt al-Mustaqīm*, August 14, 1930.

Khulusi, Safa. "Ma'ruf Al-Rusafi in Jerusalem." *Jerusalem Quarterly* 22–23 (2005).

Kimmerling, Baruch. *The Invention and Decline of Israeliness: Society, Culture and Military*. Berkeley: University of California Press, 2001.

———. *Zionism and Territory: The Socio-Territorial Dimensions of Zionist Politics*. Berkeley: Institute of International Studies, University of California, 1983.

Ḳiryat Sefer: Riva'on l-bibliografyah shel beit ha-sefarim ha-le'umi ve-ha-'universita'i be-Yerushalayim [Ḳiryat Sefer: Bibliographic quarterly of the Jewish national and university library]. Vol. 24. Jerusalem: Hebrew University Press Association, 1947–48.

Klein, Menachem. *Lives in Common: Arabs and Jews in Jerusalem, Jaffa and Hebron.* Translated by Haim Watzman. London: Hurst & Company, 2014.

Klein, Samuel, Joseph Klausner, and Naḥum Slouschz. "Le-Yuvalo shel mar David Yellin" [The jubilee of Mr. David Yellin]. *Bulletin of the Jewish Palestine Exploration Society* 1, no. 2 (1933): 1–4.

Knar, Naḥamah. "Nitsige ha-sefardim ve-yehude ha-mizraḥ ba-asifat ha-nivḥarim ha-reshonah shel ha-yishuv ha-yehudi be-erets yisrael ve-ha-va'ad ha-le'umi." MA thesis, Hebrew University, 2004.

Kohen, Moshe. "First a Jerusalemite." *Jerusalem Post*, September 26, 1969.

Koplewitz, Immanuel. "Arabic in Israel: The Sociolinguistic Situation of Israel's Arab Minority." *International Journal of the Sociology of Language* 1992, no. 98 (1992): 29–66.

Krämer, Gudrun. *A History of Palestine: From the Ottoman Conquest to the Founding of the State of Israel.* Translated by Graham Harman and Gudrun Krämer. Princeton, NJ: Princeton University Press, 2008.

Krauss, Samuel. Review of *Erets Yisrael u-shekhenoteha: Entsiḳlopedyah ge'ografit-hisṭorit le-Erets Yisrael, Suriyah ya-ḥatsi ha-'i Sinai. Zeitschrift des Deutschen Palästina-Vereins (1878–1945)* 46, no. 3–4 (1923): 228–31.

Kressel, Getzel. *Erets Yisrael ve-toldoteha: madrikh bibliografi, ha-sifrut ha-'ivrit 'al Erets Yisrael* [The land of Israel and its history: A bibliographic guide]. Tel Aviv: Makhon Mazkeret, 1980.

———. "Sokolow, Naḥum." In *Encyclopaedia Judaica*, edited by Michael Berenbaum and Fred Skolnik, 747–49. Detroit: Macmillan Reference USA, 2007.

Lacquer, Walter. *The History of Zionism.* New York: Holt, Rinehart, and Winston, 2003.

Landau, Jacob M. "Hebrew and Arabic in the State of Israel: Political Aspects of the Language Issue." *International Journal of the Sociology of Language* 67 (1987): 117–33.

Lane, Edward William. *The Arabian Nights' Entertainments.* Boston: Little, Brown and Company, 1853.

Lang, Yoseph. *Daber 'ivrit!: Haye Eliezer Ben-Yehuda* [Speak Hebrew! The life of Eliezer Ben-Yehuda]. Vol. 1. Jerusalem: Yad Yitsḥaḳ Ben-Tsevi, 2008.

Laqueur, Walter, and Barry M. Rubin. *The Israel-Arab Reader: A Documentary History of the Middle East Conflict.* 7th ed. New York: Penguin Books, 2008.

Lasḳov, Shulamit. *Ha-Biluyim* [The Biluim]. Edited by Reuven Eshel. Jerusalem: Ha-Sifriyah ha-Tsiyonit, 1979.

Lederhendler, Eli. *The Road to Modern Jewish Politics: Political Tradition and Political Reconstruction in the Jewish Community of Tsarist Russia.* New York: Oxford University Press, 1989.

Le Strange, Guy. *Palestine under the Moslems: A Description of Syria and the Holy Land from A. D. 650 to 1500.* London: Committee of the Palestine Exploration Fund, 1890.

Lev, Efraim. "Reconstructed *materia medica* of the Medieval and Ottoman Al-Sham." *Journal of Ethnopharmacology* 80, no. 2–3 (May 2002): 167–79.

Levy, Amit. "Conflicting German Orientalism: Zionist Arabists and Arab Scholars, 1926–1938." *British Journal of Middle Eastern Studies* (2022).

Levy, Lital. "Historicizing the Concept of Arab Jews in the 'Mashriq.'" *Jewish Quarterly Review* 98, no. 4 (2008): 452–69.

———. "Jewish Writers in the Arab East: Literature, History, and the Politics of Enlightenment, 1863–1914." PhD diss., University of California at Berkeley, 2007.

———. "The Nahḍa and the Haskala: A Comparative Reading of 'Revival' and 'Reform.'" *Middle Eastern Literatures* 16, no. 3 (2013): 300–316.

Lieberman, Haim. "Tirgum Yidi bilti Yadu' shel Sefer Elef Laylah va-Laylah." *Alei Sefer: Studies in Bibliography and in the History of the Printed and the Digital Hebrew Book* (1977): 156–62.

Little, Donald P. "Mujīr Al-Dīn Al-'Ulaymī's Vision of Jerusalem in the Ninth/Fifteenth Century." *Journal of the American Oriental Society* 115, no. 2 (1995): 237–47.

Littmann, Enno. "Alf Laila wa-Laila." In *The Encyclopedia of Islam: New Edition*, edited by H. A. R. Gibb, J. H. Kramers, E. Levi-Provencal, and J. Schacht. Leiden: Brill, 1960.

"Lo tihenah shtey leshonot rishmiyot ba-Medinah." *Ha-Mashkif*, September 10, 1948.

Lunts, Avraham Moshe. *Kotel ha-ma'aravi shel har bet Elohenu: mehuto, tekhunato, ve-zikhronotav* [The Western Wall of our God's Temple Mount: Its essence, features, and memories]. Jerusalem, 1912.

———. "Matsav ha-arets bekhlal" [The general state of the land]. *Yerushalayim* 2 (1887): 168–81.

———. "Mavo" [Introduction]. *Yerushalayim* 1 (1882).

Magness, Jodi. *Jerusalem through the Ages: From Its Beginnings to the Crusades.* New York: Oxford University Press, 2024.

Mahdi, Muhsin. *The Arabian Nights.* New York: W. W. Norton and Company, 2010.

———. *The Thousand and One Nights.* Leiden: Brill, 1995.

Makdisi, Saree, and Felicity Nussbaum. *The Arabian Nights in Historical Context: Between East and West.* Oxford: Oxford University Press, 2008.

Makdisi, Ussama. *Age of Coexistence: The Ecumenical Frame and the Making of the Modern Arab World.* Berkeley, CA: University of California Press, 2019.

Maman, Aaron. *Comparative Semitic Philology in the Middle Ages: From Sa'adiah Gaon to Ibn Barūn (10th–12th c.).* Leiden: Brill, 2004.

Mandel, Neville J. *The Arabs and Zionism before World War I.* Berkeley: University of California Press, 1976.

Manor, Dory. "Aba sheli hayah mizraḥ u-Ma'rav bo-zemanit: Siḥah 'im ha-Nasi Reuven (Rubi) Rivlin" ["My father was both East and West simultaneously": A conversation with president Reuven (Ruby) Rivlin]. *Ho: Literary Magazine* 16 (2018): 13–18.

Marchand, Suzanne L. *German Orientalism in the Age of Empire: Religion, Race, and Scholarship.* Washington, DC: Cambridge University Press, 2009.

Markovitzki, Yaakov. *Be-khaf ha-kela' shel ha-ne'emanuyot: Bene ha-yishuv ba-tsava ha-Turḳi, 1908–1918* [Conflicts of loyalities: The enlistment of Palestinian Jews in the Turkish Army]. Ramat Ef'al: Ha-Merkaz le-Toldot Koaḥ ha-Magen ha-Haganah 'al shem Yisra'el Gelili, 1995.

Marks, Richard G. "Hinduism, Torah, and Travel: Jacob Sapir in India." *Shofar* 30, no. 2 (2012): 26–51.

Marlow, Louise "Among Kings and Sages: Greek and Indian Wisdom in an Arabic Mirror for Princes," *Arabica* 60, no. 1–2 (2013): 1–57.

Masalha, Nur. "Settler-Colonialism, Memoricide and Indigenous Toponymic Memory: The Appropriation of Palestinian Place Names by the Israeli State." *Journal of Holy Land and Palestine Studies* 14, no. 1 (2015): 3–57.

Mayer, Thomas. *Egypt and the Palestine Question, 1936–1945.* Berlin: K. Schwarz Verlag, 1983.

Mazza, Roberto. "The Deal of the Century? The Attempted Sale of the Western Wall by Cemal Pasha in 1916." *Middle East Studies* 57, no. 5 (2021): 696–711.

———. *Jerusalem: From the Ottomans to the British*. London: Tauris Academic Studies, 2009.

Meirovitch, Menashe. *'Etsah ve-tushiyah, o, hatsa'ah 'al devar maṭa' keramim ve-gidul gefanim be-Erets Yisrael* [Help and initiative: An offer about planting vineyards in Erets Yisrael]. Warsaw: Hayyim Kelter, 1885.

———. *Ḥevle teḥiyah: ḳovets ma'amarim nivḥarim bi-she'elot ha-yishuv ha-'ivri be-Erets Yisrael mili-fene 50 shanah ṿe-'ad perots milḥemet ha-'olam* [Pains of rejuvenation]. Edited by Yitsḥaḳ Avinery. Tel Aviv: Ḥevrat Misḥar ṿe-Ta'asiyah, 1931.

———. *Me-Bilu 'ad ya'pilū: 'al shishim ve-ḥamesh shenot he'avḳūt 'aliyah, binyan, vi-yetsirah* [Sixty-five years of struggle with immigration, building, and creation]. Edited by Yitsḥaḳ Sela'. Rishon Le-Zion: Hotsa'at ha-Teḥiyah, 1946.

———. *Me-ha-shevil el ha-derekh: kovets ma'amarim u-mikhtavim bi-she'elot ha-yishuv ha-'ivri be-Erets Yisrael* [From the trail to the road: A collection of essays and letters regarding the Hebrew settlement in the land of Israel]. Tel Aviv: Be-hotsa'at ḥevrat shṭibel ṿe-ḥever yedide ha-meḥaber, 1936.

———. "Menashe Meirovitch: aḥaron ha-biluyim ben 85." *Ha-mashkif*, June 13, 1945, 2.

———. *Mi-zikhronotav shel aḥaron ha-Biluyim* [From the memoirs of the last of Bilu members]. Jerusalem: Ha-ḳeren ha-ḳayemet le-yisrael, 1946.

———. "Tsimḥe erets ha-tsevi." *Yerushalayim* 4 (1892): 125–36.

———. "Tsimḥe erets ha-tsevi: yikhlol matsav kol ha-tsemaḥim ve-ha-neṭi'ot ha-mo'ilim asher be-erets Paleshet ve-suryah, ofen ve-seder neṭi'atam ve-to'eletam" [The Flora of the Land of Gazelles]. *Yerushalayim* 3 (1888): 177–200.

Meitlis, Ofra. *Be-derekh ha-emtsa': David Yellin—sipur ḥayim* [On the middle path: David Yellin—a life story]. Tel Aviv: Tel Aviv University Press, 2015.

Mendel, Yonatan. *The Creation of Israeli Arabic: Political and Security Considerations in the Making of Arabic Language Studies in Israel*. Hampshire: Palgrave Macmillan, 2014.

Meyuḥas, Yosef. "Mishle moreshet yildey 'Arav." *Do'ar ha-Yom*, September 13, 1935.

Moreh, Shmuel. "Oriental Literature." In *Encyclopaedia Judaica*, 15:471–74. Jerusalem: Keter Publishing, 1973.

Muslih, Muhammad Y. *The Origins of Palestinian Nationalism*. New York: Columbia University Press, 1988.

Nadan, Amos. *The Palestinian Peasant Economy under the Mandate: A Story of Colonial Bungling*. Cambridge, MA: Harvard University Press, 2006.

Natronai, Berechiah ben. *Fables of a Jewish Aesop* [Mishle shu'alim]. Translated by Moses Hadas. New York: Columbia University Press, 1967.

Natronai, Berekhiah ben. *Mishle Sshu'alim* [Fox fables]. Jerusalem: Hirsch Zuckermann, 1919.

Noy, Amos. *'Edim o mumḥim: Yehudim maskilim bene Yerushalayim ve-ha-mizraḥ bi-teḥilat ha-me'ah ha-'isrim* [Experts or witnesses: Jewish intelligentsia from Jerusalem and the Levant in the beginning of the 20th century]. Tel Aviv: Resling, 2017.

Oppenheimer, Yochai. *Me'ever lagader: ytsug ha-'Aravim ba-sipuret ha-'ivriyt v-ha-yisraelit, 1906–2005*. [Barriers: The representation of the Arab in Hebrew and Israeli fiction, 1906–2005]. Tel Aviv: 'Am 'oved, 2008.

Or, Iair G. *Bor'im signon le-dor: ha-emunot ve-ha-ide'ologyot shel metakhnene ha-lashon ha-'ivrit be-Erets Yisrael* [Creating a style for a generation: The beliefs and ideologies of Hebrew language planners]. Tel Aviv: Hidkel, 2016.

Parry, Jonathan. *Promised Lands: The British and the Ottoman Middle East.* Princeton, NJ: Princeton University Press, 2022.

Péaud, Laura. "Relire la géographie de Conrad Malte-Brun." *Annales de géographie* 701, no. 1 (2015): 99–122.

Peled, Alisa Rubin. *Debating Islam in the Jewish State: The Development of Policy toward Islamic Institutions in Israel.* Albany: SUNY Press, 2001.

Peleg, Yaron. *Orientalism and the Hebrew Imagination.* Ithaca, NY: Cornell University Press, 2005.

Penimi. "Bifnim Ha-Arets." *Ha-Po'el Ha-Tza'ir* (Jerusalem), July 29, 1909, 16.

Penslar, Derek. *Theodor Herzl: The Charismatic Leader.* New Haven, CT: Yale University Press, 2020.

———. *Zionism and Technocracy: The Engineering of Jewish Settlement in Palestine, 1870–1918.* Bloomington: Indiana University Press, 1991.

———. "Zionism, Colonialism and Postcolonialism." *Journal of Israeli History* 20, no. 2–3 (June 1, 2001): 84–98.

Petersen, Andrew, Marcus Milwright, Heather Nixon, and Peter Leach. *A Gazetteer of Buildings in Muslim Palestine: Part 1.* Jerusalem: Council for British Research in the Levant, 2001.

Piamenta, Moshe. "Hashpa'at Ha-'Aravit 'al ḥidushe Ben-Yehuda." *Leshonenu la-'am* 12 (1961): 150–58.

Polley, Gabriel. *Palestine in the Victorian Age: Colonial Encounters in the Holy Land.* London: I. B. Tauris, 2022.

Porath, Yehoshua. *The Emergence of the Palestinian-Arab National Movement, 1918–1929.* 2 vols. London: Frank Cass, 1974.

Potenza, Daniela. "Alfred Farağ's Arabian Nights: Ongoing Experimentation in Arabic Theatre." In *The Thousand and One Nights: Sources and Transformations in Literature, Art, and Science*, edited by Ibrahim Akel and William Granara, 198–215. Leiden: Brill, 2020.

Press, Yeshayahu. *Erets-Yisrael: Entsiḳlopedyah topografit-hisṭorit* [The land of Israel: Topographical-historical encyclopedia]. 2nd ed. Jerusalem: Hots'at R. Mas, 1951.

———. "Ha-yishuv ha-Yehudi bi-Yerushalayim ba-me'ah ha-tesha' 'isreh" [The Jewish settlement in Jerusalem in the nineteenth century]. *Report (World Congress of Jewish Studies)* 1 (1947): 427–33.

———. *Me'ah shanah be-Yerushalaiym: me-zikhronot 'ish Yerushalaiym* [A hundred years of Jerusalem: Memories of a Jerusalemite man]. Jerusalem: Rubin Mass, 1964.

Provence, Michael. *The Last Ottoman Generation and the Making of the Modern Middle East.* Cambridge: Cambridge University Press, 2017.

Rabbih, Ibn 'Abd. *Al-'iqd al-farīd* [The unique necklace]. Vol. 3. Beirut: Dār al-Kutub al-'ilmiyya, 1981.

Raz-Krakotzkin, Amnon. "Orientalism, Jewish Studies, and the Israeli Society: Several Observations." *Jama'ah* 3, no. 1 (1999): 34–61.

Regan, Bernard. *The Balfour Declaration: Empire, the Mandate and Resistance in Palestine.* London: Verso, 2017.

Reimer, Michael J. "Contradiction and Consciousness in 'Ali Mubarak's Description of Al-Azhar." *International Journal of Middle East Studies* 29, no. 1 (1997): 53–69.

Retso, Jan. *The Arabs in Antiquity: Their History from the Assyrians to the Umayyads.* London: Routledge, 2013.

Rivlin, Benjamin. "Rivlin, Joseph Joel." In *Encyclopaedia Judaica*, edited by Michael Berenbaum and Fred Skolnik. Vol. 17. Jerusalem: Keter Publishing, 2007.

Rivlin, Yosef Yo'el, ed. *Al-ḳuran* [The Quran]. Tel Aviv: Devir, 1936.

———. "Beit Hashem be-me'arbolet." *Hed ha-Mizraḥ*, June 2, 1950.

———. "Beit Hashem bi-me'arbolet." *Had ha-Mizraḥ*, 3 February 3, 1950.

———. *Elef Laylah va-Laylah* [One thousand and one nights]. Vol. 1. Jerusalem: Ḳeryat Sefer, 1947.

———. "Ha-mizraḥ be-yetsirotav shel Ḥaim Naḥman Bialik." *Hed ha-Mizraḥ*, July 14, 1944.

———. "Hora'at ha-Safah ha-'Aravit be-Batey ha-Sefer ha-Yehudim be-Erets Yisrael." In *Sedeh Ilan 2: Sefer Zikaron Le-Aryeh Ilan*. Jerusalem, 1967.

Robinson, Shira. *Citizen Strangers: Palestinians and the Birth of Israel's Liberal Settler State.* Stanford, CA: Stanford University Press, 2013.

Robson, Laura. *Colonialism and Christianity in Mandate Palestine.* Austin: University of Texas Press, 2011.

Roded, Ruth. "A Voice in the Wilderness? Rivlin's 1932 Hebrew Life of Muhammad." *Middle East Critique* 18, no. 1 (2009): 39–59.

Rosén, Haiim B. *A Textbook of Israeli Hebrew: With an Introduction to the Classical Language.* Chicago: University of Chicago Press, 1966.

Rosenzweig, Franz. *Ninety-Two Poems and Hymns of Yehuda Halevi.* Albany: SUNY Press, 2012.

Sabbagh-Khoury, Areej. *Colonizing Palestine: The Zionist Left and the Making of the Palestinian Nakba.* Stanford, CA: Stanford University Press, 2023.

Said, Edward W. *Orientalism.* New York: Vintage Books, 1978.

Salmon, Yosef. *Religion and Zionism: First Encounters.* Jerusalem: Hebrew University Magnes Press, 2002.

Samsonov, Gil. *Netanyahu and Likud's Leaders: The Israeli Princes.* Translated by Kaeren Fish. Abingdon, UK: Routledge, 2020.

Sapir, Eliyahu. *Ha-Arets* [The land]. Jaffa: Hotsa'at Ḳohelet, 1911.

———. "Harḥavat sefatenu ve-ha-'Aravit" [The enlargement of Hebrew and the issue of Arabic]. *Haschiloah: Litterarisch-wissenschaftliche Monatsschrift* 4 (1898): 328–35.

———. "Ha-sin'ah le-Yisrael ba-sifrut ha-'Aravit" [Israel hatred in Arabic literature]. *Ha-Schiloah* 6 (1899): 222–32.

———. *Ḳovets mi-kitve Eliyahu Sapir* [A collection of Eliyahu Sapir's writings]. Jaffa: Hotsa'at ḥevrat Anglo-Palestinah, 1913.

———. "Tsimḥe Erets Yisrael" [Plants of the land of Israel]. *Ha-ḥinukh: 'Itun Pedagugi la-Morim ve-la-Horim* 1, no. 4–5 (1911): 342–56.

Saposnik, Arieh Bruce. *Becoming Hebrew: The Creation of a Jewish National Culture in Ottoman Palestine.* New York: Oxford University Press, 2008.

———. "Europe and Its Orients in Zionist Culture before the First World War." *Historical Journal* 49, no. 4 (2006): 1105–23.

Schama, Simon. *Landscape and Memory.* New York: Alfred A. Knopf, 1995.

Schayegh, Cyrus. *The Middle East and the Making of the Modern World.* Cambridge, MA: Harvard University Press, 2017.

Scheindlin, Raymond P. "Merchants and Intellectuals, Rabbis and Poets: Judeo-Arabic Culture in the Golden Age of Islam." In *Cultures of the Jews*, edited by David Biale, 313–86. New York: Schocken Books, 2002.

Schneider, Suzanne. *Mandatory Separation: Religion, Education, and Mass Politics in Palestine.* Stanford, CA: Stanford University Press, 2018.

———. "Monolingualism and Education in Mandate Palestine." *Jerusalem Quarterly File* 52 (2013): 68–74.

Schölch, Alexander. *Palestine in Transformation, 1856–1882: Studies in Social, Economic, and Political Development.* Washington, DC: Institute for Palestine Studies, 1993.

Schorsch, Ismar. "The Myth of Sephardic Supremacy." *Leo Baeck Institute Year Book* 34, no. 1 (1989): 47–66.

Schwarz, Joseph. *Tevo'ot ha-arets* [All the produce of the land]. Edited by Abraham Moshe Lunts. Jerusalem: Abraham Moshe Lunts, 1880.

Segev, Tom. *One Palestine Complete: Jews and Arabs under the British Mandate.* New York: Henry Holt and Company, 2000.

Sellheim, Rudolf. *Die Klassisch-Arabischen Sprichwörtersammlungen: Insbesondere die des Abu 'Ubaid.* The Hague: Mouton, 1954.

———. *Kitāb al- 'Amthāl al-'Arabiyya al-Qadīma* [The book of old Arabic proverbs]. Translated by Ramaḍān 'Abd al-Tawwāb. Beirut: Mu'assasat al-Risāla, 1971.

Sellheim, R., G. M. Wickens, P. N. Boratav, J. A. Haywood, and J. Knappert. "Mathal." In *Encyclopaedia of Islam*, edited by Th. Bianquis P. Bearman, C. E. Bosworth, E. van Donzel, and W. P. Heinrichs. Leiden: Brill, 2012. doi.org/10.1163/1573-3912_islam_COM_0707.

Shafir, Gershon. *Land, Labor and the Origins of the Israeli-Palestinian Conflict, 1882–1914.* Berkeley: University of California Press, 1996.

———. "Settler Citizenship in the Jewish Colonization of Palestine." In *Settler Colonialism in the Twentieth Century: Projects, Practices, Legacies*, edited by Caroline Elkins and Susan Pedersen, 41–57. London: Routledge, 2005.

———. "Zionism and Colonialism: A Comparative Approach." In *The Israel/Palestine Question*, edited by Ilan Pappé, 72–85. London: Routledge, 1999.

Shapira, Anita. "The Fashioning of the 'New Jew' in the Yishuv Society." *Major Changes within the Jewish People in the Wake of the Holocaust*, edited by Yisrael Gutman and Avital Saf, 427–41. Jerusalem: Yad Vashem, 1996.

———. "Hirbet Hizah: Between Remembrance and Forgetting." *Jewish Social Studies* 7, no. 1 (2000): 1–62.

———. *Israel: A History.* Waltham, MA: Brandeis University Press, 2012.

———. *Land and Power: The Zionist Resort to Force, 1881–1948.* New York: Oxford University Press, 1992.

Shapiro, Joseph. *Me'ah Shanah Miḳveh-Yisrael: 630–730, 1870–1970* [A century of Miḳveh-Yisrael]. Tel-Aviv: Tarbut ṿe-ḥinukh, 1970.

Sharon, Moshe. *Corpus Inscriptionum Arabicarum Palaestinae.* Vol. 3. Leiden: Brill, 2004.

Sheehi, Stephen. *Foundations of Modern Arab Identity.* Gainesville: University Press of Florida, 2004.

Sheila, Margalit. "Milḥemet ha-Safot Ke-Tenu'a 'amamit." *Katedrah* 74 (1994): 87–119.

Sheltiel, Eli. *Pinhas Rutenberg: 'alyato u-nefilato shel "ish hazak" be-Erets Yisrael, 1879–1942* [Pinhas Rutenberg: The rise and fall of a strongman in the land of Israel, 1879–1942]. Tel Aviv: 'am 'oved, 1990.

Shenhav, Yehudah. *Ha-Tsiyonut Ve-Ha-Imperyot* [Zionism and empires]. Jerusalem: Hotsa'at ha-Ḳibuts ha-me'uḥad, 2015.

Shumsky, Dmitry. *Beyond the Nation-State: The Zionist Political Imagination from Pinsker to Ben-Gurion.* New Haven, CT: Yale University Press, 2018.

Shuqayr, Na'ūm. *Amthāl al-'awām fī Miṣr wa al-Sūdān wa al-Shām* [Proverbs of the common people in Egypt, Sudan, and al-Sham]. Edited by Muḥammad Ibrāhīm Abū Salīm. Beirut: Dār al-Jīl, 1995.

Ṣib'a, Nissim. "Aḥmad Zaki Pasha wa al-ṣuhyūniyya." *Filasṭīn* (Jaffa), November 7, 1922.

Sinanoglou, Penny. *Partitioning Palestine: British Policymaking at the End of Empire.* Chicago: University of Chicago Press, 2019.

Siton, David. "'Al tirgumav me-'Aravit." *Hed ha-Mizraḥ* (Jerusalem), December 23, 1949.

Sivan, Emanuel. "The Beginnings of the 'Fada'il al Quds' Literature." *Der Islam; Zeitschrift für Geschichte und Kultur des Islamischen Orients* 48 (1972): 100–101.

Slutsky, Yehuda. "Menashe Meirovitch." In *Ha-'Entsayklopedyah ha-'Ivrit; Kelalit, Yehudit ve-Eretsyisraelit*, 75–76. 1970.

Slutsky, Yehuda, and Benzion Dinur. "Yellin." In *Encyclopaedia Judaica*, edited by Michael Berenbaum and Fred Skolnik, 300–301. Detroit: Macmillan Reference USA, 2007.

Smilansky, Moshe, and Aryeh Samsonov. *Ha-dorkhim ba-gat: gefen ve-yayin be-Yisrael* [Walkers on wine press: Grapevine and wine in Israel]. 1957.

Smith, Anthony. "'The Land and Its People': Reflections on Artistic Identification in an Age of Nations and Nationalism." *Nations and Nationalism* 19, no. 1 (2013): 87–106.

Sokolow, Naḥum. *Erets Ḥemdah: Kolel Yedi'at Gelilot Erets ha-Ḳodesh 'al pi Gedole ha-Tayarim u-vo-gam Tamtsit Sefer ha-Masa' shel ha-Sar ha-Angli Laurence Oliphant* [A desirable land]. Warsaw: Bi-defus Yitsḥaḳ Goldman, 1885.

Soravia, Bruna. "Arabic Bibliographies." In *Encyclopaedia of Islam*, edited by Kate Fleet, Gudrun Krämer, Denis Matringe, John Nawas, and Everett Rowson. Third, 2015.

Sorek, Tamir. *Palestinian Commemoration in Israel: Calendars, Monuments, and Martyrs.* Stanford, CA: Stanford University Press, 2015.

Spencer, Scoville. "Translating Orientalism into the Arabic 'Nahda.'" *Alif: Journal of Comparative Poetics* 38 (January 1, 2018): 11–36.

Spolsky, Bernard, and Elana Goldberg Shohamy. *The Languages of Israel: Policy, Ideology, and Practice.* Clevedon, UK: Multilingual Matters, 1999.

Stein, Kenneth W. *The Land Question in Palestine, 1917–1939.* Chapel Hill: University of North Carolina Press, 1984.

Szekely, Yaffa. "Deyoḳno shel ha-Moreh ha-'Ivri be-Moshavot ha-'aliyah ha-reshonah 1881–1904" [The character of the teachers in the First Aliya colonies, 1881–1904]. *Cathedra: For the History of Eretz Israel and Its Yishuv* 84 (1997): 143–74.

Ṭahṭawī, Rifa'a Rāfi'. *Al-Kanz al-Mukhtār fī iktishāf al- 'aradī w-al-fiḥār* [The fine treasure in the discovery of land and sea]. 1833.

Tamari, Salim. "Jerusalem's Ottoman Modernity: The Times and Lives of Wasif Jawhariyyeh." *Jerusalem Quarterly File* 9 (2000): 27.

———. *Mountain against the Sea: Essays on Palestinian Society and Culture.* Berkeley: University of California Press, 2009.

———. *Year of the Locust: A Soldier's Diary and the Erasure of Palestine's Ottoman Past.* Berkeley: University of California Press, 2015.

———. "Wasif Jawhariyyeh, Popular Music, and Early Modernity in Jerusalem." In *Palestine, Israel, and the Politics of Popular Culture*, edited by Rebecca L. Stein and Ted Swedenburg, 27–50. Durham, NC: Duke University Press, 2005.

Tawfiq, Canaan. "Plant-Lore in Palestinian Superstition." *Jerusalem Quarterly* 24 (2005): 57–64.

"Tirgum Ḥadash shel agadot 'Arav." *Ha-arets*, July 18, 1947.

Tzoreff, Avi-Ram. "Beyond the Boundaries of 'The Land of the Deer': R. Binyamin between Jewish and Arab Geographies, and the Critique of the Zionist-Colonial Connection." *Jerusalem Quarterly* 82 (2020): 130–53.

———. "Reading the Arabian Nights in Modern Hebrew Literature: Judaism, Arabness and the City." *Philological Encounters* 5, no. 2 (2020): 223–53.

Veit, Raphaela. "Greek Roots, Arab Authoring, Latin Overlay: Reflections on the Sources for Avicenna's Canon." In *Vehicles of Transmission, Translation, and Transformation in Medieval Textual Culture*, edited by Robert Wisnovsky, Faith Wallis, Jamie C. Fumo, and Carlos Fraenkel. Turnhout, Belgium: Brepols Publishers, 2011.

Veracini, Lorenzo. *Israel and Settler Society.* London: Pluto Press, 2006.

———. "The Other Shift: Settler Colonialism, Israel, and the Occupation." *Journal of Palestine Studies* 42, no. 2 (2013): 26–42.

Vilnai, Ze'ev. "'Araviye Tsafa u-sefatam." *Mizraḥ u-Ma'arav* 3, no. 7 (1929).

Wexler, Paul. *The Schizoid Nature of Modern Hebrew: A Slavic Language in Search of a Semitic Past.* 4 vols. Wiesbaden: Otto Harrassowitz, 1990.

Wolfe, Patrick. "Settler Colonialism and the Elimination of the Native." *Journal of Genocide Research* 8, no. 4 (2006): 387–409.

Yaari, Abraham. *Masa'ot Erets-Yisrael.* [Voyages to the land of Israel]. Ramat Gan: Hotsa'at Masadah, 1976.

Yahuda, A. S. "Ḥalifat mikhtavim 'im Tschernichovsky 'al ha-shirah ha-'Aravit." In *'Erev ve-'Arav: 'osef miḥḳarim u-ma'amarim, shirat ha-'Aravim, zikhronot u-reshamim*, edited by A. S. Yahuda. New York: Shulsinger Bros., 1946.

———. "Nedive ve-gibure 'Arav." In *'Ever ve-'Arav*, edited by A. S. Yahuda. New York: Shlusinger Bros., 1946.

Yahuda, Abraham Shalom. *Ḳadmoniyot ha-'Arvim: bi-yeme ha-ba'arut asher li-fene Muḥammad.* [The antiquities of the Arabs]. Jerusalem, 1894.

———. "Nedive ve-gibure 'Arav" [Arab noblemen and heroes]. *Luaḥ Erets Yisrael* 2 (1896): 89–119.

———. "To'elet leshonot 'Arav le-havanat ha-Miḳra." *Zikhronot Va'ad ha-Lashon* 6 (1911): 19–23.

Yahuda, Isaac. "Binah ba-Miḳra." *Yerushalayim* 6, no. 3 (1903): 261–62.

———. "Kotel Ha-Ma'Aravi." *Zion: Me'asef ha-ḥevra ha-Erets-Yisraelit le-hisṭoryah ve-etnografyah* 3 (1929): 95–163.

———. *Mishle 'Arav: asufat mivḥar mishle bene ḳedem* [Proverbia Arabica: A collection of the sons of the Orient's proverbs]. Edited by Isaac Benjamin S. E. Yahuda. 3 vols. Jerusalem: Ha-ḥivrah ha-Erets Yisraelit le-hisṭorya ve-ithnographia, 1932.

Yahuda, Isaac Benjamin S. E. *Ha-Kotel ha-Ma'aravi: Ma'amar maḳif 'al kotlenu zeh, ma she ne'emar 'alav, u-mah she dubar bo, mi-yeme ha-ḥurban 'ad ha-yom hazeh 'im mavo ve-hashmatot* [The Western Wall: A comprehensive essay on our wall]. Jerusalem: Y. A. Weiss, 1929.

"Yedi'at Sefarim: Miḳra le-yelde bene Yisrael." *Ha-Magid*, June 13, 1889.

Yehezkiel, Abraham Shalom Le-Beit. "To'elet Lashon 'Aravit." *Ha-Melits* (Petersburg), September 11, 1894.

———. "To'elet Lashon 'Aravit." *Ha-Melits* (Petersburg), September 14, 1894, 7.

Yellin, David. *Al-Yahūd wa-Hā'iṭ al-Mabka (al-Burāq)* [Jews and the Wailing Wall (al-Burāq)]. Al-Quds: Maṭba'at Malūl, 1930.

———. *Ha-Melekh 'Umar al-No'man u-vanav: Me-sipure Elef laylah va-laylah* [The king 'Umar al-Nu'man and his sons: From the tales of one thousand and one nights]. Vol. 2. Tel Aviv: Devir, 1937.

———. "Hagadot ve-sipurim." *Ha-Tsvi* (Jerusalem), 1884.

———. *Ha-mivṭa ve-ha-ketiv be-'Ivrit: hartsa'ah ba-asefah ha-kelalit ha-shenit le-agudat ha-morim be-Erets Yisrael she-hayetah be-moshavat Gederah be-Elul 664* [The accent and writing in Hebrew]. Jerusalem: Lunts, 1904.

———. *Kitve David Yellin: yerushalayim shel temol.* [The writings of David Yellin: The Jerusalem of yesterday (letters from Jerusalem to "Hamelitz," 1896–1904)]. Edited by Benyamin Rivlin. Vol. 1. Jerusalem: Ha-Ṿa'ad le-Hotsa'at Kitve Daṿid Yellin, Hotsa'at Rubin Mass, 1972.

———. "Melitsat Yisrael 'al adamat yishma'el" [The oratory of Israel on the soil of Ishmael]." *Yerushalayim* (1891): 37–48.

———. "Melitsat Yisrael 'al adamat Yishma'el." In *Kitve David Yellin: leḥeḳer ha-shirah ha-'Ivrit be-Sefarad*, edited by A. M. Habermann, 1–12. Jerusalem: Committee for Republication of David Yellin's Writings, 1975.

———. *Mi-Dan ve-'ad Be'er Sheva'* [From Dan to Beer Sheva]. Edited by Avraham Ḥayim Elḥanani. Jerusalem: Ha-Va'ad li-Hotsaat Kitve David Yellin, 1973.

———. "Mikhtav Mr. David Yellin El 'Orekh Ha-Ṣābaḥ." *Ha-arets* (Jerusalem), December 4, 1921.

———. *Miḳra le-na're bene Yisrael* [Reading for the youth of the children of Israel]. Jerusalem, 1889.

———. *Rabenu Mosheh Ben Maymun* [Our master Moses Maimonides]. Warsaw: Toshyah, 1898.

———. "The Renaissance of the Hebrew Language in Palestine." In *Zionist Work in Palestine*, edited by Israel Cohen, 143–56. New York: Judaean Publishing Company, 1912.

———. *Sipure Elef Laylah va-Laylah* [The thousand and one nights]. Vol. 1. Odessa: Turgman, 1912.

———. "Yerushalayim li-fnay arba' Me'ot shanah." *Ha-Pardes* 2 (1894): 157–72.

Yellin, David, and Israel Abrahams. *Maimonides*. Philadelphia: Jewish Publication Society of America Philadelphia, 1903.

Zaki Pasha, Aḥmad. "Al-ṣakhra al-muqaddasa fī al-masjid al-ḥarām" [The sacred rock in Al-Aqsa Mosque]. *Al-Ma'rifa al-Miṣriyya* 2 (1931): 165–76.

———. *Taṣḥīḥ al-Aghlaṭ al-Wārida fī Difā' al-Ustādh Yalīn al-Muḥāmī 'an al-Yahūd* [Correcting errors occurred in the defense of Mr. Yellin the defender of Jews]. Al-Quds: Dār al-Aytām al-Islāmiyya, 1930.

Zank, Michael. *Jerusalem: A Brief History.* Hoboken, NJ: Wiley-Blackwell, 2018.

Zaydān, Jurjī. *Tārīkh 'Adab al-lugha al-'Arabiyya* [A history of Arabic literature]. Edited by Shawqī Dhayf. 4 vols. Cairo: Dār Al-Hilāl, 1950.

Zerubavel, Yael. *Desert in the Promised Land.* Stanford, CA: Stanford University Press, 2018.

———. "The Forest as a National Icon: Literature, Politics, and the Archaeology of Memory." *Israel Studies* 1, no. 1 (1996): 60–99.

———. "Memory, the Rebirth of the Native, and the 'Hebrew Bedouin' Identity." *Social Research* 75, no. 1 (2008): 315–52.

———. *Recovered Roots: Collective Memory and the Making of Israeli National Tradition.* Chicago: University of Chicago Press, 1995.

Zreik, Raef. "When Does a Settler Become a Native? (with Apologies to Mamdani)." *Constellations* 23, no. 3 (2016): 351–64.

Zu'bi, Nahla. "The Development of Capitalism in Palestine: The Expropriation of the Palestinian Direct Producers." *Journal of Palestine Studies* 13, no. 4 (1984): 88–109.

Zytnicki, Colette. "The 'Oriental Jews' of the Maghreb: Reinventing the North African Jewish Past in the Colonial Era." In *Colonialism and the Jews*, edited by Ethan B. Katz, Lisa Moses Leff, and Maud S. Mandel. Bloomington: Indiana University Press, 2017.

INDEX

Aaronsohn, Aaron, 140
Aaronsohn, Ran, 105, 148
Abū Ibrāhīm. *See* Meirovitch, Menasche
Abū 'Ubayd, 186
Abufarha, Nasser, 105
Agnew, John, 62
agricultural colonies, teaching of Arabic in, 119–21
agricultural practices: Arab, Jewish settlers' negative perception of, 25; Arab, reliance of Jewish settlers on, 25–26, 53–58, 148–49; and Meirovitch's relation with Arab elites, 46–53. *See also* rural settings, Jewish-Palestinian encounters in
al-'Anṭākī, Dāwūd, 113
Al-Aqsa Mosque, 90–91
al-'Aref, 'Aref, 233, 235
al-Bājūrī, Maḥmūd 'Umar, 186, 195
al-Burāq Commission, 170–74, 177
al-Burāq Wall (Ḥāiṭ al-Burāq), conflict over ownership of, 91–92
al-Burāq Wall disturbances of 1929: Jewish reactions to, 166–74; overview, 164–66; sense of otherness after, 190; Zaki Pasha and Muslim reactions to, 174–78
al-Bustānī, Buṭrus, 9, 22, 66–67
al-Dabbāgh, Muṣṭafa Murād, 280nn54, 280nn55, 280nn56
al-Dīn, Yusūf Ḍiyā, 253nn44
Alf Laylah wa-Laylah. See Arabian Nights, The
al-Ḥanbalī, Mujīr al-Dīn, 86–87, 88, 265nn99
al-Ḥaram al-Sharīf (Noble Sanctuary)/ Temple Mount, 88, 172–73. *See also* al-Burāq Wall disturbances of 1929
al-Hussein, Abdullah Ibn, 234
al-Ḥusseinī, Bashīr 'Abdelsalām, 91–92
al-Ḥusseinī, Hajj Amin, 174, 233
al-Ḥusseinī. Jamāl, 146, 174, 198
al-Ḥusseinī, Musa Kāẓim, 198
'Ali, Qaṣaṣuna al-sha'bī, 286nn67
Al-'iqd al-farīd (The unique necklace) (Rabbih), 185–86
al-'Isa, 'Isa, 47–48
al-'Isa, Yūsuf, 22
al-Jumaḥī, Muḥammad Ibn Sallām, 124
al-Khālidī, Rūḥī, 45, 52, 90–91
al-Khālidī, Yusūf Ḍiya al-Dīn, 27
al-Khālidiyya library, 43–44
Al-khiṭaṭ al-tawfiqiyya (The quarters of Tawfik) (Mubārak), 62–63
al-Khūrī, Salīm, 63
All the produce of the land (*Tevo'ot ha-arets*) (Schwarz), 261nn36
al-lamiyyat: inna al-kirām qalūl (The nobles are few) (al-Samaw'al), 127
Allenby, Edmund, 153
al-Maḍnūn bihi 'ala ghayr Ahlih (That which is to be withheld from those unworthy of it) (Yahuda), 42–43, 66–67
al-Mas'ūdī, 203
al-Mashriq, semitism in, 21–22
al-Mawāṣif, Zayn (character in *Arabian Nights*), 211, 213
al-Muqaddima (Introduction) (Ibn Khaldūn), 37–38
al-Musawi, Muhsin, 203
al-Muẓafar, 'Abd al-Qāder, 235
al-Nādī al-'Arabī (Arab Club), 235, 236
al-Nafir (Clarion) newspaper, 50

al-Qalamāwī, Suhair, 288nn81
al-Qays, Imru', 126
al-Raḥmān, Sālim 'Abd, 235
al-Rikābī, Ali Riḍa Pasha, 234
al-Ruṣāfī, Ma'rūf, 143
al-Ṣāliḥ, Sheikh Muḥammad, 185
al-Samaw'al Ibn 'Adiya' al-Yahūdī (the Jew), 125–27
al-Ṭabarī, Sheikh Ṭāher, 240, 295nn59
al-Ṭahṭawī, Rifā'a Rāfi', 66–67, 187
al-Ṭā'ī, Ḥātim (Ḥātim of Ṭayy'), 128–30
al-Tamthīl wa-al-muḥāḍara (The book of exemplification and discussion) (al-Tha'labī), 190
al-Tha'labī, Abū Manṣūr Ismā'īl, 190
al-'Ubaydī, 'Ubayd Allāh Ibn 'abd Al-Kāfī, 255nn72
al-'Umarī, Ibn Faḍl-Allah, 177
Al-'uns al-jalīl bi-tārīkh al-Quds wa-al-Khalīl (The glorious history of Jerusalem and Hebron) (al-Ḥanbalī), 86–87, 88, 265nn99
al-Yahudiyya village, 35
al-Zanjānī, 255nn72
al-Zayyāt, Aḥmad Ḥasan, 203, 217
ambivalent encounters in Late Ottoman Palestine, 23–26. *See also* Jewish-Palestinian encounters in Late Ottoman Palestine
Amthāl al-'awām fī Miṣr wa-al-Sūdān wa-al-Shām (On the proverbs of the masses in Egypt, Sudan, and Sham) (Shuqayr), 186–87
ancients (*ḳadmonim*), methods of, 55
Andalusian Jews, cultural legacy of, 122–23. *See also* Sephardi Jews
Antebi, Albert, 92
Antiquities of the Arabs, The (*Ḳadmoniyot ha-'Aravim*) (Yahuda), 28–30
anti-Semitism in late Ottoman Palestine, 36–39
anti-Zionism in late Ottoman Palestine, 34–41
appearances, proverbs related to, 196
Arab Club (al-Nādī al-'Arabī), 235, 236
Arab lands, commemorating Jewish heroes from, 178–81
Arab Nation Fund (ṣundūq al-Umma al-'Arabī), 235
"Arab noblemen and heroes" ("Nedive ve-gibure 'Arav") (Yahuda), 128–30, 132–33
Arab renaissance, 66–67, 184. *See also* nahdawi Arab intellectuals
Arabian Nights, The: background of Rivlin's translation, 208–10; cross-cultural content of, 199–200; enhancement of Hebrew through translation of, 218–22; general discussion, 223; as guide to Arabs, 213–18; Jewish past encoded in, 211–13; and Jewish rootedness in Orient, 204–8; in Jewish vernacular, 200–202; as world literature, 202–4
Arabic language: Ben-Yehuda's use of, 72, 73–75; botanical names from, expansion of Hebrew through, 104–8; cross-pollination with Hebrew, 113–17; enrichment of Hebrew lexicon through, 97–100; and hebraization of Palestine's flora, 108–13; and Hebrew Bible, 22, 133–36; Hebrew writers' knowledge of, 3; Horowitz's view of Arabic knowledge and, 158–62; instruction in Ashkenazi schools, 117–21; as linguistic source for Hebrew, 219–22; in Mandate Palestine, 141–42; Meirovitch's advocacy of learning, 49; nahdawi intellectuals and renaissance of, 66–67; poetry in, Jewish identity formation and, 124–33; prose in, and retrieval of Hebrew nativity, 122–24; recruitment of to advance Jewish objectives, 242–44; and remaking of Hebraic landscape, 100–104; revitalizing Hebrew and reshaping New Jew through, 136–37; settler colonialism and, 14; status in Israeli state, 237–41; Yahuda and, 42–44; Yellin's use of, 77, 82–83
Arabic place-names: Ben-Yehuda's use of, 73–75, 102–4; evolutionary process of

building Arabic map, 227; replacement with Hebrew place-names, 12, 13, 162, 227–30; role in identifying previous Jewish settlements, 151–52; as source for knowledge of the land, 162–64; Yellin's use of, 77
Arabic proverbs: and Biblical interpretation, 192–94; as cross-cultural discourse, 185–89; and Jewish proverbs, 198–99; as mirror of intercommunal life in Orient, 195–96; in *Mishle ʿArav*, 189–92; portrayal of Jews, 196–98
Arabic teachers' conference of 1950 (Israel), 239–41
Arab-Israeli War of 1948, 225, 231
Arabo-Islamic culture, Jewish engagement with, 4, 7–8. *See also* Hebrew Orientalism
Arabo-Islamic literary past, Hebrew construction of, 183–85, 222–24. *See also* *Arabian Nights, The*; Arabic proverbs
Arabs: *Arabian Nights* as guide to, 213–18; Arabic proverbs as providing insights into, 189–90, 195–96; conquest of Palestine in 634 CE, 117; elites, relations of Jewish settlers with, 41–53; framing of in Ben-Yahuda's history of Zionism, 241; portrayals of Jews in proverbs of, 196–98; Zionist opinions of British policy favoring, 233–34. *See also* nahdawi Arab intellectuals; Palestinian Arabs
archaeological exploration in Jerusalem, 90–91, 172
Aryan origins of *Arabian Nights*, 203–4, 288nn87
Aryan race, conceptualization of, 21
Ashkenazi Jews: Arabic instruction in schools of, 117–21; changes in relative status in Mandate Palestine, 3; and ecumenical frame, 20; fascination with *Arabian Nights* among, 200–201; and Hebrew Orientalism, 10–11; relation with Arab elites, 44–53. *See also* Zionism
assimilation, ideas of Jewish settlers on, 149–50
Association for the Exploration of the Land of Israel and Its Antiquities, 155
Association of the Eastern Bond (Jambiya al-Rābiṭa al-Sharqiyya), 174–75
atad tree, 79–82
Attal, Robert, 284nn33
authenticity, 12, 55
Avishur, Yitsḥaḳ, 201

Bakhos, Carol, 27
Balfour Declaration, 3; Arab population's reaction to, 144–45; contradictions related to, 146; differing reactions to in Palestine, 17–18; Jewish anxieties about, 152–53; Muslim-Christian Association and, 5; Zionist reactions to, 139–40, 278nn22
Bashkin, Orit, 21, 36
Baudissin, Wolf Wilhelm, 82
Baydas, Khalīl, 64–65
beards, proverbs related to, 196
Bedouins, 7, 35, 53–55
Begin, Menaḥem, 233
Beit ha-Sefer shel Ezrah (Ezrah School), 185
"Beit Hashem be-meʿ arbolet" (The Hashemite dynasty in a whirlpool) (Rivlin), 232–36
Beit Sheʿarim settlement, 155–56
Belḳind, Israel, 245; apolitical entrepreneurial agenda of, 105; *Erets Yirael shel zemanenu*, 32, 150–51, 154, 162–64; interest in Arabic and education, 119–21; Ḳiryat Sefer school and, 25, 121; on origins of Palestinian Arabs as Hebrews, 32–34, 59; relationship to Arab population promoted by, 147–49
ben Korḥa, Yehoshua, 193
Ben-Arieh, Yehoshua, 117–18
Bene ha-Mizraḥ (Sons of the East), 83
bene ḳedem (people of the East), 189, 191
Ben-Gurion, David, 227
Benvenisti, Meron, 162, 225
Ben-Yahuda, Barukh, 241

Ben-Yehuda, Eliezer: attitude towards Arabs, 39–41; as encouraging young Jews to identify with Palestine's culture, 123–24; first encounter with Palestinian Arabs, 30–31; life of, 69; as recommending Jews become Ottoman citizens, 48; relations with Arab elites, 44–46, 59; on similarities of Arabic and Hebrew, 97–98; study of Arabic by, 100–101; use of Arabic to enrich Hebrew lexicon, 99–100, 101–2; writings on geography and landscape, 69–75, 99–100, 260nn32

Ben-Ze'ev, Israel: criticism of Naming Committee by, 180–81; description of Yahuda's personality by, 42; on influence of *Mishle 'Arav*, 191; on influence of nahdawi scholars, 66; on use of Arabic for enrichment of Hebrew, 142; and use of Arabic in early Israeli state, 239–41

Ben-Zvi, Isaac, 184, 185

Beška, Emanuel, 22

Bezalel, Yitsḥaḳ, 8

Bhabha, Homi, 10

Bialiḳ, Ḥaim Naḥman, 205, 220

Bible. *See* Hebrew Bible

Biluim: attitudes toward Arabic, 119; dualistic nature of mentality of, 58–59; and ethnonationalization of Palestine landscape, 149, 151–52; objective of, 23; rebranding of as pioneers, 277nn2; views on origins of Palestinian Arabs, 27–28; as working on two fronts, 252nn16. *See also* Belḳind, Israel

"Binah ba-Miḳra" (Understanding the Hebrew Bible) essays (Yahuda), 192

Binyamin, Rabbi, 142

bitter herb (*maror*), 116–17

Blau, Joshua, 274nn152

B'nai B'rith (Children of the Covenant) order, 73, 84

Boissier, Edmond, 111

Book of compilation of medication and aliment simples, The (*Kitāb al-jāmi' li-mufradāt al-'adwiya wa al-aghdhiya*) (Ibn al-Bayṭār), 80

Book of exemplification and discussion, The (*al-Tamthīl wa-al-muḥāḍara*) (al-Tha'labī), 190

Book of pleasant gardens in describing the Holy Land, The (*Kitāb al-rawḍa al-Mu'nisa fī waṣf al-'arḍ al-Muqaddasa*) (Baydas), 64–65

Book of the land of Israel, The (*Sefer Erets Yisrael*) (Ben-Yehuda), 70–73, 75, 99–100, 259nn32

botanical nomenclature: and Biblical interpretation, 78–82; and cross-pollination between Arabic and Hebrew, 113–17; expansion of Hebrew through, 104–8; hebraization of Palestine's flora, 109–13

bravery, moral virtue of, 131–32

Brinner, William, 211

Britain. *See* Great Britain; Mandate Palestine

Brith Shalom (Covenant of Peace), 142

Burton, Richard, 211

cacti, 105

Cairo Geniza, 285nn43

Campos, Michelle U., 8, 18, 46

catastrophe (Nakba), Palestinian, 225, 231

Cemal Pasha, 92

Children of the Covenant (B'nai B'rith) order, 73, 84

Christians: Arabic proverbs as mirror of intercommunal life, 195; and British conquest of Jerusalem, 153; Christian Arab intellectuals, 47; conflicts over sacred sites in Jerusalem, 90–93; ecumenical frame, 18–20, 21, 36; importance of Jerusalem to, 87–88; literature concerning Palestine produced by, 154; maps of Holy Land, 61; Muslim-Christian Associations, 5, 144–45; opinion of Mandate Palestine, 18; resistance to Jewish immigration, 36–37

Churchill, Winston, 198

citizenship: Ottoman, 48, 90; in state of Israel, 231

civic Ottomanism, 18

Clarion (*al-Nafir*) newspaper, 50

Classes of champion poets (*Ṭabaqāt Fuḥūl al-Shu'arā'*) (al-Jumaḥī), 124
Claval, Paul, 62
clothing styles, 7
Cohen, Ephraim, 185
Cohen, Hillel, 142–43, 165–66, 170
commemorating Jewish heroes from Arab lands, 178–81
Commission on the Palestine Disturbances of August 1929 (Shaw Commission), 170–74, 177
comparative philology, 135
converts to Islam, Palestinian Arabs as, 32–34
Covenant of Peace (Brith Shalom), 142
cross-cultural content of *Arabian Nights*, 199–200
cross-cultural discourse, Arabic proverbs as, 185–89

Dahamsheh, Amer, 162
"Dallim ve-reḳim anaḥnu" (How vacuous and penurious we are!) (Meirovitch), 49
Dalman, Gustaf Hermann, 111
Deer (*ha-Tsevi*) newspaper, 44–45
Der Judenstaat (The Jewish state) (Herzl), 121
descriptive geography, increased interest in, 62–65
Die Pflanzen Palästinas (Plants of Palestine) (Dinsmore), 111
Dinsmore, John Edward, 111
Dā'irat al-ma' ārif (The dictionary of knowledge) (al-Bustānī), 67
Discourse on Arab culture (*Khutba fi adab al-'Arab*) (al-Bustānī), 9
division of Palestine, 225
Dizengoff, Meir, 110
Dolbee, Samuel, 46
Dome of the Rock, 88, 90
Dowty, Alan, 36
dual society paradigm, in Mandate Palestine, 146
Duggan, Anne, 291nn140
Duncan, James, 62

East Jordan, 233–34
ecumenical frame, 18–20, 21, 36, 181–82
Eder, David, 143, 174, 175–76
education, Jewish views of Muslim Arab, 40
Efron, John, 11
Egypt, 174, 186–87
Elmaleḥ, 181
Eloenskii, Nikolai Aleksander, 65
El-Shamy, Hasan, 126
Erets avotenū (Land of our fathers) (Yellin), 75, 76
Erets Ḥemdah (Sokolow), 75, 259nn18
erets tovah (good land), in Hebrew Bible, 74
Erets Yisrael shel zemanenu (The land of Israel in our time) (Belḳind), 33, 150–52, 154, 162–64
Erets Yisrael u-shekhenoteha (The land of Israel and its adjacent countries) (Horowitz), 158, 164
Erets-Yisrael (The land of Israel) (Press), 228–29
Erwin, Robert, 205
Esau, descendents of, 30–31
Esther, Yahuda's discussion of, 192–94
ethnography, treatment of *Arabian Nights as*, 214–15, 216–17, 218
ethnonationalization of Palestine landscape: Arabs and popular culture as source for knowledge, 156–64; commemorating Jewish heroes from Arab lands, 178–81; contesting sacred spaces (*see* Wall disturbances of 1929); general discussion, 181–82; identification of historic Jewish settlements, 154–56; Judaization of homeland, 152–54; overview, 147–52
Etzel, 233
European anti-Semitism, 36–39
European Jews: criticism of use of Arabic in Hebrew revival, 122; Hebrew writings on landscape for, 65–69; imagination of landscape, 61; and Orientalism, 11; Ottomanization of settlers, 48–49, 51–52; superiority complex of, 27–34, 40. *See also* Ashkenazi Jews; Russian Jews; Sephardi Jews

Europeans: interest in Arabic proverbs, 186; Orientalist, fascination with *Arabian Nights*, 201–2, 203–4, 216–17
Even Sapir (Sapir), 269nn60
Even-Zohar, Itamar, 9
excavations in Jerusalem, 90–91, 172
Eyal, Gil, 161
Ezra the Jew (character in *Arabian Nights*), 213
Ezrah School (Beit ha-Sefer shel Ezrah), 185

Facing forests (*Mūl ha-ye'arot*) (Yehushua), 104
faḍā'il al-Quds (Virtues of Jerusalem), 167–68, 170
Fainberg, Joseph, 58
Faisal (King of Syria), 235–37
faithfulness, moral virtue of, 125–27
familial affinity between Jews and Arabs, 27–34
Farmers' Federation (hit'aḥdut ha-'ikarim), 105
Farağ, Alfred, 287nn68
fellahin (Palestinian Arab farmers), 7, 161–62. *See also* agricultural practices; rural settings, Jewish-Palestinian encounters in
Fellman, Jack, 267nn24
Fields, Gary, 97
Filasṭīn (Palestine) newspaper, 47–48, 49–50, 51
First Aliyah: Arabic instruction in schools in Jewish settlements, 120; hierarchical coexistence after, 24–25; relations of Jewish settlers with Arabs, 34; uniqueness of immigrants of, 105
Fishman, Louis, 51–52
flora of Palestine. *See* botanical nomenclature
"Flora of the land of gazelles, The" ("Tsimḥe Erets Ha-Tsevi") (Meirovitch), 78–82, 81, 107
folkloric literature, Arabic, 199–200. *See also Arabian Nights, The*
foxes, parables of, 123–24
Frumkin, Israel Dov, 40
Furas, Yoni, 21

Galland, Antoine, 201, 203, 216
Garden of Knowledge (Rawḍat al-ma'ārif), 185
Gedera settlement, 151–52
General Zionists, 105
generosity, moral virtue of, 128–30
geography of Palestine, 150–52, 154. *See also* landscape
George, Lloyd, 146
German language instruction in Mandate Palestine, 218–19
Glorious history of Jerusalem and Hebron, The (*Al-'uns al-jalīl bi-tārīkh al-Quds wa-al-Khalīl*) (al-Ḥanbalī), 86–87, 88, 265nn99
Godfry of Bouillon, 153
Goitein, S. D., 30, 194, 284nn33, 288nn76
Goldberg, Harvey, 10
good land (*erets tovah*), in Hebrew Bible, 74
Gordon, Yehuda Leib, 99
Gordon, Yehuda Leib, 100
Governmental Naming Committee (va'adat ha shemot ha-mimshaltit) (GNC), 227–30, 293nn5
Graetz, Heinrich, 254nn61
Great Britain: Balfour Declaration, 139–40, 152–53 (*see also* Mandate Palestine); conquest of Jerusalem in 1917, 153
Great War, The (World War I), 90–93
Greater Syria, 142, 176
Gribetz, Jonathan, 45

Ha-arets (The land) (Sapir), 116, 158, 160
Habicht, Christian Maximilian, 201
Haim, Abraham, 143–44, 167
Ḥāiṭ al-Burāq (al-Burāq Wall), conflict over ownership of, 91–92. *See also* Wall disturbances of 1929
ḥakīrat ha-arets (study of the land), Horowitz's essay on, 161

Halevi, Yehuda, 5, 134
Halperin, Liora, 47, 105, 141, 251nn8
Hammer-Purgstall, Joseph von, 204
Ha-Po'el ha-Tza'ir (Young Worker) movement, 121
Ḥasanein, Fū'ād, 287nn71, 288nn87
"Hashemite dynasty in a whirlpool, The" ("Beit Hashem be-me' arbolet") (Rivlin), 232–36
Hashemite kingdom, 233–34
Ha-shomer (Watchmen's Association), 7
Hatim of Tayy' (al-Ta'i, Hatim), 128–30
ha-Tsevi (Deer) newspaper, 44–45
Hatt-i Humayun (Noble Rescript), Ottoman Empire, 9
Ha-turgman (Translator) publishing house, 205–6, 289nn100
Ḥawaja Nazar (Smilansky), 23
Haycraft Commission of Inquiry, 175–76
Hazkani, Shay, 46
Hebrew Bible: Arabic language and, 22, 133–36; Arabic proverbial lore and interpretation of, 192–94; botanical knowledge and interpretation of, 78–82; imagery of Palestine in, 151; linking flora to, 111; national identity and, 14; and origins of Palestinian Arabs, 27, 30; reconstruction of landscape in accordance with, 73–75
Hebrew construction of Arabo-Islamic literary past, 183–85, 222–24. *See also* *Arabian Nights, The*; Arabic proverbs
Hebrew language: Ben-Yehuda's referencing Arabic dialects for, 73–75; enhancement of through translation of *Arabian Nights*, 218–22; Meirovitch's writings on need for national language, 106–7; Semitic character of, 269nn58; status of in Israeli state, 237; use of Sephardi accent, 100, 101; Yellin's *Miḳra'* and, 75–78. *See also* revival of Hebrew language
Hebrew Language Committee (Va'ad ha-Lashon ha-'Ivrit), 96, 109–10, 114, 261nn42
Hebrew Orientalism: general discussion, 244–46; and life and work of Yellin, 5–9; methodologies of study, 1–5; overview, 10–11; settler colonialism and, 11–15
Hebrew place-names: institutional activities related to in Mandate period, 154–56; in Israeli state, 226–30; replacement of Arabic place-names with, 12, 13, 162, 227–30; role of existing Palestinian settlements in, 151–52; Yellin's use of, 77
Hebrew translation of *Arabian Nights* (Rivlin), 212; background of, 208–10; and enhancement of modern Hebrew, 218–22; as guide to Arab culture and society, 215–16; and Horovitz's German study of, 204; objectives of, 200–202; review of fourth volume of, 242–44
Hebrew translation of *Arabian Nights* (Yellin), 205–6, 208, 220–21, 222
Herzl, Theodor, 121, 165
hierarchical coexistence, 24–25, 251nn8
higher culture, Jewish ideas about, 150
Hilfsverein der deutschen Juden school, 185
Hissin, Haim, 277nn12
historic Jewish settlements, identification of, 151–52, 154–56
hit'aḥdut ha-'ikarim (Farmers' Federation), 105
holy sites, 90–93. *See also* Wall disturbances of 1929
homeland, creation of: construction of Jewish past in Palestine, 82–89; Hebrew writings on landscape, 65–69; Jewish imagination of, 93–94; in Mandate Palestine, 139–46; by nahdawi Arab intellectuals, 62–63; reconstruction of landscape in accordance with, 73–75. *See also* ethnonationalization of Palestine landscape; Hebrew construction of Arabo-Islamic literary past
Horovitz, Josef, 204, 214–15
Horowitz, Abraham, 158, 279nn38, 279nn40

Horowitz, Israel, 92, 93, 153–54, 156–62, 164
hospitality, moral virtue of, 130
hostility between Palestinian Arabs and Jewish settlers, 34–41
"How vacuous and penurious we are!" ("Dallim ve-reḳim anaḥnu") (Meirovitch), 49
Ḥussein, Ṭaha, 132, 286nn67

Ibn al-Bayṭār, ʿAbd Allāh Ibn Aḥmad, 80
Ibn al-Nadīm al-Yahūdī (the Jew), as title for Yahuda, 42
Ibn al-Nadīm (medieval bibliographer), 203, 255nn70
Ibn al-Najjār, Mordechai, 201–2
Ibn Ezra, Moses, 221
Ibn Khaldūn, 37–38
Ibn Manẓūr, 72
Ibn Shaddād, ʿAntar, 128–29, 131–32, 135–36
Ibrāhīm, Abū. *See* Meirovitch, Menasche
identity formation, Jewish: Arabic poetry and, 124–33; ideas of Jewish settlers about, 149–50; link between landscape and, 61–64
immigration: of Ashkenazi Jews, 10; fourth centenary of Jewish arrival in Ottoman Empire, 83–84; Ottoman policies for Jewish settlers, 67–69. *See also* First Aliyah; Second Aliyah
imperial power, positioning Zionist movement within, 232–33
Imru' al-Qays, 193
indigeneity, Jewish: and adoption of Arab agricultural practices, 53–58; Arabic prose and retrieval of, 122–24; and Arabo-Islamic literature, 198, 222–23; and assimilation of Arab culture, 7–8; and botanical knowledge and Biblical interpretation, 78–82; and Hebrew writings on landscape, 65–69; and identification of historic Jewish settlements, 155–56; in Mandate Palestine, 144; and settler colonialism, 11–15, 244–45. *See also* revival of Hebrew language
indigeneity of Palestinian Arabs, Zionist recognition of, 235
intercommunal life in Orient, Arabic proverbs as mirror of, 195–96
interconfessional relations: ecumenical frame, 2, 18–20, 21, 36; effect of British takeover of Palestine on, 18; under Ottoman rule, 67–69; relations with Arab elites, 41–53
Introduction (*al-Muqaddima*) (Ibn Khaldun), 37–38
Irwin, Robert, 213
Ishmael, Arabs as descendents of, 27, 30–31
Islam: and British conquest of Jerusalem, 153; conflicts over sacred sites in Jerusalem, 90–93; and ecumenical frame, 18–20, 21, 36; Hebrew writers' knowledge of, 3; importance of Jerusalem in, 86–88; Jewish engagement with Arabo-Islamic culture, 4, 7–8 (*see also* Hebrew Orientalism); Muslim opinions of Mandate Palestine, 18; Palestinian Arabs as Hebrew converts to, 32–34; tolerance towards Jews in, 36–37; and Wall disturbances of 1929, 164–66, 177–78
Islamic jurists (qadis), 295nn59
Islamicate civilization, 2
Israel: birth of state of, 225–26; creation of Hebrew map for, 226–30; recruitment of Arabic to advance national objectives, 242–44; status of Arabic in, 237–41; status of Arabs in early years of, 230–37
Israeli Citizenship Law of 1952, 231
Israeli Parliament (Knesset), 237–38
Israelite patriarchs, recreation of life of, 23
Issa, Rana, 22

Jabal Hārūn (Mount Hor), 74–75
Jabotinsky, Ze'ev, 208, 214, 233, 289nn100
Jacobson, Abigail, 8, 92–93, 145, 166, 173
Jaffa disturbances of 1921, 175–76
Jaffa oranges, 104–5
Jamʿiyyat al-Rābiṭa al-Sharqiyya (Association of the Eastern Bond), 174–75
Jankowski, James, 186

Jawhariyyeh, Wāṣif, 18, 19, 164–74, 271nn94
Jerusalem: British conquest of, 153; Hebrew writings in Late Ottoman era about, 90–93; holy sites, conflicts over, 90–91 (*see also* Wall disturbances of 1929); Yellin's writings about, 84–88
"Jerusalem four hundred years ago" ("Yerushalayim li-fnay arba' Me'ot shanah") (Yellin), 84–89
Jerusalemite circle, 209
Jewish identity, formation of. *See* identity formation, Jewish
Jewish National Council (Va'ad Le'umi), 167
Jewish National Fund's Naming Committee, 155–56, 162, 178–81
Jewish proverbs, 194, 198–99
Jewish state, The (*Der Judenstaat*) (Herzl), 121
Jewish-Palestinian encounters in Late Ottoman Palestine: agricultural practices and, 53–58; Jewish insights on Arab discontent, 34–41; Jewish relations with Arab elites, 41–53; Jewish views on origins of Palestinian Arabs, 27–34; overview, 23–26; Palestinian Arabs as model, 58–60
Jews: *Arabian Nights* in vernacular of, 200–202; Arabic proverbs as mirror of intercommunal life, 195–96; and ecumenical frame, 18–20, 21, 36; heroes from Arab lands, commemorating, 178–81; Judaization of homeland by, 152–54; King Faisal of Syria's attitude toward, 235–36; land acquisition by in Mandate Palestine, 140; in late Ottoman Palestine (*see* Jewish-Palestinian encounters in Late Ottoman Palestine; landscape; late Ottoman Palestine; revival of Hebrew language); national home for, construction of in Mandate Palestine, 139–46 (*see also* ethnonationalization of Palestine landscape; Hebrew construction of Arabo-Islamic literary past); past of as encoded in *Arabian Nights*, 211–13; portrayal of in Arabic proverbs, 196–98; relationship to Arab population in Mandate period, 147, 148–52, 181; reliance on Arab agricultural practices, 148–49; and settler-native analytic framework, 244–46; status of in Israeli state, 231; and Wall disturbances of 1929, 164–74, 178. *See also* Hebrew Orientalism; interconfessional relations; Zionism
Job (Bible character), 191
Jordan, Hashemite kingdom of, 233–34
Jordan River, identification of, 103
Judaization of homeland, 152–54. *See also* ethnonationalization of Palestine landscape
Judeo-Arabic, 201, 202

Kabha, Mustafa, 105
ḳadmonim (the ancients), methods of, 55
Ḳadmoniyot ha-'Aravim (The antiquities of the Arabs) (Yahuda), 28–30
Kalisman, Hilary, 141
Kalmar, Ivan Davidson, 10–11
Kāmil, Muṣṭafa, 19–20
Karlinsky, Nahum, 105
Katzenelson, Yitsḥaḳ, 205
Khazzoom, Aziza, 26, 150
Khirbet Khizeh (Yizhar), 225
Khusraw, Nāṣir, 93
Khuṭba fīadab al-'Arab (Discourse on Arab culture) (al-Bustānī), 9
Kimmerling, Baruch, 11–12
Ḳiryat Sefer school, 25, 121
Kitāb al-jāmi' li-mufradāt al-'adwiya wa al-aghdhiya (The book of compilation of medication and aliment simples) (Ibn al-Bayṭār), 80
Kitāb 'āthār al-adhār (Signs of times) (al-Khūry and Shihāda), 63
Kitāb al-rawḍa al-Mu'nisa fī waṣf al-'arḍ al-Muqaddasa (The book of pleasant gardens in describing the Holy Land) (Baydas), 64–65
Klausner, Joseph, 82–83, 96, 155–56

Klein, Samuel, 82–83
Knesset (Israeli Parliament), 237–38
knowledge of the land (*mada' ha-arets),* 157–58
knowledge of the land (*yedi'at ha-arets*): Arabs and popular culture as source for, 156–64; Ben-Yehuda's writings on, 69–75; Hebrew writings on, 65–69; settler colonialism and, 14; Yellin's writings on, 69–75
Krauss, Samuel, 279nn38

Labor Zionists (Socialist Zionists), 140
Lake Tiberius, identification of, 102–3
Land, The (*Ha-arets*) (Sapir), 116, 158, 160
land acquisition, as priority for Zionists in Mandate Palestine, 140
Land of Gilad, The (Oliphant), 259nn18
Land of Israel and its adjacent countries, The (*Erets Yisrael u-shekhenoteha*) (Horowitz), 158, 164
Land of Israel in our time, The (*Erets Yisrael shel zemanenu*) (Belḳind), 33, 150–52, 154, 162–64
Land of Israel, The (*Erets-Yisrael*) (Press), 228–29
Land of our fathers (*Erets avotenū*) (Yellin), 75, 76
landscape: Arab hostility toward settler land purchases and use, 34–41; Arabo-Islamic botanical knowledge and Biblical interpretation, 78–82; Ben-Yehuda and, 69–75; construction of Jewish past in Palestine, 82–89; expansion of Hebrew through botanical names, 104–8; hebraization of Palestine's flora, 108–13; Hebrew writings on, 7–8, 65–69; human identity and, 61–64; Jewish imagination of, 93–94; nahdawi writings on, 62–65; Ottoman love of homeland, 9; sacralization of, 111; settler colonialism and, 11–15; World War I and, 90–93; Yellin and, 75–78. *See also* ethnonationalization of Palestine landscape
Lane, Edward William, 216
Lang, Yoseph, 260nn30
language, effect of founding of Israeli state on, 237–44. *See also* Arabic language; Hebrew language; revival of Hebrew language
Language of Arabs, The (*Lisān al-'arab*) (Ibn Manẓūr), 72
language of the land (*sefat ha-arets*), 14, 78, 96. *See also* Arabic language
Language War, 218–19
late Ottoman Palestine: Arab hostility towards Jewish settlers in, 34–41; Arabic and Hebrew Bible in, 22; Arabic instruction in Ashkenazi schools in, 117–21; demographics of, 279nn44; and ecumenical frame, 2, 18–20, 21, 36; fourth centenary of Jewish arrival in Ottoman Empire, 83–84; hebraization of place-names in, 226–27; hostile Jewish-Arab relations before WWI, 90; immigration policies for Jewish settlers, 67–69; Ottomanization of European Jewish settlers, 51–52, 66; overview, 17–18; political and economic changes in, 118–19; protests against Jewish immigration in, 127; semitism in al-Mashriq, 21–22; writings on holy sites through WWI, 90–93. *See also* Jewish-Palestinian encounters in Late Ottoman Palestine; landscape; revival of Hebrew language
legends found in Arabic sources, use by Hebrew writers, 164
Leibovitz, Dov Ariel, 149
Levy, Lital, 42, 44, 144
lexicon, Hebrew, 218–22
Lilienblum, Moshe Leib, 98
Lipschitz, Eliezer Meir, 98–99, 266nn8
Lisān al-'arab (The language of Arabs) (Ibn Manẓūr), 72
literary past, Hebrew construction of Arabo-Islamic, 183–85, 222–24. *See also Arabian Nights, The*; Arabic proverbs

Lorenzo, Kamel, 63–64
lotus tree, 82
Lunts, Abraham Moshe, 67–69, 107–8, 168

mada' ha-arets (knowledge of the land), 157–58
madrasah, 185
magic, 213
Magness, Jodi, 165
Mahdi, Muhsin, 200, 204
Maimonides, Moses, 87, 89
Makdisi, Ussama, 18, 19, 36, 144
Malūl, Nissim, 170, 173, 174
Mamluk Jerusalem, 84–86
Mandate Palestine: changes in Jewish communities during, 3; conflicting opinions on, 17–18; construction of national home in, 139–46; end of, 225; hebraization of place-names in, 154–56, 162, 227–30; opposing Zionist positions toward, 232–35; Orientalist views in, 2–3; plurilingualism in, 237; status of Palestinian Arabs in, 230–31. *See also* ethnonationalization of Palestine landscape; Hebrew construction of Arabo-Islamic literary past
Mandel, Neville, 36
maps, hebraizing of. *See* place-names
maror (bitter herb), 116–17
Masalha, Nur, 154
Masālik al-ʾabṣār fī mamālik al-ʾamṣār (Voyages of eyes) (Zaki Pasha), 177
Masrūr (character in *Arabian Nights*), 211, 213
Mazar, Benjamin, 156
MCAs (Muslim-Christian Associations), 5, 144–45
Meʾasef Zion journal, 168
medieval Arabic literature, status of *Arabian Nights* in, 203
medieval Hebrew poetry, 219–20
Meirovitch, Menasche, 255nn88, 256nn106; depiction of Indigenous agricultural practices, 53–58; ideals related to agricultural colonization and language, 105–7; relation with Arab elites, 46–53, 59; use of Arabo-Islamic botanical sources, 78–82
Meyuḥas, 156, 181
Midrash, 168–70
Miḳra le-naʿre Bene Yisrael (Reading for the youth of the children of Israel) (Yellin), 75–78, 125–27
Miḳra le-yilde bene Yisrael (Reading to the children of the people of Israel) (Ben-Yehuda and Yellin), 123–24
Miḳveh Yisrael colony, 119–20
military rule of Palestinian Arabs in Israeli state, 231, 241
Mishle ʿArav (Yahuda): comprehensive approach in, 189–92; general discussion, 223; and intercommunal life in the Orient, 195–96; and interpretation of Hebrew Bible, 192–94; Jewish proverbs in, 198–99; overview, 187, 188; portrayal of Jews, 196–98
Mishnaic period, 114–15
modern Hebrew language. *See* Hebrew language; revival of Hebrew language
monolingualism, 141
Montefiore, Moses, 118
moral lessons, storytelling as medium to convey, 206, 216
moral virtues, revival of: Arabic poetry in context of Hebrew identity formation, 132–33; bravery of ʿAntar Ibn Shaddād, 131–32; faithfulness of al-Samawʾal Ibn ʿAdiyaʾ, 125–27; generosity of Ḥātim of Ṭayyʾ, 128–30; through Arabic poetry, 124–25
Moreh, Shmuel, 135
moshavoth, 23
Mount Hor (Jabal Hārūn), 74–75
Mubārak, ʿAli, 62–63
Mughrabi Quarter, claims of ownership of, 91–92
Mūl ha-yeʿarot (Facing forests) (Yehushua), 104
Muslim-Christian Associations (MCAs), 5, 144–45

Muslims: and British conquest of Jerusalem, 153; conflicts over sacred sites in Jeruselem, 90–93; and ecumenical frame, 18–20, 21, 36; Hebrew writers' knowledge of Islam, 3; importance of Jerusalem to, 86–88; Jewish engagement with Arabo-Islamic culture, 4, 7–8 (*see also* Hebrew Orientalism); opinion of Mandate Palestine, 18; Palestinian Arabs as Hebrew converts, 32–34; tolerance towards Jews, 36–37; and Wall disturbances of 1929, 164–66, 177–78; Yellin's calls to regarding excavation of sacred sites, 172–73

nabaq tree, 79–82
nahdawi Arab intellectuals: anti-Semitism among, 36–37; attention to geography and landscape, 62–65; and ecumenical frame, 19, 20; overview, 9; and renewal of Arabic language, 22; role in literary and cultural Arab renaissance, 66–67; Semitism and, 21; use of prose to rejuvenate Arabic, 122; Yahuda and, 42–44
nahdawi Jews, 66–69
Nakba (catastrophe), Palestinian, 225, 231
Naming Committee of the Jewish National Fund, 155–56, 162, 178–81
Naor, Moshe, 8, 166, 173
national home, construction of in Mandate Palestine, 139–46. *See also* ethnonationalization of Palestine landscape; Hebrew construction of Arabo-Islamic literary past
national landscape. *See* landscape
nativity, Jewish. *See* indigeneity, Jewish
natural habitat. *See* landscape
"Nedive ve-gibure 'Arav" (Arab noblemen and heroes) (Yahuda), 128–30, 132–33
New Jews: Arabic literature in construction of, 185; overview, 14; reshaping through Arabic language and literature, 136–37; as seeing themselves reflected in fellahin, 161–62; and settler-native analytic framework, 245; translation of *Nights* as proclaiming rootedness in Orient, 204–8
Nimtsuvitz, Yisrael, 58
Noble Rescript (Hatt-i Humayun), Ottoman Empire, 9
Noble Sanctuary (al-Ḥaram al-Sharīf)/ Temple Mount, 88, 172–73. *See also* al-Burāq Wall disturbances of 1929
Nobles are few, The (*al-lamiyyat: inna al-kirām qalūl*) (al-Samaw'al), 127

Oliphant, Laurence, 259nn18
olive oil production, 55–58
On the proverbs of the masses in Egypt, Sudan, and Sham (*Amthāl al-'awām fī Miṣr wa-al-Sūdān wa-al-Shām*) (Shuqayr), 186–87
One Thousand and One Nights. *See Arabian Nights, The*
oral Arabic tradition, replacement by printing, 66–67
Oriental Jews: affiliation with Zionism, 8; al-Rikābī's opinions on allowing in Transjordan, 234; Arab nationalist views of, 145–46; attitude toward Arab population in Mandate Palestine, 143–44; changes in relative status in Mandate Palestine, 3; familiarity with *Arabian Nights*, 201–2; marginalization of in Mandate period, 167; and Orientalism, 10; and Wall disturbances of 1929, 166, 167–68, 181–82
Oriental Neighbors (Jacobson & Naor), 8
Orientalism. *See* Hebrew Orientalism
Ottoman Empire: Arab hostility toward settler land purchases and use, 34–41; and ecumenical frame, 18–20, 21, 36; fourth centenary of Jewish arrival in, 83–84; immigration policies for Jewish settlers, 67–69; imperial rescript of 1856, 9; regional integration under, 142; Young Turk Revolution, 46–47, 50–51, 90. *See also* late Ottoman Palestine

Ottomanization of European Jewish settlers, 48–49, 51–52
Our master Moses Maimonides (*Rabenu Mosheh Ben Maymun*) (Yellin), 89

Palestine: British (*see* ethnonationalization of Palestine landscape; Hebrew construction of Arabo-Islamic literary past; Mandate Palestine); Ottoman (*see* Jewish-Palestinian encounters in Late Ottoman Palestine; landscape; late Ottoman Palestine; revival of Hebrew language); partition of and war after, 225. *See also* Hebrew Orientalism
Palestine (*Filasṭīn*) newspaper, 47–48, 49–50, 51
Palestine Exploration Fund, 227
Palestinian Arabs: agricultural practices of, 25, 53–58, 148–49; Arabic proverbs as providing insights into, 189–90; Arabic use by in Israeli state, 238; Ben-Yehuda's use of accounts of, 73; connection to land, 104–5; distinction between native Jews and Zionist settlers by, 198; efforts to marginalize in Mandate Palestine, 139–40; elites, relations of Jewish settlers with, 41–53; fellahin (farmers), 7, 161–62 (*see also* agricultural practices; rural settings, Jewish-Palestinian encounters in); framing of in Ben-Yahuda's history of Zionism, 241; Hebrew place-naming based on settlements of, 151–52, 155–56; hostile Jewish-Arab relations before WWI, 90; reaction to Balfour Declaration, 144–45; relationship with Jews in Mandate period, 147, 148–52; settler colonialism and, 11–15, 244–46; as source for knowledge of the land, 156–64; status in early years of Israeli state, 225, 230–37; and Wall disturbances of 1929, 164–66, 170–71, 174–78; Yellin's calls to regarding excavation of sacred sites, 172–73; and Zionism in Mandate Palestine, 142–44; Zionist distinction of Palestinian nationalists from, 173–74; Zionist opinions of British policy favoring, 233–34. *See also* Jewish-Palestinian encounters in Late Ottoman Palestine; nahdawi Arab intellectuals
Palestinian identity, complexity of, 1
Palestinian national movement (Palestinianism), 52; policy of monolingualism in, 141; Rivlin's portrayal of, 235–36; views of native Jews and foreign Zionists, 145–46; Zaki Pasha and, 175, 176; Zionist distinction of Palestinian population from, 173–74
Palmon, Joshua, 295nn59
Paran, identification of, 103–4
partition of Palestine, 225
"peaceful crusade" in Jerusalem, 90–91
Penslar, Derek Jonathan, 10–11, 27
people of the East (*bene ḳedem*), 189, 191
Petaḥ Tiḳva (Jewish settlement), 35
Pines, Michel, 149
Pines, Yehiel Michael, 24
place-names: Ben-Yehuda's use of, 73–75, 102–4; institutional activities related to in Mandate period, 154–56; in Israeli state, 226–30; replacement of Arabic with Hebrew, 12, 13, 162, 227–30; role of existing Palestinian settlements in choosing, 151–52; Yellin's use of, 77
plant names: Biblical and Arabic, use of corresponding, 78–82; and cross-pollination between Arabic and Hebrew, 113–17; expansion of Hebrew through, 104–8; hebraization of Palestine's flora, 109–13
Plants of Palestine (*Die Pflanzen Palästinas*) (Dinsmore), 111
poetry, Arabic: al-Samaw'al Ibn 'Adiya', 125–27; 'Antar Ibn Shaddād, 131–32; in context of Hebrew identity formation, 132–33; Ḥātim of Ṭayy', 128–30; reviving lost Hebrew virtues through, 124–25
popular culture, 156–64. *See also* Arabic proverbs

portrayal of Jews in Arabic proverbs, 196–98
Post, George Edward, 111
Press, Yeshayahu, 101, 226, 228–29, 242
print, importance in knowledge production, 66–67
productivization ethos, 27–28, 119
professional mourners, proverb on, 195–96
property ownership in Jerusalem, conflicts over, 91–92
Provence, Michael, 18, 19
proverbs. *See* Arabic proverbs
Psalms 119:61, 136

qadis (Islamic jurists), 295nn59
Qaṭra (Palestinian village), 151–52
Quarters of Tawfik, The (*Al-khiṭaṭ al-tawfiqiyya*) (Mubārak), 62–63
Quran, Ishmael in, 30

Rabbih, Ibn ʿAbd, 185–86
Rabenu Mosheh Ben Maymun (Our master Moses Maimonides) (Yellin), 89
race. *See* Semitism (semitic race)
Rawḍat al-maʿārif (Garden of Knowledge), 185
Raz-Krakotzkin, Amnon, 123
Reading for the youth of the children of Israel (*Miḳra le-naʿre Bene Yisrael*) (Yellin), 75–78, 125–27
"Reading the Arabian Nights in Modern Hebrew Literature" (Tzoreff), 287nn72
Reading to the children of the people of Israel (*Miḳra le-yilde bene Yisrael*) (Ben-Yehuda and Yellin), 123–24
Regan, Bernard, 146
Reḥovot colony, 35
religion: ecumenical frame, 18–20, 21, 36, 181–82; effect of British takeover of Palestine, 18; nahdawi Arab intellectuals and anti-Semitism, 36. *See also* Christians; interconfessional relations; Islam; Wall disturbances of 1929
Renan, Ernest, 21
Renan, Ernest, 204
Revisionist Zionism, 232–33, 238
revival of Hebrew language: Arabic and Hebrew cross-pollination, 113–17; and Arabic instruction in Ashkenazi schools, 117–21; Arabic poetry and Jewish identity formation, 124–33; Arabic prose and retrieval of Hebrew nativity, 122–24; enrichment of lexicon through Arabic, 97–100; expansion through botanical names, 104–8; general discussion, 136–37, 242–44; hebraization of Palestine's flora, 108–13; overview, 95–97; remaking of Hebraic landscape, 100–104; and role of Arabic in interpreting Hebrew Bible, 133–36
Rishon Le-Zion colony, 35
Rivlin, Rachel, 209
Rivlin, Yosef Yo'el; background of, 208–10; and founding of Israeli state, 226; overview, 183–85; political vision of, 213–14, 291nn136, 294nn31; and selective Zionist settler memory, 232–36; on Sephardic Jewish poetry, 219–20. *See also* Hebrew translation of *Arabian Nights* (Rivlin)
Romantic Orientalism, 168, 189
rootedness of Jews in Orient, translation of *Nights* and, 204–8
Rothschild, Edmond de, 106, 151, 152
Ruppin, Arthur, 52
rural settings, Jewish-Palestinian encounters in: agricultural practices and, 53–58; Jewish insights on Arab discontent, 34–41; Jewish relations with Arab elites, 41–53; Jewish views on origins of Palestinian Arabs, 27–34; overview, 23–26; Palestinian Arabs as model, 58–60
Russia, persecution of Jews in, 24, 39, 147
Russian Jews, 23–24, 27–28, 46–53. *See also* Biluim
Rutenberg, Pinḥas, 167

Sabbagh-Khoury, Areej, 12
sacralization of landscape, 111
sacred sites, 90–93. *See also* Wall disturbances of 1929
sacred trees, 82
Sacy, Silvestre de, 203
Said, Edward, 1, 217
Samuel, Herbert, 233, 234
Sapir, Eliyahu: countering of anti-Semitism by, 36–39, 41; and cross-pollination between Arabic and Hebrew, 113–17; *Ha-arets*, 116, 158, 160; study of Arabic, 108–9; work on flora of Palestine, 109–13
Sapir, Jacob, 108–9, 269nn60
Saposnik, Arieh Bruce, 205
Schama, Simon, 93
Schayegh, Cyrus, 142
Schlegel, Friedrich von, 204
Schneider, Suzanne, 141
schools, Arabic instruction in, 117–21
Schwarz, Joseph, 261nn36
Second Aliyah: and anti-Zionist sentiments among Arabs, 35–36; Ha-Po'el ha-Tza'ir movement, 121; relations of Jewish settlers with Arabs, 25, 34
sefat ha-arets (language of the land), 14, 78, 96. *See also* Arabic language
Sefer Erets Yisrael (The book of the land of Israel) (Ben-Yehuda), 70–73, 75, 99–100, 259nn32
Semitic character of Hebrew, 269nn58
Semitic origin of *Arabian Nights*, 204, 288nn87
Semitism (semitic race), 8, 21–22
Sephardi Jews: affiliation with Zionism, 8; Arab nationalist views of, 145–46; attitude toward Arabs in Mandate period, 143; changes in relative status of in Mandate Palestine, 3; community and schools of, 117; fourth centenary of arrival in Ottoman Empire, 83–84; marginalization of in Mandate period, 167; and Orientalism, 10; poetry of, 219–20; use of Sephardi accent, 100, 101; and Wall disturbances of 1929, 166, 167–68, 181–82
Settlement of the Holy Land (Yishuv Erets Ha-Ḳodesh) association, 149
settler colonialism: general discussion, 244–46; and Hebrew Orientalism, 11–15; selective Zionist memory of, 231–36; Sephardi and Oriental authors' adoption of settler identity, 3–4
settler-native analytic framework, 244–46
Shafir, Gershon, 12
shared traditions, Arabic proverbs as mirror of, 195–96
Shaw Commission (Commission on the Palestine Disturbances of August 1929), 170–74, 177
Sheikh Burayk (Palestinian town), 156
Shenhav, Yehudah, 17
Shihāda, Salīm, 63
Shuqayr, Na'ūm, 186–87
sidr tree, 79–82
Signs of times (*Kitāb ʿāthār al-adhār*) (al-Khūry and Shihāda), 63
Siton, David, 209, 219
Slouschz, Naḥum, 82–83
Smilansky, Moses, 23
Smilansky, Moshe, 96
Socialist Zionists (Labor Zionists), 140
Sokolow, Naḥum, 65–66, 75, 259nn18
Sons of the East (Bene ha-Mizraḥ), 83
Stein, Kenneth, 140
stereotypes, in Arabic proverbs, 197–98
Stern, Avraham (Yair), 233
stigmatization, hierarchy of, 26
"Story Told by the Jewish Physician, The" (*The Arabian Nights*), 213
storytelling, 206, 208. *See also Arabian Nights, The*
Studien zur Semitischen Religionsgeschichte (Baudissin), 82
study of the land (*ḥaḳīrat ha-arets*), Horowitz's essay on, 161
ṣundūq al-'uma al-'Arabī (Arab Nation Fund), 235

superiority complex of European Jews, 27–34, 40
supersession of Palestinian farmers, 12
Syria, 235–36

Ṭabaqāt Fuḥūl al-Shuʿarāʾ (Classes of champion poets) (al-Jumaḥī), 124
Talmud, proverbs of, 194
Tamārī, Salīm, 260nn26
Temple Mount/al-Ḥaram al-Sharīf (Noble Sanctuary), 88, 172–73. *See also* Wall disturbances of 1929
Tevoʾot ha-arets (All the produce of the land) (Schwarz), 261nn36
That which is to be withheld from those unworthy of it (*al-Maḍnūn bihi ʿala ghayr Ahlih*) (Yahuda), 42–43, 66–67
Tidhar, David, 178
"toʿelet lashon ʿAravit" (The Value of Arabic) (Yahuda), 134
toponomy. *See* place-names
Totaḥ, Musa Eliyahu, 236
Transjordan, 233–34
Translator (Ha-turgman) publishing house, 205–6, 289nn100
Tschernichovsky, Saul, 132–33, 274nn152
"Tsimḥe Erets Ha-Tsevi" (The flora of the land of gazelles) (Meirovitch), 78–82, 81, 107
Tzoreff, Avi-Ram, 287nn72

"Understanding the Hebrew Bible" ("Binah ba-Miḳra") essays (Yahuda), 192
Unique necklace, The (*Al-ʿiqd al-farīd*) (Rabbih), 185–86
urban centers, anti-Jewish sentiment in, 35–36

Vaʿad ha-Lashon ha-ʿIvrit (Hebrew Language Committee), 96, 109–10, 114, 261nn42
Vaʿad Le'umi (Jewish National Council), 167
vaʿadat ha shemot ha-mimshaltit (Governmental Naming Committee) (GNC), 227–30, 293nn5
"Value of Arabic, The" (toʿelet lashon ʿAravit) (Yahuda), 134
Veracini, Lorenzo, 12
Virtues of Jerusalem (*faḍāʾil al-Quds*), 167–68, 170
Voyages of eyes (*Masālik al-ʾabṣār fī mamālik al-ʾamṣār*) (Zaki Pasha), 177

Wall, conflict over ownership of, 91–92
Wall disturbances of 1929: Jewish reactions to, 166–74; overview, 164–66; sense of otherness after, 190; Zaki Pasha and Muslim reactions to, 174–78
War of Independence, 225, 231
Watchmen's Association (*Ha-shomer*), 7
Weil, Gustav, 201
Western travelogues to Palestine, 72
Wilderness of Paran, identification of, 103–4
wisdom literature, 123–24
Wolfe, Patrick, 11
World War I (WWI), 90–93

Yahuda, Abraham Shalom, 143, 209; discussion of ʿAntar Ibn Shaddād by, 131–32; discussion of Ḥātim of Ṭayyʾ by, 128–30; *Miḳra le-yelde bene Yisrael*, 123–24; and role of Arabic in interpreting Hebrew Bible, 133–36; theories on origins of Arabs, 28–30
Yahuda, Isaac, 209; background of, 187, 189; concerns about British colonial rule, 18; as encouraging settlers to become Ottoman citizens, 90; mentoring of Abraham Shalom, 134; overview, 183–84; relations with Arab elites, 42–44; writings on Western Wall by, 168–70. *See also Mishle ʿArav*

yedi'at ha-arets (knowledge of the land): Arabs and popular culture as source for, 156–64; Ben-Yehuda's writings on, 69–75; Hebrew writings on, 65–69; settler colonialism and, 14; Yellin's wiritngs on, 69–75
Yehushua, Abraham B., 104
Yellin, David, 209, 233; as Bene ha-Mizraḥ, 83; Ben-Yehuda's relation with, 73; book about Maimonides by, 87, 89; and construction of Jewish past in Palestine, 82–89; cooperation with Ottoman and British powers, 17; discussion of al-Samaw'al Ibn 'Adiya' by, 125–27; as encouraging young Jews to identify with Palestine's culture, 123–24; on familial affinity with Arabs, 30; general discussion, 5–9, 83; Hebrew translation of *Nights* by, 205–6, 208, 220–21, 222; on importance of Arabic to Hebrew language, 96; on importance of Hebrew language, 95; proficiency in Arabic language and culture, 82–83; recommendation to use Sephardi Hebrew accent, 101; request to purchase Wailing Wall, 92; Rivlin's parallel career path, 271nn94; and Wall disturbances of 1929, 166–67, 170–74; writings on geography and landscape, 75–78; Zaki Pasha's treatise in response to testimony of, 177–78, 179
Yerushalayim almanac (Lunts), 67–69
"Yerushalayim li-fnay arba' Me'ot shanah" (Jerusalem four hundred years ago) (Yellin), 84–89
Yishuv Erets Ha-Ḳodesh (Settlement of the Holy Land) association, 149
Yizhar, S., 225
Young Turk Revolution of 1908, 46–47, 50–51, 90
Young Worker (Ha-Po'el ha-Tza'ir) movement, 121
Zaki Pasha, Ahmad, 143; and Palestinian nationalist movement, 175, 176; perception of Zionism, 174–76; testimony on Wall disturbances of 1929, 177; treatise in response to Yellin's testimony, 177–78, 179
Zerubavel, Yael, 104
Zionism: affiliation of Sephardi and Oriental Jews with, 8; Arab hostility toward land purchases, 34–41; and assimilation of Arab culture, 7; Belḳind's focus on education contrary to, 121; and changes in relative status in Mandate Palestine, 3; and conflicts over sacred sites, 90–93; and construction of Jewish past in Palestine, 82–89; and distinction of Palestinian nationalists from Arab population, 173–74; effect of increased activity on Arab elite, 52; General, 105; and Hebrew place-naming, 162, 226–27; and Hebrew writings on landscape, 65–69; and hostile Jewish-Arab relations before WWI, 90; and imagination of landscape, 61; importance of Jewish connection to land for, 104; King Faisal of Syria's attitude toward, 235–36; in Late Ottoman era, 59; in Mandate Palestine, 139–46; and Orientalization of others, 26; Palestinian Arab opposition to, 198; policy of monolingualism in, 141; reactions to Balfour Declaration, 139–40, 278nn22; Revisionist, 232–33, 238; settler colonialism and, 11–15, 231–36; Socialist, 140; and transmission of Islamic culture into modern culture, 3; and Wall disturbances of 1929, 165, 166, 168; writings on holy sites through WWI, 90–93; Zaki Pasha's perception of, 174–76. *See also* ethnonationalization of Palestine landscape; Hebrew construction of Arabo-Islamic literary past

GPSR Authorized Representative: Easy Access System Europe - Mustamäe tee 50, 10621 Tallinn, Estonia, gpsr.requests@easproject.com

www.ingramcontent.com/pod-product-compliance
Lightning Source LLC
Chambersburg PA
CBHW030605230426
43661CB00053B/1847
* 9 7 8 0 6 9 1 2 0 2 0 3 7 *